Lecture Notes in Computer Science

Lecture Notes in Artificial Intelligence 13974

Founding Editor

Jörg Siekmann

Series Editors

Randy Goebel, *University of Alberta, Edmonton, Canada*
Wolfgang Wahlster, *DFKI, Berlin, Germany*
Zhi-Hua Zhou, *Nanjing University, Nanjing, China*

The series Lecture Notes in Artificial Intelligence (LNAI) was established in 1988 as a topical subseries of LNCS devoted to artificial intelligence.

The series publishes state-of-the-art research results at a high level. As with the LNCS mother series, the mission of the series is to serve the international R & D community by providing an invaluable service, mainly focused on the publication of conference and workshop proceedings and postproceedings.

Feng Liu · Yu Zhang · Hongzhi Kuai ·
Emily P. Stephen · Hongjun Wang
Editors

Brain Informatics

16th International Conference, BI 2023
Hoboken, NJ, USA, August 1–3, 2023
Proceedings

Springer

Editors
Feng Liu 🆔
Stevens Institute of Technology
Hoboken, NJ, USA

Yu Zhang 🆔
Lehigh University
Bethlehem, PA, USA

Hongzhi Kuai 🆔
Maebashi Institute of Technology
Maebashi, Japan

Emily P. Stephen 🆔
Boston University
Boston, MA, USA

Hongjun Wang 🆔
Stevens Institute of Technology
Hoboken, NJ, USA

ISSN 0302-9743   ISSN 1611-3349 (electronic)
Lecture Notes in Artificial Intelligence
ISBN 978-3-031-43074-9   ISBN 978-3-031-43075-6 (eBook)
https://doi.org/10.1007/978-3-031-43075-6

LNCS Sublibrary: SL7 – Artificial Intelligence

This Springer imprint is published by the registered company Springer Nature Switzerland AG
The registered company address is: Gewerbestrasse 11, 6330 Cham, Switzerland

Paper in this product is recyclable.

Preface

The International Conference on Brain Informatics (BI) series has established itself as the world's leading research conference in the field of brain informatics—an emerging interdisciplinary and multidisciplinary domain that synergizes cognitive science, neuroscience, medical science, data science, machine learning, artificial intelligence (AI), and information and communication technology (ICT) to address the interplay between human brain studies and informatics research. The 16th International Conference on Brain Informatics (BI 2023) provided an international platform for researchers and practitioners from diverse fields to showcase original research findings, exchange innovative ideas, and disseminate practical development experiences in brain informatics. The conference's primary theme – "Brain Science Meets Artificial Intelligence" – encompassed five tracks: Cognitive and Computational Foundations of Brain Science; Human Information Processing Systems; Brain Big Data Analytics, Curation, and Management; Informatics Paradigms for Brain and Mental Health Research; and Brain-Machine Intelligence and Brain-Inspired Computing.

The inception of the Brain Informatics conference series can be traced back to the WICI International Workshop on "Web Intelligence Meets Brain Informatics", held in Beijing, China, in 2006. As one of the pioneering conferences to explore the application of informatics for brain sciences, it laid the groundwork for subsequent BI conferences. The 2nd, 3rd, 4th, and 5th BI conferences were held in Beijing (China, 2009), Toronto (Canada, 2010), Lanzhou (China, 2011), and Macau (China, 2012), respectively. In 2013, the conference title evolved to Brain Informatics and Health (BIH), focusing on real-world applications of brain research in human health and well-being. BIH 2013, BIH 2014, BIH 2015, and BIH 2016 respectively took place in Maebashi (Japan), Warsaw (Poland), London (UK), and Omaha (USA). In 2017, the conference returned to its original vision, centered on investigating the brain from an informatics perspective and fostering a brain-inspired information technology revolution. Consequently, the conference name also reverted to Brain Informatics for the event held in Beijing, China, in 2017. The 2018 and 2019 editions were held in Arlington, Texas, USA, and Haikou, China, respectively.

The unforeseen challenges posed by the COVID-19 pandemic significantly impacted BI 2020, originally planned in Padua, Italy, necessitating a virtual format condensed into a one-day event. In 2021, the conference remained online due to the continued impact from the pandemic. However, to foster broader participation, the conference resumed its customary three-day schedule, comprising workshops and special sessions on day one, outstanding keynote sessions on day two, and technical sessions on day three. Based on our extensive experience in organizing both offline and online BI conferences, we successfully orchestrated a three-day hybrid conference in 2022. This innovative format co-hosted the event in Padua, Italy (in person), and Queensland, Australia (online). Notably, the BI 2022 conference was an integral part of the University of Padua's 800th-anniversary celebration.

The BI 2023 conference, held in Hoboken, New Jersey, USA, from August 1-3, 2023, marked our first completely in-person gathering after the challenging pandemic period. The conference featured high-quality papers, world-class keynote speeches, workshops, poster sessions, and special sessions, and attracted esteemed leaders in brain research and informatic technologies from various continents, including Europe, Africa, Asia, and North and South America. Our distinguished keynote speakers were Emery N. Brown, Bin He, Helen Mayberg, Paul Sajda, John Ngai, Grace M. Hwang, Vinod Goel, and Amy Kuceyeski. The proceedings of BI 2023 encompass 40 papers that offer comprehensive insights into brain informatics, bridging scales from atoms to thoughts and behaviors. These papers exemplify cutting-edge advancements in brain informatics, spanning methodologies, frameworks, techniques, applications, and case studies.

We would like to extend our heartfelt gratitude to all BI 2023 committee members for their indispensable and unwavering support. The success of BI 2023 owes much to the dedication of the Program Committee members, who diligently reviewed the conference papers. Our profound appreciation goes to the generous sponsorship from Stevens Institute of Technology, ANT-Neuro, g.tech, Medical Image Computing and Computer Assisted Intervention Society (MICCAI), Web Intelligence Consortium (WIC), International Neural Network Society, IEEE Computational Intelligence Society, and the Chinese Association for Artificial Intelligence. We also thank Springer's LNCS/LNAI team for their continuous support in coordinating and publishing this special volume. Special thanks are given to the organizing team at Stevens Institute of Technology, including Dr. Yu Gan, Ms. Joy Wilson, Ms. Frances Salvo, Ms. Leslie Jenkins, Ms. Dawne Eng, Ms. Mette Gomez, Ms. Sanika More, Ms. Meng Jiao, and Mr. Shihao Yang. We are also grateful for the tremendous support from the Interim Dean Dr. Anthony Barrese from School of Systems and Enterprises, Center for Healthcare Innovation, the Vice Provost of Research Dr. Edmund Synakowsk, and President Dr. Nariman Farvardin from Stevens Institute of Technology. We are grateful to Ning Zhong, the chair of Steering Committee and Advisory Board, for his invaluable contributions to organizing and promoting BI 2023. At last but not least, we would express our deep gratitude to all contributors and volunteers who made a resounding success of BI 2023 amid the challenging times.

August 2023

Feng Liu
Yu Zhang
Hongzhi Kuai
Emily P. Stephen
Hongjun Wang

Organization

General Chairs

Bin He — Carnegie Mellon University, USA
Stefano Panzeri — University Medical Center Hamburg-Eppendorf, Germany

Organizing Chairs

Feng Liu — Stevens Institute of Technology, USA
Hongjun Wang — Stevens Institute of Technology, USA
Emily P. Stephen — Boston University, USA
Sheraz Khan — MGH Harvard and MIT, USA
Yu Gan — Stevens Institute of Technology, USA

Program Chairs

Yu Zhang — Lehigh University, USA
Zhe Sage Chen — New York University, USA
Jordi Solé-Casals — University of Vic, Spain
Peipeng Liang — Capital Normal University, China
Islem Rekik — Istanbul Technology University, Turkey

Workshop/Special Session Chairs

Vicky Yamamoto — Keck School of Medicine of USC, USA
Xiang Li — MGH, Harvard Medical School, USA
Yusuf Cakmak — University of Otago, New Zealand
Shuqiang Wang — Shenzhen Institute of Advanced Technology, CAS, China
Yang Yang — Beijing Forestry University, China
Lu Zhang — University of Texas at Arlington, USA

Tutorial Chairs

Guihong Wan	MGH, Harvard Medical School, USA
Shouyi Wang	University of Texas at Arlington, USA
Antonia Zaferiou	Stevens Institute of Technology, USA
Xiaofu He	Columbia University, USA

Publicity Chairs

Hongzhi Kuai	Maebashi Institute of Technology, Japan
Miaolin (Melody) Fan	MGH, Harvard Medical School, USA
M. Shamim Kaiser	Jahangirnagar University, Bangladesh

CyberChair and Web Master

Hongzhi Kuai	Maebashi Institute of Technology, Japan

Advisory Board

Ning Zhong (Chair)	Maebashi Institute of Technology, Japan
Tianzi Jiang	Institute of Automation, CAS, China
Nikola Kasabov	Auckland University of Technology, New Zealand
Hesheng Liu	Harvard Medical School & Massachusetts General Hospital, USA
Guoming Luan	Sanbo Brain Hospital, China
Mufti Mahmud	Nottingham Trent University, UK
Hanchuan Peng	SEU-Allen Institute for Brain & Intelligence, China
Shinsuke Shimojo	California Institute of Technology, USA

Contents

Brain Big Data Analytics, Curation and Management

Informatics Paradigms for Brain and Mental Health Research

Brain-Machine Intelligence and Brain-Inspired Computing

**The 5th International Workshop on Cognitive Neuroscience of
Thinking and Reasoning**

Cognitive and Computational Foundations of Brain Science

Fusing Structural and Functional Connectivities Using Disentangled VAE for Detecting MCI

Qiankun Zuo[1,8], Yanfei Zhu[2(✉)], Libin Lu[3], Zhi Yang[4], Yuhui Li[5], and Ning Zhang[6,7]

[1] School of Information Engineering, Hubei University of Economics, Wuhan 430205, China
[2] School of Foreign Languages, Sun Yat-sen University, Guangzhou 510275, China
zhuyf53@mail.sysu.edu.cn
[3] School of Mathematics and Computer Science, Wuhan Polytechnic University, Wuhan 430023, China
[4] College of Electronics and Information Engineering, Sichuan University, Chengdu 610065, China
[5] Goertek Inc., Beijing 100083, China
[6] Beijing SmartDoor Technology Co., Ltd., Beijing 101399, China
[7] Beijing Zhongke Ruijian Technology Co., Ltd., Beijing 100088, China
[8] Zhuhaishi Jiexinsoftware Technology Co., Ltd., Zhuhai 519090, China

Abstract. Brain network analysis is a useful approach to studying human brain disorders because it can distinguish patients from healthy people by detecting abnormal connections. Due to the complementary information from multiple modal neuroimages, multimodal fusion technology has a lot of potential for improving prediction performance. However, effective fusion of multimodal medical images to achieve complementarity is still a challenging problem. In this paper, a novel hierarchical structural-functional connectivity fusing (HSCF) model is proposed to construct brain structural-functional connectivity matrices and predict abnormal brain connections based on functional magnetic resonance imaging (fMRI) and diffusion tensor imaging (DTI). Specifically, the prior knowledge is incorporated into the separators for disentangling each modality of information by the graph convolutional networks (GCN). And a disentangled cosine distance loss is devised to ensure the disentanglement's effectiveness. Moreover, the hierarchical representation fusion module is designed to effectively maximize the combination of relevant and effective features between modalities, which makes the generated structural-functional connectivity more robust and discriminative in the cognitive disease analysis. Results from a wide range of tests performed on the public Alzheimer's Disease Neuroimaging Initiative (ADNI) database show that the proposed model performs better than competing approaches in terms of classification evaluation. In general, the proposed HSCF model is a promising model for generating brain structural-functional connectivities and identifying abnormal brain connections as cognitive disease progresses.

© The Author(s), under exclusive license to Springer Nature Switzerland AG 2023
F. Liu et al. (Eds.): BI 2023, LNAI 13974, pp. 3–13, 2023.
https://doi.org/10.1007/978-3-031-43075-6_1

Keywords: Structural-Functional fusion · Hierarchical
representation · Disentangled learning · Graph convolutional network ·
MCI

1   Introduction

Alzheimer's disease (AD) is one of the most prevalent progressive and irreversible
degenerative disorders affecting the elderly, where the initial onset is considered
to be mild cognitive impairment (MCI). Memory loss, aphasia, and other declin-
ing brain functions represent MCI-related symptoms and are indicative of pathological changes [1]. According to literature [2], the AD conversion rate from MCI
is much higher than in normal people. In addition to making AD patients more
depressed and anxious, it also lowers their quality of life and places a heavy financial burden on their families due to the high cost of care [3]. Furthermore, there
is still no effective treatment for the illness [4]. Early diagnosis and treatment
of patients with MCI can effectively slow their progression to AD. Therefore,
developing an effective machine learning model for analyzing scanned medical
imaging and other field applications for disease detection has attracted growing
attention [5–15].

When the human brain completes a certain task, multiple brain regions need
to interact with each other, so studying cognitive diseases from the perspective
of brain connectivity is more explanatory. Brain networks are based on graph
theory, where nodes usually represent neurons or regions of interest (ROIs),
and edges represent the relationships between nodes (i.e., brain regions) [16].
Disease-related information can be conveyed in various ways by multiple modal
images [17–20]. fMRI (functional magnetic resonance imaging) records brain
activity and can reveal abnormal functional connectivity (FC) associated with
disease [21,22]. White matter fiber bundles in the brain can be recorded using
diffusion tensor imaging (DTI), which can reveal abnormal structural connectivity (SC) between different brain regions [23,24]. Compared with the traditional
imaging-based method in MCI diagnosis [25–30], the connectivity-based methods show superior performance in accuracy evaluation by graph convolutional
networks (GCN) [31,32]. Researchers either use SC or FC to perform an early
AD diagnosis clinically. For example, Zuo et al. [33] designed a transformer-based
network to construct FC from functional MRI and improve MCI diagnosis accuracy compared with empirical methods. Since both fMRI and DTI can explore
complementary information in patients, multimodal fusion has produced superior results in MCI diagnosis [34–36]. The work in [37] has proved the success
of fusing SC and FC in MCI prediction. They utilized the local weighted clustering coefficients to adaptively fuse the functional and structural information,
thus enhancing the disease diagnosis. This shows that fusing multimodal brain
networks is promising and is becoming a hot topic in cognitive disease analysis
[38–40]. However, the information from one modality may act as noise to prevent the expression of the other modality in previous approaches, which always
combine the disentangled information of multimodal information. Consequently,

minimizing the components that can have a detrimental impact on one another during the fusion process is the key to efficiently merging DTI and fMRI data.

The variational autoencoder (VAE) is one of the most generative methods [41–43] in information fusion by encoding features into latent representations,and the graph convolutional network (GCN) has a strong advantage in constructing topological features. Inspired by the observations, in this paper, a novel hierarchical structural-functional connectivity fusion (HSCF) model is proposed to construct brain structural-functional connectivity matrices and predict abnormal brain connections based on functional magnetic resonance imaging (fMRI) and diffusion tensor imaging (DTI). The main advantages of this paper are the following: (1) The prior knowledge is incorporated into the separators for disentangling each modal information by GCN, which can separate the connectivity information in topological space and is more suitable for downstream fusion. (2) The hierarchical representation fusion module is designed to effectively maximize the combination of relevant and effective features between modalities, which makes the generated structural-functional connectivity more robust and discriminative in the cognitive disease analysis. Comprehensive results on the Alzheimer's Disease Neuroimaging Initiative (ADNI) database show that the performance of the proposed model outperforms other competitive methods in terms of classification tasks.

2   Proposed Method

2.1   Disentangled VAE

The input to our framework is the graph data, where nodes represent the ROIs and edges represent the SC or FC. To simplify the description, we denote the SC and FC as the A_1 and A_2 respectively. Both SC and FC have the dimension size $N \times N$. The N represents the total number of brain regions studied in our study. The prior knowledge refers to the relative volume of anatomical brain regions, and we construct the node feature (NF) by translating each ROI's volume into a one-hot vector. The NF is denoted as X with a size of $N \times N$.

The framework is shown in Fig. 1. The disentangled VAE consists of four separators and four reconstructors. As an example, consider the distangled structural connectivity. The two separators are S_{ss} and S_{su}, where each of them takes A_1 and X as input and outputs the latent variables. The difference is that the former learns the structural-specific component (μ_{ss}, σ_{ss}), while the latter learns the universal component (μ_{su}, σ_{su}). The network structure of them contains three GCN layers: the first two layers have hidden dimensions of 64 and 32, respectively; the last layer has hidden dimensions of 16. Except for the last layer, the $ReLU$ activation function is applied to all GCN layers. The computation procedure can be defined as follows:

$$\mu_{ss}, \sigma_{ss} = S_{ss}(A_1, X); \mu_{su}, \sigma_{su} = S_{su}(A_1, X) \tag{1}$$

$$\mu_{ff}, \sigma_{ff} = S_{ff}(A_2, X); \mu_{fu}, \sigma_{fu} = S_{su}(A_2, X) \tag{2}$$

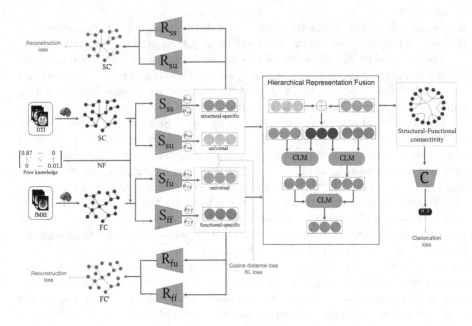

Fig. 1. The framework of the proposed HSCF using DTI and fMRI. It consists of three parts: the encoders, the decoders, and the hierarchical representation fusion.

here, each pair of latent variables has the same dimension $N \times 16$. The latent variable pairs can be considered a standard normal distribution, where we can obtain the latent representations by sampling operations. Supposing that the latent representations are Z_{ss}, Z_{su}, Z_{ff}, and Z_{fu}, we can recover the SC and FC by the reconstructors. The structure of the reconstructor has an N filter with a kernel size of 16×1. The final output is the matrix inner product, followed by a *sigmoid* activation function. The formula can be expressed by:

$$A_1' = 0.5(A_{s1} + A_{s2}) \tag{3}$$

$$A_{s1} = R_{ss}(Z_{ss}), A_{s2} = R_{su}(Z_{su}) \tag{4}$$

$$A_2' = 0.5(A_{f1} + A_{f2}) \tag{5}$$

$$A_{f1} = R_{ff}(Z_{ff}), A_{f2} = R_{fu}(Z_{fu}) \tag{6}$$

2.2   Hierarchical Representation Fusion

The disentangled representations are combined to generate structural-functional connectivity for fusing complementary information. The hierarchical representation fusion (HRF) consists of three stages: (1) fusing the universal representations to obtain phase-1 representation; (2) partially fusing the phase-1 representation with modality-specific representations using connectivity linear mapping (CLM); this stage outputs phase-2 representations; and (3) continuing to incorporate the phase-2 representations to obtain phase-3 representation. The CLM consists of a two-layer multilayer perceptron (MLP). The output dimension of each layer is the same as the latent variable. The generated structural-functional connectivity is defined as:

$$A_m = SFC = HRF(Z_{ss}, Z_{su}, Z_{ff}, Z_{fu}) \tag{7}$$

The classifier C shares the same structure with the work in [33]. The input of C is the generated SFC and NF.

2.3   Loss Functions

The Kullback-Leibler (KL) divergence and reconstruct loss must be monitored during the training process to keep the VAE-based model stable and robust. The generated structural-functional connectivity must be discriminative after disentangling and fusing the fMRI and DTI. We design four hybrid loss functions: the KL loss (L_{kl}), the reconstruct loss (L_{rec}), the distangled cosine distance loss (L_{cos}), and the classification loss (L_{cls}). They are defined as follows:

$$
\begin{aligned}
L_{kl} = &\, KL(Z_{ss}|\mathcal{N}(0,1)) + KL(Z_{su}|\mathcal{N}(0,1)) \\
&+ KL(Z_{ff}|\mathcal{N}(0,1)) + KL(Z_{fu}|\mathcal{N}(0,1))
\end{aligned} \tag{8}
$$

$$L_{rec} = ||A_1' - A_1||_2 + ||A_2' - A_2||_2 \tag{9}$$

$$L_{cos} = \frac{Z_{su} \cdot Z_{fu}}{||Z_{su}|| * ||Z_{fu}||} \tag{10}$$

$$L_{cls} = -y \cdot log(C(A_m)) \tag{11}$$

here, y is the one-hot vector that represents the truth label.

3   Experimental Results

In this study, we selected subjects with both fMRI and DTI from the Alzheimer's Disease Neuroimaging Initiative (ADNI) dataset. Three stages during the AD progression are considered: normal control (NC), early mild cognitive impairment (EMCI), and late mild cognitive impairment (LMCI). To remove the impact of the imbalanced labels, 76 subjects are selected for each stage. The GRETNA and PANDA toolboxes are utilized to preprocess the fMRI and DTI, respectively. Detailed procedures are described in the work [34]. The final outputs of the pre-processing operation are FC and SC.

The model is trained on the Ubuntu 18.04 platform with the TensorFlow tools. The optimization algorithm is Adam, where the weight decay and momentum rates are 0.01 and (0.9, 0.99). Two binary classification tasks (i.e., NC vs. EMCI and EMCI vs. LMCI) are conducted to evaluate the model's performance.

Table 1. Comparison of classification performance using different fMRI-DTI fusing methods(%).

Methods	NC vs. EMCI				EMCI vs. LMCI			
	ACC	SEN	SPE	F1	ACC	SEN	SPE	F1
DCNN	83.55	84.21	82.89	83.66	87.50	86.84	88.15	87.41
MVGCN	87.50	88.15	86.84	87.58	90.78	89.47	92.10	90.66
JNML	88.15	89.47	86.84	88.31	92.10	90.78	93.42	92.00
Ours	**90.78**	**92.10**	**89.47**	**90.90**	**93.42**	**92.10**	**94.73**	**93.33**

Three methods are introduced to compare the classification performance of FC and SC. These methods are as follows: (1) DCNN [44], (2) MVGCN [45], (3) JNML [46], and (4) Ours.

The classification results are presented in Table 1. Our model achieves the best classification performance among the compared methods. The best results for NC vs. EMCI are an ACC value of 90.78%, SEN value of 92.10%, SPE value of 89.47%, and a F1 value of 90.90%; the task of EMCI vs. LMCI yields the best results in terms of ACC (93.42%), SEN (92.10%), SPE (94.73%), and F1 (93.33%). The same phenomenon can be observed by comparing the generated SFC and the empirical SFC. As shown in Fig. 2, the generated SFCs are classified more precisely than the empirical SFCs.

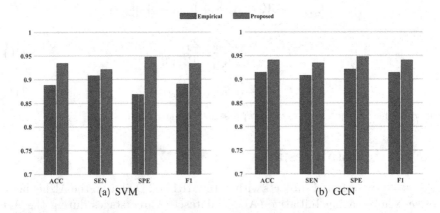

Fig. 2. Classification comparison between the generated and empirical SFCs using (a) SVM classifier, and (b) GCN classifier.

To analyze the MCI-related brain regions and connections, we average the generated SFCs for each group (i.e., NC, EMCI, and LMCI) and compute the connectivity difference between adjacent stages. Positive values indicate increased brain connections, and negative values indicate decreased brain connections. We then select important connections by setting a threshold of 75 percent quantile. These connectivity-related ROIs are displayed in Fig. 3. It shows some

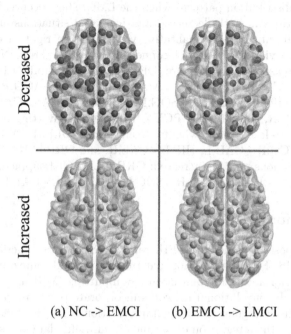

(a) NC -> EMCI   (b) EMCI -> LMCI

Fig. 3. Spatial distribution of important connectivity-related ROIs at different stages of MCI.

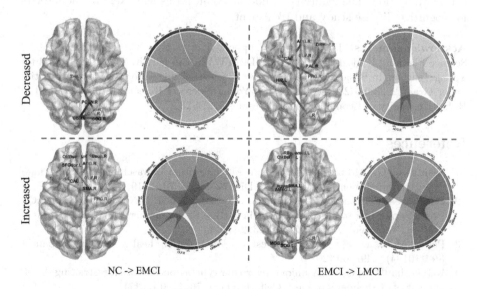

NC -> EMCI   EMCI -> LMCI

Fig. 4. Qualitative and quantitative visualization of top 5 decreased and increased connections.

abnormal ROI distribution patterns when the LMCI stage occurs. In Fig. 4, the top five connections in both decreased and increased situations are presented. The left of each subplot is a qualitative view, and the right of each subplot is a quantitative view with altered connection strength. From NC to EMCI, the top five increased connections are: ORBsup.L - ORBsup.R, PHG.R - TPO-mid.L, ACG.R - CAU.L, SFGdor.L - SMA.R, and OLF.R - ACG.R; the top five decreased connections are: CAL.L - SOG.R, PCUN.R - THA.L, CAL.L - CAL.R, LING.R - PCUN.R, and CUN.L - PCUN.R. Patients converting from EMCI to LMCI are likely to lose the following five connections: OLF.R - ACG.R, PHG.R - TPOmid.L, ACG.R - CAU.L, HIP.L - CAL.R, and ORBinf.R - PAL.R, while five other connections may be increased: ORBsup.L - ORBsupmed.L, AMYG.L - MOG.L, SMA.L - PUT.L, CAL.R - SOG.L, and CAL.L - CAL.R.

4   Conclusion

This study proposes a model named Hierarchical Structural-functional Connectivity Fusing (HSCF) to build brain structural-functional connectivity matrices and forecast abnormal brain connections by inputting fMRI and DTI. In particular, the graph convolutional networks incorporate prior knowledge into the separators for disentangling each modal information. The additional HRF module can maximize the integration of pertinent and useful data across modalities, which makes the generated structural-functional connectivity more reliable and discriminative in the analysis of cognitive diseases. Study results conducted on the public ADNI database reveal the proposed model's effectiveness in classification evaluation. The identified abnormal connections will likely be biomarkers for cognitive disease study and treatment.

Acknowledgements. This work was supported in part by the Guangdong Social Science Planning Project under Grant GD21YWW01, in part by the Special Fund for Young Teachers in Basic Scientific Research Business Expenses of Central Universities under Grant 2023qntd28, in part by the Young Doctoral Research Start-Up Fund of Hubei University of Economics under Grant XJ22BS28.

References

1. Tsentidou, G., Moraitou, D., Tsolaki, M.: Cognition in vascular aging and mild cognitive impairment. J. Alzheimers Dis. **72**(1), 55–70 (2019)
2. Davatzikos, C., Bhatt, P., Shaw, L.M., Batmanghelich, K.N., Trojanowski, J.Q.: Prediction of mci to ad conversion, via MRI, CSF biomarkers, and pattern classification. Neurobiol. Aging **32**(12), 2322 (2011)
3. Peres, M.A., et al.: Oral diseases: a global public health challenge. Lancet **394**(10194), 249–260 (2019)
4. Keren-Shaul, H., et al.: A unique microglia type associated with restricting development of Alzheimer's disease. Cell **169**(7), 1276–1290 (2017)
5. Wang, S.-Q., Li, X., Cui, J.-L., Li, H.-X., Luk, K.D., Hu, Y.: Prediction of myelopathic level in cervical spondylotic myelopathy using diffusion tensor imaging. J. Magn. Reson. Imaging **41**(6), 1682–1688 (2015)

6. Shen, Y., Huang, X., Kwak, K.S., Yang, B., Wang, S.: Subcarrier-pairing-based resource optimization for OFDM wireless powered relay transmissions with time switching scheme. IEEE Trans. Signal Process. **65**(5), 1130–1145 (2016)
7. Gibson, E., et al.: NiftyNet: a deep-learning platform for medical imaging. Comput. Methods Programs Biomed. **158**, 113–122 (2018)
8. Wang, S., Shen, Y., Zeng, D., Hu, Y.: Bone age assessment using convolutional neural networks. In: 2018 International Conference on Artificial Intelligence and Big Data (ICAIBD), pp. 175–178. IEEE (2018)
9. Wang, S., et al.: Skeletal maturity recognition using a fully automated system with convolutional neural networks. IEEE Access **6**, 29979–29993 (2018)
10. Hong, J., et al.: Brain age prediction of children using routine brain MR images via deep learning. Front. Neurol. **11**, 584682 (2020)
11. Wang, S., et al.: An ensemble-based densely-connected deep learning system for assessment of skeletal maturity. IEEE Trans. Syst., Man, Cybern.: Syst. **52**(1), 426–437 (2020)
12. Hu, S., Yu, W., Chen, Z., Wang, S.: Medical image reconstruction using generative adversarial network for Alzheimer disease assessment with class-imbalance problem. In: 2020 IEEE 6th International Conference on Computer and Communications (ICCC), pp. 1323–1327. IEEE (2020)
13. Yu, W., Lei, B., Ng, M.K., Cheung, A.C., Shen, Y., Wang, S.: Tensorizing GAN with high-order pooling for Alzheimer's disease assessment. IEEE Trans. Neural Netw. Learn. Syst. **33**(9), 4945–4959 (2021)
14. Zeng, D., Wang, S., Shen, Y., Shi, C.: A GA-based feature selection and parameter optimization for support tucker machine. Procedia Comput. Sci. **111**, 17–23 (2017)
15. Zuo, Q., Pun, C. M., Zhang, Y., Wang, H., Hong, J.: Multi-resolution spatiotemporal enhanced transformer denoising with functional diffusive gans for constructing brain effective connectivity in MCI analysis. arXiv preprint: arXiv:2305.10754 (2023)
16. Zuo, Q., Lei, B., Shen, Y., Liu, Y., Feng, Z., Wang, S.: Multimodal representations learning and adversarial hypergraph fusion for early Alzheimer's disease prediction. In: Ma, H., et al. (eds.) PRCV 2021. LNCS, vol. 13021, pp. 479–490. Springer, Cham (2021). https://doi.org/10.1007/978-3-030-88010-1_40
17. Wang, S., Shen, Y., Chen, W., Xiao, T., Hu, J.: Automatic recognition of mild cognitive impairment from MRI images using expedited convolutional neural networks. In: Lintas, A., Rovetta, S., Verschure, P.F.M.J., Villa, A.E.P. (eds.) ICANN 2017. LNCS, vol. 10613, pp. 373–380. Springer, Cham (2017). https://doi.org/10.1007/978-3-319-68600-4_43
18. Wang, S., Hu, Y., Shen, Y., Li, H.: Classification of diffusion tensor metrics for the diagnosis of a myelopathic cord using machine learning. Int. J. Neural Syst. **28**(02), 1750036 (2018)
19. Hong, J., Yu, S.C.-H., Chen, W.: Unsupervised domain adaptation for cross-modality liver segmentation via joint adversarial learning and self-learning. Appl. Soft Comput. **121**, 108729 (2022)
20. Lei, B., et al.: Predicting clinical scores for Alzheimer's disease based on joint and deep learning. Expert Syst. Appl. **187**, 115966 (2022)
21. Hirjak, D., et al.: Multimodal magnetic resonance imaging data fusion reveals distinct patterns of abnormal brain structure and function in catatonia. Schizophr. Bull. **46**(1), 202–210 (2020)
22. Zuo, Q., et al.: Brain functional network generation using distribution-regularized adversarial graph autoencoder with transformer for dementia diagnosis (2023)

23. Honey, C.J., et al.: Predicting human resting-state functional connectivity from structural connectivity. Proc. Natl. Acad. Sci. **106**(6), 2035–2040 (2009)
24. Zuo, Q., et al.: Hemisphere-separated cross-connectome aggregating learning via VAE-GAN for brain structural connectivity synthesis. IEEE Access **11**, 48493–48505 (2023)
25. Wang, S., Wang, H., Shen, Y., Wang, X.: Automatic recognition of mild cognitive impairment and Alzheimers disease using ensemble based 3D densely connected convolutional networks. In: 2018 17th IEEE International Conference on Machine Learning and Applications (ICMLA), pp. 517–523. IEEE (2018)
26. Hu, S., Yuan, J., Wang, S.: Cross-modality synthesis from MRI to PET using adversarial U-net with different normalization. In: 2019 International Conference on Medical Imaging Physics and Engineering (ICMIPE), pp. 1–5. IEEE (2019)
27. Wang, S., Wang, H., Cheung, A.C., Shen, Y., Gan, M.: Ensemble of 3D densely connected convolutional network for diagnosis of mild cognitive impairment and Alzheimer's disease. In: Wani, M.A., Kantardzic, M., Sayed-Mouchaweh, M. (eds.) Deep Learning Applications. AISC, vol. 1098, pp. 53–73. Springer, Singapore (2020). https://doi.org/10.1007/978-981-15-1816-4_4
28. Hu, S., Lei, B., Wang, S., Wang, Y., Feng, Z., Shen, Y.: Bidirectional mapping generative adversarial networks for brain MR to pet synthesis. IEEE Trans. Med. Imaging **41**(1), 145–157 (2021)
29. Yu, W., et al.: Morphological feature visualization of Alzheimer's disease via multidirectional perception GAN. IEEE Trans. Neural Netw. Learn. Syst. (2022)
30. You, S. et al.: Fine perceptive GANs for brain MR image super-resolution in wavelet domain. IEEE Trans. Neural Netw. Learn. Syst. (2022)
31. Lei, B., et al.: Diagnosis of early Alzheimer's disease based on dynamic high order networks. Brain Imaging Behav. **15**, 276–287 (2021)
32. Zuo, Q., Lei, B., Zhong, N., Pan, Y., Wang, S.: Brain structure-function fusing representation learning using adversarial decomposed-VAE for analyzing MCI. arXiv preprint: arXiv:2305.14404 (2023)
33. Zuo, Q., Lu, L., Wang, L., Zuo, J., Ouyang, T.: Constructing brain functional network by adversarial temporal-spatial aligned transformer for early AD analysis. Front. Neurosci. **16**, 1087176 (2022)
34. Zuo, Q., Lei, B., Wang, S., Liu, Y., Wang, B., Shen, Y.: A prior guided adversarial representation learning and hypergraph perceptual network for predicting abnormal connections of Alzheimer's disease. arXiv preprint: arXiv:2110.09302 (2021)
35. Zong, Y., Jing, C., Zuo, Q.: Multiscale autoencoder with structural-functional attention network for Alzheimer's disease prediction. In: Yu, S., et al. (eds.) PRCV 2022. Lecture Notes in Computer Science, vol. 13535, pp. 286–297. Springer, Cham (2022)
36. Hong, J., Zhang, Y.-D., Chen, W.: Source-free unsupervised domain adaptation for cross-modality abdominal multi-organ segmentation. Knowl.-Based Syst. **250**, 109155 (2022)
37. Yu, S., et al.: Multi-scale enhanced graph convolutional network for early mild cognitive impairment detection. In: Martel, A.L., et al. (eds.) MICCAI 2020. LNCS, vol. 12267, pp. 228–237. Springer, Cham (2020). https://doi.org/10.1007/978-3-030-59728-3_23
38. Hu, S., Shen, Y., Wang, S., Lei, B.: Brain MR to PET synthesis via bidirectional generative adversarial network. In: Martel, A.L., et al. (eds.) MICCAI 2020. LNCS, vol. 12262, pp. 698–707. Springer, Cham (2020). https://doi.org/10.1007/978-3-030-59713-9_67

39. Liu, L., Wang, Y.-P., Wang, Y., Zhang, P., Xiong, S.: An enhanced multi-modal brain graph network for classifying neuropsychiatric disorders. Med. Image Anal. **81**, 102550 (2022)

40. Zhang, L., et al.: Deep fusion of brain structure-function in mild cognitive impairment. Med. Image Anal. **72**, 102082 (2021)

41. Wang, S.-Q.: A variational approach to nonlinear two-point boundary value problems. Comput. Math. Appl. **58**(11–12), 2452–2455 (2009)

42. Mo, L.-F., Wang, S.-Q.: A variational approach to nonlinear two-point boundary value problems. Nonlinear Anal. Theory Methods Appl. **71**(12), e834–e838 (2009)

43. Kingma, D.P., et al.: An introduction to variational autoencoders. Found. Trends® Mach. Learn. **12**(4), 307–392 (2019)

44. Atwood, J., Towsley, D.: Diffusion-convolutional neural networks. In: Advances in Neural Information Processing Systems, vol. 29 (2016)

45. Zhang, X., He, L., Chen, K., Luo, Y., Zhou, J., Wang, F.: Multi-view graph convolutional network and its applications on neuroimage analysis for Parkinson's disease. In: AMIA Annual Symposium Proceedings, vol. 2018, p. 1147. American Medical Informatics Association (2018)

46. Lei, B., et al.: Self-calibrated brain network estimation and joint non-convex multitask learning for identification of early Alzheimer's disease. Med. Image Anal. **61**, 101652 (2020)

Modulation of Beta Power as a Function of Attachment Style and Feedback Valence

Dor Mizrahi[✉], Ilan Laufer, and Inon Zuckerman

Department of Industrial Engineering and Management, Ariel University, Ariel, Israel
dor.mizrahi1@msmail.ariel.ac.il, {ilan1,inonzu}@ariel.ac.il

Abstract. Attachment theory is concerned with the basic level of social connection associated with approach and withdrawal mechanisms. Consistent patterns of attachment may be divided into two major categories: secure and insecure. As secure and insecure attachment style individuals vary in terms of their responses to affective stimuli and negatively valanced cues, the goal of this study was to examine whether there are differences in Beta power activation between secure and insecure individuals to feedback given while performing the arrow flanker task. An interaction emerged between Attachment style (secure or insecure) and Feedback type (success or failure) has shown differences in Beta power as a function of both independent factors. These results corroborate previous findings indicating that secure and insecure individuals differently process affective stimuli.

Keyword: Attachment theory · EEG · Beta band power · Flanker task

1 Introduction

Attachment theory is concerned with the basic level of social connection associated with approach and withdrawal mechanisms [1–4]. Consistent patterns of attachment may be divided into two major categories: secure and insecure. While the insecure category may be further divided into three separate attachment styles ("anxious preoccupied", "dismissive avoidant" and "fearful avoidant") [2] in this paper we will focus only the main division into the two basic classes, secure and insecure. Previous research indicates that secure and insecure attachment style individuals vary in terms of their responses to affective stimuli and negatively valanced social cues Specifically, the goal of this study is to show differences between secure and insecure attachment styles in Beta power activation in the context of a simple cognitive task, i.e., the arrow flanker task. Beta band power is a frequency range in EEG recordings that typically falls between 12–30 Hz and is associated with cognitive and motor functions.

Previous findings show that the Beta band power is implicated in high-level cognitive processes, such as the processing of affective stimuli and executive function tasks [5, 6]. Hence, we expect to see differences between secure and insecure attachment styles following the valence of the feedback associated with task performance. To that end, we have recorded EEG from participants while they were engaged in performing the flanker task. Then, based on their score on an attachment questionnaire we have compared

F. Liu et al. (Eds.): BI 2023, LNAI 13974, pp. 14–20, 2023.
https://doi.org/10.1007/978-3-031-43075-6_2

between the two classes of secure and insecure attachment based on the relative Beta power extracted from the EEG signals.

2 Experimental Design

The study comprised two stages. In the first stage, 96 participants filled out the ECR-R questionnaires [7], composed of 36 items. In the second stage, based on the analysis of the ECR-R data, 27 players out of the 96 were invited to the EEG lab to conduct the second part of the experiment in such a way as to create an equal sample from all the different attachment style groups. In this stage, players were engaged in performing 60 trials of the arrow flanker task [8] while the EEG was recorded from their scalp]. The experimental protocol was approved by the institution's IRB committee. All participants signed an informed consent form to participate in the study.

2.1 Stage 1–Assessment of Secure and Insecure Attachment Styles Based on the ECR-R

In the first stage, 96 students filled out the ECR-R questionnaire which has two dimensions: anxiety and avoidance. Figure 1(A) shows the distribution of the ECR-R values. The x-axis denotes the avoidance dimension while the y-axis the anxiety dimension. The values of each of the scales range from 1 to 7. Participants who obtain low values in both dimensions of the ECR-R are considered to have a secure attachment style, whereas those participants who obtain high values on both scales are fearful avoidants (or disorganized). Following the results of the distribution of the ECR-R questionnaire, we have clustered the data into the four main attachment styles using the k-means clustering algorithm [9] on the basis of the elbow method [10]. The analysis of the results (Fig. 1A, B) revealed that the optimal number of clusters is k = 4, as can be seen in Fig. 1(B). This number of clusters is in accordance with the four different attachment classifications reported in the scientific literature (e.g. [3]).

In an overview of the clusters appearing in Fig. 1B, it can be seen that the cluster of the green dots represents players characterized by secured attachment, while all other players (denoted by blue, red and purple dots) are considered to be insecure. Noteworthily, the clustering results shown in the scatterplot are corroborated by the distribution of attachment styles in the population [11].

2.2 Stage 2–EEG Recording While Performing Success and Failure Tasks

Twenty-seven participants out of the 36 that were initially recruited participated in the second stage of the study. The distribution of this study population into attachment styles was as follows: 7 belonged to the avoidant group (#0), 6 belonged to the secure group (#1), 9 belonged to the anxious group (#2) and 5 belonged to the fearful avoidant group (#3).

In this stage, the players were engaged in performing the flanker task [12]. One of four possible configurations of the arrow's flanker task (see Fig. 2) was presented for a duration of 1 s. The players were instructed to indicate the direction of a centrally located

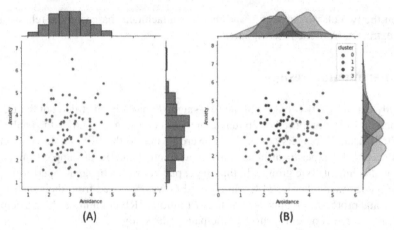

(A)   (B)

Fig. 1. Attachment results of the ECR-R questionnaire. (A) Unclustered results (B) Clustered results

arrow (the target) flanked by non-target stimuli by pressing the corresponding right or left arrow on the keyboard. Each player was presented with 60 flanker trials divided into 3 blocks of 20 trials each. In the first and third blocks, the player had to press the keyboard arrow that was congruent with the direction of the target arrow. However, in the second block, participants had to press the keyboard arrow pointing to the opposite direction of the target. Feedback was provided at the end of each trial by changing the color of the feedback message that appeared on a subsequent slide. For correct trials the word "correct" appeared in green, whereas for incorrect trials the word "incorrect" appeared in red for a duration of 1 s. In between trials, participants were asked to focus their gaze at a gray cross situated in the middle of a black screen, for a random duration of 0.5 to 1.5 s, uniformly distributed.

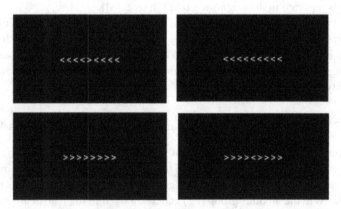

Fig. 2. Possible flanker task screens

The EEG signals were acquired by a 16 channels active EEG amplifier (g.USBAMP, by g.tec, Austria) with a sampling frequency of 512 [Hz] according to the 10–20 international system. Electrode impedance was kept under 5 [Kohm] during the entire experiment and was monitored by the OpenVibe [13] processing and recording software. Participants underwent a training session which allowed them to get familiar with the experimental procedure.

3 Results

Noise and artifacts were removed from the EEG data using a conventional pipeline comprising filtration (band pass [1,32] Hz), re-referencing to the average reference and ICA. Finally, the EEG was divided into 1-s epochs from the onset of feedback (success or failure). Since he frontal lobe electrodes are known to be implicated in cognitive processing we have focused our analyses on the frontal and prefrontal electrodes (Fp1, F7, Fp2, F8, F3 and F7), (e.g., [14–18]) (Fig. 3).

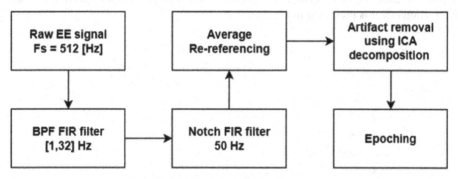

Fig. 3. EEG preprocess scheme

To estimate the relative beta power of each EEG epoch, we have based on the Discrete Wavelet Transform (DWT) [19–22]. The discrete wavelet transform (DWT) is a mathematical tool used in signal processing for analyzing and decomposing signals into different frequency components. The DWT is performed by convolving the signal with a set of wavelet filters that are scaled and translated versions of a mother wavelet function. The resulting coefficients are then down sampled to obtain a lowerresolution version of the signal. This process is repeated iteratively on the lowerresolution signal, generating a multiresolution representation of the signal. In this process, as illustrated in Fig. 4, we inserted an EEG signal with a sampling frequency of 64 Hz, whereby implementing a 3-level DWT, we decomposed it into the four frequency components, Delta, Theta, Alpha, and Beta. We finally calculated the power of each frequency component and normalized them to get the relative energy of each frequency.

A two-way ANOVA with Attachment Style (secure or insecure) and Feedback Type (success or failure) as independent factors and relative Beta power as the dependent variable was computed. The results revealed a statistically significant interaction between attachment style and feedback type ($F (1, 1596) = 8.906$, $p = 0.0109$). Also, simple main

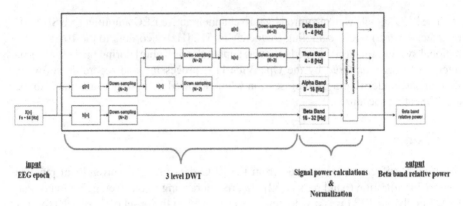

Fig. 4. Beta relative band power extraction scheme

effects analysis showed that Attachment Style and Feedback Type each had a statistically significant effect on EEG relative beta power ($p < 0.001$, $p < 0.05$, respectively). The interaction effect is presented in Fig. 5.

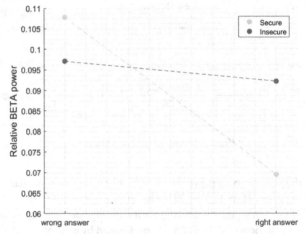

Fig. 5. The interaction between Attachment Style (secure or insecure) and Feedback Type (success or failure)

4   Conclusions and Future Work

In this study we sought to examine whether there are differences in relative Beta band power between secure and insecure attachment style individuals. To that end participants were engaged in performing the arrow flanker task [18 in neuroIS2] and were given feedback (success or failure) following each trial. Since secure and insecure individuals vary in their responses to affective stimuli [5, 6] we investigated the differences in relative Beta band power between secure and insecure attachment styes. For that purpose, we have designed a two-stage experiment. In the first stage, participants filled out an attachment style questionnaire, and those participants that were the best exemplars of secure or insecure attachment also participated in the second stage of the study where they performed the arrow flanker task with feedback while EEG was simultaneously recorded from their scalp. The effect of attachment style (secure, insecure) and feedback type (success or failure) on relative Beta power was examined.

The significant interaction between Attachment style and Feedback Type. In both attachment styles there is a decline in relative Beta power in successful compared to unsuccessful trials. However, the interaction s due to a more rapid decline in the secure attachment style compared to only a moderate decline in the insecure attachment style. Moreover, in unsuccessful trials the average relative Beta power associated with the secure attachment style is higher than the corresponding value of insecure attachment, whereas the opposite trend exists for successful trials. These results corroborate previous findings showing that the Beta power is implicated in differential responses to affective stimuli [37, 38, 40 58 in Memories paper] and that secure and insecure individuals differently process the valence of affective stimuli [23]. Moreover, the relative consistent response associated with the insecure attachment style may suggests that insecure individuals may use a defense mechanism that inhibits a heightened emotional response to a negative valence cue [24].

There are several avenues for future research. First, additional features other than the relative Beta band power of the EEG should be investigated, such as, spatialbased [25], or time domain-based features [26, 27]. Second, a denser network of electrodes could allow investigating the brain sources associated with affective responses of secure and insecure attachment styles. Finally, it would be interesting to utilize machine learning techniques to predict the attachment style based on electrophysiological features in a broader context. For example, a wider range of stimuli could be used to induce the affective responses such as emotional faces and voices.

References

1. Fearon, R.P., Roisman, G.I.: Attachment theory: progress and future directions. Curr. Opin. Psychol. **15**, 131–136 (2017)
2. Hazan, C., Shaver, P.: Romantic love conceptualized as an attachment process. J. Pers. Soc. Psychol. **52**, 511 (1987)
3. Cassidy, J., Shaver, P.R.: Handbook of Attachment: Theory, Research, and Clinical Applications. Rough Guides (2002)
4. Freeman, H., Brown, B.B.: Primary attachment to parents and peers during adolescence: differences by attachment style. J. Youth Adolesc. **30**, 653–674 (2001)
5. Farina, B., et al.: Della: memories of attachment hamper EEG cortical connectivity in dissociative patients. Eur. Arch. Psychiatry Clin. Neurosci. **264**, 449–458 (2014)
6. Nasiriavanaki, Z., et al.: Anxious attachment is associated with heightened responsivity of a parietofrontal cortical network that monitors peri-personal space. NeuroImage Clin. 30, 102585 (2021). AD
7. Fraley, R.C., Waller, N.G., Brennan, K.A.: An item response theory analysis of self-report measures of adult attachment. J. Personal. Soc. Psychol. **78**, 350 (2000)
8. Ridderinkhof, K.R., Wylie, S.A., van den Wildenberg, W.P.M., Bashore, T.R., van der Molen, M.W.: The arrow of time: advancing insights into action control from the arrow version of the Eriksen flanker task. Attention, Percept. Psychophys. **83**, 700–721 (2021)

9. Jain, Anil K.: Data clustering: 50 years beyond K-means. In: Daelemans, W., Goethals, B., Morik, K. (eds.) ECML PKDD 2008. LNCS (LNAI), vol. 5211, pp. 3–4. Springer, Heidelberg (2008). https://doi.org/10.1007/978-3-540-87479-9_3

10. Kodinariya, T.M.: Review on determining number of cluster in K-means clustering. Int. J. Adv. Res. Comput. Sci. Manag. Stud. **1**, 90–95 (2013)

11. Magai, C., Cohen, C., Milburn, N., Thorpe, B., McPherson, R., Peralta, D.: Attachment styles in older European American and African American adults. J. Gerontol. Ser. B Psychol. Sci. Soc. Sci. **56**, S28–S35 (2001)

12. Brunetti, M., Zappasodi, F., Croce, P., Di Matteo, R.: Parsing the Flanker task to reveal behavioral and oscillatory correlates of unattended conflict interference. Sci. Rep. **9**, 1–11 (2019)

13. Renard, Y., et al.: Openvibe: an open-source software platform to design, test, and use brain–computer interfaces in real and virtual environments. Presence Teleoperators Virtual Environ. **19**, 35–53 (2010)

14. Mizrahi, D., Laufer, I., Zuckerman, I.: Topographic analysis of cognitive load in tacit coordination games based on electrophysiological measurements. In: Davis, F.D., Riedl, R., vom Brocke, J., Léger, P.-M., Randolph, A.B., Müller-Putz, G. (eds.) NeuroIS 2021. LNISO, vol. 52, pp. 162–171. Springer, Cham (2021). https://doi.org/10.1007/978-3-030-88900-5_18

15. Gartner, M., Grimm, S., Bajbouj, M.: Frontal midline theta oscillations during mental arithmetic: effects of stress. Front. Behav. Neurosci. **9**, 1–8 (2015)

16. Boudewyn, M., Roberts, B.M., Mizrak, E., Ranganath, C., Carter, C.S.: Prefrontal transcranial direct current stimulation (tDCS) enhances behavioral and EEG markers of proactive control. Cogn. Neurosci. **10**, 57–65 (2019)

17. Laufer, I., Mizrahi, D., Zuckerman, I.: An electrophysiological model for assessing cognitive load in tacit coordination games. Sensors. **22**, 477 (2022)

18. Mizrahi, D., Zuckerman, I., Laufer, I.: the effect of social value orientation on theta to alpha ratio in resource allocation games. Information **14**, 146 (2023)

19. Jensen, A., la Cour-Harbo, A.: Ripples in Mathematics: The Discrete Wavelet Transform. Springer, Heidelberg (2001)

20. Rioul, O., Duhamel, P.: Fast algorithms for discrete and continuous wavelet transforms. IEEE Trans. Inf. theory. **38**, 569–586 (1992)

21. Shensa, M.J.: The discrete wavelet transform: wedding the a trous and Mallat algorithms. IEEE Trans. Signal Process. **40**(10), 2464–2482 (1992)

22. Mizrahi, D., Zuckerman, I., Laufer, I.: Analysis of Alpha Band Decomposition in Different Level-k Scenarios with Semantic Processing. In: Mahmud, M., He, J., Vassanelli, S., van Zundert, A., Zhong, N. (eds.) Brain Informatics. BI 2022. LNCS, vol. 13406, pp. 65–73. Springer, Cham (2022). https://doi.org/10.1007/978-3-031-15037-1_6

23. Grecucci, A., Theuninck, A., Frederickson, J., Job, R.: Mechanisms of social emotion regulation: From neuroscience to psychotherapy. In: Handbook of Emotion Regulation. Nova Publishers (2015)

24. Békés, V., Aafjes-van Doorn, K., Spina, D., Talia, A., Starrs, C.J., Perry, J.C.: The relationship between defense mechanisms and attachment as measured by observer-rated methods in a sample of depressed patients: a pilot study. Front. Psychol. 4152 (2021)

25. Zuckerman, I., Mizrahi, D., Laufer, I.: EEG pattern classification of picking and coordination using anonymous random walks. Algorithms. **15**, 114 (2022)

26. Al-Fahoum, A.S., Al-Fraihat, A.A.: Methods of EEG Signal Features Extraction Using Linear Analysis in Frequency and Time-Frequency Domains. ISRN Neurosci (2014)

27. Mizrahi, D., Laufer, I., Zuckerman, I.: Level-K classification from EEG signals using transfer learning. Sensors. **21**, 7908 (2021)

Harneshing the Potential of EEG in Neuromarketing with Deep Learning and Riemannian Geometry

Kostas Georgiadis[1]([✉]) [iD], Fotis P. Kalaganis[1] [iD], Vangelis P. Oikonomou[1] [iD], Spiros Nikolopoulos[1] [iD], Nikos A. Laskaris[2] [iD], and Ioannis Kompatsiaris[1] [iD]

[1] Centre for Research and Technology Hellas, Information Technologies Institute (ITI), Thermi-Thessaloniki, Greece
kostas.georgiadis@iti.gr
[2] AIIA-Lab, Informatics Dept, AUTH, NeuroInformatics.Group, Thessaloniki, Greece

Abstract. Neuromarketing exploits neuroimaging techniques to study consumers' responses to various marketing aspects, with the goal of gaining a more thorough understanding of the decision-making process. The neuroimaging technology encountered the most in neuromarketing studies is Electroencephalography (EEG), mainly due to its non-invasiveness, low cost and portability. Opposed to typical neuromarketing practices, which rely on signal-power related features, we introduce an efficient decoding scheme that is based on the principles of Riemannian Geometry and realized by means of a suitable deep learning (DL) architecture (i.e., SPDNet). We take advantage of a recently released, multi-subject, neuromarketing dataset to train SPDNet under the close-to-real-life scenario of product selection from a supermarket leaflet and compare its performance against standard tools in EEG-based neuromarketing. The sample covariance is used as an estimator of the 'quasi-instantaneous', brain activation pattern and derived from the multichannel signal recorded while the subject is gazing at a given product. Pattern derivation is followed by proper re-alignment to reduce covariate shift (inter-subject variability) before SPDNet casts its binary decision (i.e., "Buy"-"NoBuy"). The proposed decoder is characterized by sufficient generalizability to derive valid predictions upon unseen brain signals. Overall, our experimental results provide clear evidence about the superiority of the DL-decoder relatively to both conventional neuromarketing and alternative Riemannian Geometry-based approaches, and further demonstrate how neuromarketing can benefit from recent advances in data-centric machine learning and the availability of relevant experimental datasets.

Keywords: Neuromarketing · Riemannian Geometry · Deep Learning · SPDNet · Electroencephalography · BCIs

This work was a part of project NeuroMkt, co-financed by the European Regional Development Fund of the EU and Greek National Funds through the Operational Program Competitiveness, Entrepreneurship and Innovation, under the call RESEARCH CREATE INNOVATE (Project code T2EDK-03661).

F. Liu et al. (Eds.): BI 2023, LNAI 13974, pp. 21–32, 2023.
https://doi.org/10.1007/978-3-031-43075-6_3

1 Introduction

Neuromarketing refers to the field of studying consumer behavior by taking advantage of neuroimaging techniques [16,25]. The conceptualization of neuromarketing by researchers and practitioners is the aftereffect of their efforts to obtain a more thorough understanding regarding the process of consumer decision-making. Neuromarketing's rapid advancement in the recent years is attributed to the credence that traditional marketing practices, such as focus groups, questionnaires, interviews, and behavioral metrics, are insufficient in capturing the wide variety of aspects involved in consumer behavior. Indeed, traditional practices are cost-effective, scalable, and easy to interpret, however, they lack in terms of generalizability and predictive power. As a matter of fact, participants' responses may be inaccurate, unreliable, biased, or influenced by others' opinions (particularly in the case of focus groups) [20].

Electroencephalography (EEG) is the most commonly used neuroimaging method in neuromarketing studies due to its non-invasiveness, portability, cost effectiveness, and high temporal resolution. Although EEG has lower spatial resolution than other neuroimaging technologies, its aforementioned characteristics compensate for this limitation. Neuromarketing is a passive form of Brain-Computer Interface (BCI) that monitors the user's cognitive states, such as attention, mental workload, and memorization, rather than serving as an alternative communication or control pathway, which is the case for active and reactive BCIs (e.g. [13]).

Typically, EEG-based neuromarketing studies employ signal-power related features of neuroscientific intelligibility in order to examine the consumers' responses to marketing stimuli. Among those features, the most commonly anticipated indices are those of approach-withdrawal, mental workload, attention, and memorization. In essence approach-withdrawal (AW) is an index that quantifies the hemispheric asymmetry of α activity in the prefrontal cortex [26]. As AW is a contralateral phenomenon, the increased left or right frontal activity usually indicates the approach and withdrawal effect respectively. Mental workload, which can be interpreted as the effort invested by consumers while making decisions, is quantified by the strength of θ activation in the prefrontal/frontal areas [9]. In a similar manner, the memorization process [26] is known to affect the decision making process as the selection of familiar products is more probable. On the contrary, the attention index is studied both at a single-subject level [1] and at a population level [14], with the latter being widely known as inter-subject correlation. Moreover, the emotional aspect is also considered pivotal in the decision making process and consequently several neuromarketing studies have employed emotional indices in this direction [22]. Finally, there are a series of studies that employ fusion techniques to combine the aforementioned indices (e.g. [14,23]).

Instead of employing naive signal-power features, recent developments in EEG decoding are oriented towards more sophisticated approaches that encapsulate the functional interactions between distinct brain rhythms (i.e. cross-frequency coupling) and the functional dependencies across the distributed cortical networks (by means of various connectivity measures). Among the wide spectrum of functional connectivity estimators spatial covariance matrice (SCM) stands out as the most computationally efficient, since it inherits the advantage of parallel computation (all pairwise relations are recovered within one step) and can be easily adapted for deriving evolving connectivity patterns. SCMs provide a first glance at the underlying correlation networks while simultaneously incorporate signal power features (i.e., the signal energy levels at the individual sensors are tabulated along the main diagonal of the SCM matrix). By exploiting the fact that SCMs are symmetric and positive definite (SPD), principles of Riemannian Geometry can be employed to study and decode EEG signals in their SCM form. Although typical neuromarketing studies usually rely on statistical tests in order to examine the possibility of predicting consumers' responses from EEG features, our recent study [12] demonstrates that Riemannian geometry holds the potential of achieving state of the art results in the field.

In this study, we aim to advance our previous work [12] by combining the strength of Riemannian Geometry with the increasingly-documented, high predictive power of SPDNet [15], a Riemannian geometry-based deep learning architecture. Although SPDNet has been employed with success in the past for several EEG decoding tasks (e.g., motor imagery [19], emotion recognition [27], etc.), this is the first time that it is exploited in the context of neuromarketing. The employment of SPDNet in our work is enabled by a large-scale dataset that was recently made publicly available by our research group and contains multiple trials of multichannel EEG signals from 42 participants, hence, constituting the employment of deep learning approaches both feasible and fruitful.

As demonstrated in the Results sections, our approach is capable of predicting whether a participant would buy or not a particular product solely from EEG activity. In particular, by adopting a Riemannian alignment procedure [29], we manage to tackle this problem in a subject independent manner, which is in direct contrast with the widely adopted strategy of deploying personalized classifiers. The proposed decoder exhibits state of the art performance, that surpasses both conventional Riemannian geometry approaches and typical neuromarketing approaches. This in turn makes our approach more robust and appropriate for practical applications with the potential of minimizing calibration times.

The remainder of this paper is organized as follows: Section 2 describes the selected dataset and the corresponding preprocessing steps, Sect. 3 presents the proposed methodology, Sect. 4 is dedicated to the obtained results, while Sect. 5 discusses the added value and limitations of this work and identifies potential future extensions.

2   NeuMa Dataset and Preprocessing

The NeuMa dataset[1] that includes the experimental data of 42 individuals (23 males - 19 females, aged 31.5 ± 8.84), while browsing a digital supermarket brochure, was selected for the evaluation of the proposed decoding framework. Participants were engaged in a realistic shopping scenario, where they had to

---

[1] https://doi.org/10.6084/m9.figshare.22117124.v3.

select (by pressing the left click) the products they intended to buy. In particular, a series of 6 brochure pages were presented to the participants, each including 24 different products belonging to the same product category. Participants could freely browse among the 6 provided brochure pages, with the selection of products being unrestricted both in terms of quantity and total cost. The process resulted in having all products included in the brochure labeled as "Buy" or "NoBuy" depending on whether the product was selected by the participant or not. Prior to the recording process, subjects were thoroughly informed regarding the experiment and provided their written informed consent (approved by CERTH's Ethical Committee, Ref. No. ETH.COM-68). A more detailed description of the experimental protocol alongside with the corresponding EEG data can be found here [11].

Brain activity was recorded, via 21 dry sensors placed according to the 10–20 International System, namely Fp1, Fp2, Fz, F3, F4, F7, F8, Cz, C3, C4, T7/T3, T8/T4, Pz, P3, P4, P7/T5, P8/T6, O1, O2, A1 and A2 via Wearable Sensing's DSI 24[2]. The sampling frequency was 300 Hz and the impedance for all electrodes was set below $10K\Omega$ prior to the experiment's initiation.

Prior to the analysis, the recorded EEG signals were subjected to a two-stage offline preprocessing. Firstly, raw EEG signals were bandpass filtered within [0.5–45] Hz using a 3rd-order zero-phased Butterworth filter. Then, artifactual activity was removed using in sequence Artifact Subspace Reconstruction (ASR) [21] and FORCe [8].

Besides brain activity, ocular activity was also registered using Tobii Pro Fusion eye tracker, with a sampling frequency of 120 Hz and the eye movement traces were used for the trial definition/segmentation process. More specifically, a single trial is defined as the time a participant was observing a product, which is equivalent to the time the participant's gaze was located within the boundaries of each product image. Single trials of duration less than one second were considered insufficient to convey information about δ brain rhythm and were consequently discarded [6].

3   Methodology

3.1   Riemannian Geometry Preliminaries

Let $\mathbf{X}_i \in \mathbb{R}^{E \times t}, i = 1, \ldots, n$ be a single trial EEG response, also referred to as epoch, where E denotes the number of electrodes and t the number of time samples. Each $\mathbf{X}_i$ is accompanied by a label $y_i \in \{0, 1\}$ that corresponds to two distinct brain states (or performed tasks; in our case corresponding to "Buy"-"NoBuy"). Moving from the time domain, each EEG epoch (assuming zero mean signals) can also be described by the corresponding SCM $\mathbf{C}_i = \frac{1}{t-1}\mathbf{X}_i\mathbf{X}_i^\top \in \mathbb{R}^{E \times E}$, where $(\cdot)^\top$ denotes the transpose operator. By definition and under sufficiently large t to guarantee a full rank covariance matrix, spatial covariance matrices are symmetric positive definite (SPD) that lie on a

---

[2] https://wearablesensing.com/dsi-24/.

Riemannian manifold instead of a vector space (e.g. scalar multiplication does not hold on the SPD manifold).

3.2   Riemannian Alignment

While SCMs can provide information rich representations regarding EEG responses, their relative placement over the Riemannian manifold may significantly differ among subjects and even recording sessions of the same subject. In detail, it is possible for a subject's SCMs to be concentrated at a different area over the same manifold. This problem, usually referred as the covariate shift phenomenon, can significantly harness the performance of deep learning architectures, like SPDNet. To alleviate this problem Zanini et al. [29] proposed a Riemannian alignment process, that in essence re-alings all SCMs around the same reference point. Consequently, the alignment process requires the identification of a unique reference point in the Riemannian manifold, known as center of mass (or geometric mean) for a given set of SCMs. This point is being identified by minimizing the sum of squared Affine Invariant Riemannian Metric (AIRM)-induced distances [24] (which offers equivalence between the sensor and the source space) as follows, with an iterative process (due to the lack of a closed form solution) and is known as the Karcher/Fréchet mean [3]:

$$\bar{\mathbf{B}} = argmin_{\mathbf{P}\in Sym_s^+} \sum_{i=1}^{n} \delta^2(\mathbf{C_i}, \mathbf{P}) \tag{1}$$

where n denotes the number of SCMs, δ refers to the AIRM-induced Riemannian distance and $\mathbf{P}$ being any given point residing on Riemannian manifold.

Finally, once the center of mass has been identified (Eq. 1), each SCM can now be re-alligned as follows:

$$\mathbf{C}_i^A = \bar{\mathbf{B}}^{-1/2}\mathbf{C}_i\bar{\mathbf{B}}^{-1/2} \tag{2}$$

3.3   The SPDNet Architecture

As its name states, SPDNet is a deep learning architecture designed for processing data represented as SPD matrices [15]. The SPDNet architecture is based on the idea of representing SPD matrices as points on a Riemannian manifold, which is a space that can be locally treated as an Euclidean space but has a nontrivial global structure. The key idea behind SPDNet is that the convolution and pooling operations are performed on the Riemannian manifold rather than in Euclidean space. This allows the architecture to take into account the intrinsic geometry of SPD matrices when processing them. In the following, the main components of SPDNet are briefly described, while a more detailed description can be found here [15]:

– BiMap Layer: A special type of layer that is designed to preserve the Riemannian structure of SPD matrices while reducing their dimensionality.

- ReEig Layer: A layer designed to improve performance by introducing a non-linearity.
- LogEig Layer: A layer that maps the input SPD matrices onto an Euclidean space.
- A fully connected layer that maps the output of the previous layer to the desired output.

The BiMap layer transforms the input SPD matrices into new SPD matrices by means of a bilinear mapping. In more detail, this layer applies a transformation matrix $\mathbf{W}$ to the input SPD matrix, $\mathbf{C}$, using the bilinear mapping $\mathbf{WCW}^{\top}$. This mapping results in dimensionaly reduced SPD matrices. In order to ensure that the resulting output will maintain the SPD property of the input matrix while being dimensionaly reduced, $\mathbf{W}$ is required to be a row full-rank matrix. In essence, the BiMap Layer can be considered as a special type of pooling layer in the SPDnet architecture that uses bilinear pooling to preserve the Riemannian structure of SPD matrices while reducing their dimensionality.

The ReEig layer applies diagonalization to SPD matrices by computing the eigendecomposition of each matrix. However, instead of applying any other non-linear function to the eigenvalues, the ReEig layer applies a ReLU (Rectified Linear Unit) activation function to the eigenvalues. The ReLU function is a commonly used activation function in deep learning that has been shown to improve the performance of neural networks. It simply sets all negative values to zero, while leaving positive values unchanged. In the context of SPD matrices, applying the ReLU function to the eigenvalues has the effect of setting all close-to-zero eigenvalues to a positive value. This has the advantage of enforcing strong positive definiteness on the diagonalized matrices while introducing a non-linearity in order to increase the networks performance.

The LogEig layer performs the logarithmic mapping of the input SPD data. This mapping converts the SPD matrix to a tangent space vector (typically at the Identity matrix) by applying the logarithm operation at the eigenvalues of the SPD matrix. Such an operation can be thought of as a vector that describes how the SPD matrix deviates from the identity matrix. Among the useful properties of the logarithmic mapping (e.g., distance preservation and invariance to affine transformations), it is employed in the context of machine learning since it essentially reduces the SPD manifold to a flat space where Euclidean operation can be deployed.

The fully connected layer in SPDnet is a standard layer that is commonly used in neural networks. However, unlike the fully connected layer in a standard feedforward neural network, the fully connected layer in SPDnet operates on the vectorized form of the input SPD matrices, rather than on the raw feature vectors. In other words, the input to the fully connected layer in SPDnet is a vectorized SPD matrix, which is obtained by flattening the matrix into a vector. The fully connected layer then applies a matrix multiplication to this vector, followed by a bias term and an activation function. The output of this layer is a vector of activations that can be passed to the next layer in the network. The fully connected layer in SPDnet is typically used as the final layer in the network, where it maps the low-dimensional SPD matrix representations obtained from the previous layers to the desired output space. However, in our setting considering that we are dealing with a classification task, the final layer of the employed architecture is a softmax layer. Finally, we note that the network was trained using a stochastic gradient descent optimization algorithm on Stiefel manifolds, as proposed in [15].

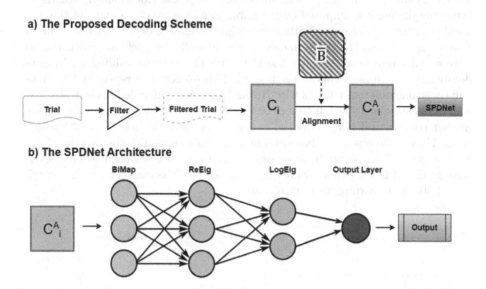

Fig. 1. The proposed decoding scheme (a), and the employed SPDNet architecture (b).

3.4   The Proposed Decoding Framework for Neuromarketing

The proposed decoder brings the Riemannian related notions and the deep learning architecture of SPDNet described in the previous subsections into the neuromarketing EEG setting. It aims to differentiate the consumers' brain activity between the state during which a product is selected and the opposite state. Figure 1 graphically illustrates the proposed decoding pipeline and the SPDNet architecture in the upper and lower panel respectively. In some detail, all single trials (i.e. trials from all subjects) are first bandpass filtered within 1–45 Hz, aiming to capture the entire spectrum of brain states (e.g., approach/withdrawal and memorization) that can affect the decision making process [16]. Then SCMs are formulated and re-aligned within the Riemannian manifold as described in Subsects. 3.1 and 3.2 respectively. Finally, SPDnet is employed to process the corresponding re-aligned SPD representations for each instantiation of the train/test split. It is important to note here, that while for the training data the alignment process can be easily performed using Eq. (2), the process is not as straightforward regarding the test data, as SCMs arising from the test set must be firstly placed within a pre-learned embedding using the "out of sample extension" algorithm [2].

4   Results

The proposed decoder was trained on SCMs derived from Neuma dataset. Its efficiency and efficacy is demonstrated under a dichotomic, "Buy"-"NoBuy", scenario. A 10-fold cross validation scheme was employed for its thorough evaluation. In this validation scheme, the dataset is being split into ten equal parts and iteratively one part is being used for testing purposes. Additionally, aiming to overcome the barriers imposed by the unbalanced nature of the dataset (i.e. the number of trials labeled as "NoBuy" was higher than the ones labeled as "Buy") that would harness the performance of any classification scheme, both classes were equally represented before the initiation of the cross validation, by randomly sub-sampling the majority class [5]. This process was repeated 100 times and each time different trials of the "NoBuy" class were included in the train/test split. This approach was followed in order to ensure that the obtained results are neither coincidental nor attributed to the particular selection of the "NoBuy" trials. Hence, the reported classification results correspond to the average of the aforementioned procedure, leading ultimately to a fair evaluation scheme. Concerning the SPDNet hyperparameters we note that it is employed with a batch size of 30 and a learning rate set to 0.01.

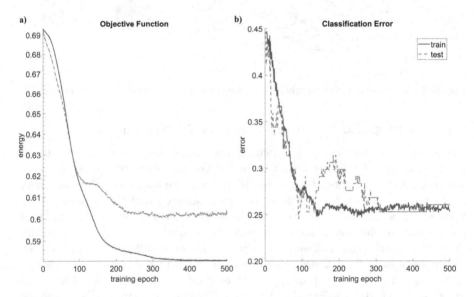

Fig. 2. (a) The convergence curve for the proposed decoding scheme and (b) the corresponding error/accuracy curve.

Figure 2 showcases the accuracy curve and convergence curve of the proposed decoding scheme for an indicative instatiation of the 10-fold cross validation scheme. It is evident that after a few training epochs the decoder's performance is stabilized between 70% and 75% and that it can converge well approximately within the same number of epoches (i.e. the classification error becomes stable only when the objective function is also stabilized). It is important to note here that similar trends are also observed in the majority of the train/test instatiations, therefore it is safe to assume that approximately 300 epochs would suffice for the training process.

Figure 3 presents the classification accuracy for the "Buy"-"NoBuy" scenario for the proposed decoder and, in addition, for a classifier that incorporates well-established neuromarketing EEG-based indices and two other popular Riemannian Geometry classifiers [7,18]. In the former case typical features, like approach-withdrawal and attention, were fused and fed to a Support Vector Machine (SVM), with the approach being referred as EEG-Fusion [14]. In the latter case, the R-kNN (Riemannian k-nearest neighbor: similarly to the classical kNN examines the geodesic distances between SCMs) and the Tangent Space SVM (that classifies SCMs in the Euclidean tangent space delineated by the barycenter of all the SCMs) are used.

It is apparent, that the only approach that can be characterized as competitive to the proposed decoding scheme is the Tangent Space SVM, that reaches a mean accuracy of 67.72% compared to the 72.18% accuracy of the proposed decoder, with the observed difference being statistically significant at a P-value of 0.01. The rest of the approaches employed for comparisons are significantly outperformed by the proposed decoding scheme and their performance cannot be characterized as competitive, considering that both barely surpass the random level. In detail, the EEG-Fusion approach yields an accuracy of 52.75%, while the corresponding accuracy for the R-kNN is 51.96%.

5   Discussion

Riemannian Geometry receives continuously increasing attention within the signal processing and machine learning communities, as the provided framework for processing SCMs alleviates a series of problems, like non-stationarity or subject/session variability, encountered in typical signal analytic pipelines. Within the same context, the adaptation of the information-rich SCM descriptors and consequently of Riemannian geometry concepts by the neuroscientific community has led to the design of robust brain decoding schemes.

Despite the well documented potential of the Riemannian Geometry, its application in neuromarketing-related data remains limited. This alongside with the findings of our recent paper [12] that showcased the potential of Riemannian geometry to achieve state of the art performance on neuromarketing data, fueled the present study. In particular, we examined here the conceptual blending of Riemmanian geometry with deep learning, as realized in SPDNet with the scope of designing a robust decoding scheme that can detect the preferences of consumers. The proposed decoder was introduced in the binary setting of the "Buy"-"NoBuy" scenario, with the former referring to products that were selected (i.e. bought) and the latter to the ones that were dismissed. By exploiting an information-rich multi-subject dataset (i.e. a total of 42 subjects), in

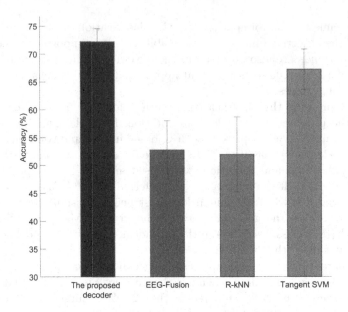

Fig. 3. Classification performance in the "Buy"-"NoBuy" scenario.

conjunction with Riemannian alignment process (see Subsect. 3.2), the feasibility of reliable decoding was demonstrated for the SPDNet. The proposed decoder outperformed standard classifiers operating within the Riemannian framework and a classifier that operates on standard neuromarketing descriptors. Moreover, the added value of proposed decoder stems from the fact that it can be characterized as global, considering that it operates on EEG data from several subjects opposed to previous studies where personalized decoding schemes that lack generalizability are explored (e.g. [9,12]).

At this point, it is important to note that only one dataset was selected for the validation of the proposed decoder. This decision was imposed by the scarcity of publicly available neuromarketing datasets, as to the best of our knowledge, besides the selected dataset there are only two extra datasets that can be freely accessed [14,28]. However, both datasets, include a limited amount of trials that constitute the use of SPDNet impractical without employing proper data augmentation procedures (e.g. [17]). Therefore, the generation of artificial data and its incorporation in the proposed decoding pipeline could be considered as potential future extensions of this study.

Another potential future extension of this work could be the reduction of the SCMs' size, by identifying and selecting the most informative subset of sensors (e.g. [10,18]) or by combining sensors' information via approaches like spatial filters [4]. This could not only lead to improved performance but also to fastest computations, and consequently decreased computational cost. In the same direction, frequency ranges that may carry more descriminative information regarding the SCM formulation can be explored. Finally, exploring the potential of the proposed decoder in a multi-class scenario would be also particularly interesting. The modification steps required to do so seem feasible, as the generated SCMs (for all classes) will reside in a common Riemannian manifold and SPDNet is capable of handling efficiently data arising from multiple classes.

References

1. Ali, A., et al.: EEG signals based choice classification for neuromarketing applications. In: Kumar, P., Obaid, A.J., Cengiz, K., Khanna, A., Balas, V.E. (eds.) A Fusion of Artificial Intelligence and Internet of Things for Emerging Cyber Systems. ISRL, vol. 210, pp. 371–394. Springer, Cham (2022). https://doi.org/10.1007/978-3-030-76653-5_20
2. Bengio, Y., Paiement, J.f., Vincent, P., Delalleau, O., Roux, N., Ouimet, M.: Out-of-sample extensions for LLE, isomap, MDS, eigenmaps, and spectral clustering. In: Advances in Neural Information Processing Systems, vol. 16 (2003)
3. Bini, D.A., Iannazzo, B.: Computing the Karcher mean of symmetric positive definite matrices. Linear Algebra Appl. **438**(4), 1700–1710 (2013)
4. Blankertz, B., Tomioka, R., Lemm, S., Kawanabe, M., Muller, K.R.: Optimizing spatial filters for robust EEG single-trial analysis. IEEE Signal Process. Mag. **25**(1), 41–56 (2007)
5. Branco, P., Torgo, L., Ribeiro, R.P.: A survey of predictive modeling on imbalanced domains. ACM Comput. Surv. (CSUR) **49**(2), 1–50 (2016)
6. Cohen, M.X.: Analyzing Neural Time Series Data: Theory and Practice. MIT press, Cambridge (2014)
7. Congedo, M., Barachant, A., Bhatia, R.: Riemannian geometry for EEG-based brain-computer interfaces; a primer and a review. Brain-Comput. Interfaces **4**(3), 155–174 (2017)
8. Daly, I., Scherer, R., Billinger, M., Müller-Putz, G.: Force: fully online and automated artifact removal for brain-computer interfacing. IEEE Trans. Neural Syst. Rehabil. Eng. **23**(5), 725–736 (2014)
9. García-Madariaga, J., Moya, I., Recuero, N., Blasco, M.F.: Revealing unconscious consumer reactions to advertisements that include visual metaphors. a neurophysiological experiment. Front. Psychol. **11**, 760 (2020)
10. Georgiadis, K., Adamos, D.A., Nikolopoulos, S., Laskaris, N., Kompatsiaris, I.: A graph-theoretic sensor-selection scheme for covariance-based motor imagery (MI) decoding. In: 2020 28th European Signal Processing Conference (EUSIPCO), pp. 1234–1238. IEEE (2021)
11. Georgiadis, K., Kalaganis, F.P., Riskos, K. et al.: NeuMa - the absolute neuromarketing dataset en route to an holistic understanding of consumer behaviour. Sci. Data **10**, 508 (2023). https://doi.org/10.1038/s41597-023-02392-9
12. Georgiadis, K., Kalaganis, F.P., Oikonomou, V.P., Nikolopoulos, S., Laskaris, N.A., Kompatsiaris, I.: Rneumark: a Riemannian EEG analysis framework for neuromarketing. Brain Inform. **9**(1), 22 (2022)
13. Georgiadis, K., Laskaris, N., Nikolopoulos, S., Kompatsiaris, I.: Exploiting the heightened phase synchrony in patients with neuromuscular disease for the establishment of efficient motor imagery bcis. J. Neuroeng. Rehabil. **15**(1), 1–18 (2018)
14. Hakim, A., Klorfeld, S., Sela, T., Friedman, D., Shabat-Simon, M., Levy, D.J.: Machines learn neuromarketing: improving preference prediction from self-reports using multiple EEG measures and machine learning. Int. J. Res. Mark. **38**(3), 770–791 (2021)

15. Huang, Z., Van Gool, L.: A Riemannian network for SPD matrix learning. In: Proceedings of the AAAI Conference on Artificial Intelligence, vol. 31 (2017)
16. Kalaganis, F.P., Georgiadis, K., Oikonomou, V.P., Laskaris, N.A., Nikolopoulos, S., Kompatsiaris, I.: Unlocking the subconscious consumer bias: a survey on the past, present, and future of hybrid EEG schemes in neuromarketing. Front. Neuroergonomics **2**, 11 (2021)
17. Kalaganis, F.P., Laskaris, N.A., Chatzilari, E., Nikolopoulos, S., Kompatsiaris, I.: A data augmentation scheme for geometric deep learning in personalized brain-computer interfaces. IEEE Access **8**, 162218–162229 (2020)
18. Kalaganis, F.P., Laskaris, N.A., Chatzilari, E., Nikolopoulos, S., Kompatsiaris, I.: A Riemannian geometry approach to reduced and discriminative covariance estimation in brain computer interfaces. IEEE Trans. Biomed. Eng. **67**(1), 245–255 (2019)
19. Kobler, R., Hirayama, J.i., Zhao, Q., Kawanabe, M.: SPD domain-specific batch normalization to crack interpretable unsupervised domain adaptation in EEG. In: Advances in Neural Information Processing Systems, vol. 35, pp. 6219–6235 (2022)
20. MacKenzie, S.B., Podsakoff, P.M.: Common method bias in marketing: causes, mechanisms, and procedural remedies. J. Retail. **88**(4), 542–555 (2012)
21. Mullen, T.R., et al.: Real-time neuroimaging and cognitive monitoring using wearable dry EEG. IEEE Trans. Biomed. Eng. **62**(11), 2553–2567 (2015)
22. Naser, D.S., Saha, G.: Influence of music liking on EEG based emotion recognition. Biomed. Signal Process. Control **64**, 102251 (2021)
23. Oikonomou, V.P., Georgiadis, K., Kalaganis, F., Nikolopoulos, S., Kompatsiaris, I.: A sparse representation classification scheme for the recognition of affective and cognitive brain processes in neuromarketing. Sensors **23**(5), 2480 (2023)
24. Pennec, X., Fillard, P., Ayache, N.: A Riemannian framework for tensor computing. Int. J. Comput. Vision **66**, 41–66 (2006)
25. Rawnaque, F.S., et al.: Technological advancements and opportunities in neuromarketing: a systematic review. Brain Inform. **7**, 1–19 (2020)
26. Vecchiato, G., et al.: Neurophysiological tools to investigate consumer's gender differences during the observation of tv commercials. Comput. Math. Methods Med. **2014** (2014)
27. Wang, Y., Qiu, S., Ma, X., He, H.: A prototype-based SPD matrix network for domain adaptation EEG emotion recognition. Pattern Recogn. **110**, 107626 (2021)
28. Yadava, M., Kumar, P., Saini, R., Roy, P.P., Prosad Dogra, D.: Analysis of EEG signals and its application to neuromarketing. Multimedia Tools Appl. **76**, 19087–19111 (2017)
29. Zanini, P., Congedo, M., Jutten, C., Said, S., Berthoumieu, Y.: Transfer learning: a Riemannian geometry framework with applications to brain-computer interfaces. IEEE Trans. Biomed. Eng. **65**(5), 1107–1116 (2017)

A Model of the Contribution of Interneuron Diversity to Recurrent Network Oscillation Generation and Information Coding

Gabriel Matías Lorenz[1,2,3]([✉]) [iD], Pablo Martínez-Cañada[4] [iD], and Stefano Panzeri[1,3] [iD]

[1] Istituto Italiano di Tecnologia, Rovereto, Italy
gabriel.lorenz@iit.it
[2] Department of Pharmacy and Biotechnology, University of Bologna, Bologna, Italy
[3] Department of Excellence for Neural Information Processing, University Medical Center Hamburg-Eppendorf (UKE), Hamburg, Germany
s.panzeri@uke.de
[4] Department of Computer Engineering, Automation and Robotics, University of Granada, Granada, Spain
pablomc@ugr.es

Abstract. Spiking neural network models that have studied how oscillations are generated by recurrent cortical circuits and how they encode information have been focused on describing the encoding of information about external sensory stimuli carried by feed-forward inputs in a two-population circuit configuration that includes excitatory cells and fast-spiking interneurons. Here we extend these models to explore the contribution of different classes of cortical interneurons to cortical oscillations. We found that in our extended model, the feed-forward stimulus is still mainly encoded in the gamma frequency range, consistent with earlier works using a single interneuron type. However, we also found that the information carried by different regions of the gamma frequency range was larger than the sum of the information carried by the two individual frequencies. This shows that the power values at different frequencies carried information about the feedforward input in a synergistic way. This is in contrast to previous models with only one interneuron type, which mainly led to redundant information between frequencies in the gamma range. These results suggest that interneuron diversity has useful properties for enriching the encoding of information in the gamma frequency range.

Keywords: Local Field Potential · Neural Circuit · Neural Network Model · Adaptive Exponential Integrate-and-Fire Neuron Model

1 Introduction

Oscillations are a ubiquitous feature of neural activity, which are thought to serve several important brain functions [5,9,10,23,30]. One of the functions that have been imputed to oscillations is the participation in the encoding of information from the sensory environment. Several experimental studies have demonstrated that cortical oscillations, especially in sensory areas, encode sensory information by modulating their power as a function of the sensory stimuli [4,5,18,19]. Especially in visual cortices, the most information is carried by the power of gamma-band (40–100 Hz) oscillations. Experimental evidence [11] shows that the generation of these oscillations within recurrent circuits mainly relies on fast-spiking parvalbumin-expressing (PV) inhibitory neurons and their interaction with excitatory pyramidal neurons. Previous theoretical and computational studies of gamma oscillations typically included excitatory neurons and a single type of inhibitory neurons. The model of this inhibitory neuron did not specify or differentiate the type of interneuron being modeled, but that was loosely matched to the properties of fast-spiking PV neurons. These models could explain the generation of gamma oscillations exhibiting realistic spectral features, and could also explain the privileged encoding of information from the sensory periphery by the power of activity in the gamma band [3,8,10,16,24,25].

Despite its success, recurrent network modeling based on a single undifferentiated interneuron type ignores the contribution of individual interneuron cell types to cortical oscillations and information coding. Besides the fast-spiking PV neurons considered above, these interneuron types include somatostatin-expressing (SOM) and vasoinstestinal peptide-expressing (VIP) neurons [14].

In this work, we address these questions about the role of different interneuron types in network-level oscillatory information coding by extending previous modeling work on information encoding by recurrent networks [12,25]. Specifically, we develop a recurrent network model containing excitatory neurons and SOM and VIP, as well as PV interneurons (Fig. 1). We then analyze the behavior of this model to understand how the interaction between these types of neurons affects oscillations and their encoding of information. Using a conductance-based spiking neural network model adapted from [20], we computed the local field potential (LFP) and measured the mutual information between the external stimuli and the power generated by the network at each frequency.

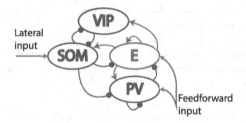

Fig. 1. The network is composed of 500 neurons (400 excitatory neurons, 50 PV neurons, 25 SOM neurons, and 25 VIP neurons). There are two types of input that we change across simulations: a feed-forward excitatory input to E and PV neurons and a lateral one only targeting SOM neurons. There is also a background input that is kept constant across simulations

2 Methods

2.1 Network Model

We implemented a spiking network of a recurrent cortical circuit that follows the characteristics of mouse visual cortex V1 [20,31]. Besides the excitatory pyramidal population (E), we included three distinct inhibitory neurons. Parvalbumin-expressing neurons (PV) have strong recurrent connections within themselves and excitatory neurons. Somatostatin-expressing (SOM) neurons inhibit all neuron types except themselves, are preferentially excited by horizontal cortical connections [1] and have a causal role in feedback- and horizontal-mediated suppression [1,2,36,37]. Vasointestinal peptide-expressing (VIP) neurons form the third largest population of inhibitory cell subtypes and preferentially inhibit SOM neurons.

Besides the inputs from recurrent connectivity, neurons in the network receive also an external stimulus signal S mimicking the effect of feedforward sensory inputs from the thalamus that targets E and PV neurons. We also include a lateral input rate that only targets SOM neurons [1,31]. Both the stimulus and the lateral input were implemented as a Poisson process (240 Poisson sources) with a time-independent rate. The spike rate of the feed-forward input varied from 2 to 8 Hz/cell with steps of 2 Hz/cell and the lateral input was set to either to 2 or 4 Hz/cell.

The neurons were simulated using an adaptive exponential integrate-and-fire (aEIF) neuron model. This model is a relatively simple one, yet it reproduces the experimental qualitative properties of gamma oscillations and the different firing patterns of cortical dynamics [7,8]. The following equation defines the evolution of the membrane potential V:

$$C\frac{dV}{dt} = I(t) - w(t) - g_L \cdot (V(t) - E_L) + g_L \cdot \Delta_T \cdot e^{\frac{V(t)-V_{th}}{\Delta_T}}. \qquad (1)$$

We took the parameter values from [7,20]. The resting membrane potential E_L was set to -60 mV. The membrane capacitance C was set to 180 pF in excitatory neurons and 80 pF in inhibitory neurons. The leak conductance g_L is set as 6.25 nS in excitatory neurons and 5 nS in inhibitory neurons. The slope parameter Δ_T was set to 0.25 mV for PV neurons and 1 mV otherwise. The threshold potential V_{th} was set to -45 mV in excitatory neurons and -40 mV in all three types of inhibitory neurons.

The adaptation variable $w(t)$ evolved according to the following equation

$$\tau_w \frac{dw}{dt} = a(V(t) - E_L) - w(t), \qquad (2)$$

where τ_w was set to 150 ms, and a to 4 nS [7]. Whenever the membrane potential reached 20 mV, a spike event was detected, the membrane potential was set to the reset voltage $V_{reset} = -70$ mV and the neuron did not spike for a refractory period of $t_{ref} = 2$ ms. The spike event also increases w by an amount $b = 80$ pA [7]. In the case of PV neurons, the adaptation w is set to zero [15].

The synaptic currents were modeled as $I_{syn} = g_{syn}(t) \cdot (V(t) - E_{syn})$, where $g_{syn}(t)$ is the synaptic conductance and E_{syn} is the reversal potential. The conductance $g_{syn}(t)$ was modeled as a double exponential (beta synapses) [33]:

$$g(t) = \frac{g_0}{\tau_d - \tau_r} \left(e^{-\frac{t-\tau_l}{\tau_d}} - e^{-\frac{t-\tau_l}{\tau_r}} \right), \tag{3}$$

where τ_l is the latency time, set to 1 ms. The time constants τ_r and τ_d are the rise and decay times of the post-synaptic conductance. For connections from pyramidal and PV neurons, τ_r is set to 0.5 ms, and 1 ms otherwise. The decay time τ_d was set to 2 ms for connections from pyramidal neurons, 3 ms for PV neurons, and 4 ms otherwise. The values of g_0 were chosen to match the post-synaptic current amplitudes in the visual cortex [20,31] and are reported in Table 1.

Table 1. Table of the conductance values for each connection between two populations. The values are set in nS and the columns indicate the population of the presynaptic neuron and the rows, the post-synaptic one.

	E	PV	SOM	VIP
E	1.66	136.4	68.2	0
PV	5.0	136.4	45.5	0
SOM	0.83	0	0	136.4
VIP	1.66	27.3	113.6	0

The network model was adapted from [20], removing for simplicity the orientation tuning and synaptic plasticity. It comprises 500 neurons: 400 pyramidal, 50 PV neurons, 25 SOM neurons, and 25 VIP neurons. The probability of connection between neurons belonging to different population classes is shown in Table 2, chosen in accordance with connectivity measurements in visual cortex [20,31].

Table 2. Table of the connection probability for any pair of neurons between two populations. The columns indicate the population of the presynaptic neuron and the rows, the post-synaptic one.

	E	PV	SOM	VIP
E	0.1	0.6	0.6	0
PV	0.6	0.6	0.6	0
SOM	0.6	0	0	0.4
VIP	0.6	0.1	0.6	0

The neurons in the network receive a third type of input that we named background input. The background input targets all neurons in the network model and sets the network in a regime of minimal spiking and gamma band oscillations, made by a constant input rate plus noise. The constant input rates are set as $(r_{0E}, r_{0P}, r_{0S}, r_{0V}) = (2.0, 0.33, 0.66, 0.25)$ Hz/cell. The noise was set as a slow-varying Ornstein-Uhlenbeck process, whose power spectrum is constant until 10 Hz, after which it decays.

For all three types of inputs, the random Poisson sources generating the stochastic input made excitatory synapses to the network's neurons with the same synaptic parameters that we used for the excitatory recurrent synapses.

For each combination of feed-forward and lateral stimulus values, we generated 50 simulations of 2.5 s with a time step of 0.1 ms using the NEST simulator module in Python [17]. The first half second of the simulations was discarded to ensure stationary dynamics.

Cortical oscillations are usually measured with Local Field Potentials (LFPs) [16]. However, LFPs are generated mostly by dendrosomatic dipoles whose computation cannot be obtained by our point-like neurons because generating these dipoles would require spatially extended neurons. However, we have demonstrated in previous work that the LFP generated by a network can be approximated simply and with high accuracy (approximately 90% of variance) by the sum of the absolute values of the synaptic current of all types of neurons, both excitatory and inhibitory [23, 25]. This proxy is based on the geometrical arrangement of the pyramidal neurons in the cortex [9, 22–25]. We thus computed LFPs from our simulated network of point-like neurons using this proxy.

2.2   Information-Theoretic and Spectral Analysis of Simulated Network Activity

For each simulation, we computed the power spectral density (PSD) of the LFP signal with the multitaper method using the Chronux package [26].

We used mutual information [13, 35] to measure the information about the stimulus carried by the LFP power at each frequency f. Mutual information between a stimulus feature S and the LFP power at a given frequency R_f is defined as follows:

$$I(S; R_f) = \sum_s \sum_{r_f} P(r_f, s) \log_2 \frac{P(r_f, s)}{P(r_f)P(s)}. \tag{4}$$

where $P(r_f, s)$ is the joint probability of presenting stimulus s and observing response r_f, and $P(r_f)$, $P(s)$ are the marginal probabilities. For the numerical evaluation, following our previous work [23], we binned computed probabilities by binning the responses in 3 equi-populated bins [21], and by using a Panzeri-Treves bias correction [28, 29] to remove the sampling bias. To study how different frequency bands complemented each other for information coding, we also computed (in similar ways) the information $I(S; R_{f_1}, R_{f_2})$ that was jointly encoded by the observation of the power at two different frequencies f_1 and f_2. To understand if power at different bands carried similar or different information about the stimulus, we also calculated their information synergy, defined as the difference between the information jointly carried by two frequencies and the sum of the information carried by the different frequencies, as follows [27,32,34]:

$$Syn(R_{f_1}, R_{f_2}) = I(S; R_{f_1}, R_{f_2}) - I(S; R_{f_1}) - I(S; R_{f_2}). \tag{5}$$

Note that this quantity is also termed Co-Information [6,38]. Unlike more sophisticated quantities based on the Partial Information Decomposition [6,38], it computes the total effect or synergy vs redundancy without further tearing apart the two. If $Syn(R_{f_1}, R_{f_2})$ is negative, then the responses at frequencies f_1 and f_2 are carrying predominantly redundant information. If instead $Syn(R_{f_1}, R_{f_2})$ is positive, the information carried by the two frequencies is predominantly synergistic and it would mean that the frequency pair has a fraction of information on the stimulus that cannot be accessed by each frequency value separately. Both the joint and synergistic information were computed with the shuffling technique from [28] which provides a conservative estimation of synergy.

3   Results

As an intuitive demonstration of how the network responds to the feed-forward stimulus, Fig. 2 shows the power spectrum of the local field potential (LFP) changes for different values of the feed-forward (S) input rates. All spectra show two local peaks. The first peak is at approximately 30 Hz (in the high-beta/low-gamma frequency band), and the second peak lies between 60 and 80 Hz in the gamma frequency band. The feed-forward input strength modulates mostly the frequencies in the gamma range. The power in the gamma range appeared to be more consistently modulated by the feedforward stimulus than the beta band power, across different values of the lateral input. This suggests that power in the gamma range may carry information about the feed-forward stimulus, as found in real data in visual cortices [18] and in earlier models with just one inhibitory class [25]. Importantly, the power at frequencies below the gamma peak frequency was modulated in different ways than the power of the frequencies above the gamma peak frequency. This suggests that power at different frequencies in the gamma range may carry some complementary information about the feed-forward stimulus.

To quantify this intuition in rigorous terms, we next computed and determined the mutual information carried by the LFP about the feed-forward stimulus. We express this as a function of frequency by calculating the mutual information $I(S; R_f)$ between the feed-forward S stimulus rates and the power R_f at the frequency f of the LFP spectrum. Information was higher in the gamma frequency range. The information had two peaks, one at approximately 55 Hz, just below the peak of the gamma power, and one at approximately 90 Hz, just above the peak of the gamma power. This is different from earlier recurrent network models, which had only one peak of gamma information which was located in

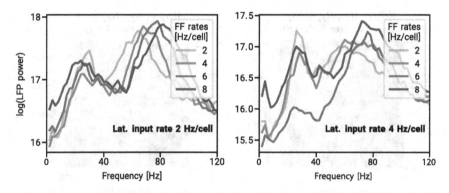

Fig. 2. LFP spectra for different values of the feed-forward (S) input rates. Left: Spectra computed with a lateral input value of 2 Hz/cell. Right: Spectra computed with a lateral input value of 4 Hz/cell.

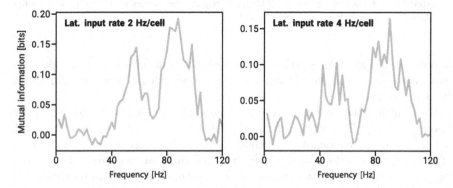

Fig. 3. The mutual information $I(S; R_f)$ that the power of the LFP carries about the strength S of the feed-forward stimulus. Left: values of $I(S; R_f)$ when using as the value of the lateral input rate 2 Hz/cell. Right: values of $I(S; R_f)$ when the lateral input has a rate of 4 Hz/cell.

approximate correspondence with the peak of the gamma power [12, 22, 25]. The values of the information peaks were slightly modulated by the strength of the lateral input, but similar structures were observed across changes in the lateral input (Fig. 3).

The presence of two information peaks at different frequencies and the fact that the feed-forward stimulus modulates differently the LFP power above and below the peak power frequency prompted us to study how much information could be gained by observing simultaneously in the same trial the power at two different frequencies. To investigate this, in Fig. 4 we report for each pair of frequencies f_1, f_2 the joint information $I(S; R_{f_1}, R_{f_2})$ that they carry about the feed-forward stimulus S. Interestingly, we found that the highest joint information value was reached when considering one frequency around the first gamma-band information peak and a frequency around the second gamma-band infor-

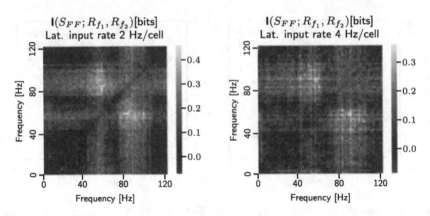

Fig. 4. The joint information $I(S; R_{f_1}, R_{f_2})$ that the LFP power of each pair of frequencies carries about the feed-forward stimulus S. Left: values of $I(S; R_{f_1}, R_{f_2})$ when the lateral input rate has strength 2 Hz/cell. Right, the values of $I(S; R_{f_1}, R_{f_2})$ when the lateral input rate has a value of 4 Hz/cell.

mation peak. This suggests that the power of frequencies above or below the frequency with the highest gamma power carries complementary information about the stimuli.

To quantify this, in Fig. 5 we report for each pair of frequencies f_1, f_2 the synergy $Syn(R_{f_1}, R_{f_2})$ of the information of the two frequencies about the feed-forward stimulus. We found that, while the pairs of frequencies around the same information peak carried largely redundant information (negative values of synergy), pairs with one frequency around one information peak and one frequency around the other information peak carried synergistic information (positive synergy values; joint information larger than the sum of the two information values). The two regions with high redundancy along the diagonal have different sizes as expected from the different widths of the information peaks at the single frequency level, see Fig. 3. Importantly, these patterns of synergy were not found in earlier modeling work with just one class of interneurons [25], in which we found only redundant information shared across frequencies in the gamma range.

4   Discussion

We used computer simulations of the dynamics of recurrent networks of spiking neurons to study if interneuron diversity affects network-level information coding. Several previous studies investigated how different interneuron subpopulations affect network dynamics [20,36,37]. However, none of these studies examined the effect of interneuron types on information encoding in single frequencies or in multiple frequencies. While a straightforward prediction would be that adding cell diversity may enrich the information processing capabilities of the network, it would be more difficult to predict from intuition only without the

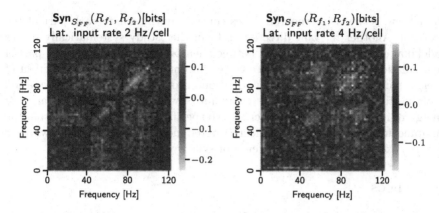

Fig. 5. The amount of synergistic information $Syn(R_{f_1}, R_{f_2})$ that each pair of LFP powers at different frequencies f_1 and f_2 carries about the feed-forward stimulus S. Left: values of $Syn(R_{f_1}, R_{f_2})$ when using a lateral input rate of 2 Hz/cell. Right: values of synergy when using a lateral input rate of 4 Hz/cell.

support of systematic simulations exactly how information coding at each frequency is affected, and how the patterns of information synergy and redundancy across bands are affected. Our main result was that a network with diverse types of interneurons has different and richer information encoding dynamics than a network with only one interneuron type, with patterns of synergy of encoding across frequencies that were not observed in less diverse networks.

One main result that we confirmed from previous studies of simpler networks is that we found was that, as reported in some previous experimental studies [5], the frequencies with the highest power were not necessarily those with the highest information or input modulation. Indeed, the frequencies that had the highest information were those above or below the frequency of the peak of the gamma power.

However, the main difference with respect to previous models was that oscillations in different frequency ranges (below or above the frequency with the peak gamma power) within the gamma band were differentially modulated by the strength of the feed-forward input to the network. In the model of [25] that includes only one un-differentiated interneuron type, the spectrum of network oscillations is modulated redundantly by the feedforward input at frequencies above 40 Hz, with no combination of frequencies in the power spectrum contributing synergistically to encode the input firing rate. This comparison leads us to attribute the formation of across-frequency synergistic information patterns to interneuron diversity.

In future work, it will be interesting to analyze datasets with field potential responses to different kinds of stimuli and see the extent to which the synergy of information across frequencies is realized, and which behavioral function it may serve. The differential and synergistic modulation by the feed-forward input of different frequencies within the gamma range suggests that different types of interactions between interneuron types control and modulate each part of the spectrum. Another relevant direction is to further study systematically in our model how each type of interaction between neuron classes regulates each part of the oscillation spectrum. Also, since the co-information expresses a net effect of synergy/redundancy, examining information encoding with partial information decompositions [38] would help us characterize whether overall redundancy or synergy of information encoding across two specific frequencies results from the simultaneous presence of different degrees of redundancy and synergy, or whether it results exclusively from the presence of synergy or redundancy.

References

1. Adesnik, H., Bruns, W., Taniguchi, H., Huang, Z.J., Scanziani, M.: A neural circuit for spatial summation in visual cortex. Nature **490**(7419), 226–231 (2012)
2. Angelucci, A., Bijanzadeh, M., Nurminen, L., Federer, F., Merlin, S., Bressloff, P.C.: Circuits and Mechanisms for Surround Modulation in Visual Cortex. Annu. Rev. Neurosci. **40**(1), 425–451 (2017)
3. Barbieri, F., Mazzoni, A., Logothetis, N.K., Panzeri, S., Brunel, N.: Stimulus dependence of local field potential spectra: experiment versus theory. J. Neurosci. **34**(44), 14589–14605 (2014)
4. Belitski, A., et al.: Low-frequency local field potentials and spikes in primary visual cortex convey independent visual information. J. Neurosci. **28**(22), 5696–5709 (2008)
5. Belitski, A., Panzeri, S., Magri, C., Logothetis, N.K., Kayser, C.: Sensory information in local field potentials and spikes from visual and auditory cortices: time scales and frequency bands. J. Comput. Neurosci. **29**(3), 533–545 (2010)
6. Bertschinger, N., Rauh, J., Olbrich, E., Jost, J., Ay, N.: Quantifying unique information. Entropy **16**(4), 2161–2183 (2014)
7. Brette, R., Gerstner, W.: Adaptive exponential integrate-and-fire model as an effective description of neuronal activity. J. Neurophysiol. **94**(5), 3637–3642 (2005)
8. Brunel, N., Wang, X.J.: What determines the frequency of fast network oscillations with irregular neural discharges? I. Synaptic dynamics and excitation-inhibition balance. J. Neurophysiol. **90**(1), 415–430 (2003)
9. Buzsáky, G., Anastassiou, C.A., Koch, C.: The origin of extracellular fields and currents – EEG, ECoG, LFP and spikes. Nat. Rev. Neurosci. **13**(6), 407–420 (2012)
10. Buzsáky, G., Draguhn, A.: Neuronal oscillations in cortical networks. Science **304**(5679), 1926–1929 (2004)
11. Cardin, J.A., et al.: Driving fast-spiking cells induces gamma rhythm and controls sensory responses. Nature **459**(7247), 663–667 (2009)
12. Cavallari, S., Panzeri, S., Mazzoni, A.: Comparison of the dynamics of neural interactions between current-based and conductance-based integrate-and-fire recurrent networks. Front. Neural Circ. **8**, 12 (2014)
13. Cover, T.M., Thomas, J.A.: Information theory and statistics. Elements Inf. Theory **1**(1), 279–335 (1991)
14. DeFelipe, J., et al.: New insights into the classification and nomenclature of cortical GABAergic interneurons. Nat. Rev. Neurosci. **14**(3), 202–216 (2013)
15. Descalzo, V.F., Nowak, L.G., Brumberg, J.C., McCormick, D.A., Sanchez-Vives, M.V.: Slow adaptation in fast-spiking neurons of visual cortex. J. Neurophysiol. **93**(2), 1111–1118 (2005)

16. Einevoll, G.T., Kayser, C., Logothetis, N.K., Panzeri, S.: Modelling and analysis of local field potentials for studying the function of cortical circuits. Nat. Rev. Neurosci. **14**(11), 770–785 (2013)
17. Gewaltig, M.O., Diesmann, M.: NEST (NEural simulation tool). Scholarpedia **2**(4), 1430 (2007)
18. Henrie, J.A., Shapley, R.: LFP power spectra in V1 cortex: the graded effect of stimulus contrast. J. Neurophysiol. **94**(1), 479–490 (2005)
19. Kayser, C., König, P.: Stimulus locking and feature selectivity prevail in complementary frequency ranges of V1 local field potentials. Eur. J. Neurosci. **19**(2), 485–489 (2004)
20. Litwin-Kumar, A., Rosenbaum, R., Doiron, B.: Inhibitory stabilization and visual coding in cortical circuits with multiple interneuron subtypes. J. Neurophysiol. **115**(3), 1399–1409 (2016)
21. Magri, C., Whittingstall, K., Singh, V., Logothetis, N.K., Panzeri, S.: A toolbox for the fast information analysis of multiple-site LFP, EEG and spike train recordings. BMC Neurosci. **10**(1), 81 (2009)
22. Martínez-Cañada, P., Ness, T.V., Einevoll, G.T., Fellin, T., Panzeri, S.: Computation of the electroencephalogram (EEG) from network models of point neurons. PLOS Comput. Biol. **17**(4), e1008893 (2021)
23. Martínez-Cañada, P., Noei, S., Panzeri, S.: Methods for inferring neural circuit interactions and neuromodulation from local field potential and electroencephalogram measures. Brain Inform. **8**(1), 27 (2021)
24. Mazzoni, A., Lindén, H., Cuntz, H., Lansner, A., Panzeri, S., Einevoll, G.T.: Computing the local field potential (LFP) from integrate-and-fire network models. PLOS Comput. Biol. **11**(12), e1004584 (2015)
25. Mazzoni, A., Panzeri, S., Logothetis, N.K., Brunel, N.: Encoding of naturalistic stimuli by local field potential spectra in networks of excitatory and inhibitory neurons. PLoS Comput. Biol. **4**(12), e1000239 (2008)
26. Mitra, P.: Observed Brain Dynamics. Oxford University Press, Oxford (2007)
27. Panzeri, S., Schultz, S.R., Treves, A., Rolls, E.T.: Correlations and the encoding of information in the nervous system. Proc. R. Soc. London Ser. B: Biol. Sci. **266**(1423), 1001–1012 (1999)
28. Panzeri, S., Senatore, R., Montemurro, M.A., Petersen, R.S.: Correcting for the sampling bias problem in spike train information measures. J. Neurophysiol. **98**(3), 1064–1072 (2007)
29. Panzeri, S., Treves, A.: Analytical estimates of limited sampling biases in different information measures. Netw. Comput. Neural Syst. **7**(1), 87 (1996)
30. Pesaran, B., et al.: Investigating large-scale brain dynamics using field potential recordings: analysis and interpretation. Nat. Neurosci. **21**(7), 903–919 (2018)
31. Pfeffer, C.K., Xue, M., He, M., Huang, Z.J., Scanziani, M.: Inhibition of inhibition in visual cortex: the logic of connections between molecularly distinct interneurons. Nat. Neurosci. **16**(8), 1068–1076 (2013)
32. Pola, G., Thiele, A., Hoffmann, K.P., Panzeri, S.: An exact method to quantify the information transmitted by different mechanisms of correlational coding. Netw. Comput. Neural Syst. **14**(1), 35–60 (2003)
33. Roth, A., van Rossum, M.C.W.: Modeling synapses. In: De Schutter, E. (ed.) Computational Modeling Methods for Neuroscientists. The MIT Press (2009)
34. Schneidman, E., Bialek, W., Berry, M.J.: Synergy, redundancy, and independence in population codes. J. Neurosci. **23**(37), 11539–11553 (2003)
35. Shannon, C.E.: A mathematical theory of communication. Bell Syst. Tech. J. **27**(3), 379–423 (1948)

36. Urban-Ciecko, J., Barth, A.L.: Somatostatin-expressing neurons in cortical networks. Nat. Rev. Neurosci. **17**(7), 401–409 (2016)
37. Veit, J., Hakim, R., Jadi, M.P., Sejnowski, T.J., Adesnik, H.: Cortical gamma band synchronization through somatostatin interneurons. Nat. Neurosci. **20**(7), 951–959 (2017)
38. Williams, P.L., Beer, R.D.: Nonnegative Decomposition of Multivariate Information. arXiv preprint arXiv:1004.2515 (2010)

Measuring Stimulus-Related Redundant and Synergistic Functional Connectivity with Single Cell Resolution in Auditory Cortex

Loren Koçillari[1,2,3](✉) , Marco Celotto[1,2,4] , Nikolas A. Francis[5] ,
Shoutik Mukherjee[6] , Behtash Babadi[6] , Patrick O. Kanold[7] ,
and Stefano Panzeri[2]

[1] Istituto Italiano di Tecnologia, 38068 Rovereto, Italy
{loren.kocillari,marco.celotto}@iit.it
[2] Department of Excellence for Neural Information Processing, Center for Molecular
Neurobiology (ZMNH), University Medical Center Hamburg-Eppendorf (UKE),
Falkenried 94, 20251 Hamburg, Germany
s.panzeri@uke.de
[3] Department of Neurophysiology and Pathophysiology, University Medical Center
Hamburg-Eppendorf (UKE), 20246 Hamburg, Germany
[4] Department of Pharmacy and Biotechnology, University of Bologna,
40126 Bologna, Italy
[5] Department of Biology and Brain and Behavior Institute, University of Maryland,
College Park, MD 20742, USA
cortex@umd.edu
[6] Department of Electrical and Computer Engineering, Institute for Systems
Research, University of Maryland, College Park, MD 20742, USA
{smukher2,behtash}@umd.edu
[7] Department of Biomedical Engineering and Kavli Neuroscience Discovery Institute,
Johns Hopkins University, Baltimore, MD 21205, USA
pkanold@jhu.edu

Abstract. Measures of functional connectivity have played a central
role in advancing our understanding of how information is communi-
cated within the brain. Traditionally, these studies have focused on identifying redundant functional connectivity, which involves determining
when activity is similar across different sites. However, recent research
has highlighted the potential importance of also identifying synergistic
connectivity-that is, connectivity that gives rise to information not contained in either site alone. Here, we measured redundant and synergistic
functional connectivity with individual-neuron resolution in the primary
auditory cortex of the mouse during a perceptual task. Specifically, we
identified pairs of neurons that exhibited directed functional connectivity
between them, as measured using Granger Causality. We then used Partial Information Decomposition to quantify the amount of redundant and
synergystic information carried by these neurons about auditory stimuli. Our findings revealed that functionally connected pairs carry proportionally more redundancy and less synergy than unconnected pairs,

F. Liu et al. (Eds.): BI 2023, LNAI 13974, pp. 45–56, 2023.
https://doi.org/10.1007/978-3-031-43075-6_5

suggesting that their functional connectivity is primarily redundant in nature. Furthermore, we observe that the proportion of redundancy is higher for correct than for incorrect behavioral choices, supporting the notion that redundant connectivity is beneficial for behavior.

Keywords: Functional connectivity · Redundancy · Synergy · Auditory perception

1   Introduction

Functional connectivity (FC) has emerged as a mainstream concept and a fundamental tool to understand how networks in the brain communicate, and how functional interactions between networks or between neurons shape the dynamics and functions of the brain [4,6,7,9,21]. Most of these traditional measures of FC focused on redundant connectivity, by measuring (for example, through linear cross-correlations) the similarity of activity at different sites. However, recent studies have begun to highlight the importance of another type of FC - synergistic connectivity. This type of connectivity focuses on how variations of the interaction between activity at different sites create information that is not present at each site alone [14,21,29,32]. While the presence and merits of redundant connectivity have been extensively documented [4,7,31], it remains unclear whether synergistic interactions are prominent and how they contribute to functions.

An additional question regards the spatial scale at which both redundant and synergistic interactions are expressed. Most studies of FC investigated it at a coarse scale, such as that obtained with fMRI or EEG [5,11–13,19]. The organization of FC at the smaller spatial scale of population recordings with single-cell resolution is less understood.

In this study, we address some of these open questions regarding synergistic and redundant FC. First, we address their relationship with respect to a widely used FC measure, Granger Causality (GC) [26,28], between the activities of different neurons. This measure of FC is interesting because, unlike simple measures of FC based on cross-correlation, it considers not only the similarity of activity but also the strength and directionality of information transmission. GC can, in principle, capture redundant FC because the process of transmission causes sharing of information between the sending and the receiving site. However, it can also correspond to synergistic FC. For example, if transmission varies across sensory stimuli, FC can create sensory information not available in each node individually. Second, we use precise information theoretic measures to quantify redundancy and synergy related to the encoding of important sensory variables (in this case, features of auditory stimuli). These measures, based on the theory of Partial Information Decomposition (PID) [33], have the advantage of separating redundancy from synergy, something that simpler measures [25] used in recent studies [8,18] cannot do. Third, we study synergy and redundancy with neuron resolution, using the primary auditory cortex (A1) of the mouse brain as an experimental model. Fourth, we explore the potential impact of synergy and redundancy on sensory processing by studying how they vary between cases of correct and incorrect perceptual discrimination.

2 Experimental Task and Single Neuron Stimulus Information

To investigate the relationship between FC and the presence of synergistic and redundant information with single-neuron resolution, we focused on the activity of the mouse primary auditory cortex during a sound discrimination task. We reanalyzed a previously published dataset [8] in which the activity of several tens to a few hundreds of neurons was recorded simultaneously using *in vivo* 2P calcium imaging (Ca^{2+}) from A1 L2/3 neurons in transgenic CBA × Thy1-GCaMP6s F1 mice during a pure-tone discrimination task (Fig. 1A).

The experimental task was structured as follows. After a pre-stimulus interval of 1 s, head-fixed mice were exposed to either a low frequency (7 or 9.9 kHz) or a high frequency (14 or 19.8 kHz) tone for a period of 1 s. Mice were trained to report their perception of the sound stimulus by their behavioral choice, which consisted of licking a waterspout in the post-stimulus interval (0.5 to 3 s from stimulus onset) after hearing a low-frequency tone (target tones) and holding still after hearing high-frequency tones (non-target tones). Calcium imaging was used to continuously acquire the fluorescence signals from individual A1 L2/3 neurons during the task with a sampling frequency of 30 Hz.

We used Shannon mutual information [24, 27] to compute the stimulus information carried by each neuron about the stimulus category (low vs high-frequency tones) in each imaging time frame (Fig. 1B, top plot). Stimulus information is defined as follows:

$$I(S; R_i) = \sum_{s \in S, r_i \in R} p(s, r_i) \log_2 \frac{p(s, r_i)}{p(s)p(r_i)} \tag{1}$$

where i indexes the neurons and $p(s, r_i)$ denotes the joint probability of observing in a given trial the activity r_i of neuron i and the value s of the stimulus variable S. $p(r_i) = \sum_s p(s, r_i)$ and $p(s) = \sum_{r_i} p(s, r_i)$ are the marginal probabilities. We estimated $p(s, r_i)$ using the direct method [15].

The activity r_i of neuron i was inferred following the same approach described in [8]. Briefly, we first deconvolved the single-trial calcium fluorescence traces of each neuron to infer the spiking activity (Fig. 1B, bottom plot). We then used a sliding window approach (a sliding window of 10 time frames with time-steps of 1 time frame) to binarize the spiking activity into 0 and 1, where 1 denotes spiking activity higher than zero. We then computed the time-resolved stimulus information on these neural responses. Finally, we subtracted the average stimulus information computed in the pre-stimulus interval from the stimulus information time-courses, which enabled us to remove the bias in the information that occurred for the limited number of trials [22].

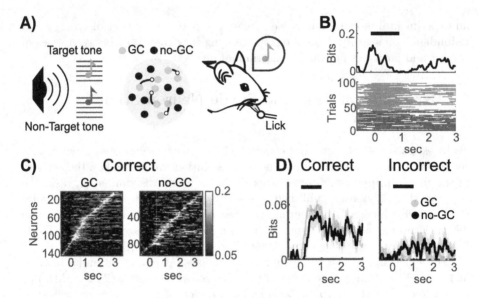

Fig. 1. Stimulus information in mouse auditory cortex during a tone discrimination task. A) Mice performed a go/no-go tone discrimination task while the activity of A1 L2/3 neurons were monitored with two-photon calcium imaging. In response to a target tone (low-frequency, in orange) mice had to lick a waterspout and not to lick for non-target tones (high-frequency, in blue). Granger Causality analysis revealed sparsely connected networks of cells in A1 L2/3 [8]. We classified neurons as GC (purple) and no-GC (black) depending on whether or not they formed a GC link. B) Example of the stimulus information time-course for a single neuron. We computed the time-resolved stimulus information as the mutual information (top plot) between the auditory stimuli (low-/high-frequency tones) and the spike activity across trials. In the raster plot (bottom plot) we color-coded and sorted the spiking activity based on the tone that occurred across trials. C) Stimulus information time-course for GC neurons (left map) and no-GC neurons (right map) in correct trials only. We then sorted the peaks of stimulus information for each neuron to tile the trial time. D) Population-averaged stimulus information for GC (in purple) and no-GC (black) neurons in case of correct and incorrect trials separately. (Color figure online)

Following our previous study [8], we first analyzed the entire dataset (2792 neurons recorded from 34 sessions) to identify those neurons that carried significant task-related information. Neurons were defined as carrying task-related information if they carried statistically significant stimulus information (defined as in Eq. 1 above), significant choice information (defined as in Eq. 1 above but replacing the stimulus presented in the given trial with the behavioral choice of the animal in the trial), and intersection information, defined as the amount of sensory information encoded in neural activity that is used to inform the behavioral choice [20] and computed using PID [23]. The statistical significance of each information measure was computed using a non-parametric permutation test at $p < 0.1$. The requirement of all three non-independent tests being satis-

fied simultaneously was empirically estimated, resulting in a false discovery rate
of 1% [8]. We found a subset of 475/2790 neurons that transiently and sequentially carried significant task-relevant information [8]. Using methods described
in [8,28] we next performed a Granger causality (GC) analysis on the selected
subset of neurons. We picked the 20 neurons with the peak intersection information with the shortest latencies in 12 of 34 sessions and found that they formed
sparse functional networks that transmitted redundant task-relevant information across the trial time (Fig. 1A) [8]. Of these 240 neurons, 144 formed GC
connections with other neurons in the network and were termed GC neurons
hereafter. The remaining 96 neurons, which did not form GC connections with
other neurons, were termed no-GC neurons hereafter.

We used information-theoretic measures to map the stimulus information
dynamics of individual neurons. We first considered information in trials in
which the mouse made correct perceptual discriminations to understand whether
GC neurons and no-GC neurons encoded information differently during correct
behavior. The stimulus information time-courses, plotted in (Fig. 1C) after sorting neurons by their peak information timing, showed sequential information
coding across the population in both GC and no-GC neurons. Neurons in both
classes had similar amounts of information at peak, the main difference being
that GC-connected neurons had peak information earlier in the trial (during
the stimulus presentation), while no-GC neurons carried information later in
the trial (after stimulus presentation) (Fig. 1C). The sequential nature of their
activation suggests that information is represented throughout the trial only at
the population level, motivating our later information analyses at the neural
population level.

To investigate what aspects of neural activity may be key for performing
correct perceptual judgements, we assessed how information about the auditory
stimulus category was encoded in trials in which the animal judged the stimulus
either correctly or incorrectly. For simplicity, we averaged the stimulus information across neurons (Fig. 1D). Importantly, we found that in incorrect trials, the
stimulus information dropped for both populations across the entire trial time,
suggesting that the stimulus information that both GC and no-GC neurons
encode is used for the behavioral choice. Importantly, all information quantities
computed during correct discriminations were calculated on random subsets of
correct trials with the same size as the number of incorrect trials in the same
session. With this equalized sub-sampling, we could fairly compare the amount
of information encoded in correct and the incorrect trials, thereby controlling for
potential artefacts introduced by different amounts of limited-sampling bias [22].

3   PID for Measuring Synergy and Redundancy

The above analysis considered the single-neuron correlates of correct and incorrect perceptual discriminations with the directed FC. We next asked how these
properties relate to the emergent properties of population coding. This requires
computing stimulus information from more than one neuron.

As in our previous study [8], we estimated the total stimulus information that was jointly carried by pairs of neurons, following a time-lagged approach (Fig. 2A). We first identified for each neuron the peak times of task-related information, i.e., the time frames when intersection information time-courses peaked. We then computed the time-lagged stimulus information carried jointly by the activity of each pair of neurons as follows:

$$I(S; R_i, R_j) = \sum_{s \in S, r_i \in R_i, r_j \in R_j} p(s, r_i, r_j) \log_2 \frac{p(s, r_i, r_j)}{p(s)p(r_i, r_j)} \tag{2}$$

where $p(s, r_i, r_j)$ denotes the probability of simultaneously observing in the same trial the value s of the stimulus category and the joint responses r_i and r_j of neurons i and j at the time frames of their peak of task-related information. In our previous work [8], we investigated the nature of redundant and synergistic interactions in pairs of neurons by computing the so-called co-information [2,17], defined as the difference between the total stimulus information that was jointly carried by both neurons (Eq. 2 above) and the sum of the information carried by the single neurons individually (Eq. 1 above):

$$CoInfo(S; R_i; R_j) = I(S; R_i, R_j) - (I(S; R_i) + I(S; R_j)) \tag{3}$$

If $CoInfo(S; R_i; R_j)$ is positive, then the pair of neurons carries overall more information than expected by summing the information carried by the neurons individually. Thus, a positive sign of this quantity is interpreted as predominant synergy, and a negative sign as predominant redundancy. However, it has been shown that co-information conflates two non-negative pieces of information which properly and separately quantify synergy and redundancy [33]. Indeed, there could be cases when co-information is low, but synergy and redundancy are both high [10]. In simple terms, redundancy (the area in red in the Venn diagram in Fig. 2B) quantifies the amount of information that both neurons carry independently about the stimulus, while synergy (the area in green in the Venn diagram in Fig. 2B) is the amount of information that can be accessed when observing both neuronal responses simultaneously but is not carried individually by any neuron.

To determine the specific contributions of synergy and redundancy to the total joint information, we used the formalism of PID [33]. PID allows breaking down the joint mutual information that two or more source variables carry about a target variable into non-negative and well-interpretable pieces of information. An important insight coming from this decomposition is that $CoInfo$ is the difference between two distinct pieces of information that can be quantified separately:

$$CoInfo(S; R_i; R_j) = Syn(S : R_i, R_j) - Red(S : R_i, R_j) \tag{4}$$

where $Red(S : R_i, R_j)$ is the redundant information which is present in both neuron R_i and neuron R_j, and $Syn(S : R_i, R_j)$ is the synergistic information carried only by the joint response of the two neurons. To compute $Red(S :$

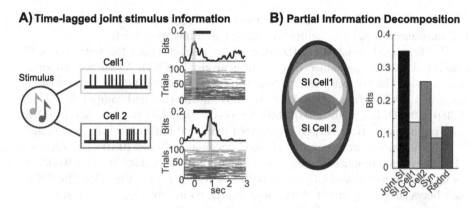

Fig. 2. Partial information decomposition of the time-lagged joint stimulus information. A) Time-lagged joint stimulus information is defined as the mutual information that the neural responses of two cells at their information time peaks (yellow and cyan vertical bars in the raster plots) jointly carry about the stimulus. We colour-coded and sorted trials in the raster plots based on the stimulus category (low vs high-frequency tones). B) The joint stimulus information can be decomposed into the non-negative components of synergy, redundancy, and the stimulus information of each cell (Venn diagram on the left). The bar plot on the right shows the amount of the joint stimulus information for the pair of cells in panel A) (black bar), stimulus information of both cells (yellow and cyan colors), the synergistic (green bar), and redundant (red bar) components. (Color figure online)

R_i, R_j) and $Syn(S : R_i, R_j)$ we used the definition provided by [3], where the two terms are computed by solving a constrained convex optimization problem in the space of the trivariate probability distributions $Q(S, R_i, R_j)$. To numerically solve this optimization problem, we used the *BROJA_2PID* python package [16]. In this way, we decomposed the joint stimulus information into the synergy, redundancy, and individual neuron stimulus information.

4   Measuring Stimulus-Related Synergy and Redundancy in Auditory Cortex

In our previous study [8] we found an overall redundancy of task-related information in correct trials and an overall synergy in incorrect trials for both pairs of neurons having a GC link and pairs of neurons not having a GC link, suggesting that redundancy is relevant for the behavioural choice. Following [8], we labelled neuronal pairs as GC-connected if they shared at least one GC link and as GC-unconnected otherwise. Since we employed the conflated measure of co-information in [8], the above levels of redundancy in correct trials could arise in distinct scenarios: redundancy is higher in correct rather than in incorrect trials, synergy is lower in correct than in incorrect trials, or a combination of the two. To separate the amounts of stimulus-related synergistic and redundant interactions, we thus employed the formalism of PID. We next performed the stimulus-related PID analysis in the two separate groups of GC-connected and GC-unconnected pairs of neurons in correct and incorrect trials.

We first performed the PID analysis in correct trials for both the GC-connected and GC-unconnected pairs of neurons (Fig. 3A). Again, we randomly sub-sampled the correct trials to equalize the number of incorrect trials (average over 100 repetitions). The joint stimulus information had comparable values $(0.386 \pm 0.002 \text{bits}, 0.402 \pm 0.012 \text{bits}$ for no-GC and GC pairs respectively) in both populations. However, GC-connected pairs had higher levels of redundancy $(0.121 \pm 0.006 \text{bits})$ compared to the GC-unconnected ones $(0.105 \pm 0.001 \text{bits})$, while they had similar amounts of synergy $(0.097 \pm 0.001 \text{bits}, 0.093 \pm 0.003 \text{bits}$ for GC-unconnected and GC-connected pairs respectively) (Fig. 3A). The difference between synergy and redundancy, i.e., the co-information (Eq. 4), showed a prevalence of redundant information in both populations, but the GC-connected pairs were more redundant $(-0.027 \pm 0.006 \text{bits})$ than GC-unconnected pairs $(-0.007 \pm 0.001 \text{bits})$.

We next quantified the fraction of redundancy and synergy by normalizing each term with respect to the total joint mutual information. We found that GC-connected pairs had proportionally more redundancy and less synergy (red= 0.292 ± 0.01, syn= 0.239 ± 0.007), compared to GC-unconnected ones (red= 0.262 ± 0.001, syn= 0.261 ± 0.001) (Fig. 3A). Finally, the normalized co-information showed that GC-connected pairs neurons had much higher redundancy (-0.053 ± 0.013) than GC-unconnected pairs (-0.001 ± 0.002). Our results suggest that GC-connected pairs of neurons have more redundant than synergistic functional connections.

Next, we investigated whether larger amounts of redundancy and lower amounts of synergy could be beneficial for task performance and behavioral accuracy. We computed the PID in incorrect trials (Fig. 3B). The joint stimulus information in incorrect trials was only about $\sim 30\%$ of what it was in correct trials $(0.130 \pm 0.002 \text{bits}, 0.123 \pm 0.014 \text{bits}$ for no-GC and GC pairs respectively). Redundancy in incorrect trials had a value of $(0.01 \pm 0.001 \text{bits}, 0.012 \pm 0.004 \text{bits}$ for no-GC and GC pairs respectively), which is proportionally ten times smaller than that of correct trials, while synergy dropped to $(0.063 \pm 0.002 \text{bits}, 0.053 \pm 0.007 \text{bits}$ for no-GC and GC pairs respectively), proportionally only half of that in correct trials. Co-information showed positive values, i.e. more synergy than redundancy, in both GC-unconnected and GC-connected pairs $(0.053 \pm 0.002 \text{bits}, 0.04 \pm 0.007 \text{bits})$. Fractional redundancy was just $\sim 10\%$ of the total information, whereas fractional synergy was $\sim 45\%$ of it (Fig. 3B). Moreover, we did not find significant differences in the normalized co-information between GC-unconnected and GC-connected pairs on incorrect trials $(0.382 \pm 0.008, 0.304 \pm 0.044)$. Our results suggest that only the redundant FC associated with GC links is useful for correct sensory discriminations.

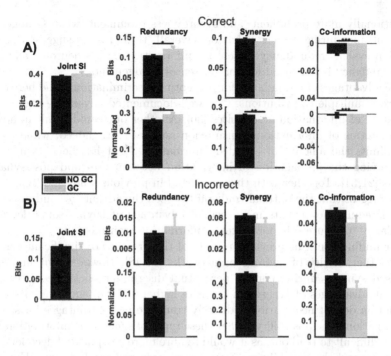

Fig. 3. Redundancy and synergy in auditory cortex. A) Redundancy and synergy PID computed in correct trials. From left to right: time-lagged joint stimulus information (SI), redundancy, synergy, and co-information for GC-connected (purple) and GC-unconnected pairs of neurons (black). For synergy, redundancy and co-information, the top plots show values in bits and the bottom plots show values normalised by the joint stimulus information. B) As in panel A), but in the case of incorrect trials. Bar plots show mean ± SEM across pairs. Statistics were made with a Wilcoxon rank-sum test (*p < 0.05, **p < 0.01, ***p < 0.001). (Color figure online)

5 Discussion

In this study, we teased apart the relationship between FC and stimulus-related synergy and redundancy with single-neuron resolution in the auditory mouse cortex during a perceptual discrimination task. We deliberately considered one specific, widely-used type of directed FC measure, Granger Causality. Unlike other measures such as the Pearson correlation between the activity of two neurons, Granger Causality can in principle be related to redundancy and synergy. Our findings revealed that Granger FC between A1 L2/3 neurons was accompanied by proportionally higher levels of redundancy and lower levels of synergy compared to pairs of neurons that were not linked with a Granger FC. Moreover, we found that the levels of redundancy were higher in both populations in correct behavioral choices compared to incorrect ones. Our results suggest that both synergy and redundancy coexist across the population, regardless of whether or not they are Granger connected and of whether or not the mouse makes correct or incorrect perceptual discriminations. However, redundancy becomes proportionally more prominent, and synergy less prominent, when Granger FC is present and during correct behavior. Overall, these results suggest that FC creates prevalent redundancy of sensory information across neurons, and that this redundancy is beneficial for correct sensory judgements.

The advantages of redundancy for perceptual discrimination found here could arise from multiple contributions. One well-documented advantage regards the integration of information across sites [30]. Another one could result in advantages in terms of information transmission and readout. Indeed, while redundancy limits the amount of encoded information [1], it has benefits in terms of improving the propagation of information between pre- and post-synaptic neurons [21,31]. Together with those reported in previous studies [8,21,31], our results suggest that the optimal trade-off between the advantages and disadvantages of redundancy results in an overall advantage of having some degree of redundancy to secure safe downstream information transmission.

Our finding confirms previous reports of the presence of significant synergy between the activity of neurons or networks [14,18]. However, our finding of decreased synergy during correct perceptual discrimination suggests that the potential advantages of synergy in terms of higher levels of encoding of sensory information do not necessarily or directly translate into advantages for sensory discrimination. One possibility is that these types of synergistic information may be more difficult to read out, as it would require more complicated decoders that may be beyond the capabilities of some downstream neural circuits. However, given that presence of synergy has been well documented, another possibility, to be explored in future studies, is that synergy may not be needed for the simple perceptual tasks we consider but that it could become more important for more complex behaviors.

From the theoretical perspective, previous studies that investigated synergy and redundancy between neurons or networks employed a measure of co-information which conflates synergy with redundancy, measuring only their net effect [8,25]. With respect to these studies, we made the advance of using a more refined measure that teased apart redundancy from synergy, which allowed us the important step forward of being able to measure separately their relationship with both FC and the accuracy of behavior. With respect to other studies considering redundancy and synergy, but not relating it to information content about variables of cognitive interest [14], we made progress by measuring redundancy and synergy of information about variables, such as sensory stimuli, which have a well-defined meaning and role in terms of perceptual functions. We hope that our work contributes to creating a neuroinformatics framework that can help researchers to study the patterns of synergy and redundancy about external stimuli and pinpoint their contribution to behavior and functions.

In conclusion, our findings suggest that correct behavior is associated with a pervasive presence of redundant information in functionally connected neural networks. Further research is needed to better understand the contributions of synergy and redundancy in different contexts.

References

1. Averbeck, B.B., Latham, P.E., Pouget, A.: Neural correlations, population coding and computation. Nat. Rev. Neurosci. **7**, 358–366 (2006)
2. Bell, A.J.: The co-information lattice. In: 4th International Symposium on Independent Component Analysis and Blind Signal Separation (ICA2003), pp. 921–926 (2003)
3. Bertschinger, N., Rauh, J., Olbrich, E., Jost, J., Ay, N.: Quantifying unique information. Entropy **16**(4), 2161–2183 (2014)
4. Biswal, B., Zerrin Yetkin, F., Haughton, V.M., Hyde, J.S.: Functional connectivity in the motor cortex of resting human brain using echo-planar MRI. Magn. Reson. Med. **34**(4), 537–541 (1995)
5. Deco, G., Ponce-Alvarez, A., Mantini, D., Romani, G.L., Hagmann, P., Corbetta, M.: Resting-state functional connectivity emerges from structurally and dynamically shaped slow linear fluctuations. J. Neurosci. **33**(27), 11239–11252 (2013)
6. Engel, A.K., Gerloff, C., Hilgetag, C.C., Nolte, G.: Intrinsic coupling modes: multiscale interactions in ongoing brain activity. Neuron **80**(4), 867–886 (2013)
7. Fox, M.D., Snyder, A.Z., Vincent, J.L., Corbetta, M., Van Essen, D.C., Raichle, M.E.: The human brain is intrinsically organized into dynamic, anticorrelated functional networks. Proc. Natl. Acad. Sci. U.S.A. **102**(27), 9673–9678 (2005)
8. Francis, N.A., Mukherjee, S., Koçillari, L., Panzeri, S., Babadi, B., Kanold, P.O.: Sequential transmission of task-relevant information in cortical neuronal networks. Cell Rep. **39**(9), 110878 (2022)
9. Greicius, M.D., Krasnow, B., Reiss, A.L., Menon, V.: Functional connectivity in the resting brain: a network analysis of the default mode hypothesis. Proc. Natl. Acad. Sci. U.S.A. **100**(1), 253–258 (2003)
10. Griffith, V., Koch, C.: Quantifying synergistic mutual information. In: Prokopenko, M. (ed.) Guided Self-Organization: Inception. ECC, vol. 9, pp. 159–190. Springer, Heidelberg (2014). https://doi.org/10.1007/978-3-642-53734-9_6
11. van den Heuvel, M.P., Hulshoff Pol, H.E.: Exploring the brain network: a review on resting-state fMRI functional connectivity. Eur. Neuropsychopharmacol. **20**(8), 519–534 (2010)
12. Honey, C.J., et al.: Predicting human resting-state functional connectivity from structural connectivity. Proc. Natl. Acad. Sci. U.S.A. **106**(6), 2035–2040 (2009)
13. Lachaux, J.P., Rodriguez, E., Martinerie, J., Varela, F.J.: Measuring phase synchrony in brain signals. Hum. Brain Mapp. **8**(4), 194–208 (1999)
14. Luppi, A.I., et al.: A synergistic core for human brain evolution and cognition. Nat. Neurosci. **25**(6), 771–782 (2022)
15. Magri, C., Whittingstall, K., Singh, V., Logothetis, N.K., Panzeri, S.: A toolbox for the fast information analysis of multiple-site LFP, EEG and spike train recordings. BMC Neurosci. **10**, 1–24 (2009)
16. Makkeh, A., Theis, D.O., Vicente, R.: BROJA-2PID: a robust estimator for bivariate partial information decomposition. Entropy **20**(4), 271 (2018)
17. McGill, W.J.: Multivariate information transmission. Psychometrika **19**, 97–116 (1954)
18. Nigam, S., Pojoga, S., Dragoi, V.: Synergistic coding of visual information in columnar networks. Neuron **104**(2), 402–411 (2019)
19. Nolte, G., Bai, O., Wheaton, L., Mari, Z., Vorbach, S., Hallett, M.: Identifying true brain interaction from EEG data using the imaginary part of coherency. Clin. Neurophysiol. **115**(10), 2292–2307 (2004)

20. Panzeri, S., Harvey, C.D., Piasini, E., Latham, P.E., Fellin, T.: Cracking the neural code for sensory perception by combining statistics, intervention, and behavior. Neuron **93**(3), 491–507 (2017)
21. Panzeri, S., Moroni, M., Safaai, H., Harvey, C.D.: The structures and functions of correlations in neural population codes. Nat. Rev. Neurosci. **23**(9), 551–567 (2022)
22. Panzeri, S., Senatore, R., Montemurro, M.A., Petersen, R.S.: Correcting for the sampling bias problem in spike train information measures. J. Neurophysiol. **98**(3), 1064–1072 (2007)
23. Pica, G., et al.: Quantifying how much sensory information in a neural code is relevant for behavior. In: 31st Conference on Neural Information Processing Systems (NIPS 2017), pp. 3686–3696 (2017)
24. Quian Quiroga, R., Panzeri, S.: Extracting information from neuronal populations: information theory and decoding approaches. Nat. Rev. Neurosci. **10**(3), 173–185 (2009)
25. Schneidman, E., Bialek, W., Berry, M.J.: Synergy, redundancy, and independence in population codes. J. Neurosci. **23**(37), 11539–11553 (2003)
26. Seth, A.K., Barrett, A.B., Barnett, L.: Granger causality analysis in neuroscience and neuroimaging. J. Neurosci. **35**(8), 3293–3297 (2015)
27. Shannon, C.E.: A mathematical theory of communication. Bell Syst. Tech. J. **27**(3), 379–423 (1948)
28. Sheikhattar, A., et al.: Extracting neuronal functional network dynamics via adaptive Granger causality analysis. Proc. Natl. Acad. Sci. U.S.A. **115**(17), E3869–E3878 (2018)
29. Sporns, O.: The complex brain: connectivity, dynamics, information. Trends Cogn. Sci. **26**(12), 1066–1067 (2022)
30. Tononi, G., Sporns, O., Edelman, G.M.: A measure for brain complexity: relating functional segregation and integration in the nervous system. Proc. Natl. Acad. Sci. U.S.A. **91**(11), 5033–5037 (1994)
31. Valente, M., et al.: Correlations enhance the behavioral readout of neural population activity in association cortex. Nat. Neurosci. **24**(7), 975–986 (2021)
32. Varley, T.F., Sporns, O., Schaffelhofer, S., Scherberger, H., Dann, B.: Information-processing dynamics in neural networks of macaque cerebral cortex reflect cognitive state and behavior. Proc. Natl. Acad. Sci. U.S.A. **120**(2), e22076771, 20 (2023)
33. Williams, P.L., Beer, R.D.: Nonnegative decomposition of multivariate information. arXiv preprint arXiv:1004.2515 (2010)

Fusing Simultaneously Acquired EEG and fMRI via Hierarchical Deep Transcoding

Xueqing Liu$^{(\boxtimes)}$ and Paul Sajda

Columbia University, New York, NY 10027, USA
{xl2556,psajda}@columbia.edu

Abstract. Functional magnetic resonance imaging (fMRI) and electroencephalography (EEG) are neuroimaging modalities that offer complementary strengths and weaknesses in terms of spatial and temporal resolution. In this study, we propose a hierarchical deep transcoding model for fusing simultaneous EEG-fMRI data to recover a high spatiotemporal resolution latent neural source space. The model utilizes a cyclic Convolutional Neural Network (CNN) architecture to generate the latent source space through a deep transcoding process. The model is interpretable and capable of extracting meaningful features such as hemodynamic impulse response functions (HRF) from the data. We demonstrate the effectiveness of the model by applying it to an auditory oddball task dataset, showing strong correlations between the EEG transcoded from fMRI and actual EEG recordings, as well as substantial overlap between activation maps generated from fMRI transcoded from EEG and real fMRI data. The model also recovers the HRF and enables the interpretation of spatial and temporal patterns in the latent source space. Overall, our hierarchical deep transcoding model provides a valuable tool for integrating EEG and fMRI data, offering enhanced spatiotemporal resolution and interpretability for neuroimaging studies.

Keywords: Simultaneous EEG-fMRI · hierarchical deep transcoding · cyclic Convolutional Neural Network

1 Introduction

Functional magnetic resonance imaging (fMRI) and electroencephalography (EEG) are two prominent neuroimaging modalities that provide complementary information about brain activity. fMRI offers full-brain coverage with relatively high spatial resolution, typically at the millimeter level, but it has limited temporal resolution due to the sluggishness of the hemodynamic response [1]. On the other hand, EEG measures electrical signals recorded from electrodes placed on the scalp, providing high temporal resolution in the millisecond range, but with lower spatial resolution compared to fMRI [2].

F. Liu et al. (Eds.): BI 2023, LNAI 13974, pp. 57–67, 2023.
https://doi.org/10.1007/978-3-031-43075-6_6

Given the strengths and weaknesses of these two modalities, simultaneous acquisition of EEG and fMRI data has emerged as a promising approach to leverage their advantages and compensate for their limitations. By combining the rich temporal information from EEG and the detailed spatial information from fMRI, it becomes possible to obtain a more comprehensive understanding of brain activity.

In this study, we propose a novel model for recovering the latent neural source space with high spatiotemporal resolution through the transcoding of simultaneous EEG/fMRI data. The goal is to generate a latent source space that captures neural activity patterns at the millimeter and millisecond scales. Our approach utilizes a hierarchical deep transcoding process based on a cyclic Convolutional Neural Network (CNN), as illustrated in Fig. 1.

An important feature of our proposed model is its interpretability, distinguishing it from being a mere "black box" approach. It is designed to extract meaningful features from the data, such as hemodynamic impulse response functions (HRF), which provide insights into the underlying neural processes. By unraveling the latent source space, our model facilitates the interpretation and understanding of the neural dynamics captured by the combined EEG/fMRI data.

In this paper, we present the architecture and implementation details of our model, followed by a comprehensive evaluation of its performance using both simulated and real EEG/fMRI data. The results demonstrate the effectiveness of our approach in recovering high-resolution neural activity patterns and extracting interpretable features from the multimodal data.

Overall, this study contributes to the growing body of literature on multimodal neuroimaging and provides a novel approach for combining EEG and fMRI data to enhance spatiotemporal resolution and interpretability. Our proposed model holds promise for advancing our understanding of brain function and supporting various applications in neuroscience and clinical research.

2   Hierarchical Deep Transcoding for Modality Fusing

Figure 1.a illustrates the overall pipeline of the hierarchical deep transcoding model, which consists of two stages, forming a hierarchy. In the first stage, the model is trained at the group level using data from the entire subject population. This training aims to achieve an intermediate spatiotemporal resolution. The group level EEG estimated source exhibits higher spatial resolution than the original EEG but lower spatial resolution than the desired super-resolution latent source space (equivalent to the spatial resolution of the original fMRI data). Similarly, the group level fMRI estimated source shows higher temporal resolution than the original fMRI but lower temporal resolution than the desired super-resolution latent source space (equivalent to the temporal resolution of the original EEG data).

The second stage involves training a subject level model using each subject's individual data to ultimately reach the millimeter/millisecond resolution of the

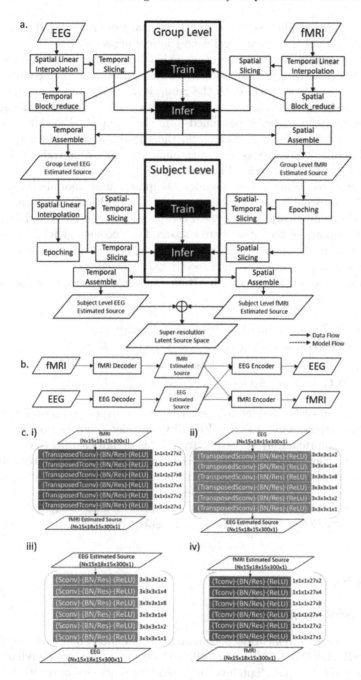

Fig. 1. a. Framework of hierarchical deep transcoding for fusing simultaneous EEG/fMRI: Both the group level model and subject level model are cyclic convolutional transcoders as shown in b. **b.** Framework of a cyclic convolutional transcoder: The transcoder is made up of an fMRI decoder, an EEG encoder, an EEG decoder and an fMRI encoder. **c.** Detailed structure of the i) fMRI decoder, ii) EEG decoder, iii) EEG encoder, iv) fMRI encoder. In group level transcoders, batch-normalization layers are used, while in subject level transcoders, residual layers are used instead.

latent source space. The cyclic convolutional transcoder, depicted in Fig. 1.b, serves as the core of the hierarchical deep transcoding structure. The concept of "neural" transcoding involves generating a signal of one neuroimaging modality from another by decoding it into a latent source space and then encoding it into the other measurement space. Both the group level model and the subject level model are designed as cyclic convolutional transcoders. However, the subject level model cannot be simply fine-tuned from the group level model since their inputs are of different scales. Therefore, the subject level model requires re-initialization of the parameters during training and cannot be trained on top of the parameters of the group level model.

The cyclic convolutional transcoder comprises four modules: the fMRI decoder, fMRI encoder, EEG decoder, and EEG encoder. Drawing inspiration from digital communications and video compression, both EEG and fMRI are viewed as encodings of the latent source space. The decoders generate the latent source space from the encoding (EEG/fMRI), while the encoder maps the latent source space into the measurement space (EEG or fMRI).

To train these models, a loss function is employed, given by $loss_{total} = \sum_{i=1}^{4} loss_i$, where:

- fMRI-to-EEG transcoding loss: $loss_1 = \sum_{i=1}^{n}(E_i - \hat{E}_i)^2$
- EEG-to-fMRI transcoding loss: $loss_2 = \sum_{i=1}^{n}(F_i - \hat{F}_i)^2$
- fMRI-to-fMRI cycle consistency loss: $loss_3 = \sum_{i=1}^{n}(F_i - \hat{F}'_i)^2$
- EEG-to-EEG cycle consistency loss: $loss_4 = \sum_{i=1}^{n}(E_i - \hat{E}'_i)^2$

The fMRI or EEG decoder consists solely of transpose temporal or spatial convolutional layers, while the fMRI or EEG encoder comprises only temporal or spatial convolutional layers, respectively. This design ensures that the fMRI encoder or decoder applies temporal transformation solely to the original fMRI data, while the EEG encoder or decoder applies spatial transformation only to the original EEG data. This rule applies to both the group level and subject level models. This particular design not only preserves the temporal or spatial information of EEG or fMRI by the model respectively but also yields an interpretable model.

3   Results

3.1   Transcoding Results

We applied our hierarchical deep transcoder to simultaneously acquired EEG (64 channel) and fMRI (3T) data collected during an auditory oddball task. The auditory oddball paradigm involves presenting sequences of repetitive sound stimuli, occasionally interrupted by a deviant sound stimulus, while the subject is required to respond to the oddball stimuli by pressing a button. This well-studied experimental paradigm allows us to evaluate our method and validate our findings against existing approaches.

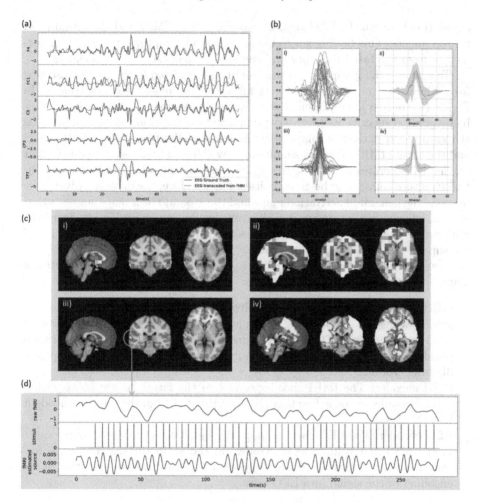

Fig. 2. a. EEG transcoded from fMRI compared with the EEG ground truth. **b.** HRF extracted from data by the group level fMRI encoder. **c.** Activation map generated from fMRI estimation generated from EEG for ii) standard and iv) oddball stimulus compared with the correspondent i) standard tone fMRI activation map and iii) oddball fMRI activation map ground truth. **d.** fMRI estimated source generated by group level fMRI decoder of one voxel in the auditory cortex.

To gain a comprehensive understanding of our model, we conducted additional analyses focusing on the auditory oddball dataset. Since our group-level cyclic convolutional transcoder serves as an end-to-end structure for EEG-to-fMRI and fMRI-to-EEG transcoding, we can utilize the trained model to infer fMRI from EEG and EEG from fMRI when only one modality is available. In Fig. 2a, we present an example of EEG channels inferred from fMRI data for a subject on which the model was not trained. Notably, we observe a strong correlation between the EEG signals transcoded from fMRI and the actual EEG measurements. This finding suggests that our model captures meaningful information from the fMRI modality and successfully reconstructs EEG signals.

To evaluate the group-level activation maps generated from fMRI transcoded from EEG data, we selected subjects for which the model was not trained. In Fig. 2c (ii) and (iv), we present the activation maps for the standard and oddball stimuli, respectively. We observe significant overlap and correlation between the group-level activation maps generated from EEG-transcoded fMRI (ii/iv) and the actual fMRI acquired simultaneously (i/iii). These results indicate that our model generates a latent source space that captures the underlying generative structure connecting both modalities. Furthermore, the observed divergence between the generated activation maps and the ground truth maps suggests that certain information is captured exclusively by one modality, emphasizing the importance of subject-specific differences in achieving precise reconstruction of the super-resolution latent source space.

The functionality of each module in the group-level cyclic convolutional transcoder can be interpreted as follows:

- fMRI decoder: The fMRI decoder solves the fMRI blind deconvolution problem, allowing for the decoding of the latent source space from fMRI data.
- EEG decoder: The EEG decoder addresses the EEG blind signal separation problem, enabling source localization from channel-wise EEG recordings to a 3D brain volume.
- fMRI encoder: The fMRI encoder convolves the latent source space with a hemodynamic response function (HRF) estimated from the data to encode it into fMRI data.
- EEG encoder: The EEG encoder maps the signal from the latent source space in the 3D brain volume to electrodes on the scalp surface through a forward head model (lead field matrix) estimated from the data, resulting in the encoding of the signal into EEG data.

The interpretability of our model's structure is a key design feature, allowing us to examine the representation specific to the functionality of each module. For instance, in Fig. 2d, we selected a voxel in the auditory cortex (indicated by the green circle) from the fMRI recording (referred to as "raw fMRI") and applied deconvolution using the fMRI decoder of the group level model. By doing so, we obtained the "fMRI estimated source" plot, which was then plotted relative to the stimulus. Remarkably, the resulting plot demonstrated that the peaks align with the auditory tones, with the standard tone represented in blue and the oddball tone in orange. This observation validates the ability of our model to capture and represent the neural responses associated with specific stimuli.

Simultaneously, the fMRI encoder performs a convolution process to generate fMRI estimations from the latent source space. Leveraging this process, we successfully extracted the hemodynamic response function (HRF) from the fMRI encoder by inputting a unit impulse response. The recovery of the HRF is illustrated in Fig. 2b. Specifically, Fig. 2b (i) presents the HRFs extracted from 19 fMRI encoders for the group level models that were retrained using a leave-one-subject-out approach. In contrast, Fig. 2b (ii) depicts the mean of these HRFs, accompanied by a 95% confidence interval. Notably, while each retrained model may converge to a different local minimum, all HRF estimates exhibit a typical time scale of 20–30 s, characterized by an initial dip followed by an overshoot. This consistent pattern across the HRF estimates reinforces the reliability of our model's ability to capture the underlying hemodynamic response dynamics. It is worth mentioning that we conducted the same analysis on a completely different experiment and a simultaneous EEG/fMRI dataset, yielding analogous results presented in Fig. 2b (iii) and (iv).

These findings highlight the robustness and generalizability of our approach across different datasets and experimental conditions. The successful recovery of the HRFs further demonstrates the capacity of our model to capture and represent the neurovascular coupling phenomena in response to various stimuli. By effectively decoding the fMRI data and extracting meaningful information, our model contributes to our understanding of the underlying neural processes and their relationship to the measured hemodynamic signals.

3.2   Recovery of the Latent Source Space

Our approach introduces a novel aspect whereby the latent representation in our transcoder can be interpreted as a spatiotemporal neural source space, providing insights into brain activity at the spatial resolution of fMRI (2 mm) and the temporal resolution of EEG (100 Hz). The resultant source space is illustrated in Fig. 3, enabling us to make several intriguing observations.

Firstly, Fig. 3i displays a representative spatial distribution of source deactivation occurring at 450 ms after an oddball stimulus. This deactivation pattern spreads across regions such as the prefrontal cortex, posterior cingulate cortex, temporal pole, and others. Importantly, this finding aligns with previous fMRI-only analyses conducted for the auditory oddball task [3]. However, our contribution lies in associating this deactivation with a specific time point, namely 450 ms after the stimulus. This temporal association enhances our understanding of the dynamics of brain activity during the oddball task and provides valuable insights into the underlying cognitive processes involved.

Moving on to Fig. 3i, we observe representative time frames of the thresholded Z-maps depicting the activation for both oddball and standard trials. At 350 ms after an oddball stimulus, significant activation is observed in the parietal lobe, as highlighted by the circled region. In contrast, this activation pattern is not seen for standard stimuli. Additionally, at approximately 400 ms after the onset of the oddball stimuli, we notice significant activation in the left motor cortex, specifically in the region corresponding to the right hand's index finger representation. Conversely, for standard stimuli, activation is observed in the primary auditory cortex, similar to the activation observed for oddball stimuli, but no activation is observed in the motor cortex. These findings are consistent with the experimental task, as participants only respond to oddball stimuli with a right-handed button press. The temporal resolution of the source space enables

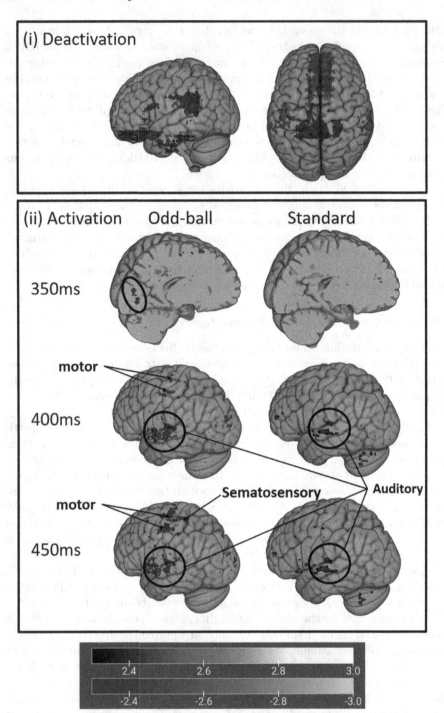

Fig. 3. Representative time frames of (i) deactivation and (ii) activation (uncorrected Z-maps) in the spatiotemporal latent source space.

us to differentiate the motor activation at 400 ms from the somatosensory activation at 450 ms, which arises due to the button press. This fine-grained temporal discrimination provides valuable insights into the neural dynamics associated with different aspects of the task.

The results presented in Fig. 3 offer compelling evidence of the utility of our approach in recovering the latent source space and unraveling the spatiotemporal dynamics of brain activity during the auditory oddball task. By combining fMRI and EEG data, our method sheds light on the neural processes underlying stimulus processing, cognitive engagement, and motor responses, thereby enriching our understanding of the complex interplay between brain regions and their temporal dynamics.

4   Conclusion

In this study, we have presented a novel hierarchical deep transcoding model designed for the fusion of simultaneously acquired EEG-fMRI data. Our model offers interpretability and represents a symmetric approach for EEG/fMRI fusion, addressing the need for a comprehensive understanding of brain activity across multiple modalities [4].

Through extensive experiments, we have demonstrated the efficacy of our model in generating one modality from another while effectively resolving the latent neural source space. The interpretability of our model enables us to gain insights into the functionality of each module and understand the representations specific to different aspects of brain activity.

By leveraging the capabilities of our model, we have successfully generated fMRI estimations from EEG data and vice versa. The accurate generation of one modality from the other signifies the robustness and reliability of our approach in capturing the complex relationships between EEG and fMRI signals. Furthermore, our model's ability to resolve the latent neural source space provides valuable information about the spatiotemporal dynamics of brain activity, enhancing our understanding of the underlying neural processes.

The development of our hierarchical deep transcoding model represents a significant step forward in the field of EEG-fMRI fusion. The model's interpretability and symmetric nature contribute to its versatility and applicability in various research domains, enabling researchers to explore the intricate interactions between electrical and hemodynamic signals in the human brain.

In conclusion, our work demonstrates the potential of our hierarchical deep transcoding model as a powerful tool for integrating EEG and fMRI data. By leveraging the complementary strengths of these modalities, our model opens up new avenues for investigating brain function and provides a valuable framework for future studies aiming to unravel the complex mechanisms underlying brain activity.

5   Broader Impact

The development of our model has the potential to significantly impact the field of neuroimaging by addressing cost and accessibility limitations associated with traditional fMRI scans. A single fMRI scan can be expensive, with costs ranging from $600 to $1200, and the initial investment for fMRI equipment, including necessary support costs, can exceed $3 million. In contrast, electroencephalography (EEG) offers high temporal resolution but lower spatial resolution and is much more affordable, with scan costs typically below $10 and equipment costs around $50,000.

By leveraging our model, which can reconstruct fMRI data from EEG recordings and vice versa, we present a computationally-driven approach that has the potential to significantly reduce the cost of obtaining fMRI images. This could enable researchers and clinicians to generate fMRI-like information from affordable EEG recordings, thereby democratizing access to functional brain imaging. By reducing the financial barrier associated with fMRI scans, our model may have a positive broader impact by making functional brain imaging more accessible to researchers and healthcare providers, especially those with limited resources or in resource-constrained settings.

However, it is important to acknowledge that the potential cost reduction of fMRI scans through our model could have implications for the development and usage of traditional MRI technology. The availability of a low-cost alternative that can generate fMRI-like images from EEG data might lead to a decrease in demand for traditional fMRI scans. This could potentially impact the market for MRI machines and related technologies, which have historically played a significant role in advancing medical diagnostics and research. Therefore, it is essential for stakeholders in the field to carefully consider the potential consequences and ensure a balanced approach that maximizes the benefits of both EEG and fMRI technologies.

Furthermore, our model's ability to improve source localization accuracy for EEG has significant implications for brain-computer interface (BCI) applications. EEG is a widely used modality in BCI research due to its ease of operation and lower cost compared to other imaging techniques. By enhancing the accuracy of source localization, our model could contribute to advancements in BCI systems, enabling more precise and reliable brain activity measurements. This has the potential to open up new possibilities in various fields, such as assistive technologies, neurorehabilitation, and human-computer interaction, where accurate and real-time monitoring of brain activity is crucial.

In conclusion, our model's potential for cost reduction in fMRI scans and its impact on EEG-based source localization accuracy in BCI applications highlight the broader implications of our research. While offering the prospect of increased accessibility to functional brain imaging, it is essential to carefully consider the potential consequences and engage in responsible and ethical adoption to ensure that the benefits are maximized and any potential negative impacts are mitigated.

Acknowledgements. This work is supported by the Army Research Laboratory under Cooperative agreement number W911NF-10-2-0022 and a Vannevar Bush Faculty Fellowship from the US Department of Defense (N00014-20-1-2027).

References

1. Huettel, S.A., Song, A.W., McCarthy, G., et al.: Functional magnetic resonance imaging. Sinauer Associates Sunderland, MA, vol. 1 (2004)
2. Niedermeyer, E., da Silva, F.L.: Electroencephalography: Basic Principles, Clinical Applications, and Related Fields. Lippincott Williams & Wilkins, Philadelphia (2005)
3. Wolf, D.H., et al.: Auditory oddball fMRI in schizophrenia: association of negative symptoms with regional hypoactivation to novel distractors. Brain Imaging Behav. **2**(2), 132–145 (2008)
4. Philiastides, M.G., Tu, T., Sajda, P.: Inferring macroscale brain dynamics via fusion of simultaneous EEG-fMRI. Annu. Rev. Neurosci. **44**(1), 1–20 (2021)

Investigations of Human Information Processing Systems

Decoding Emotion Dimensions Arousal and Valence Elicited on EEG Responses to Videos and Images: A Comparative Evaluation

Luis Alfredo Moctezuma[1]([✉]), Kazuki Sato[1], Marta Molinas[2], and Takashi Abe[1]

[1] International Institute for Integrative Sleep Medicine (WPI-IIIS), University of Tsukuba, Tsukuba, Ibaraki, Japan
luisalfredomoctezuma@gmail.com
[2] Department of Engineering Cybernetics, Norwegian University of Science and Technology, Trondheim, Norway

Abstract. This study aims to compare the automatic classification of emotions based on the self-reported level of arousal and valence with the Self-Assessment Manikin (SAM) when subjects were exposed to videos or images. The classification is performed on electroencephalographic (EEG) signals from the DEAP public dataset, and a dataset collected at the University of Tsukuba, Japan. The experiments were defined to classify low versus high arousal/valence using a Convolutional Neural Network (CNN). The obtained results show a higher performance when the subjects were exposed to videos, i.e., using DEAP dataset we obtained an area under the receiver operating characteristic (AUROC) of 0.844 ± 0.008 and 0.836 ± 0.009 to classify low versus high arousal/valence, respectively. In contrast, when subjects were stimulated with images, the obtained performance was 0.621 ± 0.007 for both, arousal and valence classification. The obtained difference was confirmed by testing the experiments using a method based on the Discrete Wavelet Transform (DWT) for feature extraction and classification using random forest. Using image-based stimulation may help to better understand low and high arousal/valence when analyzing event-related potentials (ERP), however, according to the obtained results, for classification purposes, the performance is higher using video-based stimulation.

Keywords: Emotion classification · Electroencephalography (EEG) · Convolutional Neural Networks (CNN) · Discrete Wavelet Transform (DWT)

1 Introduction

Emotions play an important role in our social structure, personal life, human working ability, and mental health, etc. They can be triggered in response to stimuli, and are regulated and guided by our brain [1,2].

F. Liu et al. (Eds.): BI 2023, LNAI 13974, pp. 71–82, 2023.
https://doi.org/10.1007/978-3-031-43075-6_7

This work considers the dimensional space-based classification model, which holds that emotions are not discrete, and that the similarity and difference between emotions are represented according to their distance in the dimensional space. It proposes that all affective states arise from two fundamental neuro-physiological systems, one related to valence (a pleasure-displeasure continuum) and the other to arousal, or alertness (related to the perceived intensity of an event) [3,4].

Based on arousal and valence, researchers have proposed automatic methods to classify the elicited emotions while a subject is exposed to different stimuli. The response to stimuli is measure using electroencephalography (EEG), and then the EEG signals are used to classify if the emotion belongs to a low or high arousal/valence. Emotion recognition can be useful in different domains and EEG-based applications including education, security, mental health and general healthcare [5–7].

The Self-Assessment Manikin (SAM) is a non-verbal and image-oriented questionnaire that is used to measure the affective reaction of the subject to a stimulus, i.e., we can expose a subject to emotional videos/film clips or images, and then using SAM, it is possible to measure the elicited emotion in terms of arousal and Valence [8]. Current EEG-based approaches in the state-of-the-art uses mainly public datasets like DEAP, MAHNOB-HCI, SEED (SEED, SEED-IV, SEED-V, SEED-FRA, SEED-GER), DREAMER [9–14]. Most of them measure the elicited emotion in terms of negative, positive, neutral or happy, sad, angry, and fear, and a few of them with **arousal and valence** and dominance.

Automatic classification approaches include the use of classical machine learning (ML) such as Support Vector Machine (SVM), naive Bayes, random forest, as well as Deep Learning (DL) [15,16]. A proposed Convolutional Neural Network (CNN) architecture called EEGNet has been tested for different EEG-related task classification, including emotion classification, and it has shown higher accuracies than some ML-based classifiers [7,17].

Recent approaches include the use of methods for pre-processing and feature extraction, as well as the use of raw data as input to ML/DL architectures. The Discrete Wavelet Transform (DWT) as been used to decompose the EEG signals into different sub-bands, extract a set of statistical values per sub-band, then apply Principal Component Analysis (PCA) to reduce the set of features, and use the obtained values as input to SVM, obtaining accuracies above 80% [18].

A previous research explored the use of multi-objective optimization for channel selection, and the reported performance using in some subjects of DEAP dataset was up to 86% and 92% to classify low versus high arousal/valence using a CNN [7].

For the interest of this work, Table 1 present an overview of relevant approaches where the emotions were measured in terms of arousal and valence. The presented approaches use the DEAP and DREAMER dataset, and the reported performance is about 94% using all the EEG channels in the classification process, and 89% using only one channel.

Table 1. Related works using emotion classification in terms of Arousal and Valence

Dataset, reference	Method	Result
DEAP, 32 subjects, 32 channels with 512 Hz, 60-s **videos** [7]	low vs high arousal/valence using CNN (2 s segments).	Using only 1ch. **Arousal**: up to 86%. **Valence**: up to 92%
DEAP [19]	CNN, Sparse Autoencoder and DNN	**Arousal**: 89.4%. **Valence**: 92.9%
DEAP [18]	Three features per DWT sub-band (3.5 s segments). PCA to reduce the features, and SVM for classification.	Up to 80%
DEAP [20]	4D-convolution recurrent neural network	**Arousal**: 94.58. **Valence**: 94.22
DREAMER, 23 subjects, 14 channels with 128 Hz, 60-s **videos** [13]	Common Average Reference (CAR), 3 sub-bands, apply PSD to each sub-band	**Arousal** : 62.4%. **Valence**: 62.2%

This study analyzes two datasets for low versus high arousal/valence classification, one using video and the other images for emotion elicitation. We compare the performance of the same classification process in both datasets and using the EEG channels in common.

First, we tested a CNN in the DEAP dataset, where the arousal/valence values were reported by the subjects. Then, we use the CNN to classify the subject's report in a private dataset that was collected while the subjects were exposed to images from the International Affective Picture System (IAPS) and the Open Affective Standardized Image Set (OASIS) [21–23], to later compare the performance of the same dataset but using the defined values in IAPS/OASIS instead of subjects report.

This is relevant because using IAPS/OASIS values may contribute to future work for creating subject-independent models, since presenting the same image to different subjects may report different SAM values. As in our previous research in EEG-related tasks [7,24], we compare both datasets using a pre-processing step, DWT-based feature extraction method and random forest classifier.

2 Materials and Methods

2.1 Description and Preprocessing of the Datasets

The first dataset was collected in the International Institute for Integrative Sleep Medicine (WPI-IIIS) at University of Tsukuba, Japan. It consists of EEG recordings from 16 subjects using 12 EEG channels (Polymate Pro MP6100, Miyuki

Giken, Tokyo, Japan) with a sample rate of 1000 Hz located according to the 10–20 international system: F3, F4, C3, C4, O1, O2, Fpz, Fz, Cz, Pz, M1 and M2, and Fcz as reference. The data collection of the WPI-IIIS dataset was approved by the ethics committee of the University of Tsukuba [25].

The followed protocol consisted on presenting 420 images from IAPS/OASIS during 1.5 s, this duration allows for conscious processing of the subjects but maintains an adequate level of difficulty, as it was done in other related research [26]. The WPI-IIIS dataset collected EEG data before, during, and after sleep, all repeated under two different conditions that were different only for sleep data (presenting ODOR or AIR during Rapid Eye Movement (REM) sleep). Sleep EEG data were collected for purposes other than those of this paper, therefore we did not consider it for the analysis. The protocol before sleep was collected 420 epochs per condition in two sessions (210 per session), and only one session after sleep (420 images).

Friedman test revealed no difference in the valence and arousal between the two conditions, either before or after sleep [25], therefore, for the design of the experiments, we have separated the dataset into two sets, before (pre) and after sleep (post). In this way, we obtain **840 epochs before** (210 × 2 sessions × two conditions) and **840 after sleep** (420 × two conditions) per subject [25]. The EEG channels were re-referenced to $(M1 + M2)/2$, then, we applied a notch filter at 50 Hz, and a band-pass frequency filter from 0.1–45 Hz.

We also used the well-known DEAP dataset, which consists of EEG recordings from 32 subjects, using 32 EEG electrodes of the Biosemi ActiveTwo system, with a sample rate of 512 Hz and located according to the 10–20 international system. The followed protocol for emotion stimulation consisted on presenting 40 60-s music videos, that subjects rated in terms of **valence, arousal, like/dislike,** and **dominance** using SAM [9].

For the defined experiments using DEAP dataset, we have used 2-s instances, since the classification performance is higher than with other segment size [7]. We obtained 800 instances per subject (60-s, 30 instances per video), however in some subjects the number is lower or higher, as it is shown in [7].

The authors applied preprocessing on the DEAP dataset, and it consists of down-sampling at 128 Hz, electrooculography (EOG) artifact removal, a 4–45 Hz band-pass frequency filter, then they applied CAR [9].

For the experiments, we considered the 9 channels in common between both datasets: F3, F4, C3, C4, O1, O2, Fz, Cz, and Pz. We separated the EEG signals from a given subject into Training with 60% of the dataset, validation 20% and test set 20%. For DEAP dataset, each participant signed a consent form and filled out a questionnaire prior to the experiment. All the procedures were performed in accordance with the relevant guidelines and regulations or in accordance with the Declaration of Helsinki [9].

2.2   CNN-Based Classification

Previous research has shown that CNN outperforms other methods based on classical machine learning algorithms for emotion classification [7, 15–17]. Based on this, we used a compact CNN architecture called EEGNet, which can be summarized as follows: **Block 1** performs two convolutional steps in sequence. First, it fits a *2D convolutional filter*, with the filter length chosen to be half the sampling rate, resulting in feature maps that contain different band-pass frequencies of the EEG signal. Then, a *Depthwise convolution* that learns a spatial filter, is applied. It applies a *Batch Normalization* along the feature map dimension before applying the *exponential linear unit (ELU)* nonlinearity, and to help regularize it uses the *Dropout* technique. After that, it applies an *average pooling* layer to reduce the sampling rate and regularize each spatial filter by using a maximum norm constraint of 1. **Block 2** uses a *Separable Convolution*, which is a *Depthwise Convolution* followed by *Pointwise Convolutions*.

Lastly, an Average Pooling layer for dimension reduction is used, and the features are managed by a softmax classification with N = 2 units, where N is the number of classes.

The loss function was categorical cross-entropy, and the network was optimized with the *Adam* algorithm. Based on previous research, we considered a maximum of 200 epochs for training the CNN models [7]. We applied the Early stopping callback in Keras to interrupt training when the validation accuracy has stopped improving.

2.3   DWT-Based Feature Extraction and ML for Classification

Previous research has considered decomposing the EEG signals into different sub-bands and then extracting a set of features, and in some cases, it has shown high performance. To analyze how it works on the tested datasets, we applied DWT to decompose the EEG signals into 5 sub-bands (4 arrays of detail coefficients and 1 approximation), then for each sub-band we computed 10 features: Skewness, Kurtosis, Instantaneous energy, Teager energy, Hjort mobility, Hjort complexity, Selvik fractal dimension, Higuchi fractal dimension, Katz fractal dimension, Petrosian fractal dimension [7,24].

The obtained features from all the EEG channels were used as input to different classifiers and validated using 10-fold cross-validation. We only report the results obtained with random forest, with which the highest performance was achieved.

For both cases, using either CNN or DWT-based feature extraction, we have validated the model's performance using the accuracy, Fscore, Precision, Recall, and area under the receiver operating characteristic (AUROC).

3   Results

The following set of experiments were performed, aiming to classify the EEG signals into two classes: **low versus high arousal**, and also **low versus high valence**. The experiments were carried out considering the 9 EEG channels in common between WPI-IIIS and DEAP dataset. All the experiments were considered using the EEG data from one subject at the time, and the average performance is reported.

3.1   Video-Based Emotion Elicitation

We used the EEG signals of the DEAP dataset to create a model per subject and classify Low versus High Arousal, as well as Low versus High Valence. After the pre-processing, the EEG signals from each of the 60-s videos were divided into 2-s segments, and then use it as input to the CNN.

Figure 1 shows the distribution of the 60-s instances from all the subjects in terms of arousal/valence, with values from 1–9. It also shows where most of the instances are concentrated (see the maximum values in the color scale), and the number of videos in each quadrant, which are used to divide the classes: Low ($<= 5$) versus High (>5) arousal/valence. This shows that the classes are slightly unbalanced, i.e., 572 and 708 for Low and High arousal, and 543 and 737 for low versus high valence.

The models were trained and validated using the accuracy metric (Training acc and Validation acc). Once each of the models were trained, the test sets were used and the performance was evaluated using the five metrics defined above (Acc, Fscore, Precision, Recall and AUROC). The obtained results are presented in Fig. 2.

The obtained results shown that the performance in the training, test and validation sets are consistent, and the standard deviation is similar among them. In the case of the AUROC, it is shown a higher performance, and the stan-

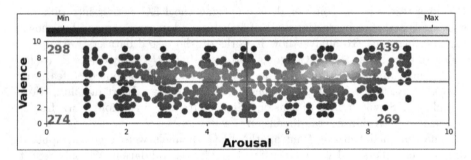

Fig. 1. Distribution of arousal and valence rating values for the videos presented to all the subjects in the DEAP dataset

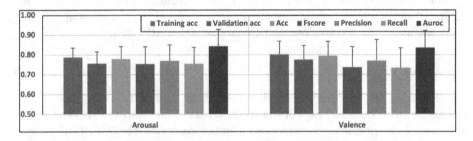

Fig. 2. CNN-based low versus high arousal/valence classification using 9 channels of DEAP dataset.

dard deviation is also higher, obtaining up to 0.93, for both, low versus high arousal and low versus high valence. Which means that selecting accurately a new threshold, the other metrics may increase.

3.2 Image-Based Emotion Elicitation, Labels Using Subject's Report

As in the case of DEAP dataset, here we considered the level of Arousal and Valence reported by the subjects when they were exposed to the IAPS/OASIS images. After the pre-processing of the 1.5-s instances and class labeling, the data of each subject was used as input to the same CNN architecture to classify low versus high arousal, and low versus high valence. The obtained results are presented in Fig. 3.

As it was explained in Sect. 2.1, the dataset contains EEG signals collected before (PRE) and after sleep (POST). Taking advantage of this, we performed the experiment considering the signals PRE, POST and also joining BOTH. The obtained results for low versus high arousal/valence are presented in Fig. 3.

The results have shown a clear different performance across the used metrics, but still higher than random. This indicates that there is a difference in the low and high arousal/valence, but not enough or clear in the majority of the instances.

The difference between the training and validation performance is larger in the case of Valence than Arousal, in all cases, PRE, POST or BOTH. The performance obtained with the test set (Acc, Fscore, Precision, Recall and AUROC) is lower than in the training and validation (Training acc and Validation acc), which indicates that the generalization is poor, and the CNN didn't learn correctly.

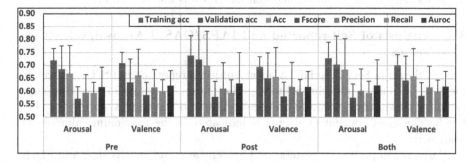

Fig. 3. CNN-based classification of the self-reported level of arousal and valence for labelling the WPI-IIIS dataset

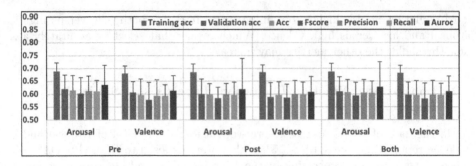

Fig. 4. CNN-based classification using the IAPS/OASIS arousal and valence values for labelling the WPI-IIIS dataset

3.3 Image-Based Emotion Elicitation, Labels Using IAPS/OASIS Values

To study if the difference between the subject's reported values and the associated arousal/valence value in the IAPS/OASIS dataset affect the performance, this experiment considered the same conditions as in Sect. 3.2, but the labels are defined by the arousal/valence values in the IAPS/OASIS dataset.

The set of experiments also considered the subset of data from PRE, POST and BOTH, and the obtained results are presented in Fig. 4.

It is shown that the performance for the different configurations is lower than defining the labels with the subject's report. In general, the performance decreased 3–4%, which indicates that it is possible to define the labels using the proposed values in the IAPS/OASIS dataset.

Figure 4 shown that the different reported metrics are more stable (except the accuracy of the trained models), and similar among them. In contrast, using subject's report, the variation between metrics was higher (see Fig. 3).

3.4 Analysis of Self-reported and IAPS/OASIS Arousal/valence Values

As it is shown in Sect. 3.2 and 3.3, using subject's report or IAPS/OASIS values for data labeling, results in different performance. To analyze it, we compared the distribution of the arousal/valence values, and the results are presented in Fig. 5. The most concentrated area is indicated at the maximum value of the color scale.

We also computed the correlation for each case, and as it is shown in Fig. 6, in the case of the Arousal the correlation is 0.49, which indicates that subject's reports are different from the arousal/valence values in the IAPS/OASIS dataset.

In the best case, the correlation between subject's report and IAPS/OASIS values was 0.776 for arousal and 0.86 for valence. In the worst case, the correlation was 0.178, and 0.509, for arousal and valence, respectively. This indicates that some subjects responded similar values than the one in IAPS/OASIS, but in some cases the values are different, specially in the case of Arousal.

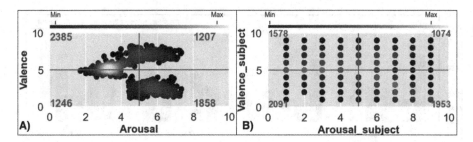

Fig. 5. Distribution of self-reported arousal and valence rating values for the images presented to all the subjects in the WPI-IIIS dataset.

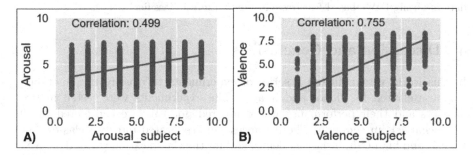

Fig. 6. Correlation of the self-reported arousal and valence values with the values from IAPS/OASIS dataset

3.5 DWT-Based Features to Classify Low Versus High Arousal

The objective of this experiment is to show an overview of the performance obtained using DWT-based features and then use them as input to random forest, which used 10-fold cross-validation and the defined datasets with 9 EEG channels. Different algorithms were tested, but only the one with the highest performance is presented. The obtained results are presented in Fig. 7.

Previous research has shown that for emotion classification, the CNN outperform a DWT-based feature extraction method [7]. To explore if this applies also for image-based stimulation, as well as to confirm the difference found in the previous experiments, we performed a set of experiments to classify low versus high arousal in both datasets for comparison purposes, but as it has been shown in previous experiments, the performance is similar for both, arousal and valence.

The obtained performance is lower using DWT-based features and random forest classifier than with the CNN, but the performance is still higher with DEAP dataset (i.e., using video-based stimulation instead of image-based stimulation). It is shown that the metrics are more stable in the DEAP dataset, but in the case of the WPI-IIIS the performance of the trained model is higher than in the test and validation sets.

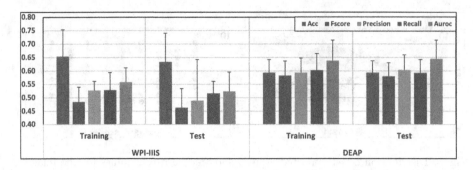

Fig. 7. Comparison of low versus high arousal classification in WPI-IIIS and DEAP datasets using DWT-based features and random forest classifier

4 Discussion and Conclusions

In this work, we conducted a series of experiments to classify the emotional response elicited by videos and images. The experiments were tested in two datasets and their performance was compared, for this, we considered the 9 EEG channels in common. The instances were separated into two classes, low ($<=5$) and high (>5) arousal/valence, and for the classification we used a CNN.

The experiments suggest that when stimulating the emotions using videos, the classification performance is higher than using images from IAPS/OASIS.

The image-based stimulation was during 1.5 s, while the video-base stimulation was during 40 s. If the objective of a study is ERP analysis, the presentation of images may be clearer than in the case of the videos, where the emotion will vary along the 40-s videos. This is because the evoked potential may not be at the start of the video in all the cases.

In the case of video-based stimulation, the reported emotion by the subject may be clearer or more associated to the presented video than to the images, since the emotion is clarified during some seconds, instead of reporting the first impression as it may occur in the case of presenting images. This is apparent in the WPI-IIIS dataset, where the originally associated values to the images in the IAPS/OASIS dataset are not correlated to the subject's report, specially for arousal (correlation: 0.499, see Fig. 6).

The obtained results with DEAP dataset are more stable in the different metrics used than in the WPI-IIIS dataset. All the experiments were performed using a common set of 9 channels, which were selected based on the available channels of the WPI-IIIS dataset, however, previous research has shown that if we select the channels using an automatic method, the results may improve [7]. In that way, we could exploit the spatial filters inherent in the CNN. For instance, using the 32 EEG channels from the DEAP dataset, we can obtain 0.94 ± 0.6 accuracy for both low versus high, arousal/valence. In the case of the WPI-IIIS, using all the available channels, the performance does not increase significantly, i.e., 1–2% in the different experiments.

The obtained results show that considering the IAPS/OASIS values instead of subject's report, don't help to increase the performance, but rather it is lower.

However, to propose a subject-independent model, it is necessary to consider a method that include the analysis of actual values from a dataset, as well as subject's report.

As it is shown in Fig. 5, in the case of low versus high valence, the most crowded part in the distribution is around the value 5, which means that subjects reported a neutral emotion, and this may be the reason for decreasing the classification performance. In the case of DEAP, the distribution of the reported values, is slightly higher than Neutral for the same case of Valence.

Considering subject's report, it would not be possible to propose a subject-independent model, but as this study suggests, it would be possible to design the labels based on the values from the used dataset. Future work, will evaluate this by testing both approaches for labeling, stimulating the emotions using videos.

There are differences in the protocols followed for data collection that may influence the performance comparison, such as the use of different devices, acquisition time, etc., in this sense, future research will control all these factors to draw further conclusions.

Recently, some approaches have tested the Bidirectional long-short term memory(Bi-LSTM) for EEG-based applications [27], however, preliminary results with DEAP and the WPI-IIIS dataset show that Bi-LSTM performance is lower than using EEGNet or DWT-based features and ML models, but further analyzes testing new architectures will be tested in future work.

Acknowledgement. This work was supported by JSPS Postdoctoral Fellowship for Research in Japan: Fellowship ID P22716, and JSPS KAKENHI: Grant number JP22K19802 and JP20K03493.

References

1. Reeck, C., Ames, D.R., Ochsner, K.N.: The social regulation of emotion: an integrative, cross-disciplinary model. Trends Cogn. Sci. **20**(1), 47–63 (2016)
2. James, W.: What is an emotion? Mind **9**, 188–205 (1884)
3. Russell, J.A.: A circumplex model of affect. J. Pers. Soc. Psychol. **39**(6), 1161 (1980)
4. Dalgleish, T.: The emotional brain. Nat. Rev. Neurosci. **5**(7), 583–589 (2004)
5. Liu, Y., Fu, G.: Emotion recognition by deeply learned multi-channel textual and EEG features. Futur. Gener. Comput. Syst. **119**, 1–6 (2021)
6. Daily, S.B., et al.: Affective computing: historical foundations, current applications, and future trends. Emot. Affect Hum. Factors Hum.-Comput. Interact. 213–231. Elsevier (2017)
7. Moctezuma, L.A., Abe, T., Molinas, M.: Two-dimensional CNN-based distinction of human emotions from EEG channels selected by multi-objective evolutionary algorithm. Sci. Rep. **12**(1), 1–15 (2022)
8. Bradley, M.M., Lang, P.J.: Measuring emotion: the self-assessment manikin and the semantic differential. J. Behav. Ther. Exp. Psychiatry **25**(1), 49–59 (1994)
9. Koelstra, S., et al.: DEAP: a database for emotion analysis; using physiological signals. IEEE Trans. Affect. Comput. **3**(1), 18–31 (2011)

10. Soleymani, M., Lichtenauer, J., Pun, T., Pantic, M.: A multimodal database for affect recognition and implicit tagging. IEEE Trans. Affect. Comput. **3**(1), 42–55 (2011)
11. Duan, R.-N., Zhu, J.-Y., Lu, B.-L.: Differential entropy feature for EEG-based emotion classification. In: 2013 6th International IEEE/EMBS Conference on Neural Engineering (NER), pp. 81–84. IEEE (2013)
12. Zheng, W.-L., Zhu, J.-Y., Lu, B.-L.: Identifying stable patterns over time for emotion recognition from EEG. IEEE Trans. Affect. Comput. **10**(3), 417–429 (2017)
13. Katsigiannis, S., Ramzan, N.: DREAMER: a database for emotion recognition through EEG and ECG signals from wireless low-cost off-the-shelf devices. IEEE J. Biomed. Health Inform. **22**(1), 98–107 (2017)
14. Zheng, W.-L., Liu, W., Lu, Y., Lu, B.-L., Cichocki, A.: Emotionmeter: a multimodal framework for recognizing human emotions. IEEE Trans. Cybern. **49**(3), 1110–1122 (2018)
15. Lotte, F., et al.: A review of classification algorithms for EEG-based brain-computer interfaces: a 10 year update. J. Neural Eng. **15**(3), 031005 (2018)
16. Roy, Y., Banville, H., Albuquerque, I., Gramfort, A., Falk, T.H., Faubert, J.: Deep learning-based electroencephalography analysis: a systematic review. J. Neural Eng. **16**(5), 051001 (2019)
17. Lawhern, V.J., Solon, A.J., Waytowich, N.R., Gordon, S.M., Hung, C.P., Lance, B.J.: EEGNet: a compact convolutional neural network for EEG-based brain-computer interfaces. J. Neural Eng. **15**(5), 056013 (2018)
18. Placidi, G., Di Giamberardino, P., Petracca, A., Spezialetti, M., Iacoviello, D.: Classification of emotional signals from the deap dataset. Int. Congress Neurotechnol. Electron. Inform. **2**, 15–21. SCITEPRESS (2016)
19. Liu, J., et al.: EEG-based emotion classification using a deep neural network and sparse autoencoder. Front. Syst. Neurosci. **14**, 43 (2020)
20. Shen, F., Dai, G., Lin, G., Zhang, J., Kong, W., Zeng, H.: EEG-based emotion recognition using 4D convolutional recurrent neural network. Cogn. Neurodyn. **14**(6), 815–828 (2020)
21. Lang, P., Greenwald, M.: The international affective picture system standardization procedure and initial group results for affective judgments: Technical report 1a, The Center for Research in Psychophysiology, University of Florida (1988)
22. Lang, P.J., Bradley, M.M., Cuthbert, B.N., et al.: International affective picture system (IAPS): affective ratings of pictures and instruction manual. Center for the Study of Emotion & Attention Gainesville, FL, NIMH (2005)
23. Kurdi, B., Lozano, S., Banaji, M.R.: Introducing the open affective standardized image set (OASIS). Behav. Res. Methods **49**, 457–470 (2017)
24. Moctezuma, L.A.: Towards Universal EEG systems with minimum channel count based on Machine Learning and Computational Intelligence. PhD thesis, Department of Engineering Cybernetics, Norwegian University of Science and Technology (2021)
25. Sato, K.: Targeted memory reactivation during rem sleep selectively enhances brain responses to unpleasant images. Master's thesis, International Institute for Integrative Sleep Medicine (WPI-IIIS), University of Tsukuba (2023)
26. Groch, S., Wilhelm, I., Diekelmann, S., Born, J.: The role of rem sleep in the processing of emotional memories: evidence from behavior and event-related potentials. Neurobiol. Learn. Mem. **99**, 1–9 (2013)
27. Ma, S., Cui, J., Chen, C.-L., Xiao, W., Liu, L.: An improved Bi-LSTM EEG emotion recognition algorithm. J. Netw. Intell. **7**(3), 623–639 (2022)

Stabilize Sequential Data Representation via Attraction Module

Petr Kuderov[1,2,3](✉) , Evgenii Dzhivelikian[2] , and Aleksandr I. Panov[1,3]

[1] AIRI, Moscow, Russia
kuderov@airi.net
[2] Moscow Institute of Physics and Technology, Dolgoprudny, Russia
[3] Federal Research Center "Computer Science and Control" of the Russian Academy of Sciences FRC CSC RAS, Moscow, Russia

Abstract. Artificial intelligence systems operating in the sequential decision making paradigm are inevitably required to do effective spatio-temporal processing. The memory models for such systems are often required not just to memorize the observed data stream, but also to encode it so it is possible to separate dissimilar sequences and consolidate similar ones. Moreover, for solving complex problems, it is advantageous to have the ability to treat sequences as unit abstractions, which imposes restrictions on the topology of the representation space and the information contained in the representations themselves. In this paper, we propose a method for encoding sequences that allows efficient memorization, but at the same time retains the degree of similarity between sequences. We based our approach on the combination of biologically-inspired temporal memory and spatial attractor that stabilize temporal coding. The experiments performed on synthetic data confirm the coding efficiency and allow us to identify promising directions for further development of methods.

Keywords: Sequential memory · Spatio-temporal abstractions · Spatial pooler · Temporal memory · Spatial attractor

1 Introduction

In the paradigm of sequential decision-making, artificial intelligence (AI) systems must perform spatio-temporal processing effectively. Memory models for these systems must not only memorize observed data streams, but also encode them in order to differentiate dissimilar sequences and combine similar ones. Such models, when combined with the ability to treat sequences as unit abstractions, are critical for solving complex problems because they allow operating at different scales of space and action and, as a result, significantly reduce the solution search space by reusing high-level abstractions (such as trajectories, objects or skills). This constrains the representation space's topology and the information contained in the representations.

© The Author(s), under exclusive license to Springer Nature Switzerland AG 2023
F. Liu et al. (Eds.): BI 2023, LNAI 13974, pp. 83–95, 2023.
https://doi.org/10.1007/978-3-031-43075-6_8

Many successful sequential memory models in Machine Learning are inspired by what we know about the human brain [4, 24]. It is not by coincidence, because for our brains a continuous sequential stream of stimuli is a natural type of input, and evolution has trained them to make spatio-temporal processing effective [12, 13]. Therefore, we believe that biologically plausible models of memory can help us not only understand how the human brain works, but also develop better models for artificial systems. However, collaboration between ML and computational neuroscience in combining disparate models and ideas are complicated because in Machine Learning biological plausibility is not a constraint.

In this work, we propose the biologically inspired memory model for effective spatio-temporal processing in order to memorize sequential data and form their abstractions, where the latter is expressed via the ability to retain sequences' mutual similarity in the memory latent state representations. Our model has several components: the spatial encoder block, the sequence memory, and the attractor block consisting of spatial and associative attractors. We evaluate the model in two regimes: when the input dataset is static and when it varies during the course of learning. The results confirm that the attractor block helps the sequential memory learn sequences significantly faster and forces it to form semantically meaningful representations reflecting the truth input data similarity, while the spatial encoder block benefits the memory's ability to generalize and reuse learned representations.

2 Related Works

Sequence processing and memorization tasks are common in Machine Learning. The models based on the transformer architecture are the most successful in modern Deep Learning [15, 24]. Their self-attention mechanism is proved to be effective for attentive context aggregation. However, the main drawback of the vanilla transformer architecture is the requirement to attend to the whole context at once, which is not available in online sequence processing. This is only partially remedied in transformer architectures with memory, which processes the input sequence by chunks called segments and either accumulates context in memory slots or attends to the hidden state of the previous time step [3, 5, 7].

The more biologically plausible models are recurrent memory models [6, 17]. Working in an online fashion, they learn to effectively encode sequences in their latent state and attend to past information when new data arrives. The most prominent of such models in classical ML is LSTM [14], which, however, employs a biologically implausible backpropagation-through-time algorithm for weight updating. LSTM is successfully used for modeling a huge variety of time series data [26], however, some variants of the Hidden Markov Model (HMM) may give a better performance on long sequences [8]. Moreover, in contrast to deterministic artificial neural networks (ANNs), probabilistic HMM-like models can deal effectively with missing data and probabilistic multi-step predictions.

The fast weights approach [1] extends recurrent memory models like LSTM, which stores the context in its hidden state, with the fast network accumulating the short-term context in its weights via the Hebbian-like plasticity rule. As the result, such a model benefits from the extended quadratic capacity of the fast weights network to store more information about the recent past. It is also shown that the effects of applying the fast network copy the transformers self-attention mechanism and therefore provide a fine-grained attentive short-term context-dependent processing. Given that the In-Context Learning for transformer architectures results in the weights matrix difference similar to the weights of the fast network, we believe that this approach itself is a promising direction to link the power of self-attention from the offline transformer architectures to online memory models. Moreover, the fast weights networks are attractor networks—after storing memories they become attractor states supporting pattern completion on retrieval. It means that they tend to consolidate similar memories together bringing generalization properties to the memory. In our model, the attractor module is loosely inspired by the fast weights approach and is expected to integrate representations of similar sequences.

Attractors are traditionally used for modeling working memory [2,25] and activity of the neocortex [19]. Despite their high capacity properties (due to distributed storing of information in weights), attractors mostly lose temporal information and aren't suitable for sequence modeling. Therefore, the integration of auto-associative attractor dynamics and temporal context formation is a promising direction, which we investigate in the proposed model.

There are also several key aspects worth mentioning that distinguish our model from the models based on ANNs in terms of biological plausibility. First of all, in our model neurons interact with discrete binary spikes, not floating-point valued data. Second, the model works with sparse distributed representations. Also, we use a multi-compartment model of a neuron with active dendrites—in addition to feedforward connections, modulating contextual connections are defined, and the connections themselves are combined into dendritic segments. Finally, we use local Hebbian learning instead of non-biological backpropagation.

3   Background

In this work, we study the spatio-temporal memory model inspired by HTM [11, 16] and HIMA frameworks [9], which is based on a discrete three-compartment computational model of a pyramidal neuron with active dendrites of the cerebral cortex and hippocampus (see Fig. 1A). In our model, neurons communicate through binary synapses—all inputs and outputs of the model are presented as binary patterns. The connections have real-valued weights and are trained by the Hebbian rule. Depending on the algorithm, synaptic weights determine either the binary ability to transmit information between connecting neurons, on the basis of the threshold function, or determine the strength of this transmission.

The dendritic synapses of the neuron are grouped into compartments, and within them, into segments. The proximal basal compartment has a single segment that is responsible for the direct input of the neuron. The distal basal and apical compartments can have multiple segments. Each segment sets the unit of

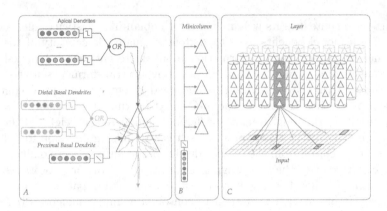

Fig. 1. Hierarchical Temporal Memory framework. **A.** Pyramidal neuron model. **B.** A group of neurons organized into a minicolumn. Neurons within a minicolumn share the same receptive field. **C.** Minicolumns organized into a layer share the same feedforward input, however, they may have different receptive fields.

neuron activation—it becomes active based on the activity of its receptive field, regardless of the activity of other segments. Neurons themselves are organized into ensembles called minicolumns (see Fig. 1B). The neurons of the minicolumn share receptive field represented by a common proximal basal segment and, therefore, recognize the same feedforward input pattern. At a higher level, ensembles are organized into layers (see Fig. 1C). Belonging to a layer determines the difference between the distal and apical compartments: the distal compartment contains intra-layer synapses, while the apical compartment contains inter-layer synapses.

The activity of neurons is determined by two parallel factors: the relative ability of minicolumns to recognize an incoming spatial pattern and the threshold ability of neurons to recognize spatiotemporal patterns in the context arriving at the distal and apical compartments. Apical and distal basal dendrite NMDAR spikes are believed to raise neuron potential near to firing threshold, leading to shorter latency of action potential (AP) by driving proximal input and stimulus selectivity of the neuron [21,23]. Neurons with faster APs inhibit other neurons through inhibitory interneurons [22], representing sparse coding of context.

In our work, the memory algorithm is constructed using two basic blocks: a spatial pooler and a temporal memory. Spatial Pooler (SP) is a neural network algorithm capable of encoding input stimuli patterns using an unsupervised learning method similar to the local Hebbian rule. The main function of SP is the spatial specialization of the receptive fields of proximal basal dendritic segments through kWTA (k winners take all) inhibition [18], resulting in a sparse distributed representation (SDR), which means that only a small percentage of neurons are active at any moment and the semantics is spread across them. There is evidence, that mammal brains might employ an analogous strategy for coding, which is efficient and noise tolerant [10]. Another algorithm, Temporal

Memory (TM), describes the sequential memory realized through recurrent connections via distal basal compartments of pyramidal neurons in the superficial cortex layer [11]. As stated before, distal basal and apical dendrites activity and minicolumnar inhibition lead to the coding of intracolumnar contextual activity of neurons that precede stimulus input. In the case of recurrent connections, this coding reflects the previous sequence of stimuli, analogously to the hidden state of the recurrent neural network [20].

4 Methods

4.1 Sequence Memory Model

In this work we propose a sequence memory model that consists of three blocks: 1) the spatial encoder for the input sequence elements, 2) the sequence memory itself, and 3) the memory hidden state attractor. An illustration of the model is shown in Fig. 2.

The spatial encoder (SE) is an optional block implemented with the Spatial Pooler algorithm. It accepts an SDR of the current observation o_t and transforms (encodes) it to another SDR—a latent observation vector z_t. The Spatial Pooler algorithm is highly efficient at retaining input patterns pairwise similarity—it clusterizes close input patterns and, on the other hand, separates not-so-close

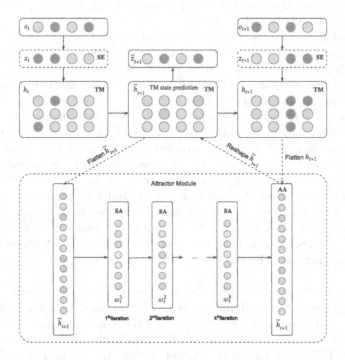

Fig. 2. Schematic view of the sequence memory model and the processing.

patterns by adapting to the average degree of similarity between patterns in the input stream. Due to this property, we expect it to help clusterize/separate entire sequences as well resulting in the easier memorization task for the sequence memory. However, if an input stream has already been encoded appropriately in terms of sparsity and topology semantics, using an additional encoder is just redundant. On the other hand, since SE learns online, the output representation can be highly unstable during the learning process. Therefore, it is also interesting to study the sequence memory ability to learn under such conditions. In our experiments, we tested both scenarios: with and without spatial encoder block.

The second block represents sequence memory itself and is implemented with a high-order temporal memory (TM). Given feedforward SDR z_t, TM updates its hidden state h_t, which is then used then to predict the next hidden state $\tilde{h}_{t+1}$. The high efficiency of temporal memory is largely due to the ability to represent the context of the observed element of a sequence, which is the sequence's prefix, in a unique way. While the TM algorithm efficiently separates different contexts, it is much less efficient at representing similar contexts with similar latent states. For the task of perfect memorization of near-symbolic sequences, this is not a desirable property. But for the tasks that require sequence abstraction and generalization, this property is a major drawback.

To improve the consolidation of similar contexts, we use the attractor module. It is an attractor network operating in the TM latent state space with the purpose of correcting TM predictions. It is expected to push predictions to the strongest memories that are close to them. The attractor block has two parts: spatial attractor and associative attractor.

A spatial attractor (SA) is a neural network similar to a spatial encoder as it is also implemented with the Spatial Pooler algorithm. It gets the flattened vector of the predicted TM hidden state SDR $\tilde{h}_{t+1}$ as input and transforms it recurrently k times—that is, the output from the spatial attractor w_t^i is fed to itself as an input, and so on k times. The role of the spatial attractor in the learning process is to form stable representations for the recurring observed vectors. Since these vectors are hidden states of temporal memory, they represent sequences (or their prefixes). It is expected that the spatial attractor trained with the Hebbian rule forms an attractor network in which representations corresponding to the observed recurring sequences act as attractors. This could allow us to integrate contexts corresponding to similar sequences.

The SDR w_t^k obtained after SA processing is expected to correct the temporal memory prediction $\tilde{h}_{t+1}$. However, the SA output no longer corresponds to the columnar structure (topology) of the temporal memory as SA learns without supervision. Therefore, the attractor block has a second part—the associative attractor.

The associative attractor (AA) is an associative memory, which is implemented with the first-order Temporal Memory algorithm. AA learns the inverse mapping from the space of representations of the spatial attractor back to the TM latent state space. Similar to TM, the associative attractor also learns to predict the TM's next hidden states, but it gives the SA output SDR w_t^k as a feedforward input. The AA prediction SDR is then used as a replacement correction to the TM prediction $\tilde{h}_{t+1}$.

On the next timestep, after observing the next element of a sequence, the mismatch between the next feedforward signal z_{t+1} and the final TM prediction $\tilde{h}_{t+1}$ forms a supervision learning signal used by both TM and AA, and the learning step is performed.

It is worth noticing that the resulting attractor module is an autoencoder with the SA playing the role of encoder and AA playing a role of a decoder. It is also worth pointing out that SA in the attractor block is optional, that is k could be set to zero. For both cases $k = 0$ and $k > 0$, we expect the associative attractor to also have properties of an attractor network (hence the name) because due to the lag between TM and AA learning (note that the attractor block learns over what TM has already learned), it will act as an additional regularizing filter. While we expected the radius of attraction in AA to be small and mostly for increased noise robustness, the experiment results were a bit surprising for us. In our experiments we tested both versions with $k > 0$ and $k = 0$.

4.2 Quality Metrics

To evaluate the model sequence processing and memorization ability we are concerned with the learning speed and the ability to retain sequence information accumulated in the memory latent state. We use the model prediction anomaly as a metric for the learning speed. Applied to temporal memory, anomaly measures the mismatch between two SDR representing TM prediction about the hidden state $\tilde{h}$ and the actual hidden state h:

$$\text{Anomaly}(h, \tilde{h}) = 1 - \text{Precision}(h, \tilde{h}) = 1 - \frac{|h \cap \tilde{h}|}{|h|}. \tag{1}$$

We also use a pairwise similarity error to measure TM's ability to retain sequence information (pairwise relation between observed sequences). We calculate similarity error as an absolute value of the difference between two similarities—of two input representations and their corresponding output representations. That is, we compute a mean absolute similarity error for the set of testing sequences S—an average value of the similarity error for each pair of testing sequences:

$$\text{SimilarityMAE}(S) = \frac{1}{|S|^2} \sum_{0 \leq i,j < |S|} |\text{sim}_{ij}^{\text{in}} - \text{sim}_{ij}^{\text{out}}|, \tag{2}$$

where $\text{sim}_{ij}^{\text{in}}$ and $\text{sim}_{ij}^{\text{out}}$ are similarities between i-th and j-th sequences' input and output representations correspondingly.

The question of how to measure similarity between two sequences is not obvious and is inherently task-dependent. Because some tasks require strict ordering of sequence elements, similarity is reduced to average elementwise similarity (the average fraction of intersection between corresponding SDR elements). Other tasks have less stringent ordering requirements, which in the extreme case reduces to the similarity of activation distributions or binary unions of sequence elements. Most tasks may necessitate soft ordering, which could be reflected by a balanced version of these extremes—average distribution similarity accumulated over a fixed window or as an exponential moving average distribution. We chose an average elementwise similarity metric for our study because we do not specifically test our model against sequence reordering. However, we also compared the alternative version to the distribution and found that they were very close. We only include results for the average elementwise similarity metric version in this paper.

5   Experiments

The proposed memory model is tested in two experimental setups using synthetically generated sequential data. As the proposed model has several optional components we test all their combinations. In both experimental setups, we examine the ability of the model to memorize sequences while maintaining the degree of pairwise similarity between sequences in the latent state.

Data Generation. For the first experiment, we generate 10 pseudo-random symbolic sequences of length 20 from an alphabet A of size 200 with controlled varying degrees of elementwise similarity between sequences. For it, we first generate a single symbolic sequence, which then acts as a seed. After that, we generate the rest 9 sequences as augmentations of the seed sequence with various target similarities. That is, for each generated sequence we define a target similarity between the seed and itself, find the required number of positions to be changed to match the required similarity, then select random elements for it, and finally replace these elements with the different random characters from the alphabet A. Generating data this way we can test our model on a set of sequences with various degrees of pairwise similarity (note that we only control similarity between the single seed sequence and the rest, not between all pairs, otherwise it would greatly complicate the generation process).

After generating the set of symbolic sequences, we encode them into SDR sequences. For that, we generate a mapping for each alphabet character $a \in A$ to a random SDR of size 500 with 10 active (=non-zero) elements, which corresponds to 2% sparsity.

5.1   Stationary Sequences Set Memorization

In the first experiment, we test the model's ability to memorize generated sequences. This also assesses the ability of the model to maintain the degree of pairwise similarity of the input data in its hidden states. In this experiment the tested models repeatedly observe the dataset—each sequence is observed a single time for each of the 50 epochs. Results provided in this section are averaged over 15 different random seeds. Also, provided TM anomaly plots are smoothed with the running average window of size 10.

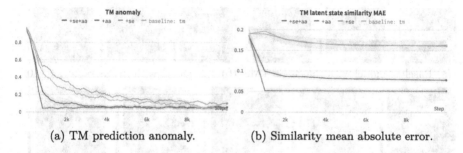

(a) TM prediction anomaly.   (b) Similarity mean absolute error.

Fig. 3. The associative attractor (+aa) significantly increases the learning speed and the similarity transfer of the temporal memory (baseline: tm). We also include the comparison of the results with the spatial encoder added to both versions (+se and +se+aa) as they show how the spatial encoder's online learning instability affects the early stage of the sequence learning process.

Figure 3 shows that the associative attractor helps TM to learn sequences significantly faster while retaining much more of the pairwise sequence information. It also proves our expectations that the SE block could decrease learning speed as it introduces encoding instability in the early stages of learning. While the version with the associative attractor still learns significantly faster than both tm and +aa variants, its ability to preserve similarity is also significantly damaged compared to the version to the version without SE block, which is not the case for the baseline. However, AA helps TM deal with the input encoding instability faster than it does it alone.

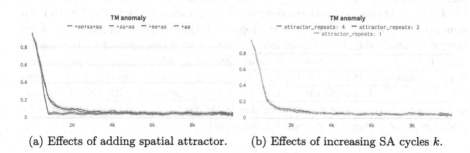

(a) Effects of adding spatial attractor.   (b) Effects of increasing SA cycles k.

Fig. 4. The number of spatial attractor recurrent cycles k shows no effect on model performance. Left: a single SA cycle (+sa+aa and +se+sa+aa) does not affect performance of the model with the associative attractor regardless of the spatial encoder inclusion. Right: increasing the number of cycles also does not affect +se+sa+aa model performance.

Figure 4 shows that for all model block combinations, the resulting performance does not depend on the spatial attractor and the number of its cycles k. This result was the most surprising for us, however, we did not manage to find an explanation for such behavior.

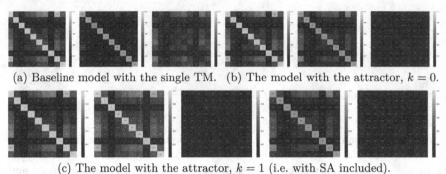

(a) Baseline model with the single TM.   (b) The model with the attractor, $k = 0$.

(c) The model with the attractor, $k = 1$ (i.e. with SA included).

Fig. 5. Similarity matrices for the models tested on a single dataset. a-b) Left to right: input similarity matrix, TM latent state similarity matrix, TM similarity error. c) Left to right: input similarity matrix, SA output w_t^1 similarity matrix, SA similarity error, TM latent state similarity matrix, TM similarity error.

Finally, to assess the qualitative contribution of the attractor block to the learned TM latent state representations we analyzed the pairwise similarity matrices of the input dataset and the resulted TM latent states (Fig. 5). Results for the baseline model (Fig. 5.a) prove our expectations that the TM alone is not able to learn latent state space meaningful topology and that TM hidden state encoding is close to hash encoding. Resulted TM similarity matrix is almost diagonal with the similarity preserved only for very similar sequences. Compared to it, TM supported with the attractor block (with and without spatial attractor, Fig. 5.b-c) retains the similarity matrix much more precisely for the entire similarity spectrum. This means the proposed attractor block forces TM to form semantically meaningful latent state representations with continuous topology. We also provide the similarity matrix for representations formed by the spatial attractor (Fig. 5.c, center pair). It shows that while SA generally preserves similarity it tends to overstate it (compare matrix 2 and 4). Interestingly, this does not prevent TM from learning latent state representations with this overstatement negated. And even more surprising is the fact that the resulted similarity matrices for $k = 0$ and $k = 1$ are almost equal.

5.2   Varying Sequences Set Memorization

The second experiment extends the first one by introducing the changes to the input dataset over the course of the learning. In this experiment, we generate the set of 50 sequences exactly the same way as we do for the first experiment. However, we split the dataset into 5 distinct subsets by 10 sequences and present each one for 10 subsequent epochs to the model. Thus, the whole experiment consists of 5 stages, where each stage is identical in structure to the first experiment and the same metrics are evaluated. With this experiment, we study the model's ability to adapt to input distribution changes, and generalize and reuse learned representations.

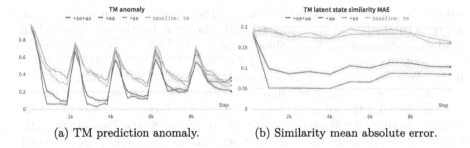

(a) TM prediction anomaly.   (b) Similarity mean absolute error.

Fig. 6. Model versions with the associative attractor (+aa and +se+aa) adapt to the dataset changes significantly faster than versions without AA (baseline: tm and +se). However, their performance degrades during the course of learning.

Results in Fig. 6 confirm the results from 5.1 that the associative attractor helps TM learn faster and retain a larger portion of the similarity. However, in this setup, the models with AA face performance degradation during the course of learning. Given the gradual increase of similarity error, TM learns to be less resistant to the difference between sequences and to filter them out. As the anomaly spikes after the sequence set changes do not decrease, it is a sign of over-generalization, which means it does not help the model to adapt. Conversely, this testing setup shows a potential benefit of including the spatial encoder in the model, as by effectively adapting to the input average similarity it helps separate input patterns and alleviate such crude model generalization. The lower anomaly spikes indicate a more effective reuse of the learned representations.

6   Conclusion and Discussion

In this work, we proposed a biologically inspired memory model that is able to effectively memorize sequential data while retaining sequences' mutual similarity in their latent state representations. The proposed model consists of several optional components—the spatial encoder block and the attractor block consisting of spatial and associative attractors—that support a sequence memory based on a temporal memory algorithm. We tested the model with different combinations of its optional components in two regimes—when the input dataset is static and when it varies during the course of learning—to show how each component contributes to the model performance.

The spatial encoder, due to the online learning algorithm, introduces input encoding instability for the sequence memory in the early stages of learning and leads to a learning speed decrease. However, as it is able to adapt to an average input patterns similarity, the spatial encoder positively contributes to the model generalization and helps it form effective representations that can be reused when the input dataset changes over time.

The attractor block significantly speeds up sequence learning. It also significantly changes the learned sequence memory hidden state representations by making them reflect the context similarity. This brings the sequence memory an ability to consolidate similar contexts, while also retaining the sequence mutual information. Surprisingly for us, these effects are due to the associative attractor alone, while the spatial attractor itself does not add any value to the proposed model. We expected that the associative attractor will work as an attractor network but did not expect it will have such effects. Nevertheless, we still believe that the spatial attractor itself has potential, for example as a short-term self-attention module that is analogous to Fast Weights networks. We did not study attentive mechanisms of the spatial attractor in this work and plan to further investigate it in future works.

In our study, we set a narrow notion for the sequence similarity by meaning only the elementwise similarity, which requires strict element ordering. As we pointed out in Sect. 4.2, different tasks require different meanings of the sequence similarity relating to their element's ordering. Therefore, in future works, we plan to investigate the model's ability to match and join similar sequences with softer or even controllable sequence ordering requirements.

References

1. Ba, J., Hinton, G.E., Mnih, V., Leibo, J.Z., Ionescu, C.: Using fast weights to attend to the recent past. In: Lee, D., Sugiyama, M., Luxburg, U., Guyon, I., Garnett, R. (eds.) Advances in Neural Information Processing Systems, vol. 29. Curran Associates, Inc. (2016)

2. Barak, O., Tsodyks, M.: Working models of working memory. Curr. Opin. Neurobiol. **25**, 20–24 (2014). theoretical and computational neuroscience

3. Bessonov, A., Staroverov, A., Zhang, H., Kovalev, A.K., Yudin, D., Panov, A.I.: Recurrent memory decision transformer. arXiv preprint arXiv:2306.09459 (2023)

4. Botvinick, M.M., Plaut, D.C.: Short-term memory for serial order: a recurrent neural network model. Psychol. Rev. **113**(2), 201 (2006)

5. Burtsev, M.S., Kuratov, Y., Peganov, A., Sapunov, G.V.: Memory transformer. arXiv preprint arXiv:2006.11527 (2020)

6. Cho, K., et al.: Learning phrase representations using RNN encoder-decoder for statistical machine translation. arXiv preprint arXiv:1406.1078 (2014)

7. Dai, Z., Yang, Z., Yang, Y., Carbonell, J., Le, Q.V., Salakhutdinov, R.: Transformer-xl: attentive language models beyond a fixed-length context. arXiv preprint arXiv:1901.02860 (2019)

8. Dedieu, A., Gothoskar, N., Swingle, S., Lehrach, W., Lázaro-Gredilla, M., George, D.: Learning higher-order sequential structure with cloned HMMs (2019)

9. Dzhivelikian, E., Latyshev, A., Kuderov, P., Panov, A.I.: Hierarchical intrinsically motivated agent planning behavior with dreaming in grid environments. Brain Inform. **9**(1), 8 (2022)

10. Graham, D., Field, D.: Sparse coding in the neocortex. Evol. Nerv. Syst. **3** (2007). https://doi.org/10.1016/B0-12-370878-8/00064-1

11. Hawkins, J., Ahmad, S., Cui, Y.: A theory of how columns in the neocortex enable learning the structure of the world. Front. Neural Circuits **11**, 81 (2017). https://doi.org/10.3389/fncir.2017.00081

12. Heeger, D.J.: Theory of cortical function. Proc. Natl. Acad. Sci. **114**(8), 1773–1782 (2017). https://doi.org/10.1073/pnas.1619788114

13. Himberger, K.D., Chien, H.Y., Honey, C.J.: Principles of temporal processing across the cortical hierarchy. Neuroscience **389**, 161–174 (2018). 8
14. Hochreiter, S., Schmidhuber, J.: Long short-term memory. Neural Comput. **9**, 1735–80 (1997). https://doi.org/10.1162/neco.1997.9.8.1735
15. Jaegle, A., Gimeno, F., Brock, A., Vinyals, O., Zisserman, A., Carreira, J.: Perceiver: general perception with iterative attention. In: International Conference on Machine Learning, pp. 4651–4664. PMLR (2021)
16. Kuderov, P., Panov, A.: Planning with hierarchical temporal memory for deterministic Markov decision problem. In: Rocha, A.P., Steels, L., Herik, J.V.D. (eds.) Proceedings of the 13th International Conference on Agents and Artificial Intelligence, vol. 2, pp. 1073–1081. SCITEPRESS - Science and Technology Publications (2021). https://doi.org/10.5220/0010317710731081
17. Miconi, T.: Biologically plausible learning in recurrent neural networks reproduces neural dynamics observed during cognitive tasks. Elife **6**, e20899 (2017)
18. Oster, M., Douglas, R., Liu, S.C.: Computation with spikes in a winner-take-all network. Neural Comput. **21**(9), 2437–2465 (2009)
19. Rolls, E.T., Mills, W.P.C.: Computations in the deep vs superficial layers of the cerebral cortex. Neurobiol. Learn. Mem. **145**, 205–221 (2017)
20. Rumelhart, D.E., Hinton, G.E., Williams, R.J.: Learning internal representations by error propagation. Technical report, California Univ San Diego La Jolla Inst for Cognitive Science (1985)
21. Smith, S.L., Smith, I.T., Branco, T., Häusser, M.: Dendritic spikes enhance stimulus selectivity in cortical neurons in vivo. Nature **503**(7474), 115–120 (2013). https://doi.org/10.1038/nature12600
22. Staiger, J.F., Petersen, C.C.H.: Neuronal circuits in barrel cortex for whisker sensory perception. Physiol. Rev. **101**(1), 353–415 (2021). https://doi.org/10.1152/physrev.00019.2019
23. Stuart, G.J., Spruston, N.: Dendritic integration: 60 years of progress. Nat. Neurosci. **18**(12), 1713–1721 (2015). https://doi.org/10.1038/nn.4157
24. Vaswani, A., et al.: Attention is all you need. Adv. Neural Inf. Process. Syst. **30** (2017)
25. Whittington, J.C., et al.: The Tolman-Eichenbaum machine: unifying space and relational memory through generalization in the hippocampal formation. Cell **183**(5), 1249-1263.e23 (2020)
26. Yu, Y., Si, X., Hu, C., Zhang, J.: A review of recurrent neural networks: LSTM cells and network architectures. Neural Comput. **31**(7), 1235–1270 (2019)

Investigating the Generative Dynamics of Energy-Based Neural Networks

Lorenzo Tausani[1,2], Alberto Testolin[1,2] (ORCID), and Marco Zorzi[2,3](✉) (ORCID)

[1] Department of Mathematics, University of Padova, 35141 Padua, Italy
alberto.testolin@unipd.it
[2] Department of General Psychology and Padova Neuroscience Center, University of Padova, 35141 Padua, Italy
marco.zorzi@unipd.it
[3] IRCCS San Camillo Hospital, 30126 Venice Lido, Italy

Abstract. Generative neural networks can produce data samples according to the statistical properties of their training distribution. This feature can be used to test modern computational neuroscience hypotheses suggesting that spontaneous brain activity is partially supported by top-down generative processing. A widely studied class of generative models is that of Restricted Boltzmann Machines (RBMs), which can be used as building blocks for unsupervised deep learning architectures. In this work, we systematically explore the generative dynamics of RBMs, characterizing the number of states visited during top-down sampling and investigating whether the heterogeneity of visited attractors could be increased by starting the generation process from biased hidden states. By considering an RBM trained on a classic dataset of handwritten digits, we show that the capacity to produce diverse data prototypes can be increased by initiating top-down sampling from chimera states, which encode high-level visual features of multiple digit classes. We also find that the model is not capable of transitioning between all possible digit states within a single generation trajectory, suggesting that the top-down dynamics is heavily constrained by the shape of the energy function. We also study the generative dynamics on a more challenging dataset containing pictures of faces, showing that the exploration of stable states also partially depends on complexity of the training data distribution.

Keywords: Energy-based models · Spontaneous brain activity · Generative models

1 Introduction

One frontier of modern neuroscience is understanding the so-called *spontaneous brain activity*, which arises when the brain is not engaged in any specific task [1]. This intrinsic activity accounts for most of brain energy consumption [2], and has

Supported by grant RF-2019-12369300 from the Italian Ministry of Health.

been studied using electrophysiological recordings [3], electroencephalography [4] and functional magnetic resonance imaging [5].

A recently proposed computational framework [6] suggests that spontaneous activity could be interpreted as top-down computations that occur in *generative models*, whose goal is to estimate the latent factors underlying the observed data distribution [7]. This framework entails a strong connection between spontaneous and task-related brain activity: when performing a task, the generative model would focus on maximizing accuracy in the task of interest, while during rest the model would reproduce task-related activation patterns and use them for the computation of generic spatiotemporal priors that summarize a large variety of task representations with a low dimensionality [6]. This is in agreement with modeling work suggesting that the brain at rest is in a state of maximum metastability [8], where brain regions are organized into quasi-syncronous activity, interrupted by periods of segregation, without getting caught in attractor states [9].

Deep learning models are increasingly used to simulate the activity of biological brains and explore the principles of neural computation [10,11]. For example, deep networks have been used to reproduce some functional properties of cortical processing, particularly in the visual system [12], as well as to simulate a variety of cognitive functions (e.g., [13–15]) and their progressive development [16,17]. However, it is not well understood whether existing deep learning architectures could capture key signatures of spontaneous brain activity.

Here we propose to investigate the (spontaneous) generative dynamics of a well-known class of generative models called Restricted Boltzmann Machines (RBMs), which are a particular type of energy-based neural networks rooted in statistical physics [18]. The RBM is an undirected graphical model formed by two layers of symmetrically connected units. Visible units encode the data (e.g., pixels of an image), whereas hidden units discover latent features through unsupervised generative learning [18]. In RBMs, sampling from the hidden states leads to generating visible states that correspond to trained patterns, but these configurations represent local energy minima (i.e., attractors) that are difficult to escape. Indeed, large energy barriers need to be crossed to go from one (stable) visible state to another, which makes these transitions very difficult [19].

Our approach aims at finding constrained initializations of hidden states that could induce the network into metastable sample generation, thus simulating the dynamics of spontaneous activity in the brain. We quantify this as the number of well-formed visible states explored in a generation round, identified by a trained neural network classifier, avoiding to get caught in attractor states. In the first set of simulations, we exploit the method described in [14] to sample visual patterns starting from hidden states derived by inverting a classifier trained to map internal representations into one-hot encoded labels. As a test bed, we use the classical MNIST dataset of handwritten digits [20]. Next, we describe two variations of the original method that combine features of different digits to produce "biased" hidden states away from attractor basins, which should be capable of exploring more states during the generation process. Our results indicate that such biased states indeed increase state exploration compared to classical label biasing with digit labels. However, no hidden state is capable of inducing the exploration of all digits in a single generation round, suggesting that the RBM in its classic version is not capable of mimicking the continuous and heterogeneous state exploration demonstrated by biological brains. We also analyse the generative dynamics emerging when the RBM is trained on the CelebA dataset of human faces [21]. State exploration is even less pronounced in such case, suggesting that the generative dynamics also tightly depends on the training data distribution, that is, on the inherent similarity between the stable attractors that are created in the energy function.

2   Materials and Methods

2.1   Datasets

Our main simulations are based on the classic MNIST dataset [20], which contains images of 28×28 pixels representing handwritten digits from 0 to 9, encoded in 8-bit grayscale (values from 0 to 255, normalized between 0 and 1). It encompasses a training set of 60000 examples and a testing set of 10000 examples. Although this is a medium-sized dataset with a limited number of classes, it allows us to more clearly characterize the generative dynamics by measuring the number of different states visited during top-down sampling. In the Appendix we also discuss some simulations obtained using the more complex CelebA dataset containing pictures of human faces [21]. The project code is available at[1].

2.2   Restricted Boltzmann Machines

Boltzmann machines are energy models composed of two different kinds of units: *visible units*, which are used to provide input data (e.g. pixels of an image) and *hidden units*, which are used to extract latent features by discovering higher-order interactions between visible units [18]. In RBMs there are no hidden-to-hidden and visible-to-visible connections: the only connections are between the visible and hidden units, which can be considered as two separate layers of a bipartite, fully-connected graph [22]. Neurons in a Boltzmann machine are conceptualized as stochastic units, whose activity is the result of a Bernoullian sampling with activation probability $P(\sigma_i = 1)$ defined as follows:

$$P(\sigma_i = 1) = \frac{1}{1 + e^{-\Delta E_i/T}} \tag{1}$$

where ΔE_i is the difference in the energy of the system caused by the change in the state of the unit i, and T is the temperature parameter that acts as a noise factor. Given a set of training data $\mathcal{D} = \left\{ x^{(i)} \right\}_{i=1}^{n}$ the parameters θ of an RBM (that is, the weights connecting the units and the biases) are updated by

---

[1] https://github.com/CCNL-UniPD/Generative_dynamics.

maximizing the likelihood $p(\mathcal{D}|\theta)$, where $p(\mathcal{D}|\theta)$ is the Boltzmann distribution with temperature $T = 1$. Training is performed by gradient ascent, usually adopting the contrastive divergence training algorithm, which exploits Monte Carlo Markov chain methods to estimate the gradient update [23].

Model Architecture and Training Details. In our study, we used an RBM with 784 visible units (that is, equal to the vectorization of single MNIST examples ($28 \times 28 = 784$)) and 1000 hidden units. The RBM was trained with 1 step contrastive divergence and learning rate $\eta = 0.1$ for both weights and biases (hidden and visible). The parameter update also included a momentum term γ to speed up the training. Following standard practice [24] γ was equal to 0.5 in the first 5 training epochs and 0.9 in successive iterations. Furthermore, the parameter update was decreased by the value of the parameter of interest in the previous training iteration multiplied by a decay factor equal to 0.0002. Both hidden and visible biases were initialized equal to 0, while connection weights were initialized with random numbers sampled from a zero-mean normal distribution with standard deviation equal to 0.1. The model was trained for 100 epochs following a batch-wise approach, with batch size $= 125$. Learning was monitored using a root mean square error loss function. In the Appendix we also discuss preliminary explorations obtained when considering hidden units with continuous activation, though in such case the generation quality degrades quickly during top-down sampling.

Top-Down Sampling from RBM. Data generation was performed at the end of the RBM training phase. To generate smoother images, during top-down sampling visible units were not binarized, thus assuming continuous values between 0 and 1. Hidden units were instead binarized through Bernoulli sampling. Data patterns were generated following the *label biasing* procedure described in [14], where examples are generated top-down from a hidden state vector $H_{\text{Label biasing}}$ obtained through the inversion of a linear classifier trained to classify the digit class from its hidden representation.

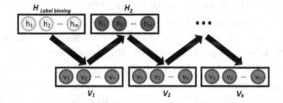

Fig. 1. Illustration of the label biasing generation procedure. A hidden state vector $H_{\text{Label biasing}}$ is obtained using the linear projection method [14]. Then from $H_{\text{Label biasing}}$ a visible vector V_1 is generated. The process is repeated k times, where k is the desired number of generation steps.

A *generation step* is defined as a single generation of a visible state (generated sample) from a hidden state. The generated sample is then used to instantiate the hidden state of the next generation step. In the first generation step, the activation of the visible layer A_V is computed as the matrix multiplication between $H_{\text{Label biasing}}$ and the transposed weight matrix W of the RBM model. The result of the operation is added to the visible bias b_V:

$$A_V = (H_{\text{Label biasing}} \cdot W^T) + b_V \tag{2}$$

The first visible state V_1 is computed as the output of a sigmoid activation function taking as input A_V divided by the temperature T:

$$V_1 = \sigma(\frac{A_V}{T}) \tag{3}$$

In the following generation steps, the hidden state H_s is computed as follows:

$$H_s \sim Bernoulli\left(p = \sigma(\frac{V_{s-1} \cdot W + b_H}{T})\right) \tag{4}$$

where V_{s-1} is the visible state of the previous reconstruction step and b_H is the hidden bias. The consequent visible states are computed following the same procedure described for step 1 (Fig. 1).

2.3   Digit Classifier

In order to establish whether top-down generation resulted in well-formed image patterns over visible units, we trained a classifier to identify digit classes taking as input the patterns generated by the RBM. We used a VGG-16 classifier, which is a convolutional architecture widely used in image classification [25]. The model was adapted from[2] and was made up of 4 VGG block units, followed by 3 fully connected layers and a final softmax layer. Unlike (see footnote 2), the final fully connected layer outputted a vector of 11 entries (i.e., the number of MNIST classes plus one special class representing non-digit samples), which was then processed by a softmax layer. Softmax output was used to classify the example and estimate the uncertainty of the network in the classification, which was measured by calculating the entropy of the softmax output.

The classifier was trained on the MNIST dataset, with grayscale images resized to 32×32 pixels. The training set was made up of 113400 examples: 54000 were extracted from the MNIST training set, while the remaining 59400 represented non-digit examples. This was done to exclude random classifications when the network was exposed to unrecognizable digits, which is a situation that often occurs during spontaneous top-down sampling in energy-based models. Among these non-digit examples, 5400 were composed of scrambled digit images, while the remaining 54000 were training set examples with a random

---

[2] https://colab.research.google.com/drive/1IN0HD7-ljlPFtsbstfxLSKWvg2y2ndmO?
usp=sharing.

number of adjacent active pixels (i.e. intensity >0) masked. The choice of this method for producing non-digits was motivated by empirical observation of cases in which the RBM generation produced objects that could not be identified as digits by a human observer. Learning was monitored through a validation set made up of the remaining 6000 examples of the MNIST training set. Testing was done on the 10000 images of the MNIST test set. The model was trained using minibatches of size 64, with stochastic gradient descent and learning rate $\eta = 0.01$ with cross-entropy loss. The model was trained for 20 epochs, selecting the model resulting in the highest validation accuracy (99,3%).

2.4 Generativity Metrics

In order to measure the diversity and stability of the generative dynamics of the model, we implemented several metrics to characterize changes in visual and hidden activation during top-down sampling. The idea is that the model should develop attractor states in correspondence to digit representations, which are then dynamically visited during spontaneous generation of sensory patterns.

For each generation step, the classifier evaluated the class (i.e. digit from 0 to 9 and non-digit case) of the sample produced. The *number of states visited* was defined as the number of different digits visited during the generation process, without including the non-digit state. Multiple visits to the same state (i.e., same digit recognized by the classifier) during a single generation trajectory were counted as 1. A related metric was the number of generation steps (*state time* in short) in which the sample remained in each digit state, including the non-digit state. This index measures the stability of each attractor state. Finally, we measured the *number of transitions* occurring during the generation process. A transition was defined as the change in classification of a sample from one state to another (transitions to the non-digit state were not included in this quantification). Transitions between states, including the non-digit state, were also used to estimate a *transition matrix* of the entire generation procedure (i.e., taking into account all samples and all generation steps). The aim of the transition matrix was to estimate the probability during the generation process to transition from one digit (or non-digit) state to another. The transition matrix was estimated by counting all transitions from one state to another, normalized by the total number of transitions from that particular state.

For each label biasing vector used, 100 samples were generated. For each sample, a generation period of 100 generation steps was performed. Measures are reported together with standard error of the mean.

3 Results

The classifier accuracy decreased as a function of the generation step for all digits (average classifier accuracy - step 100: 11.2%, Fig. 2b), except for the digit zero, which only saw a moderate decrease (classifier accuracy (digit: 0) - step 100: 86.0%). This indicated that the samples were significantly distorted during the generation period, inducing more errors in the classifier (examples of sample generation from each digit are shown in Fig. 2a). In accordance with this, the average classification entropy increased during the generation period, showing a high anticorrelation with the classifier accuracy ($\rho = -0.999$). Interestingly, all digits showed a similar percentage of active units in the hidden layer through-out the generation process, keeping active only $14 - 22\%$ of the units (average percentage of active units - step 1: $14.964 \pm 0.079\%$, average percentage of active units - step 100 : $21.892 \pm 0.054\%$, n = 10 digits, Fig. 2c), which is in line with previous results suggesting the emergence of sparse coding in RBM models [26].

On average, in each generation period 1.78 ± 0.21 states were visited, with 2.90 ± 0.54 transitions between states (Fig. 2d, n = 1000). The transition matrix shows that most transitions occur within the same class of digits (average prob-ability of transition within the same digit: 0.87 ± 0.02, $n = 10$, Fig. 2f), while the probabilities for a digit state to transition to another digit state are low, almost never exceeding 0.01 (0.012 ± 0.002, n = 110). This, combined with the small number of transitions per generation period, suggests that state transitions are sharp and that oscillations between two states are extremely rare. Non-digits transition almost invariably to themselves: when a sample transitions to a non-digit, it hardly ever gets out of it in the following generation steps. The conse-quences of this attractor-like behavior of non-digits states is that all digits except 0 spend the majority of the generation period as non-digits (average non-digit state time between digits (0 excluded): 76.09 ± 4.21, n = 9 digits, Fig. 2e).

A limitation of the "single digit" label biasing approach described in the previous paragraph is that it does not allow to explore heterogeneous sensory states, as highlighted by the small number of digit states visited on average in a single generation period (Fig. 2d). This might be due to the fact that label biasing forces the RBM to start the generation from a hidden state close to an attractor basin corresponding to the prototype of the selected digit, thus limiting the exploration of other states during top-down sampling. A way to overcome this issue could be to bias the network toward *chimera states*, for example by starting the generation from a hidden state mixing different digit representations. The hypothesis is that this could increase state exploration by decreasing the probability of stranding the generation process in a specific attractor.

We implemented two methods to obtain such chimera states, both based on the observation that the distributions of the activations of the hidden states produced through label biasing are right-skewed, with a long tail of outliers at the upper end of the distribution (see Fig. 3a). This suggests that for each state there are only a few active hidden units. In the first method (*intersection method*), chimera states between two digits were computed by activating (i.e. $h = 1$) only the units in common between the highest k active units of the label biasing vectors of the two digits, while the others were set to 0. Given that we observed that the percentage of active hidden units remained constrained in a small range during the generation process (Fig. 2c), we decided to set k equal to the rounded down average number of active hidden units in the first step of generation (i.e. 149). In the second method (*double label biasing*), instead of using a one-hot encoded label for label biasing (see [14] for details), we utilized a binary vector with two active entries (i.e. = 1) that corresponded to the digits of the desired chimera state. The resulting $H_{\text{Label biasing}}$ was then binarized, keeping active only the top k most active units (also here $k = 149$). Generativity (quantified as the average number of states visited in a generation period) was characterized in all intersections of two digits (100 samples per digit combination, Fig. 3b,d). Examples of chimera state generations are shown in Fig. 3c,e.

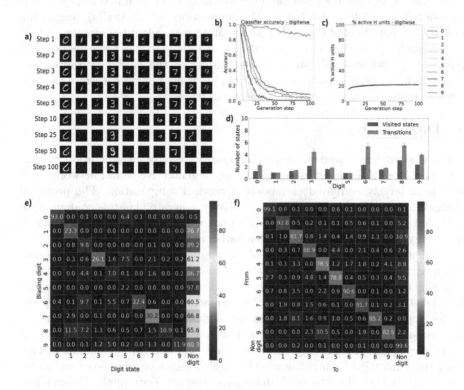

Fig. 2. Characterization of sample generation. **a)** Examples of digit generations over sampling steps. **b)** Classifier accuracy and **c)** average percentage of active hidden units as a function of generation step. **d)** Average number of visited states and states transitions per generation period for different label biasing digits. **e)** Average state time per each digit state (columns) for different label biasing digits (rows). **f)** Transition matrix estimated from all generated data. Each entry represents the probability of transition from one state (rows) to another (columns).

Interestingly, both techniques induced higher state exploration than the classic label biasing generation method (average number of visited states between chimera states - intersection method: 2.951 ± 0.099, average number of visited states between chimera states - double label biasing: 2.104 ± 0.122; $n = 45$ combinations of two digits), although only the intersection method state exploration was significantly higher than the classical label biasing (Mann-Whitney U test (one-sided): $p = 6.703 \cdot 10^{-5}$ (intersection method), $p = 0.139$ (double label biasing)). Some combinations of digit states (e.g. $\{6,9\}$) seemed to induce particularly high state exploration with both methods; however, the correlation between the number of visited states in the two methods was mild ($\rho = 0.334$, n = 45 combinations of two digits). Both methods also induced a significant drop in non-digit state time (average non-digit state time - intersection method: 12.156 ± 2.272, Mann-Whitney U test (one-sided): $p = 2.338 \cdot 10^{-5}$; average non-digit state time - double label biasing: 25.032 ± 4.215, Mann-Whitney U test (one-sided): $p = 5.054 \cdot 10^{-4}$; n = 45 combinations of two digits), suggesting that the increase in exploration leads to visiting more plausible sensory states.

Interestingly, in simulations based on the CelebA dataset the model only generated plausible visible states corresponding to the biased categories (see Appendix), suggesting that more structured input data might constrain the top-down sampling toward more stable activation states.

4   Discussion

In this work we introduced an original framework to study the generation dynamics of restricted Boltzmann machines, a class of generative neural networks that have been largely employed as models of cortical computation. The proposed method exploits label biasing [14] to iteratively generate plausible configuration of hidden and visible states, thus allowing to explore the attractor landscape of the energy function underlying the generative model.

To demonstrate the effectiveness of our approach, we characterized the generation dynamics of an RBM trained on a classical dataset of handwritten digits, exploring different sampling strategies to maximize state exploration. The standard label biasing approach initiate the generation of class prototypes from the hidden representation of single digits; our simulations show that this strategy can produce high-quality digit images, but does not allow to explore multiple states during the generative process. We thus explored the possibility of initiating the generation from chimera states, which might be considered as "meta-stable" states that allow to reach different attractors. Both methods developed (intersection method and double label biasing) indeed increased the number of states visited during the generation process, also significantly diminishing the non-digit state time. Nevertheless, the estimated transition matrices indicated that the non-digit state generally acts as a strong attractor, from which the system is unable to escape. This suggests that the generative dynamics of RBMs might not fully mimic the spontaneous dynamics observed in biological brains, which appear more flexible and heterogeneous.

Future work should explore more recent version of RBMs, for example the Gaussian-Bernoulli RBM [27], which is capable of generating meaningful samples even from pure noise and might thus develop more interesting generation dynamics. It might also be important to investigate methods to escape or modulate the influence of spurious (e.g., non-digit) attractors in the generation process. Another interesting research direction could be to explore datasets involving natural images, which would increase model realism and might allow to more systematically test neuroscientific hypotheses [6].

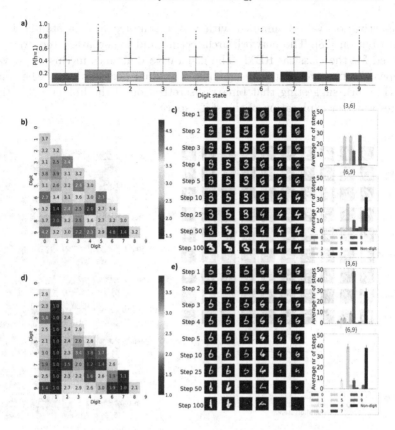

Fig. 3. Characterization of generation using chimera states. **a)** Distribution of activation probability of hidden units of label biasing vectors of each digit. **b)** Average number of visited states for each chimera state of two digits using the intersection method. **c)** Example generation periods with intersection method with two chimera states ({3,6} (columns 1 to 3) and {6,9} (columns 4 to 6)). Average digit state times are shown in bar plots. **d)** Average number of visited states using the double label biasing method. **e)** Example generation periods with two example double label biasing chimera states ({3,6} (columns 1 to 3) and {6,9} (columns 4 to 6)).

Finally, a systematic comparison with neuroscientific data will be a crucial and essential step to assess the adequacy of energy-based neural networks in capturing realistic patterns of intrinsic brain dynamics.

A   Appendix

A.1   RBM with Continuos Hidden Units

We also investigated the generation dynamics in RBMs using continuous hidden units with a Rectified Linear Unit (ReLU) activation function. In such architecture, continuous activations are obtained by applying the ReLU function to the pre-activation values summed with values sampled from a standard normal distribution [28]. The network architecture and hyperparameters were the same used for the classical RBM. The generative dynamics in this RBM variant appears somewhat static, resembling a gradual degradation of the initial image (Fig. 4a), suggesting that binary discretization of the hidden activations promotes a better exploration of the state space.

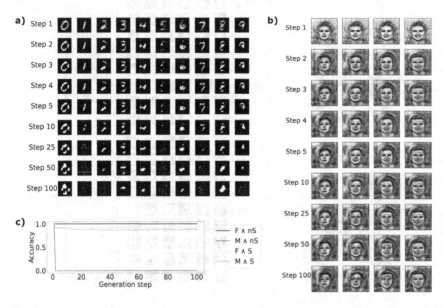

Fig. 4. a) Sample generation in RBM with ReLU activation function. **b)** Representative generations (one per column) for each label biasing class (from left to right: *female not smiling (F∧nS), male not smiling (M∧nS), female smiling (F∧S), male smiling (M ∧ S)*). **c)** Accuracy of the classifier as a function of the generation step.

A.2 Generation Dynamics Emerging from the CelebA Dataset

To study the RBM generative dynamics on a more naturalistic dataset, we performed some simulations using the CelebA dataset, which consists of over 200,000 images of celebrity faces labeled with 40 binary attributes [21]. Following common practice, images were resized to 64 × 64 pixels, converted to grayscale and then binarized using the Sauvola-Pietikinen algorithm [29,30]. Images were divided into four categories based on the combined values of the attributes *male/female* and *smiling/not smiling*. To avoid class imbalance, the training set was undersampled so that each class had an equal number of examples (27256 examples per class). The RBM had 4096 visible units and 5000 hidden units. The other training hyperparameters were kept the same as in the MNIST simulations. We used a pre-trained ResNet18 classifier to categorize visible states

[31], which was finetuned for 20 epochs on the binarized CelebA images. The classifier achieved a validation accuracy of 97.8%. Examples of generation with label biasing (Fig. 4b) show that the method is successful in inducing the appropriate initial state, but the generation process appears static, with only few transitions occurring (average number of visited states: 1.425 ± 0.255, average number of state transitions: 1.475 ± 0.265, n = 400, Fig. 4c).

References

1. Mitra, A., et al.: Spontaneous infra-slow brain activity has unique spatiotemporal dynamics and laminar structure. Neuron **98**(2), 297–305 (2018)
2. Mitra, A., Raichle, M.E.: How networks communicate: propagation patterns in spontaneous brain activity. Philos. Trans. R. Soc. B Biol. Sci. **371**(1705), 20150546 (2016)
3. Pan, W.-J., Thompson, G., Magnuson, M., Majeed, W., Jaeger, D., Keilholz, S.: Broadband local field potentials correlate with spontaneous fluctuations in functional magnetic resonance imaging signals in the rat somatosensory cortex under isoflurane anesthesia. Brain Connect. **1**(2), 119–131 (2011)
4. Tortella-Feliu, M., Morillas-Romero, A., Balle, M., Llabrés, J., Bornas, X., Putman, P.: Spontaneous EEG activity and spontaneous emotion regulation. Int. J. Psychophysiol. **94**(3), 365–372 (2014)
5. Leuthardt, E.C., et al.: Resting-state blood oxygen level-dependent functional MRI: a paradigm shift in preoperative brain mapping. Stereotact. Funct. Neurosurg. **93**(6), 427–439 (2015)
6. Pezzulo, G., Zorzi, M., Corbetta, M.: The secret life of predictive brains: what's spontaneous activity for? Trends Cogn. Sci. **25**(9), 730–743 (2021)
7. Parr, T., Friston, K.J.: The anatomy of inference: generative Models and brain structure. Front. Comput. Neurosci. **12**, 90 (2018)
8. Deco, G., Kringelbach, M.L., Jirsa, V.K., Ritter, P.: The dynamics of resting fluctuations in the brain: metastability and its dynamical cortical core. Sci. Rep. **7**(1), 1–14 (2017)
9. Tognoli, E., Kelso, J.A.S.: The metastable brain. Neuron **81**(1), 35–48 (2014)
10. Richards, B.A., et al.: A deep learning framework for neuroscience. Nat. Neurosci. **22**(11), 1761–1770 (2019)
11. De Schutter, E.: Deep learning and computational neuroscience. Neuroinformatics **16**(1), 1–2 (2018)
12. Yamins, D.L., DiCarlo, J.J.: Using goal-driven deep learning models to understand sensory cortex. Nat. Neurosci. **19**(3), 356–365 (2016)
13. Stoianov, I., Zorzi, M.: Emergence of a 'visual number sense' in hierarchical generative models. Nat. Neurosci. **15**(2), 194–196 (2012)
14. Zorzi, M., Testolin, A., Stoianov, I.P.: Modeling language and cognition with deep unsupervised learning: a tutorial overview. Front. Psychol. **4**, 515 (2013)
15. Testolin, A., Stoianov, I., Zorzi, M.: Letter perception emerges from unsupervised deep learning and recycling of natural image features. Nat. Hum. Behav. **1**(9), 657–664 (2017)
16. Testolin, A., Zou, W.Y., McClelland, J.L.: Numerosity discrimination in deep neural networks: initial competence, developmental refinement and experience statistics. Dev. Sci. **23**(5), e12940 (2020)

17. Zambra, M., Testolin, A., Zorzi, M.: A developmental approach for training deep belief networks. Cogn. Comput. **15**(1), 103–120 (2022)
18. Ackley, D.H., Hinton, G.E., Sejnowski, T.J.: A learning algorithm for Boltzmann machines. Cogn. Sci. **9**(1), 147–169 (1985)
19. Roussel, C., Cocco, S., Monasson, R.: Barriers and dynamical paths in alternating Gibbs sampling of restricted Boltzmann machines. Phys. Rev. E **104**(3) (2021)
20. Lecun, Y., Bottou, L., Bengio, Y., Haffner, P.: Gradient-based learning applied to document recognition. Proc. IEEE **86**(11), 2278–2324 (1998)
21. Liu, Z., Luo, P., Wang, X., Tang, X.: Deep learning face attributes in the wild. In: 2015 IEEE International Conference on Computer Vision (ICCV) (2015)
22. Goodfellow, I., Bengio, Y., Courville, A.: Deep Learning. The MIT Press, Cambridge, MA, USA (2016)
23. Hinton, G.E.: Training products of experts by minimizing contrastive divergence. Neural Comput. **14**(8), 1771–1800 (2002)
24. Testolin, A., Stoianov, I., De Filippo De Grazia, M., Zorzi, M.: Deep unsupervised learning on a desktop PC: a primer for cognitive scientists. Front. Psychol. **4** (2013)
25. Simonyan, K., Zisserman, A.: Very deep convolutional networks for large-scale image recognition. arXiv abs/1409.1556 (2014)
26. Testolin, A., De Filippo De Grazia, M., Zorzi, M.: The role of architectural and learning constraints in neural network models: a case study on visual space coding. Front. Comput. Neurosci. **11**, 13 (2017)
27. Liao, R., Kornblith, S., Ren, M., Fleet, D. J., Hinton, G.: Gaussian-Bernoulli RBMs Without Tears. arXiv abs/2210.10318 (2022)
28. Nair, V., Hinton, G.E.: Rectified linear units improve restricted Boltzmann machines. In: Proceedings of the 27th International Conference on Machine Learning (ICML-10), pp. 807–814 (2010)
29. Sauvola, J., Pietikäinen, M.: Adaptive document image binarization. Pattern Recognit. **33**, 225–236 (2000)
30. Fernandez-de-Cossio-Diaz, J., Cocco, S., Monasson, R.: Disentangling representations in restricted Boltzmann machines without adversaries. Phys. Rev. X **13** (2023)
31. He, K., Zhang, X., Ren, S., Sun, J.: Deep residual learning for image recognition. In: 2016 IEEE Conference on Computer Vision and Pattern Recognition (CVPR) (2016)

Exploring Deep Transfer Learning Ensemble for Improved Diagnosis and Classification of Alzheimer's Disease

Tanjim Mahmud[1]([📧])[iD], Koushick Barua[1], Anik Barua[1], Sudhakar Das[1],
Nanziba Basnin[2], Mohammad Shahadat Hossain[3][iD], Karl Andersson[4][iD],
M. Shamim Kaiser[5][iD], and Nahed Sharmen[6]

[1] Rangamati Science and Technology University, 4500 Rangamati, Bangladesh
tanjim_cse@yahoo.com
[2] Leeds Beckette University, Leeds, UK
[3] University of Chittagong, Chittagong, Bangladesh
[4] Pervasive and Mobile Computing Laboratory, Lulea University of Technology,
S-931 87, Skelleftea, Sweden
[5] Institute of Information Technology, Jahangirnagar University, Dhaka, Bangladesh
[6] Chattogram Maa-O-Shishu Hospital Medical College, Chittagong, Bangladesh

Abstract. Alzheimer's disease (AD) is a progressive and irreversible
neurological disorder that affects millions of people worldwide. Early
detection and accurate diagnosis of AD are crucial for effective treatment and management of the disease. In this paper, we propose a transfer learning-based approach for the diagnosis of AD using magnetic resonance imaging (MRI) data. Our approach involves extracting relevant
features from the MRI data using transfer learning by alter the weights
and then using these features to train pre-trained models and combined
ensemble classifier. We evaluated our approach on a dataset of MRI
scans from patients with AD and healthy controls, achieving an accuracy of 95% for combined ensemble models. Our results demonstrate the
potential of transfer learning-based approaches for the early and accurate diagnosis of AD, which could lead to improved patient outcomes
and more effective management of the disease.

Keywords: Alzheimer's disease · Transfer learning · Magnetic
resonance imaging(MRI) · Ensemble model

1 Introduction

Alzheimer's disease (AD) is a progressive and irreversible neurological disorder
that affects millions of people worldwide [1]. The disease is characterized by
cognitive and memory impairments, which can have a significant impact on the
quality of life of patients and their families [1,2]. Early detection and accurate
diagnosis of AD are crucial for effective treatment and management of the disease. Medical imaging techniques, such as magnetic resonance imaging (MRI),

© The Author(s), under exclusive license to Springer Nature Switzerland AG 2023
F. Liu et al. (Eds.): BI 2023, LNAI 13974, pp. 109–120, 2023.
https://doi.org/10.1007/978-3-031-43075-6_10

are commonly used to aid in the diagnosis of AD. However, the interpretation of MRI data can be challenging and time-consuming, requiring specialized expertise [3–5].

In recent years, machine learning-based approaches have emerged as a promising tool for the diagnosis of AD using MRI data. Machine learning algorithms can automatically extract relevant features from medical imaging data and use these features to train classifiers that can accurately distinguish between patients with AD and healthy controls [6,7]. This can significantly improve the accuracy and efficiency of AD diagnosis, leading to better patient outcomes and more effective management of the disease [8–10].

In this paper, we propose a deep learning-based approach for the diagnosis of AD using MRI data. Our approach involves extracting relevant features from MRI data using pre-trained models, only altering the weights of the last layer from which predictions are derived. Training with some pre-trained models and combined ensemble model classifier to distinguish between patients with AD and healthy controls. We evaluate our approach on a dataset of MRI scans from patients with AD and healthy controls, demonstrating its potential for the early and accurate diagnosis of AD. The proposed approach has the potential to improve the accuracy and efficiency of AD diagnosis, leading to better patient outcomes and more effective management of the disease.

The research objectives of our study were to develop and evaluate a deep learning-based approach for the diagnosis of Alzheimer's disease (AD) using medical imaging data, such as magnetic resonance imaging (MRI) scans. Our approach aimed to automate the interpretation of medical imaging data and improve the accuracy and efficiency of AD diagnosis, leading to more effective treatment and management of the disease.

The key contributions of our study were:

1. Our method includes training with different pre-trained models to automatically extract relevant elements from medical imaging data.
2. With high accuracy, sensitivity, and specificity, we evaluated our method using a dataset of medical imaging scans from AD patients and healthy controls.
3. Our study adds to the growing corpus of research on the application of pre-trained deep learning-based methods for the analysis of medical imaging data in the diagnosis of AD. Our method could lead to better patient outcomes and a higher standard of living for patients and their families by increasing the effectiveness and accuracy of AD diagnosis.

The rest of the paper is organized as follows. In Sect. 2, we displayed the related works. The suggested methodology is provided in Sect. 3. Section 4 also displays the analysis and outcomes of the experiment. The summary of our research is found in Sect. 5, the final section.

2   Related Works

Alzheimer's disease (AD) is a growing public health concern that affects millions of people worldwide. Early detection and accurate diagnosis of AD are essential for effective treatment and management of the disease. Consequently, we investigated and evaluated the accuracy of the Alzheimer's disease diagnosis made by BRBES [8] using data on blood gene expression. We used a gradient-free strategy to enhance the BRBES because prior research had shown the drawbacks of gradient-based optimization. We have also made an effort to address the issue of class inequality using the utility parameters discovered by BRBES [1]. [2] demonstrated the use of cutting-edge ML classifiers in the 4-way categorization of Alzheimers' disease. They showed an ensemble classifier based on ML models which achieved an accuracy of 94.92%. In paper [3] showed deep ensemble based model with four tasks for categorizing Alzheimer's disease, three binary categorizations, and one multi-class categorization task. The proposed technique produced 92.3% accuracy for the multi-class-classification task. Several studies have explored the use of ensemble models for the diagnosis of AD using MRI data. For example, in a study [4], a deep learning-based ensemble model approach was proposed for the diagnosis of AD using MRI data. The authors used a ensembles model with pre-trained model to extract relevant features from the MRI data and achieved an accuracy of 86%. In another study [5], a deep learning-based approach was proposed for the classification of AD using structural MRI data. The authors used a GLCM method and ensemble learning to distinguish between patients with AD and healthy controls, achieving an accuracy of 93%. The use of ANN achieves an overall test accuracy of 0.9196 whereas two ensemble techniques, namely gradient boosting and voting classifier achieve an overall test accuracy of 0.857 and 0.8304 which acquired in paper [6]. In paper [9] shows some experiments where the AD classification accuracy of the MCENN model is comparable when using high- and low-resolution brain images, suggesting the insensitivity of the MCENN to image resolution has an accuracy of 88%. In paper [10,11] has a combination of 3D convolutional networks and local transfer learning, and that for the prognostic prediction of AD is 89%,93.6% and 87.78% respectively by using pre-trained 3D convolutional network-based architectures. In a recent study [12], a deep learning-based approach was proposed for the diagnosis of AD using MRI data. The authors used a feature selection algorithm to extract relevant features from the MRI data and then trained deep learning analysis in 3238 participants worldwide where accuracy is 91.6%.

3   Proposed Methodology

To carry out our experiment, we must go through several stages. The workflow is described in detail below. The workflow diagram shown in Fig. 2, differnt transfer learning operation shown in Fig. 3 and ensemble model operation shown in Table-2.

3.1 Dataset Collection

Data is the primary component required to execute any kind of machine learning and deep learning experiment [13]. To diagnose Alzheimers' disease, the OASIS-2 dataset for MRI scan from Kaggle [14] was retrieved. It contained 4 classes and 6400 images. The 6400 images in the OASIS-2 collection have a size of 176 × 208. The images for each class are shown in Fig. 1 and Table-1.

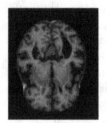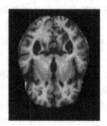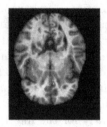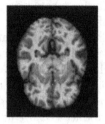

Fig. 1. Different brain MRI images for Alzheimer's disease stages from left to right "Mild Dementia", "Moderate Dementia", "Non Demented" and "Very Mild Dementia"

Table-1 shows how the four class images are separated into an imbalance formation. According to the table, there appears to be a considerable imbalance in the dataset across all classes. The biased level comprises 3200 images, and it is difficult to correctly classify all the levels in traditional learning because they are not all the same number. As a result, several transfer learning models and ensemble models are employed to categorize all of the levels accurately [10,15].

Table 1. Dataset statisics

Class Name	No. of Images
Mild Dementia	896
Moderate Dementia	64
Non Demented	3200
Very Mild Dementia	2240

3.2 Splitting Dataset

To categorize or predict any machine learning project using an algorithm, the dataset must be split. As a result, the OASIS dataset is divided into three parts: training, testing, and validation. We can conclude from Fig. 1 and Table-1 that there is a major data imbalance in the dataset. We used 80% of the total images for training and 20% for testing and validation when partitioning the dataset [16,17].

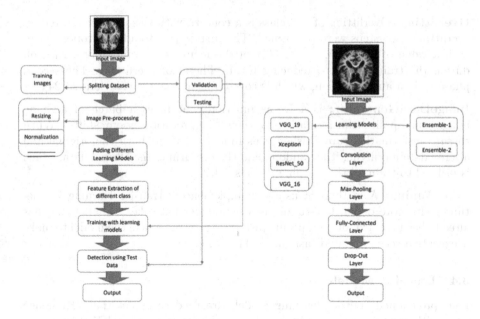

Fig. 2. Workflow diagram

Fig. 3. Pre-trained learning models setup

3.3 Image Pre-processing

Image pre-processing is a technique for performing operations on an image in order to improve it or extract relevant information from it. Image resizing, normalization, and overfitting are used to improve image experience shown in Fig. 2 [18].

Image Resizing: The entire set of images, including training, testing, and validation, is downsized to 224×224, while the primitive size was 176×208. The picture size for transfer learning models was 224×224 with RGB values also for ensemble models [19].

Normalization: When data is normalized (re-)scaled, it is projected into a preset range. (i.e. usually [0, 1] or [−1, 1]). To normalize all picture data, use the same techniques (CNN and transfer learning) on them, as described in Eq.:1 and typically performed as follows:

$$img = \frac{1}{255.0} \tag{1}$$

The pixel values between 0 and 1 are normalized [20,21].

Data Augmentation: By creating additional data points from existing data, a group of techniques known as "data augmentation" can be used to artificially enhance the amount of data. We used data augmentation to get new data points through deep learning pre-trained models [22,23].

Overfitting: Overfitting of one class is a concern with this dataset. To reduce overfitting, two steps were performed. The first step is to add a dropout layer with a value of 0.5. As a result, 50% of the neurons are randomly turned off during the training phase, reducing the likelihood of overfitting. The second phase is data augmentation, which is covered in the next subsection [23, 24].

ImageDataGenerator: is a Keras function that takes a batch of training images and applies transformations to them. (i.e., rotation, zoom, shifts). When these transformations are finished, this function returns both the original and altered data modifying it at random, and then returning the altered data, which is utilized to train all the learning models [24, 25].

Fine Tuning: A method of using or implementing transfer learning is fine-tuning. In more detail, fine-tuning is a technique that takes a model that has already been trained for one specific task and tunes or tweaks the model to make it execute a second related task [5, 6, 8, 11, 14, 20].

3.4   Learning Models

Four pre-trained transfer learning models are used to detect the MRI image issue with greater accuracy. Figure 3 depicts the operation of VGG19, Xception, ResNet50, and VGG16.All of the pre-trained models have a Convolution layer with two fully connected layers, and the softmax layer has been adjusted to (224, 224) to be compatible with this model by freezing the layers, and the learning rate has been set to 0.0001. For the optimizer, the stochastic gradient descent algorithm (SGD) was utilized [5, 6, 8, 11, 24, 26–28].

Table 2. Proposed ensemble-2 model description

Model Content	Details
Input Image size	$224 \times 224 \times 3$
ResNet50(Sequential 1)	
VGG16(Sequential 2)	
Second Convolution Layer	32 filters, Size= 3×3, ReLu, Padding='Same'
Second Max Pooling Layer	Pooling Size: 2×2
Third Convolution Layer	64 filters, Size= 3×3, ReLu, Padding='Same'
Third Max Pooling Layer	Pooling Size: 2×2
Fourth Convolution Layer	128 filters, Size= 3×3, ReLu, Padding='Same'
Fourth Max Pooling Layer	Pooling Size: 2×2
Fully Connected Layer	4096 nodes, ReLU
Dropout Layer	50% Neurons dropped randomly
Dense_1 Layer	8320 nodes, ReLu
Dense_2 Layer	516 nodes, ReLu
Output Layer	4 nodes, Softmax activation
Optimization Function	Adam optimization
Learning Rate	0.001
Loss Function	Categorical Cross Entropy

3.5   Ensemble Models

An approach to machine learning called an ensemble model combines various other models in the prediction process [29]. Base estimators are the name given to these models. The difficulties in creating a single estimator technically can be overcome via ensemble models. We used two ensemble models which are:

Ensemble-1: After running all of the transfer learning models provided in table-3, the greatest accuracy is 84%. We explored two Ensemble models, ensemble-1 and ensemble-2, to enhance accuracy, with the ensemble-1 model incorporating VGG19 and the Xception model containing 9,871,848 trainable parameters. Table-3 shows that the ensemble-1 model has a 93% higher accuracy than the rest of the transfer learning models. However, ensemble-2, reported in the following ensemble-2, attained 95% accuracy [3–5, 10–12].

Ensemble-2: Ensemble-2 model incorporates with ResNet50 and VGG16 model together with 6,207,976 trainable parameters. We created a table names Table-2 where model description has been given so that it provides higher accuracy among all the model. Table-2 shows the model description [3–5, 10–12].

4   Result and Analysis

In this part, we will go over the results of our model. The overall experiment done in "Google-Colab" where Provided "GPU" is "Tesla-K80". The model is trained with 80% of the information and evaluated with the remaining 20%. A comparison of the different models is presented here. As classification matrices [30], Accuracy, Precision, Recall, and the macro F1 score were computed in order to assess the model without bias.

Table 3. Model evaluation

Model_Name	Accuracy	Precision	Recall	F1_Score
VGG19	84%	82%	84%	83%
Xception	79%	80%	79%	79%
ResNet50	83%	82%	84%	83%
VGG16	84%	83%	81%	84%

Table 4. Model evaluation with ensemble

Ensemble_Model_Name	Accuracy	Precision	Recall	F1_Score
Ensemble-1	93%	92%	91%	90%
Ensemble-2	95%	91%	89%	93%

This part examines the performance of our models in experiments using the OASIS dataset for MRI scan. The deep learning model was used to evaluate results on datasets with and without image recurrence. In a batch size of 16,

The validation error was calculated by multiplying the training accuracy, training error, and validation accuracy for each period. We used an adaptive momentum (Adam) algorithm with a learning rate (LR) of 0.001 and a categorical cross entropy loss function. Using an annealing method with an LR, the optimizer was modified to converge more quickly and closely to the global minimum. We dynamically reduced the LR each time to maintain the advantage of a quicker computation time with a high LR.

Every five epochs, depending on the veracity of the validation. We chose to use the "ReduceLROnPlateau" function from "Keras.callbacks" to cut the LR in half if the validation loss did not decrease after five iterations.

Table-3 and 4 display the results of our trial after fine tuning the accuracy, precision, recall, and f1 score. According to Table-3, the acuracy for pre-trained models is 0.84 for the VGG19 and VGG16, 0.83 for ResNet50, and 0.79 for Xception. In Table 3, precision, recall, and F1 result are displayed beside accuracy. The pre-trained models' accuracy and validation accuracy, loss and validation loss curves are shown in Fig. 4, Fig. 5, Fig. 6 and Fig. 7 where the VGG19's training loss is 0.835 and validation loss is 1.125 shown in Fig. 4. The training loss and validation loss for the Xception model are 0.703 and 1.137 shown in Fig. 5. The training and validation loss for two additional models are ResNet50 and VGG16, are 0.935 and 1.1898 as well as 0.694 and 1.162, shown in Fig. 6 and Fig. 7 respectively.

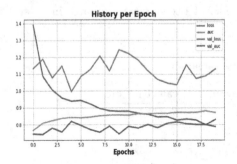 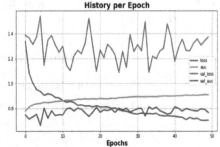

Fig. 4. Acc and loss curve for VGG19   **Fig. 5.** Acc and loss curve for Xception

Since the accuracy of the aforementioned transfer learning models didn't improve, we attempted an ensemble model in addition to them. Therefore, the VGG19 and xception(ensemble-1) model are ensembled. Model has 9,871,848 trainable parameters after fine tuning the inclusion of a few layers. The model evaluation has a good image in Table 4 after 30 successful epochs. ResNet50 and VGG16(ensemble-2), another ensemble model, have a trainable parameter

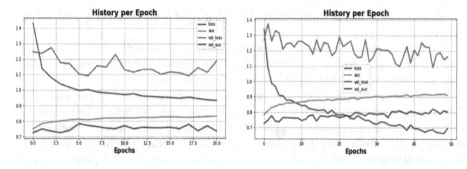

Fig. 6. Acc and loss curve for ResNet50   **Fig. 7.** Acc and loss curve for VGG16

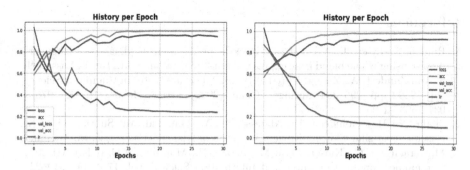

Fig. 8. Acc and loss curve, Ensemble-1   **Fig. 9.** Acc and loss curve, Ensemble-2

count of 6,207,976 after fine tuning. Following 30 successful epochs, the ensemble model assessment is presented in Table-4.

Accuracy and validation accuracy of VGG19+Xception(ensemble-1) is 0.99 and 0.93 and for ResNet50+VGG16(ensemble-2) model is 0.98 and 0.95 respectively shown in Table 4. Loss and validation loss curves are shown in Fig. 8, where the VGG19+Xception(ensemble-1)'s training loss is 0.2367 and validation loss is 0.3855. The training loss and validation loss for the ResNet50+VGG16 model(ensemble-2) are 0.0973 and 0.33, shown in Fig. 9.

5 Conclusion and Future Work

In this study, we investigated the use of ensemble deep transfer learning for enhanced Alzheimer's disease detection and classification. The ensemble model outperformed the individual deep transfer learning model, according to our findings. On a dataset of MRI scans from AD patients and healthy controls, we tested our methodology and found that an ensemble of ResNet50 and VGG16(ensemble-2) had an accuracy of 95%. The ensemble model exhibited more precision, sensitivity, and specificity than the other models. Our findings suggest that enhancing Alzheimer's disease diagnosis and classification by ensemble deep transfer learning can be a promising strategy. The promise of deep transfer learning ensemble based techniques for the diagnosis of AD using MRI data is thus highlighted by our study.

We believe that our proposed approach, have the potential to revolutionize how AD is recognized and classified, leading to improved patient outcomes and a greater standard of life for patients and their families.

In the future, we can focus on improving the performance of the ensemble deep transfer learning model. One approach that could be used is investigating additional classifying approaches [31–34] and optimizing the model combination [35–40]. Additionally, larger datasets can be used to train the model and judge its generalizability. The model can be improved to predict the progression of Alzheimer's disease and the effectiveness of different treatments.

References

1. Raihan, S.M., et al.: A belief rule based expert system to diagnose Alzheimer's disease using whole blood gene expression data. In: Mahmud, M., He, J., Vassanelli, S., van Zundert, A., Zhong, N. (eds.) BI 2022. Lecture Notes in Computer Science, vol. 12892, pp. 295–304. Springer, Cham (2022). https://doi.org/10.1007/978-3-031-15037-1_25

2. Shaffi, N., Hajamohideen, F., Abdesselam, A., Mahmud, M., Subramanian, K.: Ensemble classifiers for a 4-way classification of Alzheimer's disease. In: Mahmud, M., Ieracitano, C., Kaiser, M.S., Mammone, N., Morabito, F.C. (eds.) AII 2022. Communications in Computer and Information Science, vol. 1724, pp. 219–230. Springer, Cham (2022). https://doi.org/10.1007/978-3-031-24801-6_16

3. Ismail, W.N., Fathimathul Rajeena, P.P., Ali, M.A.S.: A meta-heuristic multi-objective optimization method for Alzheimer's disease detection based on multi-modal data. Mathematics 11(4), 957 (2023). https://doi.org/10.3390/math11040957

4. An, N., et al.: Deep ensemble learning for Alzheimer's disease classification. J. Biomed. Inf. 105, 103411 (2021). https://doi.org/10.1016/j.jbi.2020.103411

5. Islam, J., Zhang, Y.: A novel deep learning based multi-class classification method for Alzheimer's disease detection using brain MRI data. In: Zeng, Y., et al. (eds.) Brain Informatics. Lecture Notes in Computer Science, vol. 10654, pp. 213–222. Springer, Cham (2017). https://doi.org/10.1007/978-3-319-70772-3_20

6. Bandyopadhyay, A., et al.: Alzheimer's disease detection using ensemble learning and artificial neural networks. In: Santosh, K., Goyal, A., Aouada, D., Makkar, A., Chiang, Y.Y., Singh, S.K. (eds.) RTIP2R 2022. Communications in Computer and Information Science, vol. 1704, pp. 12–21. Springer, Cham (2023). https://doi.org/10.1007/978-3-031-23599-3_2

7. Salehi, A.W., et al.: A CNN model: earlier diagnosis and classification of Alzheimer disease using MRI. In: 2020 International Conference on Smart Electronics and Communication (ICOSEC) (2020). https://doi.org/10.1109/icosec49089.2020.9215402

8. Sethi, M., Ahuja, S.: Alzheimer disease classification using MRI images based on transfer learning. In: Innovations in Computational and Computer Techniques, ICACCT-2021 (2022). https://doi.org/10.1063/5.0108540

9. Liu, C., et al.: Monte Carlo ensemble neural network for the diagnosis of Alzheimer's disease. Neural Netw. 159, 14–24 (2023). https://doi.org/10.1016/j.neunet.2022.10.032

10. Savaş, S.: Detecting the stages of Alzheimer's disease with pre-trained deep learning architectures. Arab. J. Sci. Eng. **47**, 2201–2218 (2022). https://doi.org/10.1007/s13369-021-06131-3

11. Agarwal, D., et al.: Transfer learning for Alzheimer's disease through neuroimaging biomarkers: a systematic review. Sensors **21**(21), 7259 (2021). https://doi.org/10.3390/s21217259

12. Zhang, Y., Li, H., Zheng, Q.: A comprehensive characterization of hippocampal feature ensemble serves as individualized brain signature for Alzheimer's disease: deep learning analysis in 3238 participants worldwide. Eur. Radiol. 1–13 (2023). https://doi.org/10.1007/s00330-023-09519-x

13. Ouchicha, C., et al.: A novel deep convolutional neural network model for Alzheimer's disease classification using brain MRI. Autom. Control. Comput. Sci. **56**(3), 261–271 (2022). https://doi.org/10.3103/s0146411622030063

14. Kaggle: Alzheimers' Dataset (2023). www.kaggle.com/datasets/tourist55/alzheimers-dataset-4-class-of-images

15. Feng, C., et al.: Deep learning framework for Alzheimer's disease diagnosis via 3D-CNN and FSBI-LSTM. IEEE Access **7**, 63605–63618 (2019). https://doi.org/10.1109/access.2019.2913847

16. Bangyal, W.H., et al.: Constructing domain ontology for Alzheimer disease using deep learning based approach. Electronics **11**(12), 1890 (2022). https://doi.org/10.3390/electronics11121890

17. Anbarjafari, G.: Introduction to image processing (2023).https://www.sisu.ut.ee/imageprocessing/book/1

18. GeeksforGeek: Image Resizing using OpenCV (2023), https://www.geeksforgeeks.org/image-resizing-using-opencv-python/

19. Stakeoverflow: normalization in image processing (2023). https://stackoverflow.com/questions/33610825/normalization-in-image-processing

20. Ashtari-Majlan, M., Seifi, A., Dehshibi, M.M.: A multi-stream convolutional neural network for classification of progressive MCI in Alzheimer's disease using structural MRI images. IEEE J. Biomed. Health Inf. **26**(8), 3918–3926 (2022). https://doi.org/10.1109/JBHI.2022.3155705

21. Ji, H., et al.: Early diagnosis of Alzheimer's disease using deep learning. In: Proceedings of the 2nd International Conference on Control and Computer Vision (2019). https://doi.org/10.1145/3341016.3341024

22. Francis, A., Pandian, I.A.: The Alzheimer's disease neuroimaging initiative. Early detection of Alzheimer's disease using local binary pattern and convolutional neural network. Multimed. Tools Appl. **80**, 29585–29600 (2021). https://doi.org/10.1007/s11042-021-11161-y

23. Warnita, T., Inoue, N., Shinoda, K.: Detecting Alzheimer's disease using gated convolutional neural network from audio data. arXiv preprint arXiv:1803.11344 (2018). https://doi.org/10.21437/interspeech.2018-1713

24. Nawaz, A., Anwar, S.M., Liaqat, R., Iqbal, J., Bagci, U., Majid, M.: Deep convolutional neural network based classification of Alzheimer's disease using MRI data. In: IEEE 23rd International Multitopic Conference (INMIC), Bahawalpur, Pakistan, pp. 1–6 (2020). https://doi.org/10.1109/INMIC50486.2020.9318172

25. Raju, M., Gopi, V.P., Anitha, V.S., et al.: Multi-class diagnosis of Alzheimer's disease using cascaded three dimensional-convolutional neural network. Phys. Eng. Sci. Med. **43**, 1219–1228 (2020). https://doi.org/10.1007/s13246-020-00924-w

26. AbdulAzeem, Y., Bahgat, W.M., Badawy, M.: A CNN based framework for classification of Alzheimer's disease. Neural Comput. Appl. **33**, 10415–10428 (2021). https://doi.org/10.1007/s00521-021-05799-w

27. Lanjewar, M.G., Parab, J.S., Shaikh, A.Y.: Development of framework by combining CNN with KNN to detect Alzheimer's disease using MRI images. Multimed. Tools Appl. **82**, 12699–12717 (2023). https://doi.org/10.1007/s11042-022-13935-4
28. Mahmud, T., Barua, A., Begum, M., Chakma, E., Das, S., Sharmen, N.: An improved framework for reliable cardiovascular disease prediction using hybrid ensemble learning. In 2023 International Conference on Electrical, Computer and Communication Engineering (ECCE), pp. 1–6. IEEE (2023)
29. Mahmud, T., et al.: Reason based machine learning approach to detect Bangla abusive social media comments. In: Vasant, P., Weber, G.W., Marmolejo-Saucedo, J.A., Munapo, E., Thomas, J.J. (eds.) ICO 2022. Lecture Notes in Networks and Systems, vol. 569. Springer, Cham (2022). https://doi.org/10.1007/978-3-031-19958-5_46
30. Mahmud, T., et al.: A decision concept to support house hunting. Int. J. Adv. Comput. Sci. Appl. **13**(10) (2022). https://doi.org/10.14569/ijacsa.2022.0131091
31. Das, S., et al.: Deep transfer learning-based foot no-ball detection in live cricket match. Comput. Intell. Neurosci. **2398121**, 12 (2023). https://doi.org/10.1155/2023/2398121
32. Hossain, M.S., Habib, I.B., Andersson, K.: A belief rule based expert system to diagnose dengue fever under uncertainty. In: 2017 Computing Conference, pp. 179–186. IEEE (2017)
33. Mahmud, T., et al.: An optimal learning model for training expert system to detect uterine cancer. Procedia Comput. Sci. **184**, 356–363 (2021)
34. Islam, D., Mahmud, T., Chowdhury, T.: An efficient automated vehicle license plate recognition system under image processing. Indonesian J. Electr. Eng. Comput. Sci. **29**(2), 1055–1062 (2023)
35. Hossain, M.S., Rahaman, S., Kor, A.L., Andersson, K., Pattinson, C.: A belief rule based expert system for datacenter PUE prediction under uncertainty. IEEE Trans. Sustain. Comput. **2**(2), 140–153 (2017)
36. Patwary, M.J.A., Akter, S., Mahmud, T.: An expert system to detect uterine cancer under uncertainty. IOSR J. Comput. Eng. (IOSR-JCE), e-ISSN, 2278–0661 (2014)
37. Hossain, M.S., Rahaman, S., Mustafa, R., Andersson, K.: A belief rule-based expert system to assess suspicion of acute coronary syndrome (ACS) under uncertainty. Soft. Comput. **22**(22), 7571–7586 (2018)
38. Mahmud, T., Hossain, M.S.: An evidential reasoning-based decision support system to support house hunting. Int. J. Comput. Appl. **57**(21), 51–58 (2012)
39. Mahmud, T., Rahman, K.N., Hossain, M.S.: Evaluation of job offers using the evidential reasoning approach. Glob. J. Comput. Sci. Technol. **13**(D2), 35–44 (2013)
40. Islam, M.M., Mahmud, T., Hossain, M.S.: Belief-rule-based intelligent decision system to select hospital location. Indonesian J. Electr. Eng. Comput. Sci. **1**(3), 607–618 (2016)

Brain Big Data Analytics, Curation and Management

Effects of EEG Electrode Numbers on Deep Learning-Based Source Imaging

Jesse Rong[1], Rui Sun[1], Yuxin Guo[2], and Bin He[1(✉)]

[1] Department of Biomedical Engineering, Carnegie Mellon University, Pittsburgh, PA 15213, USA
bhe1@andrew.cmu.edu

[2] Neural Computation Program, Carnegie Mellon University, Pittsburgh, PA 15213, USA

Abstract. Electrophysiological source imaging (ESI) allows spatio-temporal imaging of brain activity and functional connectivity with high density EEG. The relationship between the performance of ESI methods and the number of scalp EEG electrodes has been a topic of ongoing investigation. Research has shown that high-density EEG is necessary for obtaining accurate and reliable ESI results using conventional ESI solutions, limiting their applications when only low-density EEG is available. In recent years, deep learning-based ESI methods have demonstrated strong performance by learning spatiotemporal patterns of brain activities directly from data. In this work, we examined the effect of the EEG electrode numbers on a recently proposed Deep Learning-based Source Imaging Framework (DeepSIF). We evaluated the ESI performance with 16, 21, 32, 64, and 75 channel EEG configurations using DeepSIF and conventional ESI methods in computer simulations. Our findings suggest that DeepSIF can provide accurate estimations of the source location and extent across various numbers of channels and noise levels, outperforming conventional methods, which indicates its merits for wide applications of ESI, especially for centers/labs without high density EEG devices.

Keywords: Electrophysiological Source Imaging · Source Localization · Deep Neural Networks · Electrode Number · EEG

1 Introduction

Electroencephalography (EEG) is a non-invasive technique that records the electrical activity of the brain by placing a limited number (typically up to a few hundred) of electrodes on the scalp. It provides real-time, direct measurement of neural activity with high temporal resolution and whole brain coverage, making it a valuable tool for studying the dynamics of brain function and dysfunction. However, several factors limit the spatial resolution of EEG, mainly due to the blurring effect of the volume conduction [1, 2], limited scalp sampling, and low signal-to-noise ratio (SNR). Electrophysiological source imaging (ESI) seeks to estimate the spatiotemporal distribution of brain electrical

---

J. Rong and R. Sun—Equal Contribution.

© The Author(s), under exclusive license to Springer Nature Switzerland AG 2023
F. Liu et al. (Eds.): BI 2023, LNAI 13974, pp. 123–132, 2023.
https://doi.org/10.1007/978-3-031-43075-6_11

sources using scalp recorded EEG [1]. It can significantly enhance the spatial resolution of EEG and allows researchers and clinicians to localize and image specific brain areas associated with certain cognitive processes or neurological disorders [3–6].

Evidence has emphasized the importance of using high-density EEG as opposed to low-density EEG, as they provide more accurate source localization results [7–11]. Utilizing a larger number of sensors offers better spatial coverage of the scalp, resulting in a more detailed representation of the scalp potential distribution. This increased coverage helps to reduce the ill-posedness of the ESI problem and improve the accuracy and reliability of the ESI results [11, 12]. However, more electrodes lead to higher cost associated with acquiring and maintaining high-density EEG systems, as well as longer preparation times for EEG recordings. In many clinical centers, high density EEG systems are unavailable due to these reasons. Routine clinical recordings often rely on low-density EEG systems, typically using no more than 32 channels or even fewer [9, 13]. This practical constraint makes it crucial to develop and optimize ESI methods that can effectively utilize low-density EEG data.

Deep learning-based ESI methods have shown considerable potential in recent years [14–19]. The use of deep learning can implicitly learn source-field distributions from a wide variety of data, resulting in a more accurate and robust ESI estimate. A large amount of training samples has enabled such methods to show excellent performance in computer simulations, particularly under challenging conditions for conventional ESI methods, such as low SNR or deep sources. These studies used an array of sensor channels in real data analysis, without examining the impact of the number of channels on the model performance.

In this study, we investigated the effect of electrode numbers on a recently proposed method, deep learning-based source imaging framework (DeepSIF) [20, 21], using 16-, 21-, 32-, 64-, and 75-channel configurations. We compared the results with two conventional benchmark methods: standardized low resolution brain electromagnetic tomography (sLORETA) [22] and linearly constrained minimum variance (LCMV) beamformer [23]. Our findings demonstrated that DeepSIF can provide robust performance across different numbers of channels at various SNR levels. This study highlights the versatility and adaptability of DeepSIF in handling varying sensor densities while maintaining accuracy and reliability. These advancements could potentially contribute to the ongoing progress in understanding brain functions, diagnosing neurological disorders, and developing effective treatment plans.

2 Materials and Methods

2.1 DeepSIF Outline

DeepSIF [20] is a spatiotemporal electrophysiological source imaging method based on biophysically constrained neural mass models and deep learning techniques. The source space is segmented into subregions, each represented by a neural mass model (NMM), specifically, the Jansen-Rit model [24, 25]. The NMM is a generative model inspired by neurophysiology and biophysics, which employs a set of nonlinear differential equations to describe local interactions among neural subpopulations. The Jansen-Rit model is versatile, as it can simulate brain signals similar to resting-state brain activity and spike-like activities resembling interictal spike signals with different parameter sets. Subregions can be grouped using a region growing method to form a source patch with various sizes and shapes. Thus, realistic synthetic sources with different source sizes, locations and interictal spike waveforms can be generated by interconnected NMM networks. This synthetic brain signal and its corresponding scalp signal serve as training data for the deep neural network. The neural network takes multi-channel EEG signals as inputs and produces activities in each brain region as outputs. Details regarding building the source models with NMM and the region growing method can be found in [20].

2.2 Synthetic Data Generation for Different Electrode Configuration

Five electrode configurations were included in this study based on the 10–10 and 10–20 system, including 75 channels, 64 channels, 32 channels, 21 channels, and 16 channels, respectively. Fsaverage5 in Freesurfer [26] was used as the head model, and its cortical surface was used as the source space. It was segmented into 994 regions. A leadfield matrix using 75-channel electrode configurations was first generated using the boundary element model in Brainstorm [27]. Four more leadfield matrices were subsequently generated by downsampling the 75-channel leadfield matrix according to the specific electrode configuration.

A training dataset was generated for each electrode configuration. They contained the same source space activity, which is two source patches generating various waveforms of interictal spike activities. The source space signal was projected to the sensor space with different leadfield matrices and Gaussian white noise was added to the EEG signals to maintain an SNR of 5, 10, 15, or 20 dB. Each training dataset contains a total of 310,128 pairs of sources and EEG signals. A DeepSIF model was trained for each training set, resulting in five models in total.

Testing data was generated following the same pipeline as the training data. For each electrode configuration, two testing datasets were generated, each with a size of 4,000. The first had only one active source, while the second had two simultaneously active sources. This resulted in testing data sizes of 8,000 samples of sources and EEG pairs for each electrode configuration.

2.3 DeepSIF Model Training

The deep neural network contains the spatial module and the temporal module. The spatial module is composed of 5 fully connected layers with skip connections similar to a ResNet [28]. The input size for the spatial module equals to the number of EEG electrodes, and the last output layer size is 500. The temporal filter is composed of three Long Short-Term Memory (LSTM) layers [29]. The first LSTM layer has an input size of 500 and output size of 994, and other layers have the same input and output size of 994. Mean square error loss was the loss function and Adam optimizer with a weight decay of 1e-6 and a learning rate of 3e-4 was used. The model was trained on one NVIDIA Tesla V100 GPU at Pittsburgh Supercomputing Center [30]. More details and network architecture illustration can be found in the original DeepSIF paper [20].

2.4 Model Evaluation

The output of each ESI method was evaluated at its peak activation. The threshold was determined using Otsu's threshold technique [31]. The estimated source regions were regions with activation values exceeding Otsu's threshold. The performance of the estimated source regions was then evaluated by comparing them with the ground truth source regions.

To determine the localization error, we calculated the average error between the estimated regions and the ground truth regions. Specifically, we computed the Euclidean distance between each ground truth region $J_{groundtruth,i}$ and its closest region in the estimated regions $J_{estimated}$, and then averaged these distances. We performed a similar calculation to measure the error from the estimated regions to the ground truth regions, using the Euclidean distance between each estimated region $J_{estimated,i}$ and its closest region in the ground truth regions $J_{groundtruth}$. The localization error is defined as the average of these two errors. An illustration of the error calculation can be found in Fig. 1.

The overlap between the estimated regions and the ground truth regions is represented by $A_{overlap} = A_{groundtruth} \cap A_{estimated}$. We employed two metrics to assess the accuracy of the identification and its dependence on the source size: recall and precision. Recall is the ratio of the overlapping area to the ground truth area, $A_{overlap}/A_{groundtruth}$, and indicates the proportion of correctly identified ground truth regions. Precision is the ratio of the overlapping area to the estimated area, $A_{overlap}/A_{estimated}$, and penalizes overestimation of the source regions.

The performance of the DeepSIF model was also compared with two classical ESI methods, sLORETA and LCMV, calculated using MNE-Python [27].

3 Results

Figure 1 illustrates the relationship between the number of electrodes and three ESI methods: DeepSIF, sLORETA and LCMV. DeepSIF shows strong robustness to changes in electrode number, maintaining a median localization error of around 2 mm across all configurations studied. The precision and recall values are both above 0.8 for all configurations, indicating a good overlap between the DeepSIF estimation and the ground truth. Conversely, the localization error of sLORETA and LCMV increases significantly when the electrode number is reduced, especially when it drops below 32 channels. Additionally, DeepSIF model outperforms both sLORETA and LCMV in most metrics, except for recall, where it has a slightly lower performance than LCMV. The difference between DeepSIF and LCMV in recall value is only about 0.1 and LCMV's precision is approximately 0.6 lower than DeepSIF, indicating that LCMV's favorable recall performance is achieved at the expense of overly diffused estimation.

The comparison results are further shown in a single source example in Fig. 2. The estimation produced by the DeepSIF model shows a more focused estimation compared to both sLORETA and LCMV. Additionally, the estimation of the DeepSIF model remains consistent across different electrode configurations, whereas the estimation of sLORETA becomes increasingly diffused as the number of electrodes decreases.

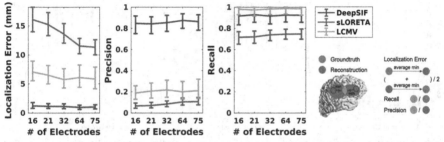

Fig. 1. Effect of EEG electrode numbers on ESI performance for a single source. Metric evaluation and comparison of DeepSIF, sLORETA, and LCMV are shown across different electrode configurations. The median value is plotted against the number of electrodes. The error bar represents the 25th and 75th percentile.

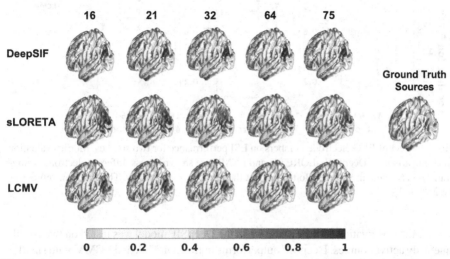

Fig. 2. Source estimation examples for a single source by the DeepSIF model, sLORETA, and LCMV for each electrode configuration. The colorbar shows the normalized source magnitude, and the simulated source is in green. SNR = 5 dB.

We conducted further analysis of the DeepSIF model by examining its performance across different SNR levels. Our results show that for each electrode configuration, the DeepSIF model produces a similar distribution of metric scores across different SNRs. While we observed a slight overall increase in localization error and a slight overall decrease in precision and recall at an SNR of 5, these differences are not significant (Fig. 3).

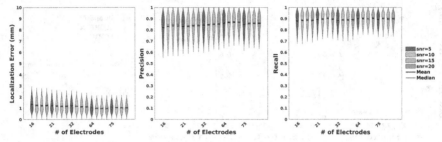

Fig. 3. DeepSIF Performance for imaging a single source at different signal-to-noise ratios. The metric distributions demarcated within the 10th to 90th percentile are plotted.

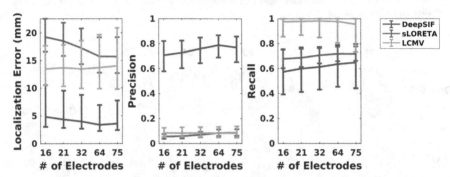

Fig. 4. Effect of EEG electrode numbers on ESI performance for two sources. Metric evaluation and comparison of DeepSIF, sLORETA, and LCMV are shown across different electrode configurations. The median value is plotted against the number of electrodes. The error bar represents the 25th and 75th percentile.

Similar observations can be made when the DeepSIF model was tested on two simultaneously active sources. DeepSIF outperforms both sLORETA and LCMV, with smaller localization errors and greater precision in all electrode configurations. However, as the number of electrodes decreases, we observe an increase in localization errors and a decrease in precision and recall for all ESI methods (Fig. 4). This is anticipated as the interference between two sources makes it more challenging to distinguish multiple sources with limited spatial coverage. However, DeepSIF can still provide relatively consistent results with two simultaneous sources. Figure 5 shows an example that the DeepSIF model produces consistent estimations of the true sources across all electrode configurations. On the other hand, both sLORETA and LCMV showed decreased performance when imaging the two concurrent source configuration, especially when fewer electrodes are used. When using 75 electrodes, sLORETA shows diffused estimates on the left frontal cortex, while LCMV estimates were shifted away from the ground truth on the frontal cortex.

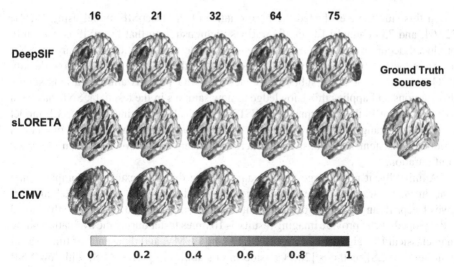

Fig. 5. Source estimation examples for two sources by the DeepSIF, sLORETA, and LCMV for each electrode configuration. SNR = 5 dB.

4 Discussion

Many ESI studies have shown the importance of using high-density EEG to achieve accurate ESI results [7–11]. However, standard clinical recordings frequently employ low-density EEG systems ($<= 32$ channels) due to increased cost and time for high density EEG [9, 13]. There is a clinical need to develop an accurate ESI method capable of providing spatiotemporal source estimates from low-density EEG data.

Deep learning-based ESI has gained increasing attention in recent years [14–19]. These data-driven approaches aim to learn the mapping relationship between the brain and scalp from data. Given the rich information contained in the large amount of training data and the expressive representation power of deep neural networks, deep learning-based ESI methods have the ability to incorporate more information into the inverse solution compared to conventional model-based methods. Studies have demonstrated that deep learning-based ESI methods can maintain consistent performance under challenging conditions, such as extremely low SNR signals [16] or sources located deep within the brain [14], using 64–128 channel recordings in computer simulations, because the neural network has learned similar conditions from the training data. Studies also suggested that evoked potential imaging results are concordant with physiological understandings in healthy subjects using 32-electrode EEG [14] or 59-electrode EEG [19]. The DeepSIF model was rigorously validated in 75-electrode EEG configuration [20] and 102-, 148-channel MEG configurations [21] for imaging interictal spike activity in a large cohort of epilepsy patients and it demonstrated superior ability to accurately identify the epileptogenic zone. However, there is no systemic investigation regarding the relationship between the number of electrodes and the model performance for these deep learning-based-ESI methods.

In this study, we evaluated the performance of the DeepSIF model using 16, 21, 32, 64, and 75 channel EEG configurations, demonstrating that DeepSIF consistently produced accurate results across different electrode configurations and various SNR levels, outperforming conventional ESI methods. As the model is trained on low-density EEG data, it captures the subtle differences in EEG patterns among various source distributions and applies this knowledge to new samples in the test data. SNR has been a critical factor in the performance of ESI methods [7]. By testing the DeepSIF model across a wide range of SNRs (5–20 dB), our results show that the DeepSIF model can produce consistent and robust results across different SNR levels for each electrode configuration.

Admittedly, it is the large amount and training data and extensive computational time during the training phase, which is not required for conventional ESI methods, that gives DeepSIF an advantage over conventional ESI methods. However, once the model is developed, it can provide imaging results 5–10 times faster during the evaluation phase than classical ESI algorithms like sLORETA and LCMV, and thousands of times faster than iterative ESI methods [20]. Considering its ability to perform ESI with low SNR and low spatial sampling, DeepSIF holds the potential for real-time ESI applications across various research and clinical settings.

While we have demonstrated DeepSIF's ability to provide robust imaging with varying numbers of sensors and SNR levels in computer simulations, a thorough validation with real data is essential, to truly establish its value. Previous research has shown that deep learning-based ESI methods can produce reasonable source distributions from low-density EEG recordings with 29 channels [17] or 32 channels [14]. However, no quantitative evaluation has been performed to assess the performance of such methods when using low-density EEG data. Moreover, a quantitative comparison between low- and high-density EEG across a group of subjects is also necessary for determining the efficacy of low-density EEG for source localization. Therefore, the immediate next steps for this study will involve conducting a thorough quantitative evaluation of the DeepSIF method using low-density EEG data, as well as comparing its performance with high-density EEG data in the same subjects. These analyses will help us better understand the value of low-density EEG in localizing brain activity, and if the use of DeepSIF will remove the need for high density EEG for accurate ESI imaging in real subjects. The simulation results from our study suggest that the DeepSIF model holds promise for accurately localizing brain activity using fewer electrodes than traditional ESI methods. This is particularly important for studies with a limited number of electrodes, such as routine EEGs performed in many clinical settings. The successful implementation of DeepSIF in these situations could lead to more efficient and cost-effective EEG assessments, ultimately benefiting both patients and healthcare.

Acknowledgment. This work was supported in part by National Institutes of Health grants NS096761, EB021027, AT009263, MH114233, EB029354, and NS124564, and by a gift from the Pittsburgh Health Data Alliance. R.S. was supported in part by a Fellowship from the Center for Machine Learning and Health.

References

1. He, B., Sohrabpour, A., Brown, E., Liu, Z.: Electrophysiological source imaging: a noninvasive window to brain dynamics. Annu. Rev. Biomed. Eng. **20**, 171–196 (2018). https://doi.org/10.1146/annurev-bioeng-062117-120853
2. Grech, R., Cassar, T., Muscat, J., et al.: Review on solving the inverse problem in EEG source analysis. J. Neuroeng. Rehabil. **5**, 1–33 (2008). https://doi.org/10.1186/1743-0003-5-25
3. Lopes da Silva, F.: EEG and MEG: relevance to neuroscience. Neuron **80**, 1112–1128 (2013)
4. Sohrabpour, A., Cai, Z., Ye, S., et al.: Noninvasive electromagnetic source imaging of spatiotemporally distributed epileptogenic brain sources. Nat. Commun. **11**, 1946 (2020). https://doi.org/10.1038/s41467-020-15781-0
5. Ye, S., Yang, L., Lu, Y., et al.: Contribution of ictal source imaging for localizing seizure onset zone in patients with focal epilepsy patients. Neurology **96**, e366–e375 (2020). https://doi.org/10.1212/WNL.0000000000011109
6. Cai, Z., Sohrabpour, A., Jiang, H., et al.: Noninvasive high-frequency oscillations riding spikes delineates epileptogenic sources. Proc. Natl. Acad. Sci. **118**, e2011130118 (2021). https://doi.org/10.1073/pnas.2011130118
7. Lu, Y., Yang, L., Worrell, G.A., He, B.: Seizure source imaging by means of FINE spatio-temporal dipole localization and directed transfer function in partial epilepsy patients. Clin. Neurophysiol. **123**, 1275–1283 (2012). https://doi.org/10.1016/j.clinph.2011.11.007
8. Lantz, G., Grave de Peralta, R., Spinelli, L., et al.: Epileptic source localization with high density EEG: how many electrodes are needed? Clin. Neurophysiol. **114**, 63–69 (2003). https://doi.org/10.1016/S1388-2457(02)00337-1
9. Brodbeck, V., Spinelli, L., Lascano, A.M., et al.: Electroencephalographic source imaging: a prospective study of 152 operated epileptic patients. Brain **134**, 2887–2897 (2011). https://doi.org/10.1093/brain/awr243
10. Michel, C.M., Lantz, G., Spinelli, L., et al.: 128-channel EEG source imaging in epilepsy: clinical yield and localization precision. J. Clin. Neurophysiol. **21**, 71–83 (2004). https://doi.org/10.1097/00004691-200403000-00001
11. Sohrabpour, A., Lu, Y., Kankirawatana, P., et al.: Effect of EEG electrode number on epileptic source localization in pediatric patients. Clin. Neurophysiol. **126**, 472–480 (2015). https://doi.org/10.1016/J.CLINPH.2014.05.038
12. Song, J., Davey, C., Poulsen, C., et al.: EEG source localization: Sensor density and head surface coverage. J. Neurosci. Methods **256**, 9–21 (2015). https://doi.org/10.1016/j.jneumeth.2015.08.015
13. Michel, C.M., Brunet, D.: EEG source imaging: a practical review of the analysis steps. Front Neurol **10**, 325 (2019). https://doi.org/10.3389/fneur.2019.00325
14. Hecker, L., Rupprecht, R., Tebartz Van Elst, L., Kornmeier, J.: ConvDip: a convolutional neural network for better EEG source imaging. Front Neurosci **15**, 569918 (2021). https://doi.org/10.3389/fnins.2021.569918
15. Wei, C., Lou, K., Wang, Z., et al.: Edge sparse basis network: a deep learning framework for EEG source localization. In: Proceedings of the International Joint Conference on Neural Networks, pp 1–8 (2021)
16. Huang, G., Liu, K, Liang, J., et al.: Electromagnetic source imaging via a data-synthesis-based convolutional encoder–decoder network. IEEE Trans. Neural Netw. Learn. Syst. 1–15 (2022https://doi.org/10.1109/TNNLS.2022.3209925
17. Jiao, M., Wan, G., Guo, Y., et al.: A graph fourier transform based bidirectional long short-term memory neural network for electrophysiological source imaging. Front. Neurosci. **16**, 867466 (2022). https://doi.org/10.3389/FNINS.2022.867466

18. Bore, J.C., Li, P., Jiang, L., et al.: A long short-term memory network for sparse spatiotemporal EEG source imaging. IEEE Trans. Med. Imaging **40**, 3787–3800 (2021). https://doi.org/10.1109/TMI.2021.3097758

19. Dinh, C., Samuelsson, J.G., Hunold, A., et al.: Contextual MEG and EEG source estimates using spatiotemporal LSTM networks. Front. Neurosci. **15**, 119 (2021). https://doi.org/10.3389/FNINS.2021.552666/BIBTEX

20. Sun, R., Sohrabpour, A., Worrell, G.A., He, B.: Deep neural networks constrained by neural mass models improve electrophysiological source imaging of spatiotemporal brain dynamics. Proc. Natl. Acad. Sci. **119**, e2201128119 (2022). https://doi.org/10.1073/PNAS.2201128119

21. Sun, R., Zhang, W., Bagić, A., He, B.: Personalized Deep Learning based Source Imaging Framework Improves the Imaging of Epileptic Sources from MEG Interictal Spikes. bioRxiv 2022.11.13.516312 (2022). https://doi.org/10.1101/2022.11.13.516312

22. Pascual-Marqui, R.D.: Standardized low resolution brain electromagnetic tomography (sLORETA): technical details. Methods Find Exp. Clin. Pharmacol. **24**(Suppl D), 5–12 (2002)

23. Van Veen, B.D., Van Drongelen, W., Yuchtman, M., Suzuki, A.: Localization of brain electrical activity via linearly constrained minimum variance spatial filtering. IEEE Trans. Biomed. Eng. **44**, 867–880 (1997). https://doi.org/10.1109/10.623056

24. Jansen, B.H., Rit, V.G.: Electroencephalogram and visual evoked potential generation in a mathematical model of coupled cortical columns. Biol. Cybern. **73**, 357–366 (1995). https://doi.org/10.1007/BF00199471

25. Wendling, F., Bellanger, J.J., Bartolomei, F., Chauvel, P.: Relevance of nonlinear lumped-parameter models in the analysis of depth-EEG epileptic signals. Biol. Cybern. **83**, 367–378 (2000). https://doi.org/10.1007/s004220000160

26. Fischl, B.: FreeSurfer. Neuroimage **62**, 774–781 (2012)

27. Tadel, F., Baillet, S., Mosher, J.C., et al.: Brainstorm: a user-friendly application for MEG/EEG analysis. Comput. Intell. Neurosci. (2011). https://doi.org/10.1155/2011/879716

28. He, K., Zhang, X., Ren, S., Sun, J.: Deep residual learning for image recognition. In: Proceedings of the IEEE Conference on Computer Vision and Pattern Recognition, pp 770–778 (2016)

29. Hochreiter, S., Schmidhuber, J.: Long short-term memory. Neural Comput. **9**, 1735–1780 (1997). https://doi.org/10.1162/neco.1997.9.8.1735

30. Towns, J., Cockerill, T., Dahan, M., et al.: XSEDE: accelerating scientific discovery. Comput. Sci. Eng. **16**, 62–74 (2014). https://doi.org/10.1109/MCSE.2014.80

31. Otsu, N.: A threshold selection method from gray-level histograms. IEEE Trans. Syst. Man Cybern. **9**, 62 (1996)

Graph Diffusion Reconstruction Network for Addictive Brain-Networks Identification

Changhong Jing, Changwei Gong, Zuxin Chen, and Shuqiang Wang[✉]

Shenzhen Institutes of Advanced Technology, Chinese Academy of Sciences,
Shenzhen, China
{ch.jing,cw.gong,zx.chen3,sq.wang}@siat.ac.cn

Abstract. Functional Magnetic Resonance Imaging(fMRI) can reveal complex patterns of brain functional changes. The exploration of addiction-related brain connectivity can be more precise with fMRI data. However, it is still difficult to obtain addiction-related brain connectivity effectively from fMRI data due to the complexity and non-linear characteristics of brain connections. Therefore, this paper proposed a Graph Diffusion Reconstruction Network (GDRN), which could capture addiction-related brain connectivity from fMRI data of addicted rats. The diffusion reconstruction module effectively maintained the unity of data distribution by reconstructing the training samples. This module enhanced the ability to reconstruct nicotine addiction-related brain networks. Experiments on the nicotine addiction rat dataset show that the proposed model can effectively explore nicotine addiction-related brain connectivity.

Keywords: Brain connectivity · Graph diffusion · Nicotine addiction · Generative learning

1 Introduction

Addiction is a disease characterized by seeking compulsive drugs. Smoking addiction is not only the most common drug addiction behavior in humans worldwide [1], but also considered to be one of the leading causes of death and disease in the world [2]. Clinical studies have shown that long-term exposure to nicotine can lead to changes in brain structure and function [3]. However, few studies have focused on the changes in global brain functional networks caused by long-term exposure to nicotine, which are associated with severe damage to brain circuits, especially in acute nicotine withdrawal. To better understand smoking behavior and help improve the treatment of nicotine addiction, key functional connectivity and mechanisms of addiction that are altered by acute nicotine withdrawal and recovery need to be identified.

F. Liu et al. (Eds.): BI 2023, LNAI 13974, pp. 133–145, 2023.
https://doi.org/10.1007/978-3-031-43075-6_12

Imaging studies have revealed neurochemical and functional changes in the brains of addicted individuals, providing new insights into the mechanisms of addiction. Functional magnetic resonance image (fMRI) is currently our most powerful tool [4] for non-invasive functional imaging of the whole brain [5]. The development of magnetic resonance imaging has transformed the study of neuroanatomy, enabling for the first time well-contrasted in vivo experiments in different brain regions. The brain network is divided into different brain regions by anatomical structure and connected together, and the functional brain network shows its complex neuron communication and signal transmission mode. Thanks to the advancement of modern imaging technology and advanced medical image analysis methods [6], the pattern of this complex neural signal can be analyzed from functional images, which reveals neuronal activities related to behavior and cognition, as well as brain diseases.

In brain imaging computing, artificial intelligence technology [7,8] based on machine learning [9] can effectively improve the efficiency [10,11] of doctors' treatment and the accuracy of diagnosis. Convolutional neural networks reduce the dimensionality of medical image data through convolution operators, which can effectively identify patterns in neuroimaging. Generative adversarial strategies [12] can simulate the real distribution of data, reduce the interference caused by noise, and enhance the robustness of the model. Generative artificial intelligence [13–15] can be applied to brain network analysis to help better understand the function and structure of the brain [16]. In brain network analysis, generative artificial intelligence [17] can be used to generate simulated data to explore different types of neurons and connections between neurons, which can help to better understand brain networks [18]. It can also be used to simulate the transmission of signals between neurons to help better understand the interaction and information transmission between neurons [19]. Generative artificial intelligence can be used in neuroimaging to help better interpret neuroimaging data and provide information about the structure and function of brain networks [20]. Generative artificial intelligence can be used to denoise and de-artifact fMRI data, thereby improving the accuracy and reliability of brain network analysis [21]. Generative artificial intelligence has broad application prospects in brain network analysis, which can help to better understand the function and structure of the brain, and provide new opportunities and methods for neuroscience research [22].

Related Work. The strategy of generative adversarial learning [23,24] can be easily applied to the field of brain imaging [25,26]. Conte [27] et al. developed a GAN based on the pix2pix framework for a brain tumor segmentation model. Pan [28] et al. designed a disease image-specific network framework (DSNet) to model the specificity of disease images with spatial cosine implicits. Bo [29] et al. developed a multi-tracer PET synthesis model for the task of generating multi-tracer PET volumes that can generate multi-tracer PET from single-tracer PET. Jiao [30] et al. study the cross-modal generation task of MRI and propose an end-to-end self-supervised GAN model for MRI synthesis.

With the rapid development of diffusion models in the field of cross-modal generation, more and more studies have applied diffusion models to the field of brain imaging research. Wolleb [31] adopted a DDIM-based anomaly detection model to achieve anomaly detection tasks for brain tumor images. In the anomaly detection task, compared with mainstream methods such as FP-GAN and VAE, it can be found that better results can be obtained at the same duration level. Pinaya [32] used DDPM/DDIM to realize the detection and segmentation of diseases such as brain tumors and cerebral hemorrhage, and performed better than Transformer on synthetic data and real data. DDPM/DDIM shows better performance on disease tasks such as brain tumor and cerebral hemorrhage. Khader [33] proposed a diffusion model Medical Diffusion applied to 3D images for 3D brain image generation. Chung [34] et al. used score-based accelerated MRI reconstruction to produce highly accurate results on the MRI reconstruction task. However, the existing methods are still difficult to effectively obtain the brain connections related to nicotine addiction from fMRI images.

To address the above issues, this paper proposed a graph diffusion reconstruction network (GDRN) to capture brain connections associated with nicotine addiction from fMRI data of addicted rats. The diffusion reconstruction module effectively maintains the unity of the data distribution in the latent space by reconstructing the training samples. This module enhances the reconstruction of nicotine addiction-related brain networks, allowing the model to learn more subtle distribution differences. This allows the model to effectively capture addiction-related brain connections.

2   Method

In order to generate more effective addiction-related brain networks, so as to capture the characteristics of addiction and finally detect addiction-related brain connections, a reconstruction network with graph diffusion is proposed for the generation of addiction-related brain connections. The overall architecture of the framework is shown in Fig. 1, which includes functional brain network construction, brain network diffusion reconstruction module and addiction-related brain connection detector. The following mainly introduces the proposed brain network diffusion reconstruction module.

From a probabilistic modeling point of view, the key defining characteristic of a generative model is that it is trained in such a way that its samples $\tilde{x} \sim p_\theta(\tilde{x})$ come from the same distribution $x \sim p_\theta(x)$ as the training data distribution. Energy-based models do this by defining an unnormalized probability density over the state space. However, if these methods perform Markov Chain Monte Carlo (MCMC) sampling during both training and inference, a slow iterative process is required. The Denoising Diffusion Probabilistic Models (DDPMs) define a forward diffusion phase. In this method, the input data is gradually perturbed in several steps by adding Gaussian noise, and then learns the backdiffusion process. Data is recovered by reversing this noise process.

Diffusion models have strong pattern coverage and quality of generated samples. This brain network diffusion reconstruction module combines and applies

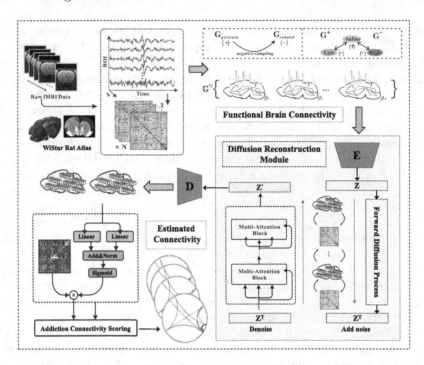

Fig. 1. The structure of the proposed Graph Diffusion Reconstruction Network.

this technique to the generation of addiction-related brain networks. The ability to effectively extract latent variables with the help of diffusion models captures addiction-related representations for the detection of addiction-related brain connections in the next step.

Inspired by DDPM, this module also adopts the diffusion forward process and reverse diffusion process when reconstructing addiction-related brain networks. The model was used to generate the addiction brain network of rats in the normal saline group, the low-concentration nicotine group, and the high-concentration nicotine group.

In the forward process, given the initial observation value $x_0 \sim q(x_0)$, it is defined as a Markov chain and a diffusion process is performed. And update the conditional probability of the current sample x_t at each time step. Finally, from the conditional probabilities at all time steps, the probability density function for $_0$ can be calculated. Taking $\alpha_t = 1 - \beta_t$ and $\bar{\alpha}_t = \prod_{s=0}^{t} \alpha_s$ as the premise, in order to be able to sample any step of the noise latency under the input x_0 condition, the forward formula can be expressed as follows:

$$q\left(\mathbf{x}_t \mid \mathbf{x}_0\right) = N\left(\mathbf{x}_t; \sqrt{\bar{\alpha}_t}\mathbf{x}_0, \left(1 - \bar{\alpha}_t\right)\mathbf{I}\right) \tag{1}$$

$$\mathbf{x}_t = \sqrt{\bar{\alpha}_t}\mathbf{x}_0 + \sqrt{1 - \overline{\alpha_l}}\epsilon \tag{2}$$

where $\mathbf{I}$ is the identity matrix $\mathcal{N}(x; \mu, \sigma)$ representing the normal distribution with mean μ and covariance σ.

In the backward pass, the forward pass is reversed to get a sample from $q(x_0)$. For this purpose, it has the following formula:

$$p_\theta(\mathbf{x}_{0:T}) = p(\mathbf{x}_T) \prod_{t=1} p_\theta(\mathbf{x}_{t-1} \mid \mathbf{x}_t) \tag{3}$$

$$p_\theta(\mathbf{x}_{t-1} \mid \mathbf{x}_t) = \mathcal{N}(\mathbf{x}_{t-1}; \mu_\theta(\mathbf{x}_t, t), \Sigma_\theta(\mathbf{x}_t, t)) \tag{4}$$

In order to train this model, let $p(x_0)$ learn the real data distribution $q(x_0)$, and also optimize the following variational upper bound according to the idea and theory of DDPM:

$$\mathbb{E}[-\log p_\theta(\mathbf{x}_0)] \leq \mathbb{B}_q\left[-\log \frac{p_\theta(\mathbf{x}_{0:T})}{q(\mathbf{x}_{1:T} \mid \mathbf{x}_0)}\right]$$

$$= \mathbb{E}_q\left[-\log p(\mathbf{x}_T) - \sum_{t \geq 1} \log \frac{p_\theta(\mathbf{x}_{t-1} \mid \mathbf{x}_t)}{q(\mathbf{x}_t \mid \mathbf{x}_{t-1})}\right] \tag{5}$$

$$= -L_{\text{VL.B}}$$

Consistent with DDMP, this module chooses to let the network of the inverse process output random variables ϵ, and use the predictive random variable method to train a model $\epsilon_\theta(x_t, t)$ to predict ϵ, so the final loss function can be simplified as:

$$L_{\text{simple}} = E_{t, x_0, \epsilon}\left[\|\epsilon - \epsilon_\theta(x_t, t)\|^2\right] \tag{6}$$

Thus, through the diffusion forward process and reverse diffusion process, this model can obtain the addiction-related brain network through training, and learn the representation distribution of rat brain networks of different categories (normal saline, low concentration, high concentration).

3   Experiments

The fMRI data sets used in the experiment were divided into three groups, and the functional brain network was constructed from three different groups of rat fMRI scan data. After the original fMRI image data were preprocessed, the time series signals of the brain regions were extracted from the fMRI images according to the Wistar rat brain atlas. The functional connectivity matrix for each rat brain was obtained using Pearson correlation coefficients to calculate correlations between brain region time series. The following two evaluation groups were established: (1) high vs. saline, and (2) low vs. saline.

Implementation Detail. The PyTorch backend was used to implement the proposed GDRN. One Nvidia GeForce RTX 3090 was used to speed up the network's training. The learning rate was set to 0.001, and the training epoch was set to 1000.

This study explores the brain networks that generate the resulting differences from nicotine injections. Inputting different types of rat brain network data, the model can use the learned information to generate more realistic network data. It was effective in alleviating the small-sample problem of addiction in rats. Classification experiments were carried out on the results, and the results are shown in the Fig. 2. Experiments have verified that the model has good classification performance.

The model proposed in this paper can generate different types of brain networks, that is, reconstruct the functional connectivity matrix of the saline group, the low nicotine group, and the high nicotine group. As shown in Fig. 3, it shows the brain connections with the most obvious differences between the high concentration group and the normal saline group under different experimental settings. Figure 4 shows the most prominent brain connections between the low-concentration nicotine group and the saline group.

The experimental results are then analyzed from the perspective of brain connectivity. The most apparent brain connections in the high-concentration and saline groups were: (optic pathways_R, pituitary_R), (diagonal domain_R,

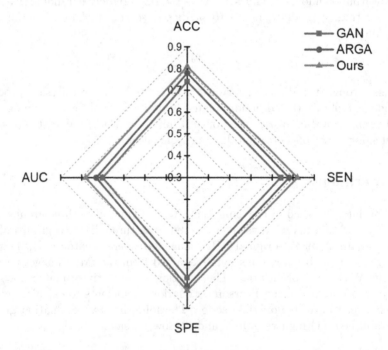

Fig. 2. Performance of different models on datasets. Experimental results show that the proposed model outperforms other comparison methods.

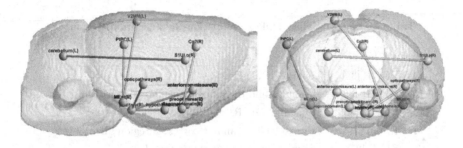

Fig. 3. The brain connectivity with the most obvious differences between high concentration and normal saline.

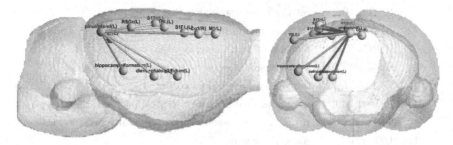

Fig. 4. The brain connectivity with the most obvious differences between low concentration and normal saline.

cingulate cortex, area 2_R), (hypothalamus_R, pituitary_R), (parietal cortex, posterior area, caudal part_L, medial entorhinal cortex_L), (pituitary_R, anterior commissure_R), (preoptic area_L, diagonal domain_R), (anterior commissure_L, diagonal domain_L), (primary somatosensory cortex, upper lip region_R, cerebellum_L), (anterior commissure_L, preoptic area_R), (secondary visual cortex, mediomedial area_L, medial entorhinal cortex_R).

The most apparent brain connections in the low concentration and normal saline groups were: (pineal gland_L, diencephalon_L), (retrosplenial granular cortex, c region_L,pineal gland_L), (pineal gland_L, pallidum_L), (pineal gland_L, primary somatosensory cortex, hindlimb region_L), (secondary visual cortex, lateral area_L, pineal gland_L), (hippocampal formation_L, pineal gland_L), (pineal gland_L, primary motor cortex_L), (pineal gland_L, primary somatosensory cortex, forelimb region_L), (pineal gland_L, primary somatosensory cortex, trunk region_L), (pineal gland_L, cingulate cortex, area 1_R).

Table 1 and Table 2 show the Top 15 brain regions with the most significant performance under different experimental settings. Brain regions with high weights can be found to be strongly associated with prior studies of addiction, and the visualization of these brain regions is shown in the Fig. 5. We can find that there is a certain consistency in the distribution of these brain regions and brain connections. The same low-concentration group is concentrated in the

Table 1. Low vs. Saline TOP 15 Addiction-Related Brain Regions.

High vs. Saline

149	PG_L [35]	pineal gland_L
14	GD_R [36]	granular and dysgranular insular cortex_R
148	PG_R [35]	pineal gland_R
71	RSGb_L	retrosplenial granular cortex, b region_L
73	S1_L [37]	primary somatosensory cortex_L
25	RSGb_R	retrosplenial granular cortex, b region_R
87	V1M_L	primary visual cortex, monocular area_L
26	RSGc_R	retrosplenial granular cortex, c region_R
72	RSGc_L	retrosplenial granular cortex, c region_L
67	PtPC_L [38]	parietal cortex, posterior area, caudal part_L
34	S1Sh_R [37]	primary somatosensory cortex, shoulder region_R
56	DLEnt_L [39]	dorsolateral entorhinal cortex_L
48	AIV_L [40]	agranular insular cortex, ventral part_L
80	S1Sh_L [37]	primary somatosensory cortex, shoulder region_L
111	DD_L [41]	diagonal domain_L

Table 2. High vs. Saline TOP 15 Addiction-Related Brain Regions.

High vs. Saline

142	Pit_R [42]	pituitary_R
110	DD_R [41]	diagonal domain_R
64	MEnt_L	medial entorhinal cortex_L
105	AC_L	anterior commissure_L
111	DD_L [41]	diagonal domain_L
48	AIV_L [40]	agranular insular cortex, ventral part_L
103	SN_L [43]	substantia nigra_L
146	OP_R	optic pathways_R
104	AC_R	anterior commissure_R
133	PA_L [44]	preoptic area_L
18	MEnt_R	medial entorhinal cortex_R
143	Pit_L [42]	pituitary_L
132	PA_R [44]	preoptic area_R
141	BNST_L [45]	bed nucleus of the stria terminalis_L
140	BNST_R [45]	bed nucleus of the stria terminalis_R

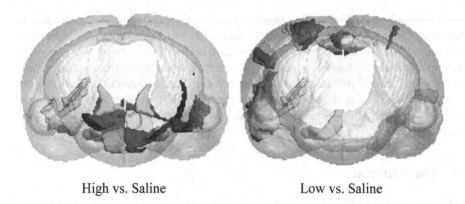

High vs. Saline   Low vs. Saline

Fig. 5. The brain regions with the most obvious differences between different groups.

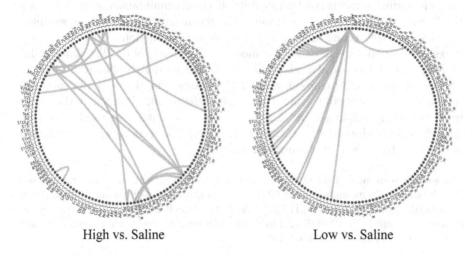

High vs. Saline   Low vs. Saline

Fig. 6. Nicotine addiction-related brain connections. The most pronounced brain connections at different nicotine concentrations. The threshold is set here.

upper left part of the brain, while the high-concentration group is concentrated in the middle and lower parts of the brain. The left and right brains are relatively balanced, which is consistent with the previous conclusions match.

It can be seen from the Fig. 6 that the brain connections affected by low-concentration nicotine are concentrated in the upper left of the brain and have strong aggregation. The brain connections affected by high concentrations of nicotine are concentrated in the lower right of the brain, which is relatively uniform. This has a lot to do with the mechanism of nicotine's influence on the brain. When the concentration is low, it preferentially affects some areas, and then spreads outward and finally affects most of the brain areas.

The study found that the brain regions and brain connections related to nicotine addiction at different concentrations have certain similarities, and these regions or connections can be confirmed in existing literature, which can prove the validity of the model. Moreover, compared with the normal saline group, there are certain differences in the most obvious brain connections between different concentrations. From another perspective, different addiction-related connections suggest that different doses may also correspond to different addiction mechanisms.

4   Conclusion

This paper proposed a graph diffusion reconstruction network (GDRN) to capture brain connectivity associated with nicotine addiction from fMRI data in rats. The diffusion reconstruction module effectively maintains the unity of data distribution in the latent space through the reconstruction of training samples, and enhances the reconstruction ability of nicotine addiction-related brain networks. This module can make the model learn more subtle distribution differences and global correlations. This allows the model to effectively capture addiction-related brain connections. GDRN shows remarkable performance in nicotine-related connection generation. Most of the results obtained by the model are validated by existing work in neuroscience. The remaining results are considered as yet undiscovered nicotine-related brain connections and regions that can be used to explore mechanisms of addiction.

Acknowledgements. This work was supported by the National Natural Science Foundations of China under Grant 62172403, the Distinguished Young Scholars Fund of Guangdong under Grant 2021B1515020019, the Excellent Young Scholars of Shenzhen under Grant RCYX20200714114641211 and Shenzhen Key Basic Research Project under Grant JCYJ20200109115641762.

References

1. Hartmann-Boyce, J., Chepkin, S.C., Ye, W., et al.: Nicotine replacement therapy versus control for smoking cessation. Cochrane Database Syst. Rev. (5) (2018)
2. Beaglehole, R., Bates, C., Youdan, B., et al.: Nicotine without smoke: fighting the tobacco epidemic with harm reduction. Lancet **394**(10200), 718–720 (2019)
3. Quach, B.C., Bray, M.J., Gaddis, N.C., et al.: Expanding the genetic architecture of nicotine dependence and its shared genetics with multiple traits. Nat. Commun. **11**(1), 5562 (2020)
4. Heeger, D.J., Ress, D.: What does fMRI tell us about neuronal activity? Nat. Rev. Neurosci. **3**(2), 142–151 (2002)
5. Allen, E.A., Damaraju, E., Plis, S.M., et al.: Tracking whole-brain connectivity dynamics in the resting state. Cereb. Cortex **24**(3), 663–676 (2014)
6. Hu, S., Lei, B., Wang, S., et al.: Bidirectional mapping generative adversarial networks for brain MR to PET synthesis. IEEE Trans. Med. Imaging **41**(1), 145–157 (2021)

7. Wang, S., Shen, Y., Zeng, D., et al.: Bone age assessment using convolutional neural networks. In: 2018 International Conference on Artificial Intelligence and Big Data (ICAIBD), pp. 175–178. IEEE (2018)
8. Wang, S.Q., Li, X., Cui, J.L., et al.: Prediction of myelopathic level in cervical spondylotic myelopathy using diffusion tensor imaging. J. Magn. Reson. Imaging **41**(6), 1682–1688 (2015)
9. Hu, S., Yuan, J., Wang, S.: Cross-modality synthesis from MRI to PET using adversarial U-net with different normalization. In: 2019 International Conference on Medical Imaging Physics and Engineering (ICMIPE), pp. 1–5. IEEE (2019)
10. Shen, Y., Huang, X., Kwak, K.S., et al.: Subcarrier-pairing-based resource optimization for OFDM wireless powered relay transmissions with time switching scheme. IEEE Trans. Signal Process. **65**(5), 1130–1145 (2016)
11. Lei, B., Liang, E., Yang, M., et al.: Predicting clinical scores for Alzheimer's disease based on joint and deep learning. Exp. Syst. Appl. **187**, 115966 (2022)
12. Hu, S., Yu, W., Chen, Z., et al.: Medical image reconstruction using generative adversarial network for Alzheimer disease assessment with class-imbalance problem. In: 2020 IEEE 6th International Conference on Computer and Communications (ICCC), pp. 1323–1327. IEEE (2020)
13. Wang, S., Hu, Y., Shen, Y., et al.: Classification of diffusion tensor metrics for the diagnosis of a myelopathic cord using machine learning. Int. J. Neural Syst. **28**(02), 1750036 (2018)
14. Wang, S., Shen, Y., Chen, W., Xiao, T., Hu, J.: Automatic recognition of mild cognitive impairment from MRI images using expedited convolutional neural networks. In: Lintas, A., Rovetta, S., Verschure, P.F.M.J., Villa, A.E.P. (eds.) ICANN 2017. LNCS, vol. 10613, pp. 373–380. Springer, Cham (2017). https://doi.org/10. 1007/978-3-319-68600-4_43
15. Zeng, D., Wang, S., Shen, Y., et al.: A GA-based feature selection and parameter optimization for support tucker machine. Procedia Comput. Sci. **111**, 17–23 (2017)
16. Wang, S., Wang, H., Shen, Y., et al.: Automatic recognition of mild cognitive impairment and Alzheimer's disease using ensemble based 3d densely connected convolutional networks. In: 2018 17th IEEE International Conference on Machine Learning and Applications (ICMLA), pp. 517–523. IEEE (2018)
17. Mo, L.F., Wang, S.Q.: A variational approach to nonlinear two-point boundary value problems. Nonlinear Anal. Theory Methods Appl. **71**(12), e834–e838 (2009)
18. Wang, S., Wang, X., Shen, Y., et al.: An ensemble-based densely-connected deep learning system for assessment of skeletal maturity. IEEE Trans. Syst. Man Cybern.: Syst. **52**(1), 426–437 (2020)
19. Yu, W., Lei, B., Wang, S., et al.: Morphological feature visualization of Alzheimer's disease via multidirectional perception GAN. IEEE Trans. Neural Netw. Learn. Syst. (2022). https://doi.org/10.1109/TNNLS.2021.3118369
20. Lei, B., Yu, S., Zhao, X., et al.: Diagnosis of early Alzheimer's disease based on dynamic high order networks. Brain Imaging Behav. **15**, 276–287 (2021)
21. Yu, S., et al.: Multi-scale enhanced graph convolutional network for early mild cognitive impairment detection. In: Martel, A.L., et al. (eds.) MICCAI 2020. LNCS, vol. 12267, pp. 228–237. Springer, Cham (2020). https://doi.org/10.1007/978-3-030-59728-3_23
22. Hu, S., Shen, Y., Wang, S., Lei, B.: Brain MR to PET synthesis via bidirectional generative adversarial network. In: Martel, A.L., et al. (eds.) MICCAI 2020. LNCS, vol. 12262, pp. 698–707. Springer, Cham (2020). https://doi.org/10.1007/978-3-030-59713-9_67

23. Goodfellow, I., Pouget-Abadie, J., Mirza, M., et al.: Generative adversarial networks. Commun. ACM **63**(11), 139–144 (2020)
24. Pan, S., Hu, R., Long, G., et al.: Adversarially regularized graph autoencoder for graph embedding. In: Proceedings of the 27th International Joint Conference on Artificial Intelligence, pp. 2609–2615 (2018)
25. You, S., Lei, B., Wang, S., et al.: Fine perceptive GANs for brain MR image super-resolution in wavelet domain. IEEE Trans. Neural Netw. Learn. Syst. (2022). https://doi.org/10.1109/TNNLS.2022.3153088
26. Yu, W., Lei, B., Ng, M.K., et al.: Tensorizing GAN with high-order pooling for Alzheimer's disease assessment. IEEE Trans. Neural Netw. Learn. Syst. **33**(9), 4945–4959 (2021)
27. Conte, G.M., Weston, A.D., Vogelsang, D.C., et al.: Generative adversarial networks to synthesize missing t1 and flair MRI sequences for use in a multisequence brain tumor segmentation model. Radiology **299**(2), 313–323 (2021)
28. Pan, Y., Liu, M., Xia, Y., et al.: Disease-image-specific learning for diagnosis-oriented neuroimage synthesis with incomplete multi-modality data. IEEE Trans. Pattern Anal. Mach. Intell. **44**(10), 6839–6853 (2021)
29. Zhou, B., et al.: Synthesizing multi-tracer PET images for Alzheimer's disease patients using a 3d unified anatomy-aware cyclic adversarial network. In: de Bruijne, M., et al. (eds.) MICCAI 2021. LNCS, vol. 12906, pp. 34–43. Springer, Cham (2021). https://doi.org/10.1007/978-3-030-87231-1_4
30. Jiao, J., Namburete, A.I., Papageorghiou, A.T., et al.: Self-supervised ultrasound to MRI fetal brain image synthesis. IEEE Trans. Med. Imaging **39**(12), 4413–4424 (2020)
31. Wolleb, J., Bieder, F., Sandkuhler, R.: Diffusion models for medical anomaly detection. In: Wang, L., Dou, Q., Fletcher, P.T., Speidel, S., Li, S. (eds.) MICCAI 2022. Lecture Notes in Computer Science, vol. 13438, pp. 35–45. Springer, Cham (2022). https://doi.org/10.1007/978-3-031-16452-1_4
32. Pinaya, W.H., Graham, M.S., Gray, R.: Fast unsupervised brain anomaly detection and segmentation with diffusion models. In: Wang, L., Dou, Q., Fletcher, P.T., Speidel, S., Li, S. (eds.) MICCAI 2022. Lecture Notes in Computer Science, vol. 13438, pp. 705–714. Springer, Cham (2022). https://doi.org/10.1007/978-3-031-16452-1_67
33. Khader, F., Mueller-Franzes, G., Arasteh, S.T., et al.: Medical diffusion - denoising diffusion probabilistic models for 3d medical image generation. arXiv preprint arXiv: Arxiv-2211.03364 (2022)
34. Chung, H., Ye, J.C.: Score-based diffusion models for accelerated MRI. Med. Image Anal. **80**, 102479 (2022)
35. Mizutani, H., Yamamura, H., Muramatsu, M., et al.: Spontaneous and nicotine-induced Ca2+ oscillations mediated by Ca2+ influx in rat pinealocytes. Am. J. Physiol.-Cell Physiol. **306**(11), C1008–C1016 (2014)
36. Keeley, R.J., Hsu, L.M., Brynildsen, J.K., et al.: Intrinsic differences in insular circuits moderate the negative association between nicotine dependence and cingulate-striatal connectivity strength. Neuropsychopharmacology **45**(6), 1042–1049 (2020)
37. Claus, E.D., Blaine, S.K., Filbey, F.M., et al.: Association between nicotine dependence severity, BOLD response to smoking cues, and functional connectivity. Neuropsychopharmacology **38**(12), 2363–2372 (2013)
38. Giessing, C., Thiel, C.M., Rosler, F., et al.: The modulatory effects of nicotine on parietal cortex activity in a cued target detection task depend on cue reliability. Neuroscience **137**(3), 853–864 (2006)

39. Perry, E.K., Morris, C.M., Court, J.A., et al.: Alteration in nicotine binding sites in Parkinson's disease, Lewy body dementia and Alzheimer's disease: possible index of early neuropathology. Neuroscience **64**(2), 385–395 (1995)

40. Pushparaj, A., Kim, A.S., Musiol, M., et al.: Involvement of the rostral agranular insular cortex in nicotine self-administration in rats. Behav. Brain Res. **290**, 77–83 (2015)

41. Levin, E.D., Hall, B.J., Rezvani, A.H.: Heterogeneity across brain regions and neurotransmitter interactions with nicotinic effects on memory function. Neurobiol. Genet. Nicotine Tob., 87–101 (2015)

42. Nega, S., Marquez, P., Hamid, A., et al.: The role of pituitary adenylyl cyclase activating polypeptide in affective signs of nicotine withdrawal. J. Neurosci. Res. **98**(8), 1549–1560 (2020)

43. Dehkordi, O., Rose, J.E., Millis, R.M., et al.: GABAergic neurons as putative neurochemical substrate mediating aversive effects of nicotine. J. Alcohol. Drug Depend. **6**(2) (2018)

44. Saint-Mleux, B., Eggermann, E., Bisetti, A., et al.: Nicotinic enhancement of the noradrenergic inhibition of sleep-promoting neurons in the ventrolateral preoptic area. J. Neurosci. **24**(1), 63–67 (2004)

45. Qi, X., Guzhva, L., Yang, Z., et al.: Overexpression of CRF in the BNST diminishes dysphoria but not anxiety-like behavior in nicotine withdrawing rats. Eur. Neuropsychopharmacol. **26**(9), 1378–1389 (2016)

MR Image Super-Resolution Using Wavelet Diffusion for Predicting Alzheimer's Disease

Guoli Huang[1], Xuhang Chen[1,2], Yanyan Shen[1], and Shuqiang Wang[1(✉)]

[1] Shenzhen Institutes of Advanced Technology, Chinese Academy of Sciences,
Shenzhen, China
sq.wang@siat.ac.cn
[2] University of Macau, Macau, China

Abstract. Alzheimer's disease (AD) is a neurodegenerative disorder that exerts a substantial influence on individuals worldwide. Magnetic resonance imaging (MRI) can detect and track disease progression. However, the majority of MRI data currently available is characterized by low resolution. The present study introduces a novel approach for MRI super-resolution by integrating diffusion model with wavelet decomposition techniques. The methodology proposed in this study is tailored to address the issue of restricted data availability. It utilizes adversarial training and capitalizes on the advantages of denoising diffusion probabilistic model (DDPM), while simultaneously avoiding the problem of diversity collapse. The proposed method incorporates wavelet decomposition within the latent space to augment the resilience and efficiency of generative models. The experimental findings demonstrate the superior efficacy of our proposed model in contrast to alternative techniques, as indicated by the SSIM and FID metrics. Moreover, our methodology has the potential to enhance the precision of Alzheimer's disease assessment.

Keywords: MR image super-resolution · diffusion model · discrete wavelet transformation · Alzheimer's disease assessment

1 Introduction

Alzheimer's disease (AD) is a widely prevalent form of dementia that impacts a significant number of individuals globally. At present, there exists no definitive remedy for AD. Therefore, it is imperative to conduct additional research on methods that can alter the trajectory of the disease and impede its advancement. The acquisition of imaging biomarkers is of utmost importance in enhancing our understanding of the disease and evaluating the efficacy of suggested interventions [1]. Magnetic Resonance Imaging (MRI) has emerged as a potential imaging biomarker and has demonstrated significant utility in the diagnosis of neurodegenerative disorders [2].

F. Liu et al. (Eds.): BI 2023, LNAI 13974, pp. 146–157, 2023.
https://doi.org/10.1007/978-3-031-43075-6_13

However, due to the limitations of instruments and experiments, a considerable part of the clinical MR images have low resolution, which may lead to wrong disease detection results [3,4]. The same situation occurs in AD diagnosis, and the images lack sufficient details to reflect AD patients [5–7]. Small changes in brain structure that make it difficult to distinguish between normal and abnormal brains. In order to deal with this ubiquitous challenge, image super-resolution has been extended from natural images to medical imaging. In recent years, research has proved that a variety of methods can significantly upscale the resolution of MR image, and there has a obvious breakthrough in the task of single image super-resolution (SISR) based on machine learning. A Wavelet-based Generative Adversarial Network (GAN) approaches achieve state-of-the-art metrics for this task [8]. Despite the success of GANs in this field, they are inherently difficult to train and often mode collapse, [9] pointed out that Denoising Diffusion Probabilistic Model (DDPM) is a viable alternative to GANs in super-resolution tasks to generate high quality image without above problems.

In this paper, we propose the first application of the Wavelet-based Diffusion model in the super-resolution of MR images from Alzheimer's disease. Based on the conditional diffusion model, our wavelet diffusion model samples a set of high-resolution MR images and is conditioned on the Wavelet decomposition and downsampling state of these MRI images. A Wavelet Unet module is designed to fuse the multiscale information of discrete Wavelet transformations to maintain the model's sensitivity to subspace. Compared with the original Diffusion and GAN models, the Wavelet Diffusion has a faster sampling speed and more stable training. The experiments demonstrate that our model achieves comparable results in the MR images super-resolution task of Alzheimer's disease and proves its effectiveness in improving the performance of the AD disease classification [10].

The main contributions of this paper are outlined as follows:

1. We propose a diffusion model based on DDGAN for MR image super-resolution. Specifically, the denoising process is specifically designed to avoid diversity collapse while leveraging adversarial training and DDPMs' benefits. The utilization of wavelet decomposition in the latent space has been employed to improve the resilience and efficiency of generative models.
2. We have adapted our redesigned U-net with Freq-aware mechanism to a wavelet-based diffusion model that prioritizes in-depth analysis of low-frequency components in medical images.
3. The experimental results indicate that the wavelet diffusion model has significant potential to improve AD diagnosis [11] in MRI disease based on the super-resolution processing of MR image (Figs. 3 and 5).

2   Related Work

2.1   Super-Resolution in MR Image

Super-Resolution (SR) is a widely researched technique used in Magnetic Resonance (MR) imaging to improve the spatial resolution of low-resolution images. Better image quality is critical to making informed medical diagnoses and has several applications in medical research, including Alzheimer's disease (AD) diagnosis [12], brain tumor detection, and vascular imaging [13]. Recent studies have demonstrated the potential of generative models in creating high-quality SR images [14].

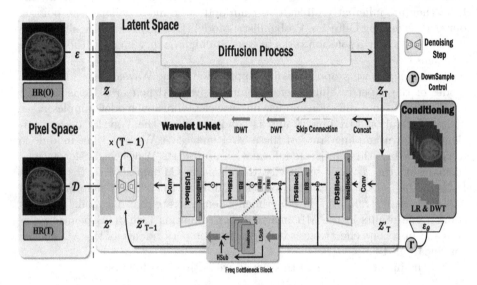

Fig. 1. Illustration of Wavelet-embedded diffusion model. The model consists of several building blocks, including a down-sampling block, a wavelet decomposition block, a frequency bottleneck block, and several residual blocks.

However, super-resolution generating for MR images remains challenging, particularly in balancing resolution and noise suppression. One approach to address this challenge is by employing discrete wavelet transform (DWT) methods, which have shown promise in improving MR images' resolution. In general, wavelet-based models leverage residual learning by combining the 2D DWT with deep learning [15,16]. The use of wavelet prior for driving models in medical imaging tasks is both streamlined and effective, which inspires ongoing research focuses on model design, incorporating different loss functions, or using differ learning strategy to generate high-quality SR images in medical imaging [8,9].

2.2   Generative Models for Medical Assessment

Generative models continue to gain popularity in medical image analysis and show promise for improving medical assessment through image processing, generation, and enhancement. Generative adversarial network (GAN) [17] and variational autoencoder (VAE) [18] are often used in medical image analysis tasks. These methods focus on the improvement of upstream data quality for corresponding tasks, including Bidirectional Mapping MRI-PET cross-modal conversion [19], Clinical Brain MRI samples data synthesis [20], which can be used for tasks such as lesion detection and classification, modeling of disease progression, and risk stratification [12].

GANs, VAEs and diffusion models (DDPMs) are types of generative models that use probabilistic modeling to obtain latent code representations of input data [21–23]. This endows the data with more features for processing or enhancement. Diffusion methods are generally considered more complex than VAEs in mathematical modeling, which is considered has more application prospects [24–32].

3   Method

3.1   Diffusion Forward Process

The general diffusion model follows a round-trip diffusion (forward) process and denoise (reverse) process. The forward diffusion process comprises thousands of time steps. During this process, each input z_0 undergoes a gradual conversion into Gaussian noise by following the data distribution $p(z_0)$. A closed form of the posterior probability of the diffused image or latent z_t [33] at any given time step t exists:

$$q(z_t|z_0) = \mathcal{N}(z_t; \sqrt{\bar{\alpha}_t}z_0, (1 - \bar{\alpha}_t)\mathbf{I}) \tag{1}$$

here $\alpha_t = 1 - \beta_t$, $\bar{\alpha}_t = \prod_{s=1}^{t} \alpha_s$, and $\beta_t \in (0,1)$ is defined to be small through a variance schedule which can be learnable or fixed at timestep t in the forward process. In a random Gaussian noise $\epsilon \sim \mathcal{N}(0, \mathbf{I})$:

$$z_t = \sqrt{\bar{\alpha}}z_0 + \sqrt{1 - \bar{\alpha}}\epsilon \tag{2}$$

where all latent variables $\{z_t\}_1^T$ have the same dimension as z_0 and ϵ. Usually, the variance β_t is constrained to be small enough to ensure $q(z_{t-1}|z_t)$ following a Gaussian distribution.

3.2   Adapt Wavelet Domain in Denoising Process

In this section, we illustrate how to integrate DWT and IDWT into our forward process 2. Given an input gray image in latent form, represented as $x \in \mathbb{R}^{3 \times H \times W}$, we partition it into a low-frequency and high-frequency set of subbands by DWT, which concatenated into a single unit for the denoising stage. These

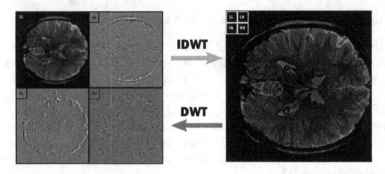

Fig. 2. Discrete wavelet transform (DWT) and Inverse discrete wavelet transform (IDWT) of one example MR image.

subbands are then concatenated and represented as a matrix, $y \in \mathbb{R}^{12 \times \frac{H}{2} \times \frac{W}{2}}$. Following this, the input is projected into the channel (D) through the first linear layer.

During the denoising (reverse) process, the generator takes input in the form of a tuple that consists of variable z_t and latent variable z_t'. z_t' is obtained by sampling the Gaussian distribution $\mathcal{N}(0, \mathbf{I})$ at timestep t to approximate the original variable z_0. Thus, the model predicts a noisy sample z_{t-1}' by drawing from a tractable posterior distribution $q(z_{t-1}|z_t, z_0')$. This procedure computes the output as follows: $z_0' = G(z_t, z_t', t)$.

Adversarial Objective. According to the DDGAN architecture, the discriminator plays a key role in distinguishing between the real pairs (z_{t-1}, z_t) and the fake pairs (z_{t-1}', z_t).

$$
\begin{aligned}
\mathcal{L}_{adv}^{G} &= -\log(D(z_{t-1}', z_t, t)), \\
\mathcal{L}_{adv}^{D} &= -\log(D(z_{t-1}, z_t, t)) + \log(D(z_{t-1}', z_t, t)).
\end{aligned}
\tag{3}
$$

$$
\mathcal{L}_{rec} = \|y_0' - y_0\|.
\tag{4}
$$

$$
\mathcal{L}^{G} = \mathcal{L}_{adv}^{G} + \lambda \mathcal{L}_{rec}.
\tag{5}
$$

In addition to the adversarial objective in Eq. 3, we add a reconstruction term to not only impede the loss of frequency information but also preserve the consistency of wavelet subbands. The Eq. 4 is formulated as an L1 loss between a generated image and its ground-truth. The overall objective of the generator in Eq. 5 is a linear combination of adversarial loss and reconstruction loss (λ is a hyper-parameter with a default value of 1).

3.3 Denoising Wavelet U-Net Structure

The main denoising (sampling) part in the structure of our proposed wavelet-embedded process. It follows the UNet structure of [34] with M down-sampling and M up-sampling blocks plus skip connections between blocks of the same resolution, with M predefined. Instead of using the normal downsampling and upsampling, we replace them with frequency-aware blocks.

Frequency-aware Blocks. The designed architecture comprises frequency-aware blocks drawing on the properties of the wavelet transform, our approach leverages up and down sampling for better conditioning results. The downsampling block receives conditioning features ε_i, latent $z't$, and embedding time step t, which are processed via a sequence of residual layers to obtain Down features and high-frequency subbands. The frequency bottleneck block, located in the middle stage, includes two frequency bottleneck blocks and one attention block in between. Each frequency bottleneck block first divides the feature map ε_i into a low-frequency subband $\varepsilon_{i,ll}$ and the concatenation of high-frequency subbands $\varepsilon_{i,H}$. Next, the processed low-frequency feature map and the original high-frequency subbands $\varepsilon_{i,H}$ are transformed back to the original space via Inverse Wavelet Transform (IWT). The upsampling block receives these returned subbands serve as additional feature input based on frequency cues, allowing the model to concentrate on learning intermediate feature representations of low-frequency subbands while preserving the high-frequency details.

As a result, our model utilizes high-frequency data present in the wavelet spectrum to improve the level of detail in synthesized images. Additionally, the model operates on the latent form of the original image, reducing computation by a factor of 4 or more due to spatial dimension reduction [35]. Consequently, our sampling process requires significantly fewer computational resources compared to standard diffusion methods.

4 Experiments

4.1 Data Preparation

Data used in preparation of this article were obtained from the Alzheimer's Disease Neuroimaging Initiative (ADNI) database. ADNI is a longitudinal multicenter study designed to develop clinical, imaging, genetic, and biochemical biomarkers for the early detection and tracking of Alzheimer's disease (AD). The whole ADNI dataset consists of ADNI1, ADNIGO, ADNI2 and ADNI3. We adopted [8,36] for experiment, selected ADNI2 dataset, which consists 169 Alzheimer' of MR raw data labeled in Normal Control (NC), Early Mild Cognitive Impairment (EMCI), Mild Cognitive Impairment (MCI), Late Mild Cognitive Impairment (LMCI), and AD groups, 27600 pairs of T1-weighted MR images with size of (192×192) and along transverse axis are adopted for experiment, 70% MR images are utilized for training, 20% are utilized for validation, the 10% for test.

4.2 Implementation and Training Detail

In the experiment, we implemented Wavelet Diffusion model based on DDGAN [37] with the same training configuration. The experiment were trained on 4 Nvidia RTX 3090 GPUs. In the WaveDiff training process, a batch size of 32, 2 ResNet blocks per scale, and an initial number of channels of 128. The learning rates of the generators and discriminators were set as 1×10^{-4} and 5×10^{-4}, respectively. The settings used for the comparison of our proposed method with other existing methods are the same as those described in their respective original papers. Furthermore, we set up these methods in our dataset environment to ensure fair and accurate performance comparison.

4.3   Evaluation Metrics

We use Frechet Inception Distance (FID) to measure the feature distance between two images and evaluate the perceptual quality of super-resolution MR images. In addition, we utilize Peak Signal-to-Noise Ratio (PSNR) and Structural Similarity Index (SSIM) as commonly used standard evaluation metrics. It has been reported that high PSNR values do not necessarily guarantee high visual quality, and PSNR is may inaccurate for evaluating image quality with respect to the visual. To address this issue, PSNR and SSIM measure objective image quality, whereas FID assesses visual image quality from a human perspective.

4.4   Experimental Results

As depicted in Fig. 4, we presents various sample types that were evaluated on the same test sample. The results show that two types of interpolation-based

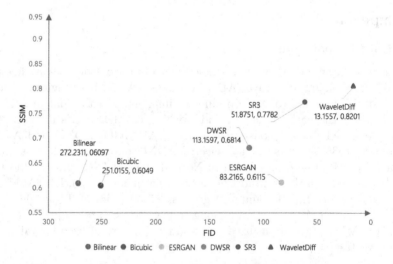

Fig. 3. Comparison with different categories of super-resolution methods: interpolation based methods (Bilinear, Bicubic), GAN based method (ESRGAN), wavelet based methods (DWSR), Diffusion method (SR3) on SSIM and FID metrics. The SSIM and FID values are evaluated on all group of ADNI2 with scale factor ×4.

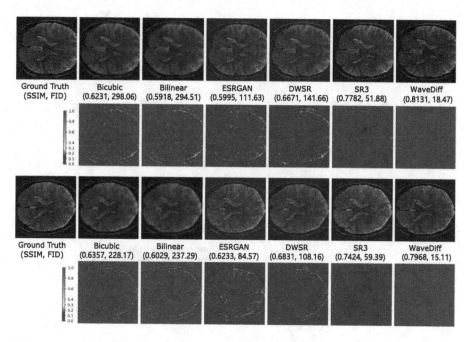

Fig. 4. Error map Comparison with different categories of super-resolution methods with scale factor ×4.

methods produce oversmoothed images. Although the GAN-based approach, ESRGAN, reproduces rich textures, it lacks structural consistency with the input. In contrast, the general method based on wavelet significantly improves the index, but there remains a significant error with the actual image. Compared to other methods, both Diffusion-based models can complete the super-resolution reconstruction task. However, WaveDiff offers an advantage of combining the model and wavelet technology, resulting in a better super-resolution effect. A heatmap reflecting the absolute difference under each super-resolution legend was also included in the study. It revealed that WaveDiff has less variance than competing methods. Furthermore, the study conducted a feasibility assessment on MRI disease diagnosis based on the ADNI dataset. The support vector machine with the RBF kernel was implemented as the classifier for the experiment. Prior to classification, principal component analysis was conducted, and 200 principal factors were extracted. The performance of classification was evaluated by accuracy, recall, precision, F1 score, and AUC score. The study results indicated that super-resolution MR images generated by Wavelet Diffusion significantly improved the classification performance, as shown in Fig. 5 and Table 1.

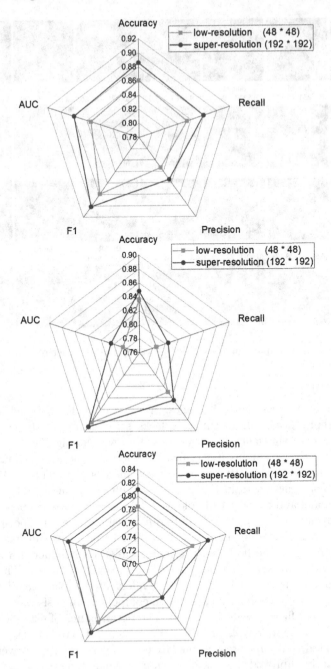

Fig. 5. Comparison of auto-diagnosis performance with low-resolution MR images (48×48) and super-resolution MR images (192 × 192). The classification performance is measured with accuracy, recall, precision, f1 score and auc score. (a), (b), and (c) illustrates the auto-diagnosis performance of (NC and MCI), (AD and MCI), and (AD and NC), respectively.

Table 1. Quantitative evaluation for super-resolution performance on ADNI2.

Scale	Metrics	Method					
		Bicubic	Bilinear	ESRGAN	DWSR	SR3	WaveDiff
×2	PSNR	27.4957	27.6820	27.6074	N/A	28.371	**28.8190**
	SSIM	0.8269	0.7894	0.8546	N/A	0.9121	**0.9226**
	FID	104.22	124.53	48.41	N/A	20.17	**12.10**
×4	PSNR	25.2539	24.8464	21.8490	23.2888	26.6793	**27.1522**
	SSIM	0.6408	0.6097	0.6115	0.6800	0.7782	**0.8201**
	FID	251.01	272.23	83.21	113.16	51.87	**13.15**
×8	PSNR	22.8815	22.7049	17.8975	N/A	19.0759	**20.9527**
	SSIM	0.4528	0.4412	0.3463	N/A	0.5659	**0.7563**
	FID	318.74	403.33	98.03	N/A	73.60	**50.59**

5   Conclusion

In this research, we introduce a new approach for MRI super-resolution through the utilization of wavelet diffusion model. The methodology utilized in this study is founded on the principles of deep residual learning and incorporates a solitary level 2D discrete wavelet transform for the purpose of extracting four sub-bands from a given input image. Subsequently, a deep residual network is trained with diffusion process regarding the correlation between low-resolution and high-resolution wavelet coefficients. Furthermore, our research explored both guided diffusion and adversarial learning theories for the reconstruction of MR images through the utilization of wavelet-based up-down sampling guidance. The findings of our study indicate that wavelet diffusion has the potential to serve as a viable technique for MR images super-resolution in Alzheimer's disease area. Subsequent research endeavors may investigate the utilization of this methodology in more medical imaging modalities or its integration with additional biomarkers to enhance diagnostic and therapeutic efficacy.

Acknowledgement. This work was supported by the National Natural Science Foundations of China under Grant 62172403, the Distinguished Young Scholars Fund of Guangdong under Grant 2021B1515020019, the Excellent Young Scholars of Shenzhen under Grant RCYX20200714114641211 and Shenzhen Key Basic Research Project under Grant JCYJ20200109115641762.

References

1. Hu, S., Yuan, J., Wang, S.: Cross-modality synthesis from MRI to pet using adversarial u-net with different normalization. In: International Conference on Medical Imaging Physics and Engineering, pp. 1–5. IEEE (2019)
2. Yu, W., et al.: Morphological feature visualization of Alzheimer's disease via multidirectional perception GAN. IEEE Trans. Neural Netw. Learn. Syst. (2022)

3. Wang, S.Q., Li, X., Cui, J.L., Li, H.X., Luk, K.D., Hu, Y.: Prediction of myelopathic level in cervical spondylotic myelopathy using diffusion tensor imaging. J. Mag. Reson. Imaging **41**(6), 1682–1688 (2015)

4. Wang, S., Shen, Y., Zeng, D., Hu, Y.: Bone age assessment using convolutional neural networks. In: International Conference on Artificial Intelligence and Big Data, pp. 175–178. IEEE (2018)

5. Wang, S., Shen, Y., Chen, W., Xiao, T., Hu, J.: Automatic recognition of mild cognitive impairment from MRI images using expedited convolutional neural networks. In: Lintas, A., Rovetta, S., Verschure, P.F.M.J., Villa, A.E.P. (eds.) ICANN 2017. LNCS, vol. 10613, pp. 373–380. Springer, Cham (2017). https://doi.org/10.1007/978-3-319-68600-4_43

6. Wang, S., Wang, H., Shen, Y., Wang, X.: Automatic recognition of mild cognitive impairment and Alzheimer's disease using ensemble based 3d densely connected convolutional networks. In: International Conference on Machine Learning and Applications, pp. 517–523. IEEE (2018)

7. Lei, B., et al.: Predicting clinical scores for Alzheimer's disease based on joint and deep learning. Expert Syst. Appl. **187**, 115966 (2022)

8. You, S., et al.: Fine perceptive GANs for brain MR image super-resolution in wavelet domain. IEEE Trans. Neural Netw. Learn. Syst. (2022)

9. Saharia, C., Ho, J., Chan, W., Salimans, T., Fleet, D.J., Norouzi, M.: Image super-resolution via iterative refinement. IEEE Trans. Pattern Anal. Mach. Intell. (2022)

10. Wang, S., Hu, Y., Shen, Y., Li, H.: Classification of diffusion tensor metrics for the diagnosis of a myelopathic cord using machine learning. Int. J. Neural Syst. **28**(02), 1750036 (2018)

11. Lei, B., et al.: Diagnosis of early Alzheimer's disease based on dynamic high order networks. Brain Imaging Behav. **15**, 276–287 (2021)

12. Yu, W., Lei, B., Ng, M.K., Cheung, A.C., Shen, Y., Wang, S.: Tensorizing GAN with high-order pooling for Alzheimer's disease assessment. IEEE Trans. Neural Netw. Learn. Syst. **33**(9), 4945–4959 (2021)

13. Wang, S., et al.: Diabetic retinopathy diagnosis using multichannel generative adversarial network with semisupervision. IEEE Trans. Autom. Sci. Eng. **18**(2), 574–585 (2020)

14. Hu, S., Yu, W., Chen, Z., Wang, S.: Medical image reconstruction using generative adversarial network for Alzheimer disease assessment with class-imbalance problem. In: International Conference on Computer and Communications, pp. 1323–1327. IEEE (2020)

15. Qin, Q., Dou, J., Tu, Z.: Deep ResNet based remote sensing image super-resolution reconstruction in discrete wavelet domain. Pattern Recognit Image Anal. **30**, 541–550 (2020)

16. Dou, J., Tu, Z., Peng, X.: Single image super-resolution reconstruction with wavelet based deep residual learning. In: Chinese Control And Decision Conference, pp. 4270–4275. IEEE (2020)

17. Goodfellow, I., et al.: Generative adversarial nets. In: Advances in Neural Information Processing Systems, pp. 2672–2680 (2014)

18. Rezende, D.J., Mohamed, S.: Variational inference with normalizing flows. In: International Conference on Machine Learning, pp. 1530–1538. PMLR (2015)

19. Hu, S., Lei, B., Wang, S., Wang, Y., Feng, Z., Shen, Y.: Bidirectional mapping generative adversarial networks for brain MR to pet synthesis. IEEE Trans. Med. Imaging **41**(1), 145–157 (2021)

20. Hu, S., Shen, Y., Wang, S., Lei, B.: Brain MR to PET synthesis via bidirectional generative adversarial network. In: Martel, A.L., et al. (eds.) MICCAI 2020. LNCS, vol. 12262, pp. 698–707. Springer, Cham (2020). https://doi.org/10.1007/978-3-030-59713-9_67

21. Ho, J., Jain, A., Abbeel, P.: Denoising diffusion probabilistic models. Adv. Neural. Inf. Process. Syst. **33**, 6840–6851 (2020)

22. Kingma, D., Salimans, T., Poole, B., Ho, J.: Variational diffusion models. Adv. Neural. Inf. Process. Syst. **34**, 21696–21707 (2021)

23. Wang, S.Q.: A variational approach to nonlinear two-point boundary value problems. Comput. Math. Appl. **58**(11–12), 2452–2455 (2009)

24. Wolleb, J., Bieder, F., Sandkühler, R., Cattin, P.C.: Diffusion models for medical anomaly detection. In: Medical Image Computing and Computer-Assisted Intervention (2022)

25. Xiang, T., Yurt, M., Syed, A.B., Setsompop, K., Chaudhari, A.: Ddm2: self-supervised diffusion MRI denoising with generative diffusion models. In: International Conference on Learning Representations (2023)

26. Cui, Z., et al.: Self-score: self-supervised learning on score-based models for MRI reconstruction. IEEE Trans. Med. Imaging abs/2209.00835 (2022)

27. Peng, C., Guo, P., Zhou, S.K., Patel, V.M., Chellappa, R.: Towards performant and reliable undersampled MR reconstruction via diffusion model sampling. In: Medical Image Computing and Computer-Assisted Intervention (2022)

28. Xie, Y., Li, Q.: Measurement-conditioned denoising diffusion probabilistic model for under-sampled medical image reconstruction. In: Medical Image Computing and Computer-Assisted Intervention (2022)

29. Song, Y., Shen, L., Xing, L., Ermon, S.: Solving inverse problems in medical imaging with score-based generative models. In: International Conference on Learning Representations (2022). https://openreview.net/forum?id=vaRCHVj0uGI

30. Chung, H., Ye, J.C.: Score-based diffusion models for accelerated MRI. Med. Image Anal. **80**, 102479 (2022)

31. Kim, B., Ye, J.C.: Diffusion deformable model for 4d temporal medical image generation. In: Wang, L., Dou, Q., Fletcher, P.T., Speidel, S., Li, S. (eds.) MICCAI 2022. Lecture Notes in Computer Science, vol. 13431, pp. 539–548. Springer, Cham (2022). https://doi.org/10.1007/978-3-031-16431-6_51

32. Pinaya, W.H., et al.: Fast unsupervised brain anomaly detection and segmentation with diffusion models. In: Wang, L., Dou, Q., Fletcher, P.T., Speidel, S., Li, S. (eds.) MICCAI 2022. Lecture Notes in Computer Science, vol. 13438, pp. 705–714. Springer, Cham (2022). https://doi.org/10.1007/978-3-031-16452-1_67

33. Rombach, R., Blattmann, A., Lorenz, D., Esser, P., Ommer, B.: High-resolution image synthesis with latent diffusion models. In: IEEE/CVF Conference on Computer Vision and Pattern Recognition, pp. 10684–10695 (2022)

34. Song, Y., Sohl-Dickstein, J., Kingma, D.P., Kumar, A., Ermon, S., Poole, B.: Score-based generative modeling through stochastic differential equations. arXiv preprint arXiv:2011.13456 (2020)

35. Wallace, B., Gokul, A., Ermon, S., Naik, N.: End-to-end diffusion latent optimization improves classifier guidance. arXiv preprint arXiv:2303.13703 (2023)

36. Lei, B., et al.: Deep and joint learning of longitudinal data for Alzheimer's disease prediction. Pattern Recognit. **102**, 107247 (2020)

37. Xiao, Z., Kreis, K., Vahdat, A.: Tackling the generative learning trilemma with denoising diffusion GANs. arXiv preprint arXiv:2112.07804 (2021)

Classification of Event-Related Potential Signals with a Variant of UNet Algorithm Using a Large P300 Dataset

Maryam Khoshkhooy Titkanlou$^{(\boxtimes)}$ and Roman Mouček

Department of Computer Science and Engineering, University of West Bohemia, 306 14 Plzen, Czech Republic
{maryamkh,moucek}@kiv.zcu.cz

Abstract. Event-related potential signal classification is a really difficult challenge due to the low signal-to-noise ratio. Deep neural networks (DNN), which have been employed in different machine learning areas, are suitable for this type of classification. UNet (a convolutional neural network) is a classification algorithm proposed to improve the classification accuracy of P300 electroencephalogram (EEG) signals in a non-invasive brain-computer interface. The proposed UNet classification accuracy and precision were 64.5% for single-trial classification using a large P300 dataset of school-aged children, including 138 males and 112 females. We compare our results with the related literature and discuss limitations and future directions. Our proposed method performed better than traditional methods.

Keywords: event-related potentials · P300 · classification · UNet

1 Introduction

The brain-computer interface (BCI) can be defined as an emerging human-computer interaction technique that enables direct communication between the electrical activity in the brain and an external device [1]. A non-invasive, relatively low-cost electrophysiological method that measures brain activity with a high temporal resolution is electroencephalography (EEG). An EEG-based event-related potential (ERP) is a signal that can detect high-level cognitive activity in the brain stimulated by specific events, which has various applications, such as object detection [2, 3], and medical diagnosis [4, 5].

In this study, we concentrated on the visual P300 ERP, which is simple to set up and widely used in developing BCIs compared to other BCI paradigms. P300 refers to a spike in activity that occurs 300 ms after the target stimulus is presented. There is a challenge in classifying the P300 events with sufficient accuracy to facilitate effective communication. Classifiers are designed to distinguish between two types of brain responses: those triggered by the stimuli a user is focused on (target) and those caused by other stimuli the user is attempting to ignore (non-target). Preprocessing, feature extraction and classification are typical processing steps for P300 component detection.

F. Liu et al. (Eds.): BI 2023, LNAI 13974, pp. 158–166, 2023.
https://doi.org/10.1007/978-3-031-43075-6_14

Early researchers usually used traditional machine learning algorithms as classifiers in order to distinguish P300 signals; for example, linear discriminant analysis (LDA) [6] and support vector machine (SVM) can be used to classify selected ICA (independent component analysis) [7] and PCA (principal component analysis) [8] components. Using such approaches entails intense preprocessing and the extraction of well-established features, which can lead to poor performance due to their limited representation. Recently, deep neural networks have been extensively used by scholars to extract features automatically [9]. Since feature extraction is one of the most challenging parts of processing EEG/ERP data, the most important objective of many experiments is to eliminate the feature extraction process using deep neural networks. The dataset that we used was utilized in the following four references. In [10], spiking neural networks (SNN) were created to classify event-related components. Vareka [3] applied a convolutional neural network (CNN) to P300 BCI data and then compared this model with traditional baseline models. He also used a recurrent neural network (RNN) [11] since EEG signals have a temporal nature and concluded that the accuracy of RNN was lower than CNN.

Furthermore, a comparison of deep learning models for classifying P300 events was presented by Selvasingham [12]. This paper's primary contribution is evaluating a variant of UNet algorithm for classifying P300 BCI data. The UNet architecture consists of an encoder-decoder structure, which results in a U-shape. This network includes down-sampling, up-sampling, and skip connection segments. In order to recover the spatial information lost during down-sampling, features are passed from the encoder path to the decoder path using skip connections. Although this network structure was designed for 2D image segmentation tasks, it would be an effective tool for signal classification since its excellent adaption to 1D time-series data has been demonstrated [13]. Ultimately, a type of UNet was compared with literature.

This paper is organized into four sections and a reference section. Material and method are presented in Sect. 2, and after that, Sect. 3 compares the results of our UNet model with the literature. Finally, a discussion and conclusion are provided in Sect. 4.

2 Material and Method

2.1 State-of-the-Art

Classification of P300 BCI data has long been a popular area of study. Several studies have focused on machine learning algorithms for ERP detection. The linear support vector machine (SVM), the stepwise linear discriminant analysis (SWLDA), the Fisher's linear discriminant analysis (LDA), and the Gaussian kernel support vector machine (nSVM) were all compared on eight healthy participants in [14]. It was determined that SWLDA and LDA produced the best overall results. Reference [15] pro- vided evidence that Bayesian linear discriminant analysis (BLDA) and LDA could be better than other classification algorithms. In [16], five types of unsupervised machine learning algorithms, including (Isolation Forest (IsoF), DBScan, Local Outlier Factor (LOF), One-class SVM (1SVM), and Hierarchical Clustering (H-C1)), were applied to a dataset that used eight channels.

On the other hand, deep learning techniques have made progress in analyzing EEG signals. A compact convolutional neural network architecture (EEGNet) was created in

[17] and is utilized to classify EEG signals. Long short-term memory (LSTM) network was employed by [18] to extract temporal characteristics for epileptic seizure prediction. Reference [19] combined CNN and LSTM to extract global features that increased the classification accuracy of EEG signals. In [20], a novel Multi-Attention Convolutional Recurrent model (MACRO) for EEG-based event-related potential (ERP) detection in the subject-independent scenario was proposed. The multi-attention mechanism is integrated to focus on the most discriminative EEG data channels and temporal periods, while the recurrent convolutional network is built to capture the spatial-temporal properties. The UNet network, besides these DL algorithms, has demonstrated a high capability in extracting local and global features [13]. In [21], novel DL architectures have been proposed for EEG-based vigilance detection: 1D-UNet and 1D-UNet- LSTM.

A Full Convolutional Network (FCN) based encoder-decoder network is the UNet architecture, where the encoder and decoder components are symmetric. Long skip links between the encoder and decoder blocks are also included in the network. As UNet can extract important information, we use this method to classify ERP signals. This kind of signal segmentation aims to label each segment of a signal with a corresponding class of what is being represented. In this paper, we assign a label of zero to non-target classes and a label of one to target classes.

2.2 Data Acquisition

A multi-subject P300 dataset [22] contains EEG data from a brain-computer interface experiment called Guess the Number (GTN). To conduct the experiment, the experimenter asks participants to select an arbitrary number between 1 and 9 and focus on it (i.e., this number is the target stimulus). The subject is exposed to visual stimuli, which include digits 1–9 appearing randomly on the monitor, while the experimenters record the EEG signal and try to guess the target number from event-related potential waveforms. This paper gathered data from 250 participating school-age children (between ages 7–17) in Czech elementary and secondary schools. To reduce preparation time, only three EEG channels were recorded (Fz, Cz, Pz). Children participate in the experiment intentionally.

2.3 Preprocessing and Feature Extraction

The following steps of data preprocessing were applied to the dataset:

1. ERP trials were extracted from each participant of the experiments. These epochs, which are available in [22], are connected with two stimuli, one of them was the number that the person was focusing on (the target) and the other one was randomly chosen from the other numbers that ranged from 1 to 9 (the non-target). A time window of 1200 ms was used, starting 200 ms before the stimulus and ending 1000 ms after it. The prestimulus interval of -200 to 0 ms was considered for baseline correction. This resulted in an 11 532 $\times$ 3 $\times$ 1200 (number of epochs $\times$ number of EEG channels x number of samples) data matrix.
2. The amplitude threshold was set to 100 μV according to common guidelines (such as in [23]) to avoid epochs that have been significantly affected, usually by eye blinks. Therefore, approximately one-third of epochs were removed.

The feature extraction method was based on averaging time intervals of interest, and the averages across all EEG channels were combined (windowed means feature extraction, WM). The time window for P300 BCIs is typically between 300 ms and 500 ms after the stimulus, which was split into 20 equal segments. Consequently, the feature vectors' dimension was reduced to 60 using three EEG channels. As a final step, the mean and variance were adjusted to zero for these feature vectors.

2.4 Classification

Before classification, 25% of the samples were separated for testing purposes, and the remaining 75% was utilized for training. For optimizing parameters, 500 iterations of Monte Carlo cross-validation (CV) were performed. After each cross-validation, the outcomes of the holdout testing set were determined, and the meaning of the results was taken at the end of the processing. The 1D-UNet model (a kind of Convolutional Neural Network (CNN)) used in this paper was implemented in Keras. The network has a u- shaped architecture because it has both contracting and expansive paths. The path that contracts is a typical convolutional network consisting of repeated convolutions, rectified linear units (ReLU), and max-pooling operations. The spatial information is decreased, while feature information is increased during the contraction. Using a series of up-convolution and concatenation, the expansive pathway integrates high-resolution characteristics from the contracting path with feature and spatial information. This method is designed to get the most validation subsets in terms of classification performance.

Figure 1 displays our proposed UNet structure and its layers which consists of 56 layers. The encoder includes conv1d, batch normalization, leaky relu, and max pooling layers. The decoder consists of upsampling, concatenate, conv1dtranspose, batch normalization, and leaky relu layers. We use flatten, dropout, and dense layers for the final layers. For the first four dense layers, the relu function is employed, and for the final dense layer, the softmax function is used. The following hyperparameters remained constant across all experiments:

- The results of the Adam optimizer are generally better than other optimization algorithms, have faster computation time, and require fewer parameters for tuning, so the Adam optimizer was applied.
- Binary cross entropy loss function is preferred for classification, while mean squared error (MSE) is one of the best choices for regression.
- The learning rate value was 0.001, the recommended value for getting started with training.
- Epoch was 500, and the batch size was 1200 since the accuracy was less than 60% for smaller batch sizes.

To evaluate the quality of classification, we calculated accuracy and precision metrics.

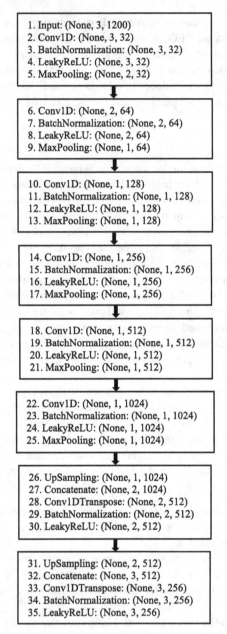

Fig. 1. The implemented architecture of our proposed UNET (Number of trainable parameters which can be used to control certain properties of the training process is 4,398,074)

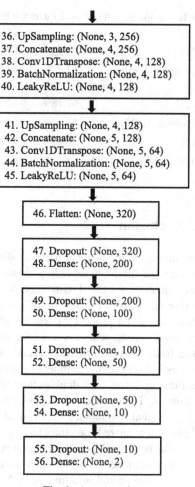

Fig. 1. (*continued*)

3 Results

The primary objective of the current research was to apply a type of 1D-UNet for the classification of P300 BCI data. Raw ERP epochs were used for this model (with the dimensionality of 3×1200) from three EEG channels (Fz, Cz, Pz). The accuracy and precision of this model were 64.5% in the single trial, which was the best result after modifying the hyperparameters. The comparison of our proposed method with previous methods is shown in Table 1, which contains the accuracy and precision of each model applied to this dataset. The result we achieved is comparable with state-of-the-art.

Table 1. Comparison of our model with the literature

Method	Accuracy	Precision
The proposed method (UNet)	**64.5%**	**64.5%**
CNN [3]	62.18%	62.76%
SNN (variant 1) [10]	63.43%	64.47%
RNN [11]	56.92%	57.61%
EMOTION_DEEP_LSTM [12]	63.71%	63.71%

4 Discussion and Conclusion

Our findings demonstrate that some models can perform slightly better on this classification task. After reviewing the literature regarding signal classification, to enhance preprocessing and feature extraction for the classification of EEG signals, we proposed an appropriate DL structure that allows for the use of global location and context at the same time. The architecture of our proposed UNet model includes an encoder network followed by a decoder network, which is used for the ERP classification of a multi-subject P300 dataset from 250 children. The encoder network (contracting path) halves the spatial dimensions and doubles the number of filters (feature channels) at each encoder block. Likewise, the decoder network doubles the spatial dimensions and halves the number of feature channels. The encoder and decoder network connect via a link. Since our dataset is an EEG signal, we replace the original 2D convolutions with 1D convolutions that have been characterized, i.e., the 1D-UNet. A combination of UNet, drop- out and dense layers was beneficial for classification performance.

After adjusting the hyperparameters, our model's accuracy and precision were 64.5%. Although UNet needs more spatial information in the data using more channels to perform better, as shown in Table 1, the result of our method was higher than previous models applied to this dataset. Alternatively, one of the limitations of this dataset is that it is not large enough for UNet to prove its advantages, so data augmentation could be an appropriate technique to solve this problem. Although UNet can achieve better accuracy in such tasks, its optimal depth is unknown, so other researchers can try different UNet models or combine them with other algorithms. The preprocessed data is available in [22].

Acknowledgment. This work was supported by the University specific research project SGS-2022–016 Advanced Methods of Data Processing and Analysis (project SGS-2022–016).

References

1. Wolpaw, J.R., Birbaumer, N., McFarland, D.J., Pfurtscheller, G., Vaughan, T.M.: Brain–computer interfaces for communication and control. Clin. Neurophysiol. **113**, 767–791 (2002)
2. Wang, Y., et al.: An iterative approach for EEG-Based rapid face search: a refined retrieval by brain computer interfaces. IEEE Trans. Auton. Ment. Dev. **7**, 211–222 (2015)
3. Vařeka, L.: Evaluation of convolutional neural networks using a large multi-subject P300 dataset. Biomed. Signal Process. Control. **58**, 101837 (2020)
4. Hope, C., et al.: High throughput screening for mammography using a human-computer interface with rapid serial visual presentation (RSVP). In: SPIE (2013)
5. Cai, Q., Gao, Z., An, J., Gao, S., Grebogi, C.: A graph-temporal fused dual-input convolutional neural network for detecting sleep stages from EEG signals. IEEE Trans. Circuits Syst. II Express Briefs **68**, 777–781 (2021)
6. Blankertz, B., Lemm, S., Treder, M., Haufe, S., Müller, K.-R.: Single-trial analysis and classification of ERP components — A tutorial. Neuroimage **56**, 814–825 (2011)
7. Xu, N., Gao, X., Hong, B., Miao, X., Gao, S., Yang, F.: BCI Competition 2003—data set IIb: enhancing P300 wave detection using ICA-based subspace projections for BCI applications. IEEE Trans. Biomed. Eng. **51**, 1067–1072 (2004)
8. Hashmi, M.F., Kene, J.D., Kotambkar, D.M., Matte, P., Keskar, A.G.: An efficient P300 detection algorithm based on kernel principal component analysis-support vector machine. Comput. Electr. Eng. **97**, 107608 (2022)
9. Sadeghibakhi, M., Pourreza, H., Mahyar, H.: Multiple sclerosis lesions segmentation using attention-based CNNs in FLAIR images. IEEE J. Transl. Eng. Health Med. **10**, 1–11 (2022)
10. Honzik, V., Moucek, R.: Spiking neural networks for classification of brain-computer interface and image data. In: 2021 IEEE International Conference on Bioinformatics and Biomedicine (BIBM), pp. 3624–3629. IEEE (2021)
11. Vařeka, L.: Comparison of convolutional and recurrent neural networks for the P300 detection. In: Proceedings of the 14th International Joint Conference on Biomedical Engineering Systems and Technologies, pp. 186–191. SCITEPRESS - Science and Technology Publications (2021)
12. Selvasingham, S., Denecke, K.: Classifying numbers from EEG data – which neural network architecture performs best? In: Healthcare of the Future 2022, pp. 103–106. IOS Press (2022)
13. Jimenez-Perez, G., Alcaine, A., Camara, O.: U-Net architecture for the automatic detection and delineation of the electrocardiogram. IEEE (2019)
14. Krusienski, D.J., et al.: A comparison of classification techniques for the P300 Speller. J. Neural. Eng. **3**, 299–305 (2006)
15. Manyakov, N.V., Chumerin, N., Combaz, A., Van Hulle, M.M.: Comparison of classification methods for P300 brain-computer interface on disabled subjects. Comput. Intell. Neurosci. **2011**, 1–12 (2011)
16. Akhter, R., Ahmad, F., Beyette, F.R.: Automated detection of ERP artifacts of auditory oddball paradigm by unsupervised machine learning algorithm. In: 2022 IEEE Conference on Computational Intelligence in Bioinformatics and Computational Biology (CIBCB), pp. 1–8. IEEE (2022)
17. Lawhern, V.J., Solon, A.J., Waytowich, N.R., Gordon, S.M., Hung, C.P., Lance, B.J.: EEGNet: a compact convolutional neural network for EEG-based brain–computer interfaces. J. Neural. Eng. **15**, 056013 (2018)
18. Tsiouris, KM, Pezoulas, V.C., Zervakis, M., Konitsiotis, S., Koutsouris, D.D., Fotiadis, D.I.: A long short-term memory deep learning network for the prediction of epileptic seizures using EEG signals. Comput. Biol. Med. **99**, 24–37 (2018)

19. Gao, Z., Yuan, T., Zhou, X., Ma, C., Ma, K., Hui, P.: A deep learning method for improving the classification accuracy of SSMVEP-based BCI. IEEE Trans. Circ. Syst. II Express Briefs **67**, 3447–3451 (2020)
20. Lan, Z., Yan, C., Li, Z., Tang, D., Xiang, X.: MACRO: multi-attention convolutional recurrent model for subject-independent ERP detection. IEEE Signal Process. Lett. **28**, 1505–1509 (2021)
21. Khessiba, S., Blaiech, A.G., Ben Khalifa, K., Ben Abdallah, A., Bedoui, M.H.: Innovative deep learning models for EEG-based vigilance detection. Neural Comput. Appl. **33**, 6921–6937 (2021)
22. Mouček, R., Vařeka, L., Prokop, T., Štěbeták, J., Brůha, P.: Event-related potential data from a guess the number brain-computer interface experiment on school children. Sci. Data. **4**, 160121 (2017)
23. Luck, S.J.: An Introduction to the Event-Related Potential Technique, 2nd edn. The MIT Press, Cambridge (2005)

Dyslexia Data Consortium Repository: A Data Sharing and Delivery Platform for Research

Roshan Bhandari[1], Rishikesh V. Phatangare[1], Mark A. Eckert[2], Kenneth I. Vaden[2], and James Z. Wang[1(✉)]

[1] School of Computing, Clemson University, Clemson, SC, USA
{rbhanda,rphatan,jzwang}@g.clemson.edu
[2] Department of Otolaryngology - Head and Neck Surgery, Medical University of South Carolina, Charleston, SC, USA
{eckert,vaden}@musc.edu

Abstract. Specific learning disability of reading, or dyslexia, affects 5–17% of the population in the United States. Research on the neurobiology of dyslexia has included studies with relatively small sample sizes across research sites, thus limiting inference and the application of novel methods, such as deep learning. To address these issues and facilitate open science, we developed an online platform for data-sharing and advanced research programs to enhance opportunities for replication by providing researchers with secondary data that can be used in their research (https://www.dyslexiadata.org). This platform integrates a set of well-designed machine learning algorithms and tools to generate secondary datasets, such as cortical thickness, as well as regional brain volume metrics that have been consistently associated with dyslexia. Researchers can access shared data to address fundamental questions about dyslexia and development, replicate research findings, apply new methods, and educate the next generation of researchers. The overarching goal of this platform is to advance our understanding of a disorder that has significant academic, social, and economic impacts on children, their families, and society.

Keywords: Dyslexia Data Consortium · Privacy Protection · Data Quality Evaluation · Deep Learning · Neuroimaging datasets

1 Introduction

This paper discusses the design and implementation of a web-based data-sharing and research collaboration platform, the Dyslexia Data Consortium repository (https://www.dyslexiadata.org), to address the increasing demand for online resources to facilitate data sharing among researchers to address fundamental questions about dyslexia, which affects 5–17% of the population in the United States [3,19,22]. The ultimate goal of this platform is to promote the replication

F. Liu et al. (Eds.): BI 2023, LNAI 13974, pp. 167–178, 2023.
https://doi.org/10.1007/978-3-031-43075-6_15

of research findings, disseminate new ideas on processing and analysis of dyslexia datasets, and educate the next generation of researchers.

In the last two decades, researchers have conducted extensive neuroimaging studies to advance understanding of the neurobiological reasons for and consequences of dyslexia, leading to a large amount of data scattered across different research and clinical sites. These datasets can be beneficial to future researchers, and they can inspire innovation and novel methods that further benefit the improvement of human health [11,24]. Jean et al. highlight several reasons for sharing neuroimaging datasets [18], including rapid advances in understanding brain structure and function, enhanced research rigor, and cost reduction. The NIH has also issued a new Data Management and Sharing (DMS) policy [17], effective January 25, 2023, to promote the sharing of scientific data. A portal or platform where researchers can share data efficiently will promote research collaboration and dissemination, increase scientific integrity, and promote innovation.

Many data-sharing platforms, such as neurovault.org [9] and brainmap.org [14], are currently used by researchers to share their neuroimaging datasets. However, these platforms are not specifically engineered for area-specific research, and some of them, such as Kaggle [12], are more generic data-sharing sites. Ideally, researchers would consolidate data and meta-data for studies of specific disorders into a single platform and develop search tools to facilitate dataset searching and retrieval.

There are several data and usability considerations for a well-designed data-sharing platform. First, retrospective datasets from different research sites vary in how to format information and how to collect the measurements. It is desirable to automatically convert and store heterogeneous datasets into a commonly adopted format. Second, research datasets require de-identification before they can be shared. Data-sharing platforms must verify that the uploaded datasets do not contain personal information. For example, recognizable facial features can be observed in rendered structural MRI scans of the head [20]. Third, researchers may be interested in secondary measures, such as brain volume, that were not included with the raw dataset and would ideally be measured consistently across studies. These issues were considered in our design and development of the web-based Dyslexia Data Consortium repository platform.

The subsequent sections are organized as follows: After presenting the high-level overview of the Dyslexia Data Consortium repository platform and summarizing its main functions in Sect. 2, we discuss the implementation details of the essential components, including data processing, storage, and sharing, data quality assurance, secondary data generation, and brain structure metric estimation in Sect. 3, 4, and 5. Finally, we present our concluding remarks Sect. 6.

2 System Overview

The Dyslexia Data Consortium repository is a web-based platform developed using Python and the Django web framework. Various software packages and

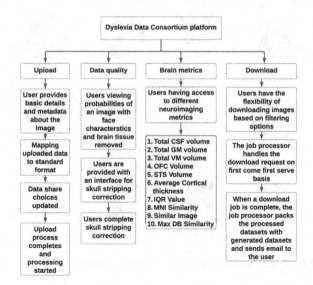

Fig. 1. System features on Dyslexia Data Consortium platform. CSF: cerebrospinal fluid; GM: gray matter; WM: white matter; OFC: orbitofrontal cortex; STS: superior temporal sulcus; IQR: image quality rating; MNI: Montreal Neurological Institute; DB: database.

computing resources are utilized in the backend to achieve different functions, including MATLAB [15] for image processing, the Clemson Palmetto Supercomputer for distributed processing, and the TensorFlow library [1] to train machine learning models. In addition to the data sharing functions such as MRI file uploading, downloading, and data quality checks, this platform provides new methods for data analysis that researchers and trainees can use in their studies. Figure 1 highlights different features available in the Dyslexia Data Consortium platform. Figure 2 shows the central user interface, a dashboard providing a set of buttons linking to individual function modules.

While the professional credentials and justification thresholds for accessing the platform are modest, users must request access and communicate how they want to use the resources. Users must also complete a data use agreement (DUA) that specifies the conditions under which the data can be used, with a vision towards protecting privacy and respecting dataset contributor requests about how their data are shared. This DUA is a template from the Federal Demonstration Partnership used to facilitate data sharing. Users access the DUA and upload the DUA with their institutional approval through the platform to facilitate data access.

Fig. 2. Dashboard for Dyslexia Data Consortium platform.

3 Data Sharing and Storage

3.1 Data De-Identification

Even when data is collected from human subjects with consent to share data, it is advisable to share de-identified data in open-access repositories. While the risk of re-identification needs consideration and will differ across topic areas, some neuroimaging datasets may have greater risk for re-identification if the images can be rendered to visualize a face, which can be a barrier to data sharing and requires careful consideration [19].

Skull-stripping tools [21,23] are commonly used to remove the facial and skull features from MRI scans. Due to the heterogeneity of these images (varying in sizes, shapes, contrast, orientation, etc.), parameter fine-tuning is often necessary to ensure that voxels representing the face have been removed. Skull-stripping tools may also inadvertently remove image voxels representing brain tissue and thus affect data quality. Additional user time and effort are often necessary to inspect the skull-stripped images visually for quality assurance. To limit the human effort invested in quality control, we have developed a deep learning model to assist with data quality assurance. This deep learning model estimates the probability that the skull-stripped MRI scans include recognizable facial features. It also calculates the probability that the skull-stripping process has accidentally removed image voxels representing brain tissues for quality control. Thus, the deep learning model directs contributors to images that may need attention to ensure de-identification and those with poor image quality. These deep learning models have been integrated into the Dyslexia Data Consortium platform with an interactive data reprocessing procedure to facilitate the effort to ensure privacy and ensure data quality for images in the repository.

The value of neuroimaging data is augmented by accompanying behavioral and demographic data. Providing a map between the new participant identification labels and the de-identified neuroimaging data file names can be time-consuming and prone to user error, particularly for large datasets. We developed the De-Identification Toolbox [24], which allows researchers to de-identify MRI scans and link the de-identified images with their associated behavioral and demographic information through a user-friendly pipeline. The toolbox automatically creates a reverse mapping table locally to trace the de-identified data back to their original datasets and ensure that new ID labels are correctly matched across files and variables. We also designed the De-Identification Toolbox to allow researchers to upload their data to the Dyslexia Data Consortium platform. After finishing the de-identification of a dataset, a data sharing page pops up in the De-Identification Toolbox. Users enter their username and password in the Dyslexia Data Consortium platform, enter the title and description, select the image type, and select the upload button. The De-Identification Toolbox prepares a zip file containing the images to be uploaded by the user, creates an HTTP POST request to send the data to the consortium platform. The datasets are finally processed and saved within the consortium platform.

3.2 Web Interface for Data Upload

For researchers who choose not to use the De-Identification Toolbox to share their datasets, the Dyslexia Data Consortium platform provides a user-friendly web interface for uploading de-identified datasets. Currently, the platform processes images in NIFTI format. Users can choose to upload a single image, multiple images at once, or a zip folder/tar file containing a group of images. Because the consortium server uses image modality-specific back-end scripts to process different types of images, users must specify the image type (functional, anatomical, diffusion, etc.) during uploading to ensure that the server invokes the correct scripts to process the uploaded data. A separate upload box is provided for users to upload text file data, such as accompanying behavioral and demographic data.

The data-sharing platform expects data to be in Brain Imaging Data Structure (BIDS) format [10]. If the uploaded data does not meet the BIDS requirements, the user interface redirects to a page where the users can edit the variable names to make them BIDS-compliant. This process ensures that all data is stored in BIDS format. We also obtain a confirmation from the user that they have the institutional approval to share the de-identified data before completing the uploading process. Users can specify how they want the consortium to share their data. Data can be shared with all users, with only a specific group of users, or private and accessible only to that user who may be interested in using the platform to generate secondary datasets for their research. Figure 3 explains the upload process in a workflow diagram.

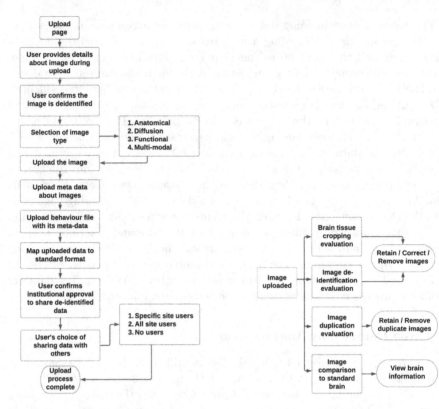

Fig. 3. Uploading Process flow diagram.   **Fig. 4.** Data quality evaluation process.

3.3 Web Interface for Data Downloading

When a user clicks the download button in the dashboard, it leads to a download page that displays a list of available datasets through the Dyslexia Data Consortium. This page provides a search interface including various filtering options with which users can narrow their selections, by demographic variables, for example. Once a user selects a group of datasets and submits a download request, the system will create a download job and put the request in a queue to wait for processing. The job processor handles the download requests on a first-come-first-serve basis. When the data is ready, the job processor zips the processed datasets with generated secondary data and sends an email to the user with a link to download the requested datasets.

3.4 BIDS Compliance

Researchers at various institutions may arrange complex neuroimaging datasets in different formats or directory structures. A well-designed data-sharing platform must organize the neuroimaging and corresponding behavioral data into a specific directory schema using a precise naming convention to ensure researchers understand data content easily. BIDS provides a simple and easy way to organize neuroimaging and behavioral data, including naming conventions for structural, diffusion, and functional brain images and the associated behavioral data. According to BIDS standards, users create separate folders for different subjects. The folder name must have a unique identifier, for example, sub-01, sub-02, etc. Under the subject folder, there are multiple folders to place anatomical, functional, or diffusion images. In addition, a tab-separated file called "participants.tsv" is used to store the details about the participants. While we encourage researchers who contribute their dyslexia datasets to the Dyslexia Data Consortium to use BIDS conventions to organize the data before uploading them to the platform, we provide the researchers with the flexibility to upload data using their in-house format. As discussed in Sect. 3.2, we have developed a user interface and proper backend scripts to convert the uploaded data into BIDS format.

4 Quality Evaluation of Shared Datasets

Figure 4 highlights different data quality measures provided by the data sharing and delivery platform, including image de-identification evaluation, brain tissue cropping probability, image duplication detection, and atypical image identification, as discussed in the following subsections.

4.1 Deep Learning Model for Data Quality Assurance

As discussed earlier, researchers often spend much time visually examining skull-stripped images for quality assurance. To ease the burden of inspecting every skull-stripped image for quality assurance, we developed a deep learning model to perform data quality assurance. This deep learning model can determine whether the skull-stripped MRI images retain recognizable facial features (identification information) or if image voxels representing brain tissue have been removed. A web interface is designed to present the data quality evaluation results and to allow users to reprocess the images to achieve better quality. In this web interface, we highlight the rows representing the images with a high probability of failed de-identification or missing brain tissue voxels. Users can click a view button to enlarge the image for a clearer view of the possibly problematic image. With this web interface, users only need to review and possibly reprocess the highlighted images, thereby limiting the need to browse through all images to evaluate image quality. Once the user identifies a problem with an image, the web interface provides options to upload a new image for that case, remove the image from the data set, retain the image if there is no identifiable face found after human inspection, or select an alternative image from a group of images skull-stripped by the system automatically. For images flagged by the system as having brain tissue voxels removed, the user can remove the image from the consortium database if there is a significant loss of brain tissue voxels or replace the image by re-uploading a new image. For images with minimal to no loss of brain tissue voxels based on visual examination, the user may keep it in the consortium database using the "retain the image" option if the user determines that the image quality is acceptable.

4.2 Image Duplication

Researchers may upload the same image more than once to the Dyslexia Data Consortium platform, unaware of the erroneous duplicate image in their dataset or repeated measures for a participant within or across different research sites. To identify a potential case duplication within and across datasets, we conduct a similarity analysis for each uploaded image with all data in the database using the Check Sample Homogeneity function from the CAT12 toolbox [8]. A higher correlation coefficient between two images indicates a higher degree of structural similarity and a higher probability of image duplication.

4.3 Unusual Images

In addition to performing quality assurance for the skull-stripped and uploaded images, the consortium platform provides the users with information about the contrast-to-noise ratio of an image and its similarity measure compared to a standard brain template, which helps the users to identify images with noise artifact and unusual brain morphology, respectively. The latter can have direct relevance to the topic of study. For example, we identified images of cases with bilateral perisylvian syndrome and pericallosal lipoma in the Dyslexia Data Consortium repository [4,7]. Identifying these unusual images can be challenging in a large dataset. For this reason, we use the CAT12 Check Sample Homogeneity code to compare each uploaded and normalized gray matter image to the MNI gray matter template. This process provides a metric for how similar/dissimilar an image is relative to the MNI template. This can help to identify images with unusual morphology or those were not segmented or normalized accurately.

5   Secondary Dataset Generation

One of the benefits of joining the Dyslexia Data Consortium and sharing data is that members can use the Clemson University's Palmetto supercomputer to process data and obtain secondary datasets.

Each structural image is processed using SPM12 [25] and CAT12 software [8] to generate segmented gray and white matter images in native and normalized template space, cortical thickness data, and data quality metrics. Here, we use the default image processing parameters to increase the likelihood that an image will be appropriately segmented and facilitate methods replication, given that researchers often use default settings in these software packages. While not currently implemented, there are plans to enable users to select age and sex-matched templates to optimize segmentation and normalization for the demographic of their datasets.

5.1   Secondary Data Generation Process

After evaluating the quality of the uploaded images, the consortium server creates parallel jobs on Clemson's Palmetto cluster to generate the secondary datasets. The consortium server uses a jobs API to initiate the processes on the Palmetto cluster. The parameters passed to the Palmetto cluster by the consortium server include information like the names of the MRI files that need to be processed and the location of the files from where the cluster nodes can retrieve them. Figure 5 shows a series of parallel processing steps for generating the secondary datasets on the Palmetto cluster and the interactions between the dyslexia consortium server and the Palmetto cluster. Once the data is ready, the job process uploads the data to the Palmetto cluster for parallel processing. Upon receiving the data, the Palmetto cluster uses MATLAB scripts on multiple nodes to generate the secondary datasets in parallel. Finally, the secondary datasets are zipped into a single file and sent to the consortium server.

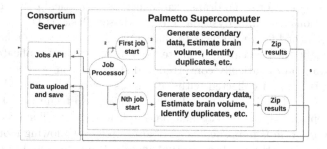

Fig. 5. Stepwise representation of parallel processing of secondary datasets in Palmetto. Numbering indicates the order of image processing.

5.2   Brain Volume Estimation

Studies of reading disability have demonstrated atypical morphology in multiple brain regions [2,13,16]. The data sharing and delivery platform provides brain structure metrics for brain regions consistently reported to exhibit atypical morphology in reading disability cases compared to controls. For example, gray matter volume in the superior temporal sulcus (STS) and orbitofrontal cortex (OFC) has been consistently associated with dyslexia [6]. The Dyslexia Data Consortium platform uses the SPM12 functions: SPM_VOL and SPM_READ _VOLS [25], to calculate the STS and OFC gray matter volumes and save them in the database based on spatial results masks from a previous reading disability study [5]. Figure 6 demonstrates this regional brain volume estimation process. The consortium platform also offers a user interface for researchers to retrieve these volumes stored in the database.

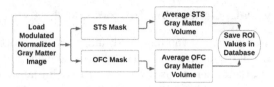

Fig. 6. Brain volume estimation process. Secondary data are generated for users to replicate previous dyslexia findings for superior temporal sulcus (STS) and orbitofrontal cortex (OFC) regions where lower gray matter volume has been observed in people with dyslexia.

6   Conclusion

Data-sharing initiatives can increase scientific integrity and experimental rigor and potentially improve our understanding of many clinical and basic science topics. By leveraging neuroimaging studies and combining retrospective datasets, our data-sharing platform can dramatically increase statistical power for various research questions regarding dyslexia. The web-based Dyslexia Data Consortium platform is designed for researchers to share data and receive secondary data in return to benefit their research, promote data discovery, and replicate previous findings. Data is automatically converted and stored in compliance with protocols such as BIDS and collected with safeguards for data privacy through the integration of the De-identification Toolbox, which also facilitates the integration of different data types into a single data upload package. The Dyslexia Data Consortium platform is published as an open-source tool allowing more features to be integrated into the platform so that investigators interested in developing data repositories for other areas of study can benefit from the work described here. The code is available at: https://github.com/bioinformatics-AI/dyslexia_ website and the Dyslexia Data Consortium repository is accessible at https:// dyslexiadata.org/.

Acknowledgements. This work was supported (in part) by NIH Eunice Kennedy Shriver National Institute of Child Health and Human Development (R01 HD 069374) and the National Science Foundation (NSF) DBI (1759856), and was conducted in a facility constructed with support from Research Facilities Improvement Program (C06 RR 014516) from the NIH/National Center for Research Resources. The funding agencies had no role in study design, data collection and analysis, decision to publish, or preparation of the manuscript. Clemson University is acknowledged for the generous allotment of computing resources on Palmetto cluster. Please see www.dyslexiadata.org for more information about the Dyslexia Data Consortium, including the contributors who provided the data for this study.

References

1. Abadi, M.: TensorFlow: learning functions at scale. In: Proceedings of the 21st ACM SIGPLAN International Conference on Functional Programming, p. 1. ACM (2016). https://doi.org/10.1145/2951913.2976746

2. Casanova, M.F., Araque, J., Giedd, J., Rumsey, J.M.: Reduced brain size and gyrification in the brains of dyslexic patients. J. Child Neurol. **19**, 275–281 (2004). https://doi.org/10.1177/088307380401900407. http://journals. sagepub.com/doi/10.1177/088307380401900407
3. Consortium, D.D., et al.: Common brain structure findings across children with varied reading disability profiles. Sci. Rep. 7, 6009 (2017). https://doi.org/10.1038/ s41598-017-05691-5. http://www.nature.com/articles/s41598-017-05691-5
4. Eckert, M.A., Berninger, V.W., Hoeft, F., Vaden, K.I.: A case of bilateral peri-sylvian syndrome with reading disability. Cortex **76**, 121–124 (2016). https://doi. org/10.1016/j.cortex.2016.01.004. https://www.sciencedirect.com/science/article/ pii/S0010945216000071
5. Eckert, M.A., Berninger, V.W., Vaden, K.I., Gebregziabher, M., Tsu, L.: Gray matter features of reading disability: a combined meta-analytic and direct analy-sis approach. ENeuro 3, ENEURO.0103–15.2015 (2016). https://doi.org/10.1523/ ENEURO.0103-15.2015. https://www.eneuro.org/lookup/doi/10.1523/ENEURO. 0103-15.2015
6. Eckert, M.A., Berninger, V.W., Vaden, K.I., Gebregziabher, M., Tsu, L.: Gray matter features of reading disability: a combined meta-analytic and direct analysis approach (1, 2, 3, 4). ENeuro 3, ENEURO.0103–15.2015 (2016). https://doi.org/ 10.1523/ENEURO.0103-15.2015
7. Eckert, M.A., Vaden, K.I., Roberts, D.R., Castles, A.: A pericallosal lipoma case with evidence of surface dyslexia. Cortex **117**, 414–416 (2019). https://doi. org/10.1016/j.cortex.2019.02.027. https://www.sciencedirect.com/science/article/ pii/S0010945219300966
8. Gaser, C., Dahnke, R., Thompson, P.M., Kurth, F., Luders, E., Initiative, A.D.N.: CAT – a computational anatomy toolbox for the analysis of struc-tural MRI data (2022). https://doi.org/10.1101/2022.06.11.495736. https://www. biorxiv.org/content/10.1101/2022.06.11.495736v1
9. Gorgolewski, K.J., et al.: Neurovault.org: a web-based repository for collecting and sharing unthresholded statistical maps of the human brain. Front. Neuroin-formatics **9**, 8 (2015). https://doi.org/10.3389/fninf.2015.00008. http://journal. frontiersin.org/article/10.3389/fninf.2015.00008/abstract
10. Gorgolewski, K.J., et al.: The brain imaging data structure, a format for orga-nizing and describing outputs of neuroimaging experiments. Sci. Data **3**, 160044 (2016). https://doi.org/10.1038/sdata.2016.44. https://www.nature.com/articles/ sdata201644
11. Irani, F., Platek, S.M., Bunce, S., Ruocco, A.C., Chute, D.: Functional near infrared spectroscopy (fNIRS): an emerging neuroimaging technology with impor-tant applications for the study of brain disorders. Clin. Neuropsychologist **21**, 9–37 (2007). https://doi.org/10.1080/13854040600910018. http://www.tandfonline. com/doi/abs/10.1080/13854040600910018
12. Kaggle: Your machine learning and data science community. https://kaggle.com
13. Kronbichler, M., Wimmer, H., Staffen, W., Hutzler, F., Mair, A., Ladurner, G.: Developmental dyslexia: gray matter abnormalities in the occipitotemporal cor-tex. Hum. Brain Mapp. **29**, 613–625 (2008). https://doi.org/10.1002/hbm.20425. http://doi.wiley.com/10.1002/hbm.20425
14. Laird, A.R., et al.: The brainMap strategy for standardization, sharing, and meta-analysis of neuroimaging data. BMC Res. Notes **4**, 349 (2011). https://doi.org/10. 1186/1756-0500-4-349. https://bmcresnotes.biomedcentral.com/articles/10.1186/ 1756-0500-4-349

15. MathWorks: MATALAB. https://www.mathworks.com/products/matlab.html
16. Menghini, D., et al.: Structural correlates of implicit learning deficits in subjects with developmental dyslexia. Ann. New York Acad. Sci. **1145**, 212–221 (2008). https://doi.org/10.1196/annals.1416.010. http://doi.wiley.com/10.1196/annals.1416.010
17. NIH: 2023 NIH data management and sharing policy. https://oir.nih.gov/sourcebook/intramural-program-oversight/intramural-data-sharing/2023-nih-data-management-sharing-policy
18. Poline, J.B., et al.: Data sharing in neuroimaging research. Front. Neuroinformatics **6**, 9 (2012). https://doi.org/10.3389/fninf.2012.00009. http://journal.frontiersin.org/article/10.3389/fninf.2012.00009/abstract
19. Rodgers, B.: The identification and prevalence of specific reading retardation. Br. J. Educ. Psychol. **53**, 369–373 (1983). https://doi.org/10.1111/j.2044-8279.1983.tb02570.x. http://doi.wiley.com/10.1111/j.2044-8279.1983.tb02570.x
20. Schwarz, C.G., et al.: Identification of anonymous MRI research participants with face-recognition software. New Engl. J. Med. **381**, 1684–1686 (2019). https://doi.org/10.1056/NEJMc1908881. http://www.nejm.org/doi/10.1056/NEJMc1908881
21. Shattuck, D.W., Leahy, R.M.: BrainSuite: an automated cortical surface identification tool. Med. Image Anal. **6**, 129–142 (2002). https://doi.org/10.1016/S1361-8415(02)00054-3. https://linkinghub.elsevier.com/retrieve/pii/S1361841502000543
22. Siegel, L.S.: Perspectives on dyslexia. Paediatr. Child Health **11**, 581–587 (2006). https://doi.org/10.1093/pch/11.9.581. https://academic.oup.com/pch/article-lookup/doi/10.1093/pch/11.9.581
23. Smith, S.M.: BET: Brain extraction tool (2013). https://fsl.fmrib.ox.ac.uk/fsl/fslwiki/BET
24. Song, X., et al.: De-identification toolbox – a data-sharing tool for neuroimaging studies. Front. Neurosci. **9**, 325 (2015). https://doi.org/10.3389/fnins.2015.00325. http://journal.frontiersin.org/Article/10.3389/fnins.2015.00325/abstract
25. SPM: Statistical parametric mapping. https://www.fil.ion.ucl.ac.uk/spm/

Conversion from Mild Cognitive Impairment to Alzheimer's Disease: A Comparison of Tree-Based Machine Learning Algorithms for Survival Analysis

Alessia Sarica[✉] [ID], Federica Aracri [ID], Maria Giovanna Bianco [ID],
Maria Grazia Vaccaro [ID], Andrea Quattrone [ID], and Aldo Quattrone [ID]

Neuroscience Research Center, Department of Medical and Surgical Sciences,
Magna Graecia University, 88100 Catanzaro, Italy
sarica@unicz.it

Abstract. Prediction of conversion from Mild Cognitive Impairment (MCI) to Alzheimer's disease (AD) is usually performed with Machine Learning (ML) supervised approaches. However, typical ML classifiers are not able to provide information on time and risk to AD conversion. Survival Analysis statistical methods as Cox Proportional Hazard (CPH) give this information and can handle censored data, but they were designed for small dataset and do not perform well on heterogeneous feature space. ML survival algorithms overcome these limitations, and in particular tree-based models showed promising results on biomedical data. Thus, we applied Random Survival Forest (RSF), Conditional Survival Forest (CSF) and Extra Survival Trees (XST) on demographic, clinical and neuroimaging data of stable and progressive MCI patients from ADNI to evaluate their accuracy in predicting time-to-AD and to stratify MCI patients based on their risk grade. Moreover, we quantitatively compared their feature importance with Rank-Biased Overlap (RBO), a similarity measure between rankings. RSF showed highest *c*-index (0.87), followed by CSF and XST (0.85), while CPH had worst performance (0.83). According to RSF, CSF and XST, high-risk group had probability of AD conversion within 48 months respectively of 76.9%, 74.8% and 72.3%. Most predictive features (FAQ, mPACCdigit, mPACCtrailsB) were in nearly same order, where highest RBO was between CSF and XST (80%), while RSF had low similarity with CSF (66.3%) and XST (67.5%). Our findings suggested that tree-based survival models represent an optimal compromise between performance and interpretability when predicting time-to-event and assessing individual risk score of conversion from MCI to AD.

Keywords: survival analysis · random survival forest · machine learning · MCI conversion · dementia prediction

1 Introduction

Alzheimer's disease (AD) is the most common form of dementia among the elderly, representing 60%-70% of the cases worldwide [1]. The diagnosis of AD is based on clinical, neuropsychological and neuroimaging evaluation [2], but at early stages, its diagnosis is challenging because symptoms could fall between normal aging changes and early dementia [1]. It has been estimated that patients affected by Mild Cognitive Impairment (MCI), which is a heterogeneous condition characterized by subjective cognitive complaints, have a cumulative risk to progress to AD of 33.6% [3].

Artificial Intelligence (AI) and Machine Learning (ML) has been widely employed for the early diagnosis of AD [4] and for the prediction of progression from MCI to AD [5], reaching excellent accuracy together with good interpretability and explainability [6]. Typical ML algorithms used with these aims are supervised learning approaches, thus they are not able to consider the time to AD conversion and they do not provide any information about the risk of progression from MCI to AD. Moreover, ML classification is not capable to handle the censoring that occurs when the event of interest is not observed for some subjects before the study is terminated [7].

Survival analysis is a statistic field that was born to predict the time to an event by incorporating censored data [7]. Cox Proportional Hazard [8] (CPH) is widely applied in survival studies, but it was designed for small datasets and it does not scale well to high dimension [9]. To overcome these limitations, ML algorithms were adapted to handle censoring and to predict the time to an event with optimal performance also on high-dimensional and heterogeneous data [9, 10]. Among novel ML survival methods, those based on decision trees and Random Forest (RF) [4, 11] showed promising results on biomedical dataset [12, 13]. The strength of tree-based survival models relies on the independence from data distribution, on their capability of handling multicollinearity together with their intrinsic feature selection that supports the interpretability of ML findings [14]. Three of the most used tree-based survival methods are Random Survival Forest (RSF) [15], Conditional Survival Forest (CSF) [16] and Extra Survival Trees (XST) [17], which adapt each one differently RF principles for growing and splitting decision trees to predict time to event and risk of occurrence. Recently, RSF was applied for dementia prediction together with CPH and other ML boosted algorithms [9], but its performance was never compared with other tree-based models, and most importantly, no study assessed the similarity among their feature importance.

For these reasons, the main aims of the present work were: (i) to evaluate the performance of RSF, CSF and XST on demographic, clinical and neuroimaging data in predicting time and risk of conversion from MCI to AD, using CPH accuracy as benchmark; (ii) to study the individual predictions of RSF, CSF and XST, and to stratify MCI patients by risk grades (low, medium, and high) according to their conversion to AD risk score; (iii) to study feature importance produced by RSF, CSF and XST, and to quantitatively compare them through the Rank-Biased Overlap (RBO) [18], a similarity measure between rankings [19].

1.1 Related Works

The prediction of diagnosis conversion from MCI to AD has been usually treated as a supervised problem using ML classifiers to discriminate between stable MCI (sMCI) and progressive MCI patients (pMCI, who will convert to AD) [5, 6]. Survival analysis with ML algorithms is a relatively novel field and very few works investigated its application on dementia data [9, 10, 20, 21]. Orozco-Sanchez et al. [10] used four different Cox regression models on brain Magnetic Resonance Imaging (MRI) to assess the rate of conversion from MCI to AD, where the best model reached a c-index of 0.84. A deep learning-based method was introduced by Nakagawa et al. [20], which was applied on gray matter measures of MCI patients and outperformed CPH with a c-index of 0.75. Spooner et al. [9] investigated dementia prediction performance on high-dimensional clinical dataset of ten ML survival approaches, among which ElasticNet, a penalized Cox regression model, had the highest performance (0.93). In a very recent work by Mirabnahrazam et al. [21], a deep learning-based survival model, which extends CPH, predicted the time-to-conversion to AD with a c-index of 0.831 on a dataset with MRI, genetic, demographic and cognitive data.

2 Materials and Methods

2.1 Dataset Preparation

Data used in the preparation of this article were obtained from the Alzheimer's Disease Neuroimaging Initiative (ADNI) database (adni.loni.usc.edu). The ADNI was launched in 2003 as a public-private partnership, led by Principal Investigator Michael W. Weiner, MD. The primary goal of ADNI has been to test whether serial magnetic resonance imaging (MRI), positron emission tomography (PET), other biological markers, and clinical and neuropsychological assessment can be combined to measure the progression of Mild Cognitive Impairment (MCI) and early Alzheimer's disease (AD).

Table file DXSUM_PDXCONV_ADNIALL was filtered to include patients who converted from MCI to AD (progressive MCI, pMCI) and who did not convert their diagnosis overtime maintaining their baseline diagnosis as stable MCI (sMCI). Binary variable *event* was created to trace whether the *event* or the *censorship* occurred, where its value is 1 for the diagnosis conversion from MCI to AD (pMCI), 0 otherwise (sMCI). Variable visit code (VISCODE) was transformed into the variable *time* of event/censorship occurrence, which value corresponds to the number in months after the baseline visit (follow-up at m06, m12, m18, m24, m36, m48) [10]. Patients' demographic, clinical, cognitive, and neuroimaging data at baseline was obtained from table ADNIMERGE.

Final dataset consists of 216 sMCI and 171 pMCI, and features were: *demographic variables* age, gender (PTGENDER), education levels (PTEDUCAT), ethnicity (PTETHCAT), race (PTRACCAT), marital status (PTMARRY); *biomarker* APOE4 allele genotype, i.e., presence of APOE gene that makes the ApoE4 protein, associated with late-stage AD; *cognitive and neuropsychological assessment* Clinical Dementia Rating Sum of Boxes (CDRSB); Alzheimer's Disease Assessment Scale (ADAS), item 11 and 13, and Delayed Word recall (Q4); Mini-Mental State Examination (MMSE);

Rey Auditory Verbal Learning Test (RAVLT), immediate, learning, forgetting and percent forgetting; Logical Memory Delayed Recall (LDELTOTAL); Digit Symbol Substitution (DIGITSCOR); Trails B (TRABSCOR); Functional Activities Questionnaire (FAQ); ADNI modified Preclinical Alzheimer's Cognitive Composite (PACC) with Digit Symbol Substitution (mPACCdigit); ADNI modified Preclinical Alzheimer's Cognitive Composite (PACC) with Trails B (mPACCtrailsB); *neuroimaging measures* MRI volumes of ventricles, hippocampus, whole brain, entorhinal cortex, fusiform, middle temporal gyrus (MidTemp) and total intracranial volume (ICV), calculated with Freesurfer[1]. Categorical variables (PTGENDER, PTETHCAT, PTRACCAT, PTMARRY) were converted to numerical data with the One-Hot Encoding approach [9], also called dummy coding (python function *get_dummies()* on Pandas *dataframe*).

ADNI, as well as other international databases, have the problem of missing data, so here, to avoid reducing sample size, we employed the missForest (MF) algorithm to impute missing data [22]. MissForest is based on the Random Forest (RF) classification method [4], and it can handle any type of input data (continuous and categorical) by making as few as possible assumptions about the structural aspect of the dataset [22].

2.2 Statistical Analysis

Differences between patients' groups in age and years of education were assessed with one-way analysis of variance (ANOVA), differences in distributions of categorical variables were evaluated with Chi-square test, analysis of covariance (ANCOVA) was employed with age and gender as covariates for comparing clinical and cognitive variables, while ANCOVA with age, gender and ICV as covariates for neuroimaging features (significant at $p < 0.05$). Collinearity among features was also evaluated and redundant variables were removed if Pearson's correlation coefficient was $r > 0.60$ or $r < -0.60$. All statistical analyses were performed with Python 3.8 and the package scikit-learn 1.1.3.

2.3 Machine Learning Models for Survival Analysis

The aim of Survival Analysis is to assess when an event is likely to happen or to predict the time-to-event such as the time of progression to AD. Survival Analysis could handle censored data, that is situations when the event of interest is not observed until the study is terminated, as in the case of stable MCI patients. The waiting time until an event occurs is defined as a positive random variable T and given its probability density function $f(t)$, the cumulative distribution function is $F(t) = P_r[T < t] = \int_{-\infty}^{t} f(u)du$. The probability $S(t)$ that the event of interest has not occurred by some time t is $S(t) = 1 - F(t) = P_r[T > t]$. The hazard function $h(t)$ denotes the approximate probability that an event occurs in the small interval $[t, t + dt)$, while the cumulative hazard function $H(t)$ is the integral of the hazard function over the interval $[0;t]$. For discrete time interval subdivided in J parts, the risk score of a sample x is calculated as $r(x) = \sum_{i=1}^{J} H(t_j, x)$.

Cox Proportional Hazard (CPH) [8] is a semi-parametric approach that focuses on modeling the hazard function as $h(t, \vec{x_i}) = h_0(t)\eta(\vec{x_i})$, where $h_0(t)$ is the unknown

---

[1] https://freesurfer.net/.

baseline hazard function, $\eta\left(\overrightarrow{X_i}\right)$, is the risk function usually defined as a linear representation and $\overrightarrow{x_i}$ is the observed feature vector.

Random Survival Forest (RSF) [15] follows the same principles of RF for growing decision trees using bootstrapping and when splitting tree nodes a random feature selection is applied. In particular, a predictor x and a split value c are selected at each node from a collection of randomly chosen predictor variables. Each individual sample i is assigned to the right node if $x_i \leq c$ or to left node if $x_i > c$. Then, the value of the logrank is calculated to test the null hypothesis that there is no difference between the two groups (sMCI and pMCI) in the probability of the event [15].

In Conditional Survival Forest (CSF) [16], the objective function is given by testing the null hypothesis that there is independence between the response and the predictor. For splitting tree nodes, CSF first computes the logrank score and its associated p-value for each predictor variable x. Then, it selects the predictors with the smallest p-value, which must be also less than a specified value α [16]. If no predictor can be used, no split is performed.

Extra Survival Trees (XST) [17] is an extension of the Extremely Randomized trees model. XST applies the same objective function of RSF, but differently from RSF that uses the unique values of x to find the best split, it draws the split value from a uniform distribution over the interval $[min(x), max(x)]$.

Survival analysis was conducted with python package PySurvival[2] by Fotso et al. (2019), which implements ML models described above, while plots were created by modifying the original functions of PySurvival with package seaborn 0.12.2.

First, dataset without collinear features was randomly split with a static seed into training and test sets (80%–20%) stratified by the column *event*. Then, optimal values of hyperpameters that maximized the performance were found through 5-fold cross-validation (*cv*) on training set [9, 12], as follows:

- **CPH**: $lr = $ 1e-04, $l2_reg = $ 1e-04, $init_method = $ 'zeros';
- **RSF**: $num_trees = $ 200, $max_features = $ 'sqrt', $min_node_size = $ 5;
- **CSF**: $num_trees = $ 200, $max_features = $ 'sqrt', $alpha = $ 0.07, $minprop = $ 0.1, $min_node_size = $ 5;
- **XST**: $num_trees = $ 200, $max_features = $ 'sqrt', $min_node_size = $ 5, $num_random_splits = $ 80.

The performance of ML algorithms was evaluated on test set with the concordance index (*c*-index) [23]. The *c*-index represents a generalization of the area under the ROC curve (AUC) for survival analysis models, which can take into account censored data. Its value provides the model discrimination power, and when it is close to 1, the model has an almost perfect discriminatory power, while if it is close to 0.5 (random prediction), it has no ability to discriminate between low- and high-risk subjects. Mean and standard deviation of *c*-index calculated with *cv* during hyperparameter tuning on training set was also reported. The Integrated Brier-score (IBS) [24] was used to evaluate the accuracy of predicted survival function across multiple timepoints on test set. It is calculated as the average squared distances between the actual survival status and the predicted survival probability, and its value is between 0 and 1, where 0 is for a perfect model while a

---

[2] https://square.github.io/pysurvival/.

cut-off limit of 0.25 is considered as critical [24]. Actual survival function was obtained using the Kaplan-Meier estimator and compared with predicted survival function through Root Mean Square Error (RMSE) and median/mean absolute error, as well as visually compared by plotting curves one against other.

Individual predictions done on test set by RSF, CSF and XST were used to manually stratify MCI patients in risk groups (low, medium, and high) according to their conversion to AD risk score. For each risk grade, the probability curve of conversion from MCI to AD per timepoint was calculated through the estimation of cumulative density function.

Feature importance on training set by the three tree-based approaches were estimated with normalized permutation and quantitatively compared with the Rank-Biased Overlap (RBO) [18]. RBO is a similarity measure between incomplete, top-weighted and indefinite rankings, which has been recently introduced for estimating the overlap between ML feature importance at different depths d (number of the top variables in the ranking) [19]. RBO assumes values in the range [0, 1], where 0 means disjoint, and 1 means identical.

3   Results

Demographic, clinical and imaging data of dataset prior to imputation were reported in Table 1, together with missingness percentage and statistical results. sMCI and pMCI patients had significantly different values in almost all features, except for age, gender, education level, RAVLT forgetting and ICV ($p > 0.05$).

Figure 1 depicts correlation matrix of complete dataset after imputation, (Fig. 1A) and of dataset without collinear features (Fig. 1B) used for ML analysis (22 features in total).

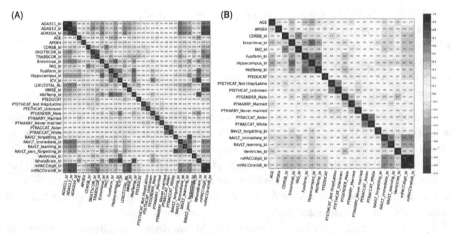

Fig. 1. Correlation matrix of (A) all original features; (B) features after removing redundant variables with $r > 0.6$ or $r < -0.6$.

ML algorithms showed similar and optimal values of c-index on test set and on training set with cv, although the best performance was obtained by RSF (0.87, 0.783 ± 0.03), followed by CSF (0.85, 0.781 ± 0.02) and XST (0.85, 0.782 ± 0.02), while CPH had the worst performance (0.83, 0.776 ± 0.03). IBS score were 0.14 for CPH, and 0.11 for RSF, CSF, and XST.

Table 1. Demographic, clinical and imaging data of sMCI and pMCI patients.

	sMCI (216)	pMCI (171)	Miss (%)	p-value
Age	74.8 ± 7.4	74.7 ± 6.9	0.0	0.65[a]
Gender (M/F)	144/72	105/66	0.0	0.28[b]
Education level	15.4 ± 3.1	15.8 ± 2.9	0.0	0.26[a]
APOE4 (0/1/2)	120/76/20	56/88/27	0.0	**<.001[b]**
CDRSB	1.4 ± 0.8	1.85 ± 0.9	0.0	**<.001[c]**
ADAS11	10.4 ± 4.3	13.1 ± 4.1	0.0	**<.001[c]**
ADAS13	16.7 ± 6.2	21.3 ± 5.4	0.77	**<.001[c]**
ADASQ4	5.5 ± 2.2	7.1 ± 1.9	0.0	**<.001[c]**
MMSE	27.3 ± 1.8	26.6 ± 1.7	0.0	**<.001[c]**
RAVLT_immediate	33.6 ± 9.9	27.3 ± 6.4	0.0	**<.001[c]**
RAVLT_learning	3.8 ± 2.5	2.7 ± 2.1	0.0	**<.001[c]**
RAVLT_forgetting	4.5 ± 2.4	4.9 ± 2.1	0.0	0.1[c]
RAVLT_perc_forgetting	59.3 ± 33.1	78.7 ± 26.9	0.25	**<.001[c]**
LDELTOTAL	4.6 ± 2.7	3.0 ± 2.7	0.0	**<.001[c]**
DIGITSCOR	38.8 ± 10.8	34.2 ± 10.8	0.25	**<.001[c]**
TRABSCOR	118.5 ± 64.8	147.2 ± 79.3	1.0	**<.001[c]**
FAQ	2.4 ± 3.5	5.5 ± 4.9	0.77	**<.001[c]**
mPACCdigit	-6.3 ± 3.1	-8.76 ± 2.8	0.0	**<.001[c]**
mPACCtrailsB	-6.4 ± 3.2	-8.86 ± 3.1	0.0	**<.001[c]**
Ventricles	42297.1 ± 24293.2	47201.5 ± 23132.8	1.5	**0.002[d]**
Hippocampus	6722.7 ± 1025.4	6014.1 ± 1020.9	19.1	**<.001[d]**
WholeBrain	1011262.1 ± 104469.7	980820.5 ± 113713.5	1.3	**0.008c**
Entorhinal	3548.8 ± 731.5	3015.9 ± 713.8	19.1	**<.001[d]**
Fusiform	16894.5 ± 2193.8	15733.7 ± 2471.7	19.1	**<.001[d]**
MidTemp	19597.4 ± 2678.6	17524.6 ± 2980.4	19.1	**<.001[d]**
ICV	1580838.1 ± 164668.7	1571086.5 ± 174884.8	0.0	0.928[c]
Occurrence of event/censorship (sMCI = 0, pMCI = 1) per time point (in months):				
m06	20	22		
m12	17	47		
m18	21	35		
m24	31	36		
m36	109	27		
m48	18	4		

[a] One-way ANOVA. [b] Chi-square test. [c] ANCOVA with age and gender in covariates. [d] ANCOVA with age, gender and ICV in covariates. In bold significant result at $p < 0.05$

It could be noted from plots comparing actual and predicted survival curves (Fig. 2 A-D on the left) that prediction accuracy of all models decreased while time progresses. In other words, predicted number of MCI patients at risk of AD differs more from actual number as timespan reaches 36 months after baseline visit. CPH had a drop in performance also between the 12th and 24th month. Regarding the prediction error per each timepoint (Fig. 2A-D on the right), CPH, RSF, CSF and XST never exceeded the IBS cut-off (dotted red line), although they all showed a global maximum at the 24th month.

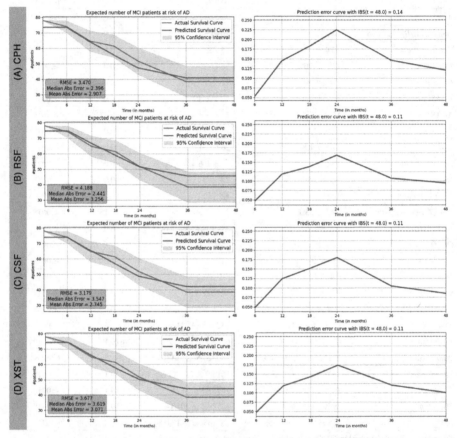

Fig. 2. Performance on test set of ML survival algorithms. Plots over time of expected number of MCI patients at risk of conversion to AD on the left and of prediction error curve calculated with integrated Brier score (IBS, critical cut-off limit of 0.25 in red) on the right. Root Mean Square Error (RMSE) and median and mean absolute error are also reported. (Color figure online)

The risk distributions provided by tree-based models together with the MCI patients stratification by risk grade were depicted in Fig. 3. Cumulative density functions showed that low-, medium- and high-risk groups had probabilities of conversion from MCI to AD within 48 months respectively of 21.4%, 41.9% and 76.9% according to RSF (Fig. 3A), 36.0%, 42.2% and 74.8% according to CSF (Fig. 3B), and 31.4%, 54.1% and 72.3% according to XST (Fig. 3C).

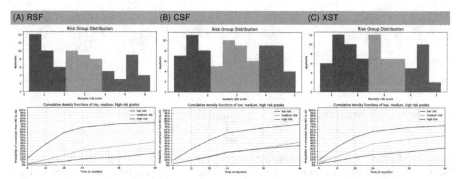

Fig. 3. Low- (in green), medium- (in orange) and high-risk (in red) groups distribution of (A) Random Survival Forest (RSF); (B) Conditional Survival Forest (CSF); (C) Extra Survival Trees (XST). Top: distribution of MCI patients based on their risk score of conversion to AD. Bottom: plot of cumulative density functions of risk grades, i.e., probability of conversion to AD over time per risk group. (Color figure online)

Feature importance rankings of tree-based survival models were reported in Fig. 4A, where the first ten features (FAQ, MidTemp, mPACCdigit, mPACCtrailsB, RAVLT immediate, Enthorinal, Fusiform, Hippocampus, CDRSB and RAVLT forgetting), were the same across algorithms, although in different order.

RBO curves of pairwise comparisons between feature importance by raising the depth d were depicted in Fig. 4B. The most similar variable rankings were those produced by CSF and XST (Fig. 4B in teal), with an overlapping of 100% when considering only the first feature (mPACCdigit) and a RBO above 80% up to the first ten variables. RSF variable ranking showed low similarity compared with both CSF (maximum of 66.3% with the first eight features, Fig. 4B yellow curve) and XST (maximum of 67.5% with the first eight features, Fig. 4B purple curve).

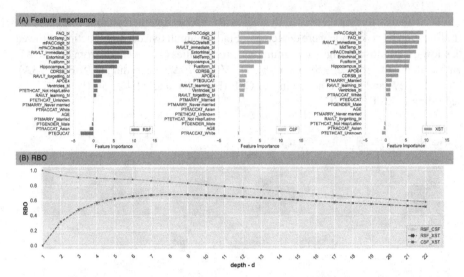

Fig. 4. (A) Feature importance (normalized permutation) of the tree-based survival algorithms, RSF, CSF and XST; (B) RBO curves of variable rankings comparison between RSF and CSF (in yellow), RSF and XST (in purple), CSF and XST (in teal), for increasing values of depth d, i.e. increasing number of important features considered. (Color figure online)

4   Discussion and Conclusions

In the present work, tree-based ML survival algorithms were applied on demographic, clinical and neuroimaging data for the prediction of time and risk of conversion from MCI to AD. We found that RSF had the highest accuracy (c-index 0.87) compared with CSF and XST (0.85), and all the tree-based models outperformed CPH (0.83). We stratified the MCI patients into low-, medium- and high-risk groups, where the high-risk patients had probability to progress to AD within 48 months comparable across models (> 72%). Moreover RSF, CSF and XST had similar feature importance rankings up to the first ten variables, as quantitatively assessed through RBO.

Our findings confirmed that ML survival models can improve the prediction power of CPH on dementia data [9, 10, 20, 21]. Moreover, our RSF accuracy (0.87) was higher than in similar studies on AD progression, 0.84 by [10], 0.75 by [20] and 0.831 by [21], while it was lower than in the work by Spooner et al. (0.93) [9], who used also longitudinal data rather than baseline data alone as in the present and other three studies. Here, RSF, CSF and XST models were robust and stable as showed by 5-fold cv c-index and by the low IBS score, but they had a drop of prediction accuracy between the 36th and 48th month after baseline visit (Fig. 2). This is probably due to the low number of event occurrences at the last two timepoints and to the imbalance between event and censorship occurrence (Table 1).

Regarding the stratification of MCI patients by risk grades, CSF model proved unable to separate the low and medium risk group, showing similar probability of conversion in all timepoints (Fig. 3B), suggesting the presence of two risk groups – low and high – rather than three. The stability of the three tree-based models was demonstrated also by their similarity in feature importance [19], where CSF and XST had the most similar rankings (RBO above 80%), while RSF had lower overlap with the other two models. In detail, the first ten predictive variables were similar across algorithms and consisted in six cognitive tests and four neuroimaging measures. As in Spooner et al. [9], we found that FAQ, mPACCdigit, mPACCtrailsB and RAVLT immediate were among the most important questionnaire and neuropsychological tests for assessing the time and risk of AD progression. FAQ evaluates instrumental activities of daily living, and it is used to differentiate MCI from AD since functional changes are found early in dementia. The mPACCdigit and test mPACCtrailsB measures respectively working memory and performance of processing speed, while RAVLT immediate assesses the total acquisition/learning in episodic memory [2]. The most important MRI derived measures were middle temporal gyrus, entorhinal, fusiform and hippocampus volumes, which are all brain regions well-known for their involvement in dementia [2].

Our work has two main limitations related to the dataset itself from ADNI. First limitation regards the variable *time*, which had imbalanced distribution of event/censorship occurrences per timepoint. Indeed, no study demonstrated the stability of tree-based ML survival approaches on imbalanced groups. Thus, we cannot exclude that the feature importance was biased toward the characteristics of the majority class (sMCI). The other issue related to the dataset is that we did not use longitudinal data of MCI patients to avoid high missingness, but we might expect an improvement of the prediction accuracy with features at different timepoints. As minor issue, it should be reported that ADNI provides MRI and demographics data with confounding factors such as different scanner and coil, as well as sex, age, and racial difference, thus a further study with harmonization is necessary to reduce this bias.

In conclusions, our findings suggested that ML survival methods represent a reliable tool for the prediction of time and risk to conversion from MCI to AD. Moreover, in addition to excellent performance, ML survival algorithms based on Random Forest as RSF, provide good interpretability of the findings through the feature importance, giving a characterization of the main demographic, clinical and neuroimaging variables associated with the AD progression.

References

1. Alzheimer's Association: 2018 Alzheimer's disease facts and figures. Alzheimer's & Dementia **14**, 367–429 (2018)
2. Sarica, A., et al.: MRI asymmetry index of hippocampal subfields increases through the continuum from the mild cognitive impairment to the Alzheimer's disease. Front. Neurosci. **12**, 576 (2018)
3. Mitchell, A.J., Shiri-Feshki, M.: Rate of progression of mild cognitive impairment to dementia–meta-analysis of 41 robust inception cohort studies. Acta. Psychiatr. Scand. **119**, 252–265 (2009)
4. Sarica, A., Cerasa, A., Quattrone, A.: Random forest algorithm for the classification of neuroimaging data in Alzheimer's disease: a systematic review. Front. Aging. Neurosci. **9**, 329 (2017)
5. Sarica, A., Cerasa, A., Quattrone, A., Calhoun, V.: Editorial on special issue: machine learning on MCI. J. Neurosci. Meth. **302**, 1–2 (2018)

6. Sarica, A., Quattrone, A., Quattrone, A.: Explainable boosting machine for predicting Alzheimer's disease from MRI hippocampal subfields. In: Mahmud, M., Kaiser, M.S., Vassanelli, S., Dai, Q., Zhong, N. (eds.) BI 2021. LNCS (LNAI), vol. 12960, pp. 341–350. Springer, Cham (2021). https://doi.org/10.1007/978-3-030-86993-9_31

7. Klein, J.P., Moeschberger, M.L.: Survival Analysis: Techniques for Censored and Truncated Data. Springer, New York (2003)

8. Cox, D.R.: Regression models and life-tables. J. Roy. Stat. Soc.: Ser. B (Methodol.) **34**, 187–202 (1972)

9. Spooner, A., et al.: A comparison of machine learning methods for survival analysis of high-dimensional clinical data for dementia prediction. Sci. Rep. **10**, 20410 (2020)

10. Orozco-Sanchez, J., Trevino, V., Martinez-Ledesma, E., Farber, J., Tamez-Peña, J.: Exploring survival models associated with MCI to AD conversion: a machine learning approach. bioRxiv 836510 (2019)

11. Breiman, L.: Random forests. Mach. Learn. **45**, 5–32 (2001)

12. Jung, J.O., et al.: Machine learning for optimized individual survival prediction in resectable upper gastrointestinal cancer. J. Cancer Res. Clin. Oncol. **179**, 1691–1702 (2022)

13. Chen, Z., et al.: Random survival forest: applying machine learning algorithm in survival analysis of biomedical data. Zhonghua yu Fang yi xue za zhi [Chin. J. Prev. Med.] **55**, 104–109 (2021)

14. Sarica, A.: Editorial for the special issue on "machine learning in healthcare and biomedical application." Algorithms **15**, 97 (2022)

15. Ishwaran, H., Kogalur, U.B., Blackstone, E.H., Lauer, M.S.: Random survival forests (2008)

16. Wright, M.N., Dankowski, T., Ziegler, A.: Unbiased split variable selection for random survival forests using maximally selected rank statistics. Stat. Med. **36**, 1272–1284 (2017)

17. Geurts, P., Ernst, D., Wehenkel, L.: Extremely randomized trees. Mach. Learn. 63, 3-42 (2006)

18. Webber, W., Moffat, A., Zobel, J.: A similarity measure for indefinite rankings. ACM Trans. Inf. Syst. (TOIS) **28**, 1–38 (2010)

19. Sarica, A., Quattrone, A., Quattrone, A.: Introducing the rank-biased overlap as similarity measure for feature importance in explainable machine learning: a case study on Parkinson's disease. In: Mahmud, M., He, J., Vassanelli, S., van Zundert, A., Zhong, N. (eds.) Brain Informatics. BI 2022. Lecture Notes in Computer Science, vol. 13406, pp. 129–139. Springer, Cham (2022). https://doi.org/10.1007/978-3-031-15037-1_11

20. Nakagawa, T., et al.: Prediction of conversion to Alzheimer's disease using deep survival analysis of MRI images. Brain Commun. **2**, fcaa057 (2020)

21. Mirabnahrazam, G., et al.: Alzheimer's disease neuroimaging, I.: predicting time-to-conversion for dementia of Alzheimer's type using multi-modal deep survival analysis. Neurobiol. Aging. **121**, 139–156 (2023)

22. Stekhoven, D.J., Buhlmann, P.: MissForest–non-parametric missing value imputation for mixed-type data. Bioinformatics **28**, 112–118 (2012)

23. Uno, H., Cai, T., Pencina, M.J., D'Agostino, R.B., Wei, L.-J.: On the C-statistics for evaluating overall adequacy of risk prediction procedures with censored survival data. Stat. Med. **30**, 1105–1117 (2011)

24. Steyerberg, E.W., et al.: Assessing the performance of prediction models: a framework for traditional and novel measures. Epidemiology **21**, 128–138 (2010)

Predicting Individual Differences from Brain Responses to Music: A Comparison of Functional Connectivity Measures

Arihant Jain[1]([⊠])⬭, Petri Toiviainen[2]⬭, and Vinoo Alluri[1]⬭

[1] International Institute of Information Technology, Hyderabad, Hyderabad, India
`arihant.jain@research.iiit.ac.in`
[2] Finnish Centre for Interdisciplinary Music Research, Department of Music, Art, and Culture Studies, University of Jyvaskyla, Jyväskylä, Finland

Abstract. Individual differences are known to modulate brain responses to music. Recent neuroscience research suggests that each individual has unique and fundamentally stable functional brain connections irrespective of task. Our study aims to identify individual differences such as gender and musical expertise from brain responses to music. Thirty-six participants' functional Magnetic Resonance Imaging (fMRI) responses were measured while listening to three 8-min-long musical pieces representing different musical styles. They were analyzed using various temporal and spectral functional connectivity (FC) measures. These FC measures were compared to identify the one that captured the most variation associated with gender and musical expertise. Subsequently, the measures were used to classify distinct population groupings using a binary Support Vector Machine (SVM). Our results revealed that Coherence, a spectral-domain FC measure, captured the maximum variation for musical stimuli. However, in classifying individuals based on gender and musical expertise, a composite measure outperformed any single measure and had above-chance accuracy. This suggests that each FC measure captures different aspects of the relationship between brain regions and is influenced by the level of analysis (group or individual) and the task, such as similarity analysis or classification. Further ramifications of the findings are discussed.

Keywords: Individual differences · fMRI · Naturalistic paradigm · Functional connectivity · Classification

1 Introduction

Individual differences such as age, gender, personality, musical expertise, and empathy are known to modulate responses to music. This has been observed both in behavioral studies as well as neuroimaging studies [2,6,19,27,31]. Studies have also shown that each individual has a unique functional brain network

F. Liu et al. (Eds.): BI 2023, LNAI 13974, pp. 191–202, 2023.
https://doi.org/10.1007/978-3-031-43075-6_17

that is dominated by common principles and individual features and is independent of the task they perform [18]. Gratton et al. (2018) also concluded that functional networks are suitable for measuring consistent individual features and hence can be used to identify an individual across activities. Mohanty et al. (2020) compared various measures that characterize the brain's functional connections for age-based classification and prediction of behavioral data. Since it has been established behaviorally and neurologically that individual differences dictate musical responses and hence preferences, one can hypothesize that we can identify these differences from neural responses. However, it has to be shown whether this holds in a naturalistic paradigm in which the subject performs a continuous task like music listening [3], simulating real-life experiences.

Gender differences in structural brain connections have been discovered in studies. Male brains are better at intrahemispheric communication, while female brains are better at interhemispheric communication [23]. These structural differences which arise at a young age translate to functional differences in adulthood. Few behavioral studies have looked into gender as a critical factor in determining musical preferences [19,27]. Evidence suggests that women prefer "softer" musical types like mainstream pop, while males prefer "harder" styles like rock [28]. This implies that such differences can manifest as differences in brain connectivity patterns during music listening. However, whether these gender differences can be predicted from brain responses to continuous music listening has to be shown.

Musical expertise is also known to cause structural and functional changes in the brain [2,4,13]. Musicians demonstrate changes in grey and white brain matter, which correlates with the onset and the intensity of training [22]. Several studies have identified differences in functional connectivity that arise due to musical expertise during continuous music listening [1,2,26]. To date, only one study has aimed at predicting the musicianship class of an individual from neural activations from naturalistic music listening [33]. However, their approach did not focus on functional brain connections or how brain regions functioned in an integrated manner.

Our study focuses on whether these unique functional brain networks can be used to identify individuals based on differences such as gender and musical expertise. We measure participants' functional magnetic resonance imaging (fMRI) responses while listening to musical pieces to study these differences in brain mechanisms. fMRI responses capture changes in blood oxygen level-dependent (BOLD) levels at the voxel level. We then study the interconnection between voxels via functional connectivity (FC). Traditionally, FC is defined as the similarity of brain signals from two regions, whether they possess direct anatomical connections. Signals from two anatomically separated brain regions may appear correlated under a traditional notion of similarity, such as Pearson's correlation, indicating that the regions are functionally connected in the brain [10,20,34,36]. However, recent studies have demonstrated that Pearson's Correlation alone does not provide complete FC characterization [25]. There exist several alternative measurements that can capture interactions between the brain in various ways. As a result, combining numerous complementing metrics or selecting a subset of them is a better alternative. We used nine FC measures that capture different aspects of statistical dependence, such as temporal and spectral domain information, similarities and dissimilarities, and linear and non-linear dependencies for our research. These measures were chosen to study which best captures the maximum variation of functional networks in brain responses to music. Subsequently, we compared these measures to identify which one best classified distinct population groups such as males-females, musicians-nonmusicians, and combined population groups.

2   Methods

2.1   Participants

The data set used was part of a broader project, "Tunteet," and is used in a range of previous studies [2,9,33,40]. It involves various tests and neuroimaging, and neurophysiological measures. Thirty-six healthy participants with no history of neurological or psychological disorders participated in the fMRI experiment. The participant pool consisted of 18 musically trained (9 females, age 28.2 ± 7.8 years) and 18 untrained participants (10 females, age 29.2 ± 10.7). The two groups were comparable for gender, age distribution, cognitive measures (Processing Speed and Working Memory Index Scores from the WAIS- WMS III), and socioeconomic status (Hollingshead's Four-Factor Index). The musicians' group was homogeneous regarding the duration of their musical training and years of active instrument playing.

2.2   Stimulus and Task

Participants were asked to listen to three instrumental pieces: (a) Adios Nonino by Astor Piazzolla (tango nuevo); (b) Stream of Consciousness by Dream Theater (progressive rock); and (c) Rite of Spring (comprising the first three episodes from Part I: Introduction, Augurs of Spring, and Ritual of Abduction) by Igor Stravinsky (modern classical). They are further referred to as stimuli 1, 2, and 3, respectively. Each piece belonged to a different genre (to allow for generalization of the obtained findings), did not contain lyrics (to avoid the confounding effects of semantics), and was roughly around 8 min long. Participants were also asked to rate their liking of each of the three pieces on a discrete 5-point scale.

2.3   fMRI Data Acquisition and Preprocessing

Participants' brain responses were acquired while listening to the musical stimuli presented in a counterbalanced order. Their only task was to attentively listen to the music delivered via MR-compatible insert earphones while keeping their eyes open. MRI data were collected at the Advanced Magnetic Imaging Centre, Aalto University, Finland. Thirty-three oblique slices (FoV: 192 mm × 192 mm,

64×64 matrix, interslice skip $= 0$ mm) were acquired every 2 s, with echo time $= 32$ ms and voxel size $= 2 \times 2 \times 2\,\text{mm}^3$ using a single-shot gradient echo-planar imaging (EPI) sequence, providing whole-brain coverage for each participant. fMRI scans were preprocessed on Matlab using SPM8, VBM5, and custom scripts. Normalization to MNI segmented tissue template was carried out. Head movement-related components were regressed out, followed by spline interpolation and filtering (Fig. 1).

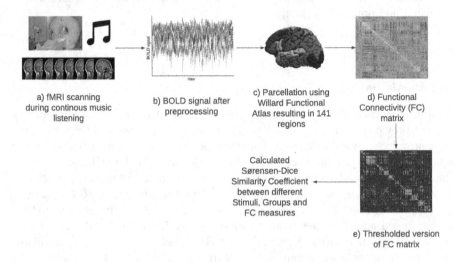

a) fMRI scanning during continous music listening

b) BOLD signal after preprocessing

c) Parcellation using Willard Functional Atlas resulting in 141 regions

d) Functional Connectivity (FC) matrix

Calculated Sørensen-Dice Similarity Coefficient between different Stimuli, Groups and FC measures

e) Thresholded version of FC matrix

Fig. 1. An overview of our similarity pipeline

2.4   Calculating FC Measures

BOLD time courses were extracted from preprocessed fMRI data for each stimulus in 141 regions based on a standard functional (Willard) Atlas [36]. We use various temporal and spectral measures to capture different statistical dependence aspects between two BOLD signals, including linear and non-linear dependencies, as described in Mohanty et al. (2020). We use the following temporal measures: Pearson's [15] and Spearman's Correlation [5], Cityblock, Euclidean and Earth Mover's Distance (EMD) [32], Cross-Correlation [8], Dynamic Time Warping (DTW) [29], and Mutual Information [35]; spectral measure Coherence [17]; and spectro-temporal measures: Instantaneous Phase Synchrony (IPS) [16] and Wavelet Coherence [21]. The measures were then compared across various stimuli to examine the consistency of information offered by the FC measures and their utility in determining individual differences.

For each FC measure, we obtain a symmetrical functional connectivity matrix of size 141×141 for each stimulus for each individual. Each entry in the matrix represents FC between the corresponding pair of brain regions. All the FC analyses were performed using MATLAB.

2.5   Similarity Coefficient Analysis

FC matrices were then averaged across multiple groups: a) 18 musicians, b) 18 non-musicians, c) 17 males, d) 19 females, and e) all 36 individuals to generate group-level mean FC matrices. Each element in the mean FC matrix was obtained by computing the mean of FC values in the cell of each of the corresponding individual matrices in the group. The mean group-level FC matrices were subsequently thresholded to obtain a binary adjacency matrix. We used four thresholding methods: a) standard deviation higher and lower than the overall mean (mean $\pm$ c*std, where c = 1 and 2) [25], and b) average degree thresholding (S = 2.5 and S = 4) [24,37,39].

The hence obtained binary adjacency matrices were then averaged across all the subjects and compared between three stimuli by calculating the Sørensen-Dice similarity coefficient [11,38]. We averaged FC matrices for three stimuli within groups (a) to (d) and compared musicians to non-musicians and males to females by calculating the same similarity coefficient. Additionally, we averaged across all stimuli and subjects for each FC measure and calculated the similarity coefficient to compare various FC measures (Fig.2).

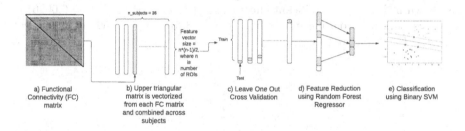

Fig. 2. An overview of our classification pipeline

2.6   Feature Selection and Classification

The upper triangular matrices (of size $\frac{n(n-1)}{2}$, where n = 141 regions) were used to generate feature vectors, which were combined across subjects (feature vector size = 36 x $\frac{n(n-1)}{2}$) to form the training data.

We employed leave-one-out cross-validation to maximize the size of the training dataset before performing feature selection. To reduce redundant features and noise, we applied feature selection using a Random Forest Regressor (RFR) [7,14] ensemble, which provides feature importance in terms of weights. RFR was performed with the default number of trees, implemented using Python's scikit-learn toolbox [30]. A meta-transformer (SelectFromModel) was used to select features based on their importance weights. The threshold value for feature selection was set to the mean weight.

Finally, we used a binary support vector machine (SVM) classifier from the scikit-learn toolbox for classification. The classification accuracy was calculated using the leave-one-out strategy. The average accuracy was determined by evaluating the classification label (i.e., musical expertise or gender) across all the left-out subjects. We repeated this process for each of the eleven FC measures and three stimuli and compared the results.

3   Results

3.1   Liking Ratings

We first examine differences in liking ratings specific to gender and musical expertise. To this end, we perform a non-parametric alternative to a two-way ANOVA called the permuted Wald-type statistic (WTP) [12] on the liking ratings wherein one factor represents gender while the other represents musical expertise. WTP was used because the liking ratings violated the normality and homogeneity of variance assumptions for parametric ANOVA. WTP analysis revealed a significant main effect of musical expertise across all three stimuli (QN = 5.877 for stimulus 1, QN = 4.89 for stimulus 2, QN = 5.699 for stimulus 3, all p < 0.05). As shown in Fig. 3a, a significant effect of gender (QN =10.622, p = 0.0026) is observed, and a borderline interaction (QN = 3.813, p = 0.059) with musical expertise for Stimulus 1.

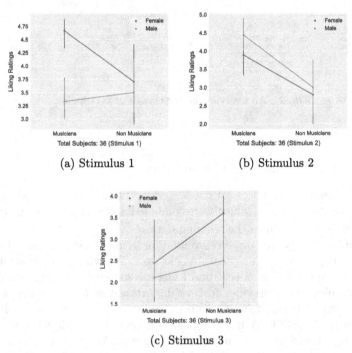

(a) Stimulus 1   (b) Stimulus 2

(c) Stimulus 3

Fig. 3. Point plot for liking ratings grouped by musical expertise and gender for all three stimuli.

Table 1. Similarities measured by Sørensen-Dice similarity coefficient between different stimuli and groups. **Note:** Threshold method used to generate adjacency matrices is mean ± std.

FC Measure	Stimulus			Mus vs NonMus	Males vs Females
	1 vs 2	2 vs 3	1 vs 3		
Cityblock Distance	0.88	0.89	0.89	0.83	0.81
Coherence	0.71	0.71	0.70	0.68	0.69
Cross Correlation	0.85	0.88	0.87	0.82	0.77
DTW	0.87	0.87	0.85	0.79	0.73
EMD	0.88	0.89	0.89	0.82	0.80
Euclidean Distance	0.89	0.89	0.89	0.83	0.81
IPS	0.74	0.74	0.74	0.70	0.71
Mutual Information	0.85	0.87	0.89	0.83	0.82
Pearson Correlation	0.82	0.84	0.83	0.78	0.78
Spearman Correlation	0.82	0.83	0.82	0.78	0.77
Wavelet Coherence	0.75	0.76	0.78	0.73	0.71

3.2 FC Similarities Between Different Stimuli, Groups and Measures

Overall, the results were highly consistent across different threshold methods, with minimal differences observed between the different methods. We report results for one standard deviation higher and lower than the mean FC value. As can be seen in Table 1, the spectral measure, Coherence, captures maximum variation, as evidenced by the low Sørensen-Dice coefficient. In contrast, the temporal measures show a more significant overlap. Additionally, it was noted that IPS followed Coherence and then Wavelet Coherence in terms of the level of similarity observed across different threshold methods. This pattern is similar across stimuli and groups.

Figure 4 shows a high similarity between Cityblock Distance, Earth Mover's Distance (EMD), and Euclidean Distance. They all are dissimilarity measures and calculate distances between two points, with EMD being an exception since it represents the minimum cost of converting one distribution into the other. The least similarity is observed between Cityblock Distance and Mutual Information, which suggests that they capture different aspects of functional connectivity. Pearson's and Spearman's Correlation are highly similar, as expected since they are both correlation-based measures. In addition, the spectral measure, Coherence, demonstrates high similarity with these two most commonly used temporal measures of FC.

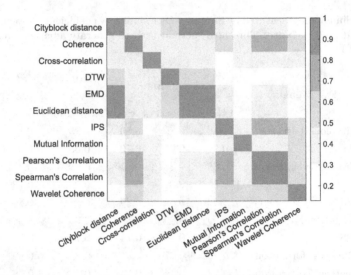

Fig. 4. Similarities measured by Sørensen-Dice similarity coefficient between FC measures averaged across all stimulus and subjects. Note: Threshold method used to generate adjacency matrices is mean ± std.

3.3   Classification

Fig. 5 shows the classification results. As can be seen, no single FC measure particularly performed consistently better than the rest. Furthermore, the composite method, which concatenates all FC measures, almost always had higher accuracy than individual measures. This is most likely because the composite measure includes additional FC measures, which could increase the discriminatory power of any one measure and produce more precise results.

Notably, in classifying individuals based on musical expertise, most functional connectivity measures perform better for stimulus 3 than others. For example, the Mutual Information achieves an accuracy of 66.67% for stimulus 3 but only 52.78% for stimulus 1 and 47.22% for stimulus 2. Similarly, EMD achieves an accuracy of 61.11% for stimulus 3 but only 52.78% for stimuli 1 and 2.

In classification based on gender, the composite measure has the highest accuracy across all three stimuli, with an average accuracy of 73.48%. The IPS measure also shows high accuracy, particularly for stimulus 2, where it achieves an accuracy of 72.22%. On the other hand, some measures like coherence and wavelet coherence have relatively low accuracy.

4   Discussion

Our study achieved comparable results to the non-FC-based approach on the same dataset in Saari et al. (2018), which reported a classification accuracy of 77%. Using functional connectome during continuous music listening to classify gender and musical expertise is a novel approach as it leverages the functional

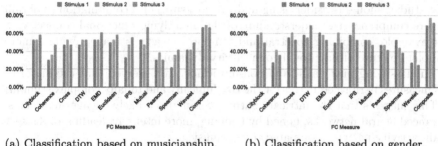

(a) Classification based on musicianship.   (b) Classification based on gender.

Fig. 5. Classification accuracy for all three stimuli and FC measures.

connectivity measures to capture different statistical dependencies between two BOLD signals, including linear and non-linear dependencies. Our exploration of several FC measures for the same also reveals novel insights. The findings are explained in the context of earlier research.

Behaviorally, the differences observed in liking ratings align with previous research. Precisely, the main effect of musical expertise on liking ratings for all stimuli reflects the findings from Greenberg et al. (2015), which concluded that musical preferences are a personality trait. Females preferred the tango (stimulus1) and modern classical (stimulus3) pieces over males, although males preferred the progressive rock piece (stimulus 2). This is in line with previous studies that have found that females prefer more "mellow" musical styles with negative emotions and greater emotional depth, while males tend to prefer "harder" or "intense" styles [19].

The spectral measure, Coherence, consistently demonstrated the least similarity and captured maximum variation across stimuli and groups compared to temporal measures. This suggests that different measures capture information that may vary depending on the task or activity carried out while capturing the brain responses. For instance, the low similarity in Coherence and other spectro-temporal measures (IPS and Wavelet Coherence) may suggest that these measures are better suited for capturing dynamic changes in functional connectivity over time. In contrast, temporal measures may better capture more stable, long-term functional connectivity. This suggests that for analyses at a group level, temporal measures provide a more reliable and robust characterization of the FC patterns. These measures can be used in further studies to minimize the impact of individual variations and highlight the significant features that define the group.

The comparison of all FC measures in classifying individuals based on gender and musical expertise aligns with the findings of Mohanty et al. (2020). There was no single FC measure that consistently outperformed others. However, a composite measure - a combination of all measures obtained by concatenation followed by a feature selection procedure was relatively more consistent and, in most cases, performed better than the rest of the measures. This suggests that studies should consider using multiple measures or a combination to obtain a more comprehensive understanding of the underlying functional connectivity. For example, combining spectral and temporal measures may provide a more complete picture of functional connectivity dynamics.

In classifying musicians from non-musicians, we observed that the majority FC measures performed better for the rhythmically and tonally complex stimulus 3. This suggests that the intricate nature of stimulus 3 likely engages musicians' advanced neural networks, honed by training, more intensely, leading to distinct brain activity patterns compared to non-musicians.

To conclude, while our research was confined to a dataset of 36 people, which also explains the low accuracy results of binary SVM-based classification, albeit employed in multiple previous studies to investigate various phenomena, it nevertheless was comparable to the existing methods of classifying musical expertise. This research can be expanded in the future to investigate which regions contribute to classification, shedding light on the essential functional connections related to musical expertise and gender.

References

1. Alluri, V., et al.: Musical expertise modulates functional connectivity of limbic regions during continuous music listening. Psychomusicology: Music Mind Brain 25(4), 443–454 (2015)
2. Alluri, V., Toiviainen, P., Burunat, I., Kliuchko, M., Vuust, P., Brattico, E.: Connectivity patterns during music listening: evidence for action-based processing in musicians. Hum. Brain Mapp. 38(6), 2955–2970 (2017)
3. Alluri, V., Toiviainen, P., Jääskeläinen, I.P., Glerean, E., Sams, M., Brattico, E.: Large-scale brain networks emerge from dynamic processing of musical timbre, key and rhythm. NeuroImage 59(4), 3677–3689 (2012)
4. Angulo-Perkins, A., Aubé, W., Peretz, I., Barrios, F.A., Armony, J.L., Concha, L.: Music listening engages specific cortical regions within the temporal lobes: differences between musicians and non-musicians. Cortex 59, 126–137 (2014)
5. Best, D.J., Roberts, D.E.: Algorithm AS 89: the upper tail probabilities of Spearman's rho. Appl. Stat. 24(3), 377 (1975)
6. Bonneville-Roussy, A., Rentfrow, P.J., Xu, M.K., Potter, J.: Music through the ages: trends in musical engagement and preferences from adolescence through middle adulthood. J. Pers. Soc. Psychol. 105(4), 703–717 (2013)
7. Breiman, L.: Random forests. Mach. Learn. 45(1), 5–32 (2001)
8. Buck, J.R., Daniel, M.M., Singer, A.: Computer explorations in signals and systems using MATLAB. Prentice Hall (2002)
9. Burunat, I., Brattico, E., Puoliväli, T., Ristaniemi, T., Sams, M., Toiviainen, P.: Action in perception: prominent visuo-motor functional symmetry in musicians during music listening. PLOS ONE 10(9), e0138238 (2015)
10. Damoiseaux, J.S., et al.: Consistent resting-state networks across healthy subjects. Proc. Natl. Acad. Sci. 103(37), 13848–13853 (2006)
11. Dice, L.R.: Measures of the amount of ecologic association between species. Ecology 26(3), 297–302 (1945)
12. Friedrich, S., Brunner, E., Pauly, M.: Permuting longitudinal data in spite of the dependencies. J. Multivar. Anal. 153, 255–265 (2017)

13. Gaser, C., Schlaug, G.: Brain structures differ between musicians and non-musicians. J. Neurosci. **23**(27), 9240–9245 (2003)
14. Geurts, P., Ernst, D., Wehenkel, L.: Extremely randomized trees. Mach. Learn. **63**(1), 3–42 (2006)
15. Gibbons, J.D., Chakraborti, S.: Nonparametric statistical inference. In: Lovric, M. (eds.)International Encyclopedia of Statistical Science, pp. 977–979. Springer, Heidelberg (2011). https://doi.org/10.1007/978-3-642-04898-2_420
16. Glerean, E., Salmi, J., Lahnakoski, J.M., Jääskeläinen, I.P., Sams, M.: Functional magnetic resonance imaging phase synchronization as a measure of dynamic functional connectivity. Brain Connectivity **2**(2), 91–101 (2012)
17. González, A.G., Rodríguez, J., Sagartzazu, X., Schumacher, A., Isasa, I.: Multiple coherence method in time domain for the analysis of the transmission paths of noise and vibrations with non stationary signals. In: Proceedings of ISMA 2010 (2010)
18. Gratton, C., et al.: Functional brain networks are dominated by stable group and individual factors, not cognitive or daily variation. Neuron **98**(2), 439–452 (2018)
19. Greenberg, D.M., Baron-Cohen, S., Stillwell, D.J., Kosinski, M., Rentfrow, P.J.: Musical preferences are linked to cognitive styles. PLOS ONE **10**(7), e0131151 (2015)
20. Greicius, M.D., Krasnow, B., Reiss, A.L., Menon, V.: Functional connectivity in the resting brain: a network analysis of the default mode hypothesis. Proc. Natl. Acad. Sci. **100**(1), 253–258 (2002)
21. Grinsted, A., Moore, J.C., Jevrejeva, S.: Application of the cross wavelet transform and wavelet coherence to geophysical time series. Nonlinear Process. Geophys. **11**(5/6), 561–566 (2004)
22. Imfeld, A., Oechslin, M.S., Meyer, M., Loenneker, T., Jancke, L.: White matter plasticity in the corticospinal tract of musicians: a diffusion tensor imaging study. NeuroImage **46**(3), 600–607 (2009)
23. Ingalhalikar, M., et al.: Sex differences in the structural connectome of the human brain. Proc. Natl. Acad. Sci. **111**(2), 823–828 (2013)
24. Laurienti, P.J., Joyce, K.E., Telesford, Q.K., Burdette, J.H., Hayasaka, S.: Universal fractal scaling of self-organized networks. Phys. A: Stat. Mech. Appl. **390**(20), 3608–3613 (2011)
25. Mohanty, R., Sethares, W.A., Nair, V.A., Prabhakaran, V.: Rethinking measures of functional connectivity via feature extraction. Sci. Rep. **10**(1), 1298 (2020)
26. Niranjan, D., Toiviainen, P., Brattico, E., Alluri, V.: Dynamic functional connectivity in the musical brain. In: Liang, P., Goel, V., Shan, C. (eds.) BI 2019. LNCS, vol. 11976, pp. 82–91. Springer, Cham (2019)
27. North, A.C.: Individual differences in musical taste. Am. J. Psychol. **123**(2), 199–208 (2010)
28. North, A.C., Hargreaves, D.J., O'Neill, S.A.: The importance of music to adolescents. Br. J. Educ. Psychol. **70**(2), 255–272 (2000)
29. Paliwal, K., Agarwal, A., Sinha, S.S.: A modification over Sakoe and Chiba's dynamic time warping algorithm for isolated word recognition. Sig. Process. **4**(4), 329–333 (1982)
30. Pedregosa, F., et al.: Scikit-learn: machine learning in Python. J. Mach. Learn. Res. **12**, 2825–2830 (2011)
31. Rentfrow, P.J., Gosling, S.D.: The do re MI's of everyday life: the structure and personality correlates of music preferences. J. Pers. Soc. Psychol. **84**(6), 1236–1256 (2003)

32. Rubner, Y., Tomasi, C., Guibas, L.J.: The earth mover's distance as a metric for image retrieval. Int. J. Comput. Vision **40**, 99–121 (2004)

33. Saari, P., Burunat, I., Brattico, E., Toiviainen, P.: Decoding musical training from dynamic processing of musical features in the brain. Sci. Rep. **8**(1), 708 (2018)

34. Salvador, R., Suckling, J., Coleman, M.R., Pickard, J.D., Menon, D., Bullmore, E.: Neurophysiological architecture of functional magnetic resonance images of human brain. Cereb. Cortex **15**(9), 1332–1342 (2005)

35. Shannon, C.E.: A mathematical theory of communication. Bell Syst. Tech. J. **27**(3), 379–423 (1948)

36. Shirer, W.R., Ryali, S., Rykhlevskaia, E., Menon, V., Greicius, M.D.: Decoding subject-driven cognitive states with whole-brain connectivity patterns. Cereb. Cortex **22**(1), 158–165 (2011)

37. Simpson, S.L., Bowman, F.D., Laurienti, P.J.: Analyzing complex functional brain networks: fusing statistics and network science to understand the brain. Stat. Surv. **7**, 1 (2013)

38. Sørensen, T., Sørensen, T., Biering-Sørensen, T., Sørensen, T., Sorensen, J.T.: A method of establishing group of equal amplitude in plant sociobiology based on similarity of species content and its application to analyses of the vegetation on Danish commons (1948)

39. Telesford, Q.K., Simpson, S.L., Burdette, J.H., Hayasaka, S., Laurienti, P.J.: The brain as a complex system: using network science as a tool for understanding the brain. Brain Connectivity **1**(4), 295–308 (2011)

40. Toiviainen, P., Burunat, I., Brattico, E., Vuust, P., Alluri, V.: The chronnectome of musical beat. NeuroImage **216**, 116191 (2020)

Multiplex Temporal Networks for Rapid Mental Workload Classification

Arya Teymourlouei[1](✉), Joshua Stone[2], Rodolphe Gentili[3], and James Reggia[1]

[1] Department of Computer Science, University of Maryland, College Park, MD 20742, USA
ateymo2@terpmail.umd.edu, reggia@umd.edu
[2] Department of Electrical and Computer Engineering, University of Maryland, College Park, MD 20742, USA
jstone14@terpmail.umd.edu
[3] Department of Kinesiology, University of Maryland, College Park, MD 20742, USA
rodolphe@umd.edu

Abstract. The automated classification of a participant's mental workload based on electroencephalographic (EEG) data is a challenging problem. Recently, network-based approaches have been introduced for this purpose. We seek to build on this work by introducing a novel feature extraction method for mental workload classification which uses multiplex networks formed from visibility graphs (VGs). The VG algorithm is an effective method for transforming a time series into a complex network representation. To analyze multivariate EEG time series, we construct multiplex temporal networks (MTNs), structures which contain the VGs of multiple EEG channels. We examine the tendency of layers in an MTN to share the same edges, referred to as layer entanglement. Using layer entanglement metrics as inputs, a support vector machine (SVM) classifier achieved an average 97% accuracy, 0.07 loss, and 99% F1 score in discrimination between two levels of cognitive workload based on EEG data. The findings presented here extend the findings from other recent studies that examined the prediction of mental workload. This work suggests that multiplex networks and layer entanglement can provide potential metrics for assessing mental workload with application to passive brain-computer interfaces.

Keywords: Multiplex network · layer entanglement · classification · mental workload · passive brain-computer interface (pBCI) · electroencephalography (EEG)

1 Introduction

Cognitive computational neuroscience has rapidly progressed with the use of functional brain imaging techniques, such as EEG, functional magnetic resonance imaging, and positron emission tomography [1]. Researchers have investigated many aspects of human cognitive and cognitive-motor behavior including learning, working memory, motor planning, and mental workload [2, 3]. In particular, the study of mental workload has

F. Liu et al. (Eds.): BI 2023, LNAI 13974, pp. 203–214, 2023.
https://doi.org/10.1007/978-3-031-43075-6_18

found applications in prosthetic devices [4], human-robot teaming [5], and passive brain-computer interfaces (pBCI) [6]. A pBCI makes use of brain dynamics to assess the cognitive state when performing a task. To ensure the usefulness of a robust pBCI, we require a method to classify the workload of a human user rapidly and accurately. In this research, we propose a novel method for workload prediction which studies the structural properties of multiplex temporal networks formed from EEG time series.

In recent work [7], we filtered EEG signals into five frequency ranges, and then transformed these signals into visibility graphs (VGs). The VG algorithm maps a univariate time series signal into a complex network. The random forest classifier that we used achieved a 92% accuracy. The approach in [7] differed from existing methods [6, 8, 9] in that the properties of the cortical signal were regionally extracted, as opposed to a representation that captures interactions between brain regions (known as functional connectivity).

The primary limitation of the work in [7] is that EEG classification was performed based on an entire 2.5-min signal. A robust pBCI must be able to classify mental workload in a much shorter period of time. A recent EEG study on pBCI performed online classification with 30 s of signal [6]. Another pBCI study used a windowed-means approach, taking 8 windows of 0.05 s each [8]. The existing graph-based methodology is not able to accurately discriminate workload in such a time frame. Therefore, we expand on the work in [7] by proposing a new feature extraction method for mental workload classification. The methodology addresses the problem by using 5-s fragments of publicly available EEG data for classification.

Our methodology is to form a structure which contains the VGs of EEG channels, defined as a multiplex temporal network (MTN). In this structure, all graphs have identical nodes, because they correspond to the same time points on the signal. Each VG in the MTN is defined as a layer of the structure. In this work, we examine the tendency of layers of the MTN to share the same edges. That is, two corresponding nodes in two different layers have the same edge connecting them. The property of common edges between graphs in the MTN is defined as *layer entanglement*. Layer entanglement quantifies the similarity of layers in the MTN. We compute several metrics related to layer entanglement and use them as features for a support vector machine (SVM) classifier. We demonstrate here that the new method's mental workload classification accuracy is high even though it is based on much shorter 5 s EEG samples.

2   Background

2.1   Mental Workload

The EEG examination of mental workload has primarily been conducted through the assessment of regional cortical activity by means of spectral power. Previous work has observed that greater levels of mental workload led to an elevation of theta power (4–8 Hz) and an attenuation of alpha power (8–13 Hz) in various cortical regions [9]. More recently, methods which use connectivity to investigate the brain dynamics underlying mental workload have been proposed [10]. These approaches consider functional networks, where nodes are understood as brain regions, and edges between nodes signify a relationship between the regions. An example is in [10], which investigated the betweenness centrality of a multiplex brain network using wavelet bicoherence. The results of [10] found an increase in mental workload leads to stronger brain connectivity in higher frequencies.

2.2 Brain-Computer Interfaces

BCI is defined as a system that collects brain dynamics, performs analysis, and translates them into a state which is sent to an output device for use [11]. There are two types of BCI, passive and active. In active BCI, the user aims to control an external device (e.g., a computer cursor) by modifying their own cortical dynamics. Conversely, in pBCI the brain dynamics are recorded and processed to monitor specific user's mental states and determine what action should be taken accordingly. This work focuses on pBCI. One of the main challenges of pBCI is having a robust method for determining the brain state of the user. In the case of mental workload and EEG, the pBCI must be able to use the EEG signals to determine whether the user's mental workload level is high or low. This entire decoding process (from signal collection to quantification) must be executed quickly to avoid any delay in the user's state assessment when completing the task.

2.3 Multiplex Networks

Multiplex networks are structures which contain multiple graphs, where each graph contains the same nodes (only edges differ). Each graph is represented as a layer of the multiplex network. Such structures are useful for many problems in neuroscience. In this work, the construction of graphs from EEG time series is done by the VG algorithm. In previous work, networks were restricted to univariate time series [7]. Each VG accounts for the signal of one EEG channel. However, it is common in EEG applications to use more than one electrode. In the cases where multiple electrodes are used, EEG signals are a multivariate time series problem. It is often more powerful to represent a multivariate time series as one network. Each layer of the network represents one of the time series. Multiplex networks allow for a more in-depth analysis of the interactions between layers in the network.

A simple example of a multiplex network with two layers is presented in Fig. 1. Each layer in this toy example contains seven nodes where each node represents a single data point of an associated time series (not defined here). An edge between two nodes is formed by the criterion imposed by the natural VG algorithm. Each layer in the network represents one VG, associated with one EEG time series. Two nodes in both layers having the same edge signifies that the corresponding time series have a similar structure at the location of those data points. The corresponding points need not be identical, just similar enough that an edge is formed in both time series. Since this is a multiplex network, both layers share identical nodes, only intra-layer edges vary. In Fig. 1, we see the notion of coupling edges between the same nodes across different layers. We do not consider them further here because they lack the intuitive meaning in some other applications.

Many of the structural properties which are unique to multiplex networks exploit coupling edges. An example is the multiplex clustering coefficient, defined in [12]. However, another powerful structural property is the number of edges which layers

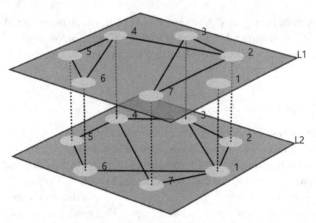

Fig. 1. A toy example of a multiplex network with two layers. Both layers of the network contain the same nodes, however edges in each layer can vary. Coupling edges (dashed lines) are presented for illustrative purposes, but our work does not consider them.

share – commonly called edge overlap or layer entanglement. In our example in Fig. 1, we see several edges are common between the two layers. The set $S = \{\{5, 6\}, \{5, 4\}, \{3, 2\}\}$ contains the edges which are common between the two layers (therefore, entanglement of $S = 3$). Entanglement is a structural property which does not require coupling edges; therefore, it is suitable for this problem. It is a measure of the similarity between layers in a multiplex network. In the context of this methodology, layer entanglement quantifies the similarity of the VGs.

3 Methodology

The entire methodology is summarized in Fig. 2.

3.1 Mental Workload Task

In a pBCI, the user uses the assistance of a computer system to complete a task. The guidelines for systems, assistance, and tasks vary greatly by the application of the pBCI. In the context of mental workload, the task generally involves lower-demand versus higher-demand mental states. Experimental designs will follow this paradigm by creating task designs where one condition seeks to elicit low mental workload, and other(s) seek to generate high(er) workload. A popular study which follows this model is the Simultaneous Task EEG Workload (STEW) dataset [13]. The STEW dataset was collected under a low and high workload where participants did not execute any task and performed the Simultaneous Capacity Multi-Tasking task (SIMKAP), respectively [13]. SIMKAP is a cognitive task which involves completing several tasks at once. The tasks were checking for matching numbers, checking a telephone book, and checking a calendar. For each participant in STEW, data was collected as three minutes of at-rest and in-task channel data. After data collection, 30 s were removed from both conditions for each participant [13]. The total remaining time was 150 s.

In the STEW dataset, the mental workload of the participants was evaluated using EEG to determine cortical activity. There were 14 electrodes used in data collection, which were AF3, AF4, F3, F4, F7, F8, FC5, FC6, P7, P8, T7, T8, O1, and O2. To reduce computational complexity, in our study features were only calculated for 10 of the 14 channels. AF3, AF4, FC5, and FC6 were omitted. Raw EEG data was preprocessed with a Butterworth filter (1–40 Hz) and linear trends were removed. The EEG signals were segmented into 5-s windows. Then, the five typical frequency bands (δ, θ, α, β, γ) were extracted by means of band-pass filtering.

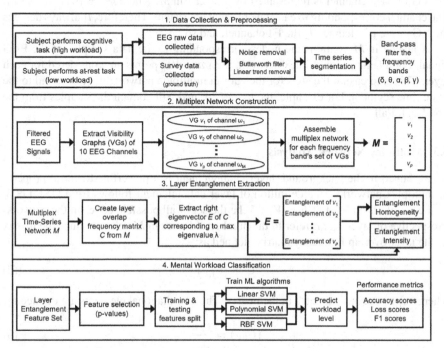

Fig. 2. Diagram of the methodology used for feature extraction. The collected EEG data is processed and prepared for transformation into graphs. The graphs for all channels are then assembled into an MTN, whose properties are extracted. These are fed to ML classifiers which then predict the level of workload taken by the EEG.

3.2 Network Construction

We use the natural VG algorithm to map an EEG signal into a network. VGs have been shown to effectively represent EEG signals of epilepsy [14], alcoholism [15], and mental workload [16]. The notion of visibility is intuitive. Two arbitrary samples on a time series have visibility if there is a straight line which connects them, which does not intersect any samples in between them. For a formal definition of visibility, we recall the original criterion from [17]. Consider two data points i and j, with associated values z_i and z_j, and an arbitrary point z_k. The data points i and j are represented as nodes in a graph, and are connected with a single edge if:

$$z_k < z_i + (z_j - z_i)\frac{k - i}{j - i} \ \forall \, k \in (i, j) \tag{1}$$

From this definition, we can construct VGs for each of the preprocessed EEG channels. To represent the VGs of multiple channels in one structure, a multiplex network is used. Let M be a multiplex network with 10 layers, one for the VG of EEG channel. Then, the VG of each channel is represented by a layer l in M, where $M = \{l_1, l_2, \ldots, l_{10}\}$. The channel corresponding to each layer is kept consistent. Therefore, l_1 always denotes the VG of the F3 channel, l_2 the F4 channel, and so on.

A layer l in M contains the nodes corresponding to the data samples of the EEG signal. For a temporal multiplex network, the *same* data points are considered for each layer. This is to ensure the VGs for the current multiplex network all correspond to the same time segment. For example, the first M formed will contain the samples from the first 5 s, for all layers.

3.3 Multiplex Network Analysis

As explained in the background, layer entanglement is a powerful structural property of multiplex networks. The definition of layer entanglement follows from [18]. Let V be the set of all nodes. Let $E = V \times V$ be the set of all possible edges in the network, irrespective of layer. Let L refer to the number of layers in M. We introduce the matrix C, the layer overlap frequency matrix, defined as:

$$C = \left(C_{l,l'}\right) \tag{2}$$

where $\left(C_{l,l'}\right)$ denotes an entry in the matrix. The non-diagonal elements are defined as:

$$\left(C_{l,l'}\right) = \frac{p_{l,l'}}{p_{l,l}} \tag{3}$$

where $p_{l,l'}$ refers to the number of edges that l and l' have in common, and $p_{l,l}$ refers to the number of edges in layer l. The diagonal elements of the matrix C are defined as:

$$\left(C_{l,l}\right) = \frac{p_{l,l}}{|E|} \tag{4}$$

where $|E|$ refers to the maximum possible number of edges in the layer l (this value would be the same for all layers, since all layers contain the same nodes). The layer entanglement vector is defined as the normalized, right eigenvector e associated with the *maximum* eigenvalue λ of the matrix C. An entry e_l in e is the entanglement of the layer l in M.

From the entanglement vector e and entanglement index λ, we can define several other measurements which extract more general observations of the multiplex network. These help to characterize the overall entanglement of a network (as opposed to e, where the entanglement values of each layer are isolated). The entanglement homogeneity, denoted *EH*, is a cosine similarity. It measures the similarity of the entanglement of each layer [12]. It is defined as:

$$EH = \frac{n \cdot e}{\|n\|\|e\|} \in [0, 1] \tag{5}$$

where $n = [1, 1, ..., 1]$ refers to a vector of size *L*. Entanglement intensity is a measure of the amount of edge overlap in a multiplex network. The entanglement intensity, denoted *EI*, is defined as:

$$EI = \frac{\lambda}{L} \tag{6}$$

The layer entanglement vector, entanglement homogeneity, and entanglement intensity are computed for the constructed MTNs. These three metrics are used as the inputs to the ML classifier, which is explained in Sect. 3.5. All graphs are directed. The direction of an edge is determined by the *y*-values of the associated data points, where the starting node always has the larger *y*-value.

3.4 Feature Selection

The multiplex network metrics introduced in the previous section form the features of our classification procedure. However, redundant features were first removed using a feature selection process. The data was evaluated for normality using a Shapiro-Wilk test. Features which followed a normal distribution were then tested for significance using a paired t-test. Otherwise, significance was assessed with a Wilcoxon test. Features which showed a statistically significant difference ($p < 0.01$) between low and high mental workload were selected as input to the ML algorithm.

3.5 Classification

Features were fed to an SVM classifier, using a 5-fold cross-validation procedure. SVM is a popular ML model for neuroscience applications [15, 16]. In the results, we used three variants of SVM. All parameters are the same except for the kernel function. The linear function, polynomial (degree = 3) function, and radial-based function (RBF) are used. All classifiers are implemented in Scikit-Learn [19]. The regularization parameter varied from 0.92–0.98, depending on the SVM variant. We evaluate the performance of the SVM using three metrics: accuracy, loss, and F1. The accuracy is the percentage of correct predictions. Loss measures the magnitude of incorrect predictions. The F1 score is the harmonic mean of the precision and recall of the ML model [19].

The goal of a prediction model in pBCI is to classify the mental workload of one participant only. Cross-participant classification is also generally avoided due to differences between participants. For these reasons, we separate the classification procedure for each participant (n = 48) in the STEW data [13]. Each participant completed 150 s of at-rest and in-demand tasks. We segment the 150-s signal into 5-s windows. So, for each participant, there are 30 windows to classify. This is done for both low and high workload, so in total, it will be 60 windows per participant, or a total of 2880 samples total. 5-fold cross validation is performed during classification.

4 Results

In the results sections we focus on the layer entanglement metrics as a discriminator between low and high mental workload. The classification performance is assessed. Figures were generated with Python 3.10.4 using Matplotlib [20] and Seaborn [21] plotting packages.

4.1 Classification Performance

In this section we study the performance of three different SVM-based classifiers (variations of the kernel; linear, polynomial, radial-based function) trained to predict two levels of mental workload. All three figures presented in this section use point plots to illustrate the performance distribution for all STEW participants [21]. The position of the dot represents the mean value (accuracy, loss, or F1 score). The error bars indicate the standard error from the mean [21]. To reduce the Type I error, the false discovery rate (FDR; *Benjamini–Hochberg* procedure) was employed to correct for multiple comparisons. Figure 3 presents the point plot for accuracy scores of the three ML classifiers.

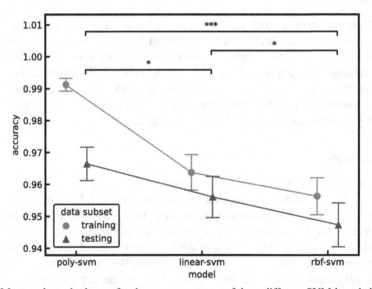

Fig. 3. Mean and standard error for the accuracy scores of three different SVM-based classifiers (variations of the kernel; linear, polynomial, radial-based function) to predict mental workload. Scores are computed for each participant (n = 48). 5-fold cross-validation is used. Statistical significance is denoted as follows: $*p < 0.05$, $***p < 0.001$.

Figure 3 depicts the average accuracy of the SVM with the polynomial kernel is near 97% for testing data. The SVM with the linear kernel had an average testing accuracy of 95.6%. The SVM with the RBF kernel an average accuracy of 94.7% using testing data. There was a slightly significant decrease in testing accuracy between polynomial and linear SVM ($p = 0.012$) and linear and RBF SVM ($p = 0.034$). There was a more significant decrease in testing accuracy from polynomial to RBF SVM ($p = 0.0006$).

In Fig. 4, the mean loss scores for both training and testing data are shown to be below 0.1 for the polynomial SVM. The SVM with the linear kernel had an average testing loss of 0.25. The average testing loss was 0.20 for the SVM with RBF kernel. There was a statistically significant increase in testing loss between the polynomial and linear SVM ($p < 0.0001$) and polynomial and RBF SVM ($p < 0.0001$). A slight decrease in testing loss was also observed from linear to RBF SVM ($p = 0.042$).

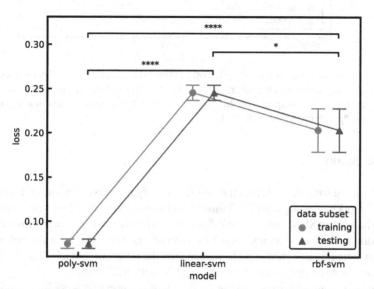

Fig. 4. Mean and standard error for the loss scores of three different SVM-based classifiers (variations of the kernel; linear, polynomial, radial-based function) to predict mental workload. Scores are computed for each participant (n = 48). 5-fold cross-validation is used. Statistical significance is denoted as follows: *$p < 0.05$, ****$p < 0.0001$.

Figure 5 depicts that the F1 scores were high for all three variants of the SVM. The SVM with the polynomial kernel had an average testing F1 of 99%, and for the linear kernel it was 96.3%. For the SVM trained with RBF kernel, the testing F1 score was 95.8%. For both training and testing data, the polynomial SVM had the least standard error. Comparison of F1 scores in testing data between linear and RBF SVM ($p = 0.032$) showed a slightly significant decrease. There was a much more significant decrease in testing F1 scores between polynomial and linear SVM ($p < 0.0001$) and polynomial and RBF SVM ($p < 0.0001$).

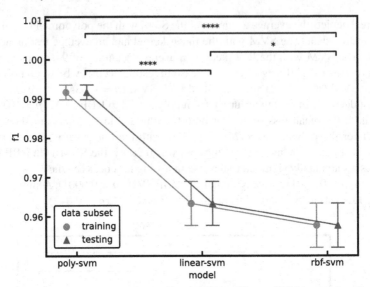

Fig. 5. Mean and standard error for the F1 scores of three different SVM-based classifiers (variations of the kernel; linear, polynomial, radial-based function) to predict mental workload. Scores are computed for each participant ($n = 48$). 5-fold cross-validation is used. Statistical significance is denoted as: $*p < 0.05$, $****p < 0.0001$.

5   Discussion

In this work we have introduced a method for classifying between a low and high level of mental workload using a 5-s EEG time period and reported the results obtained using three variants of an SVM classifier. We demonstrated that our method performs well with three scoring metrics (accuracy, loss, F1). Overall, the results suggest the polynomial SVM had a significantly better performance than the other two models. The SVM with linear kernel also slightly outperformed the SVM with RBF kernel.

In this work, we addressed a major limitation of our previous work [7], that the processing time window for classification was too large, thus preventing any future pBCI applications which require small processing time periods. The results of this methodology extend previous studies that focused on predicting the changes in mental workload [6, 7, 15]. Critically, the proposed approach exceeded the performance of some previous prediction models. For example, the study in [6] had an average accuracy of 75%, whereas here we recorded 97%. In our own previous work, the best accuracy we achieved was 92% [7].

The purpose of this work is to enable rapid classification of mental workload, for use by pBCI. This has many clinical and biomedical applications. For example, it was previously suggested that in space exploration, workload is one of the factors impacted by long-term space habitation [22]. Another prior work suggested that environmental factors in space may be responsible for astronauts' difficulty in maintaining high cognitive performance [23]. Thus, pBCI may be able to serve as a countermeasure to the challenges faced by astronauts related to cognition and workload.

While our results are encouraging in terms of using the ML approach taken here for real-time pBCI applications, there are still some remaining challenges. One concern is the number of layers in the MTNs, which corresponds to the number of EEG channels used. The computational complexity of computing MTN-based metrics increases significantly when the number of layers becomes significantly large. Specifically, the computation of the number of overlapping edges between two layers in the MTN is an $O(n)$ operation (n = number of edges). So, it may be beneficial to reduce the number of EEG channels processed for classification. However, this can lead to reduced ML performance. In addition, the layer entanglement metrics must be tested on other cognitive and cognitive-motor tasks to determine its effectiveness in other scenarios. In practical applications, it may prove useful to classify the mental workload into more than two classes.

Future efforts should focus on testing the use of layer entanglement as a biomarker to classify in real-time various levels of mental workload to verify whether it can be used in pBCI. Also, layer entanglement could be complemented by other EEG features resulting in multiple markers to provide a robust prediction model of mental workload. Beyond BCI applications, the method introduced here also can also serve in a more basic science context to examine the cognitive-motor mechanisms underlying mental workload to further understand the human adaptive behavior.

Acknowledgments. This work was supported by funding from the Maryland Space Grant Consortium and the University of Maryland College of Computer, Mathematical, and Natural Sciences Alumni Network.

References

1. Kriegeskorte, N., Douglas, P.: Cognitive computational neuroscience. Nat. Neurosci. **21**(9), 1148–1160 (2018)
2. Sylvester, J., Reggia, J., Weems, S., Bunting, M.: Controlling working memory with learned instructions. Neural Netw. **41**, 23–38 (2013)
3. Hauge, T., Katz, G., Davis, G., Huang, D., Reggia, J., Gentili, R.: High-level motor planning assessment during performance of complex action sequences in humans and a humanoid robot. Int. J. Soc. Robot. **13**(5), 981–998 (2021)
4. Gaskins, C., et al.: Mental workload assessment during simulated upper extremity prosthetic performance. Arch. Phys. Med. Rehabil. **99**(10), e33 (2018)
5. Edmonds, M., et al.: A tale of two explanations: enhancing human trust by explaining robot behavior. Sci. Robot. **4**(37), eaay4663 (2019)
6. Aricò, P., et al.: Adaptive automation triggered by EEG-based mental workload index: a passive brain-computer interface application in realistic air traffic control environment. Front. Hum. Neurosci. **10**, 539 (2016)
7. Teymourlouei, A., Gentili, R., Reggia, J.: Decoding EEG signals with visibility graphs to predict varying levels of mental workload. In: 57th Annual Conference on Information Sciences and Systems, IEEE (2023)
8. Zander, T., et al.: Evaluation of a dry EEG system for application of passive brain-computer interfaces in autonomous driving. Front. Hum. Neurosci. **11**, 78 (2017)
9. Shaw, E., et al.: Cerebral cortical networking for mental workload assessment under various demands during dual-task walking. Exp. Brain Res. **237**, 2279–2295 (2019)

10. Makarov, V., et al.: Betweenness centrality in multiplex brain network during mental task evaluation. Phys. Rev. E **98**(6), 062413 (2018)
11. Shih, J., Krusienski, D., Wolpaw, J.: Brain-computer interfaces in medicine. Mayo Clin. Proc. **87**(3), 268–279 (2012)
12. Battiston, F., Nicosia, V., Latora, V.: Structural measures for multiplex networks. Phys. Rev. E **89**(3), 032804 (2014)
13. Lim, W., Sourina, O., Wang, L.: STEW: Simultaneous task EEG workload data set. IEEE Trans. Neural Syst. Rehabil. Eng. **26**(11), 2106–2114 (2018)
14. Zhu, G., Li, Y., Wen, P.: Analysing epileptic EEGs with a visibility graph algorithm. In: International Conference on Biomedical Engineering and Informatics, pp. 432–436 (2012)
15. Zhu, G., Li, Y., Wen, P., Wang, S.: Analysis of alcoholic EEG signals based on horizontal visibility graph entropy. Brain Inform. **1**(1), 19–25 (2014)
16. Zhu, G., Zong, F., Zhang, H., Wei, B., Liu, F.: Cognitive load during multitasking can be accurately assessed based on single channel electroencephalography using graph methods. IEEE Access **9**, 33102–33109 (2021)
17. Lacasa, L., Luque, B., Ballesteros, F., Luque, J., Nuno, J.: From time series to complex networks: the visibility graph. Proc. Natl. Acad. Sci. **105**(13), 4972–4975 (2008)
18. Škrlj, B., Renoust, B.: Layer entanglement in multiplex, temporal multiplex, and coupled multilayer networks. Appl. Netw. Sci. **5**(1), 1–34 (2020)
19. Pedregosa, F., et al.: Scikit-learn: Machine learning in Python. J. Mach. Learn. Res. **12**, 2825–2830 (2011)
20. Hunter, J.: Matplotlib: A 2D graphics environment. Comput. Sci. Eng. **9**(03), 90–95 (2007)
21. Waskom, M.: Seaborn: Statistical data visualization. J. Open Source Softw. **6**(60), 3021 (2021)
22. De la Torre, G.: Cognitive neuroscience in space. Life **4**(3), 281–294 (2014)
23. Mhatre, S., et al.: Neuro-consequences of the spaceflight environment. Neurosci. Biobehav. Rev. **132**, 908–935 (2022)

Super-Resolution MRH Reconstruction for Mouse Models

Juhyung Ha[1], Nian Wang[2,3], Surendra Maharjan[2], and Xuhong Zhang[1(✉)]

[1] Computer Science Department, Luddy School of Informatics, University of Indiana, Bloomington 47408, USA
{juhha,zhangxuh}@indiana.edu
[2] Department of Radiology and Imaging Sciences, Indiana University, Indianapolis 46202, USA
{nianwang,smaharj}@iu.edu
[3] Stark Neurosciences Research Institute, Indiana University, Indianapolis 46202, USA

Abstract. Magnetic Resonance Imaging (MRI) has been widely used in pathology research and plays a vital role in clinical diagnoses. However, obtaining high-resolution MRI stays a significant challenge as the process is restrained by the hardware capacity, sampling time, signal-to-noise ratio (SNR), and subject comfort. Compared to MRI, Magnetic Resonance Histology (MRH) is more costly as it has a higher spatial resolution. Deep learning models have recently succeeded in MRI Super-Resolution (SR) reconstruction from Low-Resolution (LR) images. However, it is still hard to overcome artifacts during the restoration process. The models usually have limitations in the high-frequency component representations, which can reflect finer details as in MRH images. In this work, we propose an imaging restoration framework that can conduct SR reconstruction for the whole mouse brain MRH images, and the model is based on a deep dense network. We first synthesized LR images from HR ones to train the proposed model, and then we quantitatively compared the model performance with existing methods proposed for the human brain and natural images. Finally, we demonstrated the superior visual reconstruction and interpretation of the proposed model compared to prior works.

Keywords: MRH · MRI · Whole Mouse Brain Image · Super-resolution · Image Restoration · Dense Networks

1 Introduction

Brain connectomes encode information from many sources (synapses, neurons, axons) over many scales (nanometer to millimeter) and have tremendous potential to advance our knowledge of the brain [2, 29]. Because of the importance of connectomes in characterizing the structural and functional relationships among the brain's partitions, the connectome is an active area of investigation in brain research [3,28]. Recent advances in clinical MRI have produced more efficient imaging protocols, novel image processing, and statistical learning algorithms using independent, multiscale approaches to interrogate and validate functional and structural connectomes in the brain [42,53,55]. In animal studies, magnetic resonance histology (MRH) has recently been used to bridge the gap between MR and retroviral injection by acquiring a mesoscale connectome of the whole mouse brain at a spatial resolution more than 12,000 times greater than the resolution used in the best human Diffusion Tensor Imaging (DTI) studies [6], which is one of the most popular MRI techniques in brain research as well as in clinical practice. However, using a specially fixed postmortem mouse specimen, it can take up to 10 days to scan the subject continuously and undisturbed in a 9.4 T magnet [42], and a 10-day scan cannot serve as a routine protocol. Extensive studies have been conducted in both clinical and preclinical domains on the complex tradeoffs between the spatial resolution, the number of samples in diffusion q-space, scan time, and the reliability of the resultant data.

More recently, deep-learning-based models have been developed to convert LR MRI images to their SR counterparts for natural images [9,10]. In the biomedical field, many works focused on human brain image conversions [11–13,21,31–38,40,56]. Recently, authors in [5] utilized RealESRGAN to conduct resolution conversion, and RealESRGAN is one of our baseline models. Human brain MRI images usually have much lower resolutions than MRH, and most are at a scale of mm^3. Technically, methods proposed for SR reconstruction on the human brain can be summarized into two groups: Generative Adversarial Network (GAN) [14]-based and non-GAN-based models. By conducting a clinical evaluation on GAN-based and non-GAN-based methods, the authors of [38] found there was a quality trade-off for anatomical structures and lesions: with the GANs being more accurate in restoring images of anatomical structures but less accurate in restoring lesions, while non-GANs showed the opposite tendency. Compared to the human brain image conversion, there are fewer works on animal models, and the limited number of works are more focused on microscopy and pathology images [19,30,39,57].

In this work, we propose a framework that can restore whole mouse brain SR images from LR ones. At the same time, comparing the existing methods, the proposed work can handle the high-frequency components better by adopting a dense-block-based network architecture. We also adopted spectral normalization [27] to stabilize the training dynamics.

The main contributions of this paper are as follows: 1) To our best knowledge, this is a pioneering work on SR image restoration based on MRH images of whole mouse brain models. The techniques for our data acquisition are different from conventional MRI techniques, which makes our imaging data with very high spatial resolution and accuracy; 2) Extensive experiments show the superior image quality of the proposed method compared to existing models based on a recently proposed metric [54], which matches more human judgments comparing to traditional metrics. Additionally, a human expert confirmed this conclusion. Codes will be publicly available.

2 Dataset

Data Acquisition. Animal experiments were carried out in compliance with the Indiana University Institutional Animal Care and Use Committee. Six WT mice and five 5xFAD mice (Jackson Laboratory, Bar Harbor, ME) were used for image scans [44,45]. MR images of the specimens were acquired on a 30-cm bore 9.4T magnet (Bruker BioSpec 9430, Billerica, MA) with a maximum gradient strength of 660 mT/m on each axis. A high-sensitivity cryogenic RF surface receive-only coil was used for signal reception (Bruker CryoProbe) [8]. A 3D gradient echo (GRE) pulse sequence was used for acquisition. The scans were performed at the spatial resolutions of 50 μm^3 and 25 μm^3 [26], and we take the 25 μm^3 ones as the ground truth with HR.

Image Registration. We conducted the image registration process for the HR images through a post-acquisition pipeline. The MR images were registered to the mouse brain atlas using Advanced Normalization Tools (ANTs), described in our previous studies in detail [46–48].

3 Methodology

The synthesized images will be used for downstream analysis like neurodegenerative analysis. The quality can impact the diagnostic decision-making. Therefore, good image synthesis for our application should capture both resolution and contrast difference between LR and HR images in global, low-frequency contrast, and local, high-frequency details. Notably, it is critical to capture small structural changes in the brain and reconstruct the multi-frequency image details without introducing artifacts. To achieve these goals, we chose to adopt the residual-in-residual dense block (RRDB) [43] for the base blocks used in the model, which is also the basic building block for the baseline model RealESR-GAN [50]. The entire framework includes two component: a Dense Network as the image generator network and a Convolution Neural Network (CNN) as an image discriminator.

3.1 Proposed Method

The proposed model is based on residual-in-residual dense block (RRDB) [43], as shown in Fig. 1. Additionally, we adopted the GAN-network-based training strategy, which includes a discriminator network to distinguish authentic real images from synthesized ones. The discriminator network can help the generator to synthesize high-quality SR images.

Dense Block Based Image Generator. The RRDB [43] was designed intentionally to remove the batch normalization as it can introduce unpleasant artifacts and limit the generalization ability. In our framework, we incorporated

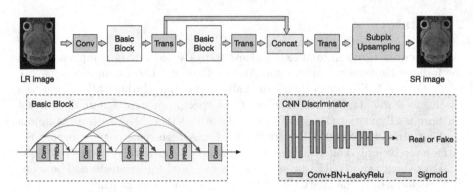

Fig. 1. An overview of the proposed SR network for MRH images. The framework contains 2 basic dense blocks which have multiple residual connections. It also has components for feature map compression, concatenation and also upsampling. The framework can output SR images with high quality.

2 basic blocks, which combine multi-level residual network and dense connections. Additionally, there are 3 "trans" components and 1 "concat" component. The "trans" component can comprise the input feature map along its channel, and the "concat" component can concatenate two feature maps. Before the last output layer, we did a sub-pixel upsampling. The upsampling component will produce an output SR image with the desired size.

CNN Based Image Discriminator. A discriminator network is adopted in our framework during the training process to recognize synthesized images from the real ones. This network consists of a sequence of multiple convolutional layers and fully connected layers. The convolutional layers first create 2D feature maps based on the input images, then flatten the feature maps to 1D vectors. Finally, fully connected layers take the 1D vectors as input and generate binary classification outputs.

Objective Function. We included the following losses in the model training process: pixel loss, perceptual loss [18] and adversarial loss. The pixel loss is an L2 loss between the generated SR image and HR ground truth. The perceptual loss is an L2 loss between feature maps of VGG19. The adversarial follows definition in [14].

3.2 K-Space Image Degradation

K-space truncation is often applied to realistically generate synthetic low-resolution images as matching pairs of high-resolution ones [23]. The method is an extension of the concept of Fourier space well known in MR imaging, where the center of k-space holds low-spatial-frequency information (image contrast). In contrast, the periphery of k-space contains high-spatial-frequency information (image details). This method has been widely used for many applications in the medical imaging field [4,16,23,24]. Here we also adopted this image degradation to generate paired low-resolution images for the 25 μm^3 ones. Then the synthetic ones were used for model training and representation learning purpose. In this application, we synthesized a 100 μm^3 counterpart image for each 25 μm^3 slice, and the scaling factor is 4× (as for brain MRI, 100 μm^3 is a common image resolution [7,51,52]).

3.3 Baseline Models

To make a better evaluation of the proposed method, we conducted the same experiments with the following baseline models: MedSRGAN [15] and SuperMRI [22], which are recently proposed to perform SR tasks on medical images; Additionally, we compared our proposed model with the state-of-the-art method for natural image SR, RealESRGAN [50].

- **MedSRGAN**: The model includes a Residual Whole Map Attention Network (RWMAN) as its generator network for extracting valuable information through different channels, as well as paying more attention to meaningful regions. In addition, a weighted sum of losses were fused to form a multi-task loss function during the MedSRGAN training. The model was trained and evaluated on 242 thoracic CT scans and 110 brain MRI scans.
- **SuperMRI**: This recent work incorporates feature-importance and self-attention methods to improve the model interpretability. The model combines the advantages of both CNNs and GAN-based networks [14], and those of data fusion, to upsample clinical low-resolution whole MRI scans. The data fusion schema can simultaneously upsample three MRI sequences, including T1-weighted, T2-weighted, and fluid-attenuated inversion recovery.
- **RealESRGAN**: The model was proposed to overcome multiple real-world imaging degradations and artifacts. The low-resolution imaging synthesis process includes leveraging classical and also high-order degradation models. The high-order models aim to combat unknown noises and complex artifacts. This model has been widely used for image super-resolution tasks [5,41,58].

3.4 Evaluation Metrics

We evaluated our proposed model against the following metrics: SSIM, MS-SSIM, PSNR, UIQI [49], and LPIPS [54]. Let an image size be $N \times N$,

- Structural Similarity Index Measure (**SSIM**): SSIM is used to measure the similarity between two images. Suppose μ_x, σ_x^2 are the mean and variance of window x, and μ_y, σ_y^2 are the mean and variance of window y. σ_{xy} is the covariance of x and y. c_1 and c_2 are two small numerical values to stabilize the division. Then SSIM is defined as:

$$\text{SSIM}(x,y) = \frac{(2\mu_x\mu_y + c_1)(2\sigma_{xy} + c_2)}{(\mu_x^2 + \mu_y^2 + c_1)(\sigma_x^2 + \sigma_y^2 + c_2)} \tag{1}$$

- Multi-scale Structural Similarity Index Measure (**MS-SSIM**): MS-SSIM is an advanced form of SSIM conducted over multiple scales through multiple stages of sub-sampling.
- Peak Signal-to-Noise Ratio (**PSNR**): Let MSE be the mean squared error, and PSNR (in dB) is then defined based on MSE:

$$PSNR = 20 \cdot \log_{10}(MAX_I) - 10 \cdot \log_{10}(MSE) \tag{2}$$

with MAX_I is the maximum possible pixel value of the image. PSNR is commonly used to quantify reconstruction quality for images and video subject to lossy compression.
- Universal Image Quality Index (**UIQI**): The UIQI aims to model any image distortion as a combination of three factors: loss of correlation, luminance distortion, and contrast distortion. The UIQI is defined based on the means and variances of the two compared images:

$$UIQI = \frac{4\sigma_{xy}\mu_x\mu_y}{(\sigma_x^2 + \sigma_y^2)(\mu_x^2 + \mu_y^2)} \tag{3}$$

The dynamic range of **UIQI** is $[-1,1]$, and the best value 1 is achieved when the two images are identical.
- Learned Perceptual Image Patch Similarity (**LPIPS**): The authors in [54] proposed a new metric for image quality evaluation because of disagreement between human judgments and traditional metrics, like PSNR, SSIM, FSIM, etc. They then presented LPIPS based on high-level features learned from deep neural networks, and details can be found in [54].

The first three metrics are commonly used for bio-medical images, and the fourth one is more popular for natural image evaluation.

4   Experiments and Results

With the synthesized LR images, we trained our proposed model on 4 Nividia A60 GPUs. The image size of each mouse sample is $512 \times 720 \times 304$, and the model was implemented with PyTorch packages. After around 700 epoch iterations, the model converges.

4.1   Implementation Details

The proposed model was trained for $1,000$ epoches with an image batch size of 24. Each training batch consisted of randomly selected pairs of downsampled input and target images with a size of 24×24 and 96×96 respectively. We adopted the Adam optimizer [20] with a starting value of 0.001. For loss calculation, we adopted the pixel-wise mean absolute error loss, VGG perceptual loss, and adversarial loss with corresponding weights at 1.0, 1.0 and 0.01. Our generator was configured with 64 as the base number of channels for each basic block, as shown in Fig. 1, and incorporated 8 modules within these basic blocks. We adopted Parametric Rectified Unit (PRElu) as the activation function.

During the experiments, we explored several normalization methods, including batch normalization [17], layer normalization [1], and spectral normalization [25]. We found that spectral normalization can stabilize the training process, so we adopted it for our task. The model needs to conduct an upsampling at the final output layer as it converts low-resolution images to high-resolution ones, and we adopted pixel shuffling to reduce artifacts like checkerboard artifacts. We adopted the 5-fold cross-validation strategy for the model training process.

4.2 Quantitative Analysis for Model Performance Comparison

We compared our proposed model with the baselines according to the evaluation metrics defined in Sect. 3.4, and Table 1 shows the results.

Based on the results shown in the table, our proposed model achieved the best performance according to LPIPS, and MedSRGAN is the best one on 3 out of the 5 metrics. Among these metrics, LPIPS is more aligned with human interpretation comparing to others, as defined in [54]. RealESRGAN, on the other hand, achieved the best performance on SSIM.

It is unsurprising that according to the 3 traditional metrics, MedSRGAN is the top model. As [54] explained the traditional ones are simple, shallow functions and fail to account for many nuances of human perception. Visually, MedSRGAN and SuperMRI introduced more artifacts compared to RealESRGAN and our model. To verify the intuition, we showed the SR results (100 groups of images, and each group contains SR images from MedSRGAN, SuperMRI, RealESRGAN, and ours) to an experienced radiologist. This expert confirmed that RealESRGAN and our model produced SR images with higher quality. Compared to RealESRGAN, our model results better on the 4 out 5 metrics.

Table 1. Comparison of super-resolution results between our proposed model and the baselines. The comparing metrics include SSIM, MS-SSIM, PSNR, UIQI, and LPIPS. ↑ means the higher the better and ↓ means the lower the better.

Models	SSIM↑	MS-SSIM↑	PSNR↑	UIQI↑	LPIPS↓
MedSRGAN	0.709 ± 0.096	**0.931 ± 0.039**	**27.870 ± 2.896**	**0.202 ± 0.074**	0.259 ± 0.048
SuperMRI	0.523 ± 0.251	0.754 ± 0.274	18.436 ± 5.613	0.142 ± 0.097	0.338 ± 0.133
RealESRGAN	**0.754 ± 0.080**	0.909 ± 0.051	25.999 ± 2.886	0.167 ± 0.070	0.204 ± 0.044
Ours	0.659 ± 0.107	0.918 ± 0.041	27.269 ± 2.500	0.184 ± 0.072	**0.184 ± 0.034**

4.3 The Super-Resolution Results

Figure 2 shows SR results generated by the proposed model and the baselines. From the figure, both SR results generated from MedSRGAN and SuperMRI

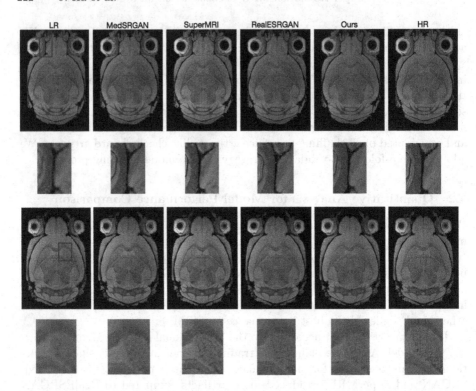

Fig. 2. SR examples generated from our proposed model and baselines. The first row is an example of WT mouse and the second row is zoomin of a local region. The third row is an example of a 5xFAD mouse and last row is zoomin of a local region. The coloumns correspond to LR, MedSRGAN, SuperMRI, RealESRGAN, proposed model, and HR. Zoomin for better visualization.

have obvious ringing and overshot artifacts. RealESRGAN produces better-quality images, but it additionally introduces white spot artifacts, as shown in the second row fourth column. The resolution of the neuroimages has been significantly increased using the proposed dense network, and compared to other baselines, the proposed model generated fewer artifacts in the generated SR images.

5   Conclusion

In this paper, we demonstrate a dense network for SR task on whole mouse brain Magnetic Resonance Histology images. The images have a resolution of 25 μm^3, which is much higher than common MRI images and requires reconstruction for fine details. We first utilized K-space to downsample the HR images and synthesized our LR training data with a downsampling factor of 4. We then adopted a dense network architecture for the resolution conversion. We compared the proposed model with several existing methods, including the ones used for the medical field and natural images. The results show that deep learning models can generate realistic SR natural images and are also useful for medical imaging analysis. To make the full potential of these models, fine-tuning is necessary as there exists a data gap between natural and medical images. The proposed model increases the LR image quality considerably, which can provide a helpful computer-aided diagnosis and decision.

Two directions can be further explored, including research purpose and clinical practice setting. For research purposes, potential adjustments on network architecture can be further explored to improve SR image quality; In clinical practice, it is necessary to integrate domain knowledge for different application scenarios and real-world settings.

Acknowledgements. This work was supported by Indiana University Internal Research Seed Fund, and in part by the NIH R01 NS125020, Indiana Center for Diabetes and Metabolic Diseases Pilot and Feasibility Grant, Roberts Drug Discovery Fund & TREAT-AD Center Grant.

References

1. Ba, J.L., Kiros, J.R., Hinton, G.E.: Layer Normalization. arXiv:1607.06450 (2016)
2. Bargmann, C.I., Marder, E.: From the connectome to brain function. Nat. Meth. **10**(6), 483–490 (2013)
3. Baldoli, C., et al.: Maturation of preterm newborn brains: a fMRI-DTI study of auditory processing of linguistic stimuli and white matter development. Brain Struct. Funct. **220**(6), 3733–3751 (2015)
4. Block, K.T., Uecker, M., Frahm, J.: Suppression of MRI truncation artifacts using total variation constrained data extrapolation. Int. J. Biomed. Imaging (2008)
5. Cao, Y., Kuai, H., Peng, G.: Enhancing the MR neuroimaging by using the deep super-resolution reconstruction. In: Mahmud, M., He, J., Vassanelli, S., van Zundert, A., Zhong, N. (eds.) BI 2022. LNCS, vol. 13406, pp. 184–194. Springer, Cham (2022). https://doi.org/10.1007/978-3-031-15037-1_16
6. Calabrese, E., Badea, A., Cofer, G., Qi, Y., Johnson, G.A.: A diffusion MRI tractography connectome of the mouse brain and comparison with neuronal tracer data. Cereb. Cortex **25**(11), 4628–4637 (2015)
7. Calamante, F., et al.: Super-resolution track-density imaging studies of mouse brain: comparison to histology. Neuroimage **115**, 202–213 (2012)
8. Crater, S., Maharjan, S., Qi, Y., Zhao, Q., Cofer, G., Cook, J.C., et al.: Resolution and b value dependent structural connectome in ex vivo mouse brain. Neuroimage **255**, 119199 (2022)
9. Dong, C., Loy, C.C., He, K., Tang, X.: Image super-resolution using deep convolutional networks. IEEE Trans. Pattern Anal. Mach. Intell. **38**(2), 295–307 (2016)
10. Dong, C., Loy, C.C., Tang, X.: Accelerating the super-resolution convolutional neural network. In: Leibe, B., Matas, J., Sebe, N., Welling, M. (eds.) ECCV 2016. LNCS, vol. 9906, pp. 391–407. Springer, Cham (2016). https://doi.org/10.1007/978-3-319-46475-6_25
11. Du, J., Wang, L., Liu, Y., Zhou, Z., He, Z., Jia, Y.: Brain MRI super-resolution using 3D dilated convolutional encoder-decoder network. IEEE Access **8**, 18938–18950 (2020)

12. Ebner, M., et al.: An automated framework for localization, segmentation and super-resolution reconstruction of fetal brain MRI. NeuroImage **206**, 116324 (2020)
13. Feng, C.M., Wang, K., Lu, S., Xu, Y., Li, X.: Brain MRI super-resolution using coupled-projection residual network. Neurocomputing **456**, 190–199 (2021)
14. Goodfellow, I., et al.: Generative adversarial networks. arXiv:1406.2661 (2014)
15. Gu, Y., Zeng, Z., Chen, H., et al.: MedSRGAN: medical images super-resolution using generative adversarial networks. Multimed. Tools Appl. **79**, 21815–21840 (2020)
16. Guo, J.Y., Kholmovski, E.G., Zhang, L., Jeong, E.K., Parker, D.L.: k-space inherited parallel acquisition (KIPA): application on dynamic magnetic resonance imaging thermometry. Magn. Reson. Imaging **24**(7), 903–915 (2006)
17. Ioffe, S., Szegedy, C.: Batch normalization: accelerating deep network training by reducing internal covariate shift. arXiv:1502.03167 (2015)
18. Johnson, J., Alahi, A., Fei-Fei, L.: Perceptual losses for real-time style transfer and super-resolution. In: Leibe, B., Matas, J., Sebe, N., Welling, M. (eds.) ECCV 2016. LNCS, vol. 9906, pp. 694–711. Springer, Cham (2016). https://doi.org/10.1007/978-3-319-46475-6_43
19. Kim, J., Kim, G., Li, L., et al.: Deep learning acceleration of multiscale super resolution localization photoacoustic imaging. Light Sci. Appl. **11**, 131 (2022)
20. Kingma, D., Ba, J.: Adam: a method for stochastic optimization. In: ICLR (2015)
21. Li, Z., Yu, J., Wang, Y., Zhou, H., Yang, H., Qiao, Z.: DeepVolume: brain structure and spatial connection-aware network for brain MRI super-resolution. IEEE Trans. Cybern. **51**(7), 3441–3454 (2021)
22. Li, B.M., et al.: Deep attention super-resolution of brain magnetic resonance images acquired under clinical protocols. Front. Comput. Neurosci. **16**, 887633 (2022)
23. Luo, J., Zhu, Y., Li, W., Croisille, P., Magnin, I.E.: MRI reconstruction from 2D truncated k-space. J. Magn. Reson. Imaging **35**(5), 1196–206 (2012)
24. Luo, J., Zhu, Y., Magnin, I.: Phase correction-based singularity function analysis for partial k-space reconstruction. Magn. Reson. Imaging **26**(6), 746–53 (2008)
25. Miyato, T., Kataoka, T., Koyama, M., Yoshida, Y.: Spectral normalization for generative adversarial networks. arXiv:1802.05957 (2018)
26. Maharjan, S., Tsai, A.P., Lin, P.B., Ingraham, C., Jewett, M.R., Landreth, G.E., et al.: Age-dependent microstructure alterations in 5xFAD mice by high-resolution diffusion tensor imaging. Front Neurosci. **16**, 964654 (2022)
27. Miyato, T., Kataoka, T., Koyama, M., Yoshida, Y.: Spectral normalization for generative adversarial networks. In: ICLR (2018)
28. Mukai, J., et al.: Molecular substrates of altered axonal growth and brain connectivity in a mouse model of schizophrenia. Neuron **86**(3), 680–695 (2015)
29. Oh, S.W., et al.: A mesoscale connectome of the mouse brain. Nature **508**(7495), 207–214 (2014)
30. Park, H., Na, M., Kim, B., et al.: Deep learning enables reference-free isotropic super-resolution for volumetric fluorescence microscopy. Nat. Commun. **13**, 3297 (2022)
31. Pham, C.H., Ducournau, A., Fablet, R., Rousseau, F.: Brain MRI super-resolution using deep 3D convolutional networks. In: ISBI, pp. 197–200 (2017)
32. Pham, C.H., et al.: Multiscale brain MRI super-resolution using deep 3D convolutional networks. Comput. Med. Imaging Graph. **77**, 101647 (2019)
33. Delannoy, Q., et al.: SegSRGAN: super-resolution and segmentation using generative adversarial networks - application to neonatal brain MRI. Comput. Biol. Med. **120**, 103755 (2020)

34. Quan, T., Nguyen-Duc, T., Jeong, W.: Compressed sensing MRI reconstruction using a generative adversarial network with a cyclic loss. IEEE Trans. Med. Imaging **37**(6), 1488–1497 (2018)
35. Song, L., et al.: Deep robust residual network for super-resolution of 2D fetal brain MRI. Sci. Rep. **12**(1), 1–8 (2022)
36. Sui, Y., Afacan, O., Jaimes, C., Gholipour, A., Warfield, K.: Scan-specific generative neural network for MRI super-resolution reconstruction. IEEE Trans. Med. Imaging **41**(6), 1383–1399 (2022)
37. Suwannasak, A., Yarach, U., Chatnuntawech, I.: Improving brain volume measurement workflow using combination of compressed sensing MRI and deep learning based super-resolution at 1.5T clinical scanner. J. Med. Imaging Radiat. Sci. Suppl. 1, **53**, S10–S11 (2022)
38. Terada, Y., et al.: Clinical evaluation of super-resolution for brain MRI images based on generative adversarial networks. Inform. Med. Unlocked **32**, 101030 (2022)
39. Urban, B.E., et al.: In vivo super resolution imaging of neuronal structure in the mouse brain. IEEE Trans. Biomed. Eng. **65**(1), 232–238 (2018)
40. Wang, L., Zhu, H., He, Z., Jia, Y., Du, J.: Adjacent slices feature transformer network for single anisotropic 3D brain MRI image super-resolution. Biomed. Sig. Process. Control **72**, 103339 (2022)
41. Wang, Y., Liang, Z., Wang, L., Yang, J., An, W., Guo, Y.: Learning a degradation-adaptive network for light field image super-solution (2022). https://doi.org/10.48550/arXiv.2206.06214
42. Wang, N., et al.: Whole mouse brain structural connectomics using magnetic resonance histology. Brain Struct. Funct. **223**, 4323–4335 (2018)
43. Wang, X., et al.: ESRGAN: enhanced super-resolution generative adversarial networks. In: ECCVW (2018)
44. Wang, N., Cofer, G., Anderson, R.J., Qi, Y., Liu, C., Johnson, G.A.: Accelerating quantitative susceptibility imaging acquisition using compressed sensing. Phys. Med. Biol. **63**(24), 245002 (2018)
45. Wang, N., Zhuang, J., Wei, H.J., Dibb, R., Qi, Y., Liu, C.L.: Probing demyelination and remyelination of the cuprizone mouse model using multimodality MRI. J. Magn. Reson. Imaging **50**(6), 1852–65 (2019)
46. Wang, N., et al.: Variability and heritability of mouse brain structure: microscopic MRI atlases and connectomes for diverse strains. NeuroImage **222**, 117274 (2020)
47. Wang, N., White, L.E., Qi, Y., Cofer, G., Johnson, G.A.: Cytoarchitecture of the mouse brain by high resolution diffusion magnetic resonance imaging. NeuroImage. **216**, 116876 (2020)
48. Wang, N., et al.: Integrating multimodality magnetic resonance imaging to the Allen Mouse brain common coordinate framework. NMR Biomed. **36**, 5 (2023)
49. Wang, Z., Bovik, A.C.: A universal image quality index. IEEE Sig. Process. Lett. **9**(3), 81–84 (2002)
50. Wang, X., Xie, L., Dong, C., Shan, Y.: Real-ESRGAN: training real-world blind super-resolution with pure synthetic data. In: 2021 IEEE/CVF International Conference on Computer Vision Workshops (ICCVW), Montreal, BC, Canada, pp. 1905–1914 (2021)
51. Wu, D., Zhang, J.Y.: In vivo mapping of macroscopic neuronal projections in the mouse hippocampus using high-resolution diffusion MRI. Neuroimage **125**, 84–93 (2016)
52. Zhang, J.Y., et al.: Mapping postnatal mouse brain development with diffusion tensor microimaging. NeuroImage **26**(4), 1042–1051 (2005)

53. Zhang, H., Schneider, T., Wheeler-Kingshott, C.A., Alexander, D.C.: NODDI: practical in vivo neurite orientation dispersion and density imaging of the human brain. NeuroImage **61**(4), 1000–1016 (2012)
54. Zhang, R., Isola, P., Efros, A.A., Shechtman, E., Wang, O.: The unreasonable effectiveness of deep features as a perceptual metric. arXiv:1801.03924 (2018)
55. Zingg, B., et al.: Neural networks of the mouse neocortex. Cell **156**(5), 1096–1111 (2014)
56. Zhao, C., Dewey, B.E., Pham, D.L., Calabresi, P.A., Reich, D.S., Prince, J.L.: SMORE: a self-supervised anti-aliasing and super-resolution algorithm for MRI using deep learning. IEEE Trans. Med. Imaging **40**(3), 805–817 (2021)
57. Zhao, F., Zhu, L., Fang, C., Yu, T., Zhu, D., Fei, P.: Deep-learning super-resolution light-sheet add-on microscopy (Deep-SLAM) for easy isotropic volumetric imaging of large biological specimens. Biomed. Opt. Express **11**(12), 7273–7285 (2020)
58. Zhu, Z., Lei, Y., Qin, Y., Zhu, C.: IRE: improved image super-resolution based on real-ESRGAN. IEEE Access **11**, 45334–45348 (2023)

Bayesian Time-Series Classifier for Decoding Simple Visual Stimuli from Intracranial Neural Activity

Navid Ziaei[1] , Reza Saadatifard[2], Ali Yousefi[2], Behzad Nazari[1],
Sydney S. Cash[3], and Angelique C. Paulk[3(✉)]

[1] Department of Electrical and Computer Engineering, Isfahan University of
Technology (IUT), Isfahan, Iran
[2] Department of Computer Science, Worcester Polytechnic Institute (WPI),
Worcester, MA 01609, USA
[3] Department of Neurology, Massachusetts General Hospital and Harvard Medical
School, Boston, MA 02114, USA
APAULK@mgh.harvard.edu

Abstract. Understanding how external stimuli are encoded in distributed neural activity is of significant interest in clinical and basic neuroscience. To address this need, it is essential to develop analytical tools capable of handling limited data and the intrinsic stochasticity present in neural data. In this study, we propose a straightforward Bayesian time series classifier (BTsC) model that tackles these challenges whilst maintaining a high level of interpretability. We demonstrate the classification capabilities of this approach by utilizing neural data to decode colors in a visual task. The model exhibits consistent and reliable average performance of 75.55% on 4 patients' dataset, improving upon state-of-the-art machine learning techniques by about 3.0%. In addition to its high classification accuracy, the proposed BTsC model provides interpretable results, making the technique a valuable tool to study neural activity in various tasks and categories. The proposed solution can be applied to neural data recorded in various tasks, where there is a need for interpretable results and accurate classification accuracy.

Keywords: Bayesian analysis · Neural decoding · Interpretable modeling

1 Introduction

Neuroscientists have long sought methods to decode neural activity in hopes of restoring movement and communication for individuals with neurological injuries [28], including stroke, spinal cord injury, brain trauma, and neurodegenerative diseases (e.g., Amyotrophic Lateral Sclerosis, ALS) using brain-computer interfaces (BCIs). Significant progress has been made in motor control [15], with advances also seen in the realms of speech [2], mood, and decoding neural activity corresponding to visual stimuli [11,14,16]. Despite these discoveries, BCIs

F. Liu et al. (Eds.): BI 2023, LNAI 13974, pp. 227–238, 2023.
https://doi.org/10.1007/978-3-031-43075-6_20

remain primarily in research endeavors, facing hurdles in terms of costs, risks, and technological challenges [36]. The critical components of a BCI system involve feature extraction and accurate classification of neural activity related to different tasks or sensory input. However, several challenges exist in achieving highly accurate classifiers, including selecting the most informative and well-reasoned neural features and developing an interpretable classifier capable of utilizing limited datasets [3]. An interpretable classifier elucidates key neural signal features, like specific frequency bands or time periods, crucial for task performance. This insight enhances our understanding of the neural mechanisms. Addressing these challenges is further complicated by the prohibitively large number of features used to decode neural activity. Features might encompass raw neural data, which include the measured voltage from single or multiple electrode contacts in non-invasive techniques such as electroencephalography (EEG), and invasive methods like intracranial EEG (iEEG) or blood-oxygen-level-dependent (BOLD) signal in functional MRI. Many researchers have suggested a variety of features derived from these neural recordings. These could range from simple statistical metrics of the signal in time or frequency domain, like mean, median, standard deviations, kurtosis, and skewness to more sophisticated features such as Common Spatial Patterns (CSPs) [7], Higher-Order Crossing (HOC) features [22], Hjorth features [20], and Auto-Regressive (AR) coefficients [33]. As the EEG signal is non-stationary [34], time-frequency domain methods such as wavelet transform (WT) have been used for feature extraction as well [23]. In addition to the types of features used, there can be multiple streams of the same data represented by different electrode channels. Many researchers employ data reduction techniques to handle this redundancy of information, such as Principal Component Analysis (PCA), Independent Component Analysis (ICA), or linear discriminant analysis (LDA) [32]. Another approach in data analysis focuses on selecting the most informative channels relative to the target classification task. This can be achieved through channel selection techniques, which can be categorized as either classifier-dependent (including wrapper and embedded-based methods) or classifier-independent (such as filter-based methods) [1]. In summary, different neural activity features can yield varied inferences, not always enhancing the understanding of encoding mechanisms. Thus, refining feature extraction and selection are essential for deriving relevant information that deepens our comprehension of brain processes. Once features are chosen, classification commences, with considerable recent work involving deep-learning-based classifier models. While deep learning frameworks such as Convolutional Neural Networks [9] and Recurrent Neural Networks [25] have been applied to the decoding and classification of EEG signals to identify stimuli [5], these methods might not be as applicable to invasive neural recordings like iEEG. This is primarily due to the limited availability of iEEG data compared to non-invasive EEG data. The drawbacks of these models include, 1) lack of interpretability, which corresponds to difficulty in identifying the necessary features for classification in many deep learning models, and 2) the requirement of vast amounts of data in the training phase of these models, which may not always be possible to collect when dealing with invasive recordings like iEEG [26]. Consequently, the limited data in invasive neural recordings necessitates the exploration of alternative methods that can effectively handle such constraints while maintaining accurate classification and interpretability. In this study, we propose the Bayesian Time-Series Classifier (BTsC) model, designed to address the above-mentioned challenges. The BTsC allows us to identify the minimum number of channels necessary for stimulus classification from neural data. Furthermore, it enables the selection of neural features from different electrodes that provide optimal classification power, as well as the determination of the precise time period following a stimulus required for accurate stimulus classification. The proposed model can be trained effectively with limited data by leveraging the dynamics of local field potential (LFP) signals in two frequency subbands. Our proposed BTsC model employs a wrapper-based technique and greedy search in selecting channels and features for optimal classification. The pipeline of feature selection and classification used in the model can be applied to other classifiers, including Support Vector Machine (SVM) [29], Long Short-Term Memory (LSTM) [10], Naïve Bayes [24], etc. We applied this model to decode the presence of one or the other visual stimulus using LFP neural activity from multiple neural nodes' activity, where our model shows high accuracy in classifying simple stimuli. In the following, we first outline our method of feature extraction from LFP signals and the development of the BTsC for stimulus decoding. Next, we assess the BTsC model's performance and compare it with other machine learning models. Lastly, we discuss our findings' implications for brain information processing and the potential applications of our model.

2   Material and Methods

2.1   Dataset and Behavioral Task

Four participants performed the visual stimulus task, while LFP was recorded from 278 sites via intracranial stereo EEG (Fig. 1-A). Intracranial EEG recordings were made over the course of clinical monitoring for spontaneous seizures. Participants were implanted with multi-lead depth electrodes (also known as stereotactic EEG, sEEG) [6]. All patients voluntarily participated after fully informed consent according to NIH guidelines, as monitored by the Massachusetts General Brigham (formerly Partners) Institutional Review Board (IRB). Participants were informed that participation in the tests would not alter their clinical treatment and that they could withdraw at any time without jeopardizing their clinical care. The Flicker task consisted of 100 trials where participants were presented with a red fixation cross for 0.5 s on a grey background (Fig. 1-B). This was followed by the appearance of a single black or white square on the same grey background. The duration of the square varied randomly between 2 to 4 s. The color of the square for each trial was randomly selected from a sequence of black or white with equal chance. Participants were instructed to focus on the red fixation cross and count the number of black or white squares presented to enhance engagement.

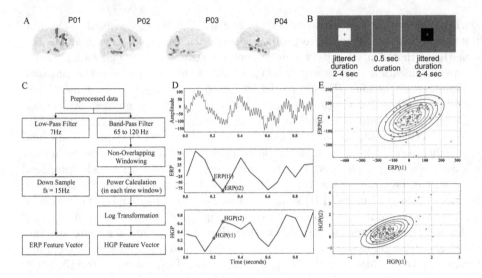

Fig. 1. Data Overview: (A) shows the electrode placement in four participants, (B) illustrates the Flicker Task paradigm performed in 100 trials, (C) outlines the steps for feature extraction, (D) displays the preprocessed single trial signal (top), ERP features (middle), and HGP features (bottom) extracted from the LTP02-LTP03 electrode for patient P04, and (E) presents a scatter plot of ERP (top) and HGP (bottom) features at times t1 and t2 for all trials recorded from the same electrode, indicating a Gaussian distribution.

2.2 Data Preprocessing: Intracranial LFP Data

Data analysis was performed using custom analysis code in MATLAB and Field-trip, an open-source software implemented in MATLAB [21]. All data were subsequently decimated to 1000 Hz, demeaned relative to the entire recording, and line noise and its harmonics up to 200 Hz were removed by subtracting the band-passed filtered signal from the raw signal. Channels with excessive line noise or which had no discernible signal were removed from the analysis. In addition, we removed pathological channels with interictal epileptiform discharges (IEDs) using an automatic IED detection algorithm [13] (version v21, default settings except -h at 60; http://isarg.fel.cvut.cz). We removed channels that had detected IEDs greater than 6.5 IEDs/minute The remaining electrodes were subsequently bipolar re-referenced relative to nearest neighbors to account for volume conduction.

2.3 Extracting Neural Features for Decoding

We focus on two categories of features known to encode stimulus information, namely the low-frequency event-related potentials (ERPs) and the high gamma power (HGP) following image onset (see Fig. 1-C). For the ERP neural features, we filter the LFP in the theta (3–7 Hz) and delta (0–3 Hz) frequency bands [35] using a low-pass filter with a cut-off frequency of 7 Hz. By applying the low-pass filter, we conform to the Nyquist-Shannon sampling theorem, which allows us to down-sample the filtered data to 15 Hz without losing crucial information. This results in 15 features (each feature being an individual time step) for ERP signals per electrode. Each sample of the ERP feature vector includes a weighted average of multiple samples of the original time series data in a specific time interval. Under the central limit theorem assumption, we can assume that each element of these vectors follows a normal distribution. As HGP has also been shown to encode visual stimuli [19,35], we band-pass filter the LFP from 65 to 120 Hz. Power is then calculated in 67-ms nonoverlapping windows after stimulus onset, generating the same number of features per each channel as the ERP. A subsequent step involves using a log transformation. This transformation compresses the range of high values and expands the range of low values, resulting in a distribution that is more symmetric and closer to a normal distribution. This justifies its use as an input feature vector to our model [4]. In the procedure described, each LFP recording channel results in two feature vectors, one for ERP and one for HGP, each represented as a time series. We model these vectors as multivariate normal distributions for use in the BTsC model, which we'll discuss further in the next section.

2.4   Bayesian Time-Series Classifier (BTsC)

In Sect. 2.3, we described how ERP and HGP feature vectors are acquired from each LFP recording channel. To simplify the description, we assume that each channel is associated with a single feature vector, and we refer to the classifier trained on this feature vector as a single-channel classifier. This simplification does not compromise the broader applicability of the model. To present the BTsC model, we start by detailing the single-channel classifier's construction and the process of determining optimal time periods. We then discuss combining single-channel classifiers into a multi-channel classifier and selecting the minimum subset of classifiers needed for maximum accuracy. The BTsC aims to determine the fewest feature vectors necessary for effective stimulus classification. Single-channel classifier. Let us assume that the pre-processed neural recording for the cth electrode is represented by the feature vector defined by $\mathbf{x}^c = \{\mathbf{x}_1^c, \mathbf{x}_2^c, \dots, \mathbf{x}_d^c\}$, where d is the length of observation period, and $\mathbf{x}_i{}^c$ is the ith sample of the feature vector for the ith time interval after the stimulus onset. As discussed in Sect. 2.3, we assume that each element of $\mathbf{x}^c$ follows a normal distribution. We further assume the joint distribution of $\mathbf{x}^c$ follows a multivariate normal, where the dependency across time points allows us to characterize the temporal dynamics of observed neural features. For the model, we build the conditional distribution of $\mathbf{x}^c$ given stimulus, $I \in \{0, \dots, k\} \equiv \{(stimulus1, \dots, stimulusK)\}$. The conditional distribution of $\mathbf{x}^c$ is defined by:

$$\mathbf{x}^c | I \sim \mathcal{N}(\mu_I^c, \Sigma_I^c) \tag{1}$$

$$p(\mathbf{X} = \mathbf{x}^c | I) = \frac{1}{(2\pi)^{d/2} |\Sigma_I^c|^{1/2}} \exp\left(-\frac{1}{2}(\mathbf{x}^c - \mu_I^c)^T \Sigma_I^{c-1}(\mathbf{x}^c - \mu_I^c)\right) \tag{2}$$

where μ_I^c and Σ_I^c are the mean and covariance of $\mathbf{x}^c$ given stimuli I. Given μ_I and Σ_I, we can construct a Bayesian classifier to compare the posterior probabilities of different stimuli. The assigned class is the one with the highest posterior probability, defined by:

$$\forall j \neq k : L(I = k \mid \mathbf{X} = \mathbf{x}^c) \geq L(I = j \mid \mathbf{X} = \mathbf{x}^c) \tag{3}$$

$L(I \mid \mathbf{X} = \mathbf{x}^c)$ corresponds to the posterior distribution of stimulus I, given the observed neural features, defined by:

$$L(I \mid \mathbf{X} = \mathbf{x}^c) \propto p(\mathbf{X} = \mathbf{x}^c \mid I)p(I) \tag{4}$$

where $p(I)$ is the stimulus prior probability. To build our single-channel classifier, we require only the mean and covariance of each neural recording ($\mathbf{x}^c$) per stimulus. Using the training dataset $\mathcal{D}$, we find the mean and covariance matrix for each time series. To obtain a robust estimation of the covariance matrix, the number of required samples must be on the order of d^2. Estimating the covariance matrix can result in a biased estimation given the limited training data [18]. Our solution is to find the minimum length of the observation ($d_{minimal}^c$) starting from the onset, providing the highest accuracy with the cross-validated result. Using this approach, we can address the limited training dataset in our estimation of the covariance matrix. In the case of the multivariate normal distribution, we can obtain the marginal distribution of a subset of the neural data; any marginalized distribution remains a multivariate normal. With this in mind, we can examine the posterior of each class of data as a time-dependent function, identifying the stimulus from a subset of neural data $\mathbf{x}^c$. We denote this posterior as L_j, signifying a marginalized version of the overall posterior distribution L, but only considering the first j features $\{\mathbf{x}_1^c, \mathbf{x}_2^c, \ldots, \mathbf{x}_j^c\}$. We introduce the concept of $C_j(\mathcal{D})$, representing the cross-validated classification accuracy of our model on the dataset $\mathcal{D}$, using a marginalized posterior distribution with the first j features. For each classifier, the minimal time, denoted as $d_{minimal}^c$, is defined as follows:

$$d_{\text{minimal}}^c = \arg\max_j C_j(\mathcal{D}) \tag{5}$$

This suggests that $d_{minimal}^c$ represents the smallest set of features necessary to optimize our model's performance, in accordance with the constraints of the k-fold cross-validation method being used.

Multi-channel Classifier. We construct our BTsC model initially based on a single-channel classifier, which turns to Quadratic Discriminant Analysis (QDA) for time series [31]. In practice, we have multiple channels, with each channel having two feature vectors. Classifiers trained on these feature vectors can be combined to achieve higher classification accuracy. Equation (4) defines the classifier model for the cth feature vector. We found that the single-channel classifier accuracy is limited, and in the best case, it is about or less than 75%. To attain higher classification accuracy, we expand our single-channel QDA classifier to account for multiple channels. We employ two solutions to adapt the classifier for multi-channel neural recordings, resulting in an ensemble-based classifier that enhances accuracy and robustness. The first solution expands the model directly to multiple channels. The second solution is based on the majority voting rule of C different classifiers, where C is the number of possible channels.

Multi-channel Likelihood Method. For a multi-channel classifier, we assume that different feature vectors are conditionally independent given the stimulus. The joint conditional distribution of all recordings is defined by:

$$p(\mathbf{X}_1 = \mathbf{x}^1, \ldots, \mathbf{X}_C = \mathbf{x}^C | I) = p(\mathbf{X}_1 = \mathbf{x}^1 | I) \ldots p(\mathbf{X}_C = \mathbf{x}^C | I) \qquad (6)$$

where I represents the stimulus. We can construct each single-channel model similar to the one defined in Eq. (2). The posterior distribution for each multi-channel neural recording is defined by:

$$L(I; \mathbf{X}_1 = \mathbf{x}^1, \ldots, \mathbf{X}_C = \mathbf{x}^C) \propto p(\mathbf{X}_1 = \mathbf{x}^1 | I) \ldots p(\mathbf{X}_C = \mathbf{x}^C | I) p(I) \qquad (7)$$

Utilizing all channels in the model is not practical as some may lack informative features for classification. Also, multiplying likelihoods from all channels can complicate computation due to smaller values. Hence, identifying the most informative channels through channel subset selection is necessary for accurate classification. We will discuss this challenge in the classification subset selection section.

Maximum Voting Method. The outcomes of single-channel classifiers can be combined using the voting method to achieve higher classification accuracy. In a poll of C single-channel classifiers, each classifier contributes a vote towards a class label based on its independent prediction. The class which receives the most votes, representing the majority opinion among the classifiers, is selected as the final output class [31].

Classifiers Subset Selection. We can combine single-channel classifiers to construct a multi-channel classifier using either of these two methods. The process of selecting the optimal subset of feature vectors is based on an adaptive (or greedy) search. It begins with a single channel with the best performance using k-fold cross-validation and then examines which other channel can be added to it. All possible combinations are evaluated, and the one with the best performance is selected. Through this adaptive search, the minimal number of channels that reach the highest classification accuracy with the highest confidence can be determined with cross-validation.

3 Results

The BTsC model can be applied to different mental tasks with various features. Here, we investigated the application of BTsC in the visual task described in

Sect. 2.1. We trained the BTsC using low-frequency (ERP, $< 7Hz$) and high-frequency power (HGP; 65–120 Hz) dynamics following image onset to test if we can decode visual stimuli from across the brain at a high temporal resolution (67 ms). Then, we identified the features and time points for maximum decoding accuracy (Fig. 2). Furthermore, to validate the results obtained with the BTsC model, we compared them with the decoding outcomes of seven additional machine learning (ML) algorithms on visual stimuli. Optimal Stimulus Decoding Time and Features in the Model Following the model subset selection, we discovered that the channels and features that survived the selection criteria and contributed to the BTsC models were from multiple electrodes across multiple brain regions. BTsC enabled us to evaluate the performance of each feature vector, ERP and HGP, on individual channels and to determine the optimal timing post-image onset for superior performance. From this analysis, we discerned which regions and which features exhibited the fastest responses. Additionally, we found that combining these feature vectors leads to a boost in performance (Fig. 2-B). Upon analyzing the BTsC results for ERP, HGP, and their combined utilization, we discovered that leveraging both ERP and HGP features enhances the decoding model's accuracy in the visual task (Fig. 2-C). After identifying the time window after image onset with the peak accuracy for the single time or cumulative BTsC models, we found that the time of maximum accuracy after image onset was below 0.8 s. The accuracy at each time point and the number of utilized feature vectors are depicted in Fig. 2-D.

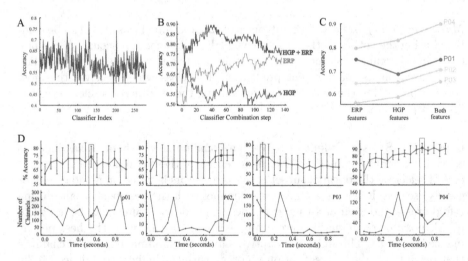

Fig. 2. Results: (A) illustrates the performance of individual classifiers. (B) shows accuracy evolution during channel combination steps for participant P05. (C) shows the comparison between the BTsC performance using ERP, HGP, and both ERP and HGP features to assess the impact of neural features. (D) displays the accuracy of the model at different time points for participants P01 to P05.

3.1 Machine Learning Decoding

To test if decoding results, which support the distributed information flow hypothesis [27] are particular to the BTsC model, we applied seven machine learning models to the same neural features (ERP and HGP) and participant data. The machine learning classifiers include SVM [29], Logistic Regression (LR) [12], Naïve Bayes (NB) [24], Random Forest (RF) [12], Multi-Layer Perceptron (MLP) [8], LSTM [10] and EEGNet [17].

4 Discussion

Our investigation has yielded significant insights into the effectiveness of the BTsC in decoding visual stimuli from intracranial EEG recordings. The BTsC model's integration of the ERP and HGP features has demonstrated a remarkable capacity for classifying visual stimuli, outperforming other machine learning models including SVM, Logistic Regression, Naïve Bayes, Random Forest, MLP, LSTM, and EEGNet. By leveraging the BTsC model, we achieved an average accuracy of 75.55% in classifying stimuli (Table 1). This is a noteworthy outcome, particularly given the inherent complexity of neural data, inter-subject variability in iEEG electrode position, and the challenges associated with decoding neural signals. Our results show that the BTsC model can effectively capture the distributed information flow within the brain, with its simplicity offering robustness against limited training data. In comparison, other methods face challenges such as overfitting, interpretability, and scalability issues. For example, complex models like EEGNet can result in overfitting due to their complex architecture, making them less reliable when dealing with limited data [5]. On the other hand, simpler models like Naïve Bayes rely on the assumption of features' independence, which is often unrealistic in real-world applications. The key feature of our model is its interpretability, essential for validating predictions and

Table 1. Performance Comparison across Different ML Techniques: The table depicts the mean and standard deviations (presented in parentheses) of 5-fold cross-validation accuracy for all models, including BTsC (L) and BTsC (V), where (L) and (V) represent combination methods using likelihood and voting, respectively.

Model	P01		P02		P03		P04	
	Acc.	F1	Acc.	F1	Acc.	F1	Acc.	F1
BTsC (L)	74.6(5)	**75.2(8)**	**73.7(4)**	**71.0(9)**	66.5(7)	62.0(8)	85.4(7)	83.1(3)
BTsC (V)	**75.1(9)**	74.3(7)	70.6(6)	69.8(9)	66.4(10)	67.3(7)	**90.0(6)**	**89.1(4)**
EEGNet	72.0(7)	73.2(9)	68.1(7)	70.1(11)	**67.4(9)**	**68.1(9)**	85.3(10)	84.2(8)
SVM	61.2(13)	65.2(8)	70.0(14)	73.0(9)	58.5(9)	51.0(10)	81.2(7)	81.1(10)
NB	70.0(6)	69.4(8)	68.7(8)	70.7(8)	51.1(11)	54.0(18)	74.8(16)	70.9(9)
RF	60.0(6)	58.5(3)	62.5(3)	63.0(3)	55.2(4)	56.1(8)	72.9(6)	71.2(5)
MLP	67.8(9)	63.2(6)	67.7(11)	68.1(9)	58.5(10)	55.9(10)	71.9(8)	72.5(7)
LR	66.2(11)	66.0(8)	67.5(7)	66.8(13)	53.1(5)	46.5(5)	75.0(12)	76.1(10)
LSTM	64.6(8)	63.2(6)	67.7(7)	64.2(9)	52.7(9)	50.0(11)	70.0(7)	71.9(11)

understanding brain functions [37]. Our BTsC model offers a clear view of which areas of the brain are encoding stimuli and at what time these features exhibit the most discriminative power. Additionally, this model possesses flexibility in utilizing diverse feature vectors and can provide insights into the specific contributions of each vector to the final outcome. In our study, we leveraged both ERP and HGP dynamical features individually and in combination within the BTsC. While both ERPs and HGP independently provided significant information for decoding visual stimuli, we found that combining these features led to a marked increase in classification accuracy. This suggests that these neural features, while independently informative, offer complementary information that enhances the decoding power when combined, reflecting the complex and distributed nature of brain processing [30]. Thus, the integration of multiple neural features could contribute to more accurate and robust models for neuroscience applications. Further expanding our research, we conducted an experiment to determine the most informative time period after image onset for training the BTsC model. This aspect is crucial, as it helps establish the optimal window for capturing the most discriminative neural features. In this experiment, we trained the BTsC model using different time windows post-image onset. Consequently, we determined the optimal time window post-image onset for training the BTsC model for each patient (Fig. 2-D). Moreover, this experiment revealed that in shorter time windows, HGP feature vectors are more involved than ERP. Despite the encouraging results, our model has limitations. The assumption of channels' independence is a significant limitation, which we intend to address in future iterations. We plan to refine our model to account for possible dependencies and correlations between features and electrodes, which could further enhance the predictive accuracy of the BTsC model.

5   Conclusion

In this study, we introduced a novel Bayesian Time-series Classifier that utilizes both low-frequency event-related potentials and high gamma power features to effectively decode visual stimuli from intracranial EEG recordings. The BTsC model identifies encoding brain areas, discriminative features, and optimal time windows, outperforming other classifiers by 3% in accuracy due to its ability to capture distributed information flow. With its demonstrated success in decoding simple visual information and accommodating individual variations, this model holds promise for applications in neuroscience and clinical settings, including brain-computer interfaces and neural prosthetics. Future research will broaden the scope to include more cognitive tasks and modalities, personalize neurotechnology through additional neural features, and explore the impact of different covariance structures on our Bayesian Time-Series Classifier model.

References

1. Alotaiby, T., El-Samie, F.E.A., Alshebeili, S.A., Ahmad, I.: A review of channel selection algorithms for EEG signal processing. EURASIP J. Adv. Signal Process. **2015**, 1–21 (2015)
2. Anumanchipalli, G.K., Chartier, J., Chang, E.F.: Speech synthesis from neural decoding of spoken sentences. Nature **568**(7753), 493–498 (2019)
3. Bashashati, A., Fatourechi, M., Ward, R.K., Birch, G.E.: A survey of signal processing algorithms in brain-computer interfaces based on electrical brain signals. J. Neural Eng. **4**(2), R32 (2007)
4. Box, G.P., Cox, D.R.: An analysis of transformations. J. Roy. Stat. Soc. **26**(21), 1–43 (1964)
5. Craik, A., He, Y., Contreras-Vidal, J.L.: Deep learning for electroencephalogram (EEG) classification tasks: a review. J. Neural Eng. **16**(3), 031001 (2019)
6. Dykstra, A.R., et al.: Individualized localization and cortical surface-based registration of intracranial electrodes. Neuroimage **59**(4), 3563–3570 (2012)
7. Falzon, O., Camilleri, K.P., Muscat, J.: The analytic common spatial patterns method for EEG-based BCI data. J. Neural Eng. **9**(4), 045009 (2012)
8. Gardner, M.W., Dorling, S.: Artificial neural networks (the multilayer perceptron)-a review of applications in the atmospheric sciences. Atmos. Environ. **32**(14–15), 2627–2636 (1998)
9. Gu, J., et al.: Recent advances in convolutional neural networks. Pattern Recogn. **77**, 354–377 (2018)
10. Hochreiter, S., Schmidhuber, J.: Long short-term memory. Neural Comput. **9**(8), 1735–1780 (1997)
11. Huth, A.G., Lee, T., Nishimoto, S., Bilenko, N.Y., Vu, A.T., Gallant, J.L.: Decoding the semantic content of natural movies from human brain activity. Front. Syst. Neurosci. **10**, 81 (2016). https://doi.org/10.3389/fnsys.2016.00081
12. James, G., Witten, D., Hastie, T., Tibshirani, R.: An Introduction to Statistical Learning, vol. 112. Springer, Heidelberg (2013). https://doi.org/10.1007/978-1-0716-1418-1
13. Janca, R., et al.: Detection of interictal epileptiform discharges using signal envelope distribution modelling: application to epileptic and non-epileptic intracranial recordings. Brain Topogr. **28**, 172–183 (2015)
14. Kay, K.N., Naselaris, T., Prenger, R.J., Gallant, J.L.: Identifying natural images from human brain activity. Nature **452**(7185), 352–355 (2008)
15. Kohler, F., Gkogkidis, C.A., Bentler, C., Wang, X., Gierthmuehlen, M., Fischer, J., Stolle, C., Reindl, L.M., Rickert, J., Stieglitz, T., et al.: Closed-loop interaction with the cerebral cortex: a review of wireless implant technology. Brain-Comput. Interfaces **4**(3), 146–154 (2017)
16. Kosmyna, N., Lindgren, J.T., Lécuyer, A.: Attending to visual stimuli versus performing visual imagery as a control strategy for EEG-based brain-computer interfaces. Sci. Rep. **8**(1), 1–14 (2018)
17. Lawhern, V.J., Solon, A.J., Waytowich, N.R., Gordon, S.M., Hung, C.P., Lance, B.J.: EEGNet: a compact convolutional neural network for EEG-based brain-computer interfaces. J. Neural Eng. **15**(5), 056013 (2018)
18. Ledoit, O., Wolf, M.: A well-conditioned estimator for large-dimensional covariance matrices. J. Multivar. Anal. **88**(2), 365–411 (2004)
19. Liu, H., Agam, Y., Madsen, J.R., Kreiman, G.: Timing, timing, timing: fast decoding of object information from intracranial field potentials in human visual cortex. Neuron **62**(2), 281–290 (2009)

20. Oh, S.H., Lee, Y.R., Kim, H.N.: A novel EEG feature extraction method using Hjorth parameter. Int. J. Electron. Electr. Eng. **2**(2), 106–110 (2014)
21. Oostenveld, R., Fries, P., Maris, E., Schoffelen, J.M.: FieldTrip: open source software for advanced analysis of MEG, EEG, and invasive electrophysiological data. Comput. Intell. Neurosci. **2011**, 1–9 (2011)
22. Petrantonakis, P.C., Hadjileontiadis, L.J.: Emotion recognition from EEG using higher order crossings. IEEE Trans. Inf. Technol. Biomed. **14**(2), 186–197 (2009)
23. Prochazka, A., Kukal, J., Vysata, O.: Wavelet transform use for feature extraction and EEG signal segments classification. In: 2008 3rd International Symposium on Communications, Control and Signal Processing, pp. 719–722. IEEE (2008)
24. Rish, I., et al.: An empirical study of the naive bayes classifier. In: IJCAI 2001 Workshop on Empirical Methods in Artificial Intelligence, vol. 3, pp. 41–46 (2001)
25. Roy, S., Kiral-Kornek, I., Harrer, S.: ChronoNet: a deep recurrent neural network for abnormal EEG identification. In: Riaño, D., Wilk, S., ten Teije, A. (eds.) AIME 2019. LNCS (LNAI), vol. 11526, pp. 47–56. Springer, Cham (2019). https://doi.org/10.1007/978-3-030-21642-9_8
26. Roy, Y., Banville, H., Albuquerque, I., Gramfort, A., Falk, T.H., Faubert, J.: Deep learning-based electroencephalography analysis: a systematic review. J. Neural Eng. **16**(5), 051001 (2019)
27. Sabesan, S., Good, L.B., Tsakalis, K.S., Spanias, A., Treiman, D.M., Iasemidis, L.D.: Information flow and application to epileptogenic focus localization from intracranial EEG. IEEE Trans. Neural Syst. Rehabil. Eng. **17**(3), 244–253 (2009)
28. Shanechi, M.M.: Brain-machine interfaces from motor to mood. Nat. Neurosci. **22**(10), 1554–1564 (2019)
29. Smola, A.J., Schölkopf, B.: A tutorial on support vector regression. Stat. Comput. **14**, 199–222 (2004)
30. Sporns, O., Tononi, G., Kötter, R.: The human connectome: a structural description of the human brain. PLoS Comput. Biol. **1**(4), e42 (2005)
31. Srivastava, S., Gupta, M.R., Frigyik, B.A.: Bayesian quadratic discriminant analysis. J. Mach. Learn. Res. **8**(6) (2007)
32. Subasi, A., Gursoy, M.I.: EEG signal classification using PCA, ICA, LDA and support vector machines. Expert Syst. Appl. **37**(12), 8659–8666 (2010)
33. Subha, D.P., Joseph, P.K., Acharya, U.R., Lim, C.M.: EEG signal analysis: a survey. J. Med. Syst. **34**, 195–212 (2010)
34. Übeyli, E.D.: Statistics over features: EEG signals analysis. Comput. Biol. Med. **39**(8), 733–741 (2009)
35. Vidal, J.R., et al.: Category-specific visual responses: an intracranial study comparing gamma, beta, alpha, and ERP response selectivity. Front. Hum. Neurosci. **4**, 195 (2010)
36. Wolpaw, J.R., Millán, J.D.R., Ramsey, N.F.: Brain-computer interfaces: definitions and principles. Handb. Clin. Neurol. **168**, 15–23 (2020)
37. Zimek, A., Filzmoser, P.: There and back again: outlier detection between statistical reasoning and data mining algorithms. Wiley Interdisc. Rev.: Data Min. Knowl. Discov. **8**(6), e1280 (2018)

Variability of Non-parametric HRF in Interconnectedness and Its Association in Deriving Resting State Network

Sukesh Kumar Das[1]([✉]) [iD], Pratik Jain[3], Anil K. Sao[2][iD], and Bharat Biswal[3][iD]

[1] Indian Institute of Technology Mandi, Mandi 175005, HP, India
skd.sentu@gmail.com
[2] Indian Institute of Technology Bhilai, Bhilai 492015, Chhattisgarh, India
anil@iitbhilai.ac.in
[3] New Jersey Institute of Technology, Newark, NJ 07102, USA
{pj44,bharat.biswal}@njit.edu

Abstract. Blood Oxygen Level-Dependent (BOLD) time course in functional magnetic resonance imaging (fMRI) is modeled as the response of the hemodynamic response function (HRF) excited by an activity-inducing signal. Variability of the HRF across the brain influences functional connectivity (FC) estimates and some approaches have been attempted to separate the HRF and activity-inducing signal from the observed BOLD signal as a blind separation problem. In this work, an approach based on homomorphic filtering is proposed to estimate a non-parametric representation of HRF in resting state fMRI. Voxel-wise and region-wise variations of correlation of the estimated HRF (both the parametric and non-parametric representation) are analyzed in different functional networks. Principal component analysis of the correlation matrix using the estimated HRF is used to analyze the interconnectedness. HRF shows higher variability for the non-parametric representation over the parametric representation. Further, the contribution of the estimated HRF is then studied in producing resting-state networks using the dictionary learning framework.

Keywords: Deconvolution · HRF variability · Resting state fMRI · Dictionary learning · Resting state networks

1 Introduction

Resting-state functional magnetic resonance imaging (rs-fMRI) is one of the popular modalities to study spontaneous neuronal behavior revealing the function of the brain. The interconnectedness in the resting brain characterizes the functional organization of the brain. The Blood Oxygen Level-Dependent (BOLD) signal, an indirect measure of neuronal activity, acquired in fMRI is modeled as [9]

$$m[n] = s[n] * h[n] + \epsilon[n], \tag{1}$$

Here, $s[n]$ is the underlying activity-inducing signal (AIS) also called as neuronal activity signal (NAS), $h[n]$ is the hemodynamic response function (HRF) associated with the vascular response evoked due to neuronal event [4], and $\epsilon[n]$ is the measurement noise. This additive noise mostly arises due to physiological activity and head movement and its effect can be mitigated using an appropriate bandpass filter in the rs-fMRI preprocessing step [1,6,7]. The HRF can vary in shape across cortical regions in the brain, across subjects, age and disease groups [5,8,11,13,16,17] due to neuronal and non-neuronal components [2]. The HRF variability and its incorrect assumption may raise significant errors in functional connectivity (FC) using observed BOLD signal [10,17,20]. In [3], the effect of the variable HRF is reduced by scaling the BOLD response using the breath-hold amplitude. The method reduces the vascular contribution to the BOLD variability but requires the acquisition of breath-hold task data. On the contrary, the deconvolution methods used in [5,12,19], do not require any additional acquisition of the data. They assume either a parametric model of the HRF or uniformity of HRF across the brain regions. The ambiguity in the case of the parametric model is that the optimal number of parameters is still unclear to represent the HRF with actual bio-physical process [18] and different parameters have a different detrimental effect on FCs [8]. This issue can be addressed using homomorphic filtering (HMF) to separate AIS and HRF from the rs-fMRI data [7]. In this work, we have analyzed the variability of interconnectedness obtained using the estimate of a non-parametric representation of the HRF in the HMF. The BOLD signal of a voxel is filtered using an appropriate cut-off quefrency (liftering) and the effect of AIS is removed so that the resultant signal will have primary information on the HRF. The variabilities of HRF across regions are analyzed using principal component analysis (PCA) of the correlation matrix obtained using the estimate of the HRF. The analysis was compared with a parametric representation of HRF [19]. As the HRF is derived regionally from fMRI conveying mechanistically relevant information about central nervous system activity [16] and can be originated from neuronal origin [2], we estimate the HRF using the HMF scheme and examine its association in deriving resting-state networks (RSNs) in the dictionary learning (DL) framework. The voxel-wise (active voxels from estimated RSNs) FC variabilities using the estimated non-parametric HRF in three dominating RSNs are also compared with the parametric representation. The non-parametric based estimate of HRF shows more variation in interconnectedness in different functional regions.

Section 2 of the paper explains the proposed method to estimate the non-parametric HRF. Section 3 describes the data and tools. Results including the variability of HRF in interconnectedness and its association with RSNs are demonstrated in Sect. 4. Finally, the discussion is explained in Sect. 5.

2   Proposed Approach

Deriving non-parametric representation of the HRF using HMF and the estimation of FC is illustrated in Fig. 1. Here, the preprocessing pipeline includes the steps used in [1,7]. The HRF is then estimated for every individual voxel using homomorphic deconvolution of the preprocessed signal. In Cepstrum domain, noise reduced signal (m_d) is expressed as [7]

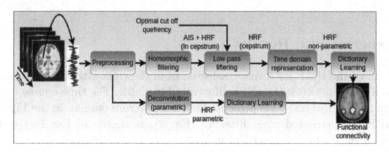

Fig. 1. Block diagram for estimation of non-parametric HRF using HMF.

$$\tilde{m}_d[n] = \tilde{s}[n] + \tilde{h}[n], \tag{2}$$

Here, the $\tilde{m}_d[n]$ is a linear sum of NAS and HRF in the cepstrum domain. The estimated HRF in the cepstrum domain can be obtained as,

$$\hat{\tilde{h}}[n] = LPL\{\tilde{m}_d[n]\}, \tag{3}$$

where LPL stands for low pass liftering. Selection of a suitable cutoff quefrency to decouple the HRF in cepstrum domain is obtained as stated in [7]. Time-domain representation of the estimated HRF is obtained by inverse Fourier transform (F^{-1}) of exponential of the Fourier transform of the estimated HRF in cepstrum domain, therefore

$$\hat{h}[n] = F^{-1}\{e^{F\{\hat{\tilde{h}}[n]\}}\}. \tag{4}$$

3   Data Description and Tools

The experiments are carried out using the resting-state data taken from the UCLA consortium for Neuropsychiatric phenomics data set[1]. A total of 40 healthy participants (age range = 21–50, 18F, 22M) are considered in this study. The functional data were acquired on a 3T Siemens Trio scanner using the following scan parameters: TR (repetition time) = 2,000 ms; TE (echo time) = 29 ms; field of view = 192 mm; flip angle = 72°; # slices (axial) = 34; slice thickness = 4 mm with gap = 0; matrix size = 64 × 64; #images = 152. The data were preprocessed using SPM12[2] software with MATLAB R2019a. The initial 4

---

[1] https://openneuro.org/datasets/ds000030/versions/00016.
[2] http://www.fil.ion.ucl.ac.uk/spm/.

time points of data from all fMRI scans across subjects were discarded to get a steady magnetization. Functional images were then realigned followed by slice time correction. Anatomical images were co-registered to functional images and it was segmented into gray matter (GM), white matter (WM), and cerebrospinal fluid (CSF). Functional images were then normalized to MNI space. The BOLD time courses are then band passed and finally, the normalized functional images were spatially smoothed with a Gaussian kernel of FWHM 5 mm × 5 mm × 5 mm.

4   Experimental Results

The result of the HMF for a voxel, selected from the right lateral parietal cortex of default mode network (DMN) is illustrated in Fig. 2. The time course $(m_d[n])$ is shown in Fig. 2(a). $m_d[n]$ is presented in the cepstrum domain in the Fig. 2(b). The HRF reconstructed after liftering (Eq. 4), is shown in Fig. 2(c) using a suitable cutoff quefrency described in [7].

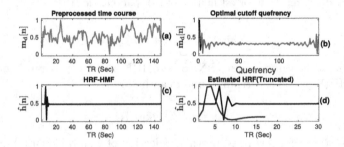

Fig. 2. Deconvolution using HMF of voxel time course, taken from the right lateral parietal cortex of DMN: (a) preprocessed time course, (b) cepstrum of $m_d[n]$ and cut off quefrency (Qc - blue vertical line), (c) reconstructed signal related to HRF, (d) estimated non-parametric HRF (truncated - black) and canonical HRF obtained from SPM (blue). (Color figure online)

4.1   ROI-Based HRF Variability in Interconnectedness

ROI (Seitzman300 functional atlas) based variability of HRF-interconnectedness was demonstrated using seven functional networks (Default mode network - DMN, Somato motor dorsal - SMD, Auditory - Au, Visual - Vis, Fronto-parietal network - FPN, Salience - Sal, Dorsal attention network - DAN) individually. They consist of 186 ROIs from the atlas and connectivity matrices were computed using the average of the estimated HRF time course from each ROI. The number of regions belonging to a network in the atlas is denoted as $n1$. Correlation matrix with $n1$ ROIs is computed using estimated HRF with the non-parametric and parametric methods respectively. Upper triangular elements of the matrices represent one observation and 40 observations are considered for

40 (N) subjects. For each of the two methods (non-parametric and parametric), a $\mathbf{H}_r \in \mathbb{R}^{N \times n_1(n_1-1)/2}$ matrix is obtained from every individual network (r). The PCA of every matrix $\mathbf{H}_r$ is performed. The estimated first three PCs, which contain most of the energy of the data, are used to get three projected coefficients for all the 40 subjects and shown in Figs. 3(a–b). It can be observed in the scatter plots that the variability is more in all 7 networks for the case of the non-parametric representation of HRF in comparison to the parametric representation.

The distribution of the connectivity matrix, $\mathbf{H}_r$ is further illustrated using eigenvalues obtained from PCA. We have computed a parameter, $\tilde{\sigma}_{ri}$, called normalized *log* of eigenvalue for the functional network, r along the ith PC. Here, $\tilde{\sigma}_{ri} = log(\sigma_{ri}/\sigma_{r1})$ for all the i, and σ_{r1} denotes the eigenvalue for the network, r along first PC. This parameter is computed for the 7 networks using the parametric and non-parametric representations of the HRF. If the distribution is spherical then all the σ_{ri} for the network, r, will be similar and $\tilde{\sigma}_{ri}$ will be a constant for all i. On the contrary, if the parameter, $\tilde{\sigma}_{ri}$ decays rapidly, distribution will be towards the ellipsoid. It is observed that the sigma of the distribution of FC using the non-parametric HRF is downward concave and they are upward concave for the case of the parametric HRF (Figs. 3(c) and (d)). It implies more variability of connectedness using HRF with the non-parametric representation. The higher variability is observed in Vis, FPN, and DMN for the non-parametric representation. Though the same trend is observed for the parametric case, the Vis shows the highest variability among the three.

4.2   RSNs Using Estimated HRF

The RSNs are obtained using the estimated HRF, computed by Eq. 4 in the framework of online dictionary learning (ODL) [6,15]. Here, the estimated HRF from multiple subjects is used to form $\mathbf{H} \in \mathbb{R}^{nm \times v}$ by temporally concatenating n number of consecutive HRF time points obtained from m number of subjects each with v number of voxels. The matrix is decomposed as

$$\mathbf{H} \approx \mathbf{DA} \;\; with \;\; \mathbf{D} \in \mathbb{R}^{nm \times k} \;\; and \;\; \mathbf{A} \in \mathbb{R}^{k \times v} . \tag{5}$$

$\mathbf{D}$ consists k dense temporal atoms (every column) and the coefficient matrix, $\mathbf{A}$ consists k sparse spatial maps (every row, 28 in this study). For the decomposition, sparsity inducing penalty is combined with the data fitting term and it leads to the following optimization problem:

$$\underset{\mathbf{D},\mathbf{A}}{\operatorname{argmin}} \|\mathbf{H} - \mathbf{DA}\|_F^2 + \lambda \| \mathbf{A}^T \|_1 \text{ s.t. } \forall j, \|\mathbf{D}_j\|_2 \leq 1. \tag{6}$$

The optimization problem (Eq. 6) with respect to the $\mathbf{D}$ and the $\mathbf{A}$ is not jointly convex and is solved by alternative minimization method [14]. FCs are obtained using preprocessed time course, estimated HRF with the ODL algorithm described in Eq. 6. We have also illustrated RSNs obtained using AIS ($s[n]$) represented by the approach followed in [7]. The six exemplary RSNs

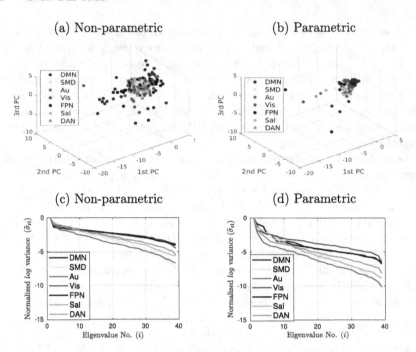

Fig. 3. Data representation of FCs (7 functional networks) in the space of the first three principal components and eigen values. FCs obtained using HRF with (a) non-parametric and (b) parametric representation. Normalized log of eigenvalues (variances) for 7 networks: FCs obtained using HRF with (c) non-parametric and (d) parametric representation.

(anterior DMN - aDMN, medial sensory-motor network - MSMN, Aud, posterior DMN - pDMN, DAN, and superior visual network - SVN) using preprocessed time course and estimated AIS, have been shown in Fig. 4 (First and Second columns). These RSNs appear symmetrically with good spatial extent using the AIS. We could critically identify the RSNs with the estimated HRF obtained using HMF. Six noisy networks named motor network (MN), right frontoparietal network (rFPN), Aud, pDMN, lingual gyrus network (LGN), and medial visual network (MVN) are identified and have been illustrated in Fig. 4 (Third column). But, only two networks - cerebellar network (CBN) and SVN were critically identified using the HRF obtained using the parametric approach [19] (Fig. 4, Fourth column).

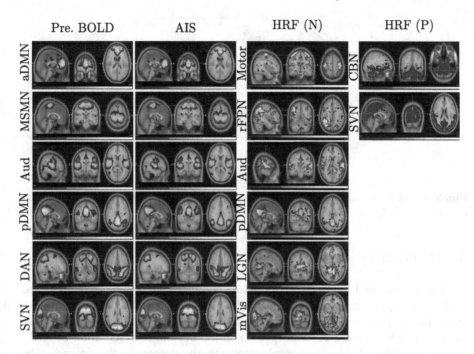

Fig. 4. Sagittal, coronal and axial views of Fcs: From top (for column 1 and 2): aDMN, MSMN, Aud, pDMN, DAN and SVN obtained with DL using conventionally preprocessed BOLD and NAS using HMF. From top (for column 3): Motor, rFPN, Aud, pDMN, LGN and MVN obtained with DL using HRF (non-parametric) estimated by HMF. From top (for column 4): CBN and SVN obtained with DL using parametric representation HRF estimated by blind deconvolution.

4.3   Voxel-Wise HRF Variability in Interconnectedness

Variability of the non-parametric and parametric [19] representation of HRF is also compared using voxel-wise interconnectedness. For this, active voxels are obtained from the three dominant RSNs named pDMN, Au, and mVis estimated with DL using the AIS (Fig. 4, Second column). Voxel-wise correlations are then obtained using the estimated parametric and non-parametric HRF from the active regions. The distribution of the HRF correlations is demonstrated in Fig. 5. The variances of the correlation for the 3 networks are (0.34, 0.35, 0.37) and (0.49, 0.50, 0.49) with parametric and non-parametric methods respectively.

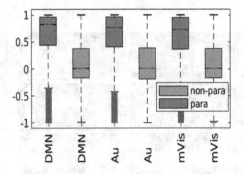

Fig. 5. Parametric and non-parametric HRF correlation distribution for 3 dominating RSNs (pDMN, Au and mVis)

5   Discussion

Finding the optimal number of parameters is difficult to define the widely used parametric representation of HRF that describes the actual biophysical process and different parameters have a different detrimental effect on FC [8,17]. This issue is addressed using HMF to get a non-parametric representation of HRF, where the effect of AIS is deemphasized via the deconvolution process. The interconnectedness in 3 dominant RSNs demonstrates higher variability using the non-parametric HRF (Fig. 5). Eigen decomposition of the correlation matrix (Sect. 4.1), obtained using the estimated HRF, across brain regions demonstrates that the variability is observed more for the non-parametric HRF in comparison with the parametric HRF (Fig. 3). The reason could be that the HRF is attempted to characterize using only three parameters and hence the variabilities are reduced. On the contrary, this constraint is realized in the non-parametric representation of HRF. The study demonstrates that the contribution of estimated HRF is inferior to that of AIS in deriving RSNs (in Fig. 4, Third column). We can critically identify only 2 RSNs (CBN and SVN) using the parametric HRF (Fig. 4, Fourth column). The RSNs are identifiable in noisy conditions and even if a few can be identified, they do not appear as integral networks. It suggests that estimated HRF insignificantly contributes to forming RSNs whereas AIS produces clear and distinct FCs [6,7]. As the ground truth of HRF is unknown, it is difficult to directly validate the estimation. One can conclude that the HRF is a confound in fMRI and can be considered an important component in its own right but assumptions made in the Eq. 1 and the selection of optimal cutoff quefrency may always not be suitable for their separation. Our study is limited to the demonstration of the variability of interconnectedness using the estimated HRF in a healthy cohort. We assume that the variability would be higher in the case of a disordered population because of neurochemical and vascular alterations.

References

1. Aggarwal, P., Gupta, A., Garg, A.: Joint estimation of hemodynamic response function and voxel activation in functional MRI data. In: Navab, N., Hornegger, J., Wells, W.M., Frangi, A.F. (eds.) MICCAI 2015. LNCS, vol. 9349, pp. 142–149. Springer, Cham (2015). https://doi.org/10.1007/978-3-319-24553-9_18
2. Bießmann, F., Murayama, Y., Logothetis, N.K., Müller, K.R., Meinecke, F.C.: Improved decoding of neural activity from fMRI signals using non-separable spatiotemporal deconvolutions. Neuroimage 61(4), 1031–1042 (2012)
3. Biswal, B.B., Kannurpatti, S.S., Rypma, B.: Hemodynamic scaling of fMRI-BOLD signal: validation of low-frequency spectral amplitude as a scalability factor. Magn. Reson. Imaging 25(10), 1358–1369 (2007)
4. Boynton, G.M., Engel, S.A., Glover, G.H., Heeger, D.J.: Linear systems analysis of functional magnetic resonance imaging in human V1. J. Neurosci. 16(13), 4207–4221 (1996)
5. Cherkaoui, H., Moreau, T., Halimi, A., Leroy, C., Ciuciu, P.: Multivariate semi-blind deconvolution of fMRI time series. Neuroimage 241, 118418 (2021)
6. Das, S., Sao, A.K., Biswal, B.: Precise estimation of resting state functional connectivity using empirical mode decomposition. In: Mahmud, M., Vassanelli, S., Kaiser, M.S., Zhong, N. (eds.) BI 2020. LNCS (LNAI), vol. 12241, pp. 75–84. Springer, Cham (2020). https://doi.org/10.1007/978-3-030-59277-6_7
7. Das, S.K., Sao, A.K., Biswal, B.: Estimation of spontaneous neuronal activity using homomorphic filtering. In: de Bruijne, M., et al. (eds.) MICCAI 2021. LNCS, vol. 12907, pp. 615–624. Springer, Cham (2021). https://doi.org/10.1007/978-3-030-87234-2_58
8. Deshpande, G., Sathian, K., Hu, X.: Effect of hemodynamic variability on granger causality analysis of fMRI. Neuroimage 52(3), 884–896 (2010)
9. Glover, G.H.: Deconvolution of impulse response in event-related bold fMRI. Neuroimage 9(4), 416–429 (1999)
10. Greve, D.N., Brown, G.G., Mueller, B.A., Glover, G., Liu, T.T.: A survey of the sources of noise in fMRI. Psychometrika 78(3), 396–416 (2013)
11. Handwerker, D.A., Ollinger, J.M., D'Esposito, M.: Variation of BOLD hemodynamic responses across subjects and brain regions and their effects on statistical analyses. Neuroimage 21(4), 1639–1651 (2004)
12. Karahanoğlu, F., Caballero-Gaudes, C., Lazeyras, F., Van De Ville, D.: Total activation: fMRI deconvolution through spatio-temporal regularization. Neuroimage 73, 121–134 (2013)
13. Liu, X., Gerraty, R.T., Grinband, J., Parker, D., Razlighi, Q.R.: Brain atrophy can introduce age-related differences in bold response. Hum. Brain Mapp. 38(7), 3402–3414 (2017)
14. Mairal, J., Bach, F., Ponce, J., Sapiro, G.: Online learning for matrix factorization and sparse coding. J. Mach. Learn. Res. 11(1) (2010)
15. Mensch, A., Varoquaux, G., Thirion, B.: Compressed online dictionary learning for fast resting-state fMRI decomposition. In: Proceedings of 13th International Symposium on Biomedical Imaging (ISBI), pp. 1282–1285. IEEE (2016)
16. Rangaprakash, D., Tadayonnejad, R., Deshpande, G., O'Neill, J., Feusner, J.D.: fMRI hemodynamic response function (HRF) as a novel marker of brain function: applications for understanding obsessive-compulsive disorder pathology and treatment response. Brain Imaging Behav. 15(3), 1622–1640 (2021)

17. Rangaprakash, D., Wu, G., Marinazzo, D., Hu, X., Deshpande, G.: Hemodynamic response function HRF variability confounds resting-state fMRI functional connectivity. Magn. Reson. Med. **80**(4), 1697–1713 (2018)
18. Sreenivasan, K.R., Havlicek, M., Deshpande, G.: Nonparametric hemodynamic deconvolution of fMRI using homomorphic filtering. IEEE Trans. Med. Imaging **34**(5), 1155–1163 (2014)
19. Wu, G., Liao, W., Stramaglia, S., Ding, J., Chen, H., Marinazzo, D.: A blind deconvolution approach to recover effective connectivity brain networks from resting state fMRI data. Med. Image Anal. **17**(3), 365–374 (2013)
20. Yan, W., Rangaprakash, D., Deshpande, G.: Aberrant hemodynamic responses in autism: implications for resting state fMRI functional connectivity studies. NeuroImage: Clin. **19**, 320–330 (2018)

BrainSegNeT: A Lightweight Brain Tumor Segmentation Model Based on U-Net and Progressive Neuron Expansion

Partho Ghose[1($\boxtimes$)], Milon Biswas[2], and Loveleen Gaur[3]

[1] Jagannath University, Dhaka 1100, Bangladesh
partho.cse.jnu@gmail.com
[2] Department of Computer Science, University of Alabama, Birmingham, USA
milon@ieee.org
[3] School of Computer Science, Taylor's University, Subang Jaya, Malaysia

Abstract. Brain tumor segmentation is a critical task in medical image analysis. In recent years, several deep learning-based models have been developed for brain tumor segmentation using magnetic resonance imaging (MRI) data. To address challenges such as high computational time and the requirement of huge storage and resources, we proposed BrainSegNet, which is a lightweight extension of U-Net with progressively expanded neurons that require fewer weights and less memory space. Unlike other DL models, our proposed model has the simplest architecture and is more accurate than other state-of-the-art methods for brain tumor segmentation. The proposed approach was extensively analyzed using the BraTS2020 benchmark dataset for segmenting brain tumors. The experimental findings demonstrate the effectiveness of the proposed system, producing a 96.01% Dice score and 95.89% mean IoU for brain tumor segmentation from brain MRI images.

Keywords: Deep learning · image segmentation · U-Net · brain tumor · MRI Images

1 Introduction

Hundreds of various forms of brain tumors afflict humans, making it one of the most fatal diseases [6]. Traditional treatments, such as surgery, chemotherapy, and radiotherapy, are mainly employed to address these conditions. Artificial intelligence (AI) [4] is gaining momentum and significance as it progresses, and can play a crucial role in brain tumor diagnosis and surgical pre-assessment procedures [30]. To assist in preoperative decisions segmenting brain tumor from medical brain image is now a cutting edge research area [21,22,29]. Researchers

F. Liu et al. (Eds.): BI 2023, LNAI 13974, pp. 249–260, 2023.
https://doi.org/10.1007/978-3-031-43075-6_22

around the world are vigorously making efforts to establish different kinds of solutions [34] for early detection for better diagnosis and one of the solutions can be the usage of deep learning approaches [7,9]. CNN-based segmentation methods have also achieved state-of-the-art performances in various tests [14,25]. The classical DL model improves the connection weight between the original neurons while analyzing lesion features in large medical images [28]. Consequently, the standard DL model [19], such as the convolutional neural network (CNN), the entire convolution networks (FCN) [18], the U-Net network, and the attention U-Net [24], has considerably improved brain tumor segmentation performance. Inspired by the successful use of CNNs in multiple medical image analysis tasks, we propose a novel lightweight high-performance model for brain tumor segmentation based on deep learning. Our approach aims to design a simple deep learning architecture for brain tumor segmentation. However, all the architectures proposed [5,14,17,20,23,25,33] for brain tumor segmentation have a complex structure that requires high computational time, more effective GPUs, large amounts of storage, and many resources.

Bare in mind these issues, we do straightforward modification of the U-Net developed by merging merits of convolutional blocks, progressive expansion layers, and residual network connections to obtain not only a better segmentation model but also reduce the parameters. The motivation behind this is to improve accuracy and, at the same time, maintain simplicity. The goal of this study is to construct a less complex CNN architecture for brain tumor segmentation, and our main contributions include the following:

1. We propose a simple U-Net architecture incorporating with progressive expansion layer, and residual network connection, referred to as BrainSegNet, that requires fewer weights and less memory space for brain tumor segmentation;
2. An extensive evaluation is done on two challenging datasets, then compared with the state-of-the-art architectures, and the evaluations show that the BrainSegNet results in outstanding performance compared to baselines.

The rest of this paper is organized as follows. A literature review of recent methodology 2. In Sect. 3, a description of the proposed system along with its data collection. Section 4.2 presents the experimental results and a comparative performance analysis are presented in Sect. 4.2.

2   Related Work

Manual tumor segmentation is subjective and time-consuming. In addition, the detection result is laborious and depends on the doctor's theoretical knowledge and practical ability. Therefore, designing an automatic and robust brain tumor segmentation system is essential to realize tumor diagnosis [1,8,10]. Various research studies have been suggested for segmenting brain tumors with deep learning methods. For example, Pius Kwao Gadosey et al. [1] proposed a lightweight model modifying the U-Net model named SD-UNet to obtain higher performance with fewer computational requirements. To reduce the computational complexity, they applied depthwise separable convolutions in their proposed network and achieved a 90.70% dice score for the brain segmentation task. However, their suggested architecture has 3.9M parameters, requiring 15.8 MB of disk space which can be further reduced. In the same year, Sergio Pereira et al. [25] presented a cascade-CNN system where they applied a 3×3 kernel to mitigate overfitting. Their approach could segment the brain MRI image into four areas: normal tissue, necrosis, edema, and enhancing tumor. According to the authors, two CNN architectures were used for better feature extraction, especially for low-grade and high-grade glioma. However, one drawback is that the operator needs manually determine the glioma grade in the early stage, which demands prior medical expertise. Besides these issues, the introduced system showed poor segmentation results for core areas in the BRATS 2015 dataset. Similarly, Havaei et al. [12] proposed another novel Cascading style to segment brain tumors automatically. This research utilized the cascade style of CNN to capture global and local contextual features to deal with imbalanced tumor labels. Moeskops et al. [21] suggested an automatic system incorporating a multi-scale CNN to segment white matter hyperintensities of presumed vascular origin (WMH) from MRI modalities. Chen et al. [5] introduced a model combing prior knowledge with DCNN to improve the captured motifs of DCNN for brain tumor sub-compartment identification.

In 2020, Zhang et al. [31] introduced an attention U-Net for the purpose of brain tumor segmentation. Their suggested architecture improved the local responses to down-sampling and the recovery effects of the up-sampling simultaneously. Furthermore, Wu et al. [29] introduced a CNN-based multi-features refinement and aggregation network (MRANet) for brain tumor segmentation. They adopted the feature fusion strategy to utilize hierarchical features in this system. Recently, Lee et al. [16] proposed an intelligent brain tissue segmentation method utilizing MR images. They partitioned the brain MRI image into small patches through a patch-wise U-Net model, and each patch was predicted separately. However, although the introduced model could overcome the limited disk space problem, the training stage showed higher computation complexity.

3 Research Methodology

3.1 U-Net

U-Net architecture [27] is one of the most popular deep-gaining knowledge of architectures used for medical image segmentation. This architecture is on the whole utilized through the research community due to the fact of its architectural variations with superior outcomes in the image segmentation tasks. In clinical image segmentation U-Net has established itself as well-known for recent proposed ideas including R2YU-Net, attention U-Net, and U-Net++. The place u-shape model is retained along with the two fundamental paths encoder and decoder. By incorporating more than a few strategies such as skip connections, attention modules, residual blocks or aggregate of them those u-net versions alter the encoder or the decoder blocks.

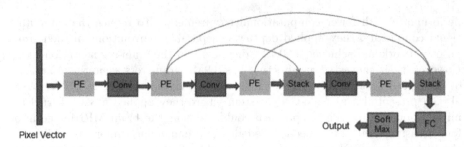

Pixel Vector

Fig. 1. Visualization of dPEN structure

3.2   dPEN: deep Progressively Expanded Network

The dPEN method takes a pixel from a multispectral image as an input vector and returns the types of objects present in the input pixel vector. Figure 1 illustrates the structure of dPEN, which is formulated as follows: four progressive expansion layers (PEL), three convolutional, three maximum-pooling, and then a fully connected layer (FC). Progressively expandable neural networks (PEN nets), developed for identifying hyperspectral images, serve as the basis of dPEN. The core idea of the dPEN paradigm is the addition of PEL, which incrementally expands each node from the input using a McClorin series expansion of a predefined nonlinear function. It is shown that the dPEN architecture is capable of extracting significant discriminative features from multispectral bands. Hence, the dPEN architecture outperforms well-known machine learning models such as random forest, support vector machine, CNN, etc.

3.3   Proposed Architecture: BrainSegNet

In this study, we propose a modified U-Net named BrainSegnet for brain tumor segmentation. BrainSegNet combines U-nets' modularity with the integration of expanded neurons using nonlinear function expansion. Our proposed architecture takes a 224 × 224 input image as input and outputs the segmented points of interest shown in Fig. 2. The U-Net's U-shape is preserved, with the encoder path on the left side and the decoder path on the right. We incorporate PEL in the encoder path only. A PEL layer, also known as PE2: progressive expansion with the first two terms in Maclaurin series expansion, is included in each residual block along with two batch normalization layers (BN), two ReLU activation layers (ReLU), two 3 * 3 2D convolutional layers (Conv 3 * 3), and a PEL layer. The enlarged area of Fig. 2 demonstrates the arrangement of the Residual PE block.

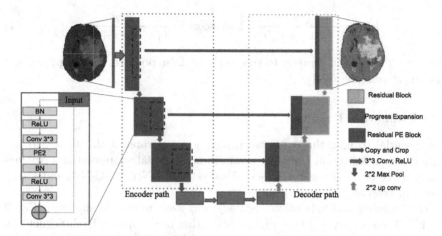

Fig. 2. The detailed illustration of the proposed BrainSegNet architecture integrated PE block with the encoder path where PE2 indicates progressive expansion with two terms.

4   Dataset and Results Evaluations

In the experiments, the training, testing, and validation datasets are all from the BraTS2020 benchmarks [2,3]. The MICCAI Brain Tumor Segmentation competition uses BraTS, a significant public dataset for multimodal brain tumor segmentation, and it is frequently utilized in research on this subject. Every year, new data are added, removed, or replaced to the dataset to enrich its scale. BraTS2020 have 369 annotated brain tumor samples for model training and 120 samples for testing. Each case includes MRI scans of four different modalities: T1-weighted (T1), T1-enhanced contrast (T1-ce), T2-weighted (T2), and T2 fluid-attenuated inversion recovery (Flair). The datasets are labeled by domain experts and contain four classes: background, necrotic and non-enhancing tumors (NCR/NET), GB-peritumoral edema (ED), and GB-enhancing tumors (ET). The evaluation is based on three different brain tumor regions:

- Whole Tumor (WT) = NCR/NET + ED + ET
- Tumor Core (TC) = NCR/NET + ET
- Enhancing Tumor (ET)

4.1   Evaluation Metrics

To verify the efficiency of the proposed model framework, two most common metrics used in medical image segmentation, mean IoU score and Dice score are used. The corresponding formulas are given:

$$\text{IoU} = \frac{(\tau\rho)}{(f\rho + \tau\rho + f\eta)}, \text{ Dice score} = \frac{2\tau\rho}{(f\eta + 2\tau\rho + f\rho)} \qquad (1)$$

where $\tau\rho$, $f\rho$, $\tau\eta$, and $f\eta$ refer to true positive, false positive, true negative, and false negative respectively.

4.2 Evaluation Results

It is essential to note that while all images are generated with 240 × 240 resolution for training, all datasets are evaluated at native resolution. No preprocessing or post-processing is done. We also train U-Net, ResU-Net, and TransUnet and keep all the settings the same.

The training and validation accuracy and loss curves are shown in Fig. 3 and Fig. 4, respectively. These Figures show that our proposed BrainSegnet and ResUnet showed almost similar accuracy and loss, while TransU-Net depicted poor performances in both cases. In BraTS2020 dataset, BrainSegNet obtained a dice score of 97.47%, 82.33%, and 90.33% for WT, ET, and TC, respectively, and the average dice score achieved 96.01%. For the sake of comparison, we also trained some state-of-the-art models with the same setup and data distribution and the experimental results are shown in Table 1 in terms of Dice score.

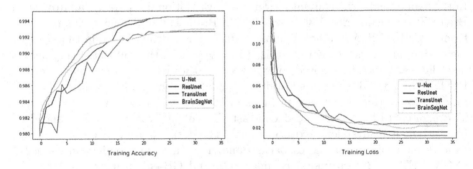

Fig. 3. Traininig accuracy and loss curves.

Generally, BrainSegNet performs well in ET, TC, and WT categories. Table 1 demonstrates that the Dice score of the BrainSegNet has a significant advantage over the conventional U-Net with less complexity. The findings indicate that the approach can segment tumors more effectively than U-Net and ResU-Net. BrainSegNet is more conducive to learning long-distance artifacts, so the effect of TC and WT category segmentation is more prominent. For ET cases, ResU-Net and Typical U-Net obtain poor results, which indicates that for brain tumor segmentation, these models cannot extract sufficient local features. However, for ET case, compared to U-Net and ResU-NeT, it performs poorly. On the other hand, Trans-Net obtains an 89.83% dice score. BrainSegNet performs exceptionally well in the ET and TC categories, demonstrating the method's superior capacity to extract both global and local features.

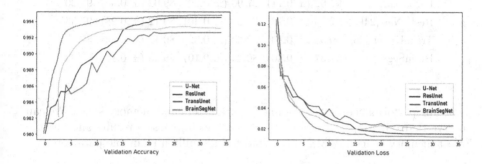

Fig. 4. Validation accuracy and loss curves.

In Table 1, the data in brackets shows the standard deviation of the proposed model segmentation outcomes. According to the table, the proposed model has a minimum classification deviation for each of the three groups. These findings suggest that the model has the best and most consistent segmentation impact and that the segmentation outcomes will not have noticeable differences. Furthermore, we can see from Table 2 that compared with U-Net and ResUet, BrainSegNet can gain 0.69% and 0.36% higher μIoU result and also has a 10.06% improvement compared to the TransU-Net model. Our model also has the minimum standard deviation among all the models mentioned in Table 2, which indicates the stability of the segmentation results of the BrainSegNet model.

Table 1. Segmentation results in terms of Dice score on BraTS 2020 dataset.

Method	Dice score (%)			
	WT	ET	TC	Avg.
U-Net [18]	96.02 ($\pm$ 0.10)	78.96 ($\pm$ 0.38)	89.72 ($\pm$ 0.30)	95.45
ResU-Net [24]	97.06 ($\pm$ 0.17)	77.85 ($\pm$ 0.39)	89.73 ($\pm$ 0.25)	95.23
TransU-Net [26]	92.38 ($\pm$ 0.10)	72.63 ($\pm$ 0.32)	79.16 ($\pm$ 0.22)	89.83
BrainSegNet	97.47 ($\pm$ 0.102)	82.33 ($\pm$ 0.125)	90.33 ($\pm$ 0.104)	96.01

Computational and Memory Requirements: The less complex methods suggested in this study are more suited for resource-constrained applications, both regarding training and deployment, for example, in portable devices. Table 3 compares the proposed architecture with three well-known architectures

Table 2. Segmentation results on the BraTS 2020 validation dataset in terms of μIoU.

Method	μIoU (%)			
	WT	ET	TC	Avg.
U-Net [18]	97.02 ($\pm$ 0.11)	77.96 ($\pm$ 0.20)	89.02 ($\pm$ 0.30)	95.20
ResU-Net [24]	97.06 ($\pm$ 0.13)	78.85 ($\pm$ 0.30)	89.12 ($\pm$ 0.28)	95.53
TransU-Net [26]	90.38 ($\pm$ 0.10)	62.63 ($\pm$ 0.32)	80.16 ($\pm$ 0.22)	87.83
BrainSegNet	97.37 ($\pm$ 0.10)	80.34 ($\pm$ 0.10)	89.53 ($\pm$ 0.10)	95.89

regarding performance vs. the volume of parameters and memory space. We can observe that our proposed BrainSegNet achieves impressive results and has the lowest memory space (18 MB) and almost ∼4.8 million trainable parameters.

Table 3. Parameters and memory requirements vs performance for several brain tumor segmentation models on BraTS2020 datset.

Model	# Params (Million)	Memory Size	μIoU (%)	Dice score (%)
U-Net	∼10.6	37.5 MB	95.45	95.20
ResU-Net	∼4.7	17.5 MB	95.23	95.53
TransU-Net	∼8.6	26 MB	89.83	87.83
BrainSegNet	∼4.8	18 MB	95.89	96.01

Visualization of Tumor Segmentation Result: In Fig. 5, a visualization of the brain tumor segmentation results is made for the BrainSegNet method. The original flair images, ground truth, all class predicted, necrotic/core, edema, and enhancing tumor are shown in the first to sixth columns, respectively. Figure 5 illustrates that the segmentation result for the WT area is the best for all the models, and the segmentation results for the two complicated edges of ET and TC are pretty different. Our model shows more accurate outcomes compared with Ground Truth for detail segmentation.

4.3   Comparison with Existing State-of-the-Art

Table 4 presents the comparative insights of few recent similar research based on DL methods. Based on this performance metrics in the comparative analysis, BrainSegNet method is the most suitable for a image segmentation of Brain tumor.

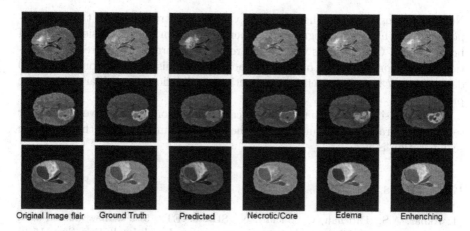

Original Image flair   Ground Truth   Predicted   Necrotic/Core   Edema   Enhenching

Fig. 5. Visualization of MRI Brain tumor image segmentation results of the proposed model.

Table 4. Comparison with recent state-of-the-art on brain tumor segmentation based on DL methods. For comparisons, we used μIoU and Dice score as performance metrics. Here ET = Enhancing tumor; WT = Whole tumor; TC = Tumor core.

Author	architecture	Dataset	Mean IoU (%)			Dice score (%)		
			WT	TC	ET	WT	TC	ET
Ranjbarzadeh et al. [26]	Cascade CNN model and distance-wise attention	BraTS2013	NA	NA	NA	92	87	91
Jiang et al. [15]	Multi-resolution fusion network based on inception U-Net (MRF-IUNet)	BraTS 2019	89.98	74.12	88.05	90.04	76.96	92.22
Zhang et al. [32]	Multi-encoder net (ME-Net)	BraTS 2020	NA	NA	NA	88	73	70
Guan et al. [11]	Encoder-decoder(AGSE-VNet)	BraTS 2020	NA	NA	NA	85	69	78
Huang et al. [13]	multi-depth fusion module based on V-Net structure	BraTS 2018	NA	NA	NA	80.0	75.0	71.0
Lee et al. [16]	DCNN (sparse-multi-OCM and dense-multi-OCM)	BraTS 2015,2017	NA	NA	NA	92	92	93
Proposed Method	BrainSegNet	BraTS2020	96.84	97.78	89.53	97.76	95.30	90.36

5   Conclusion

In this study, we proposed a novel segmentation system, a new variant of the U-Net architecture named BrainSegNet, which can automatically segment diseased tissues in brain MRI images. The model efficiently combines U-Net with PEN to accurately and efficiently segment tumors from brain MRI. Experimental outcomes demonstrate that our proposed system performs better in brain tumor MRI image segmentation than state-of-the-art methods (such as U-Net, ResU-

Net, and TransBTS). Furthermore, the visualization results show that the proposed system has a good segmentation performance for all three lesion regions of brain tumors. Comparisons with recent research on brain tumor area segmentation also demonstrate that our method achieves promising results on BraTs2020 datasets, indicating its potential for practical applications in auxiliary diagnostic procedures.

Further research may analyze the efficacy of additional distinctive features for segmenting brain tumors and explore the suggested method for other semantic segmentation issues.

References

1. Akbar, A.S., Fatichah, C., Suciati, N.: SDA-UNET2. 5D: shallow dilated with attention Unet2. 5D for brain tumor segmentation. Int. J. Intell. Eng. Syst. **15**(2) (2022)
2. Bakas, S., et al.: Advancing the cancer genome atlas glioma MRI collections with expert segmentation labels and radiomic features. Sci. Data **4**(1), 1–13 (2017)
3. Bakas, S., et al.: Identifying the best machine learning algorithms for brain tumor segmentation, progression assessment, and overall survival prediction in the brats challenge. arXiv preprint arXiv:1811.02629 (2018)
4. Biswas, M., Kaiser, M.S., Mahmud, M., Al Mamun, S., Hossain, M.S., Rahman, M.A.: An XAI based autism detection: the context behind the detection. In: Mahmud, M., Kaiser, M.S., Vassanelli, S., Dai, Q., Zhong, N. (eds.) BI 2021. LNCS (LNAI), vol. 12960, pp. 448–459. Springer, Cham (2021). https://doi.org/10.1007/978-3-030-86993-9_40
5. Chen, H., Qin, Z., Ding, Y., Tian, L., Qin, Z.: Brain tumor segmentation with deep convolutional symmetric neural network. Neurocomputing **392**, 305–313 (2020)
6. Das, S., Nayak, G.K., Saba, L., Kalra, M., Suri, J.S., Saxena, S.: An artificial intelligence framework and its bias for brain tumor segmentation: a narrative review. Comput. Biol. Med. **143**, 105273 (2022)
7. Ghose, P., et al.: Detecting COVID-19 infection status from chest X-ray and CT scan via single transfer learning-driven approach. Front. Genet. **13**, 980338 (2022)
8. Ghose, P., Sharmin, S., Gaur, L., Zhao, Z.: Grid-search integrated optimized support vector machine model for breast cancer detection. In: 2022 IEEE International Conference on Bioinformatics and Biomedicine (BIBM), pp. 2846–2852. IEEE (2022)
9. Ghose, P., Uddin, M.A., Acharjee, U.K., Sharmin, S.: Deep viewing for the identification of COVID-19 infection status from chest X-ray image using CNN based architecture. Intell. Syst. Appl. **16**, 200130 (2022)
10. Ghose, P., Uddin, M.A., Islam, M.M., Islam, M., Acharjee, U.K.: A breast cancer detection model using a tuned svm classifier. In: 2022 25th International Conference on Computer and Information Technology (ICCIT), pp. 102–107. IEEE (2022)
11. Guan, X., et al.: 3D AGSE-VNET: an automatic brain tumor MRI data segmentation framework. BMC Med. Imaging **22**(1), 1–18 (2022)
12. Havaei, M., et al.: Brain tumor segmentation with deep neural networks. Med. Image Anal. **35**, 18–31 (2017)
13. Huang, H., et al.: A deep multi-task learning framework for brain tumor segmentation. Front. Oncol. **11**, 690244 (2021)

14. Iqbal, S., Ghani, M.U., Saba, T., Rehman, A.: Brain tumor segmentation in multi-spectral MRI using convolutional neural networks (CNN). Microsc. Res. Tech. **81**(4), 419–427 (2018)
15. Jiang, Y., Ye, M., Wang, P., Huang, D., Lu, X.: MRF-IUNET: a multiresolution fusion brain tumor segmentation network based on improved inception U-net. Comput. Math. Methods Med. **2022** (2022)
16. Lee, B., Yamanakkanavar, N., Malik, M.A., Choi, J.Y.: Correction: automatic segmentation of brain MRI using a novel patch-wise u-net deep architecture. PLoS ONE **17**(2), e0264231 (2022)
17. Liu, X., Zhang, L., Li, T., Wang, D., Wang, Z.: Dual attention guided multi-scale CNN for fine-grained image classification. Inf. Sci. **573**, 37–45 (2021)
18. Long, J., Shelhamer, E., Darrell, T.: Fully convolutional networks for semantic segmentation. In: Proceedings of the IEEE Conference on Computer Vision and Pattern Recognition, pp. 3431–3440 (2015)
19. Mahbub, M.K., Zamil, M.Z.H., Miah, M.A.M., Ghose, P., Biswas, M., Santosh, K.: Mobapp4infectiousdisease: classify COVID-19, pneumonia, and tuberculosis. In: 2022 IEEE 35th International Symposium on Computer-Based Medical Systems (CBMS), pp. 119–124. IEEE (2022)
20. Maqsood, S., Damasevicius, R., Shah, F.M.: An efficient approach for the detection of brain tumor using fuzzy logic and U-NET CNN classification. In: Gervasi, O., et al. (eds.) ICCSA 2021. LNCS, vol. 12953, pp. 105–118. Springer, Cham (2021). https://doi.org/10.1007/978-3-030-86976-2_8
21. Moeskops, P., et al.: Evaluation of a deep learning approach for the segmentation of brain tissues and white matter hyperintensities of presumed vascular origin in MRI. NeuroImage Clin. **17**, 251–262 (2018)
22. Mohammed, Y.M., El Garouani, S., Jellouli, I.: A survey of methods for brain tumor segmentation-based MRI images. J. Comput. Design Eng. **10**(1), 266–293 (2023)
23. Nguyen, D.H., et al.: ASMCNN: an efficient brain extraction using active shape model and convolutional neural networks. Inf. Sci. **591**, 25–48 (2022)
24. Oktay, O., et al.: Attention U-net: learning where to look for the pancreas. arXiv preprint arXiv:1804.03999 (2018)
25. Pereira, S., Pinto, A., Alves, V., Silva, C.A.: Brain tumor segmentation using convolutional neural networks in MRI images. IEEE Trans. Med. Imaging **35**(5), 1240–1251 (2016)
26. Ranjbarzadeh, R., Bagherian Kasgari, A., Jafarzadeh Ghoushchi, S., Anari, S., Naseri, M., Bendechache, M.: Brain tumor segmentation based on deep learning and an attention mechanism using MRI multi-modalities brain images. Sci. Rep. **11**(1), 10930 (2021)
27. Ronneberger, O., Fischer, P., Brox, T.: U-net: convolutional networks for biomedical image segmentation. In: Navab, N., Hornegger, J., Wells, W.M., Frangi, A.F. (eds.) MICCAI 2015, Part III. LNCS, vol. 9351, pp. 234–241. Springer, Cham (2015). https://doi.org/10.1007/978-3-319-24574-4_28
28. Wei, D., Zhang, L., Wu, Z., Cao, X., Li, G., Shen, D., Wang, Q.: Deep morphological simplification network (MS-net) for guided registration of brain magnetic resonance images. Pattern Recogn. **100**, 107171 (2020)
29. Wu, D., Ding, Y., Zhang, M., Yang, Q., Qin, Z.: Multi-features refinement and aggregation for medical brain segmentation. IEEE Access **8**, 57483–57496 (2020)
30. Zhang, J., Jiang, Z., Dong, J., Hou, Y., Liu, B.: Attention gate resU-Net for automatic MRI brain tumor segmentation. IEEE Access **8**, 58533–58545 (2020)

31. Zhang, J., Lv, X., Zhang, H., Liu, B.: AResU-Net: attention residual u-net for brain tumor segmentation. Symmetry **12**(5), 721 (2020)
32. Zhang, W., et al.: ME-Net: multi-encoder net framework for brain tumor segmentation. Int. J. Imaging Syst. Technol. **31**(4), 1834–1848 (2021)
33. Zhao, X., Wu, Y., Song, G., Li, Z., Zhang, Y., Fan, Y.: A deep learning model integrating FCNNs and CRFs for brain tumor segmentation. Med. Image Anal. **43**, 98–111 (2018)
34. Zhu, Z., He, X., Qi, G., Li, Y., Cong, B., Liu, Y.: Brain tumor segmentation based on the fusion of deep semantics and edge information in multimodal MRI. Inf. Fusion **91**, 376–387 (2023)

Improving Prediction Quality of Face Image Preference Using Combinatorial Fusion Algorithm

Zihan Zhang[1(✉)], Christina Schweikert[2], Shinsuke Shimojo[3], and D. Frank Hsu[1]

[1] Laboratory of Informatics and Data Mining, Department of Computer and Information Science, Fordham University, York, NY 10023, USA
zzhang368@fordham.edu
[2] Division of Computer Science, Mathematics and Science, St. John's University, Queens, NY 11439, USA
[3] Division of Biology and Biological Engineering/Computation and Neural Systems, California Institute of Technology, Pasadena, CA 91125, USA

Abstract. When two face images are shown to a subject, the subject's preference choice is influenced by many factors. Although it is a challenging task, one way to detect a subject's preference is to analyze the eye movement gaze cascade in the recorded video sequence together with a set of extracted attributes (features). Combinatorial fusion algorithm (CFA) is a new information fusion and machine learning paradigm for combining multiple scoring systems using rank-score characteristic (RSC) function and cognitive diversity (CD). In this paper, we apply CFA in the analysis of the eye movement gaze cascade sequence. In particular, we characterize each of the attributes and measure the diversity between two attributes using RSC function and CD respectively. The novelty of the combinatorial fusion approach is the new paradigm of incorporating both score function and rank function as well as using both score combination and rank combination. In addition, our results demonstrate that weighted rank combination has some advantage over weighted score combination when the weight is measured using diversity strength. Since diversity strength depends only on cognitive diversity between two attributes but not on any specific sequence in the eye movement gaze cascade, our result facilitates learning and modeling in an unsupervised manner.

Keywords: Cognitive diversity · Combinatorial Fusion Algorithm · Information fusion · Preference detection · Rank-score characteristic (RSC) function

F. Liu et al. (Eds.): BI 2023, LNAI 13974, pp. 261–272, 2023.
https://doi.org/10.1007/978-3-031-43075-6_23

1   Introduction

Many factors are involved in making face image preference decisions when a subject is presented with two face images and asked to choose one face image which they believe is more attractive. For instance, in a study by Frantz [5], it was shown that there is a tendency that the subject spends longer time on the objects they favor. A research by Liao et al. [16] demonstrated that the context and the type of an image are influential on deciding whether novelty or familiarity will affect a subject's decision. Although the factors that have influences on the process of forming the face image preference decisions vary, there are some common features of the preferred face images that a subject usually considers to be more appealing, such as symmetry and typicality [15]. Other research have shown that perceptual facilitation [13,18,28] and gaze contact [4,12] are also important factors on determining the preferred image.

A "gaze cascade effect", detected and revealed by Shimojo et al. [24], demonstrates the role of gaze in the image preference formation process during a period of time towards the end of a trial. This effect happens in the situation when the subject is asked to select the more appealing face image out of two. The gaze points of a subject are evenly distributed between two face images in the beginning of the trial and eventually the subject's gaze shifts toward the face image which the subject prefers.

In our previous work [22], a set of five attributes were constructed based on the eye movement data including: A: the time spent on a face in the last 200ms of a trial, B: the total time spent on a face, C: the number of gaze points in a face, D: interest sustainability, and E: region change. It was shown that when combining different attributes to predict face image preference, the best performance achieved is 99% when precision at 100 [23]. This result indicates a possibility of overfitting, which could be caused by the fact that a significant number of tied-rankings exist in attribute A. To resolve this issue, the attribute A, in this study, has been modified as the time spent on a face in the last 3700ms of a trial. After the modification, attribute A becomes a one-to-one function.

Hsu et al. [7–10] proposed and developed the Combinatorial fusion algorithm, which is applied in this study to the eye movement data set for improving the performance of face image preference prediction as well as for determining which combinations of attributes can better detect the preference. Combinatorial fusion algorithm considers an attribute/indicator as a scoring system and it defines a rank-score characteristic (RSC) function which can characterize the scoring and ranking behavior of a scoring system [9]. Combinatorial fusion algorithm has been shown beneficial in various applications in different domains such as bioinformatics [1,17], chemical prediction [26], information retrieval [10], joint decision making [20], mobile network selection [14], stress identification [3], and virtual screening [27]. Also see Hurley et al. [11] for an extensive review.

The eye movement data set by Shimojo et al. [25] is analyzed in this study. A study by Chuk et al. [2] applied Switching Hidden-Markov Models on this data set that identified two subgroups of subjects that showed different gaze patterns and preference decisions. In terms of our previous work on this data set, we applied a multi-layer combinatorial fusion method with different machine learning models [19] and combinatorial fusion algorithm (CFA) to enhance the performance of face image preference prediction. Combinatorial fusion algorithm is also used to characterize the decision-making behavior of a prototypical subject in [21].

In Sect. 2, we include the eye movement gaze cascade data set and five attributes used in the paper. Section 3 covers combinatorial fusion algorithm while Sect. 4 covers the results and gives discussion.

2   Eye Movement Gaze Detection

In this paper, the eye movement data set by Shimojo et al. [25] is analyzed. In the experiment, there are 12 subjects participating with each of them conducting 60 trials. During each trial, a subject was shown two computer-generated face images, and each subject was asked to choose one image which he/she considered to be more attractive from the two computer-generated face images. During each trial, the gaze points of a subject on the images were tracked. The gaze points were recorded as x, y coordinates and associated with the duration of a gaze at each point (in ms). The subject's preference decision, namely, the left or the right face image that he/she preferred, was also stored. Figure 1 shows a sample trial plot that contains two faces images with the subject's gaze points [24]. A subject's preferred face image is marked in green.

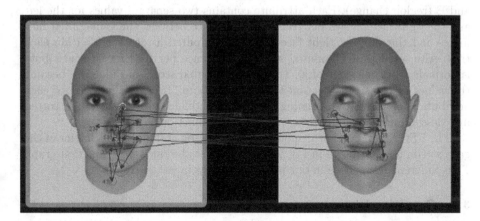

Fig. 1. A sample trial plot with subject's eye movement [24] (Color figure online)

Given the eye movement data set, a set of five attributes are constructed as follows: A: the time spent on a face in the fixed duration of 3700 ms in a trial, B: the total time spent on a face per trial, C: the number of gaze points in a face, D: interest sustainability which measures whether the length of time a subject looks at a face image in a continuous fashion increases or decreases, and E: region change which computes the number of gaze points changed between regions on one face image. The details of the process of data preprocessing and attribution formation can be found in [22]. Attributes B, C, D, and E are the same as before [19,21–23]. Attribute A is extended longer to avoid overfitting without tied-rankings. As such, the fixed duration A is obtained by moving back time until there are no ties.

3   Combinatorial Fusion Algorithm

3.1   Rank-Score Characteristic (RSC) Function

As the combinatorial fusion algorithm treats an attribute as a distinct scoring system on a set of data items, applications which contain multiple attributes can be considered as problems of multiple scoring systems. Each scoring system consists of a score function, a rank function, and a rank-score characteristic (RSC) function. The RSC function, as a key concept of CFA, can characterize the scoring and ranking behavior of a scoring system [7–11].

Let $D = \{d_1, d_2, \ldots, d_n\}$, be a set of data items. Let N be a set of natural numbers and let R be a set of real numbers. A scoring system A contains a score function from D to R, which is denoted as s_A, and a corresponding rank function from D to N, denoted as r_A. The RSC function, f_A, is defined by Hsu and Taksa [10] as:

$$f_A(i) = s_A(r_A^{-1}(i)), 1 \leq i \leq n. \tag{1}$$

Five scoring systems are formed for all attributes as stated in Sect. 2: A (fixed duration), B (total duration), C (gaze count), D (interest sustainability), and E (region change). Each attribute contains two separate values for the left and the right face images per trial. The difference between the value of left face image and the value of right face image is computed as one score within each trial. Afterwards, the computed score of difference per trial for each attribute is normalized to the scale of [0, 1]. These computed scores of difference become the values of the score function for each attribute. The rank function of each attribute is obtained by assigning the corresponding ranks to the values sorted into descending order in each attribute's score function.

The RSC functions that demonstrate the scoring and ranking behavior of the gaze attributes are shown in Fig. 2. We note that the rank-score function graph f_A is different from those in our previous studies in [19,21–23].

3.2   Cognitive Diversity

Cognitive diversity (CD) of two scoring systems A and B, proposed by Hsu et al. [7–10], is the distance between the RSC functions of A and B, i.e., f_A and f_B. To be specific, the computation of cognitive diversity between two scoring systems, A and B, is as follows:

$$CD(A, B) = d(f_A, f_B) = \sqrt{\sum_{i=1}^{n} ((f_A(i) - f_B(i))^2/n} \tag{2}$$

where n represents the number of data items.

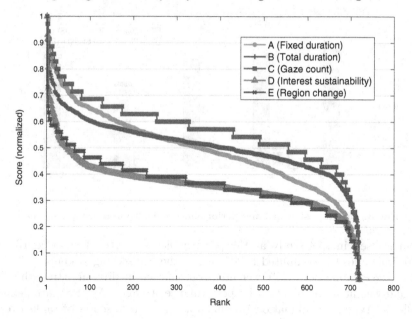

Fig. 2. Rank-score function graph for gaze attributes A, B, C, D, and E

3.3   Score Combination and Rank Combination

Multiple scoring systems can be combined by fusion each scoring function or rank function for each data item: score combination (SC) and rank combination (RC) [8]. There are multiple ways to perform score combination and rank combination, such as by taking the average of the scores and ranks of multiple scoring systems separately. Weight can also be assigned to each scoring system to compute weighted score combinations and weighted rank combinations. The assigned weight can be measured by diversity strength (DS) as well as the performance strength (PS) of each scoring system.

After computing the cognitive diversity for all scoring system pairs, diversity strength of each scoring system is the average of all cognitive diversities in which the scoring system is used. It can be used as the weight of each scoring system to combine scores and ranks of scoring systems for every data item.

Let M be a set of all scoring systems, and let A and B be two scoring systems. The following formula defines the diversity strength of a scoring system A in M:

$$DS(A) = \frac{\sum_{\substack{B \in M \\ B \neq A}} CD(A, B)}{|M| - 1} \tag{3}$$

Results of computed DS of all scoring systems are shown in Fig. 3.

Precision at m, where $m \leq n$, is measured to obtain performance strength (PS) of each scoring system. Scores in each scoring system, together with the associated choice of preferred face image, are sorted in the descending order. Precision at m is calculated as the ratio of the number of image preference chosen as left face divided by m. Precision at 300 of each individual scoring

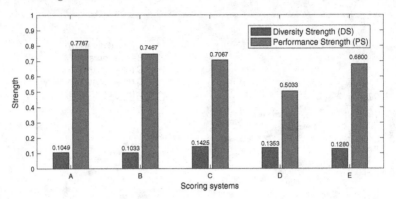

Fig. 3. Diversity strength and performance strength of scoring systems

system is used in this study as the performance strength of every attribute. Figure 3 includes the computed PS of each of the five scoring systems.

Average combination (AC), weighted combination by diversity strength (WC DS), and weighted combination by performance strength (WCPS), are defined as follows. Average combination is defined as the sum of scores of ranks over t scoring systems divided by t.

Let M denote a set of all scoring systems, where $M = \{A_1, A_2, \ldots, A_t\}$, on the set of data items $D = \{d_1, d_2, \ldots, d_n\}$. Let s_{SC} be the score function of score combinations of A_i's in M and s_{RC} be the score function of rank combinations of A_i's in M.

The formula of the weighted combination by diversity strength (formula (3)) for score combination and rank combination is defined by Eqs. (4) and (5), respectively:

$$s_{SC}(d_i) = \frac{\sum_{j=1}^t DS(A_j)(s_{A_j}(d_i))}{\sum_{j=1}^t DS(A_j)} \tag{4}$$

$$s_{RC}(d_i) = \frac{\sum_{j=1}^t \frac{1}{DS(A_j)}(r_{A_j}(d_i))}{\sum_{j=1}^t \frac{1}{DS(A_j)}} \tag{5}$$

Similarly, Eqs. (6) and (7) define the formulas of the weighted combination by performance strength (performance at precision 300) for score combination and rank combination:

$$s_{SC}(d_i) = \frac{\sum_{j=1}^t PS(A_j)(s_{A_j}(d_i))}{\sum_{j=1}^t PS(A_j)} \tag{6}$$

$$s_{RC}(d_i) = \frac{\sum_{j=1}^t \frac{1}{PS(A_j)}(r_{A_j}(d_i))}{\sum_{j=1}^t \frac{1}{PS(A_j)}} \tag{7}$$

4   Results and Discussion

4.1   Results

Table 1 presents the individual attribute's performance as a base reference for a comparison with the combined attributes' performance. Table 2 lists the result of the best performance in score combination and rank combination by each of the three combination methods. The number of all combinations of five attributes which perform equal or better than the best performing individual attribute at different level of precisions is summarized in Table 3.

Table 1. Performance of individual scoring systems

Precision@	A	B	C	D	E
100	0.8600	0.8300	0.8000	0.5100	0.7300
200	0.8000	0.7800	0.7350	0.5350	0.6950
300	0.7767	0.7467	0.7067	0.5033	0.6800

Table 2. Best performance in score combination (SC) and rank combination (RC) by average combination (AC), weighted combination by diversity strength (WCDS), and weighted combination by performance strength (WCPS).

Precision@	Score Combination			Rank Combination		
	AC	WCDS	WCPS	AC	WCDS	WCPS
100	0.8900	0.9000	0.8900	0.9100	0.9100	0.9100
200	0.8500	0.8450	0.8450	0.8500	0.8550	0.8500
300	0.7800	0.7800	0.7800	0.7833	0.7867	0.7900

Table 3. The number of combined systems performing equal or better than the top performing single system in SC and RC by AC, WCDS, and WCPS are (out of the combined systems):

Precision@	Score Combination				Rank Combination			
	AC	WCDS	WCPS	Total	AC	WCDS	WCPS	Total
100	8	7	11	26	12	12	7	31
200	9	8	11	28	10	11	7	28
300	3	2	3	8	2	2	2	6

Precisions are computed to evaluate the performance of the results by the three combination methods. Figure 4, 5 and 6 list the performance of all combined attributes by the three combination methods. Since the score function for each attribute is obtained by calculating the difference of the values between left

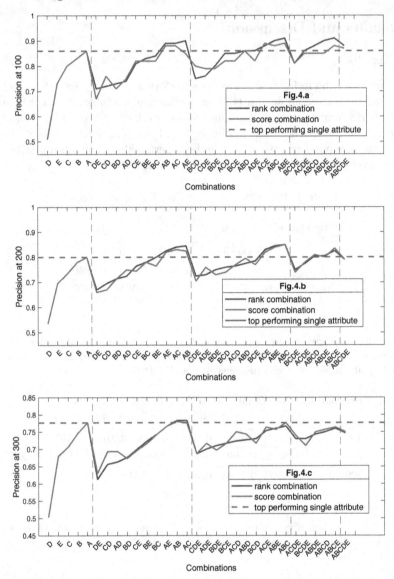

Fig. 4. Performance for average combination (AC): Performance evaluated by: a) precision @100, b) precision @200, c) precision @300.

face image and right face image, a higher score means the preferred face image is more likely to be the left image. Therefore, the preferred image as "left" is used as a reference to compute precisions. To be specific, the combined scores are sorted into descending order while the combined ranks are sorted into ascending order. Afterwards, precision at m, the ratio of the number of top m face image choice as left divided by m, is measured.

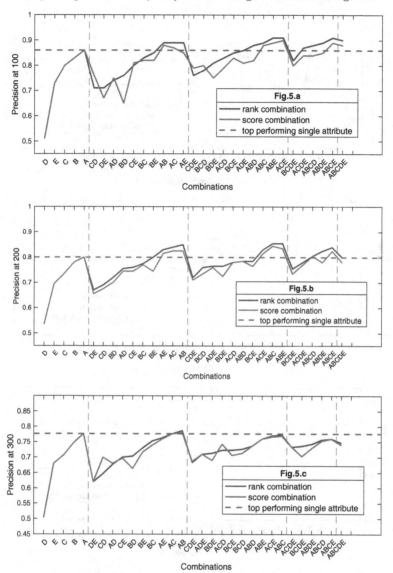

Fig. 5. Performance for weighted combination by diversity strength (WCDS): Performance evaluated by: a) precision @100, b) precision @200, c) precision @300.

In this study, precision level at 100, 200, and 300 are computed to evaluate the performance. As the result in Tables 2 and 3, it is shown that regardless of combination method, rank combinations overall achieve a better performance than score combinations. For rank combinations, weighted combination by diversity strength performs the best among the three combination methods (Table 2). For score combinations, weighted combination by performance strength is able to improve the most combined attributes.

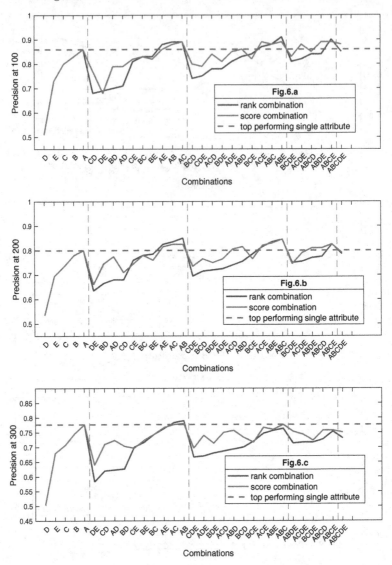

Fig. 6. Performance for weighted combination by performance strength (WCPS): Performance evaluated by: a) precision @100, b) precision @200, c) precision @300.

4.2 Discussion

Combinatorial fusion algorithm (CFA) performs both score combination in Euclidean space and rank combination in a rank space. Our score combination is equivalent to linear and weighted linear combination in Euclidean space. When combination method AC is used, rank combination is slightly better than the score combination (Table 3). Although score combination performs better than rank combination when WCPS is used, rank combination shows advantage over score combination when WCDS is used as the weight. This result is significant because: (a) WCDS is calculated under an unsupervised environment, and (b) the result supports the theoretical proof in [10] that RC(A,B) is better than SC(A,B) if scoring systems A and B are diverse (e.g., $CD(A, B) > 0$). We note that not only the diversity of attributes, but the relatively good performance of individual attributes contributes to the performance improvement by the three combination methods.

Our future works include: (a) increase the number of attributes and study their diversity [6], (b) use various diverse ML/AI models as base models and CFA for model fusion to improve data and prediction quality [26], (c) use CFA to perform deep learning on the Kemeny rank space where tied-rankings are allowed [11,19], and (d) other than precision at 100, 200, and 300, we would like to investigate when does a base model achieve its peak performance? When this happens, does the fusion method still improve the performance?

References

1. Brown, S., Hsu, D.F., Schweikert, C., Tang, Z.: ChIP-Seq analytics: methods and systems to improve ChIP-Seq peak identification. Syst. Biol.: Appl. Cancer-Relat. Res. 87–112 (2012). (H.F. Juan and S.C. Huang edited), World Scientific Publishing Company
2. Chuk, T., Chan, A.B., Shimojo, S., Hsiao, J.: Mind reading: discovering individual preferences from eye movements using switching hidden Markov models. In: Proceedings of the 38th Annual Conference of the Cognitive Science Society (2016)
3. Deng, Y., Wu, Z., Chu, C.H., Zhang, Q., Hsu, D.F.: Sensor feature selection and combination for stress identification using combinatorial fusion. Int. J. Adv. Rob. Syst. **10**(8), 306 (2013)
4. Emery, N.J.: The eyes have it: the neuroethology, function and evolution of social gaze. Neurosci. Biobehav. Rev. **24**(6), 581–604 (2000)
5. Fantz, R.: The origin of form perception. Sci. Am. **204**, 66–72 (1961)
6. Heck, M.: Presentation adaptation for multimodal interface systems: three essays on the effectiveness of user-centric content and modality adaptation. Doctoral Dissertation, University of Mannheim, Germany (2023)
7. Hsu, D.F., Chung, Y.S., Kristal, B.S.: Combinatorial fusion analysis: methods and practices of combining multiple scoring systems. In: Advanced Data Mining Technologies in Bioinformatics, pp. 32–62. IGI Global (2006)
8. Hsu, D.F., Kristal, B.S., Schweikert, C.: Rank-score characteristics (RSC) function and cognitive diversity. In: Yao, Y., Sun, R., Poggio, T., Liu, J., Zhong, N., Huang, J. (eds.) BI 2010. LNCS, vol. 6334, pp. 42–54. Springer, Heidelberg (2010). https://doi.org/10.1007/978-3-642-15314-3_5
9. Hsu, D.F., Shapiro, J., Taksa, I.: Methods of data fusion in information retreival: rank vs. score combination. DIMACS TR (2002)
10. Hsu, D.F., Taksa, I.: Comparing rank and score combination methods for data fusion in information retrieval. Inf. Retrieval **8**(3), 449–480 (2005)
11. Hurley, L., Kristal, B.S., Sirimulla, S., Schweikert, C., Hsu, D.F.: Multi-layer combinatorial fusion using cognitive diversity. IEEE Access **9**, 3919–3935 (2020)
12. Kleinke, C.L.: Gaze and eye contact: a research review. Psychol. Bull. **100**(1), 78 (1986)

13. Kunst-Wilson, W.R., Zajonc, R.B.: Affective discrimination of stimuli that cannot be recognized. Science **207**(4430), 557–558 (1980)
14. Kustiawan, I., Liu, C.Y., Hsu, D.F.: Vertical handoff decision using fuzzification and combinatorial fusion. IEEE Commun. Lett. **21**(9), 2089–2092 (2017)
15. Leopold, D.A., O'Toole, A.J., Vetter, T., Blanz, V.: Prototype-referenced shape encoding revealed by high-level aftereffects. Nat. Neurosci. **4**(1), 89–94 (2001)
16. Liao, H.I., Yeh, S.L., Shimojo, S.: Novelty vs. familiarity principles in preference decisions: task-context of past experience matters. Front. Psychol. **2**, 43 (2011)
17. Lin, K.L., et al.: Feature selection and combination criteria for improving accuracy in protein structure prediction. IEEE Trans. Nanobiosci. **6**(2), 186–196 (2007)
18. Mandler, G., Nakamura, Y., Van Zandt, B.J.: Nonspecific effects of exposure on stimuli that cannot be recognized. J. Exp. Psychol. Learn. Mem. Cogn. **13**(4), 646 (1987)
19. Schweikert, Christina, Gobin, Louis, Xie, Shuxiao, Shimojo, Shinsuke, Frank Hsu, D..: Preference prediction based on eye movement using multi-layer combinatorial fusion. In: Wang, S., et al. (eds.) BI 2018. LNCS (LNAI), vol. 11309, pp. 282–293. Springer, Cham (2018). https://doi.org/10.1007/978-3-030-05587-5_27
20. Schweikert, C., Mulia, D., Sanchez, K., Hsu, D.F.: The diversity rank-score function for combining human visual perception systems. Brain Inform. **3**(1), 63–72 (2016)
21. Schweikert, C., Shimojo, S., Glasser, H., Hendsey, R., Alsaber, R., Hsu, D.F.: Modeling prototypical preference behavior and diversity using rank score characteristic functions. In: 2022 IEEE 21st International Conference on Cognitive Informatics & Cognitive Computing (ICCI*CC), pp. 203–207 (2022). https://doi.org/10.1109/ICCICC57084.2022.10101519
22. Schweikert, C., Shimojo, S., Hsu, D.F.: Detecting preferences based on eye movement using combinatorial fusion. In: 2016 IEEE 15th International Conference on Cognitive Informatics & Cognitive Computing (ICCI* CC), pp. 336–343. IEEE (2016)
23. Schweikert, C., Shimojo, S., Zhang, Z., Tato, J., Hendsey, R., Hsu, D.F.: Improving preference detection with eye movement gaze and cognitive diversity. In: 2021 IEEE 20th International Conference on Cognitive Informatics & Cognitive Computing (ICCI* CC), pp. 98–102. IEEE (2021)
24. Shimojo, S., Simion, C., Changizi, M.A., Adams, R., Ambady, N., Nakayama, K.: Gaze and preference-orienting behavior as a somatic precursor of preference decision. Sci. Soc. Vision 151–163 (2011)
25. Shimojo, S., Simion, C., Shimojo, E., Scheier, C.: Gaze bias both reflects and influences preference. Nat. Neurosci. **6**(12), 1317–1322 (2003)
26. Tang, Y., et al.: Improving data and prediction quality of high-throughput perovskite synthesis with model fusion. J. Chem. Inf. Model. **61**(4), 1593–1602 (2021)
27. Yang, J.M., Chen, Y.F., Shen, T.W., Kristal, B.S., Hsu, D.F.: Consensus scoring criteria for improving enrichment in virtual screening. J. Chem. Inf. Model. **45**(4), 1134–1146 (2005)
28. Zajonc, R.B.: Attitudinal effects of mere exposure. J. Pers. Soc. Psychol. **9**, 1–27 (1968)

MMDF-ESI: Multi-Modal Deep Fusion of EEG and MEG for Brain Source Imaging

Meng Jiao[1], Shihao Yang[1,2], Boyu Wang[3], Xiaochen Xian[4],
Yevgeniy R. Semenov[2], Guihong Wan[2(✉)], and Feng Liu[1(✉)]

[1] School of Systems and Enterprises, Stevens Institute of Technology,
Hoboken, NJ, USA
fliu22@stevens.edu
[2] Massachusetts General Hospital, Harvard Medical School, Boston, MA, USA
gwan@mgh.harvard.edu
[3] Department of Computer Science, Western University, London, ON, Canada
[4] Department of Industrial and Systems Engineering, University of Florida,
Gainesville, FL, USA

Abstract. Electrophysiological Source Imaging (ESI) aims to reconstruct the underlying electric brain sources based on Electroencephalography (EEG) or Magnetoencephalography (MEG) measurements of brain activities. Due to the ill-posed nature of the ESI problem, faithfully recovering the latent brain sources has been a significant challenge. Classical algorithms have primarily focused on the design of regularization terms according to predefined priors derived from neurophysiological assumptions. Deep learning frameworks attempt to learn the mapping between brain source signals and scalp EEG/MEG measurements in a data-driven manner, and have demonstrated improved performance compared to the classical methods. Given that EEG and MEG can be complementary for measuring the tangential and radial electrical signals of the cortex, combining both modalities is believed to be advantageous in improving the reconstruction performance of ESI. However, the fusion of these two modalities for the ESI problem has not been fully explored in existing deep learning frameworks. In this paper, we propose a Multi-Modal Deep Fusion (MMDF) framework for solving the ESI inverse problem, termed as MMDF-ESI. Our framework integrates both EEG and MEG in a deep learning framework with a specially designed squeeze-and-excitation module. This integration of EEG and MEG is conducted at an early phase in the deep learning framework rather than on the final decision level fusion. Our experimental results show that (1) the localization accuracy of MMDF-ESI consistently outperforms that of using a single modality; (2) MMDF-ESI exhibits excellent stability, characterized by significantly smaller error variance in source reconstruction compared to benchmark methods, particularly for sources with larger extended activation areas and under low signal-to-noise ratio (SNR) conditions; (3) the evaluation on a real EEG/MEG dataset demonstrates that MMDF-ESI enables a more concentrated reconstruction, effectively recovering an extended area of underlying source activation.

F. Liu et al. (Eds.): BI 2023, LNAI 13974, pp. 273–285, 2023.
https://doi.org/10.1007/978-3-031-43075-6_24

Keywords: Brain Source Imaging · Brain Source Localization · EEG and MEG Fusion · EEG/MEG Inverse Problem · Multi-Modal Deep Learning

1 Introduction

Brain source imaging refers to the reconstruction of the underlying electrophysiological brain sources based on observed EEG or MEG recordings. It plays a fundamental role in uncovering latent brain activations and has been widely used in neuroscience studies and clinical diagnosis [1–5]. During the past decades, various algorithms have been proposed, incorporating different regularization terms that leverage assumptions about the spatio-temporal structure of the source signals [6, 7].

One seminal work introducing the ℓ_2 norm as a regularization is the minimum norm estimate (MNE) [8]. Several MNE variants, such as standardized low resolution electromagnetic tomography (sLORETA) [9] and dynamic statistical parametric mapping (dSPM) [10], have also been developed. It is worthnoting that the ℓ_2-norm based methods tend to present spatially diffuse source estimates, which may not accurately represent the true underlying activations. To promote a sparse solution, Uutela *et al.* developed the minimum current estimate (MCE) by introducing the ℓ_1 norm, which effectively reduces over-diffuse source activations [11]. Gramfort *et al.* proposed the mixed norm estimate (MxNE), where the sparse norms (ℓ_p with $p \leq 1$) were applied in the spatial domain and the ℓ_2 norm was used in the temporal domain [6]. Furthermore, Liu *et al.* introduced a graph regularization to promote intra-class similarity of the source activation [12]. Bore *et al.* proposed to apply the ℓ_p norm with $p < 1$ on the source signal and the ℓ_1 norm on the data fitting error term [13]. Babadi *et al.* showed that sparse distributed solutions to event-related stimuli could be found using a greedy subspace-pursuit algorithm [14].

The brain sources are not isolated or activated discretely. When a synchronous assemble of adjacent neurons fires simultaneously, an extended area of brain activation can be observed [15–18]. As a result, an extended area of activation is a reasonable assumption to help solve the ESI problem [19]. The first order spatial derivative [16] or fractional order spatial derivative gradient [20] design matrix can be used to find an extended source imaging. Recently, a combinatorial search method based on the mesh graph was proposed to identify the extended region of activation with provable optimality [21]. By leveraging the structural information provided by the mesh graph, this approach can effectively localize the extended activation region.

In recent years, deep learning frameworks have been proposed to solve the ESI problem. These frameworks aim to learn the mapping between the source signal and scalp EEG/MEG measurements in a data-driven way, resulting in improved performance compared to the classical methods [22–24]. Despite relying on a large amount of training data, deep learning frameworks for ESI have several advantages. Deep learning models, once trained, can provide online reconstruction of source signal following a forward pass with EEG or MEG recordings as the input. Additionally, deep learning framework is data-driven, eliminating the need for pre-specified regularization terms that can be implicitly learned. Most deep learning frameworks are based on an end-to-end architecture, which leverages convolutional neural networks (CNNs) or Long Short-Term Memory (LSTM) networks [23–25]. A model-based deep learning framework can combine the advantages of deep learning for the great approximation capability and the conventional methods for the model interpratability. Following this line, Jiao et al. proposed a model-based deep learning framework based on unrolled optimization neural network to solve the ESI problem [26].

Despite the improved performance demonstrated by deep learning frameworks and the complementary information provided by EEG and MEG, the fusion model of EEG and MEG modalities has not been fully explored for solving the ESI problem. In this study, we proposed a Multi-Modal Deep Fusion (MMDF) framework for the ESI problem, referred to as MMDF-ESI, which is built on a special design of deep learning module and a fusion of EEG and MEG modalities. The main contributions of this study are outlined as follows:

(i) We proposed a novel deep learning framework for solving the inverse problem of ESI, which utilizes the fusion of features derived from EEG and MEG measurements and enables the exploitation of the properties of two neural imaging signals for their complementary advantages.

(ii) We introduced an channel-wise attention based squeeze and excitation (SE) module to learn the weights for multiple channels, enabling the adaptive integration of the extracted features. In addition, we employed a dilated convolution filter to expand the receptive field of the network without increasing its depth, allowing better capturing of spatial dependencies.

(iii) We conducted comprehensive evaluations of the proposed MMDF-ESI framework, comparing it with benchmark methods on both synthetic and real data. The results suggest that the proposed approach outperforms benchmark methods, particularly when the source extents are large and the noise content is high.

2   Approach

2.1   Problem Statement

The ESI forward problem can be expressed as follows:

$$Y = LS + \varepsilon, \tag{1}$$

where $Y \in \mathbb{R}^{C \times T}$ represents the EEG or MEG measurements with C channels and T time points, $S \in \mathbb{R}^{N \times T}$ represents the brain sources from N regions for all the T time points, $L \in \mathbb{R}^{C \times N}$ is the *leadfield* matrix which reflects the mapping from source signals to EEG or MEG measurements, and $\varepsilon \in \mathbb{R}^{C \times T}$ denotes the measurement noise.

The ESI inverse problem is to estimate S given the EEG or MEG measurements Y and the *leadfield* matrix L. However, given that the number of source regions N always far exceeds the number of channels C, the ESI inverse problem is ill-conditioned and has an infinite number of solutions.

To find a unique solution, employing a regularization term based on prior assumptions [1,27] is of great importance. More specifically, S can be obtained by solving the following minimization problem:

$$S = \underset{S}{\arg\min} \frac{1}{2} \|Y - LS\|_F^2 + \lambda R(S), \qquad (2)$$

where $\|\cdot\|_F$ is the Frobenius norm. The first term of Eq. (2) is called *data fitting* error, which tries to explain the EEG/MEG measurements. The second term is called *regularization* term, which is imposed to restrict the solution space of Eq. (2) to obtain a unique solution.

In the past decades, the proposed algorithms for the ESI inverse problem are numerous (see the review paper [1,2] and references therein), and here we highlight two categories of frameworks in Sect. 2.2 and Sect. 2.3 that motivated our algorithm.

2.2 ESI Models with Edge Sparse Total Variation (TV)

As the cortex is discretized with 3D meshes, simply employing ℓ_1 norm on S will result in the estimated sources to be distributed discretely across the cortex rather than over an extended continuous area in the cortex. In order to promote source extents estimation, Ding proposed the TV regularization defined from the irregular 3D mesh as a sparse constraint and its definition can be found in [28]. The TV was defined to be the ℓ_1 norm of the first order spatial gradient using a linear transform matrix $V \in \mathbb{R}^{P \times N}$, where N is the number of voxels/sources, P equals the sum of the degrees of all source nodes. Similar TV definitions were also used by other researchers, such as [29,30]. Qin *et al.* [20] used a fractional-order TV term to promote "Gaussian" shape of activation. The model with sparsity and total variation constraints is given as follows:

$$S = \underset{S}{\arg\min} \frac{1}{2} \|Y - LS\|_F^2 + \alpha \|S\|_1 + \beta \|VS\|_1, \qquad (3)$$

where $\|\cdot\|_1$ represents ℓ_1 norm on both row and column of a vector or matrix. The first term is the data fitting term, the second is the sparsity term, and the third term is the total variation regularization term. Ideally, the TV regularization promotes source extents estimation.

2.3 Deep Learning Frameworks for the ESI Inverse Problem

Recently, with the popularity of deep learning, various artificial neural network (ANN)-based approaches were investigated for the estimation of brain source activities. One such framework based on convolutional neural network (CNN), called ConvDip, was proposed by Hecker *et al.* [22] to provide the reconstruction of source locations. Sun *et al.* [24] trained a deep learning-based source

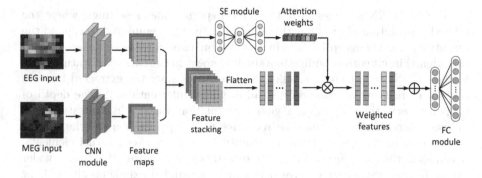

Fig. 1. The proposed framework architecture.

imaging framework (DeepSIF) with residual blocks and long short-term memory (LSTM) units to perform spatio-temporal estimation of underlying source dynamics. Craley *et al.* [31] proposed a deep architecture with 1D CNN and BiLSTM units, called SZTrack, to detect and track seizure propagation. Huang *et al.* [32] presented a data-synthesized spatiotemporally convolutional encoder-decoder network (DST-CedNet) to learn a robust mapping from EEG/MEG measurements to sources.

However, most of the developed source imaging algorithms focus on either EEG or MEG modality individually, with very few deep learning methods attempting to utilize both modalities simultaneously. In other words, the complementary of EEG and MEG is under-exploited [33–35]. It has been well-established that EEG and MEG show different sensitivities to cortical source orientation. Specifically, MEG has been shown to be less sensitive to radial components of dipolar sources, whereas EEG demonstrates sensitivity to both tangential and radial components [36]. Another characteristic of EEG is that it is highly sensitive to conductivity uncertainties. Low skull conductivity has a significant influence on the EEG inverse solution, as the electric field detected by EEG is attenuated and smeared. On the contrary, the magnetic field recorded by MEG are nearly not contaminated by these changes [37]. Thus, by leveraging the complementary strengths of EEG and MEG and applying simultaneously EEG and MEG recordings for brain source imaging in a combined fashion, it is possible to enhance the accuracy and robustness of brain source imaging algorithms, leading to improved source localization and a deeper understanding of brain activities [38,39].

2.4   Proposed Method

The proposed MMDF-ESI framework is illustrated in Fig. 1. The input design of MMDF-ESI architecture is inspired by ConvDip [22], in which EEG data at a single time point was interpolated to a matrix and utilized as the input of a 2D convolutional layer. In our study, we extend this approach by separately interpolating the EEG and MEG data to two 2D matrices according to their respective sensor montage. The two matrices from MEG and EEG are then fed into two 2D CNN modules for feature extraction.

The two CNN modules have the same hyperparameter settings, where the dilated convolution filter [40] with a dilation rate of 2 is employed to expand the receptive field. The receptive field in convolutional layers refers to the area size of the original input corresponding to a single element in the extracted feature map. Shallow CNNs tend to have smaller receptive fields since the extracted features contain more local information instead of global information. As the depth of CNN increases, the proportion of global information contains in the feature map increases accordingly, so that the receptive field expands. We use the dilated convolution in this work. There are empty "spaces" between kernel elements, which allow the convolutional kernel to directly extract information from a wider range. In this way, the receptive field can be expanded exponentially without increasing network depth, thus avoiding the increase of model parameters. The dilation rate is defined to indicate how much the kernel is widened. The normal convolution can be seen as a dilated convolution with a dilation rate of 1.

Since feature maps extracted by different CNN channels are of varied contributions to the final estimation, the squeeze-and-excitation (SE) network, which can be regarded as a self-attention module [41], is employed to fuse the features from two scenarios. In the SE network, the input layer and the output layer are set with the same number of neurons as the number of feature maps, while the hidden layer is set with less neurons according to a reduction ratio r. The SE module first aggregate the feature maps $\mathbf{U} = [\mathbf{u}_1, \mathbf{u}_2, ..., \mathbf{u}_C]$ extracted from C channels through a *squeeze* operation $\mathbf{F}_{sq}(.)$ to generate C channel descriptors:

$$z_c = \mathbf{F}_{sq}(\mathbf{u}_c) = \frac{1}{H \times W} \sum_{i=1}^{H} \sum_{j=1}^{W} u_c(i,j), \tag{4}$$

where $\mathbf{u}_c \in \mathbb{R}^{W \times H}$ refers to the c-th feature map with size of $W \times H$, z_c is the generated channel descriptor.

Then the *excitation* operation $\mathbf{F}_{ex}(.)$ is conducted to produce weights containing the channel dependencies by employing two fully connected layers:

$$\mathbf{s} = \mathbf{F}_{ex}(\mathbf{z}, \mathbf{W}) = \sigma(\mathbf{W}_2 \delta(\mathbf{W}_1 \mathbf{z})), \tag{5}$$

where $\mathbf{z} \in \mathbb{R}^{C \times 1}$ is the channel descriptor vector, $\mathbf{W}_1 \in \mathbb{R}^{\frac{C}{r} \times C}$ and $\mathbf{W}_2 \in \mathbb{R}^{C \times \frac{C}{r}}$ are two learnable mappings and r is the reduction ratio, δ is the ReLu function, σ is the sigmoid activation, $\mathbf{s} \in \mathbb{R}^{C \times 1}$ is the channel weights vector.

After the feature maps are extracted from the CNN modules, they are flattened into feature vectors. These feature vectors are then multiplied with the corresponding weights obtained by the SE module. By summing these weighted vectors, a fused feature vector is obtained. The fused feature vector, which contains the information from multiple features extracted by different channels, serves as the input of a fully connected (FC) module to estimate the brain sources. This FC module leverages the combined EEG and MEG information to make the final estimation. The multi-modal framework is so that enabled to adaptively make full use of the global spatial information from both EEG and MEG modalities.

3   Numerical Experiments

We conducted experiments to validate the effectiveness of the proposed MMDF-ESI framework on synthetic EEG and MEG data under various signal-to-noise ratios (SNRs). We further validated it on real EEG and MEG recordings for face perception.

3.1   Simulation Experiments

We first conducted experiments on synthetic data with known activation patterns.

Forward Model: To generate synthetic EEG and MEG data, we used the sample dataset from the MNE-Python toolbox [42]. The sample data were acquired with the Neuromag Vectorview MEG system (204 gradiometers and 102 magnetometers) at MGH/HMS/MIT Athinoula A. Martinos Center Biomedical Imaging. EEG data were acquired simultaneously with a 60-channel electrode cap. The original MRI dataset was obtained with a Siemens 1.5 T Sonata scanner using an MPRAGE sequence. To calculate the two leadfield matrices corresponding to EEG and MEG, a real head model was reconstructed based on the existing brain surfaces. During computation, the bad channels were excluded, and only the magnetometer channels were adopted to reduce the data size. The source space contains 1984 sources, resulting in the EEG leadfield matrix having a size of 59 by 1984 and the MEG leadfield matrix having a size of 102 by 1984.

Synthetic Data Generation: To make the synthetic data more realistic, all 1984 locations in the source space were activated in turn. Furthermore, as illustrated in Fig. 2, we used 3 different neighborhood levels (1-, 2-, and 3-level of neighborhood) to represent different sizes of source extents, then we activated the whole "patch" of sources corresponding to neighbors at different levels at the same time. The activation strength of the 1-, 2-, and 3-level adjacent regions was successively set to be 85%, 70%, and 55% of the central region. The strength of the source signal was set to be constant, then the scalp EEG and MEG data was calculated based on the forward model under different SNR settings (SNR = 40 dB, 30 dB, 20 dB, and 10 db). SNR is defined as the ratio of the signal power P_{signal} to the noise power P_{noise}: SNR $= 10 \log(P_{signal}/P_{noise})$. In total, there were 12: 3 (source extents) $\times$ 4 (SNRs) synthetic data sets (Y and S pairs).

Experimental Settings: We adopted all 12 data sets as the learning set to jointly train the proposed MMDF-ESI, then we activated 220 out of 1984 regions under different neighborhood levels, SNR settings, and activation patterns to generate the test set for model validation. The mean square error (MSE) is chosen as the loss function. The benchmark algorithms used for comparison include MNE [8], dSPM [10], sLORETA [9], ADMM [43], and ConvDip [22]. For these benchmark algorithms, we separately performed brain source localization on EEG and MEG data, next, we averaged the two scenarios source estimates as final results. All the experiments were conducted on a Windows PC with an i9

Table 1. Performance comparison between the proposed method and benchmark algorithms

SNR	Method	Source with LNs = 1		Source with LNs = 2		Source with LNs = 3	
		LE (std)	AUC (std)	LE (std)	AUC (std)	LE (std)	AUC (std)
40 dB	MNE	9.202 ± 8.301	0.995 ± 0.014	12.226 ± 8.082	0.983 ± 0.026	15.005 ± 9.154	0.970 ± 0.027
	sLORETA	**1.139 ± 3.178**	0.996 ± 0.010	6.281 ± 5.862	0.981 ± 0.027	10.092 ± 8.452	0.964 ± 0.028
	dSPM	22.236 ± 23.743	0.992 ± 0.011	27.180 ± 25.943	0.972 ± 0.031	35.481 ± 30.292	0.947 ± 0.036
	ADMM	9.949 ± 17.103	0.994 ± 0.021	11.108 ± 9.617	0.985 ± 0.038	13.647 ± 8.647	0.973 ± 0.042
	ConvDip	10.183 ± 14.089	0.998 ± 0.005	5.623 ± 5.595	0.999 ± 0.002	6.471 ± 6.540	0.999 ± 0.002
	Proposed	2.076 ± 3.940	**1.000 ± 0.000**	**0.698 ± 2.553**	**1.000 ± 0.000**	**1.271 ± 3.208**	**1.000 ± 0.001**
30 dB	MNE	7.973 ± 7.585	0.992 ± 0.022	11.588 ± 8.044	0.974 ± 0.036	13.731 ± 8.451	0.951 ± 0.039
	sLORETA	**1.027 ± 3.046**	0.995 ± 0.015	5.167 ± 5.216	0.976 ± 0.032	8.122 ± 6.246	0.950 ± 0.035
	dSPM	18.909 ± 21.068	0.991 ± 0.017	22.815 ± 22.751	0.967 ± 0.035	29.132 ± 25.786	0.933 ± 0.042
	ADMM	8.881 ± 15.701	0.994 ± 0.023	10.864 ± 9.693	0.984 ± 0.041	12.932 ± 8.974	0.971 ± 0.047
	ConvDip	10.072 ± 14.068	0.998 ± 0.005	5.369 ± 5.713	0.999 ± 0.002	6.428 ± 6.489	0.998 ± 0.002
	Proposed	1.808 ± 3.721	**1.000 ± 0.000**	**0.698 ± 2.553**	**1.000 ± 0.000**	**1.039 ± 2.968**	**1.000 ± 0.000**
20 dB	MNE	14.239 ± 20.483	0.972 ± 0.048	15.351 ± 20.993	0.925 ± 0.065	16.274 ± 17.787	0.869 ± 0.072
	sLORETA	3.613 ± 8.954	0.987 ± 0.026	6.841 ± 7.314	0.938 ± 0.051	10.448 ± 9.327	0.872 ± 0.066
	dSPM	15.356 ± 18.819	0.984 ± 0.031	17.584 ± 17.546	0.929 ± 0.058	25.121 ± 22.511	0.857 ± 0.085
	ADMM	8.480 ± 11.121	0.993 ± 0.024	10.774 ± 9.135	0.981 ± 0.043	13.691 ± 9.464	0.957 ± 0.059
	ConvDip	9.931 ± 14.227	0.998 ± 0.004	5.069 ± 5.647	0.999 ± 0.002	6.100 ± 6.370	0.998 ± 0.002
	Proposed	**1.850 ± 3.786**	**1.000 ± 0.000**	**0.716 ± 2.616**	**1.000 ± 0.000**	**1.371 ± 3.315**	**1.000 ± 0.002**
10 dB	MNE	56.266 ± 55.608	0.864 ± 0.124	64.097 ± 63.191	0.778 ± 0.120	70.787 ± 60.278	0.733 ± 0.101
	sLORETA	41.220 ± 52.494	0.876 ± 0.123	49.877 ± 57.121	0.767 ± 0.121	57.774 ± 57.160	0.710 ± 0.098
	dSPM	23.280 ± 27.462	0.887 ± 0.135	28.506 ± 28.134	0.774 ± 0.133	33.438 ± 28.953	0.711 ± 0.113
	ADMM	24.568 ± 30.248	0.958 ± 0.087	34.218 ± 39.197	0.883 ± 0.111	46.813 ± 49.630	0.824 ± 0.109
	ConvDip	10.462 ± 14.475	0.997 ± 0.006	6.270 ± 6.790	0.998 ± 0.003	7.258 ± 6.669	**0.997 ± 0.008**
	Proposed	**4.257 ± 6.211**	**0.999 ± 0.002**	**2.758 ± 4.443**	**0.999 ± 0.004**	**4.403 ± 5.102**	0.997 ± 0.009

CPU and 64 GB memory, and NVIDIA V100 with 32 GB memory was used to train deep learning models. Brain source reconstruction was then performed when results from all algorithms were available. The performance of each algorithm was quantitatively evaluated based on the following metrics:

(1) *Localization error (LE)*: it measures the Euclidean distance between two source locations on the cortex meshes.
(2) *Area under curve (AUC)*: it is particularly useful to characterize the overlap of an extended source activation pattern.

Good performance suggests when LE is close to 0 and AUC is close to 1.

The performance comparison between the proposed method and benchmark algorithms on LE and AUC is summarized in Table 1, and the boxplot figures for SNR=40 dB, 20 dB and 10 dB are given in Fig. 5. The comparison between

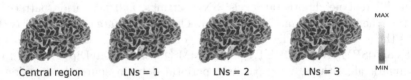

MAX

Central region   LNs = 1   LNs = 2   LNs = 3   MIN

Fig. 2. Brain source distributions with different activation levels of neighbors (LNs).

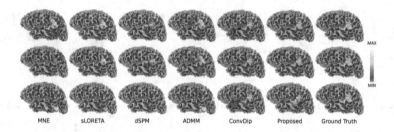

Fig. 3. Brain sources reconstruction by different ESI algorithms with 3-level of neighborhood for SNR = 40 dB (on the top row), SNR = 20 dB (on the second row) and SNR = 10 dB (on the bottom row).

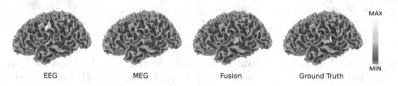

Fig. 4. Brain sources reconstruction based on unimodal and multimodal signals with 1-level of neighborhood and SNR = 40 dB.

the reconstructed source distributions with 3-level of neighborhood and 40 dB, 20 dB, and 10 dB SNR is shown in Fig. 3.

To further compare the performance of ConvDip based on single modality EEG/MEG and the proposed MMDF-ESI based on fused EEG and MEG, we provide the comparison between the reconstructed source distributions with 1-level of neighborhood and 40 dB SNR in Fig. 4.

From Table 1 and Fig. 4 and 5, we can see that:

(1) MNE, sLORETA, dSPM, and ADMM can only reconstruct the brain sources when the activated area is small and the SNR level is high. As the source range expands and the SNR decreases, a significant increase in LE and an obvious reduction in AUC can be observed. The reconstructed source distributions are no longer concentrated.

(2) By contrast, ConvDip and the proposed MMDF-ESI outperform benchmark methods in most cases. They both show excellent stability for varied neighborhood levels and SNR settings. However, MMDF-ESI has a considerable capability for large source extents and high noise levels. Compared to ConvDip, MMDF-ESI provides more concentrated source distributions.

(3) Unlike the single modality EEG or MEG, the use of combined EEG and MEG shows better performance in source localization, which manifests as more accurate and concentrated source reconstructions. This indicates that the complementary information of EEG and MEG has a significant impact on the precision of ESI inverse solutions.

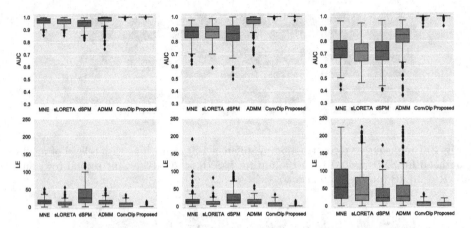

Fig. 5. Performance comparison of different algorithms on AUC (on the top) and LE (on the bottom), With single activated area and 1-level of neighborhood for SNR = 40 dB (on the left), SNR = 20 dB (on the middle) and SNR = 10 dB (on the right).

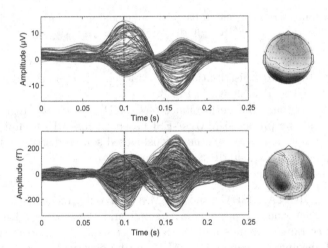

Fig. 6. Plots and topographies of averaged EEG (top) and MEG (bottom) time series.

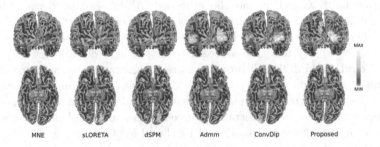

Fig. 7. Source activation patterns from both EEG and MEG recordings of the face recognition task.

3.2 Real Data Experiments

We further validated the proposed algorithm on the SPM face dataset (https://www.fil.ion.ucl.ac.uk/spm/data/mmfaces/), which contains the simultaneously acquired EEG (128-channel Biosemi system) and MEG (275-channel CTF system) recordings from the same subject. The subject underwent a face perception task that allows a basic comparison between *Faces* and *Scrambled* faces. The fMRI data were acquired using a gradient-echo EPI sequence on the Sonata. Evoked related potentials (ERP) were extracted from both the EEG and MEG measurements. We averaged these ERPs for source reconstruction by MNE, dSPM, sLORETA, ADMM, ConvDip, and the proposed MMDF-ESI. The averaged ERP are shown in Fig. 6, and the reconstructed source distributions are shown in Fig. 7.

From Fig. 7, we can see that the source area estimated by MNE, sLORETA, and dSPM is highly broad. It is worthnoting that the reconstructed source area has exceeded the scope of the visual area. By contrast, ADMM, ConvDip, and the proposed MMDF-ESI provide more sparse source reconstructions. However, compared to MMDF-ESI, the source distributions from ADMM and ConvDip cover a larger area, The proposed MMDF-ESI provides a cleaner and more accurate estimation of the visual zone.

4 Conclusion

In this study, we introduce a multi-modal deep fusion framework (MMDF-ESI) for the inverse problem of ESI. The proposed framework enjoys the advantage of combined use of simultaneously measured EEG and MEG. A SE network was introduced as a self-attention module to adaptively integrate features extracted by multiple channels. The dilated convolution was adopted to expand the receptive field. Numerical experiments demonstrated that the proposed MMDF-ESI framework performs particularly well on source extends and yields excellent stability when the SNR level is low. In the real data experiment we performed, the proposed framework provides a satisfactory reconstruction with a more concentrated source distribution than benchmark algorithms.

References

1. Michel, C.M., Murray, M.M., Lantz, G., Gonzalez, S., Spinelli, L., de Peralta, R.G.: EEG source imaging. Clin. Neurophysiol. **115**(10), 2195–2222 (2004)
2. He, B., Sohrabpour, A., Brown, E., Liu, Z.: Electrophysiological source imaging: a noninvasive window to brain dynamics. Annu. Rev. Biomed. Eng. **20**, 171–196 (2018)
3. Liu, F., Wang, S., Rosenberger, J., Su, J., Liu, H.: A sparse dictionary learning framework to discover discriminative source activations in EEG brain mapping. In: Proceedings of the AAAI Conference on Artificial Intelligence, vol. 31 (2017)
4. Liu, F., Wang, L., Lou, Y., Li, R.-C., Purdon, P.L.: Probabilistic structure learning for EEG/MEG source imaging with hierarchical graph priors. IEEE Trans. Med. Imaging **40**(1), 321–334 (2020)

5. Canuet, L., et al.: Resting-state EEG source localization and functional connectivity in schizophrenia-like psychosis of epilepsy. PloS One **6**(11), e27863 (2011)
6. Gramfort, A., Kowalski, M., Hämäläinen, M.: Mixed-norm estimates for the M/EEG inverse problem using accelerated gradient methods. Phys. Med. Biol. **57**(7), 1937 (2012)
7. Haufe, S., Nikulin, V.V., Ziehe, A., Müller, K.-R., Nolte, G.: Combining sparsity and rotational invariance in EEG/MEG source reconstruction. NeuroImage **42**(2), 726–738 (2008)
8. Hämäläinen, M.S., Ilmoniemi, R.J.: Interpreting magnetic fields of the brain: minimum norm estimates. Med. Biol. Eng. Comput. **32**(1), 35–42 (1994)
9. Pascual-Marqui, R.D., et al.: Standardized low-resolution brain electromagnetic tomography (sLORETA): technical details. Methods Find Exp. Clin. Pharmacol. **24**(Suppl D), 5–12 (2002)
10. Dale, A.M., et al.: Dynamic statistical parametric mapping: combining fMRI and MEG for high-resolution imaging of cortical activity. Neuron **26**(1), 55–67 (2000)
11. Uutela, K., Hämäläinen, M., Somersalo, E.: Visualization of magnetoencephalographic data using minimum current estimates. Neuroimage **10**(2), 173–180 (1999)
12. Liu, F., Rosenberger, J., Lou, Y., Hosseini, R., Jianzhong, S., Wang, S.: Graph regularized EEG source imaging with in-class consistency and out-class discrimination. IEEE Trans. Big Data **3**(4), 378–391 (2017)
13. Bore, J.C., et al.: Sparse EEG source localization using lapps: least absolute lP ($0 < p < 1$) penalized solution. IEEE Trans. Biomed. Eng. (2018)
14. Babadi, B., Obregon-Henao, G., Lamus, C., Hämäläinen, M.S., Brown, E.N., Purdon, P.L.: A subspace pursuit-based iterative greedy hierarchical solution to the neuromagnetic inverse problem. NeuroImage **87**, 427–443 (2014)
15. Baillet, S., Mosher, J.C., Leahy, R.M.: Electromagnetic brain mapping. IEEE Signal Process. Mag. **18**(6), 14–30 (2001)
16. Ding, L., He, B.: Sparse source imaging in electroencephalography with accurate field modeling. Hum. Brain Mapp. **29**(9), 1053–1067 (2008)
17. Liu, F., Wan, G., Semenov, Y.R., Purdon, P.L.: Extended electrophysiological source imaging with spatial graph filters. In: Wang, L., Dou, Q., Fletcher, P.T., Speidel, S., Li, S. (eds.) MICCAI 2022, Part I. LNCS, vol. 13431, pp. 99–109. Springer, Cham (2022). https://doi.org/10.1007/978-3-031-16431-6_10
18. Haufe, S., Tomioka, R., et al.: Large-scale EEG/MEG source localization with spatial flexibility. Neuroimage **54**(2), 851–859 (2011)
19. Becker, H., et al.: EEG extended source localization: tensor-based vs. conventional methods. NeuroImage **96**, 143–157 (2014)
20. Qin, J., Liu, F., Wang, S., Rosenberger, J.: EEG source imaging based on spatial and temporal graph structures. In: International Conference on Image Processing Theory, Tools and Applications (2017)
21. Wan, G., Jiao, M., Ju, X., Zhang, Y., Schweitzer, H., Liu, F.: Electrophysiological brain source imaging via combinatorial search with provable optimality. In: Proceedings of the AAAI Conference on Artificial Intelligence, vol. 37, no. 10, pp. 12491–12499 (2023)
22. Hecker, L., Rupprecht, R., van Elst, L.T., Kornmeier, J.: ConvDip: a convolutional neural network for better EEG source imaging. Front. Neurosci. **15**, 569918 (2021)
23. Jiao, M., et al.: A graph Fourier transform based bidirectional LSTM neural network for EEG source imaging. Front. Neurosci. 447 (2022)
24. Sun, R., Sohrabpour, A., Worrell, G.A., He, B.: Deep neural networks constrained by neural mass models improve electrophysiological source imaging of spatiotemporal brain dynamics. Proc. Natl. Acad. Sci. **119**(31), e2201128119 (2022)

25. Dinh, C., Samuelsson, J.G., Hunold, A., Hämäläinen, M.S., Khan, S.: Contextual meg and EEG source estimates using spatiotemporal LSTM networks. Front. Neurosci. **15**, 552666 (2021)
26. Jiao, M., Xian, X., Ghacibeh, G., Liu, F.: Extended brain sources estimation via unrolled optimization neural network. bioRxiv, pp. 2022–04 (2022)
27. Ou, W., Hämäläinen, M.S., Golland, P.: A distributed spatio-temporal EEG/MEG inverse solver. NeuroImage **44**(3), 932–946 (2009)
28. Ding, L.: Reconstructing cortical current density by exploring sparseness in the transform domain. Phys. Med. Biol. **54**(9), 2683 (2009)
29. Sohrabpour, A., Yunfeng, L., Worrell, G., He, B.: Imaging brain source extent from EEG/MEG by means of an iteratively reweighted edge sparsity minimization (IRES) strategy. Neuroimage **142**, 27–42 (2016)
30. Zhu, M., Zhang, W., Dickens, D.L., Ding, L.: Reconstructing spatially extended brain sources via enforcing multiple transform sparseness. NeuroImage **86**, 280–293 (2014)
31. Craley, J., Jouny, C., Johnson, E., Hsu, D., Ahmed, R., Venkataraman, A.: Automated seizure activity tracking and onset zone localization from scalp EEG using deep neural networks. PLoS ONE **17**(2), e0264537 (2022)
32. Huang, G., et al.: Electromagnetic source imaging via a data-synthesis-based convolutional encoder-decoder network. IEEE Trans. Neural Netw. Learn. Syst. (2022)
33. Dassios, G., Fokas, A.S., Hadjiloizi, D.: On the complementarity of electroencephalography and magnetoencephalography. Inverse Probl. **23**(6), 2541 (2007)
34. Malmivuo, J.: Comparison of the properties of EEG and MEG in detecting the electric activity of the brain. Brain Topogr. **25**, 1–19 (2012)
35. Fernando Lopes da Silva: EEG and MEG: relevance to neuroscience. Neuron **80**(5), 1112–1128 (2013)
36. Ahlfors, S.P., Han, J., Belliveau, J.W., Hämäläinen, M.S.: Sensitivity of MEG and EEG to source orientation. Brain Topogr. **23**, 227–232 (2010)
37. Ebersole, J.S., Ebersole, S.M.: Combining MEG and EEG source modeling in epilepsy evaluations. J. Clin. Neurophysiol. **27**(6), 360–371 (2010)
38. Aydin, Ü., et al.: Combined EEG/MEG can outperform single modality EEG or MEG source reconstruction in presurgical epilepsy diagnosis. PLoS ONE **10**(3), e0118753 (2015)
39. Lecaignard, F., Bertrand, O., Caclin, A., Mattout, J.: Empirical bayes evaluation of fused EEG-MEG source reconstruction: application to auditory mismatch evoked responses. Neuroimage **226**, 117468 (2021)
40. Yu, F., Koltun, V.: Multi-scale context aggregation by dilated convolutions. arXiv preprint arXiv:1511.07122 (2015)
41. Hu, J., Shen, L., Sun, G.: Squeeze-and-excitation networks. In: Proceedings of the IEEE Conference on Computer Vision and Pattern Recognition, pp. 7132–7141 (2018)
42. Gramfort, A., et al.: MNE software for processing MEG and EEG data. Neuroimage **86**, 446–460 (2014)
43. Furong, X., Liu, K., Yu, Z., Deng, X., Wang, G.: EEG extended source imaging with structured sparsity and L1-norm residual. Neural Comput. Appl. **33**(14), 8513–8524 (2021)

Rejuvenating Classical Source Localization Methods with Spatial Graph Filters

Shihao Yang[1], Meng Jiao[1], Jing Xiang[2], Daphne Kalkanis[1], Hai Sun[3],
and Feng Liu[1]([✉])

[1] School of Systems and Enterprises, Stevens Institute of Technology,
Hoboken, NJ 07030, USA
{syang57,mjiao,dkalkani,fliu22}@stevens.edu
[2] MEG Center, Division of Neurology, Cincinnati Children's Hospital Medical
Center, Cincinnati, OH, USA
[3] Department of Neurosurgery, Rutgers Robert Wood Johnson Medical School,
Brunswick, NJ, USA

Abstract. EEG/MEG source imaging (ESI) aims to find the underlying brain sources to explain the observed EEG or MEG measurement. Multiple classical approaches have been proposed to solve the ESI problem based on different neurophysiological assumptions. To support the clinical decision making, it is important to estimate not only the exact location of source signal but also the boundary of extended source activation. Traditional methods usually render over-diffuse or sparse solution, which limits the source extent estimation accuracy. In this work, we exploit the graph structure defined in the 3D mesh of the brain by decomposing the spatial graph signal into low-, medium-, and high-frequency sub-spaces, and leverage the low frequency components of graph Fourier basis to approximate the extended region of source activation. We integrate the classical source localization methods with the low frequency subspace components derived from the spatial graph signal. The proposed method can effectively reconstruct focal extent patterns and significantly improve the performance compared to classical algorithms through both synthetic data and real EEG data.

Keywords: EEG/MEG Source Imaging · Inverse Problem · Graph Signal Processing · Spatial Graph Filter

1 Introduction

EEG/MEG is a non-invasive measurement with high temporal and low spatial resolution, which collects signals on the scalp through electrodes for analysis of brain neural activity. At the same time, EEG/MEG is also a direct and real-time way to detect a spontaneous or induced activity of the brain [1]. EEG/MEG devices have the advantages of cost-effectiveness, portability, and versatility.

F. Liu et al. (Eds.): BI 2023, LNAI 13974, pp. 286–296, 2023.
https://doi.org/10.1007/978-3-031-43075-6_25

EEG, in particular, is widely recognized as a powerful tool for capturing real-time brain function by measuring neuronal processes [2]. The problem of EEG/MEG source localization can be further divided into two sub-problems, the forward and the inverse problem. The forward problem of EEG/MEG is to determine the surface potential or magnetic field strength of the scalp from a given configuration of neuronal current activity, whereas the inverse problem is defined as the reconstruction of brain activity sources from external electromagnetic signals which is also known as the EEG/MEG source imaging (ESI) problem [3]. However, the number of EEG/MEG external detection channels is far less than that of the brain sources, which makes the ESI an ill-posed problem.

In the past decades, numerous algorithms have been developed with different assumptions on the configuration of the source signal. One seminal work is minimum norm estimate (MNE) where ℓ_2 norm is used as a regularization [4], which is to explain the observed signal using a potential solution with the minimum energy. Different variants of the MNE algorithm include dynamic statistical parametric mapping (dSPM) [5] and standardized low-resolution brain electromagnetic tomography (sLORETA) [6]. The ℓ_2-norm based methods tend to render spatially diffuse source estimation. To promote a sparse solution, Uutela *et al.* [7] introduced the ℓ_1-norm, known as minimum current estimate (MCE). Also, Rao and Kreutz-Delgado proposed an affine scaling method [8] for a sparse ESI solution. q111The focal underdetermined system solution (FOCUSS) proposed by Gorodnitsky *et al.* encourages a sparse solution by introducing the ℓ_p-norm regularization [9]. Besides, Bore *et al.* also proposed to use the ℓ_p-norm regularization ($p < 1$) on the source signal and the ℓ_1 norm on the data fitting error term [10]. Babadi *et al.* [11] demonstrated that sparsely distributed solutions to event-related stimuli could be found using a greedy subspace-pursuit algorithm. Wipf *et al.* proposed a unified Bayesian learning method [12] that can automatically calculate the hyperparameters for the inverse problems under an empirical Bayesian framework and the sparsity of the solution is also guaranteed. It is worth noting that the sparse constraint can be applied to the original source signal or the transformed spatial gradient domain [13–16]. As the brain sources are not activated discretely due to the conductor property, an extended area of source estimation is preferred [17], and it has been used for multiple applications, such as somatosensory cortical mapping [18], and epileptogenic zone in focal epilepsy patients [19].

Following the early work of applying GSP to the ESI problem [20,21], in this work, we proposed to use GSP and incorporate the low frequency spatial representation for the source space and rejuvenate the classical ESI methods for the estimation of an extended area of source activation, and illustrate the importance of using GSP for an extended area of source activation.

2   Method

In this section, we start by introducing the ESI inverse problem, followed by the presentation of the graph Fourier transform (GFT). Then, we propose a improve the classical source localization methods using the low-pass spatial graph filters.

2.1   EEG/MEG Source Imaging Problem

The source imaging forward problem can be described as the format $Y = KS+E$, where $Y \in \mathbb{R}^{C \times T}$ is the EEG/MEG measurements from the scalp, C is the number of EEG/MEG channels, T is the time sequence length, $K \in \mathbb{R}^{C \times N}$ is the *leadfield* matrix which performs a linear mapping from the brain sources to the EEG/MEG electrodes on the scalp, N is the number of source locations, $S \in \mathbb{R}^{N \times T}$ represents the active source amplitudes in N source locations for all the T time points, and E is the noise which can be assumed to follow the Gaussian distribution with zero mean and identity covariance. The inverse problem is to estimate S given Y and K. Since the source number N is much larger than the electrode number C, which makes the inverse problem ill-posed, it is challenging to obtain a unique and stable solution. Thus, in order to constrain the solution space, various regularization terms were designed based on the prior assumption of the source structure. In this case, the inverse problem can be formulated as below:

$$S = \underset{S}{\mathrm{argmin}} \, \frac{1}{2} \|Y - KS\|_F^2 + \lambda R(S), \tag{1}$$

where $\| \cdot \|_F$ is the Frobenius norm, and S can be obtained by solving the minimizing problem. The first term in Eq. (1) is *datafitting* trying to explain the recorded EEG measurements. The second term is called the *regularization* term, which is imposed to find a unique solution by using sparsity or other neurophysiology inspired regularization. For example, if $R(S)$ equals ℓ_2 norm, the problem is called minimum norm estimate (MNE).

2.2   Graph Fourier Transform (GFT)

Consider an undirected graph $G = \{\mathcal{V}, A\}$ generated from the 3D mesh of cortex, where $\mathcal{V} = \{v_1, v_2, \ldots, v_N\}$ is the set of N nodes, A is the weighted adjacent matrix with entries given by the edge weights a_{ij} that represents the connection strength between node i and node j. The graph Laplacian matrix is defined as $L = D - A$, where D is the in-degree matrix with $D_{ii} = \sum_{j \neq i} A_{ij}$. Since L is a positive semi-definite matrix, its eigenvalues are all greater or equal to 0 which are usually taken as the frequency of GFT, and the associated eigenvectors $U = [u_1, u_2, \ldots, u_N]$, $U \in \mathbb{R}^{N \times N}$ can be regarded as the basis signals of GFT where any signal in the graph can be approximated as the linear combinations of basis. Thus, the graph Fourier transform for a signal S can be defined as $\tilde{S} = U^T S$, whereas the inverse graph Fourier transform is given as $S = U\tilde{S}$. Then we define normalized graph frequency (NGF) as

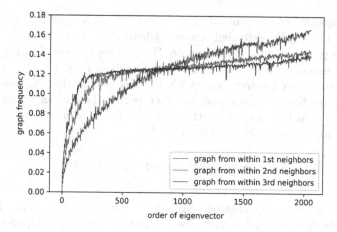

Fig. 1. Graph frequency of the eigenvectors.

$$f_G(u_i) = \frac{f_s(u_i)}{Tr(L)}, \tag{2}$$

where $Tr(L)$ is the trace of L, and $f_s(u_i)$ is defined as

$$f_s(u_i) = \sum_{m=1}^{N} \sum_{n \in \mathcal{N}(m)} \mathbb{I}(u_i(m)u_i(n) < 0)/2, \tag{3}$$

where $\mathcal{N}(m)$ represents all neighbors of node m, and $\mathbb{I}(\cdot)$ is the indicator function which equals 1 if the values of u_i on node m and n have different sign and 0 otherwise. The number of sign flip at time t indicate how many zero crossing of a basis signal within a bounded region at t.

We calculated the NGF in the whole time series within first-order neighbors, second-order neighbors, and third-order neighbors respectively. The spectrogram, which is illustrated in Fig. 1, reveals that the NGF is positively correlated with the size of the eigenvalue of L. Thus we can further separate U into low, medium, and high-frequency components according to NGF values, and reformat it as $U = [U_L, U_M, U_H]$.

2.3   Inverse Problem with Spatial Graph Filters

The existing source localization methods can be distracted by the high-frequency components and result in a spread-out solution while reconstructing the focal extend area, even the ℓ_1-norm and $\ell_{2,1}$-norm based method that is designed to promote the sparsity can hardly give a satisfying reconstruction result. Moreover, they do not take source spatial frequency correlation into consideration. The proposed method is trying to rejuvenate classical source localization methods using spatial graph filters by keeping the spatially low- and the top part of medium-frequency components $[U_L, \tilde{U}_M] \in \mathbb{R}^{N \times P}$ as a spatial graph filter to reconstruct the focally extended sources, where P is the number of frequency components preserved for reconstruction. Here we replace the S in Eq. (1) with $\tilde{U}\tilde{S}^*$ for dimensionality reduction in S and K, where $\tilde{U} = [U_L, \tilde{U}_M]$, and $\tilde{S}^* \in \mathbb{R}^{P \times T}$ is the estimated source signal with dimensionality reduction that contains smooth part of the original signal, in other words, the part of source extents. Then we can transform Eq. (1) to the problem of estimating $\tilde{S}^*$ by introducing the spatial graph filter with the form as below

$$\tilde{S}^* = \underset{\tilde{S}^*}{\operatorname{argmin}} \frac{1}{2}\|Y - K\tilde{U}\tilde{S}^*\|_F^2 + \lambda R(\tilde{S}^*), \tag{4}$$

Finally, S can be simply obtained from $\tilde{U}\tilde{S}^*$. The intuition is that the main energy of the source signal usually lies in the low-frequency components which are associated with the regions on the cortex with relatively large source extend area in a time series. Keeping the low graph frequency could promote a source extend area reconstruction and decrease the impact of the noise. Moreover, the reduced dimensional estimation in the inverse problem could further constrain the solution space and make the solution more easily solved and robust.

3   Numerical Experiments

In this section, we conducted numerical experiments to validate the effectiveness of the proposed method on synthetic EEG data under different levels of neighbors (LNs), Signal Noise Ratio (SNR) settings and further validate it on real MEG recordings from a visual-auditory test.

3.1   Simulation Experiments

We first conducted experiments on synthetic data with known activation patterns.

Forward Model: To generate synthetic EEG data, we used a real head model to compute the leadfield matrix. The T1-MRI images were scanned from a 26-year-old male subject. The brain tissue segmentation and source surface reconstruction were conducted using FreeSurfer [22]. Then a three-layer boundary element method (BEM) head was built based on these surfaces. A 128-channel BioSemi EEG cap layout was used and the EEG channels were co-registered with the head model using Brainstorm and then further validated on the MNE-Python toolbox [23]. The source space contains 1026 sources in each hemisphere, with 2052 sources combined, resulting in a leadfield matrix L with a dimension of 128 by 2052 (Fig. 2).

Synthetic Data Generation: To make the synthetic data more realistic, 200 out of 2052 locations in the source space were activated. Furthermore, as illustrated in Fig. 3, we used 3 different neighborhood levels (1-, 2-, and 3-level of the

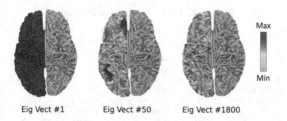

Fig. 2. Source distributions corresponding to eigenvectors with different NGFs.

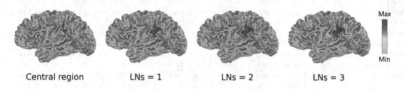

Fig. 3. Brain source distributions with different levels of neighbors (LNs).

neighborhood) to represent different sizes of source extents, then we activated the whole "patch" with different neighborhood levels at the same time. The activation strength of the 1-, 2-, and 3-level adjacent regions was successively set to be 80%, 60%, and 40% of the central region. The strength of the source signal was set to be constant, then the scalp EEG data was calculated based on the forward model under different SNR settings (SNR = 40 dB, 30 dB, 20 dB, and 10 db). SNR is defined as the ratio of the signal power P_{signal} to the noise power P_{noise}: SNR = $10 \log(P_{\text{signal}}/P_{\text{noise}})$.

In total, there were 12: 3 (source extents) × 4 (SNRs) data sets (Y and S pairs).

Experimental Settings: We adopted MNE [4], MCE [7], $\ell_{2,1}$(MxNE) [24], dSPM [5], and sLORETA [6], as benchmark algorithms for comparison. We separately performed EEG source localization based on benchmark algorithms with and without the proposed GFT-based dimensionality reduction method. Next, we performed brain source reconstruction on the results from all algorithms. All the experiments were conducted on Linux environment with CPU Intel(R) Xeon(R) Gold 6130 CPU @2.10 GHz and 128 GB memory. The performance of each algorithm was quantitatively evaluated based on the following metrics:

(1) *Localization error (LE)*: it measures the Euclidean distance between centers of two source locations on the cortex meshes.
(2) *Area under curve (AUC)*: it is particularly useful to characterize the overlap of an extended source activation pattern.

Better performance for localization is expected if LE is close to 0 and AUC is close to 1. The performance comparison between the proposed method and benchmark algorithms on LE and AUC is summarized in Table 1, and the boxplot figures for SNR = 40 dB, and 20 dB are given in Fig. 4. The comparison between

Table 1. Performance Evaluation

SNR	Method	Source with LNs = 1		Source with LNs = 2		Source with LNs = 3	
		LE (std)	AUC (std)	LE (std)	AUC (std)	LE (std)	AUC (std)
40 dB	MCE	15.028 ± 11.465	0.595 ± 0.064	15.286 ± 10.474	0.568 ± 0.031	18.656 ± 12.154	0.548 ± 0.017
	L21	16.114 ± 10.433	0.631 ± 0.096	14.993 ± 9.121	0.627 ± 0.054	15.237 ± 8.400	0.625 ± 0.052
	MNE	9.828 ± 6.455	0.992 ± 0.014	10.294 ± 6.750	0.977 ± 0.019	11.216 ± 7.452	0.961 ± 0.018
	sLORETA	7.349 ± 6.530	0.988 ± 0.018	11.504 ± 9.868	0.963 ± 0.026	15.567 ± 11.607	0.935 ± 0.025
	dSPM	33.666 ± 22.034	0.970 ± 0.027	39.868 ± 22.844	0.927 ± 0.039	47.382 ± 23.449	0.883 ± 0.043
	GFT-MCE	25.969 ± 22.269	0.975 ± 0.046	16.411 ± 14.091	0.988 ± 0.017	13.547 ± 9.922	0.983 ± 0.026
	GFT-L21	9.814 ± 7.416	0.996 ± 0.018	5.144 ± 6.607	0.999 ± 0.004	4.054 ± 6.130	0.998 ± 0.010
	GFT-MNE	3.812 ± 5.028	0.999 ± 0.001	6.526 ± 6.059	0.983 ± 0.020	7.689 ± 5.879	0.958 ± 0.023
	GFT-sLORETA	4.992 ± 4.640	0.996 ± 0.016	7.424 ± 6.144	0.971 ± 0.026	8.803 ± 6.553	0.947 ± 0.028
	GFT-dSPM	3.625 ± 5.346	0.999 ± 0.006	5.898 ± 5.374	0.992 ± 0.013	7.654 ± 6.093	0.968 ± 0.027
30 dB	MCE	14.917 ± 11.426	0.595 ± 0.065	14.779 ± 9.607	0.568 ± 0.030	18.324 ± 11.870	0.548 ± 0.017
	L21	16.460 ± 12.235	0.630 ± 0.096	14.690 ± 9.188	0.625 ± 0.053	15.330 ± 8.825	0.620 ± 0.051
	MNE	9.340 ± 6.446	0.983 ± 0.027	9.806 ± 6.493	0.958 ± 0.026	9.878 ± 6.676	0.926 ± 0.025
	sLORETA	6.358 ± 5.896	0.980 ± 0.035	8.670 ± 7.365	0.944 ± 0.036	12.347 ± 9.650	0.899 ± 0.033
	dSPM	31.885 ± 21.226	0.961 ± 0.044	36.423 ± 21.313	0.904 ± 0.053	42.922 ± 22.799	0.841 ± 0.055
	GFT-MCE	25.787 ± 22.258	0.975 ± 0.046	15.633 ± 12.640	0.989 ± 0.017	13.507 ± 9.875	0.983 ± 0.027
	GFT-L21	9.603 ± 7.393	0.996 ± 0.017	5.084 ± 6.564	0.999 ± 0.004	3.963 ± 5.874	0.998 ± 0.010
	GFT-MNE	3.236 ± 4.663	0.999 ± 0.003	5.357 ± 5.308	0.970 ± 0.030	6.921 ± 6.426	0.920 ± 0.034
	GFT-sLORETA	4.515 ± 5.990	0.994 ± 0.018	6.752 ± 6.264	0.949 ± 0.034	7.522 ± 6.589	0.902 ± 0.034
	GFT-dSPM	2.888 ± 4.292	0.999 ± 0.002	4.900 ± 5.316	0.985 ± 0.021	6.362 ± 5.907	0.946 ± 0.034
20 dB	MCE	14.655 ± 10.959	0.595 ± 0.064	14.353 ± 9.431	0.567 ± 0.031	18.302 ± 12.155	0.548 ± 0.017
	L21	16.309 ± 12.373	0.626 ± 0.099	14.087 ± 8.921	0.623 ± 0.052	16.213 ± 9.371	0.616 ± 0.044
	MNE	11.894 ± 14.620	0.951 ± 0.036	17.515 ± 23.602	0.897 ± 0.038	33.240 ± 37.552	0.846 ± 0.033
	sLORETA	7.237 ± 6.801	0.952 ± 0.051	10.639 ± 10.168	0.879 ± 0.056	19.948 ± 22.829	0.815 ± 0.043
	dSPM	27.257 ± 17.682	0.923 ± 0.070	34.975 ± 20.713	0.824 ± 0.082	41.651 ± 24.331	0.745 ± 0.074
	GFT-MCE	26.018 ± 22.997	0.976 ± 0.045	15.502 ± 12.445	0.989 ± 0.016	13.952 ± 13.063	0.983 ± 0.028
	GFT-L21	9.333 ± 7.512	0.996 ± 0.017	5.156 ± 6.540	0.999 ± 0.003	4.514 ± 6.281	0.998 ± 0.007
	GFT-MNE	3.840 ± 5.439	0.992 ± 0.019	5.630 ± 7.294	0.905 ± 0.049	10.217 ± 9.890	0.829 ± 0.042
	GFT-sLORETA	4.509 ± 6.420	0.979 ± 0.040	7.514 ± 9.787	0.873 ± 0.051	12.362 ± 12.321	0.803 ± 0.042
	GFT-dSPM	3.608 ± 4.907	0.996 ± 0.015	5.605 ± 7.311	0.941 ± 0.043	9.370 ± 8.110	0.864 ± 0.054
10 dB	MCE	15.526 ± 12.210	0.595 ± 0.061	14.247 ± 8.628	0.565 ± 0.029	17.944 ± 11.812	0.547 ± 0.017
	L21	16.434 ± 12.503	0.613 ± 0.090	15.248 ± 9.681	0.589 ± 0.051	16.307 ± 10.712	0.577 ± 0.038
	MNE	50.433 ± 47.357	0.871 ± 0.064	59.498 ± 48.871	0.804 ± 0.059	58.400 ± 46.174	0.766 ± 0.060
	sLORETA	47.815 ± 49.262	0.856 ± 0.087	59.048 ± 49.597	0.760 ± 0.082	57.989 ± 43.289	0.715 ± 0.079
	dSPM	31.356 ± 27.881	0.807 ± 0.112	37.304 ± 26.798	0.688 ± 0.101	41.865 ± 25.344	0.640 ± 0.089
	GFT-MCE	23.504 ± 16.491	0.975 ± 0.043	17.195 ± 13.654	0.988 ± 0.019	14.482 ± 11.684	0.982 ± 0.027
	GFT-L21	9.406 ± 8.054	0.996 ± 0.017	5.334 ± 5.735	0.998 ± 0.003	7.586 ± 6.490	0.948 ± 0.038
	GFT-MNE	21.581 ± 29.679	0.919 ± 0.077	28.806 ± 30.421	0.801 ± 0.067	39.258 ± 32.820	0.744 ± 0.066
	GFT-sLORETA	24.439 ± 30.874	0.891 ± 0.087	32.387 ± 31.514	0.771 ± 0.078	41.389 ± 36.626	0.729 ± 0.071
	GFT-dSPM	18.462 ± 25.356	0.937 ± 0.069	27.152 ± 30.759	0.818 ± 0.070	35.293 ± 30.785	0.750 ± 0.065

the reconstructed source distributions with a 3-level of the neighborhood and 40 dB SNR is shown in Fig. 5.

From Table 1 and Fig. 4 and 5, we can find that:

(1) MNE, MCE, $\ell_{2,1}$, sLORETA, and dSPM can only reconstruct the brain sources when the activated area is small and the SNR level is high, and even the evaluation metrics are good in this case, the reconstruction for source extend area is poor as shown in Fig. 5. As the source range expands and the SNR decreases, a significant increase in LE and an obvious reduction in AUC can be observed. The reconstructed source distributions are no longer concentrated.

(2) By contrast, the results of the rejuvenated methods outperform benchmark methods in most cases after applying the spatial graph filters. They both show good stability for varied neighborhood levels and SNR settings. Particularly, the performance of rejuvenated ℓ_1 regularization family (i.e., ℓ_1-norm

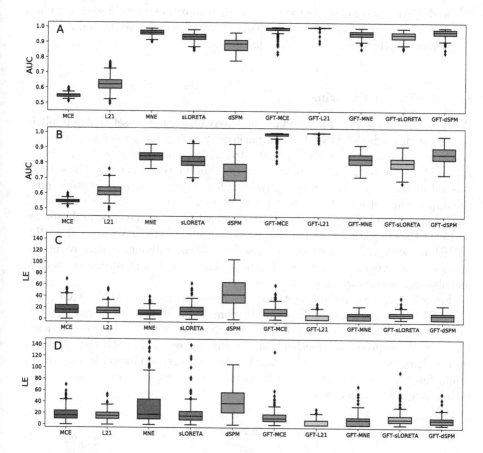

Fig. 4. Performance comparison of different algorithms on AUC and LE with 3-level of the neighborhood for SNR = 40 dB (subplot A and C), and SNR = 20 dB (subplot B and D).

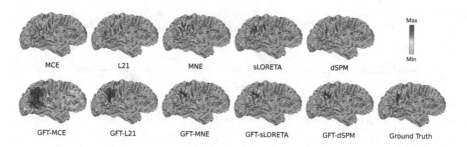

Fig. 5. Brain sources reconstruction by different ESI algorithms with the single activated area and 3-level of the neighborhood for SNR = 40 dB.

and $\ell_{2,1}$-norm) exhibits better performance on reconstructing source extents without losing its advantage in sparse focal source reconstruction and outperforms other methods in most instances.

3.2   Real Data Experiments

We further validated the proposed methodology on a real dataset that is publicly accessible through the MNE-Python package [23]. In this dataset acquirement, checkerboard patterns were presented into the left and right visual field, interspersed by tones to the left or right ear with stimuli interval 750 ms. The subject was asked to press a key with the right index finger as soon as possible after the appearance of a smiley face was presented at the center of the visual field [25]. Interictal spikes were extracted from the MEG measurements, and then we averaged these spikes for source reconstruction under MNE, MCE, $\ell_{2,1}$, dSPM, sLORETA with and without the proposed GFT-based dimensionality reduction method. The averaged spikes are shown in Fig. 6, and the reconstructed source distributions are shown in Fig. 7.

From Fig. 7, we can see that the source area estimated by MNE, MCE, $\ell_{2,1}$, sLORETA, and dSPM is highly broad. By contrast, and the rejuvenated methods provide more sparse focal source reconstructions. Moreover, the reconstructed focal for the rejuvenated methods falls primarily on areas with the strongest source signal, while others would spread to several regions. Obviously, the spatial graph filter in the rejuvenated methods promotes a concentrated and accurate estimation of the visual zone.

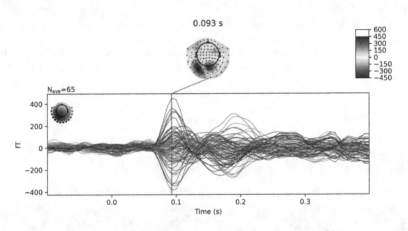

Fig. 6. Averaged MEG time series plot and topographies.

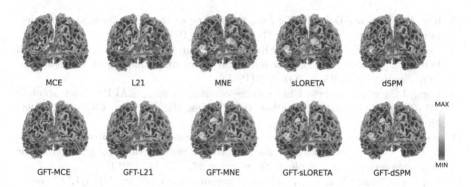

Fig. 7. Reconstructed source activation patterns from MEG data.

4 Conclusion

In this study, we rejuvenated classical source localization methods using spatial graph filters to solve the inverse problem of ESI. The proposed methodology enjoys the advantage of reconstructing focal source extents with sparsity and minimizing the impact from the noise by transforming the estimation of the source signal into an estimation of a lower dimensional latent variable in the subspace spanned by spatial frequency graph filters. Numerical experiments demonstrated that the proposed method performs particularly well on source extents, yields excellent robustness when the SNR level is low, and greatly improves the performance of the ℓ_1 family regularization. In the experiment on real data we performed, the proposed methodology provides a satisfactory reconstruction with more concentrated source distribution and more stability to noise than benchmark algorithms.

References

1. Wendel, K., et al.: EEG/MEG source imaging: methods, challenges, and open issues. Comput. Intell. Neurosci. **2009** (2009)
2. Michel, C.M., Brunet, D.: EEG source imaging: a practical review of the analysis steps. Front. Neurol. **10**, 325 (2019)
3. Huang, G., et al.: Electromagnetic source imaging via a data-synthesis-based convolutional encoder-decoder network. IEEE Trans. Neural Netw. Learn. Syst. (2022)
4. Hämäläinen, M.S., Ilmoniemi, R.J.: Interpreting magnetic fields of the brain: minimum norm estimates. Med. Biol. Eng. Comput. **32**(1), 35–42 (1994). https://doi.org/10.1007/BF02512476
5. Dale, A.M., et al.: Dynamic statistical parametric mapping: combining fMRI and MEG for high-resolution imaging of cortical activity. Neuron **26**(1), 55–67 (2000)
6. Pascual-Marqui, R.D., et al.: Standardized low-resolution brain electromagnetic tomography (sLORETA): technical details. Methods Find. Exp. Clin. Pharmacol. **24**(Suppl D), 5–12 (2002)
7. Uutela, K., Hämäläinen, M., Somersalo, E.: Visualization of magnetoencephalographic data using minimum current estimates. Neuroimage **10**(2), 173–180 (1999)

8. Rao, B.D., Kreutz-Delgado, K.: An affine scaling methodology for best basis selection. IEEE Trans. Sig. Process. **47**(1), 187–200 (1999)
9. Gorodnitsky, I.F., George, J.S., Rao, B.D.: Neuromagnetic source imaging with FOCUSS: a recursive weighted minimum norm algorithm. Electroencephalogr. Clin. Neurophysiol. **95**(4), 231–251 (1995)
10. Bore, J.C., et al.: Sparse EEG source localization using LAPPS: least absolute l-P $(0 < p < 1)$ penalized solution. IEEE Trans. Biomed. Eng. **66**(7), 1927–1939 (2018)
11. Babadi, B., Obregon-Henao, G., Lamus, C., Hämäläinen, M.S., Brown, E.N., Purdon, P.L.: A subspace pursuit-based iterative greedy hierarchical solution to the neuromagnetic inverse problem. Neuroimage **87**, 427–443 (2014)
12. Wipf, D., Nagarajan, S.: A unified Bayesian framework for MEG/EEG source imaging. Neuroimage **44**(3), 947–966 (2009)
13. Ding, L., He, B.: Sparse source imaging in electroencephalography with accurate field modeling. Hum. Brain Mapp. **29**(9), 1053–1067 (2008)
14. Sohrabpour, A., Ye, S., et al.: Noninvasive electromagnetic source imaging and granger causality analysis: an electrophysiological connectome (eConnectome) approach. IEEE Trans. Biomed. Eng. **63**(12), 2474–2487 (2016)
15. Qin, J., Liu, F., Wang, S., Rosenberger, J.: EEG source imaging based on spatial and temporal graph structures. In: International Conference on Image Processing Theory, Tools and Applications (2017)
16. Liu, F., Wang, L., Lou, Y., Li, R.-C., Purdon, P.L.: Probabilistic structure learning for EEG/MEG source imaging with hierarchical graph priors. IEEE Trans. Med. Imaging **40**(1), 321–334 (2020)
17. Baillet, S., Mosher, J.C., Leahy, R.M.: Electromagnetic brain mapping. IEEE Sig. Process. Mag. **18**(6), 14–30 (2001)
18. Cai, C., Diwakar, M., Chen, D., Sekihara, K., Nagarajan, S.S.: Robust empirical Bayesian reconstruction of distributed sources for electromagnetic brain imaging. IEEE Trans. Med. Imaging **39**(3), 567–577 (2019)
19. Becker, H., et al.: EEG extended source localization: tensor-based vs. conventional methods. Neuroimage **96**, 143–157 (2014)
20. Liu, F., Wan, G., Semenov, Y.R., Purdon, P.L.: Extended electrophysiological source imaging with spatial graph filters. In: Wang, L., Dou, Q., Fletcher, P.T., Speidel, S., Li, S. (eds.) MICCAI 2022. LNCS, vol. 13431, pp. 99–109. Springer, Cham (2022). https://doi.org/10.1007/978-3-031-16431-6_10
21. M. Jiao, et al.: A graph Fourier transform based bidirectional LSTM neural network for EEG source imaging. Front. Neurosci. **447** (2022)
22. Fischl, B.: FreeSurfer. Neuroimage **62**(2), 774–781 (2012)
23. Gramfort, A., et al.: MNE software for processing MEG and EEG data. Neuroimage **86**, 446–460 (2014)
24. Gramfort, A., Kowalski, M., Hämäläinen, M.: Mixed-norm estimates for the M/EEG inverse problem using accelerated gradient methods. Phys. Med. Biol. **57**(7), 1937 (2012)
25. Gramfort, A., Strohmeier, D., Haueisen, J., Hämäläinen, M.S., Kowalski, M.: Time-frequency mixed-norm estimates: sparse M/EEG imaging with non-stationary source activations. Neuroimage **70**, 410–422 (2013)

Prediction of Cannabis Addictive Patients with Graph Neural Networks

Shulin Wen[1], Shihao Yang[1], Xinglong Ju[2], Ting Liao[1], and Feng Liu[1(✉)]

[1] School of Systems and Enterprises, Stevens Institute of Technology,
Hoboken, NJ 07030, USA
{swen3,fliu22}@stevens.edu

[2] Department of Computer Information and Decision Management, Paul and Virginia Engler
College of Business, West Texas A&M University, Canyon, TX 79016, USA

Abstract. Neurological research is closely intertwined with public health issues, and artificial intelligence (AI) holds substantial potential in this domain. This study aims to investigate the enhancement of brain imaging classification performance in diverse populations using Graph Neural Networks (GNN) and its variants. Brain activity data are sourced from public neuroimaging databases, including functional Magnetic Resonance Imaging (fMRI) data of cannabis addicts and a healthy control group. Our results show that, compared to the healthy control group, cannabis addicts exhibit significant alterations in functional connectivity in certain brain regions. With the application of AI tools, we can distinguish the two groups based on brain imaging. We observed a significant improvement in brain imaging classification performance, and this model has achieved an accuracy rate of approximately 80%. These AI tools' robust generalizability and vast developmental potential were also highlighted. These findings not only provided a novel perspective on the role of AI in brain imaging studies but also suggested potential new strategies for addressing public health issues.

Keywords: Graph Neural Network · functional Magnetic Resonance Imaging (fMRI) · Deep Learning

1 Introduction

Brain imaging plays a critical role in the field of medicine. Advanced techniques such as Magnetic Resonance Imaging (MRI), Functional Magnetic Resonance Imaging (fMRI), Positron Emission Tomography (PET), and Computed Tomography (CT) are commonly used for detailed visualization of brain structures and functions. Combining AI tools with brain imaging data [2, 8, 19, 23], we can study the cognition of the brain and how abstract thinking ability is derived by examining the ways neurons connect and form patterns. It helps understand the brain's functional organization, study the effects of various substances or medications on the brain, and explore the neural basis of cognitive functions and emotions.

Artificial Intelligence (AI) is a revolutionary technology that is increasingly being applied in the field of medical imaging, and it has the potential to bring about significant

F. Liu et al. (Eds.): BI 2023, LNAI 13974, pp. 297–307, 2023.
https://doi.org/10.1007/978-3-031-43075-6_26

advancements on both a healthcare level and a societal level. Machine learning can be utilized for the identification of brain disorders and the creation of biomarkers to distinguish specific regions in the brain that are significantly impacted by the diseases [3]. Leveraging the data derived from smartphones and wearable devices, Graph Neural Networks (GNN) can precisely predict an individual's mental health condition [6]. By meticulously extracting individual information across multiple dimensions, such as behavioral patterns, physiological responses, and environmental interactions, Graph Neural Networks can accurately predict whether a person is at risk of developing mental health issues [12].

This paper aims to increase the classification accuracy on the selected data set [10] by utilizing Graph Neural Networks along with several enhancements for the classification of chronic marijuana use. Current research employing fMRI has discovered that chronic cannabis use leads to functional and structural changes in brain regions associated with reward processing and emotional regulation [17]. Graph Neural Networks are considered as one of the neural network types which are designed to perform tasks on graph-structured data. Graph Neural Networks are particularly useful in domains where data is naturally represented as graphs, such as the results of brain imaging scans, which produce medical images that can be used to find underlying patterns [1,7,13,15]. Many improved methods based on Graph Neural Networks have demonstrated excellent performance on various public datasets. For example, an enhanced decoding model demonstrates superior capability in deciphering cognitive states with greater accuracy [20]. By leveraging individualized functional connectivity (FC) features, the prediction models can be enhanced in both accuracy and precision [21]. Graph Neural Networks are good at recognizing complex patterns within graph-structured data. In the context of medical imaging, where data often has a complex and hierarchical structure, Graph Neural Networks can be more effective in identifying subtle patterns or anomalies that traditional neural networks might miss [22].

2   Graph Convolutional Network

Graph Convolutional Networks (GCN) and Graph Attention Networks (GAT) are two popular Graph Neural Networks (GNN), and both can be used on graph-structured data. Graph Convolutional Networks utilize convolutional operations, which are successful in social analysis, bioinformatics, and computer vision, especially in image analysis [18]. Graph Attention Networks leverage masked self-attentional layers, which utilize the neighboring nodes and specify different weights to nodes [16].

In this paper, we choose to employ Graph Convolutional Networks owing to the relatively limited size of the dataset (n = 323). The streamlined nature of Graph Convolutional Networks makes it less prone to overfitting, rendering it particularly suitable for scenarios with constrained sample sizes. Additionally, there exists no compelling evidence at present to suggest differential significance among nodes that would necessitate the attention mechanism inherent in Graph Attention Networks. Table 1 provides a comprehensive comparison elucidating the respective strengths and weaknesses of these two methodologies.

Table 1. Comparison of GNN variants: GCN and GAT

Model	Advantages	Disadvantages
Graph Convolutional Network (GCN)	1. It can model the dependencies between immediate neighbors effectively, which is beneficial in many classification tasks 2. It has a simple structure that is easy to implement	1. It has difficulty capturing higher-order interactions 2. It weighs each neighbor equally in aggregation, which may not be optimal for all datasets and tasks
Graph Attention Network (GAT)	1. It can weigh neighbors differently based on the relevance of their features to the central node, allowing for greater flexibility 2. The attention mechanism allows GATs to focus on more informative parts of the input graph	1. The computation cost can be high due to the attention mechanism, especially for graphs with many edges 2. The performance of GATs can be sensitive to the initialization and training process due to the increased model complexity

2.1 Node Feature Propagation

Graph Convolutional Networks are considered as one of the neural network architectures designed for processing graph data. In graph structures, information is represented via nodes and edges of the graph. Therefore, Graph Convolutional Networks utilize a special mechanism, known as the message passing mechanism, to propagate and update information across nodes in the graph.

The message-passing mechanism in Graph Convolutional Networks is carried out via node features across layers. For every node in the graph, we consider its neighboring nodes and aggregate the feature vectors of all neighbors of a node and then perform a linear transformation. This process can be represented with the following formula:

$$H^{(l+1)} = \sigma\left(D^{-\frac{1}{2}}AD^{-\frac{1}{2}}H^l W^l\right) \tag{1}$$

H^l is the node feature matrix at layer l, where each row represents a feature vector of a node. A is the adjacency matrix of the graph, where $A_{ij} = 1$ indicates there is an edge between node i and node j, and $A_{ij} = 0$ indicates there is no edge between the two nodes. To account for the node's own information, we usually use $A + I$, where I is the identity matrix, to represent self-loops. D is the degree matrix of A, where $D_{ii} = \Sigma_j A_{ij}$, representing the degree of node i (the number of edges that are connected to the node i). W^l is the weight matrix at layer l, which is used for linear transformation. σ is the non-linear activation function, such as ReLU, Sigmoid, tanh, Softmax, and Leaky ReLU. This formula (1) describes how information is propagated within each layer.

2.2 Aggregation and Update

In the aggregation procedure (Eq. (2)), for each node, we aggregate the information (processed through linear transformation and activation function) of all neighboring nodes. This can be seen as "passing messages" in the graph. In Eq. 2, $N(i)$ is the neighboring nodes set of node i.

$$h_{\text{aggr}(i)}^{(l+1)} = \sum_{j \in N(i)} h_j^{(l)} \tag{2}$$

In the update procedure (Eq. (3)), we use the aggregated information to update the feature vector of each node. In this way, Graph Convolutional Networks can effectively handle graph data, capture relationships between nodes, and provide effective feature representation for tasks such as graph classification, node classification, link prediction, etc.

$$h_i^{(l+1)} = \sigma \left(W^{(l)} h_{\text{aggr}(i)}^{(l+1)} \right) \tag{3}$$

3   Method

Within the scope of this study, we have adopted the methodology of Graph Neural Networks. Graph Neural Networks excel in effectively capturing the functional connectivity among different brain regions after parcellation, thereby facilitating the elucidation of physiological changes and correlations across brain regions [11]. In this study, we specifically employ Graph Convolutional Networks as our implementation approach to leverage its capabilities in modeling and analyzing the functional connectivity among different brain regions [4]. The Graph Convolutional Network model facilitates the incorporation of local neighborhood information and enables the extraction of high-level features from the graph representation of the data.

Figure 1 illustrates the deep learning pipeline of the proposed method, and there are five main steps in the framework:

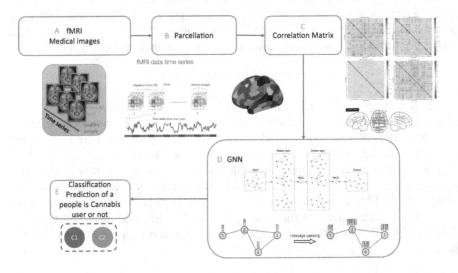

Fig. 1. Deep learning pipeline for cannabis user classification. (A) Raw fMRI data were collected from two groups of individuals. (B) The brain was divided into 90 regions using the Stanford parcellation. (C) The correlation matrix was computed to reveal the connectivity strength between different brain regions. (D) The preprocessed data was fed into the GNN neural network for training. (E) The samples were labeled and the classification results were generated.

(A): Raw fMRI data were collected from two groups of individuals. Brain activity data are sourced from public neuroimaging databases, including functional Magnetic Resonance Imaging (fMRI) data of cannabis addicts and a healthy control group.

(B): The brain was divided into 90 regions using the Stanford parcellation, and the 90 functional regions of interest were obtained over the 14 large-scale resting-state brain networks [14].

(C): The correlation matrix was computed to reveal the connectivity strength between different brain regions. The correlation value is between −1 to 1, where 0 indicates no linear relationship, 1 indicates a strong linear relationship, and −1 indicates a strong negative relationship. When the absolute value approximates 1, it indicates a strong linear relationship. When the absolute value approximates 0, it indicates a weak linear relationship. Figure 2 shows three correlation matrices of the 90 regions, one from healthy individuals, one from long-term cannabis addicts, and the differences between the two groups. The correlation matrices will

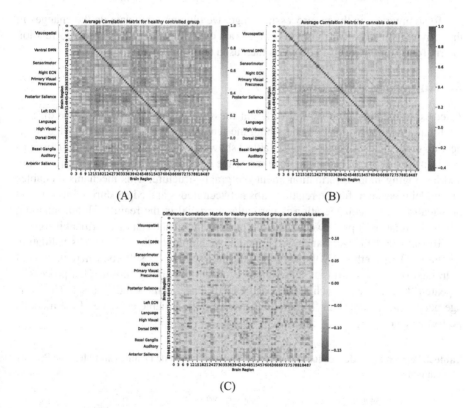

Fig. 2. There are 90 Regions of Interest (ROI) here, numbered from 0 to 89. The corresponding brain regions for each number are listed on the left side of the image. (A) The average correlation matrix of healthy individuals. (B) The average correlation matrix of long-term marijuana users. (C) The differential correlation matrix between healthy individuals and long-term marijuana users.

be the features to train the Graph Neural Network (GNN) models, and will also serve as the features to make predictions on if a person is a marijuana user or not.

(D): The preprocessed data was fed into the GNN neural network for training. In this step, the generated correlation matrices will be the features to train the Graph Neural Network binary classification models. The label for the correlation matrix is whether it is from a marijuana user or not. The correlation matrix serves as a graph to show the connections between the 90 brain regions.

(E): The samples were labeled and the classification results were generated. In this step, the predictions will be made based on the trained Graph Neural Network model from the previous step. The correlation matrix generated from a user fMRI will be the feature to be fed to the trained model, and the output of the model will be if the user is a cannabis addict or not. We will also use various metrics to measure the performance of the Graph Neural Network model. Since it is a binary classification problem, the measurements such as accuracy, AUC (area under the receiver operating characteristic curve), and F1 score, are applied.

To summarize, in the preprocessing stage, we obtained raw data on the changes in the activity intensity of various parts of the brain over time, then we derived a correlation matrix based on that. This matrix was then used to train the GNN model.

4   Numerical Experiments

After experimenting with several different message-passing mechanisms, we discovered that a method which considers both the features of the nodes and the edges connecting them yields superior results. Table 2 shows the experiment's outcome. This approach involves concatenating the features of the edge and the node, thereby preserving and leveraging more information about the graph structure. This mechanism enables the model to account for the relationships between nodes and edges during information propagation. Such consideration is particularly crucial in the realm of brain imaging, where the relationships between different parts of the image can offer critical insights.

To validate the performance of the model, we employed the k-fold cross-validation technique. This method involves splitting the data set into 'k' subsets, where the model is trained on 'k − 1' subsets and validated on the remaining subset. This process is repeated 'k' times with each subset used exactly once as the validation set. The average performance across all 'k' iterations gives a more reliable estimate of the model's performance (Fig. 3).

Table 2. Performance Metrics for Different Combinations of Node Features and Message Passing Mechanisms

	Identity			Adjacency Matrix			Degree		
	Accuracy	F1	AUC	Accuracy	F1	AUC	Accuracy	F1	AUC
Weighted Sum	60.38 ± 0.5	75.29 ± 0.4	68.90 ± 5.72	67.79 ± 2.4	76.09 ± 1.9	70.92 ± 4.5	66.89 ± 5.5	72.46 ± 3.9	71.03 ± 3.4
Edge Weight Concat	60.38 ± 0.5	75.29 ± 0.4	59.53 ± 8.0	59.75 ± 6.7	65.61 ± 11.9	65.63 ± 7.8	65.33 ± 6.9	74.33 ± 5.3	70.53 ± 5.7
Edge Node Concat	60.38 ± 0.5	75.29 ± 0.4	52.97 ± 12.1	78.33 ± 3.1	83.66 ± 2.1	84.39 ± 3.2	62.53 ± 7.0	69.63 ± 6.2	67.58 ± 9.1
Bin Concat	60.38 ± 0.5	75.29 ± 0.4	68.60 ± 5.6	64.07 ± 3.6	70.32 ± 4.7	69.54 ± 5.1	65.33 ± 3.6	74.12 ± 2.7	70.82 ± 4.4
Node Concat	60.38 ± 0.5	75.29 ± 0.4	49.72 ± 1.9	76.47 ± 2.7	79.95 ± 3.5	84.16 ± 4.9	62.85 ± 6.0	69.80 ± 5.7	65.82 ± 6.2

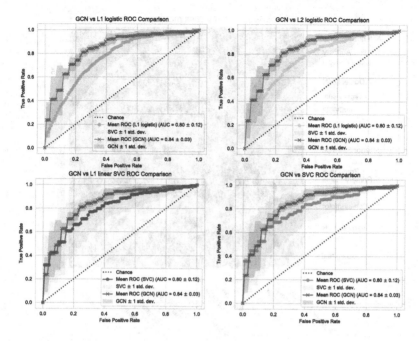

Fig. 3. ROC-Curve for GCN model, and its comparison with others.

In the evaluation of our model, we obtained an average accuracy of 78.33% with a standard deviation of 3.05%. The area under the receiver operating characteristic curve, a measure of the model's performance across all possible classification thresholds, was 84.39% with a standard deviation of 3.21%. A higher AUC indicates a better discrimination power of the classification model. This suggests that the model performs well in distinguishing between different classes. Finally, the average F1 score, which is a metric that combines both precision and recall to provide a balanced measure of a model's performance, was 83.66% with a standard deviation of 2.11%. This indicates that the model achieved a balanced performance across different classes.

Through further processing of the correlation matrix, the group t-test was conducted among these data, and the statistically significant parts were retained. Only data points with positive t-values have been retained in this analysis. The brain mapping visualization illuminates these crucial data points, indicating that the connections within these brain regions are stronger in healthy individuals and weaker in those suffering from cannabis addiction. This provides significant insights into the study of the impacts of cannabis on the nervous system (Figs. 4 and 5).

Table 3 lists a total of 20 pairs of connections which are considered to be important, and they exhibit higher levels of activity in the brains of healthy individuals.

Overall, these results demonstrate that the classification models performed well, with high accuracy, a strong discriminatory ability (as indicated by the AUC), and balanced performance across different classes (as measured by the F1-score). At the same time, it offers a predictive analysis of the potential impacts of cannabis on the brain.

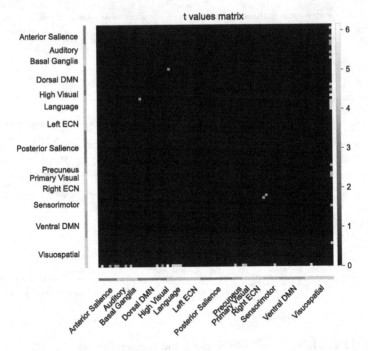

Fig. 4. Generating t value matrice with a threshold equals 0.001 on p value and t value greater than 0.

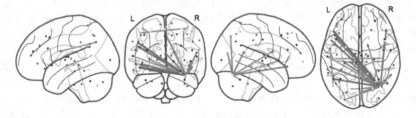

Fig. 5. The regions within the brain of healthy individuals where the connection strength is notably higher than cannabis addictive people.

Table 3. Important Brain Connections

Connection Pair	Connection Description
(1, 89)	"L anterior insula" and "R crus cerebellum - visiospatial"
(4, 89)	"R anterior insula" and "R crus cerebellum - visiospatial"
(6, 89)	"R crus cerebellum - ant_sal" and "R crus cerebellum - visiospatial"
(7, 89)	"L superior temporal/auditory" and "R crus cerebellum - visiospatial"
(10, 89)	"R striatum/thalamus" and "R crus cerebellum - visiospatial"
(12, 89)	"L inferior frontal gyrus" and "R crus cerebellum - visiospatial"
(16, 27)	"L lateral angular gyrus" and "L mid-temporal cortex"
(22, 89)	"L parahippocampal gyrus" and "R crus cerebellum - visiospatial"
(24, 89)	"L mid occipital cortex" and "R crus cerebellum - visiospatial"
(26, 89)	"L inferior frontal gyrus" and "R crus cerebellum - visiospatial"
(28, 89)	"L mid-posterior temporal cortex" and "R crus cerebellum - visiospatial"
(29, 89)	"L medial angular gyrus" and "R crus cerebellum - visiospatial"
(30, 89)	"R inferior frontal gyrus" and "R crus cerebellum - visiospatial"
(31, 89)	"R mid-temporal cortex" and "R crus cerebellum - visiospatial"
(52, 89)	"bilateral medial posterior precuneus" and "R crus cerebellum - visiospatial"
(55, 89)	"bilateral calcarine cortex" and "R crus cerebellum - visiospatial"
(56, 89)	"L LGN" and "R crus cerebellum - visiospatial"
(63, 64)	"L pre/post-central gyri" and "R pre/post-central gyri"
(67, 89)	"cerebellar vermis" and "R crus cerebellum - visiospatial"
(81, 89)	"L precentral/fronto-opercular region" and "R crus cerebellum - visiospatial"

5   Discussion and Conclusion

By applying the GNN model to the dataset, we achieved good predictive accuracy, indicating its strong versatility. In the future, we can explore more methods to optimize it, with the aim of further improving its accuracy. By incorporating these advanced techniques and methodologies, our research pushes the boundaries of current understanding and showcases the potential of AI in medical imaging, particularly in the context of brain imaging. More effort could be put into unraveling the enigmatic inner workings of machine learning's black box [5,9]. By illuminating the intricate mechanisms underlying its impressive prowess for accurate classification prediction, they can establish a profound nexus with the bedrock principles of biology and neuronal activity. This endeavor represents an unprecedented fusion of artificial intelligence and biological understanding, poised to usher in a new era of interdisciplinary research.

References

1. Bessadok, A., Mahjoub, M.A., Rekik, I.: Graph neural networks in network neuroscience. IEEE Trans. Pattern Anal. Mach. Intell. **45**(5), 5833–5848 (2022)
2. Borchardt, V., et al.: Preprocessing strategy influences graph-based exploration of altered functional networks in major depression. Hum. Brain Mapp. **37**(4), 1422–1442 (2016)

3. Chen, Z.S., Kulkarni, P.P., Galatzer-Levy, I.R., Bigio, B., Nasca, C., Zhang, Y.: Modern views of machine learning for precision psychiatry. Patterns 3(11), 100602 (2022). https://doi.org/10.1016/j.patter.2022.100602. www.sciencedirect.com/science/article/pii/S2666389922002276

4. Cui, H., et al.: BrainGB: a benchmark for brain network analysis with graph neural networks. IEEE Trans. Med. Imaging 42(2), 493–506 (2022)

5. Davatzikos, C.: Machine learning in neuroimaging: progress and challenges. Neuroimage 197, 652 (2019)

6. Dong, G., Tang, M., Cai, L., Barnes, L.E., Boukhechba, M.: Semi-supervised graph instance transformer for mental health inference. In: 2021 20th IEEE International Conference on Machine Learning and Applications (ICMLA), pp. 1221–1228. IEEE (2021)

7. Farahani, F.V., Karwowski, W., Lighthall, N.R.: Application of graph theory for identifying connectivity patterns in human brain networks: a systematic review. Front. Neurosci. 13 (2019). https://doi.org/10.3389/fnins.2019.00585. www.frontiersin.org/articles/10.3389/fnins.2019.00585

8. Gargouri, F., Kallel, F., Delphine, S., Ben Hamida, A., Lehéricy, S., Valabregue, R.: The influence of preprocessing steps on graph theory measures derived from resting state fMRI. Front. Comput. Neurosci. 12, 8 (2018)

9. Kohoutová, L., et al.: Toward a unified framework for interpreting machine-learning models in neuroimaging. Nat. Protoc. 15(4), 1399–1435 (2020)

10. Kulkarni, K.R., et al.: An interpretable connectivity-based decoding model for classification of chronic marijuana use. bioRxiv (2021). https://doi.org/10.1101/2021.05.04.442433. www.biorxiv.org/content/early/2021/05/27/2021.05.04.442433

11. Li, X., et al.: BrainGNN: interpretable brain graph neural network for fMRI analysis. Med. Image Anal. 74, 102233 (2021). https://doi.org/10.1016/j.media.2021.102233. www.sciencedirect.com/science/article/pii/S1361841521002784

12. Lu, H., Uddin, S., Hajati, F., Khushi, M., Moni, M.A.: Predictive risk modelling in mental health issues using machine learning on graphs. In: Proceedings of the 2022 Australasian Computer Science Week, pp. 168–175 (2022)

13. Sakoglu, U., Mete, M., Esquivel, J., Rubia, K., Briggs, R., Adinoff, B.: Classification of cocaine-dependent participants with dynamic functional connectivity from functional magnetic resonance imaging data. J. Neurosci. Res. 97(7), 790–803 (2019)

14. Shirer, W.R., Ryali, S., Rykhlevskaia, E., Menon, V., Greicius, M.D.: Decoding subject-driven cognitive states with whole-brain connectivity patterns. Cereb. Cortex 22(1), 158–165 (2012)

15. Sui, J., Jiang, R., Bustillo, J., Calhoun, V.: Neuroimaging-based individualized prediction of cognition and behavior for mental disorders and health: methods and promises. Biol. Psychiatry 88(11), 818–828 (2020). https://doi.org/10.1016/j.biopsych.2020.02.016. www.sciencedirect.com/science/article/pii/S0006322320301116. Neuroimaging Biomarkers of Psychological Trauma

16. Veličković, P., Cucurull, G., Casanova, A., Romero, A., Lio, P., Bengio, Y.: Graph attention networks. arXiv preprint arXiv:1710.10903 (2017)

17. Zehra, A., et al.: Cannabis addiction and the brain: a review. J. Neuroimmune Pharmacol. 13, 438–452 (2018). https://doi.org/10.1007/s11481-018-9782-9

18. Zhang, S., Tong, H., Xu, J., Maciejewski, R.: Graph convolutional networks: a comprehensive review. Comput. Soc. Netw. 6(1), 1–23 (2019)

19. Zhang, X., He, L., Chen, K., Luo, Y., Zhou, J., Wang, F.: Multi-view graph convolutional network and its applications on neuroimage analysis for Parkinson's disease. In: AMIA Annual Symposium Proceedings, vol. 2018, p. 1147. American Medical Informatics Association (2018)

20. Zhang, Y., Farrugia, N., Bellec, P.: Deep learning models of cognitive processes constrained by human brain connectomes. Med. Image Anal. **80**, 102507 (2022). https://doi.org/10.1016/j.media.2022.102507. www.sciencedirect.com/science/article/pii/S1361841522001542

21. Zhao, K., et al.: Individualized fMRI connectivity defines signatures of antidepressant and placebo responses in major depression (2022). https://doi.org/10.1101/2022.09.12.22279659

22. Zhou, J., et al.: Graph neural networks: a review of methods and applications. AI open **1**, 57–81 (2020)

23. Zhu, Y., Cui, H., He, L., Sun, L., Yang, C.: Joint embedding of structural and functional brain networks with graph neural networks for mental illness diagnosis. In: 2022 44th Annual International Conference of the IEEE Engineering in Medicine & Biology Society (EMBC), pp. 272–276. IEEE (2022)

Unsupervised Sparse-View Backprojection via Convolutional and Spatial Transformer Networks

Xueqing Liu[✉] and Paul Sajda

Columbia University, New York, NY 10027, USA
{xl2556,psajda}@columbia.edu

Abstract. Imaging technologies heavily rely on tomographic reconstruction, which involves solving a multidimensional inverse problem given a limited number of projections. Building upon our prior research [14], we have ascertained that the integration of the predicted source space derived from electroencephalography (EEG) and functional magnetic resonance imaging (fMRI) can be effectively approached as a backprojection problem involving sensor non-uniformity. Although backprojection is a commonly used algorithm for tomographic reconstruction, it often produces subpar image reconstructions when the projection angles are sparse or the sensor characteristics are non-uniform. To address this issue, various deep learning-based algorithms have been developed to solve the inverse problem and reconstruct images using a reduced number of projections. However, these algorithms typically require ground-truth examples, i.e., reconstructed images, to achieve satisfactory performance. In this paper, we present an unsupervised sparse-view backprojection algorithm that does not rely on ground-truth examples. Our algorithm comprises two modules within a generator-projector framework: a convolutional neural network and a spatial transformer network. We evaluate the effectiveness of our algorithm using computed tomography (CT) images of the human chest. The results demonstrate that our algorithm outperforms filtered backprojection significantly in scenarios with very sparse projection angles or varying sensor characteristics for different angles. Our proposed approach holds practical implications for medical imaging and other imaging modalities (e.g., radar) where sparse and/or non-uniform projections may arise due to time or sampling constraints.

Keywords: Sparse-view Backprojection · Convolutional Neural Networks · Spatial Transformer Networks

1 Introduction

In our previous study [14], convolutional neural networks (CNNs) were utilized to investigate the transcription of electroencephalography (EEG) to functional magnetic resonance imaging (fMRI) and vice versa, leveraging simultaneously

F. Liu et al. (Eds.): BI 2023, LNAI 13974, pp. 308–317, 2023.
https://doi.org/10.1007/978-3-031-43075-6_27

acquired EEG-fMRI data. The underlying hypothesis posited that the joint transcribing and predicting process could enhance the retrieval of the latent source space. A noteworthy challenge identified in this investigation pertained to the lack of ground-truth data for the source space. Subsequent analysis revealed that the predicted EEG source space and fMRI source space can be construed as two distinct projections emanating from the same underlying source space. This is similar to other medical imaging modalities, such as computed tomography (CT), rely on the acquisition of a finite number of projections using detectors (e.g., X-ray detector) and generators/sources (e.g., X-ray source). These projections are obtained by rotating the source (and/or detector) around the object of interest and capturing projections at different angles. To reconstruct the structure of the observed object, the multidimensional inverse problem needs to be solved. Furthermore, given that EEG and fMRI produce source space predictions characterized by different intensity scales, the problem can be framed as a backprojection problem that encompasses sensor non-uniformity.

Backprojection and the Fourier-domain reconstruction algorithm are two conventional and widely used methods for reconstruction. In fact, these methods are closely related, as it has been demonstrated that applying a filter in the Fourier-domain yields similar results to filtered backprojection [1]. Therefore, we refer to these methods collectively as "backprojection algorithms."

Another class of reconstruction method is iterative reconstruction [2]. Iterative reconstruction methods make strong assumptions about the scanner geometry, scanner optics, and noise statistics, and incorporate these assumptions as constraints in a multiple iteration optimization procedure.

Convolutional neural networks (CNNs) have been successfully applied to various image processing tasks, including denoising [3] and super-resolution [4]. In the context of image reconstruction via backprojection, CNNs have been used primarily as a form of image post-processing to improve signal-to-noise ratio (SNR) and image quality [5–8]. CNNs have also been incorporated into iterative reconstruction loops [9]. An innovative application of CNNs is in cases involving sparse sensors/projections. For example, in [10], an end-to-end deep learning model is proposed for reconstructing CT images with a limited number of projections, demonstrating superior reconstructions compared to conventional backprojection methods. However, their approach relies on a training set that includes high-resolution reconstructed images as the ground truth, necessitating a high density of projections and one of the conventional methods for image reconstruction from these projections.

In this paper, we introduce an unsupervised backprojection algorithm that combines a CNN and a Spatial Transformer Network (STN) [11] inspired network. Our algorithm enables sparse-view reconstruction and addresses scenarios where sensors (e.g., X-ray detectors and/or sources) exhibit non-uniform characteristics across different angles. The CNN serves as the generator, while the STN-inspired network functions as the projector within a generator-projector architecture. The original STNs introduced in [11] are capable of learning affine transformation parameters and implementing differentiable geometric transformations, making them well-suited for modification as projectors. Notably, our generator-projector architecture can be trained without relying on ground truth from high-resolution reconstructions, making it sparse-view both in terms of training and testing. We evaluate the performance of our algorithm using chest CT data and demonstrate its superiority over conventional backprojection algorithms, particularly in cases with highly sparse projections. Furthermore, we highlight substantial improvement over conventional methods when dealing with non-uniform characteristics of the sensors used for acquiring the projections.

2   Unsupervised Deep Backprojection

Figure 1 provides an overview of our framework. In this framework, sinograms are first converted to single-view backprojections, which are then inputted into a multi-layer CNN generator. The generator utilizes the sparsely measured sinograms to predict the corresponding reconstruction. Subsequently, the projector maps the generated reconstruction back to the original sinograms.

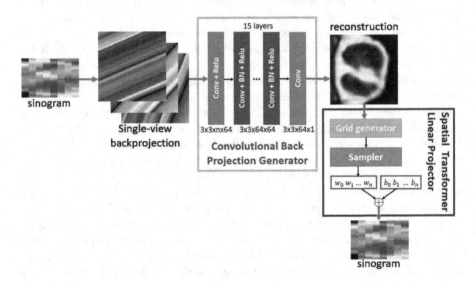

Fig. 1. Framework of the unsupervised sparse-view backprojection algorithm: Both the input and output of the network consist of sparse-view sinograms. The sinogram is initially converted into single-view backprojections, which are then utilized as input for the convolutional backprojection generator. The generator processes the input and produces the corresponding backprojection reconstruction. Subsequently, the spatial transformer linear projector takes the generated reconstruction and the transformation angle as inputs to generate a sinogram. Additionally, the projector incorporates trainable weights (w_i) and biases (b_i) to account for sensor non-uniformity.

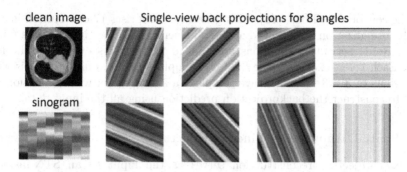

Fig. 2. Example of a high-resolution CT image (upper left), its corresponding 8-angle projection sinogram (lower left), and the single-view backprojections (right). It is important to note that the high-resolution CT image is reconstructed from hundreds of projections and typically serves as the ground truth in other deep learning-based backprojection algorithms.

2.1   Single-View Backprojections

The relationship between the data space S and its set of projections is defined by the Radon transformation:

$$Radon(S, \theta) = R_S(l(\theta), \theta) = \int_{-\infty}^{\infty} \int_{-\infty}^{\infty} S(x, y)\delta(l(\theta) - x cos\theta - y sin\theta)dxdy \quad (1)$$

where $\delta(\cdot)$ represents the Dirac delta function and $l(\theta) = xcos\theta + ysin\theta$.

In particular, a single projection p_i can be expressed as an integration of the data space S along a specific direction θ_i, using the Radon transform:

$$p_i = Radon(S, \theta_i) \quad (2)$$

A sinogram, a commonly used data structure for storing projections, is defined as an $m \times n$ matrix consisting of n projections $(p_1, p_2, p_3, ..., p_n)$ acquired from different angles $(\theta_1, \theta_2, \theta_3, ..., \theta_n)$. The objective of backprojection is to solve the inverse problem, which involves reconstructing the original data S from the sinograms generated by a limited number of projections $(p_1, p_2, p_3, ..., p_n)$.

Instead of directly using sinograms as input to a CNN, we adopt the approach of constructing single-view backprojections [10]. This process involves performing single projection backprojection and subsequently stacking the resulting backprojections. Figure 2 illustrates an example of 8-angle single-view backprojections.

2.2   Convolutional Backprojection Generator

The stacked n single-view backprojections, where n represents the number of projections, are utilized as the input with n channels for the convolutional backprojection generator.

The convolutional backprojection generator comprises 17 convolution layers. Batch normalization is employed across all layers, excluding the initial and final layers. ReLU activation functions are applied to all layers except for the last layer. Each layer, excluding the final one, employs 64 convolution kernels with dimensions of 3×3. The last layer employs a single kernel with dimensions of 3×3 to construct the backprojection prediction using all the input data.

2.3 Spatial Transformer Linear Projector

The backprojection reconstruction serves as the input to an STN-inspired linear projector, which generates predicted sinograms. The projector applies the Radon transform to the backprojection reconstruction using correspondent angles $(\theta_1, \theta_2, \theta_3, ..., \theta_n)$, as described in Eq. (3), to regenerate the sinogram prediction.

To enable gradient-based backpropagation and ensure differentiability of the Radon transformation, we employ spatial transformers introduced in [11]. The grid generator transforms the regular spatial grid of the reconstruction into a sampling grid, while the sampler produces sampled transformed data from the reconstruction at the grid points. Subsequently, a trainable linear mapping, as depicted in Eq. (4), is applied to each $\hat{p}_i$ using different w_i and b_i values. This compensates for potential sensor non-uniformity.

$$\hat{p}_i = Radon(\hat{S}, \theta_i) \tag{3}$$

$$\hat{p_i}' = w_i \hat{p}_i + b_i \tag{4}$$

The objective function, presented in Eq. (5), minimizes the mean squared error between the generated sinogram $\hat{P}' = (\hat{p_1}', ..., \hat{p_n}')$ and the sinogram ground-truth $P = (p_1, ..., p_n)$. It is worth noting that our ground-truth differs from the one used in [10]. In our case, the ground-truth refers to the sparse projections, whereas in [10], it corresponds to the high-resolution projections along with the reconstructed image. Additionally, we incorporate an l1-norm term for the predicted backprojection reconstruction $\hat{S}$ to promote sparsity.

$$l(k, w, b) = \frac{1}{n} \sum_{k=1}^{n} ||p_i - \hat{p_i}'||_2^2 + \alpha ||\hat{S}||_1 \tag{5}$$

3   Experiment and Results

We conducted an evaluation of our algorithm using a dataset comprising 43 human chest CT scans [12], which is part of The Cancer Imaging Archive (TCIA) [13]. Sinograms with 2/4/8/16 angles were generated by applying the corresponding Radon transformation to each CT slice, both with and without sensor non-uniformity. Sensor non-uniformity was introduced by multiplying each projection p_i by a weight w_i and adding a bias b_i. Both w_i and b_i were randomly

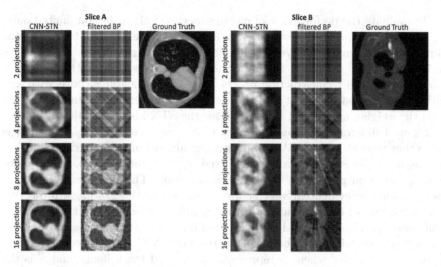

Fig. 3. Reconstruction results for the case of uniform sensors: A and B are two example slices of a reconstructed chest CT scan. For each example slice, the left most column is the reconstruction result using our algorithm, the middle column is the reconstruction result using filtered backprojection and the right image is the ground truth.

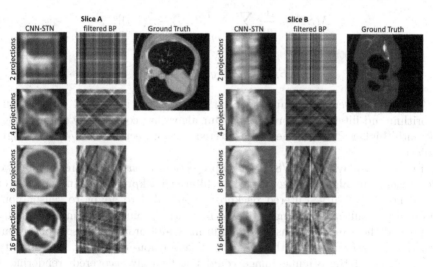

Fig. 4. Reconstruction results for the case of non-uniform sensors: A and B are two example slices of a reconstructed chest CT scan. For each example slice, the left most column is the reconstruction result using our algorithm, the middle column is the reconstruction result using filtered backprojection and the right image is the ground-truth.

generated with a standard normal distribution, and they remained constant for different slices within the same scan.

To evaluate the performance of our unsupervised algorithm on limited data, we conducted experiments where each model was trained and tested on the same subject's scan. The average number of slices per scan was found to be 80.70 ± 21.16. We compared the performance of our algorithm to filtered backprojection for the reconstruction of 2/4/8/16-angle sinograms, both with and without sensor non-uniformity. When testing without sensor non-uniformity, we fixed the weights $w_i = 1$ and bias $b_i = 0$ for the STN-inspired projector.

Figure 3 illustrates the results for two different slices using 2/4/8/16-angle projection reconstructions. We compared our algorithm to filtered backprojection assuming sensor uniformity (i.e., fixed $w_i = 1$ and $b_i = 0$). In all cases, our algorithm outperformed filtered backprojection. The superior performance was particularly evident in very sparse cases, where the 2/4-angle projection reconstructions of filtered backprojection exhibited minimal useful information, while our algorithm still produced meaningful results. To facilitate an objective comparison, we calculated the mean square error (MSE) of the reconstruction, as shown in Eq. (6), where S represents the ground truth image and $\hat{S}$ is the reconstruction. Additionally, we computed the reconstruction peak signal-to-noise ratio (PSNR) based on MSE using Eq. (7), where MAX_S denotes the maximum possible pixel value of the ground truth S.

$$MSE = \frac{1}{mn} \sum_{i=0}^{m-1} \sum_{j=0}^{n-1} [S(i,j) - \hat{S}(i,j)]^2 \qquad (6)$$

$$PSNR = 20 log_{10}(\frac{MAX_S}{\sqrt{MSE}}) \qquad (7)$$

Figure 5a presents a comparison of the reconstruction PSNR between our algorithm and filtered backprojection. Our algorithm consistently achieved significantly higher PSNR values than filtered backprojection for 2/4/8/16-angle projections.

Figure 4 displays the 2/4/8/16-angle projection reconstruction results for two slices using our algorithm compared to filtered backprojection in the case of sensor non-uniformity. Filtered backprojection failed to adapt to sensor non-uniformity, resulting in strong artifacts. In contrast, our algorithm successfully suppressed the impact of sensor non-uniformity and provided reasonable reconstructions. However, due to the presence of sensor non-uniformity, the intensity and contrast of the original image could not be fully recovered, rendering a PSNR comparison meaningless. Instead, we employed the correlation coefficient between the ground truth and reconstructed images as an evaluation metric for reconstruction performance, as depicted in Fig. 5b. Our algorithm significantly outperformed filtered backprojection, with its performance continually improving as the number of acquired projections increased. It is important to note that this improvement was not observed in the case of filtered backprojection, where performance did not enhance with additional projections in the presence of non-uniform sensors.

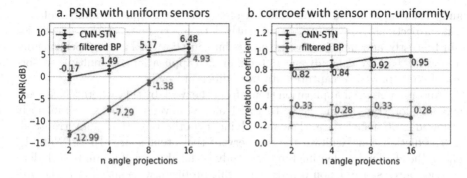

Fig. 5. Comparison of our algorithm with filtered backprojection. (a) Reconstruction PSNR of our algorithm and filtered backprojection with uniform sensors. (b) Reconstruction correlation coefficient of our algorithm and filtered backprojection with non-uniform sensors.

4   Discussion

In this paper, we introduced an unsupervised backprojection algorithm utilizing a generator-projector framework based on a convolutional neural network (CNN) and spatial transformer network (STN). Our experimental results demonstrate that our proposed algorithm achieves significantly improved performance compared to the conventional filtered backprojection algorithm. These findings highlight the effectiveness of deep learning models, such as the CNN and STN, in addressing unsupervised tasks with limited training data.

During the process, we opted to employ single-view projections as the input to the deep learning model, in contrast to using sinograms directly. This decision was motivated by the superior performance of convolutional neural networks (CNNs) in processing single-view back projections, owing to their inherent ability to handle image-like data. By virtue of their design, CNNs are specifically optimized for image processing tasks. As a result, leveraging single view back projections as input proved to be advantageous over utilizing the original sinogram in our deep learning framework.

It is worth noting, as depicted in Fig. 5(a), that our algorithm exhibits a slower increase in performance compared to filtered backprojection when the number of projections is increased under the condition of uniform sensors. With a dense set of projections, filtered backprojection still provides more accurate reconstruction results. However, our approach enables the use of methods that are constrained by a limited number of projections or arbitrary and non-uniform sensor characteristics. Therefore, our algorithm offers a valuable alternative in scenarios where the number of projections is limited or sensor characteristics are non-uniform.

Furthermore, our algorithm holds potential for broader applications, particularly in cases where sensors are sparse and non-uniform, or when ground-truth data is unavailable as required in supervised learning. For instance, radar and visual input-based reconstruction often rely on a limited number of sensors/projections. Acquiring ground-truth data for training in these scenarios can be costly and may involve extensive human effort or labeling. Sensor non-uniformity is also commonly encountered in such applications, as multiple sensors are often employed to capture data from different angles.

Another potential application stems from the work by [14], where CNNs were explored for transcribing EEG to fMRI and vice versa using simultaneously acquired EEG-fMRI data. The underlying hypothesis is that joint transcoding/prediction can facilitate the recovery of the latent source space. Notably, one of the challenges identified in that study is the absence of ground-truth data for the source space. Upon investigating this problem, we realized that the predicted EEG source space and fMRI source space can be considered as two projections of the same underlying source space. Moreover, since these two modalities yield source space predictions with different intensity scales, the problem can be framed as a backprojection problem with sensor non-uniformity. Therefore, we are currently exploring the application of our algorithm to address this neural source reconstruction problem.

In conclusion, our proposed unsupervised backprojection algorithm based on the CNN and STN framework outperforms traditional filtered backprojection in terms of reconstruction accuracy. We have shown the potential of deep learning models with a relatively small number of parameters to tackle unsupervised tasks with limited training data. The flexibility of our approach enables its application in various scenarios, including cases with sparse and non-uniform sensors and situations where ground-truth data is unavailable. Future research efforts will focus on further exploring and expanding the application of our algorithm, including its potential application in neural source reconstruction tasks.

Acknowledgements. This work is supported by the Army Research Laboratory under Cooperative agreement number W911NF-10-2-0022.

References

1. Brooks, R.A., Di Chiro, G.: Theory of image reconstruction in computed tomography. Radiology **117**(3), 561–572 (1975)
2. Beister, M., Kolditz, D., Kalender, W.A.: Iterative reconstruction methods in X-ray CT. Phys. Med. **28**(2), 94–108 (2012)
3. Zhang, K., Zuo, W., Chen, Y., Meng, D., Zhang, L.: Beyond a Gaussian denoiser: residual learning of deep CNN for image denoising. IEEE Trans. Image Process. **26**(7), 3142–3155 (2017)
4. Kim, J., Lee, J.K., Lee, K.M.: Accurate image super-resolution using very deep convolutional networks. In: Proceedings of the IEEE Conference on Computer Vision and Pattern Recognition, pp. 1646–1654 (2016)
5. Kang, E., Chang, W., Yoo, J., Ye, J.C.: Deep convolutional framelet denosing for low-dose CT via wavelet residual network. IEEE Trans. Med. Imaging **37**(6), 1358–1369 (2018)

6. Jin, K.H., McCann, M.T., Froustey, E., Unser, M.: Deep convolutional neural network for inverse problems in imaging. IEEE Trans. Image Process. **26**(9), 4509–4522 (2017)
7. Han, Y., Ye, J.C.: Framing U-Net via deep convolutional framelets: application to sparse-view CT. IEEE Trans. Med. Imaging **37**(6), 1418–1429 (2018)
8. Chen, H., et al.: Low-dose CT with a residual encoder-decoder convolutional neural network. IEEE Trans. Med. Imaging **36**(12), 2524–2535 (2017)
9. Ye, D.H., Srivastava, S., Thibault, J.-B., Sauer, K., Bouman, C.: Deep residual learning for model-based iterative CT reconstruction using plug-and-play framework. In: 2018 IEEE International Conference on Acoustics, Speech and Signal Processing (ICASSP), pp. 6668–6672. IEEE (2018)
10. Ye, D.H., Buzzard, G.T., Ruby, M., Bouman, C.A.: Deep back projection for sparse-view CT reconstruction. In: 2018 IEEE Global Conference on Signal and Information Processing (GlobalSIP), pp. 1–5. IEEE (2018)
11. Jaderberg, M., Simonyan, K., Zisserman, A., et al.: Spatial transformer networks. In: Advances in Neural Information Processing Systems, pp. 2017–2025 (2015)
12. Goldgof, D., Zhao, B., Kalpathy-Cramer, J., Napel, S.: QIN multi-site collection of lung CT data with nodule segmentations. https://doi.org/10.7937/K9/TCIA.2015.1BUVFJR7
13. Clark, K., et al.: The Cancer Imaging Archive (TCIA): maintaining and operating a public information repository. J. Digit. Imaging **26**(6), 1045–1057 (2013). https://doi.org/10.1007/s10278-013-9622-7
14. Liu, X., Sajda, P.: A convolutional neural network for transcoding simultaneously acquired EEG-fMRI data. In: 9th International IEEE EMBS Conference on Neural Engineering (NER). IEEE (2019)

Latent Neural Source Recovery via Transcoding of Simultaneous EEG-fMRI

Xueqing Liu[✉] and Paul Sajda

Columbia University, New York, NY 10027, USA
{xl2556,psajda}@columbia.edu

Abstract. Simultaneous EEG-fMRI is a multi-modal neuroimaging technique that combines the advantages of both modalities, offering valuable insights into the spatial and temporal dynamics of neural activity. In this paper, we aim to address the inference problem inherent in this technique by employing the transcoding framework. Transcoding refers to the process of mapping from a specific encoding (modality) to a decoding (the latent source space), and subsequently encoding the latent source space back to the original modality. Our proposed method focuses on developing a symmetric approach, which involves a cyclic convolutional transcoder capable of transcoding EEG to fMRI and vice versa. Importantly, our method does not rely on any prior knowledge of either the hemodynamic response function or lead field matrix. Instead, it leverages the temporal and spatial relationships between the modalities and latent source spaces to learn these mappings. By applying our method to real EEG-fMRI data, we demonstrate its efficacy in accurately transcoding the modalities from one to another, as well as recovering the underlying source spaces. It is worth noting that these results are obtained on previously unseen data, further emphasizing the robustness and generalizability of our approach. Furthermore, apart from its ability to enable symmetric inference of a latent source space, our method can also be viewed as a form of low-cost computational neuroimaging. Specifically, it allows for the generation of an 'expensive' fMRI BOLD image using 'low-cost' EEG data. This aspect highlights the potential practical significance and affordability of our approach in the field of neuroimaging research.

Keywords: Transcoding · Simultaneous EEG-fMRI · cyclic convolutional transcoder

This work is supported by the Army Research Laboratory under Cooperative agreement number W911NF-10-2-0022.

1 Introduction

Functional magnetic resonance imaging (fMRI) is a widely utilized neuroimaging modality in cognitive neuroscience and clinical psychiatric departments due to its comprehensive coverage of the entire brain at relatively high spatial resolution (in millimeters) [1]. However, fMRI's temporal resolution is somewhat limited by the sluggishness of the hemodynamic response [2]. Conversely, electroencephalography (EEG) offers high temporal resolution (in milliseconds) but suffers from low spatial resolution as it records electrical signals from scalp electrodes [3]. Simultaneously acquiring EEG and fMRI data allows for the compensation of each modality's limitations by leveraging their complementary strengths.

The fusion of EEG and fMRI using machine learning approaches has been an active research area [4–6]. A major challenge in this fusion process arises from the distinct aspects of neuronal activity captured by EEG and fMRI, resulting in biased and partially overlapping representations of the underlying neural sources [7]. An optimal cross-modal fusion method should address this challenge by (1) identifying overlapping neuronal substrates for both modalities while minimizing modality-specific bias and (2) extracting and utilizing information that is unique to each modality to optimize the fusion process.

Two approaches, EEG-informed fMRI [8–13] and fMRI-informed EEG [14], have been employed for fusing simultaneously acquired EEG-fMRI data. These approaches are asymmetrical, as they only utilize partial information from one modality to inform the analysis of the other [7]. EEG-informed fMRI involves extracting features from the EEG, such as trial-to-trial event-related potentials [8], source dipole time series [11], global EEG synchronization [9], or single-trial EEG correlates of task related activity [10,12,13], which are then convolved with a canonical hemodynamic response function (HRF) and used as input regressors in voxel-wise fMRI general linear model (GLM) analyses. However, the canonical HRF is a rough estimate of hemodynamic coupling, with significant variance reported across individuals and brain regions [15]. Conversely, fMRI-informed EEG methods employ techniques like fMRI-informed source modeling [14], which utilizes spatial prior information from fMRI to constrain EEG source localization. This process relies on complex forward and inverse models, calculated from a lead field matrix estimated based on tissue conductivity, often requiring intricate electromagnetic simulations.

To achieve a more balanced treatment of EEG and fMRI, symmetrical methods have been developed. For example, Conroy et al. [4] utilized Canonical Correlation Analysis (CCA) to transform both EEG and fMRI into the same data space. Another symmetrical approach by Oberlin et al. [5] framed the data fusion problem as an optimization problem, yet still relied on accurate HRF and lead field matrix estimates, unable to account for potential non-linearities between EEG and fMRI data.

In this paper, we propose a novel approach using simultaneously acquired EEG-fMRI data and a convolutional neural network (CNN) structure to establish the relationship between EEG and fMRI bidirectionally. Expanding upon previous work [6] in transcoder development and simulation testing, we enhance the approach by incorporating the concept of Cycle-Consistent Adversarial Networks (CycleGAN) [16]. This results in a "cyclic-CNN" architecture for transcoding EEG and fMRI data obtained from an actual EEG-fMRI experiment. Our results demonstrate that: 1) our model can reconstruct both fMRI and EEG data without prior knowledge of hemodynamic coupling or leadfield estimates; 2) the model accurately estimates the underlying HRF and head models without the need for complex electromagnetic simulations or knowledge of tissue conductivity; and 3) the model unveils the dynamics of the latent source space, enabling novel assessments of the underlying network structure that explains the observed EEG and fMRI data.

Overall, our approach offers promising capabilities for bidirectional transcoding of EEG and fMRI data, facilitating comprehensive analysis of neural activity and advancing our understanding of brain function.

2   Methods

We assessed the performance of our cyclic-CNN and transformational backprojector by analyzing simultaneously acquired EEG-fMRI data from 19 subjects. During the data collection, participants were engaged in an auditory oddball task, which involved 80% standard stimuli and 20% oddball (target) stimuli. After pre-processing, our method consists of two main steps:

- *Transcoding the Neuroimaging Data via a Cyclic-CNN:* EEG records the electrical signal from the surface of the scalp, while fMRI records the hemodynamic signals across the whole brain volume. Since EEG and fMRI capture different types of signals, we first decode these signals into a shared latent source space using a process called "neural transcoding". Neural transcoding involves generating a signal of one neuroimaging modality from another by decoding it into a latent source space and then encoding it into the new measurement space. To achieve this, we employ a cyclic Convolutional Neural Network (cyclic-CNN) as shown in Fig. 1. The cyclic-CNN generates latent source spaces estimated from EEG and fMRI independently. When transcoding fMRI to EEG, the fMRI data is first decoded to latent sources, where the fMRI decoder up-samples the original fMRI in time and transforms it into an electrical signal. Similarly, when transcoding EEG to fMRI, the EEG data is first decoded to latent sources, as the EEG decoder spatially up-samples and transforms the original EEG from channel-based surface measurements to volumetric data, while preserving the temporal information. The degree of up-sampling in this stage is constrained by computational considerations and data size, which will be discussed further in Session 2.1. Consequently, the temporal resolution of fMRI is up-sampled by a factor of 6, while the spatial resolution of EEG is up-sampled to approximately 12 mm × 12 mm × 12 mm.
- *Upsampling the Latent Source Space via a Transformational Backprojector:* To achieve our integrated source space with EEG's temporal resolution and

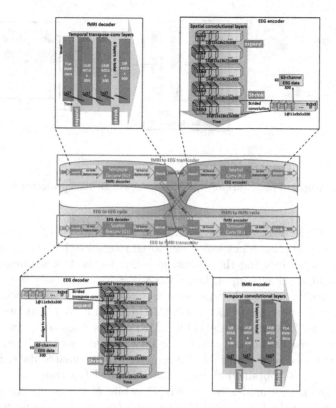

Fig. 1. Cyclic convolutional transcoder pipeline (Color figure online)

fMRI's spatial resolution, we utilize a transformational backprojector. This backprojector combines the transcoded EEG and fMRI data by up-sampling the latent source space estimated from fMRI and down-sampling the latent source space estimated from EEG. The latent source space estimated from fMRI can be considered a projection of the integrated latent source space along the time dimension, while the latent source estimated from EEG can be considered a projection along the spatial dimension. The recovery of the integrated latent source space is formulated as a sparse, two-direction unsupervised back-projection problem. We have developed a transformational backprojector that utilizes Convolutional Neural Networks (CNNs) and spatial transformer networks (STNs), as illustrated in Fig. 2.

2.1 Cyclic-CNN Transcoder

The cyclic-CNN structure, which forms the basis of our approach, draws inspiration from the cycle-GAN framework introduced by Zhu et al. [16]. In this framework, a forward mapping from the source domain (X) to the target domain (Y)

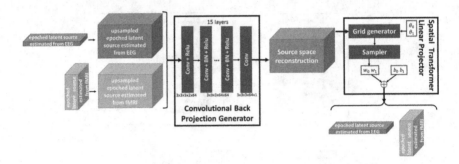

Fig. 2. Framework of the Transformational Backprojector

is defined as G: X → Y, while the reverse mapping from Y to X is defined as R: Y → X. The cycle consistency loss is employed to ensure that the reconstructed data, obtained by applying the reverse mapping to the forward-mapped data, approximates the original input, i.e., $R(G(X)) \approx X$.

In our specific setting, Y represents the latent source space, which corresponds to the pre-processed EEG (E) or fMRI (F) data. We utilize two decoding functions: G_1 for EEG signals and G_2 for fMRI signals. Conversely, two encoding functions, R_1 for EEG signals and R_2 for fMRI signals, are employed. Furthermore, we introduce several variables to represent the estimated data: $\hat{E}$ denotes the estimated EEG obtained through the fMRI-to-EEG transcoder (depicted in the top green rectangular box in Fig. 1), while $\hat{F}$ represents the estimated fMRI acquired via the EEG-to-fMRI transcoder (depicted in the bottom orange rectangular box in Fig. 1). Additionally, $\hat{E}'$ represents the estimated EEG data generated through the EEG-to-EEG cycle (depicted in the red shaded cycle in Fig. 1), and $\hat{F}'$ signifies the estimated fMRI data produced by the fMRI-to-fMRI cycle (depicted in the purple shaded cycle in Fig. 1). These variables allow for performance evaluation and analysis of different pathways within the cyclic-CNN structure.

Figure 1 depicts the integrated pipeline, illustrating the transformation process from EEG or fMRI data to the latent source space and vice versa. The conversion from data to the latent space is considered a decoding process, while the transformation from the source space to data is considered an encoding process. The four major modules in our model, namely the EEG decoder G_1, fMRI decoder G_2, EEG encoder R_1, and fMRI encoder R_2, consist of convolutional layers. Specifically, the encoder modules (EEG and fMRI encoders) comprise ordinary convolutional layers, while the decoder modules (EEG and fMRI decoders) consist of transposed convolutional layers that enable upsampling in the temporal or spatial direction, depending on the modality. It is worth noting that the EEG encoder R_1 and EEG decoder G_1 consist solely of spatial convolutional layers, whereas the fMRI decoder G_2 and fMRI encoder R_2 exclusively employ temporal convolutional layers.

With the above specifications, we introduce the EEG-to-EEG cycle consistency loss and fMRI-to-fMRI cycle consistency loss, enforcing $\hat{E}' = R_1(G_1(E)) \approx E$ and $\hat{F}' = R_2(G_2(F)) \approx F$, respectively. Similarly, we design the fMRI-to-EEG transcoder consistency loss and EEG-to-fMRI transcoder consistency loss to encourage $\hat{E} = R_1(G_2(F)) \approx E$ and $\hat{F} = R_2(G_1(E)) \approx F$, respectively. Consequently, the model can be represented by four paths, each associated with a reconstruction error term. The consistency loss terms for these paths are defined as follows:

- fMRI-to-EEG transcoding loss: $loss_1 = \sum_{i=1}^{n}(E_i - \hat{E}_i)^2$
- EEG-to-fMRI transcoding loss: $loss_2 = \sum_{i=1}^{n}(F_i - \hat{F}_i)^2$
- fMRI-to-fMRI cycle consistency loss: $loss_3 = \sum_{i=1}^{n}(F_i - \hat{F}'_i)^2$
- EEG-to-EEG cycle consistency loss: $loss_4 = \sum_{i=1}^{n}(E_i - \hat{E}'_i)^2$

with the total consistency loss being the sum of the above four losses: $loss_{total} = \sum_{i=1}^{4} loss_i$.

In the Cyclic-CNN transcoder, adjustments are made to the spatial and temporal resolutions of fMRI and EEG data to ensure computational tractability during training. These resolution adjustments have minimal impact on the transcoder's ability to process data, as long as the number of EEG channels and the temporal resolution of fMRI remain consistent throughout the decoding process.

For fMRI data, the fMRI decoder applies only a temporal transformation to the fMRI data, with the same transformation being applied to each voxel.

Similarly, for EEG data, the EEG decoder solely applies a spatial transformation.

By employing this approach, the original temporal resolution of the EEG data and the spatial resolution of the fMRI data are preserved. While the up-sampled EEG and fMRI signals facilitate feasible computation during the decoding stage, the EEG data is up-sampled spatially from 63 EEG channels to $15 \times 18 \times 15$ voxels, and the fMRI data is up-sampled temporally from a repetition time (TR) of 2.1 s to TR = 0.35 s (or a frequency of 2.86 Hz).

2.2 Transformational Backprojector

Although a compromise in resolution is necessary for feasible training and testing, our goal is to recover high-resolution estimates of latent sources in terms of both spatial and temporal aspects. The latent source space obtained from fMRI is up-sampled to a temporal resolution of 2.86 Hz, which is substantially lower than the original sampling rate of 500 Hz for EEG. Similarly, the latent sources estimated from EEG are expanded to a 3D space of dimensions $15 \times 18 \times 15$ voxels, with a voxel size of 12 mm $\times$ 12 mm $\times$ 12 mm. This spatial resolution is lower than the original spatial resolution of the acquired fMRI data, which is 2 mm $\times$ 2 mm $\times$ 2 mm.

To recover latent source space estimates at the full original resolutions of the neuroimaging data, we employ a back-projection approach. This framework is inspired by the work of [17], which introduces an unsupervised method based on a CNN and spatial transformer network for solving sparse-view back-projection without access to ground truth. Figure 2 illustrates our framework for latent source space reconstruction using simultaneous EEG-fMRI data.

Furthermore, we apply the back-projection technique on epoched data (see Experiments and Results). Specifically, the up-sampled epoched source space estimated from EEG and the epoched source space estimated from fMRI serve as two channels of input data, representing projections from an epoched integrated source space. Each time point within an epoch is treated as a data sample, and each epoch consists of 1200 ms (i.e., 600 time points), ranging from 350 ms before to 850 ms after the stimulus. A CNN is employed to perform back-projection to the epoched integrated source space, followed by a projector that projects the estimated integrated source space back to the source space estimated from fMRI in the direction θ_0 and to the source space estimated from EEG in the direction θ_1. Since temporal back-projection is already achieved through epoching, this step only involves a spatial transformation. Thus, the CNN exclusively consists of spatial convolution layers. The weights ω_0, ω_1 and biases b_0, b_1 are optimized to account for possible scale and baseline differences between the latent source space estimated from fMRI and the latent source space estimated from EEG.

3   Training and Testing

The transcoder is trained and tested using simultaneous EEG-fMRI data obtained from 19 subjects during an auditory oddball experiment [18]. A leave-one-subject-out cross-validation strategy is employed, where the sessions of the left-out subject are excluded during training. This procedure is repeated for all 19 subjects to obtain group-level results. The reported results in the subsequent sections correspond to the testing phase on the left-out subjects. Given the size of the data and the computational demands of training, the stopping criterion for model training is set to 500 epochs.

Using the aforementioned approaches, we conduct two primary analyses. The first analysis focuses on transcoding the signal from one modality to the other, specifically predicting the fMRI signal from the acquired EEG data, and vice versa. The second analysis centers around identifying the integrated source space. It is important to note that the resolution of the input data varies between these two types of analyses. In the transcoding analysis, the resolution of the EEG or fMRI data is compromised, as described earlier, to enable intensive computation. On the other hand, in the latent source space analysis, the resolution of the input data remains unchanged. The first analysis tests the model's performance on the transcoding task using pre-processed EEG and fMRI data from all subjects' sessions. The spatial and temporal resolutions of the data are adjusted to a suitable level for computationally intensive operations, as previously described. In the second analysis, which involves estimating the integrated latent source space, only the trained fMRI and EEG decoders, along with the transformational backprojector, are utilized. Thus, we investigate the recovered source space at the full resolutions of the fMRI and EEG.

In the second analysis, the epoched and up-sampled latent source space estimated from fMRI, along with the latent source space estimated from EEG, are
utilized as inputs for the transformational backprojector. The output of the
backprojector is compared with the epoched latent source space estimated from
fMRI and the latent source space estimated from EEG before upsampling. Since
the transformational backprojector is an unsupervised method, it is trained separately for each session of the epoched data to account for subject- or session-
specific differences in the leadfield. Given that only a spatial transformation is
applied, each volume is considered as one sample during training. To expedite
the training process, the models are initialized with one of the model parameters
before training for 50 epochs.

4   Results

In this section, we present the results for the two aforementioned analyses: the
performance of transcoding between modalities and the identification of the
latent integrated source space using EEG and fMRI data.

4.1   fMRI Transcoded from EEG

Figure 3 illustrates the performance of the EEG-to-fMRI transcoder using Z-
statistics maps obtained from a group-level general linear model (GLM) analysis. For each left-out subject, we generate fMRI data transcoded from the corresponding EEG data. Subsequently, we compare the activation maps between the
ground-truth fMRI and the fMRI transcoded from EEG using a GLM analysis
with standard and oddball explanatory variables. The purpose of this comparison is to assess the degree of overlap between the activation patterns obtained
from the two sources.

Figure 3 clearly demonstrates that the activation maps derived from the fMRI
transcoded from EEG exhibit substantial overlap with those obtained from the

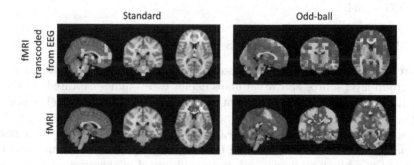

Fig. 3. Comparing fMRI transcoded from EEG and real fMRI data: fMRI transcoded
from EEG is of spatial resolution of 12 mm × 12 mm × 12 mm while real fMRI data
has a spatial resolution of 2 mm × 2 mm × 2 mm

actual acquired fMRI data. Despite the common belief that EEG source local-ization is relatively accurate only for cortical regions [19], our analysis indicates that the model is capable of localizing activations in subcortical regions as well. However, it is important to note that the activation maps obtained from the ground-truth fMRI and the fMRI transcoded from EEG are not entirely concor-dant. This discrepancy is likely attributed to the presence of activities captured by one modality but not detected by the other. Notably, our model leverages information from both modalities, even if certain information is exclusively cap-tured by one modality. This feature distinguishes our model from typical asym-metrical EEG-informed fMRI and fMRI-informed EEG analyses, where only the shared activities are exploited.

4.2   EEG Transcoded from fMRI

To assess the performance of the fMRI-to-EEG transcoder, we calculate the Pearson correlation coefficient between the EEG signal transcoded from fMRI and the real EEG signal, representing the correlation between $\hat{E}$ and E. In the cross-validation using the test subjects, out of a total of 87 runs from 19 subjects, 59 runs exhibit significant correlations at a significance level of alpha = 0.05, considering the Bonferroni correction.

Figure 4 presents the fMRI transcoded EEG from a representative channel for one of these runs. Both the ground truth EEG and the EEG transcoded from fMRI are displayed at a sampling rate of 2.86 Hz. The EEG transcoded from fMRI demonstrates a reasonable resemblance to the ground truth EEG, capturing stimulus-induced activity occurring at intervals of approximately 2 to 3 s. This observation highlights the ability of the fMRI transcoded EEG signal to recover information at higher frequencies despite the considerably lower tem-poral resolution of fMRI (TR = 2.1 s, equivalent to a sampling rate of 0.47 Hz). Moreover, the phase and amplitude of the fMRI transcoded EEG signal align with the estimated forward model of EEG, exhibiting relatively good agreement with the ground truth. These findings suggest that the transcoder learns an accurate forward model, enhancing its ability to capture the characteristics of the EEG signal.

4.3   EEG-fMRI Fused Source Space

Figure 5 illustrates representative results of the integrated source space analysis. The group-level source activation maps depict two volumes captured at 400 ms and 450 ms post-stimulus. The latent source space exhibits a spatial resolution of 2 mm × 2 mm × 2 mm and a temporal resolution of 500 Hz.

The integrated source space reveals activation patterns that are commonly associated with an auditory oddball task. Specifically, around 450 ms after the onset of the oddball stimulus, activation is observed in the primary motor cor-tex, which is known to be involved in finger movement. Preceding this activa-tion, at 400 ms, there is strong activation in subcortical regions associated with the motor system. These findings provide evidence that cortical and subcortical

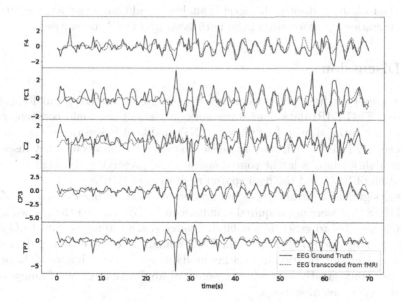

Fig. 4. Comparing EEG transcoded from fMRI and real EEG data

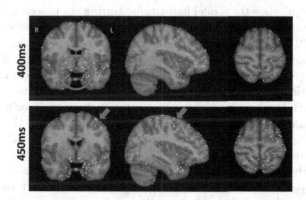

Fig. 5. EEG-fMRI integrated source space for oddball stimuli epochs: The image displays sources at two time points preceding a response (right-handed button press) for oddball epochs. Source strength is color-coded, with yellow indicating stronger activation than red. The green circle highlights subcortical regions within the motor system, including the putamen, globus pallidus, and basal ganglia elements associated with voluntary movement. The blue arrows indicate activity localized to the motor cortex specifically linked to the right hand (contralateral motor cortex).

latent sources can be resolved at a millisecond timescale, displaying consistency with the task. Importantly, this level of analysis would not be achievable without the integration of information from both EEG and fMRI modalities.

5 Discussion

In this paper, we have presented a new framework for analyzing simultaneously acquired EEG-fMRI data. Our framework consists of two main components: a cyclic convolutional neural network (CNN) capable of bidirectional transcoding between EEG and fMRI, and a transformational backprojector that fuses the two modalities into a latent source space while preserving the high temporal resolution of EEG and the high spatial resolution of fMRI.

One significant advantage of our framework is its applicability to EEG or fMRI data that were not acquired simultaneously. By utilizing the trained models, it is possible to generate the latent source space estimates from EEG data alone or transcode fMRI data to the EEG domain, thereby enabling the exploration of latent information from either modality even in the absence of the other. This flexibility greatly expands the potential applications of our framework in various experimental settings.

Compared to conventional methods that often assume linear relationships between latent sources and neuroimaging measures, as well as prior modeling of the hemodynamic responses or electromagnetic characteristics, our framework is entirely data-driven and can capture non-linear relationships. Additionally, our model treats the simultaneous acquisition of EEG-fMRI as a generative problem and optimizes the model holistically. During the process of transcoding, our model simultaneously achieves the decoding of the latent source space from EEG or fMRI, the estimation of the hemodynamic response function (HRF), and the derivation of the leadfield forward and inverse models. The resulting fused source space represents a novel neuroimaging data representation with the spatial resolution of fMRI (2 mm × 2 mm × 2 mm) and the temporal resolution of EEG (500 Hz), which surpasses the resolution previously achieved in non-invasive human brain imaging. This novel representation has the potential to serve as a powerful tool for human neuroimaging, providing a 3D data volume with high temporal resolution.

Importantly, our framework is not a black box. We have designed the model to separate spatial and temporal transformations into distinct modules based on our understanding of the underlying (linear) generative processes. The fMRI decoder, employing temporal transpose convolution, can be seen as addressing the fMRI deconvolution problem, while the fMRI encoder, composed of temporal convolutional layers, represents the data-driven generative process that maps the latent source to the measurement space using an estimated HRF. Similarly, the EEG encoder, utilizing spatial transpose convolutional layers, implements what is commonly referred to as the "forward model" in other EEG source localization methods, while the EEG decoder, consisting of spatial convolutional layers, acts as the "inverse model".

Although our framework demonstrates promising results, there are a few caveats and areas for improvement. Firstly, due to the limited data available, we trained a group-level model and used a leave-one-subject-out approach for testing. With more data per subject, it would be possible to train individual models for each subject, allowing for the learning of subject-specific HRFs and head electromagnetic characteristics. Secondly, given the computational cost of training these models, we evaluated only a limited set of hyperparameters, and further optimization is needed. These aspects represent avenues for future work to enhance the performance and applicability of our framework.

References

1. Glover, G.H.: Overview of functional magnetic resonance imaging. Neurosurg. Clin. **22**(2), 133–139 (2011)
2. Huettel, S.A., Song, A.W., McCarthy, G., et al.: Functional Magnetic Resonance Imaging, vol. 1. Sinauer Associates, Sunderland (2004)
3. Niedermeyer, E., da Silva, F.L.: Electroencephalography: Basic Principles, Clinical Applications, and Related Fields. Lippincott Williams & Wilkins (2005)
4. Conroy, B.R., Muraskin, J., Sajda, P.: Fusing simultaneous EEG-fMRI by linking multivariate classifiers. In: NIPS 2013 Workshop on Machine Learning and Interpretation in NeuroImaging (MLINI 2012), p. 6 (2012)
5. Oberlin, T., Barillot, C., Gribonval, R., Maurel, P.: Symmetrical EEG-fMRI imaging by sparse regularization. In: 2015 23rd European Signal Processing Conference (EUSIPCO), pp. 1870–1874. IEEE (2015)
6. Liu, X., Sajda, P.: A convolutional neural network for transcoding simultaneously acquired EEG-fMRI data. In: 2019 9th International IEEE/EMBS Conference on Neural Engineering (NER), pp. 477–482 (2019)
7. Jorge, J., Van der Zwaag, W., Figueiredo, P.: EEG-fMRI integration for the study of human brain function. Neuroimage **102**, 24–34 (2014)
8. Bénar, C.-G., et al.: Single-trial analysis of oddball event-related potentials in simultaneous EEG-fMRI. Hum. Brain Mapp. **28**(7), 602–613 (2007)
9. Jann, K., Dierks, T., Boesch, C., Kottlow, M., Strik, W., Koenig, T.: BOLD correlates of EEG alpha phase-locking and the fMRI default mode network. Neuroimage **45**(3), 903–916 (2009)
10. Walz, J.M., Goldman, R.I., Carapezza, M., Muraskin, J., Brown, T.R., Sajda, P.: Simultaneous EEG-fMRI reveals temporal evolution of coupling between supramodal cortical attention networks and the brainstem. J. Neurosci. **33**(49), 19212–19222 (2013)
11. Muraskin, J., et al.: Brain dynamics of post-task resting state are influenced by expertise: insights from baseball players. Hum. Brain Mapp. **37**(12), 4454–4471 (2016)
12. Muraskin, J., et al.: Fusing multiple neuroimaging modalities to assess group differences in perception-action coupling. Proc. IEEE **105**(1), 83–100 (2017)
13. Muraskin, J., et al.: A multimodal encoding model applied to imaging decision-related neural cascades in the human brain. Neuroimage **180**, 211–222 (2018)
14. Debener, S., Ullsperger, M., Siegel, M., Fiehler, K., Von Cramon, D.Y., Engel, A.K.: Trial-by- trial coupling of concurrent electroencephalogram and functional magnetic resonance imaging identifies the dynamics of performance monitoring. J. Neurosci. **25**(50), 11730–11737 (2005)

15. Handwerker, D.A., Gonzalez-Castillo, J., D'esposito, M., Bandettini, P.A.: The continuing challenge of understanding and modeling hemodynamic variation in fMRI. Neuroimage **62**(2), 1017–1023 (2012)
16. Zhu, J.-Y., Park, T., Isola, P., Efros, A.A.: Unsupervised sparse-view backprojection via convolutional and spatial transformer networks. In: Proceedings of the IEEE International Conference on Computer Vision, pp. 2223–2232 (2017)
17. Liu, X., Sajda, P.: Unsupervised sparse-view backprojection via convolutional and spatial transformer networks (2020)
18. McIntosh, J.R., Yao, J., Hong, L., Faller, J., Sajda, P.: Ballistocardiogram artifact reduction in simultaneous EEG-fMRI using deep learning. arXiv preprint arXiv:1910.06659 (2019)
19. Wolters, C.H., Anwander, A., Tricoche, X., Weinstein, D., Koch, M.A., Macleod, R.S.: Influence of tissue conductivity anisotropy on EEG/MEG field and return current computation in a realistic head model: a simulation and visualization study using high-resolution finite element modeling. Neuroimage **30**(3), 813–826 (2006)

Informatics Paradigms for Brain and Mental Health Research

Increasing the Power of Two-Sample T-tests in Health Psychology Using a Compositional Data Approach

René Lehmann[1,2]($\boxtimes$) (iD) and Bodo Vogt[2]

[1] FOM University of Applied Science, Leimkugelstraße 6, 45141 Essen, Germany
rene.lehmann@fom.de
[2] Otto-von-Guericke-University, Universitätsplatz 2, 39106 Magdeburg, Germany
{rene1.lehmann,bodo.vogt}@ovgu.de
https://www.fom.de, https://www.emwifo.ovgu.de/en/

Abstract. Increasing the statistical power of two-sample t-tests is of fundamental interest in health psychology and health economics. For example, grant funding depends on quality-adjusted life years (QALY) index values associated with a therapeutic intervention. Increasing the statistical power of t-tests corresponds to increasing effect sizes and, thus, increased grant funding and incentives. Improved psychometric profiling can help to reduce costs, improve resource usage, increase patient welfare and reduce mental health risks. Recently, the compositional structure (i.e., the Simplex) of bipolar Likert scales data was revealed pointing out the bias inherent in traditional evaluations. We propose to convert the compositional data towards the real valued interval scale using the isometric log-ratio (ilr) transformation providing unbiased parameter estimates (e.g., means, standard deviations), standards and improving psychometric patient profiling. Via simulation we show that the ilr approach increases the statistical power of the paired and unpaired two-samples t-test affecting effect size and grant funding. Re-analyzing real data we demonstrate the practical relevance of the approach. The results generalize to more complex statistical procedures, e.g. analysis of variance (ANOVA).

Keywords: bipolar scale · isometric log-ratio transformation · t-test

1 Introduction

Likert scales (LS) are widely used in psychology and medical psychometrics [1,2] to derive standards and generate psychological profiles of patients. Regarding scientific standards it is of great interest to provide assured knowledge about coherences and effects among variables and the effect size of therapeutic measures [3]. The treatment and its outcome depend on standards and on a patient's psychological profile. Suboptimal data evaluation causes possibly biased standards affecting psychological profiling and medical diagnostics. As a result, medical

F. Liu et al. (Eds.): BI 2023, LNAI 13974, pp. 333–347, 2023.
https://doi.org/10.1007/978-3-031-43075-6_29

border cases can be false positive or negative. Furthermore, suboptimal psycho-logical profiling can favour misdiagnoses, corrupt treatment plans compromising patient welfare or occasion additional treatment costs. Therefore, it is of funda-mental interest to apply statistical procedures providing large statistical power [4].

Consider the quality-adjusted life years (QALY) index approach. Measur-ing therapeutic success in health psychology focuses on pre-post-comparisons as well as comparisons of treatment groups to a control group. Obvious measures based on arithmetic means and standard deviations are Cohen's d_z, d and f [5]. Increasing statistical power implies increasing effect size and, thus, increasing QALY index values resulting in increasing grant funding. Moreover, as the sta-tistical power depends on the sample size it is possible to maintain a specific level of power while reducing the sample size, that is, sampling costs decrease.

[6] point out that the classical evaluation of bipolar Likert data using means or sums of item responses yields biased results. They emphasize the advantages of the isometric log-ratio (ilr) approach in mental health analyses and health economics. The ilr transformation proposed induces an increase of the statistical power of the well-known correlation test based on Student's t-distribution and yields unbiased standards.

According to [7] and [8], in this article psychometric variables are considered continuous and bipolar Likert data are considered compositional data underlying the Aitchison metric (Sect. 2) [6]. The compositional data space is also called the Simplex (see, e.g., [9]).

For proper understanding of the different types of scales, it is necessary to distinguish between statements (i.e., items of a questionnaire) and their corre-sponding response scale (RS) as well as a LS (i.e., a set of items represented by the sum or mean value of their corresponding responses) and the scale of a personality trait (the trait scale, TS) (i.e., the continuum of all possible man-ifestations of a trait). The RS measures the order of magnitude of a person's agreement (OMA) or disagreement (OMD) towards a statement. Associating verbal responses (e.g., ranging from "strongly disagree" to "strongly agree") with numerical values (e.g., $1, \dots, 5$) is common practice [10,11]. The LS repre-sents a model of the TS for estimating the order of magnitude of a personality trait (OMT) [12]. In the following, if not otherwise stated, the term scale refers to a bipolar scale.

2   The Compositional Structure of Bipolar Scales Data

Psychometric scales provide estimates of individual values of psychological con-structs. For example, think of the Big 5 trait openness. The items of a question-naire (e.g., the BFI-10 inventory of [13]) cover specific aspects of a psychological construct. Considering an overall value of the item responses (e.g., the arith-metic mean) provides an individual estimate of the order of magnitude of the psychological construct.

Due to imperfect knowledge, uncertainty about situations and a complex environment (see [14–16]) the psychometric scale cannot cover all individual manifestations of the psychological construct implying the existence of a limit of quantification (LOQ) [6]. For an illustration see Fig. 1.

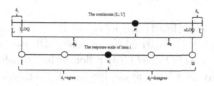

Fig. 1. The continuum [L; U] contains all possible individual manifestations μ of a construct ranging from a minimum value L (e.g., non-openness to anything) to a maximum value U (e.g., openness to everything). The complements Δ_1 and Δ_2, both represent the order of magnitude of the construct with $\Delta_1 + \Delta_2 = U - L$ (e.g., consider L = 0, U = 100, $\mu = 70$, $\Delta_1 = 70$ and $\Delta_2 = 30$). The psychometric scale consists of different items $i = 1, \ldots, I$ associated with a RS, e.g., ranging from l = "strongly disagree" to u = "strongly agree". As the items cannot cover all aspects of the construct the lower (l) and upper (u) limit of the RS are different from L and U reflecting the lower (lLOQ) and upper (uLOQ) limit of quantification. The edge area of the TS which is not covered by the items and their respective RS are named δ_l and δ_u. Any response x_i towards an item assertion reflects the OMA (d_1) and the OMD towards the item assertion (d_2). For example, let l = lLOQ = 2.5, u = uLOQ = 97.5, $x_i = 50$, $d_1 = 50$, $d_2 = 50$, $\delta_l = [0; 2.5)$ and $\delta_u = (97.5; 100])$. That is, x_i estimates the unknown value of μ.

2.1 The Compositional Structure in Brief

Concerning the TS [L; U], any limit values $L, U \in \mathbb{R}$ can be assumed as long as $L < U$ is satisfied, e.g., $L = 0$ and $U = 100$. For example $\mu_1 = 0.5$ is the midpoint of the TS $[L; U] = [0; 1]$ whereas $\mu_2 = 50$ represents the midpoint of the TS $[L; U] = [0; 100]$. μ_1 and μ_2 both represent the same order of magnitude of the trait but on different scales, so L and U can be chosen arbitrarily.

Without loss of generality consider a RS $r = \{r_1, \ldots, r_{k+1}\}$ with $r_1 = 1$, $r_{k+1} = k + 1$, $k \in \mathbb{N}$, $r_{s+1} - r_s = 1 \; \forall s \in 1, \ldots, k$ (e.g., the discrete scale $\{1, 2, 3, 4, 5\}$ of $k + 1 = 5$ categories ranging from "strongly disagree (1)" to "strongly agree (5)").

Let $p \in (0; 1)$ quantify the LOQ. Symmetric values of lLOQ and uLOQ are assumed, that is, $lLOQ = 100 \cdot p/2$ and $uLOQ = 100(1 - p/2)$. Therefore, the edge areas are also symmetric with $|\delta_l| = |\delta_u| = p/2$.

Let $x' \in \{r_1, \ldots, r_{k+1}\}$ be an observed response value and let $p \in (0; 1)$ be the LOQ. The algorithm presented transforms any response value x' towards the trait scale $[0; 100]$ with due regard to p. In the following, if not otherwise stated, assume $L = 0$, $U = 100$, $r = \{1, 2, \ldots, k + 1\}$ ($k \in \mathbb{N}$).

1. Choose $p \in (0; 1)$. Set $lLOQ = 100 \cdot p/2$ and $uLOQ = 100 \cdot (1 - p/2)$ (e.g., $p = 0.05$, lLOQ = 2.5, uLOQ = 97.5)
2. Define the *range* $:= uLOQ - lLOQ$ and the step width $sw := range/k$ (e.g., $range = 97.5 - 2.5 = 95$ and $sw = 95/4 = 23.75$).

3. Let the observed response value be $x' = r_s \in \{r_1, \ldots, r_{k+1}\}$ with $s \in \{1, \ldots, k+1\}$ (e.g., $x' = 3$ corresponds to $s = 3$).
4. Calculate the response value $x^* = lLOQ + sw \cdot (s - 1)$ (e.g., $x' = 3$ and $x^* = 2.5 + 23.75 \cdot (3 - 1) = 50$).

For example, the algorithm transforms the RS $r = \{1, 2, 3, 4, 5\}$ towards the RS* $r^* = \{2.5, 26.25, 50, 73.75, 97.5\}$ ($p = 0.05$). Please note that the bounds of r^* depend on p. $x^* \in (lLOQ; uLOQ)$ reflects the transformed OMA towards the item assertion. Any OMA value implies an OMD towards the item assertion as a complement, say $100 - x^*$. Define $x = (x_1, x_2)^T \in \mathbb{R}^2$ with $x_1 := x^*$, $x_2 := 100 - x^*$, $x_1, x_2 > 0$ and $x_1 + x_2 = 100$ where $()^T$ denotes the transpose.

Generally, the compositional data space (the Simplex) is defined as $\mathcal{S} := \{x = (x_1, \ldots, x_D)^T \in \mathbb{R}^D \mid \sum_{i=1}^{D} x_i = \kappa \in \mathbb{R}, \ x_i > 0 \ \forall \ i = 1, \ldots, D\}$. With $D = 2$ and $\kappa = 100$ x fulfills the definition of compositional data [6,17–19]. An illustration of the Simplex of bipolar scales data is presented in Fig. 2.

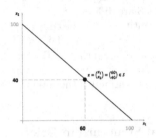

Fig. 2. The black line illustrates the Simplex of bipolar scales data. x_1 and x_2 represents the OMA and OMD towards the item assertion, respectively. The exemplary point $x = (60, 40)^T$ illustrates and OMA of 60 and an OMD of 40.

2.2   Ilr and Inverse Ilr Transformation

Any compositional data point x depends on the Aitchison metric [20]. However, most standard statistical procedures (e.g., computation of arithmetic means, Pearson correlation, (multiple) linear regression, t-tests) are based on the Euclidean metric. The ilr transformation yields interval scaled data underlying the Euclidean metric [21]. By means of the ilr and the inverse ilr, data and statistical results (e.g., mean values) can easily be (back-)transformed. The ilr transformation is defined as $ilr(x) = ilr((x_1, \ldots, x_D)^T) := (z_1, \ldots, z_{D-1})^T$ with

$$z_s = \sqrt{\frac{s}{s+1}} \ln \frac{\sqrt[s]{\prod_{j=1}^{s} x_j}}{x_{s+1}}, \quad s = 1, \ldots, D-1 \tag{1}$$

In the present case of $D = 2$ the ilr reduces to $ilr((x^*, 100 - x^*)^T) = z_1$ with

$$z_1 = \sqrt{\frac{1}{2}} \ln \frac{x^*}{100 - x^*}. \tag{2}$$

For example, the ilr transform of the RS $r^* = \{2.5, 26.25, 50, 73.75, 97.5\}$ denotes $ilr((2.5, 97.5)^T) = -2.59$, $ilr((26.25, 73.75)^T) = -0.73$, $ilr((50, 50)^T) = 0$, $ilr((73.75, 26.25)^T) = 0.73$ and $ilr((97.5, 2.5)^T) = 2.59$.

Please note that the bounds of the ilr RS depend on p because the bounds of r^* depend on p. The smaller $p \in (0, 1)$ is, the closer are the bounds of r^* to 0 and 100, respectively. Therefore, $\lim\limits_{p \to 0} \frac{r_1^*}{r_{k+1}^*} = 0$, $\lim\limits_{p \to 0} \frac{r_{k+1}^*}{r_1^*} = \infty$ and $\lim\limits_{p \to 0} \ln \frac{r_1^*}{r_{k+1}^*} = -\infty$, $\lim\limits_{p \to 0} \ln \frac{r_{k+1}^*}{r_1^*} = \infty$, i.e., the spread of the ilr RS increases as $p \to 0$.

The inverse ilr is used to back-transform any $z \in \mathbb{R}^{D-1}$ to an $x \in \mathcal{S}$ yielding the Simplex representation of the data. The inverse ilr is defined as follows. Let $z = (z_1, \ldots, z_{D-1})^T \in \mathbb{R}^{D-1}$.

$$y_s := \sum_{j=s}^{D} \frac{z_j}{\sqrt{j(j+1)}} - \sqrt{\frac{s-1}{s}} z_{s-1}; \quad z_0 := z_D := 0 \tag{3}$$

$$x_s := \kappa \cdot \frac{e^{y_s}}{e^{y_1} + \ldots + e^{y_D}}, \quad s = 1 \ldots, D \tag{4}$$

Like the ilr, the inverse ilr is simplified in the present case. The corresponding x^* is obtained by setting $z_0 := z_D := 0$ and $\kappa = 100$ with

$$x^* = 100 \cdot \frac{e^{y_1}}{e^{y_1} + e^{y_2}} \text{ with } y_1 = \sqrt{0.5} z_1 \text{ and } y_2 = -\sqrt{0.5} z_1. \tag{5}$$

Again, the complete compositional data point is given by $x = (x^*, 100 - x^*)^T$. Applying the inverse ilr transformation to the ilr RS yields the RS r^*, e.g., invilr(0.73)=73.75 in the above example.

Please note that the ilr transformation differs from the logistic transformation only by the scaling factor $\sqrt{0.5}$. Both transformations consider $\ln \frac{x^*}{100-x^*}$ in order to obtain interval scaled data. That is, mathematically they are practically identical if $D = 2$.

The idea of data evaluation is straight forward:

1. Apply the ilr transformation to obtain interval-scaled data.
2. Analyse the ilr transformed data using any appropriate statistical procedure (e.g., t-test, linear regression, Shapiro-Wilk test etc.)
3. Interpret the results on the interval scale.
4. If necessary: use the inverse ilr transformation to back-transform the results to the Simplex (e.g., apply the invilr to the arithmetic mean of ilr transformed data) and interpret.

3   Simulation Study on T-tests

In the following, if not otherwise stated, the term PAIRED (UNPAIRED) refers to the two-samples test of dependent (independent) samples. It is common practice to use Cohen's d (UNPAIRED) or d_z (PAIRED) as a measure of effect size [5].

The univariate normal distribution (see the stats package of [22]) is used for random data sampling. The simulation process is described in Fig. 3.

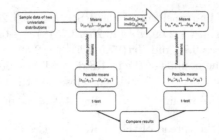

Fig. 3. After simulating values using two univariate normal distributions data are associated with their closest possible means (left-hand path). By means of the inverse ilr transformation the simulated values are transformed to the RS* and associated with their closest possible means on the original RS (right-hand path). $H_0 : \mu_1 - \mu_2 = 0$ is tested in both paths and the proportions of rejections of H_0 are obtained.

3.1   Parameters of the Simulation Study on Two-Sample T-tests

The tests considered are the UNPAIRED and the PAIRED. Welch's modification of the UNPAIRED is used if and only if the variances of the underlying data generating processes (DGPs) are unequal. It is well-known that many statistical procedures are robust against violations of the assumption of normally distributed data (e.g. the UNPAIRED and the PAIRED, see [23–25]).

Table 1 presents the parameters of the simulations. Overall, the simulations of the PAIRED (UNPAIRED) consider 240,000 (240,000) scenarios each consisting of 1,000 simulation runs.

Table 1. Parameters chosen for the PAIRED and UNPAIRED. d and d_z refer to Cohen's D [5]. $p \in (0; 1)$ quantifies the LOQ. $lLOQ$ and $uLOQ$ represent the lower and upper LOQ with $lLOQ + uLOQ = 100$. K defines the numbers of responses of the RS $r = \{1, \ldots, K\}$. The sample sizes are equal, that is, $N_1 = N_2$. I represents the numbers of items of a psychometric scale. The variances of the sampling distributions are s_{11} and s_{22} while μ_1 and μ_2 represent the expected values.

Parameter	values
Cohen's $D \in \{d, d_z\}$	$\{0.05, 0.1, 0.15, \ldots, 1\}$
p	$\{0.02, 0.04, 0.06, 0.08.0.1, 0.12, 0.14, 0.16, 0.18, 0.2\}$
$lLOQ$	$100 \cdot p/2$
$uLOQ$	$100 \cdot (1 - p/2)$
K	$\{4, 5, 6\}$
$N_1 = N_2$	$\{20, 40, 60, 80, 100\}$
I	$\{1, 2, \ldots, 8\}$
(s_{11}, s_{22})	$\{(0.5, 0.5), (0.5, 1), (0.5, 1.5), (0.5, 2), (1, 1), (1, 1.5),$ $(1, 2), (1.5, 1.5), (1.5, 2), (2, 2)\}$
μ_1	0
μ_2	$D\sqrt{(s_{11} + s_{22})/2}$

3.2   Results of the Simulation Study of T-tests

The results of the simulations concerning are summarized in Tables 2, 3 and 4. Concerning the UNPAIRED (PAIRED) please refer to and Figs. 4a–4f (Figs. 5a–5f).

Overall, the ilr approach can be considered superior to classical data evaluation. The results can be summarized as follows:

1. On average we have $\Delta Power > 0$. $\Delta Power$ is largest if $d = 0.45$ and $d_z = 0.3$ (over all values of all parameters, see Table 2).
2. As p decreases $\Delta Power$ increases (Table 3).
3. $\Delta Power$ is largest if the total variance $s^2 \in \{2.5, 3\}$ (Table 3).

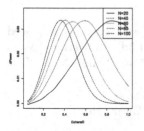

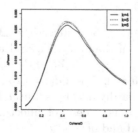

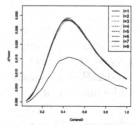

(a) $\Delta Power$ for different values of Cohen's d over all values of LOQ (p) and total variance (s^2).

(b) $\Delta Power$ for different values of Cohen's d using different LOQ values p over all values of s^2.

(c) $\Delta Power$ for different values of Cohen's d using different total variance values s^2 over all values of p.

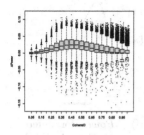

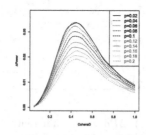

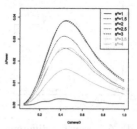

(d) $\Delta Power$ for different values of Cohen's d using different samples sizes $N_1 = N_2 = N$.

(e) $\Delta Power$ for different values of Cohen's d using different numbers of responses k.

(f) $\Delta Power$ for different values of Cohen's d using different numbers of items I.

Fig. 4. $\Delta Power$ values of the UNPAIRED

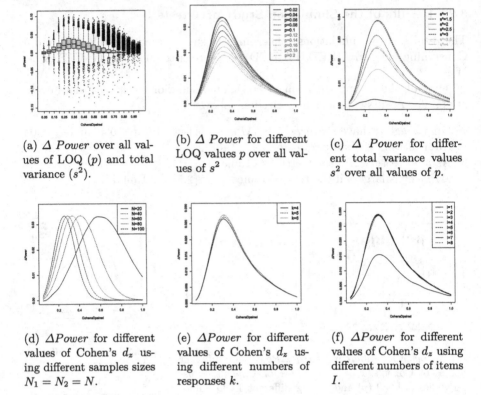

(a) Δ *Power* over all values of LOQ (p) and total variance (s^2).

(b) Δ *Power* for different LOQ values p over all values of s^2

(c) Δ *Power* for different total variance values s^2 over all values of p.

(d) $\Delta Power$ for different values of Cohen's d_z using different samples sizes $N_1 = N_2 = N$.

(e) $\Delta Power$ for different values of Cohen's d_z using different numbers of responses k.

(f) $\Delta Power$ for different values of Cohen's d_z using different numbers of items I.

Fig. 5. Δ *Power* values of the PAIRED

4. As sample sizes $N_1 = N_2 = N$ increase the $\Delta Power$ curve is displaced towards decreasing values of d and d_z (Figs. 4d and 5d). Concerning $N_1 = N_2 = 20$ $\Delta Power$ is largest if $d = 0.85$ and $d_z = 0.6$. Regarding $N_1 = N_2 = 100$ $\Delta Power$ is largest if $d = 0.35$ and $d_z = 0.25$.

5. The number of responses hardly affects $\Delta Power$ (Figs. 4e and 5e).

6. If $I > 1$ the number of items does not affect $\Delta Power$. However, $I = 1$ decreases $\Delta Power$ (Figs. 4f and 5f).

Table 2. Summary of Δ *Power* over all values of p and s^2. D refers to Cohen's d or d_z, respectively.

D	$\Delta \, Power^{UNPAIRED}$	$\Delta \, Power^{PAIRED}$
0.05	0.000	0.001
0.1	0.002	0.004
0.15	0.005	0.011
0.2	0.009	0.018
0.25	0.015	0.024
0.3	0.019	0.027
0.35	0.024	0.026
0.4	0.026	0.024
0.45	0.027	0.020
0.5	0.026	0.016
0.55	0.024	0.014
0.6	0.022	0.011
0.65	0.019	0.009
0.7	0.017	0.008
0.75	0.015	0.006
0.8	0.013	0.005
0.85	0.011	0.004
0.9	0.010	0.003
0.95	0.009	0.002
1	0.008	0.002

4   Application to Real Data

Recently, [6] re-considered the study of [11]. Applying the ilr approach to the psychometric data (e.g., the Big-Five personality traits [13], paranoia [26] and others) grouped by (un-)willingness to receive a COVID 19 vaccination (acceptance, hesitance, resistance) they generated new insights. The study considered test persons from two locations, the United Kingdom (UK) and Ireland (IRL). According to [11], the re-evaluation used pairwise two sample t-tests of independent samples (acceptance vs. hesitance, acceptance vs. resistance, acceptance vs. pooled data of hesitance and resistance).

While [11] obtained 31 (UK) and 13 (IRL) significant results out of the 2×45 t-tests of independent samples [6] obtained four (UK) and six (IRL) additional significances while losing one significance (UK) and one significance (IRL). The ilr approach yielded a total of 34 (UK) and 18 (IRL) significances. The proportion

Table 3. Summary of Δ *Power* of the UNPAIRED (PAIRED in parenthesis) for different values of the LOQ (p) over all values of the total variance s^2. D refers to Cohen's d (UNPAIRED) or d_z (PAIRED), respectively.

D	p									
	2%	4%	6%	8%	10%	12%	14%	16%	18%	20%
0.05	0.000 (0.001)	0.000 (0.001)	0.001 (0.001)	0.000 (0.001)	0.000 (0.001)	0.000 (0.001)	0.000 (0.001)	0.000 (0.001)	0.000 (0.001)	0.000 (0.001)
0.1	0.003 (0.006)	0.002 (0.006)	0.003 (0.005)	0.002 (0.005)	0.002 (0.005)	0.002 (0.004)	0.002 (0.004)	0.002 (0.004)	0.002 (0.003)	0.001 (0.003)
0.15	0.007 (0.014)	0.007 (0.014)	0.006 (0.013)	0.006 (0.012)	0.006 (0.011)	0.005 (0.011)	0.004 (0.010)	0.004 (0.008)	0.004 (0.008)	0.003 (0.007)
0.2	0.012 (0.023)	0.012 (0.022)	0.011 (0.022)	0.011 (0.020)	0.010 (0.019)	0.009 (0.017)	0.008 (0.016)	0.008 (0.014)	0.007 (0.013)	0.006 (0.012)
0.25	0.019 (0.031)	0.019 (0.030)	0.018 (0.029)	0.016 (0.027)	0.015 (0.025)	0.014 (0.023)	0.013 (0.021)	0.012 (0.020)	0.011 (0.018)	0.010 (0.016)
0.3	0.025 (0.034)	0.025 (0.033)	0.024 (0.032)	0.022 (0.031)	0.020 (0.028)	0.019 (0.026)	0.017 (0.024)	0.016 (0.022)	0.014 (0.020)	0.013 (0.019)
0.35	0.031 (0.033)	0.030 (0.033)	0.028 (0.031)	0.027 (0.029)	0.024 (0.027)	0.023 (0.025)	0.021 (0.024)	0.020 (0.022)	0.018 (0.020)	0.017 (0.019)
0.4	0.033 (0.029)	0.033 (0.028)	0.032 (0.028)	0.030 (0.026)	0.028 (0.024)	0.025 (0.023)	0.024 (0.022)	0.021 (0.020)	0.020 (0.019)	0.018 (0.017)
0.45	0.034 (0.024)	0.034 (0.024)	0.032 (0.023)	0.030 (0.022)	0.028 (0.021)	0.026 (0.020)	0.024 (0.018)	0.022 (0.017)	0.021 (0.016)	0.019 (0.015)
0.5	0.032 (0.019)	0.032 (0.020)	0.031 (0.019)	0.029 (0.018)	0.027 (0.017)	0.025 (0.016)	0.023 (0.015)	0.022 (0.014)	0.020 (0.013)	0.018 (0.012)
0.55	0.030 (0.016)	0.030 (0.016)	0.029 (0.016)	0.027 (0.015)	0.025 (0.014)	0.024 (0.013)	0.022 (0.013)	0.021 (0.012)	0.019 (0.011)	0.017 (0.010)
0.6	0.026 (0.013)	0.027 (0.014)	0.025 (0.013)	0.024 (0.012)	0.023 (0.012)	0.021 (0.011)	0.020 (0.010)	0.019 (0.010)	0.017 (0.009)	0.016 (0.009)
0.65	0.023 (0.011)	0.023 (0.011)	0.022 (0.011)	0.021 (0.010)	0.020 (0.010)	0.019 (0.009)	0.018 (0.009)	0.016 (0.008)	0.015 (0.008)	0.015 (0.007)
0.7	0.020 (0.009)	0.020 (0.009)	0.019 (0.009)	0.018 (0.009)	0.018 (0.009)	0.017 (0.008)	0.015 (0.008)	0.014 (0.007)	0.014 (0.006)	0.013 (0.006)
0.75	0.017 (0.007)	0.017 (0.008)	0.017 (0.007)	0.016 (0.007)	0.015 (0.007)	0.014 (0.006)	0.013 (0.006)	0.013 (0.006)	0.012 (0.005)	0.011 (0.005)
0.8	0.015 (0.006)	0.015 (0.006)	0.015 (0.006)	0.014 (0.006)	0.013 (0.006)	0.013 (0.005)	0.012 (0.005)	0.011 (0.005)	0.010 (0.004)	0.010 (0.004)
0.85	0.013 (0.005)	0.013 (0.005)	0.013 (0.005)	0.012 (0.005)	0.012 (0.004)	0.011 (0.004)	0.011 (0.004)	0.010 (0.004)	0.009 (0.004)	0.009 (0.003)
0.9	0.011 (0.004)	0.012 (0.004)	0.012 (0.004)	0.011 (0.003)	0.010 (0.003)	0.010 (0.003)	0.009 (0.003)	0.008 (0.003)	0.008 (0.003)	0.008 (0.003)
0.95	0.010 (0.003)	0.010 (0.003)	0.010 (0.003)	0.010 (0.003)	0.009 (0.003)	0.009 (0.002)	0.008 (0.002)	0.008 (0.002)	0.007 (0.002)	0.007 (0.002)
1.0	0.009 (0.002)	0.009 (0.002)	0.009 (0.002)	0.008 (0.002)	0.008 (0.002)	0.007 (0.002)	0.007 (0.002)	0.007 (0.002)	0.006 (0.002)	0.006 (0.002)

of significant results increased by 6.67% (UK) and 11.11% (IRL). The number of additional significances (4+6) overcomes the minor losses of significances (1+1). Ignoring the Simplex causes serious bias. Thus, the two significances lost can be interpreted as statistical type-I errors revealed by using the ilr transformation.

Table 4. Summary of Δ *Power* of the UNPAIRED (PAIRED in parenthesis) for different values of the total variance (s^2) over all values of the LOQ p. D refers to Cohen's d (UNPAIRED) or d_z (PAIRED), respectively.

D	s^2						
	1	1.5	2	2.5	3	3.5	4
0.05	0.000 (0.000)	0.000 (0.001)	0.000 (0.001)	0.001 (0.001)	0.001 (0.001)	0.000 (0.001)	0.000 (0.001)
0.1	0.000 (0.000)	0.003 (0.005)	0.002 (0.004)	0.003 (0.006)	0.003 (0.006)	0.002 (0.005)	0.001 (0.003)
0.15	0.000 (0.001)	0.006 (0.013)	0.005 (0.010)	0.007 (0.015)	0.007 (0.015)	0.005 (0.010)	0.003 (0.006)
0.2	0.001 (0.002)	0.011 (0.021)	0.009 (0.017)	0.013 (0.025)	0.013 (0.025)	0.009 (0.017)	0.006 (0.011)
0.25	0.002 (0.003)	0.017 (0.028)	0.014 (0.023)	0.021 (0.034)	0.020 (0.034)	0.014 (0.023)	0.009 (0.014)
0.3	0.002 (0.003)	0.023 (0.032)	0.019 (0.026)	0.027 (0.038)	0.027 (0.038)	0.019 (0.026)	0.012 (0.016)
0.35	0.003 (0.002)	0.028 (0.030)	0.023 (0.025)	0.033 (0.037)	0.033 (0.038)	0.023 (0.026)	0.014 (0.016)
0.4	0.003 (0.002)	0.031 (0.027)	0.025 (0.022)	0.037 (0.034)	0.037 (0.035)	0.026 (0.023)	0.016 (0.014)
0.45	0.003 (0.002)	0.031 (0.022)	0.026 (0.019)	0.038 (0.029)	0.039 (0.029)	0.026 (0.020)	0.016 (0.012)
0.5	0.002 (0.001)	0.030 (0.018)	0.025 (0.015)	0.037 (0.023)	0.038 (0.024)	0.026 (0.016)	0.016 (0.010)
0.55	0.002 (0.001)	0.028 (0.015)	0.023 (0.013)	0.035 (0.019)	0.035 (0.020)	0.024 (0.014)	0.014 (0.009)
0.6	0.002 (0.001)	0.024 (0.012)	0.021 (0.011)	0.031 (0.016)	0.032 (0.017)	0.022 (0.012)	0.013 (0.007)
0.65	0.001 (0.001)	0.021 (0.010)	0.018 (0.009)	0.028 (0.013)	0.028 (0.014)	0.019 (0.010)	0.011 (0.006)
0.7	0.001 (0.001)	0.018 (0.008)	0.016 (0.007)	0.024 (0.011)	0.025 (0.012)	0.017 (0.008)	0.010 (0.005)
0.75	0.001 (0.001)	0.016 (0.007)	0.014 (0.006)	0.021 (0.009)	0.021 (0.010)	0.015 (0.007)	0.009 (0.004)
0.8	0.001 (0.001)	0.014 (0.005)	0.012 (0.005)	0.018 (0.007)	0.019 (0.008)	0.013 (0.006)	0.008 (0.004)
0.85	0.001 (0.000)	0.012 (0.004)	0.010 (0.004)	0.016 (0.006)	0.017 (0.006)	0.012 (0.005)	0.007 (0.003)
0.9	0.001 (0.000)	0.010 (0.003)	0.009 (0.003)	0.014 (0.004)	0.015 (0.005)	0.010 (0.004)	0.006 (0.002)
0.95	0.001 (0.000)	0.009 (0.002)	0.008 (0.002)	0.012 (0.004)	0.013 (0.004)	0.009 (0.003)	0.006 (0.002)
1	0.001 (0.000)	0.008 (0.002)	0.007 (0.002)	0.011 (0.003)	0.011 (0.003)	0.008 (0.002)	0.005 (0.001)

5   Discussion, Limitations and Practical Implications

Overall, the simulations proved the ilr approach being more powerful than the classical approach. Scenarios with Δ Power > 0 were observed more often than scenarios with Δ Power < 0. Moreover, the mean gain in statistical power outweighs the potential minor losses. A mean increase of statistical power of up to 11% points is possible, see Figs. 4a and 5a.

When effect sizes d and d_z are close to 0 the statistical power is close to 0 regardless of using ilr-transformed or original-scaled data. Regarding large effect sizes the statistical power is near 1. Thus, the difference of powers Δ Power is close to 0 regardless of using ilr-transformed or original-scaled data. Concerning practically relevant moderate effect sizes we have Δ Power > 0 demonstrating the superiority of the ilr approach.

The major assumption of the ilr approach refers to the existence of the LOQ and its quantification, say p. In practice, proper selection of p is based on expert judgement because it refers to the quality of the psychometric scale. The better the psychometric procedure is, the closer p will be to 0. Assuming a high quality of the measure scale $p = 0.1$ could be reasonable. The results of the ilr transformation slightly depend on the value of p. Figures 4b and 5b show the minor influence of p on Δ Power. The smaller p the larger the value of $|\Delta Power|$ and vice versa. However, the overall influence of p seems to be negligible. Appropriate selection of p seems to be a qualitative rather than a technical task. Further research is needed to determine appropriate values of p.

Performing repeated data evaluations using different values of p could be expedient if an appropriate selection of p seems impossible. Alternatively, p could be chosen at random within reasonable bounds (e.g., using a uniform distribution on a predefined interval, e.g., $(0; 0.2)$). Another idea is to apply different proportions, e.g., $p_l > 0$ and $p_u > 0$ at both ends of the RS* where $p_l \neq p_u$ indicates differences in the order of magnitude of the LOQs at the scale ends, i.e., $|\delta_l| \neq |\delta_u|$. Overall, the selection of p will be considered in upcoming research.

The congruence of the splines of Figs. 4e and 5e indicates the number of responses $k + 1$ being a less influential parameter. That is, the mean increase of statistical power is practically identical.

Assuming normally distributed sums of ilr-transformed item responses appears to be reasonable because of the central limit theorem. Furthermore, any RS refers to a limited number of responses. Thus, applying the ilr approach also yields a limited ilr RS. Consequently, the underlying DGP must have finite variance. The convergence of means of item responses towards normality increases as the number of Items I increases. The simulations clearly show the minor influence of I as long as $I > 1$ is satisfied. The $\Delta Power$ curves are practically identical if $I > 1$ (see Fig. 4f and 5f). Thus, upcoming research should focus on $I \in \{1, 2\}$.

Another limiting factor of the simulation is the finite number of scenarios. Many more practically relevant scenarios could exist. However, it is impossible to account for every nuance (e.g., more or less heavy tailed distributions, symmetric vs. non-symmetric distributions, larger variances s_{ii} ($i \in \{1, 2\}$), different numbers of scale items $I \in \mathbb{N}$ or responses $k + 1 \in \mathbb{N}$, non-symmetric values of $lLOQ$ and $uLOQ$ concerning the scale ends). Thus far, the results appear to be plausible and generalizable towards symmetric distributions with common values of I, $k + 1$, s_{ii} and symmetric LOQ (i.e., $|\delta_l| = |\delta_u|$). Additionally, they are in accordance with the findings of [6] about the effects of the ilr approach on the well-known correlation test based on Student's t-distribution. However, further research on the influences of non-symmetric LOQ and non-symmetric DGPs on Δ Power is necessary.

The gain of statistical power contributes to the assessment of therapeutic success, especially if effects are moderate. Unbiased estimates of means and standard deviations imply more accurate standards and measures of effect size [20]. The ilr approach helps to overcome the problem of low statistical power and significance at the edge of non-significance [27–29]. The gain of statistical power is scientifically relevant, because leading journals demand powers $\geq 90\%$. Increasing the statistical power without increasing the number of test persons prevents additional collection costs. Alternatively, the number of test persons and the number of replicate studies both could be reduced contributing to ethics in medical testing and decreasing economic effort while maintaining at least the same statistical power as in classical data analysis. The ilr approach contributes to the assessment of therapeutic success. As the statistical power of the PAIRED and UNPAIRED corresponds to the effect sizes d_z and d increasing power implies increasing effect sizes [5]. That is, the estimated effect size of therapeutic measures increases. As a consequence, the QALY index value associated with a therapeutic intervention also increases affecting grant funding and incentives based on QALY index values.

The real data analyses clearly demonstrate the potential profits of the ilr approach. An overall number of 90 re-evaluations revealed 10 additional significances while losing 2 significances, i.e. an approximate increase of 7.5% of significances.

The ilr approach transforms compositional bipolar scales data towards the real valued interval scale. However, interpreting ilr transformed data is rather complicated because basically they represent the logarithm of the ratio of the OMA and the OMD [20]. That is, the ilr approach can be used to obtain unbiased effect sizes (e.g., Pearson correlations or Cohen's d, d_z) and p-values. The effect size should be back-transformed using the inverse ilr transformation to ease interpretation.

The findings of this study generalize to all fields of applications of bipolar psychometric scales, including health psychology (e.g., measurement and assessment of personality, prediction of human behaviour), neurology (e.g., cognition and pre-post-comparisons), health economics (e.g., efficacy of treatments) and econometrics (customer satisfaction and attitudes). [6] provided evidence that the ilr approach yields unbiased parameter estimates of location, scale and association increasing the statistical power of the correlation test based on Student's t-distribution. Statistical perspectives of future applications include linear regression models. Regression coefficients of continuous (binary) explanatory variables refer to Pearson correlations (Cohen's *d*). That is, the ilr approach can be used to obtain unbiased parameter estimates in linear regression models including (multivariate) analysis of (co-)variance (i.e., ANOVA and MANOVA models, moderator analysis and mediator analysis). Other application areas depending on correlations, means and standard deviations are partial least squares path modeling and factor analysis.

References

1. Edmondson, D., Edwards, Y., Boyer, S.: Likert scales: a marketing perspective. Int. J. Bus. Mark. Decis. Sci. **5**, 73–85 (2012)
2. Sullivan, G., Artino, A.: Analyzing and interpreting data from Likert-type scales. J. Grad. Med. Educ. **5**, 541–542 (2013)
3. Button, K., et al.: Confidence and precision increase with high statistical power. Nat. Rev. Neurosci. **14**, 585 (2013)
4. Button, K., et al.: Power failure: why small sample size undermines the reliability of neuroscience. Nat. Rev. Neurosci. **14**, 365–376 (2013)
5. Cohen, J.: Statistical Power Analysis for the Behavioral Sciences. Routledge, Milton Park (2013)
6. Lehmann, R., Vogt, B.: Reconsidering bipolar scales data as compositional data improves psychometric healthcare data analytics. In: Proceedings of the 56th Hawaii International Conference on System Sciences (2023)
7. Rhemtulla, M., Brosseau-Liard, P., Savalei, V.: When can categorical variables be treated as continuous? A comparison of robust continuous and categorical SEM estimation methods under suboptimal conditions. Psychol. Methods **17**, 354–373 (2012)
8. Reips, U., Funke, F.: Interval-level measurement with visual analogue scales in Internet-based research: VAS generator. Behav. Res. Methods **40**, 699–704 (2008)
9. Aitchison, J.: The Statistical Analysis of Compositional Data. Chapman (1986)
10. Pennycook, G., Epstein, Z., Mosleh, M., Arechar, A., Eckles, D., Rand, D.: Shifting attention to accuracy can reduce misinformation online. Nature **592**, 590–595 (2021)
11. Murphy, J., et al.: Psychological characteristics associated with COVID-19 vaccine hesitancy and resistance in Ireland and the United Kingdom. Nat. Commun. **12** (2021)
12. Likert, R.: A technique for the measurement of attitudes. Arch. Psychol. **22**, 5–55 (1932)
13. Rammstedt, B., John, O.: Measuring personality in one minute or less: a 10-item short version of the Big Five Inventory in English and German. J. Res. Pers. **41**, 203–212 (2007)
14. Romano, A., Mosso, C., Merlone, U.: The role of incomplete information and others' choice in reducing traffic: a pilot study. Front. Psychol. **7**, 135 (2016)
15. Loke, W.: The effects of framing and incomplete information on judgments. J. Econ. Psychol. **10**, 329–341 (1989)
16. James, J., Wood, G.: The effects of incomplete information on the formation of attitudes toward behavioral alternatives. J. Pers. Soc. Psychol. **54**, 580–591 (1988)
17. Aitchison, J., Mateu-Figueras, G., Ng, K.: Characterization of distributional forms for compositional data and associated distributional tests. Math. Geol. **35**, 667–680 (2003)

18. Aitchison, J.: A Concise Guide to Compositional Data Analysis. Department of Statistics University of Glasgow (2003)
19. Aitchison, J., Egozcue, J.: Compositional data analysis: where are we and where should we be heading? Math. Geol. **37**, 829–850 (2005)
20. Filzmoser, P., Hron, K., Reimann, C.: Univariate statistical analysis of environmental (compositional) data: problems and possibilities. Sci. Total Environ. **407**, 6100–6108 (2009)
21. Filzmoser, P., Garrett, R., Reimann, C.: Multivariate outlier detection in exploration geochemistry. Comput. Geosci. **31**, 579–587 (2005)
22. R Core Team R: A Language and Environment for Statistical Computing (2020). www.R-project.org/
23. Norman, G.: Likert scales, levels of measurement and the laws of statistics. Adv. Health Sci. Educ. **15**, 625–632 (2010)
24. Carifio, J., Perla, R.J.: Ten common misunderstandings, misconceptions, persistent myths and urban legends about Likert scales and Likert response formats and their antidotes. J. Soc. Sci. **3**, 106–116 (2007)
25. Carifio, J., Perla, R.J.: Resolving the 50 year debate around using and misusing Likert scales. Med. Educ. **42**, 1150–1152 (2008)
26. Melo, S., Corcoran, R., Shryane, N., Bentall, R.: The persecution and deservedness scale. Psychol. Psychother.: Theory Res. Pract. **82**, 247–260 (2009)
27. Simonsohn, U., Nelson, L., Simmons, J.: P-curve: a key to the file-drawer. J. Exp. Psychol. Gen. **143**, 534–547 (2014)
28. Simonsohn, U., Nelson, L., Simmons, J.: p-Curve and effect size: correcting for publication bias using only significant results. Perspect. Psychol. Sci. **9**, 666–681 (2014)
29. Simonsohn, U.: Small telescopes: detectability and the evaluation of replication results. Psychol. Sci. **26**, 559–569 (2015)

Estimating Dynamic Posttraumatic Stress Symptom Trajectories with Functional Data Analysis

Chia-Hao Shih$^{(\boxtimes)}$, Methsarani Premathilaka, Hong Xie, Xin Wang, and Rong Liu

The University of Toledo, Toledo, OH 43606, USA
chiahao.shih@utoledo.edu

Abstract. Posttraumatic stress disorder (PTSD) is a mental health condition that may develop following exposure to trauma, with diverse and complex longitudinal trajectories of symptoms during the days to months after a traumatic event. To supplement mainstream chronic PTSD research, advancing our understanding of early post-trauma longitudinal trajectories of PTSD symptoms is warranted. In the current study, we aimed to demonstrate functional data analysis (FDA), a non-parametric method which has flexibility to capture complex non-linear patterns, as a potential superior analytic tool to comprehensively examine early post-trauma longitudinal interactions among PTSD symptoms, behavioral, brain structural, and other factors. First, data from two existing longitudinal acute trauma studies were pooled. Then, trajectories of PTSD symptom, depressive symptom, and right lateral orbital frontal gyrus thickness were estimated using functional principal component analysis. Last, the temporal associations among these measures were revealed using functional regression analysis. Results showed that both cortical thickness and depressive symptoms negatively associated with PTSD symptoms post-trauma, with dynamically changing on the strength of association. These findings demonstrated FDA as a useful tool to contribute to better understanding of PTSD development and thus may improve the efficacy of individualized PTSD preventative interventions.

Keywords: trauma exposure · structural magnetic resonance imaging · depression · longitudinal analysis

1 Introduction

Traumatic experiences can result in development of posttraumatic stress disorder (PTSD), a debilitating mental health condition characterized by various symptoms including intrusive recollections of a distressing incident, avoidance of situations related to the trauma, heightened arousal, and negative changes in mood and cognition [1]. Previous studies have linked PTSD and its symptoms with behavioral and clinical factors [2, 3], as well as structural brain alterations [4, 5].

C.-H. Shih and M. Premathilaka—Contributed equally.

© The Author(s), under exclusive license to Springer Nature Switzerland AG 2023
F. Liu et al. (Eds.): BI 2023, LNAI 13974, pp. 348–356, 2023.
https://doi.org/10.1007/978-3-031-43075-6_30

Most PTSD investigations over the past decades have focused on identifying behavioral and brain abnormalities in PTSD patients [1, 2]. Yet, a few recent studies have been directed at the possibility that factors and changes, including posttraumatic stress symptoms (PTSS), behavioral, and brain structure influences, that operate during early post-trauma period, may provide a key to explain PTSD development [6–8]. Indeed, early PTSS vary and can follow longitudinal trajectories that involve persistence, remission, or absence of symptoms over days to months and longer after trauma [9, 10]. Importantly, these symptom trajectories are likely influenced by dynamically varying clinical symptoms (e.g., depression) [11, 12], structural brain changes in emotion and other brain regions [7, 8], as well as other factors including trauma types and demographic characteristics [13].

Despite these recent efforts, existing findings are often inconsistent, and PTSD symptom trajectories remain poorly understood, because existing studies are characterized by comparative differences in length of sampling intervals, variable study durations, and limited sample sizes. Additionally, existing studies often used traditional growth modeling approaches for analyzing data, which may be inadequate for discrete data, and their underlying assumptions may not be valid for real-world data, such as clinical symptoms and brain structures. As a result, it has been difficult to build a needed longitudinal understanding of progression of early post-trauma behavioral and brain changes that contribute to initial development of PTSD.

To that end, functional data analysis (FDA), a non-parametric method that has flexibility to capture complex non-linear patterns from discrete data, may provide advantages over traditional growth modeling approaches for PTSD research. In the current study, we aimed to demonstrate FDA as a potential superior analytic tool for longitudinal PTSD research. Specifically, FDA was used to analyze a sample that combined data from two existing longitudinal studies, to estimate post-trauma PTSS, depressive symptom, and brain structural measure trajectories, and to establish the associations among them.

2 Methods

2.1 Sample

The current sample included data from two existing longitudinal studies that investigated early behavioral, brain, and other factors that contribute to PTSD development after trauma exposure. Detailed descriptions of these two studies have been published previously [7, 8]. In brief, trauma survivors were contacted within 48 h of their emergency departments (ED) visits. Those who met the criteria were enrolled for follow-up assessments. Exclusion criteria included severe injuries (including traumatic brain injury), need for surgical care, history of severe neuropsychiatric problems, being under the influence of alcohol or substances during the trauma, MRI scan contradictions (such as pregnancy or ferrous implantation), or inability to read or write in English. The two studies differ on the follow-up interval and durations such that one had follow-up assessment at 2-week, 1-month, and 3-month post-trauma [7] and the other at 2-week, 3-month, 6-month, 9-month, and 12-month post-trauma [8]. Both studies were approved by the Institutional Review Board and all participants provided written informed consent.

2.2 Measures

Posttraumatic Stress Symptoms (PTSS)
The PTSD Checklist (PCL) [14, 15] was used to assess participants' PTSS at follow-up assessments. Two different versions of PCL were used in the two studies, with one examining the severity of PTSD symptom clusters as outlined in the Diagnostic and Statistical Manual (DSM)-IV (i.e., intrusive recollections, avoidant/numbing symptoms, and hyper-arousal symptoms) and the other using the DSM-V (i.e., intrusive recollection, avoidance, negative cognitions and mood, alterations in arousal or reactivity). For both versions, each item is rated on a 5-point Likert scale with higher scores reflecting more severe PTSS. Total scores from these two versions of PCL were converted to the percent of maximum possible score (POMP) [16] for further analyses.

Depressive Symptom
The Center for Epidemiologic Studies Depression Scale (CES-D) [17] and the 16-item Quick Inventory of Depressive Symptomatology (QIDS) [18] were used to assess participants' depressive symptoms at follow-up assessments. The CES-D is a 20-item questionnaire composed of six scales reflecting major facets of depression: depressed mood, feelings of guilt and worthlessness, feelings of helplessness and hopelessness, psychomotor retardation, loss of appetite, and sleep disturbance. Each item is rated on a scale of 0 to 3, with higher scores indicating the presence of more symptomatology.

The total CES-D score was calculated by summing the score for all 10 items (with reverse coding on certain items). The QIDS covers a range of symptoms including low mood, anhedonia, difficulties with sleep, appetite, energy level, concentration, psychomotor functioning, self-esteem, and thoughts of death and/or suicide. Each item is rated on a scale of 0 to 3, with higher scores reflecting more severe depression symptoms. The total QIDS score was calculated by summing the scores for all 16 items. POMP was used to convert the scores from CES-D and QIDS for further analysis.

Structural Magnetic Resonance Imaging (MRI)
High resolution T1-weighted structural MRI scans were processed using a standard automated FreeSurfer processing stream [19]. The Desikan-Killiany atlas was used to parcellate each hemisphere into 34 anatomical regions of interest (ROIs). Regional volume, average cortical thickness, and other measures were calculated for each ROI. The data underwent visual inspection using ENIGMA imaging quality control protocols (https://enigma.ini.usc.edu/protocols/imaging-protocols/), with ROIs containing segmentation or parcellation errors being excluded.

2.3 Analytical Approaches

After data aggregation and harmonization, FDA was used to analyze combined clinical and brain structural data. FDA considers every sampling element of all subjects as a random function that is defined over a single continuous post-trauma time course. Functional principal component analysis (FPCA), an extension of FDA, is an approach to determine the function (a curve over the post-trauma time course) that explains most variation. It involves non-parametric estimation of the covariance structure using all observed data from all subjects and identifying the dominant features (i.e., eigenfunctions) of the covariance matrix. This allows estimation of individual-level complex trajectories based on selected eigenfunctions. This approach can estimate individual trajectories to fit the discrete samples using available samples of other subjects to fill in temporal gaps [20, 21]. It should be noted that in FPCA, the principal components are themselves functions, whereas in traditional PCA, the principal components are vectors in the same space as the original variables. This fundamental difference comes from the fact that functional data inhabit a function space, which is infinite-dimensional.

We used FPCA to construct post-trauma progressions of PTSS, depressive symptom, and cortical thickness of right lateral orbitofrontal gyrus (LOFG). The depressive symptom score was chosen because it is the most often identified as a comorbid clinical condition with PTSD [1, 2]. Similarly, LOFG was chosen based on previous research indicating this brain region is involved in PTSD-related brain structural alteration [5]. The formulation of a progression of a measure can be expressed as:

$$U_i\left(t_{ij}\right) = \sum_{k=1}^{K} \xi_{ik}\phi_k\left(t_{ij}\right)$$

where t_{ij} denotes the available repeats (j) of the measure in subject i (from 1 to n), $\phi_k(t)$ denotes pairwise orthogonal continuous functions, and ξ_{ik} denotes the functional principal component (FPC) scores. These parameters will be estimated with all observed data using a conditional expectation method proposed in Yao et al. [21]. K is the number of FPC and was chosen by fraction of variance explained (FVE).

After the construction of progression curves of PTSS, depressive symptom, and LOFG thickness measure using FPCA, associations between these measures with PTSD symptom severity were examined using functional regression analysis (FRA) to identify relative contributions of these measures to PTSS. FRA is a statistical technique for modeling relationships between one or more functional predictors and a response. FRA offers several advantages over regular regression, for example, it can take into account the entire functional process rather than just individual points in time or space, and it can capture complex dynamic relationships that might be missed by regular regression. In the current study, PTSS trajectory was used as the dependent variable and other measures were utilized as covariates to define how these factors longitudinally affect PTSD symptoms at different times after trauma. This can be expressed as:

$$PTSS_i(t) = \beta_0(t) + \beta_1(t)Depression_i(t) + \beta\_2(t)LOFG\_i(t) + \varepsilon\_i(t)$$

where subject i's PTSS, Depression and LOFG thickness at time t are $PTSS\_i(t)$, $Depression\_i(t)$ and $LOFG\_i(t)$ respectively. $\beta\_1(t)$ is the function estimation of association between Depression and PTSS, $\beta\_2(t)$ is the function estimation of association between LOFG thickness and PTSS at time t.

3 Results

3.1 Sample Characteristics

Data from 252 trauma survivors were included in the final analyses. Participants' demographic information, baseline clinical, brain structure, and other information were summarized in Table 1.

Table 1. Sample characteristics.

	Mean (SD) or n (%)
Age	32.31 (10.99)
Sex (female)	167 (66.27%)
Race	
White/Caucasian	89 (35.32%)
Black/African American	84 (33.34%)
Bi-Racial	2 (0.8%)
Asian	2 (0.8%)
Other/Refuse to report	75 (29.76%)
Trauma type	
Motor vehicle accident	177 (70.24%)
Physical assault	58 (23.02%)
Sexual assault	11 (4.37%)
Other	6 (2.38%)
Baseline measures	
PCL	46.97 (16.31)
Depressive symptom	17.22 (10.50)
LOFG thickness	2.60 (0.15)

Note. PCL = PTSD Checklist; LOFG = lateral orbitofrontal gyrus.

3.2 Post-trauma Progressions of PTSS, Depressive Symptoms, and LOFG Thickness

Non-linear trajectories of depression symptom severity scores were modeled as functional curves to best fit to measured depression scores of each subject, using data from 252 subjects at variable time points over 120 days with 4 functional principal components (fraction of variance explained = 0.95). Eigenfunctions were estimated using observed depression scores and post-trauma days only. Figure 1 depicts PTSS trajectories from 3 randomly selected subjects (curves in different color and "x" indicates observed values).

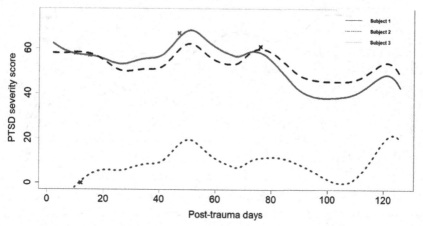

Fig. 1. Estimation of individual post-trauma stress symptom trajectories from 3 randomly selected trauma survivors. "X" indicates observed values.

The same approach was also used to model non-linear depressive symptom and brain structural measures (i.e., right LOFG thickness) over time. Figures 2 and 3 depict depressive symptom and right LOFG thickness from another 3 randomly selected subjects, respectively (curves in different color and "x" indicates observed values).

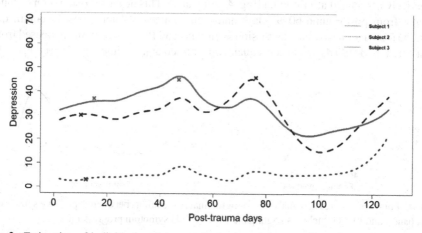

Fig. 2. Estimation of individual post-trauma depressive symptom trajectories from 3 randomly selected trauma survivors. "X" indicates observed values.

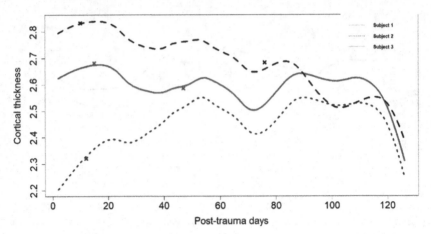

Fig. 3. Estimation of individual post-trauma right LOFG thickness trajectories from 3 randomly selected trauma survivors. "X" indicates observed values.

3.3 Functional Regression Analysis of Longitudinal Associations Between Depressive Symptoms and LOFG Thickness with PTSD Symptom Progressions

The results from FRA revealed that right LOFG thickness and PTSD symptoms were negatively associated after trauma (Fig. 4, left panel). This negative association became greater from post-trauma 60–90 days and then lessened at later times. In contrast, a positive association between depression symptoms and PTSD symptoms increased from post-trauma 40–100 days and subsequently decreased at later times (Fig. 4, right panel).

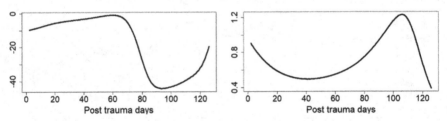

Fig. 4. Functional regression analysis of longitudinal associations between depressive symptoms (left panel) and LOFG thickness (right panel) with PTSD symptom progression.

4   Discussion

In the current study, we used FDA for analyzing data combined from two existing longitudinal acute trauma studies. Our results showed that FDA is a potentially superior analytical tool for estimating dynamic post-trauma symptom progression trajectories because it 1) makes full use of the data and can capture and retain the inherent temporal structure of the data; 2) is able to handle high-dimensional data, and 3) can model complex relationships between different functional variables and provides a more accurate and detailed understanding of the relationship in the data. Our example demonstrated how FPCA and FRA can be used to provide new insight into longitudinal associations of behavioral, brain structural, and other factors with PTSD symptoms.

Specifically, we first used FPCA to construct post-trauma progressions of brain (i.e., right LOFG thickness) and clinical (i.e., depression symptom) measures. We then used FRA to examine associations of these measures with PTSD symptoms, in which the directions of associations were in line with the current literature [1, 2, 5]. Importantly, we characterized the dynamic changing nature of these associations, where varying contributions of these two measures to the PTSS were revealed.

Despite successfully employing FDA to estimate the dynamic post-trauma trajectories of cortical brain measures, depressive symptoms, and PTSD symptoms, and exploring their interrelations, certain limitations of this study must be acknowledged. Primarily, the study predominantly involved trauma survivors from motor vehicle accidents or instances of interpersonal violence. Consequently, the results might not be generalized to survivors exposed to different forms of traumatic events. Furthermore, the FRA model incorporated merely two predictors. We anticipate that future studies, by including a wider array of relevant predictors and expanding the sample sizes, could yield more accurate and robust estimations of post-trauma progression and its associations with PTSD progression.

In summary, to supplement mainstream chronic PTSD work, advancing our understanding of early post-trauma longitudinal trajectories of PTSD symptoms is warranted. In the current study, we demonstrated FDA as a potential superior approach to achieve this goal. First, FPCA and FRA are capable of comprehensively examining early post-trauma longitudinal interactions between PTSD symptoms, behavioral, brain structural, and other factors. Additionally, FDA is a flexible analytic framework that can analyze pooled data from existing individual longitudinal studies that involved differing sampling characteristics, such as interval post-trauma before assessment, subsequent assessment intervals, and study durations. In summary, utilizing the innovative FDA approaches, researchers could contribute to a better understanding of PTSD development, improve the efficacy of individualized PTSD preventive interventions, and have a broad impact on mental health research fields.

References

1. Shalev, A., Liberzon, I., Marmar, C.: Post-traumatic stress disorder. N. Engl. J. Med. **376**(25), 2459–2469 (2017)
2. Bryant, R.A.: Post-traumatic stress disorder: a state-of-the-art review of evidence and challenges. World Psychiatry **18**(3), 259–269 (2019)
3. Scheeringa, M.S., et al.: Factors affecting the diagnosis and prediction of PTSD symptomatology in children and adolescents. Am. J. Psychiatry **163**(4), 644–651 (2006)
4. Karl, A., et al.: A meta-analysis of structural brain abnormalities in PTSD. Neurosci. Biobehav. Rev. **30**(7), 1004–1031 (2006)
5. Wang, X., et al.: Cortical volume abnormalities in posttraumatic stress disorder: an ENIGMA-psychiatric genomics consortium PTSD workgroup mega-analysis. Mol. Psychiatry **26**(8), 4331–4343 (2021)

6. McLean, S.A., et al.: The AURORA study: a longitudinal, multimodal library of brain biology and function after traumatic stress exposure. Mol. Psychiatry **25**(2), 283–296 (2020)

7. Xie, H., et al.: Relationship of hippocampal volumes and posttraumatic stress disorder symptoms over early posttrauma periods. Biol. Psychiatry: Cogn. Neurosci. Neuroimaging **3**(11), 968–975 (2018)

8. Xie, H., et al.: Adverse childhood experiences associate with early post-trauma thalamus and thalamic nuclei volumes and PTSD development in adulthood. Psychiatry Res.: Neuroimaging **319**, 111421 (2022)

9. Bryant, R.A., et al.: Trajectory of post-traumatic stress following traumatic injury: 6-year follow-up. Br. J. Psychiatry **206**(5), 417–423 (2015)

10. Galatzer-Levy, I.R., et al.: Early PTSD symptom trajectories: persistence, recovery, and response to treatment: results from the Jerusalem Trauma Outreach and Prevention Study (J-TOPS). PLoS ONE **8**(8), e70084 (2013)

11. Connor, J.P., Brier, Z.M.F., Price, M.: The association between pain trajectories with PTSD, depression, and disability during the acute post trauma period. Psychosom. Med. **82**(9), 862 (2020)

12. Zhang, J., et al.: Trajectory of post-traumatic stress and depression among children and adolescents following single-incident trauma. Eur. J. Psychotraumatol. **13**(1), 2037906 (2022)

13. Lowe, S.R., et al.: Posttraumatic stress disorder symptom trajectories within the first year following emergency department admissions: pooled results from the International Consortium to predict PTSD. Psychol. Med. **51**(7), 1129–1139 (2021)

14. Blevins, C.A., et al.: The posttraumatic stress disorder checklist for DSM-5 (PCL-5): development and initial psychometric evaluation. J. Trauma. Stress **28**(6), 489–498 (2015)

15. Weathers, F.W., et al.: The PTSD Checklist (PCL): Reliability, Validity, and Diagnostic Utility. San Antonio, TX (1993)

16. Cohen, P., et al.: The problem of units and the circumstance for POMP. Multivar. Behav. Res. **34**(3), 315–346 (1999)

17. Radloff, L.S.: The CES-D scale: a self-report depression scale for research in the general population. Appl. Psychol. Meas. **1**(3), 385–401 (1977)

18. Rush, A.J., et al.: The 16-item quick inventory of depressive symptomatology (QIDS), clinician rating (QIDS-C), and self-report (QIDS-SR): a psychometric evaluation in patients with chronic major depression. Biol. Psychiatry **54**(5), 573–583 (2003)

19. Fischl, B.: FreeSurfer. Neuroimage **62**(2), 774–781 (2012)

20. Wang, J.-L., Chiou, J.-M., Müller, H.-G.: Functional data analysis. Ann. Rev. Stat. Appl. **3**, 257–295 (2016)

21. Yao, F., Müller, H.-G., Wang, J.-L.: Functional data analysis for sparse longitudinal data. J. Am. Stat. Assoc. **100**(470), 577–590 (2005)

Comparison Between Explainable AI Algorithms for Alzheimer's Disease Prediction Using EfficientNet Models

Sobhana Jahan[1,2](✉) ⓘ, Md. Rawnak Saif Adib[3] ⓘ, Mufti Mahmud[4] ⓘ,
and M. Shamim Kaiser[5] ⓘ

[1] Department of Computer Science and Engineering, Bangladesh University
of Professionals, Dhaka, Bangladesh
sobhana@bup.edu.bd
[2] Department of Information and Communication Technology,
Bangladesh University of Professionals, Dhaka, Bangladesh
[3] Department of Computer Science and Engineering, International University
of Business Agriculture and Technology, Dhaka, Bangladesh
saifadib.cse@iubat.edu
[4] Department of Computer Science, Nottingham Trent University,
Clifton Lane, Nottingham NG11 8NS, UK
mufti.mahmud@ntu.ac.uk
[5] Institute of Information and Technology, Jahangirnagar University,
Dhaka, Bangladesh
mskaiser@juniv.edu

Abstract. Alzheimer's disease (AD) is a common form of dementia that affects brain regions that control cognition, memory, and language. Globally, more than 55 million people are suffering from dementia. Given these troubling statistics, predicting AD is critical for future medications and treatment. Mild Cognitive Impairment (MCI) is a vital stage for patients because from this stage a majority of patients turn into AD patients. Early MCI (EMCI) and Late MCI (LMCI) are vital two stages of MCI. Successful prediction of Cognitive Normal (CN), AD, MCI, EMCI, and LMCI stages is a big challenge. Although there are models for predicting these stages but all models are not near to accurate. One major concern for these lacking is not having sufficient datasets to train the model. Data augmentation can be a solution to create an abundance of MRI data. One major issue regarding Machine Learning (ML) is the black box nature. Due to this limitation, user satisfaction as well as trust in the model's prediction is missing. Explainable Artificial Intelligence (XAI) is the torchbearer approach and through this, the reason behind every decision can be observed by the user. This paper proposes a comparison between four XAI models named Gradient-weighted Class Activation Mapping (Grad-CAM), Grad-CAM++, Score-weighted CAM (Score-CAM), and Faster Score-CAM. For performing the five classes (CN, AD, EMCI, MCI, and LMCI) prediction, EfficientNet models are used because these models have performed well on the augmented dataset. Among EfficientNet models (B0-B7), EfficientNetB7 has performed the best. The testing accuracy

© The Author(s), under exclusive license to Springer Nature Switzerland AG 2023
F. Liu et al. (Eds.): BI 2023, LNAI 13974, pp. 357–368, 2023.
https://doi.org/10.1007/978-3-031-43075-6_31

and loss are 96.34% and 0.12, respectively. After that, the last layer of the EfficientNetB7 model is passed to the XAI models. Comparing the four XAI models it is observed that Grad-CAM++ and Score-CAM are better performing than others.

Keywords: Explainable AI (XAI) · Artificial Intelligence (AI) · Alzheimer's Disease (AD) · Dementia · EfficientNet · Grad CAM · Grad CAM++ · Score CAM · Faster Score CAM

1   Introduction

The most typical cause of dementia is Alzheimer's disease. Although the precise cause of Alzheimer's disease remains unclear, there are a few factors that are believed to raise your risk of getting the illness [6]. These include getting older, having the condition run in the family, untreated depression (even though it can also be one of the symptoms of Alzheimer's disease), and conditions and lifestyle choices linked to cardiovascular disease [8] and [9]. Data from population-based studies conducted across Europe reveal that the age-standardized prevalence of dementia and AD, respectively, is 6.4% and 4.4%, respectively, among adults 65 and older. The prevalence of AD was 9.7% in the study of a nationwide representative sample of Americans over the age of 70. According to estimates, 3.9% of individuals aged 60 and older worldwide have dementia, with a regional prevalence of 1.6% in Africa, 4.0% in China and the Western Pacific, 4.6% in Latin America, 5.4% in Western Europe, and 6.4% in North America. Approximately 5 million new cases of dementia are diagnosed each year, affecting more than 25 million people worldwide, the majority of whom have AD. Every 20 years, it's expected that the population of dementia sufferers will double. Mild Cognitive Impairment (MCI) is a crucial stage for patients since most patients progress from this stage into AD patients [7]. People with MCI who have abnormal results from a brain Magnetic Resonance Imaging (MRI), Positron Emission Tomography (PET) scan or a spinal fluid test for amyloid beta protein, the protein found in amyloid plaques (one of the two characteristic features of AD), are thought to have MCI as a result of AD. There are two crucial stages of MCI which are: Early MCI (EMCI) and Late MCI (LMCI) that was stated by the Alzheimer's Disease Neuroimaging Initiative (ADNI). From the ADNI-2 MCI cohort, 336 people with MCI and 294 people who were cognitively normal (CN) participated in a study conducted by EC Edmonds et al. [3].

Transfer learning is a deep learning approach that involves training a neural network model on an issue that is identical to the one that has to be addressed. Transfer learning provides the benefit of shortening a learning model's training period and lowering generalization error. The pre-trained models are often developed using sizable datasets, which serve as a common benchmark in the field of computer vision. Other computer vision tasks can use the weights derived from the models. When the training dataset is tiny, transfer learning is especially helpful. In this situation, for instance, start the weights of the new model using that from the pre-trained models. As it can be seen in a moment, transfer learning can also be used to solve issues with natural language processing. Convolutional Neural Network (CNN) models belonging to the EfficientNet family effectively expand with respect to layer depth, width, input resolution, or a blend of all of these. Using EfficientNet, it can extract features from photos that can then be fed into a classifier. Explainable Artificial Intelligence (XAI) is a useful tool for addressing the trust of the user as the decision-making features are clearly indicated in the XAI model. As a result, XAI has been recognized by AI researchers as a crucial component of reliable AI, and explainability has recently attracted more emphasis. The main objectives of this research work are:

1. To study AD and its existing prediction techniques
2. To propose an explainable model for the prediction of AD
3. To evaluate the performance of the proposed model in predicting the AD
4. To evaluate the performance of the four XAI models

The rest of the paper is organized as follows: Sect. 2 contains related works, Sect. 3 describes the background information related to the research study, Sect. 4 contains the proposed methodology, Sect. 5 describes the performance analysis, and finally Sect. 6 shows the concluding remarks.

2 Related Works

Using the benchmark ADNI dataset, Sharen et al. [13] proposed EfficietNetB7 architecture to evaluate and enhance the prediction with pre-trained weights. Layer-wise tuning entails training a predetermined set of layers using MRI images to further fine-tune the network. The proposed trained model for classifying AD achieves improved F1-score and accuracy of 0.91 and 89.7%, respectively. A deep transfer learning model was proposed by Sisodia et al. [14] to identify the various phases of Alzheimer's disease, including "Mild-Demented", "Very-Mild-Demented", "Moderate-Demented", and "No-Demented". By applying data preprocessing and augmentation techniques, the model is able to identify the appropriate class of AD. The early phases of AD are then classified and predicted using Resnet50, DenseNet201, VGG19, Xception, and EfficientNetB7 models. The best performance is noted for the DenseNet201 model, which has an accuracy of 96.59%. With validation accuracy of 93.52%, 89.77%, 95.08%, and 83.20%, respectively, the performance of the Resnet50, Xception, VGG19, and EfficientNetB7 models.

Sethi et al. [12] used an EfficientNet to classify participants as Cognitive Normal (CN) vs AD based on brain MRI scans. The Alzheimer Disease Neuroimaging Initiative (ADNI) provided the dataset for this investigation. The model was evaluated using performance parameters such as accuracy and AUC. In comparison to other current transfer learning models, the proposed model on the ADNI dataset obtained an accuracy of 91.36% and an AUC of 83%. Using the EfficientNet-B7 convolutional neural network architecture, Jahan et al. [4] provided a novel Grad-CAM-based explanation of Alzheimer's disease prediction. In this paper, the author classified the four phases of Alzheimer's disease-CN, LMCI, EMCI, and AD. The achieved accuracy for four-class classification using the basic dataset and augmented ADNI dataset is 73.47% and 91.76%, respectively.

3 Background

3.1 Prediction Model

EfficientNet. EfficientNet is a convolutional neural network design and scaling method that uses a compound coefficient to consistently scale all the dimensions of width/depth/resolution. It is a transfer learning model which is very efficient in both execution time and accuracy. There are a total of 8 versions or forms of EfficientNet starting from B0-B7 [15].

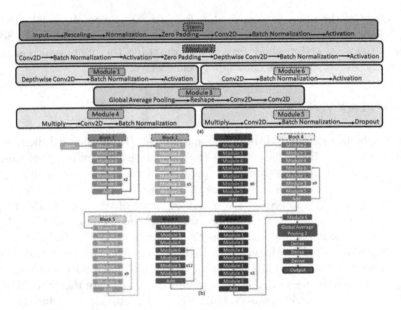

Fig. 1. Architecture of EfficientNetB7. (a) Six modules and stem of EfficientNetB7 and (b) Seven blocks of EfficientNetB7.

The EfficientNetB7 model has 873 levels in total. All 873 levels are divided into a total of seven layers. the final three levels of the last layer (seventh) were customized by inserting dense layers. The first two of those three layers are designated as Dense layers with a unit of "128" and a function for activation of "ReLu". The output layer, which is the final layer, comprises the unit value "4" and the "softmax" activation function for five-class categorization. The remaining layers of the EfficientNetB7, default model are used [5]. Figure 1 resembles the entire architecture of EfficientNetB7.

3.2 Explainable AI Algorithms

Gradient-Weighted Class Activation Mapping (Grad-CAM). Grad-CAM [10] is a post-hoc attention method, which means it produces heatmaps that is applied to an already-trained neural network once training is finished and the parameters are set. This is separate from trainable attention, which entails learning specific parameters to build attention maps as well as heatmaps during training sessions. Grad-CAM does not necessitate a specific CNN architecture. The last CNN layer of the classification model is passed through the Grad CAM [11]. Grad-CAM is a generalization of CAM (class activation mapping). Grad-CAM consists of three steps: Calculate the Gradient, Averaging Gradients to Determine Alphas or weight value, and produce the Final Grad-CAM Heatmap. Grad-CAM++ can be defined as follows: Here, W_k^c resembles weight and Y^c is the class score. W_k^c independent of the positions (i, j) of a particular activation map G^k. Z is a constant which resembles the number of pixels in the activation map.

$$W_{k-Grad-CAM}^c = 1/Z \sum_i \sum_j (\delta Y^c / \delta G_{ij}^k) \tag{1}$$

Grad-CAM++. Grad-CAM++ [1] was created with the goal of delivering better localization than Grad-CAM. While instances of an object appearing in various locations or leaving footprints in various feature maps, a simple average of the gradients at every map of features might not offer a good localization of the areas of interest because the units in every feature map may have distinct "importance" that the gradient alone does not fully capture. Grad-CAM++ is a model that is replacing the simple average of gradients at every feature map with a weighted average [2]. Grad-CAM++ can be defined as follows: Here, W_k^c resembles weight and Y^c is the class score. W_k^c independent of the positions (i, j) of a particular activation map G^k.

$$W_{k-Grad-CAM++}^c = \sum_i \sum_j \gamma_{ij}^{kc} ReLu(\delta Y^c / \delta G_{ij}^k) \tag{2}$$

Score-Weighted CAM (Score-CAM). Score CAM [16] is an attribution approach derived from the Grad CAM method. Grad CAM addressed the fundamental difficulties of the CAM approach, including its reliance on classifier architecture, gradient saturation, gradient vanishing, and false confidence issues. Score-CAM is an attribution method based on Grad CAM, however, it is a gradient-free masking XAI model. Instead of gradients, Score-CAM builds activation maps by increasing confidence. Then, for each activation map, mask the given image and determine its score. Score-CAM's pipeline is broken into two parts. Phase 1 begins with the extraction of activation maps. Each activation is then applied to the actual image as a mask to acquire its forward-passing score on the target class. The second phase is repeated N times, where N is the number of instances of activation maps. Finally, a linear mixture of activation maps and score-based weights can be used to obtain the outcome. The CNN module used in Phases 1 and 2 serves as the feature extractor. Score-CAM can be defined as follows: C() resembles the activation map B_l^k.

$$L_{Score-CAM}^c = ReLu(\sum \beta_k^c B_l^k); where : \beta_k^c = C(B_l^k) \tag{3}$$

Faster Score-CAM. While Score-CAM is an excellent method, it does take longer to process than other CAM methods. Score-CAM is more efficient when it is faster. This was accomplished by employing only the dominant channels with considerable differences as the mask image. As a result, a CAM version that is ten times faster than Score-CAM is created.

4 Proposed Methodology

4.1 Dataset Acquisition and Preparation

The Alzheimer Disease Neuroimaging Initiative-ADNI data collection is considered the gold standard for detecting Alzheimer's disease. ADNI was founded in 2003 by Dr. Michael W. Weiner and is sponsored through public-private partnerships. The ADNI is a multisite, long-term study that aims to establish clinical, genetic, imaging, and biomarkers for the early diagnosis of Alzheimer's disease. There are 1800 themes in these three databases, including ADNI 3, ADNI 2, ADNI GO, and ADNI. In this study, a subset of the ADNI dataset is utilized to train, validate, and test several CNN classifier designs. This study uses axial T2-Star weighted longitudinal MRI data from 145 AD, 493 CN, 204 EMCI, 198 MCI, and 61 LMCI. Therefore, 1,101 MRI data points are used in the base dataset.

Rotating and resizing data are used as a part of the data preprocessing. The next step was to do picture augmentation, a man-made method for expanding a training dataset by creating altered versions of the photos. This work does augmentation using a 5-unit rotation, a 0.1 width and 0.1 height shift, a horizontal flip, and 0.1 zooms. Following data augmentation, we were able to produce a collection of 10,025 data, which included 2025 CN, 2000 LMCI, 2000 EMCI, 2000 MCI, and 2000 AD. Here, 85% of the image data is used for training, and the remaining 15% is used for testing. From the training set 20% data are kept for the validation purpose.

4.2 Proposed XAI-Based Classification Architecture

The model architecture of this study work is depicted in Fig. 2. T2 star MRI images of five categories of subjects (CN, AD, EMCI, MCI, and LMCI) are used in this study. Initially, 1,101 MRI scans are used for this work. We did image rotation, scaling, and data augmentation to prepare the dataset. We used augmentation to create a large enough dataset for the EfficientNet-B7 model. After augmentation, the total number of data is 10,025 which is adequate for

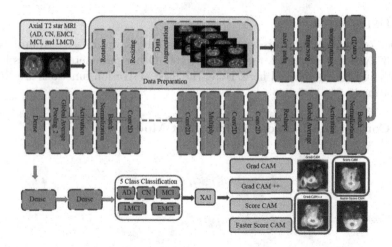

Fig. 2. The proposed model architecture for explainable Alzheimer's prediction.

the EfficientNet-B7 CNN model. The classification result was obtained after we executed the classification operation with the EfficientNet-B7 pre-trained CNN model. The 'top conv layer' which is the last layer of EfficientNetB7 is the input of the XAI model. We employed the four XAI algorithms Grad CAM, Grad CAM++, Score CAM, and Faster Score CAM to visualize the decision-making sections of the MRI images.

5 Performance Analysis

5.1 Performance Metrics

A confusion matrix is a summary of the predicted outcomes from a classification issue. We may calculate Accuracy, Precision, Recall, and F1-score from the confusion matrix by utilizing True Positive (TP), True Negative (TN), False Positive (FP), and False Negative (FN) values. The following are the rules for Accuracy, Precision, Recall, and F1-score:

$$Precision = \frac{TP}{TP + FP} \tag{4}$$

$$Recall = \frac{TP}{TP + FN} \tag{5}$$

$$Accuracy = \frac{TP + TN}{TP + TN + FN + FP} \tag{6}$$

$$F1 - score = 2 \times \frac{Precision \times Recall}{Precision + Recall} \tag{7}$$

5.2 Hyperparameters

The set of hyperparameters tuned in this study is optimizer = Adam, batch size = 32, pooling = average, and epochs = 100. Other parameters such as learning rate and loss were fixed here. Here, the used activation functions are ReLU, and softmax.

5.3 Comparison Between EfficientNet Models

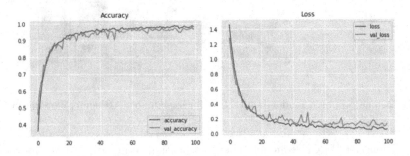

Fig. 3. Training and testing Accuracy and loss for EfficientNetB7 model.

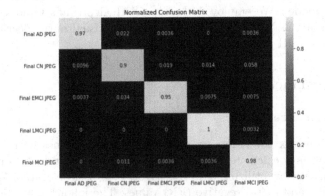

Fig. 4. Confusion matrix for EfficientNetB7 model.

Figure 3 shows the comparison between training and validation accuracy and loss. It is clearly visible that the model is well-trained. The confusion matrix is shown in Fig. 4 which is resembling the high scores through the main diagonal. So, it can be stated that the model is well-trained and tested. The class-wise Precision, Reall, and F1-score of the proposed EfficientNetB7 model are presented in Table 1. The testing accuracy and loss of the eight EfficientNet models are shown in Table 2. EfficientNetB7 is the best-performing model as it provides 96.34% accuracy and 0.12 loss. Bold-marked values are resembling the highest values. Table 3 is showing the comparison between recently published work and our proposed work. It is clear that our model is the best performing among them.

Table 1. Precision, Reall, and F1-score of the proposed EfficientNetB7 architecture.

Class	Precision	Recall	F1-score
AD	**99%**	97%	98%
CN	91%	90%	91%
EMCI	98%	95%	96%
MCI	94%	98%	96%
LMCI	98%	**100%**	**99%**

Table 2. Accuracy of eight EfficientNet models.

Model	Accuracy	Loss
EfficientNetB0	95.59%	0.19
EfficientNetB1	94.77%	0.19
EfficientNetB2	93.65%	0.15
EfficientNetB3	95.07%	0.13
EfficientNetB4	95.02%	0.20
EfficientNetB5	94.43%	0.14
EfficientNetB6	93.75%	0.18
EfficientNetB7	**96.34%**	**0.12**

Table 3. Accuracy comparison between recently published similar work and our proposed work.

Author	Model	Accuracy
Sharen et al. [13]	EfficientNetB7	91%
Sisodia et al. [14]	EfficientnetB7	83.20%
Sethi et al. [12]	EfficientNet	91.36%
Jahan et al. [4]	EfficientNetB7	91.67%
Our proposed work	EfficientNetB7	**96.34%**

5.4   XAI Result Visualization

The XAI explanation of MRI data using EfficientNetB7 is shown in Fig. 5, 6, and 7. The outputs of the four XAI methods are framed side by side to understand the exact difference between their performance. AD, CN, EMCI, MCI, and LMCI classes are classified perfectly. To evaluate the decision of XAI, each prediction result of XAI models is compared to the actual class or label. In most cases, it is found that the actual class is similar to the XAI result. Here in this paper, the XAI output of the three most difficult classifications (AD, CN, and EMCI) are discussed only. From Fig. 5, it is clear that AD is predicted properly. The performance of Grad CAM is poor than other XAI models because

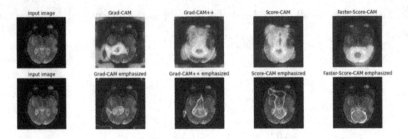

Fig. 5. XAI explanation for AD class.

Grad-CAM highlights regions of an image that a model did not actually use for prediction. For example, the Grad CAM is taking the side background of the image and the left edge of the MRI image for prediction. This means Grad-CAM is an unreliable model explanation method. Grad CAM++ and Score CAM are the best-performing XAI models because they don't create problems like Grad CAM and also Grad CAM++ and Score CAM the exact brain region which is responsible for this AD prediction. Though Faster Score-CAM is 10 times fast performing than Score CAM, in this case, Faster Score-CAM is not locating the entire responsible brain region. It is just locating a small portion of the brain responsible for the decision. So, among these four XAI models, Grad CAM is poorly performing, Faster Score CAM is average performing, and Grad CAM++ and Score CAM are the best-performing models.

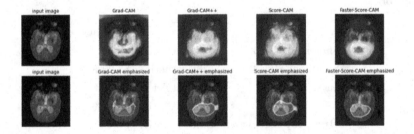

Fig. 6. XAI explanation for CN class.

Now, for CN prediction in Fig. 6, all four XAI models are well-performing as they are locating a similar region of the brain. Still, the performance of Grad CAM is a little bit poor that the other three models. Correctly classifying the EMCI is tough work to do. Here, in Fig. 7, Grad CAM is very poor performing as it is locating the background and the upper right edge of the MRI. Though the Grad CAM ++ is correctly locating the responsible brain region a bit of background is also misallocated by it. Score CAM and Faster Score CAM are good performing here in this case. So, it can be concluded that the performance of Grad CAM, Faster Score CAM, Grad CAM++, and Score CAM, and are poor, good, better, and best, respectively.

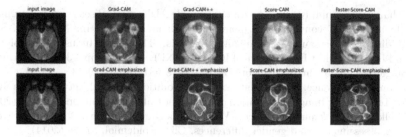

Fig. 7. XAI explanation for EMCI class.

6 Conclusion

Alzheimer's does not develop naturally as individuals become older. Since there is currently no treatment for this illness, it is crucial that we look for the early warning signs and symptoms and make every effort to reduce their severity. Additionally, more research and study will aid us in the battle against this illness. The four Explainable AI algorithms (Gradient-weighted Class Activation Mapping (Grad-CAM), Grad-CAM++, Score-weighted CAM (Score-CAM), and Faster Score-CAM) utilized in this study's prediction of Alzheimer's disease utilizing the models of EfficientNet have been compared. There are eight EfficientNet models in total. EfficientNet-B0 is the baseline network, and Efficient-B1 through B7 are obtained by scaling up the baseline network. For the patients, CN, AD, MCI, EMCI, and LMCI stages are predicted and then results are compared. The EfficientNet model with the most levels, B7, achieved the greatest results, with an accuracy of 96.34% and a loss of 0.12. The EfficientNetB7 model's final layer is then applied to the XAI models. When the four XAI models are compared, Grad-CAM++ and Score-CAM perform better than the other three. In the future, using multiple robots the XAI results should be generated and the type of explanation selection will determine which robot is most suitable to the medical examiner.

Acknowledgement. This research work is funded by the ICT Division, Bangladesh; Masters level fellowship 2020–2021 session.

References

1. Chattopadhay, A., Sarkar, A., Howlader, P., Balasubramanian, V.N.: Grad-CAM++: generalized gradient-based visual explanations for deep convolutional networks. In: 2018 IEEE Winter Conference on Applications of Computer Vision (WACV), pp. 839–847. IEEE (2018)
2. Chattopadhyay, A., Sarkar, A., Howlader, P., Balasubramanian, V.: Grad-CAM++: improved visual explanations for deep convolutional networks, arXiv preprint arXiv:1710.11063 (2018)
3. Edmonds, E.C., et al.: Early versus late MCI: improved MCI staging using a neuropsychological approach. Alzheimer's Dementia **15**(5), 699–708 (2019)

4. Jahan, S., Shamim Kaiser, M.: An explainable Alzheimer's disease prediction using EfficientNet-B7 convolutional neural network architecture. In: Majumder, S.P., Siddique, N., Hossain, M.S., Hossain, M.S. (eds.) The Fourth Industrial Revolution and Beyond: Select Proceedings of IC4IR+. LNEE, vol. 980, pp. 737–748. Springer, Singapore (2023). https://doi.org/10.1007/978-981-19-8032-9_53

5. Koonce, B., Koonce, B.: Efficientnet. In: Convolutional Neural Networks with Swift for TensorFlow: Image Recognition and Dataset Categorization, pp. 109–123 (2021)

6. Mielke, M.M., Vemuri, P., Rocca, W.A.: Clinical epidemiology of Alzheimer's disease: assessing sex and gender differences. Clin. Epidemiol. 37–48 (2014)

7. Nestor, P.J., Scheltens, P., Hodges, J.R.: Advances in the early detection of Alzheimer's disease. Nat. Med. 10(Suppl 7), S34–S41 (2004)

8. Qiu, C., Kivipelto, M., Von Strauss, E.: Epidemiology of Alzheimer's disease: occurrence, determinants, and strategies toward intervention. Dialogues Clin. Neurosci. (2022)

9. Reitz, C., Brayne, C., Mayeux, R.: Epidemiology of Alzheimer disease. Nat. Rev. Neurol. 7(3), 137–152 (2011)

10. Selvaraju, R.R., Cogswell, M., Das, A., Vedantam, R., Parikh, D., Batra, D.: Grad-CAM: visual explanations from deep networks via gradient-based localization. In: Proceedings of the IEEE International Conference on Computer Vision, pp. 618–626 (2017)

11. Selvaraju, R.R., Das, A., Vedantam, R., Cogswell, M., Parikh, D., Batra, D.: Grad-CAM: why did you say that? arXiv preprint arXiv:1611.07450 (2016)

12. Sethi, M., Ahuja, S., Singh, S., Snehi, J., Chawla, M.: An intelligent framework for Alzheimer's disease classification using efficientnet transfer learning model. In: 2022 International Conference on Emerging Smart Computing and Informatics (ESCI), pp. 1–4. IEEE (2022)

13. Sharen, H., Dhanush, B., Rukmani, P., Dhanya, D.: Efficient diagnosis of Alzheimer's disease using efficientnet in neuroimaging. In: Shaw, R.N., Das, S., Piuri, V., Bianchini, M. (eds.) ICACIT 2022. LNEE, vol. 914, pp. 211–223. Springer, Cham (2022). https://doi.org/10.1007/978-981-19-2980-9_18

14. Sisodia, P.S., Ameta, G.K., Kumar, Y., Chaplot, N.: A review of deep transfer learning approaches for class-wise prediction of Alzheimer's disease using MRI images. Arch. Comput. Methods Eng. 30, 2409–2429 (2023)

15. Tan, M., Le, Q.: EfficientNet: rethinking model scaling for convolutional neural networks. In: International Conference on Machine Learning, pp. 6105–6114. PMLR (2019)

16. Wang, H., et al.: Score-CAM: score-weighted visual explanations for convolutional neural networks. In: Proceedings of the IEEE/CVF Conference on Computer Vision and Pattern Recognition Workshops, pp. 24–25 (2020)

Social and Non-social Reward Learning Contexts for Detection of Major Depressive Disorder Using EEG: A Machine Learning Approach

Philopateer Ghattas[1], Mai Gamal[1], and Seif Eldawlatly[2,3](✉)

[1] Computer Science and Engineering Department, Faculty of Media Engineering and Technology, German University in Cairo, Cairo, Egypt
philopateer.ghattas@student.guc.edu.eg, mai.tharwat@guc.edu.eg
[2] Computer and Systems Engineering Department, Faculty of Engineering, Ain Shams University, Cairo, Egypt
seldawlatly@eng.asu.edu.eg
[3] Computer Science and Engineering Department, The American University in Cairo, Cairo, Egypt

Abstract. Major Depressive Disorder (MDD) is a leading cause of disability globally and a major cause of suicide deaths. Improving our understanding of MDD is expected to inspire better objective diagnostic and treatment tools which may decrease the burden of disease worldwide. MDD is associated with social impairments and reward processing aberrations. However, the interaction between social cognition and reward learning in MDD is not well understood. In this work, we aim to study the effect of integrating social information with reward learning in MDD using an EEG-based machine learning approach. We recorded EEG data from subjects during their participation in a reward learning experiment in social and non-social contexts. We then extracted linear and nonlinear features from the EEG data to detect MDD using Support Vector Machine (SVM) and K-Nearest Neighbors (KNN) classifiers. Our results show that the data collected during social contexts achieved broadly higher classification accuracies compared to non-social contexts reaching 80% using multi-channels. Moreover, single-channel data achieved comparable and even better accuracies than multi-channels with also superior performance in social contexts reaching 85.7%. In the sub-band classification analysis, beta and alpha bands were considerably better than theta and delta bands. Surprisingly, the non-social context had the highest accuracy in the beta band while the social context had the highest accuracy in the alpha band. The results were consistent when using single features compared to combining the features. These findings show the notable role of social information with reward processing in advancing our understanding of MDD and its subtypes which can guide the improvement of diagnostic and personalized treatment tools.

Keywords: MDD · EEG · Reward Learning · Social Cognition

© The Author(s), under exclusive license to Springer Nature Switzerland AG 2023
F. Liu et al. (Eds.): BI 2023, LNAI 13974, pp. 369–382, 2023.
https://doi.org/10.1007/978-3-031-43075-6_32

1   Introduction

Major Depressive Disorder (MDD) is a common psychiatric disorder that is a major contributor to suicide deaths. It is characterized by persistent depressed mood, lack of energy, and cognitive and social impairments [8]. MDD is a leading cause of disability, affecting approximately 300 million people globally [35] and it is expected to be the first cause of the burden of disease worldwide by 2030 [8]. Despite the huge burden caused by MDD worldwide, it is still not well understood, diagnosed, or treated due to its complexity and heterogeneity [30]. A key factor for understanding MDD is reward processing aberrations which are proposed to be a candidate mechanism of MDD pathophysiology [19] and a promising biological marker of MDD [22]. Given that most human behaviors and learning occur in social contexts and many human decisions are acquired through social learning, reward processing mechanisms in the brain are not isolated from human social cognition. This is increasingly important while studying MDD given its association with social impairments and poor social functioning [20,26]. Despite this fact, multiple studies have been focusing on reward processing in non-social contexts [13], while reward processing in social contexts is not widely assessed and its role in MDD is still unclear [12,26]. Consequently, our focus in this work is on using reward processing signals for identifying MDD not only in non-social contexts but also in social contexts. To achieve this objective, we use a machine learning approach that is applied to electroencephalography (EEG) signals. EEG has been widely used for studying MDD and developing biomarkers due to its capability to identify neurological effects of MDD on the brain [4,11,15]. EEG signals also allow for studying MDD in different frequency bands of brain activity [4,11,15] and in different brain regions based on the EEG channel locations [7]. Moreover, analysis of EEG signals using machine learning methods showed great success in better understanding and detecting MDD, especially with the development of computational psychiatry [9]. However, most of MDD studies applied machine learning to resting state EEG with limited work on EEG signals that are based on reward learning tasks [9,15].

    In this study, we aim to leverage the success of machine learning and EEG in studying reward processing in MDD in the presence and absence of social information. To our knowledge, this is the first study to investigate the interaction between reward processing and social information with EEG signals in MDD. We recorded EEG signals from 7 subjects while they were taking part in a reward learning experiment [26]. In the experiment, the subjects were making decisions in non-social and social contexts. The subjects also completed a psychometric questionnaire to measure their depressive scores. To detect and classify MDD, we extracted linear and nonlinear features from the recorded EEG signals and used them as input to Support Vector Machine (SVM) and K-Nearest Neighbors (KNN) classifiers. We did three levels of classification analysis: 1) multi-channel analysis, 2) single-channel analysis, and 3) sub-band analysis. Our results show the superiority of nonlinear features extracted during social contexts in detecting MDD compared to non-social contexts. We also present insights about the high classification performance achieved using single channels and frequency subbands. Additionally, we show the consistency of the results when using single features compared to combining the features. In summary, our work shows the association between social cognition and reward processing in MDD and their potential to provide a way for better understanding and identifying MDD.

2 Methodology

2.1 Experimental Design

We conducted a reward learning experiment which was previously presented in [26]. In the experiment, the subjects were presented with two cues, one of which had a higher reward chance. To collect as many points as possible, the subjects had to learn, by trial and error, and choose the cue with the higher reward probability. Figure 1 shows the interface developed for the experiment which demonstrates (a) the cues presented to the subject and (b) the output message corresponding to the outcome of the subject's choice. The subjects were informed that they are paired with another player in the experiment. This player is actually a simulated virtual demonstrator. The demonstrator's behavior was simulated using a reinforcement learning algorithm (Q-learning/Rescorla-Wagner model with a learning rate = 0.5 and choice temperature = 10) [26]. The generated demonstrator's behavior was held constant across all the subjects. Three different contexts/conditions were used in the experiment with different levels of social information shared with the subject. Figure 2 shows the three conditions. The first condition is the 'Private' condition which includes no information about the other player's choice. The second condition is the 'Social Choice' condition in which the choice of the other player was presented to the subject. The third and final condition is the 'Social Choice+Outcome' condition in which the choice of the other player and its outcome were presented to the subject. The experiment was divided into six blocks with two blocks for each condition and each block consists of 20 trials. In the two blocks per condition, one block had a 'stable' type and another had a 'reversal' type. In the 'stable' block type, the reward probabilities did not change during the block. In the 'reversal' type, reward probabilities were inverted across cues around the tenth trial. Before starting the experiment, the subject passes through one training block (with 20 trials) to get familiar with the experiment. After finishing the experiment, subjects were asked to answer the Hospital Anxiety and Depression Scale (HADS) questionnaire [38] to measure their depression symptoms. A HADS depression subscale score of 8 was used as the threshold to separate depressed subjects from non-depressed subjects.

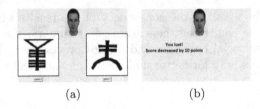

Fig. 1. Experiment's interface (a) Two cues presented to the subjects and (b) Output message corresponding to the subject's choice.

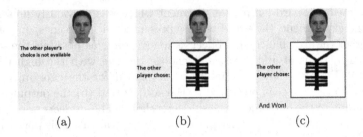

Fig. 2. Three conditions used in the experiment (a) 'Private', (b) 'Social Choice', and (c) 'Social Choice+Outcome'.

2.2 EEG Data Recording and Preprocessing

EEG signals were recorded from seven male subjects (4 non-depressed and 3 depressed) using a Unicorn Hybrid Black headset consisting of 8 channels (Fz, C3, Cz, C4, Pz, PO7, Oz, and PO8). The data was collected from the subjects while they were performing the above-mentioned experiment. The raw EEG signals were filtered using a band-pass filter of 1–30 Hz and a notch filter of 50 Hz to remove activity caused by AC power line interference [32]. After filtering, the data was annotated with the clicking events of the subjects (i.e. the time points when the subject chose one of the cues). The acquired data was then divided into epochs encompassing 0.3 s before and 1.7 s after the click event. The first 0.3 s of the epoch was used as the baseline period for baseline correction. The signals of Cz and Pz channels were found to be highly noisy and corrupted in most of the subjects' recordings, so they were removed from the analysis. Common average reference was also applied to the epochs [21]. Independent Component Analysis (ICA) [27] was then applied using the PICARD method [1]. ICA was used to remove eye movement and blinking artifacts. Finally, any epoch with an amplitude higher than 200 μV, in any of the channels, was excluded.

2.3 Feature Extraction

Multiple linear and nonlinear features have been proposed in the literature for detecting MDD from EEG [3,11]. In this study, we have focused on using different nonlinear features given their superior performance as reported by multiple studies in the literature [7,9,15,17]. Therefore, we extracted 10 nonlinear features. Additionally, we extracted one linear feature, namely Band Power (BP), due to its wide use in MDD recognition [11].

In this study, the four frequency bands we analyzed are delta (1–4 Hz), theta (4–8 Hz), alpha (8–13 Hz), and beta (13–30 Hz) [17]. For calculating the BP feature, these four bands were extracted from the filtered EEG signal and then the Welch method was used to get the Power Spectrum Density (PSD) for each band in each epoch from the six channels [6]. The 10 nonlinear features we used in this study are as follows:

1. **Katz's Fractal Dimension (KFD):** KFD is a time series fractal dimension measurement algorithm that is used to assess signal complexity and self-similarity [18].
2. **Higuchi's Fractal Dimension (HFD):** HFD quantifies fractal scaling and correlation properties in a signal [16]. It is based on the length $L(k)$ of the curve of the time series under consideration, employing a segment of k samples as a unit if $L(k)$ scales as: $L(k)$ k^{-FD}. The value of fractal dimension FD with a parameter $k_{max} = 10$ was used as presented in [16].
3. **Detrended Fluctuation Analysis (DFA):** DFA focuses on describing the self-correlation and self-affinity of the EEG signal [23].
4. **Largest Lyapunov Exponent (LLE):** LLE measures the exponential divergence or convergence of initially adjacent paths in phase space. A d-dimensional dynamical system contains d Lyapunov exponents. Mostly, the largest Lyapunov exponent is computed instead of all exponents [17].
5. **Lempel-Ziv Complexity (LZC):** LZC describes the randomness of the signal by calculating its complexity and it estimates the bandwidth of random processes [2].
6. **Correlation Dimension (CD):** CD indicates the degree of freedom of a signal with lower values indicating lower signal randomness [29]. An embedding dimension of 10 was used in this study.
7. **Sample Entropy (SampEn):** SampEn determines the signal complexity by calculating the conditional probability that two sequences of a particular length, m, similar for m points, stay similar for m points within tolerance, r, at the following data point [25].
8. **Kolmogorov Complexity (KC):** KC's purpose is to provide a metric for determining the complexity or randomness of an item [24].
9. **Determinism (DET):** DET is a recurrence quantification analysis measure representing the likelihood that two closely evolving segments of the phase space trajectory will stay close for the next time step [28].
10. **Laminarity (LAM):** LAM is a recurrence quantification analysis measure related to the probability that a state will stay constant (within the recurrence threshold error) for the next time step [28].

The 11 features were extracted at multi-channel and single-channel scales and for each band of the four frequency bands.

2.4 Classification Pipeline and Evaluation

Two classifiers were used in this work to classify input data into one of two classes: depressed or non-depressed. The two used classifiers are Support Vector Machine (SVM) and K-Nearest Neighbors (KNN), which have been widely used for the detection of MDD [9].

1. **Support Vector Machine (SVM):** A nonlinear SVM with Gaussian radial basis function (RBF) kernel was used. SVM is based on finding the hyperplane that maximizes the margin of separation. Using a nonlinear kernel such as RBF, SVM transforms the data into a higher dimensional space to find the optimal hyperplane [36].
2. **K-Nearest Neighbors (KNN):** KNN is a classification algorithm that is based on comparing the testing data point to the nearest K-nearest training data points and using majority voting to determine its label [36]. A K value of 5 was used in this study with Euclidean distance as the distance measure.

We used Leave-One-Out Cross Validation (LOOCV) for model evaluation which is also a widely used method in MDD classification [11]. LOOCV was used where, for each condition of the 3 conditions in the experiment, the data/epochs of one subject were left out as the testing data. This means that no epochs from the testing subject were included in the training data. A balanced training dataset was then used with an equal number of epochs from two depressed and two non-depressed subjects. This process was repeated for 50 iterations. In each iteration, LOOCV was used to classify each test subject out of the 7 subjects using balanced training data of 4 subjects as mentioned above. The training data in each iteration is randomly selected by, first, randomly selecting the four training subjects and, second, randomly selecting an equal number of epochs per training subject. Accordingly, the training data used for each testing subject changes, randomly, across the iterations. The predicted class of the test subject, per iteration, is indicated by the predicted class of the majority of its epochs (i.e. majority voting). The classification output in each iteration is the percentage of correctly classified subjects. Afterward, this percentage is averaged across the 50 iterations which is the final accuracy reported in this study.

3 Results

3.1 Multi-channel Analysis

The first level of our analysis is multi-channel analysis where we evaluate the classification performance for the three different conditions of our experiment using all the channels. Figure 3 shows the classification accuracies achieved using the 11 features for the 3 conditions and using both classifiers. In each classifier, the data used were the concatenated values from all the channels per feature at each condition. The figure demonstrates that the 'Social Choice' condition achieves broadly the best accuracy followed by the 'Social Choice+Outcome'

condition, and, finally, the 'Private' condition has the lowest accuracies in which
it mostly did not exceed chance-level accuracy except using very few features.
Previous work in the literature used behavioral data to show that depressive
symptoms are associated with the contexts including social information in addition to a specific association with the 'Social Choice' condition [26]. Our results
add to these previous behavioral findings by investigating the brain-signal level
and confirming the same conclusion of the association between MDD and social
information. In terms of classifiers, although, SVM and KNN show almost the
same classification trend, SVM has generally higher accuracies as found in previous studies [9,11]. For the features, most of the nonlinear features achieved
high accuracies in the social contexts better than the BP feature.

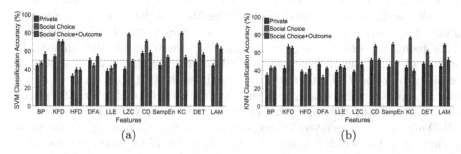

(a)   (b)

Fig. 3. Classification accuracy across features for multi-channel using (a) SVM classifier
and (b) KNN classifier. The dashed line denotes chance-level accuracy and the error
bars represent the Standard Error (SE) across the 50 iterations.

This finding is also consistent with previous results where nonlinear features were found to generally achieve higher accuracies [7,9,15,17]. In Fig. 4a,
we show the maximum accuracy achieved using SVM (given its general superior
performance) across the features in each condition. The figure confirms that the
'Social Choice' condition has the highest accuracy of 80% followed by the 'Social
Choice+Outcome' with an accuracy of 70.6% and the 'Private' condition has
the lowest accuracy of 57.7%. Multiple studies examined brain complexity in
MDD using nonlinear measures with a wide examination of KFD [5,10,33]. This
motivated our analysis of KFD. Figure 4b shows that KFD is significantly higher
in depressed subjects compared to non-depressed subjects across the three conditions (P < 0.0001, Wilcoxon rank-sum test). This agrees with the literature
in that brain complexity is higher in MDD with higher KFD [5,10]. Our results
additionally show that the brain complexity of depressed subjects is highest
in the 'Social Choice' condition with the highest KFD difference compared to
non-depressed subjects while the 'Private' condition has the lowest difference.
In sum, our results show that the presence of social information during reward
learning can provide useful insights for understanding and detecting MDD.

3.2   Single-Channel Analysis

The second level of our analysis is the single-channel analysis where we evaluate the performance of single channels in detecting MDD under the three conditions. Figure 5 shows the accuracies achieved using the 11 features with SVM and KNN for the 6 single channels. As demonstrated in the multi-channel analysis, the 'Social Choice' condition achieved higher accuracies across the features followed by 'Social Choice+Outcome', and finally the 'Private' condition. Similarly, non-linear features achieve higher accuracies than the BP for the different channels and conditions. However, as reported in [7], there is no single best nonlinear feature across the channels. To evaluate the performance of the single channels, we examined the maximum accuracy achieved using the SVM, across the features, for each channel and for each condition as shown in Fig. 6. The figure shows that all the channels succeeded in classifying MDD in the social conditions and 3 out of 6 channels passed the chance-level accuracy in the 'Private' condition. This finding agrees with previous findings from the literature that showed the success of single channels in detecting MDD with a performance close to that of multi-channels [7]. Furthermore, our results show that some single channels can achieve a better performance than multi-channels in the 'Private' condition. This indicates the importance of single-channel analysis in better detecting MDD and studying its reward-processing mechanisms. Comparing the channels' performance, C4, which lies at the central right side of the brain, was found to be the best channel, achieving an accuracy of 85.7% in the social conditions. The C4 accuracy is even higher than the maximum multi-channel accuracy achieved which was 80%. This result can be explained by the findings of recent research work which reported that the central region [7] and the right hemisphere [9,11] in the brain have a higher trend of accuracy in MDD detection.

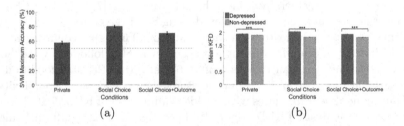

(a)   (b)

Fig. 4. Multi-channel best results and analysis in the three conditions. (a) Best accuracies achieved across the features using SVM. (b) Mean KFD across depressed and non-depressed subjects. ***P < 0.0001 (Wilcoxon rank-sum test).

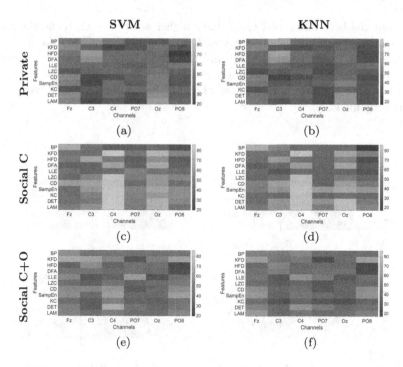

Fig. 5. SVM and KNN classification accuracies for the three conditions ('Private', 'Social Choice', 'Social Choice+Outcome') for the 6 single channels.

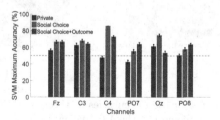

Fig. 6. Best accuracies achieved at single channels across the features using SVM.

3.3   Sub-band Analysis

The third level of our analysis is sub-band analysis where we examine the performance of the sub-bands in detecting MDD in the three conditions. Figure 7 shows the accuracies achieved using the 11 features with SVM and KNN for the 4 frequency bands. Similar to the above results, nonlinear features achieve higher accuracies than the BP except at the 'Social Choice+Outcome' condition in the beta band. There is also no single best nonlinear feature across the bands. To evaluate the performance of the sub-bands, we explored the maximum accuracy achieved, across the features, for each band, and for each condition. Figure 8 shows the maximum band accuracies using the SVM from which we can conclude that the beta and alpha bands have higher accuracies than the theta and delta bands. This result is consistent with other studies reporting the high performance of the beta band [4,9,31] and the alpha band [9,17,31] in detecting MDD. In the beta band, the accuracy of the 'Private' condition reached 81.4% which is higher than its performance when all the bands were used with multi or single channels.

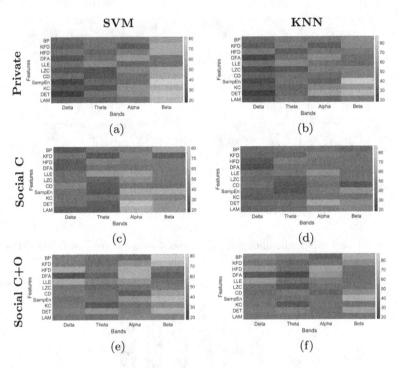

Fig. 7. SVM and KNN classification accuracies at three conditions ('Private', 'Social Choice', 'Social Choice+Outcome') at the 4 frequency bands.

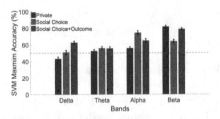

Fig. 8. Best accuracies achieved at sub-bands across the features using SVM.

This was followed by the 'Social Choice+Outcome' condition with an accuracy of 78.6% and the 'Social Choice' condition with an accuracy of 64%. The high performance of the 'Private' condition in the beta band can return to the fact that the beta band is related to reward-anticipation [14], problem solving [34], and expectancy [4]. On the other hand, the 'Social Choice' condition is the highest in the alpha band reaching 74.3% which is 10% higher than its accuracy in the beta band. This could also be because the alpha band is related to social behavior [37] and emotional processing [4,37]. These findings show the rich insights that can be provided by sub-band analysis about the reward processing of the brain in the presence and absence of social information.

3.4 Feature Combination Analysis

In the previous sections, we analyzed the classification performance using single features in three different types of analysis namely multi-channel, single-channel, and sub-band analysis. To study the consistency of the results, we examined the performance by combining the nonlinear features in the same three setups. Figure 9 shows the results of combining the features with the SVM classifier in the (a) multi-channel, (b) single-channel, and (c) sub-band setups. Figure 9a and Fig. 9b confirm the previous finding of the superiority of 'Social Choice' compared to the other two conditions. Moreover, Fig. 9b confirms that the C4 channel has the highest accuracy. Finally, Fig. 9c confirms the high accuracy achieved by the 'Private' condition in the beta band in addition to the low performance of the delta and theta bands compared to the alpha and beta bands.

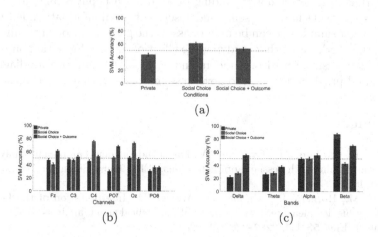

Fig. 9. SVM classification accuracies at three conditions using combined features in (a) multi-channel setup, (b) single-channel setup, (c) sub-band setup.

These results show the consistency of the findings presented in this study when using single features and combining the features. However, the performance decreased when the features are combined. This is expected because some of the features included in the combination were shown to have low accuracy when used separately. Accordingly, as part of future work, feature selection can be used to select and combine the best features which may lead to a performance increase.

4 Conclusion

In this work, our aim is to show the significant role of social cognition, accompanied by reward learning, in MDD understanding and detection. We show that MDD can be detected from EEG, using nonlinear features, in the presence of social information with higher accuracy compared to its absence in multi-channel and single-channel scales. Moreover, we demonstrate the success of single channels in MDD detection and the variability in the performance depending on the channel location. Our results are aligned with the literature findings that reported the potential superiority of the central region and right hemisphere in MDD detection. We also show that the beta and alpha bands were better in MDD detection compared to the theta and delta bands. The 'Private' condition achieved high accuracy in the beta band compared to other bands and compared to its accuracy in multi-channel and single-channel analysis. And the 'Social Choice' condition was the highest in the alpha band. In the study, we achieved high classification accuracies using single features. We also showed that combining the features led to consistent results compared to single features. For accuracy enhancement, applying feature selection and combining the best-selected features can be examined. This study is a preliminary study aiming at contributing to a better understanding of MDD's pathophysiology, its mechanisms, and subtypes in the presence and absence of social information. For future work, a bigger sample size can be used to assess the generalization of the findings. In sum, this work shows that studying the effect of social information on reward learning can push forward our understanding of MDD, improve its diagnostic process, and provide insights into novel personalized treatment mechanisms.

References

1. Ablin, P., Cardoso, J.F., Gramfort, A.: Faster independent component analysis by preconditioning with hessian approximations. IEEE Trans. Signal Process. **66**(15), 4040–4049 (2018)
2. Aboy, M., Hornero, R., Abásolo, D., Álvarez, D.: Interpretation of the Lempel-Ziv complexity measure in the context of biomedical signal analysis. IEEE Trans. Biomed. Eng. **53**(11), 2282–2288 (2006)
3. Acharya, U.R., et al.: A novel depression diagnosis index using nonlinear features in EEG signals. Eur. Neurol. **74**(1–2), 79–83 (2015)
4. de Aguiar Neto, F.S., Rosa, J.L.G.: Depression biomarkers using non-invasive EEG: a review. Neurosci. Biobehav. Rev. **105**, 83–93 (2019)
5. Akar, S.A., Kara, S., Agambayev, S., Bilgiç, V.: Nonlinear analysis of EEG in major depression with fractal dimensions. In: 2015 37th Annual International Conference of the IEEE Engineering in Medicine and Biology Society (EMBC), pp. 7410–7413. IEEE (2015)

6. Alkan, A., Kiymik, M.K.: Comparison of AR and Welch methods in epileptic seizure detection. J. Med. Syst. **30**(6), 413–419 (2006)
7. Bachmann, M., et al.: Methods for classifying depression in single channel EEG using linear and nonlinear signal analysis. Comput. Methods Programs Biomed. **155**, 11–17 (2018)
8. Bains, N., Abdijadid, S.: Major Depressive Disorder. StatPearls Publishing (2022)
9. Bashir, N., Narejo, S., Ismail, F., Anjum, M.R., Prasad, R.: A machine learning framework for major depressive disorder (MDD) detection using non-invasive EEG signals (2022)
10. Bornas, X., et al.: Complexity and irregularity in the brain oscillations of depressive patients: a systematic review. Neuropsychiatry **7**(5), 466–477 (2017)
11. Dev, A., et al.: Exploration of EEG-based depression biomarkers identification techniques and their applications: a systematic review. IEEE Access **10**, 16756–16781 (2022)
12. Frey, A.L., Frank, M.J., McCabe, C.: Social reinforcement learning as a predictor of real-life experiences in individuals with high and low depressive symptomatology. Psychol. Med. **51**(3), 408–415 (2021)
13. Frey, A.L., McCabe, C.: Impaired social learning predicts reduced real-life motivation in individuals with depression: a computational fMRI study. J. Affect. Disord. **263**, 698–706 (2020)
14. Glazer, J.E., Kelley, N.J., Pornpattananangkul, N., Mittal, V.A., Nusslock, R.: Beyond the FRN: broadening the time-course of EEG and ERP components implicated in reward processing. Int. J. Psychophysiol. **132**, 184–202 (2018)
15. Greco, C., Matarazzo, O., Cordasco, G., Vinciarelli, A., Callejas, Z., Esposito, A.: Discriminative power of EEG-based biomarkers in major depressive disorder: a systematic review. IEEE Access **9**, 112850–112870 (2021)
16. Higuchi, T.: Approach to an irregular time series on the basis of the fractal theory. Physica D **31**(2), 277–283 (1988)
17. Hosseinifard, B., Moradi, M.H., Rostami, R.: Classifying depression patients and normal subjects using machine learning techniques and nonlinear features from eeg signal. Comput. Methods Programs Biomed. **109**(3), 339–345 (2013)
18. Katz, M.J.: Fractals and the analysis of waveforms. Comput. Biol. Med. **18**(3), 145–156 (1988)
19. Keren, H., et al.: Reward processing in depression: a conceptual and meta-analytic review across fMRI and EEG studies. Am. J. Psychiatry **175**(11), 1111–1120 (2018)
20. Kupferberg, A., Bicks, L., Hasler, G.: Social functioning in major depressive disorder. Neurosci. Biobehav. Rev. **69**, 313–332 (2016)
21. Ludwig, K.A., Miriani, R.M., Langhals, N.B., Joseph, M.D., Anderson, D.J., Kipke, D.R.: Using a common average reference to improve cortical neuron recordings from microelectrode arrays. J. Neurophysiol. **101**(3), 1679–1689 (2009)
22. Mackin, D.M., Nelson, B.D., Klein, D.N.: Reward processing and depression: current findings and future directions. Neurosci. Depression 425–433 (2021)
23. Peng, C.K., Havlin, S., Stanley, H.E., Goldberger, A.L.: Quantification of scaling exponents and crossover phenomena in nonstationary heartbeat time series. Chaos Interdisc. J. Nonlinear Sci. **5**(1), 82–87 (1995)
24. Puri, D., Nalbalwar, S., Nandgaonkar, A., Wagh, A.: EEG-based diagnosis of Alzheimer's disease using Kolmogorov complexity. In: Iyer, B., Ghosh, D., Balas, V.E. (eds.) Applied Information Processing Systems. AISC, vol. 1354, pp. 157–165. Springer, Singapore (2022). https://doi.org/10.1007/978-981-16-2008-9_15

25. Richman, J.S., Moorman, J.R.: Physiological time-series analysis using approximate entropy and sample entropy. Am. J. Physiol.-Heart Circulatory Physiol. **278**, H2039–H2049 (2000)
26. Safra, L., Chevallier, C., Palminteri, S.: Depressive symptoms are associated with blunted reward learning in social contexts. PLoS Comput. Biol. **15**(7), e1007224 (2019)
27. Sanchez-Poblador, V., Monte-Moreno, E., Solé-Casals, J.: ICA as a preprocessing technique for classification. In: Puntonet, C.G., Prieto, A. (eds.) ICA 2004. LNCS, vol. 3195, pp. 1165–1172. Springer, Heidelberg (2004). https://doi.org/10.1007/978-3-540-30110-3_147
28. Schinkel, S., Dimigen, O., Marwan, N.: Selection of recurrence threshold for signal detection. Eur. Phys. J. Spec. Top. **164**(1), 45–53 (2008)
29. Shen, J., Zhao, S., Yao, Y., Wang, Y., Feng, L.: A novel depression detection method based on pervasive EEG and EEG splitting criterion. In: 2017 IEEE International Conference on Bioinformatics and Biomedicine (BIBM), pp. 1879–1886. IEEE (2017)
30. Strawbridge, R., Young, A.H., Cleare, A.J.: Biomarkers for depression: recent insights, current challenges and future prospects. Neuropsychiatric Dis. Treatment (2017)
31. Sun, S., Chen, H., Shao, X., Liu, L., Li, X., Hu, B.: EEG based depression recognition by combining functional brain network and traditional biomarkers. In: 2020 IEEE International Conference on Bioinformatics and Biomedicine (BIBM), pp. 2074–2081. IEEE (2020)
32. Tibdewal, M.N., Mahadevappa, M., Ray, A.K., Malokar, M., Dey, H.R.: Power line and ocular artifact denoising from EEG using notch filter and wavelet transform. In: 2016 3rd International Conference on Computing for Sustainable Global Development (INDIACom), pp. 1654–1659. IEEE (2016)
33. Čukić, M., López, V., Pavón, J.: Classification of depression through resting-state electroencephalogram as a novel practice in psychiatry. J. Med. Internet Res. **22**(11), e19548 (2020)
34. Watts, D., Pulice, R.F., Reilly, J., Brunoni, A.R., Kapczinski, F., Passos, I.C.: Predicting treatment response using EEG in major depressive disorder: a machine-learning meta-analysis. Transl. Psychiatry **12**(1), 332 (2022)
35. WHO: Depression and other common mental disorders: global health estimates. Technical report, World Health Organization (2017)
36. Wu, C.T., et al.: Resting-state EEG signal for major depressive disorder detection: a systematic validation on a large and diverse dataset. Biosensors **11**(12), 499 (2021)
37. Zhu, L., et al.: EEG-based approach for recognizing human social emotion perception. Adv. Eng. Inform. **46**, 101191 (2020)
38. Zigmond, A.S., Snaith, R.P.: The hospital anxiety and depression scale. Acta Psychiatr. Scand. **67**(6), 361–370 (1983)

Transfer Learning-Assisted DementiaNet: A Four Layer Deep CNN for Accurate Alzheimer's Disease Detection from MRI Images

Sultana Umme Habiba[1]($\boxtimes$)[iD], Tanoy Debnath[2][iD], Md. Khairul Islam[1][iD],
Lutfun Nahar[3], Mohammad Shahadat Hossain[4,6], Nanziba Basnin[5],
and Karl Andersson[6]

[1] Khulna University of Engineering & Technology, Khulna, Bangladesh
habiba.kuet@gmail.com
[2] Department of Computer Science and Engineering,
Green University of Bangladesh, Dhaka, Bangladesh
tanoy@cse.green.edu.bd
[3] Department of Computer Science and Engineering,
International Islamic University Chittagong, Chittagong, Bangladesh
[4] Department of Computer Science and Engineering, University of Chittagong,
Chittagong, Bangladesh
hossain_ms@cu.ac.bd
[5] Leeds Beckett University, Leeds, UK
[6] Pervasive and Mobile Computing Laboratory, Luleå University of Technology,
Luleå, Sweden
karl.andersson@ltu.se

Abstract. Alzheimer's disease is the most common type of dementia and the sixth highest cause of mortality among people over 65. Also, according to statistics, the number of deaths from Alzheimer's disease has increased dramatically. As a result, early detection of Alzheimer's disease can improve patient survival chances. Machine learning methods using magnetic resonance imaging have been utilized in the diagnosis of Alzheimer's disease to help clinicians and speed up the procedure. This research mainly focuses on Alzheimer's disease detection to overcome previous limitations. We use a publicly available dataset which contains 6400 MRI images. In order to train our dataset, we employ our suggested model, "DementiaNet", using "EfficientNet" as a feature extractor and a Deep CNN as a classifier. In order to capture all the features, this framework uses a small number of convolutional layers, which improves the effectiveness of feature learning and results in a more accurate and reliable output. In addition, to address the issue of data imbalance, we apply data augmentation to enhance the size of the minority class by considering four stages of dementia. Also, in this study, we take advantage of the transfer learning approach with the attachment of "EfficientNet", which allows our model to easily solve the overfitting problem and also

F. Liu et al. (Eds.): BI 2023, LNAI 13974, pp. 383–394, 2023.
https://doi.org/10.1007/978-3-031-43075-6_33

extract all the features in a effective way. Finally, we compare our proposed models with those reported in the literature. Our experimental results indicate that our "DementiaNet" model achieve an overall classification accuracy of 97% to detect Alzheimer from brain MRI images, exceeding all other state-of-the-art models.

Keywords: Alzheimer's disease · Convolutional Neural Network · DementiaNet · EfficientNet · MRI · Data Augmentation · Preprocessing · Feature Extraction · Transfer Learning

1   Introduction

Alzheimer's disease (AD) is the most common form of dementia that involves substantial medical attention. Early and accurate analysis of AD prognosis is required for the start of clinical progress and effective patient care [1]. Alzheimer's disease (AD) is a long-term neurobiological brain ailment that gradually destroys brain cells, causes memory and cognitive problems, and ultimately speeds up the loss of ability to carry out even the most fundamental tasks. Neuroimaging and computer-aided diagnostic methods are used by doctors to categorize AD in its early phases. According to the World Alzheimer's Association's evaluation of the most recent census, nearly 4.7 million Americans over 65 have outlived this disease. They predicted that 60 million people could be afflicted by AD during the next fifty years. Globally, Alzheimer's disease accounts for 60 to 80 percent of all dementia types. One person develops dementia every three seconds, and 60% of those cases are caused by AD. To slow down the aberrant degeneration of neurons in the brain, research on early AD diagnosis is still ongoing. Additionally, it benefits the patient's family financially and emotionally. The person with this illness experiences memory loss, strange conduct, and linguistic difficulties. It is brought on by the brain's entorhinal cortex and hippocampal areas as well as tangled bundles of neurofibrillary fibers. The patient's navigational issue and episodic memory impairment are typical initial symptoms of this condition. Memory loss, poor judgment, difficulty recognizing items, difficulty paying bills and operating a vehicle, and placing objects in strange places are some of the higher order symptoms. Improved computer-aided diagnostic tools are needed to interpret MRI images and determine whether patients have Alzheimer's disease or are healthy. Conventional deep learning algorithms perform AD classification on still raw MRI images using the cortical surface as an input to the CNN.

This research provides a methodology for extracting discriminative features using a convolutional neural network. The model is built from the ground up to better precisely classify the stages of Alzheimer's disease by decreasing its parameters and computing cost. The models are evaluated by training them on the Kaggle MRI dataset. Mild Dementia (MID), Moderate Dementia (MOD), Non-Demented (ND), and Very Mild Dementia (VMD) are the four kinds of dementia represented in the dataset. The primary goal of this inquiry was to give a list of classification accuracies as well as other performance indicators such as precision and recall. The investigation of the progression among prediction and classification of AD detection is the most significant consequence of this research study. The results show that the suggested model with fewer parameters beats all previous work models. The main contributions to this work can be summarized as follows:

- A novel "DementiaNet" architecture was developed to aid in Alzheimer's detection because this model could accurately detect Alzheimer's disease within a relatively short period of time.
- Our suggested framework "DementiaNet" employs a sufficient number of convolution filters to capture all of the essential features, increasing the efficiency of feature learning and producing a more accurate and reliable output.
- The proposed model uses transfer learning during the feature extraction stage, allowing it to take advantage of the logical weight of a successful pre-trained model to enhance performance to a greater extent.
- To ensure the quality of the input data, we have used a Gaussian filter to remove noise from the input data. By reducing the effect of noise in the MRI images, this step significantly improved the model's accuracy.
- Furthermore, we addressed the issue of class imbalance by increasing the size of the minority class through data augmentation techniques.

The rest of this work is structured as follows: Sect. 2 reviews previous investigations of AD diagnosis and classification, Sect. 3 describes the methodology for building and evaluating the proposed CNN model, Sect. 4 presents the experimental and evaluation results, and Sect. 5 concludes the paper and discusses future work.

2   Literature Review

Recent study indicates that employing multimodality data to identify and classify AD has made significant progress. Multimodality data includes positron emission tomography (PET), X-rays, MRI, computed tomography (CT), and the patient's clinical records [2]. Although MRI is more effective than CT scans in detecting Alzheimer's disease when using traditional machine learning (ML), there are a number of significant challenges associated with these techniques [3]. In recent years, significant progress has been achieved in the automatic classification of Alzheimer's disease utilizing multiple methodologies. KNN [4,5], Random Forest (RF) [6], SVM [7,8], Decision Tree (DT) [9], Deep Neural Network (DNN), CNN [10], and dynamic connectivity networks (DCN) [11] have all been used to detect AD in MRI images.

Liu et al. [12] present a method for detecting Alzheimer's disease that makes use of spectrogram information derived from voice data. This strategy can assist patients learn about the progression of their illnesses early on, allowing them to take preventive actions. AlexNet and GoogLeNet were used, and their average classification accuracies were 91.40% and 93.02%, respectively. In comparison to our work, the performance is terrible. Arco et al. [7] presented utilizing the ADNI dataset an SVM-based technique coupled with Searchlight and Principal Component Analysis (PCA). In comparison to the PCA, the Searchlight method performed well, with a maximum accuracy of 80.9%. Helaly et al. [13] used deep learning (DL) techniques (CNN and VGG16) to classify four stages of Alzheimer's disease. For each two-pair class of AD phases, different binary medical image classifications were also utilized. For 2D and 3D multiclass AD, CNN and VGG19 techniques, respectively, achieved classification accuracies of 93.61% and 95.17%, whereas VGG19 attained a classification accuracy of 97% for multiclass AD. Compared to our work, the categorization accuracy is lower.

The first transfer learning-based method for multi-class detection for stages of AD and cognitive impairment was introduced by Shanmugam et al. [14]. For training and testing on Google's GoogLeNet, AlexNet, and ResNet-18 networks, they used 6000 MRI ADNI images. The ResNet-18 network achieved the highest classification accuracy (98.63%). Kong et al. [15] developed a special PET-MRI image fusion and a 3D CNN for AD multi-classification methods using deep learning. The ADNI collection's 740 3D images in total were used. This study suggests using A3C-TL-GTO to classify MRI images and identify AD. The Alzheimer's Dataset (four picture classes) and the Alzheimer's Disease Neuroimaging Initiative (ADNI) were used to constructing and assess the A3C-TL-GTO empirical framework for automatic and precise AD classification.

In summary, the excellent capacity of pre-trained models to categorize image data in current research environments serves as the inspiration for our study. We suggest a novel method for the deep CNN-based prediction of Alzheimer's disease based on the effective global and local search capabilities of multi-objective optimization algorithms. The "DementiaNet" is used in this study to calculate and optimize a suitable CNN architectural design using a transfer learning approach based on a wide variety of hyperparameters. In order to make our work stand out, we describe the convolutional neural network parameters as a multiobjective function. This makes it easier to discover the best parameters in a given search area and overcomes the drawbacks of manual-based classifiers.

3 Methodology

This section describes our proposed methodology for Alzheimer's disease detection from MRI images as follows in Fig. 1. We utilized a transfer learning approach to leverage a pre-trained "EfficientNet" model for feature extraction, followed by training a deep convolutional neural network (CNN) as a classifier. Our motivation behind using "EfficientNet" for feature extraction was to benefit from its superior performance in image recognition tasks while reducing the computational complexity and overfitting issues commonly encountered in deep learning models. The resulting model aims to accurately distinguish between

Alzheimer's and non-Alzheimer's subjects based on the features extracted from MRI images, potentially aiding in early diagnosis and treatment of the disease.

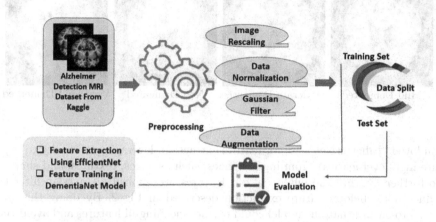

Fig. 1. Workflow Diagram For Alzheimer Detection Using "DementiaNet"

3.1 Dataset Collection and Preprocessing

We have evaluated the performance of our proposed "DementiaNet" for Alzheimer's detection on the "Alzheimer MRI Processed Dataset" collected from Kaggle. As the dataset is imbalanced, with minor sampled classes, we have applied data augmentation techniques to balance the model and improve its performance. The dataset used in this study consists of 6400 MRI images resized to 128 × 128 pixels and classified into four categories: Mild Demented, Moderate Demented, Non-Demented, and Very Mild Demented. The dataset is available on Kaggle and contains 896 images for Mild Demented, 64 images for Moderate Demented, 3200 images for Non-Demented, and 2240 images for Very Mild Demented.

In the preprocessing phase of this work, first, we have rescaled the images into 220 * 220 size as "EfficientNet" accepts images with higher resolution for better performance. After data normalization, the Gaussian filter was applied to reduce the noise of the dataset. The data augmentation technique was implemented to make a generalized model. Some sample images of our work data are given below in Table 1.

3.2 Feature Extraction Using EfficientNet

"EfficientNet" has been proven to surpass other commonly used pre-trained models in various computer vision tasks, due to its innovative scaling technique that optimizes the model's depth, width, and resolution concurrently. In our study, we

Table 1. Examples of Alzheimer MRI images from each class

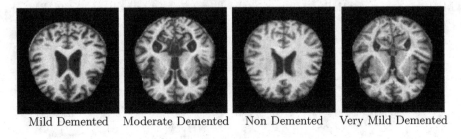

Mild Demented   Moderate Demented   Non Demented   Very Mild Demented

employed "EfficientNet" [16] for feature extraction, leveraging its ability to capture high-level features from input images, such as edges, textures, and shapes. To further improve the quality of our features, we applied a Gaussian filter to reduce noise before feature extraction described in Fig 2. By doing this, we aimed to ensure that our model could extract meaningful features and avoid the inclusion of irrelevant information from the input images. Our feature extraction method involves a combination of convolutional, pooling, and activation layers that are designed to progressively extract more complex and abstract features from the input images.

Fig. 2. Feature Extraction Using Transfer Learning By "EfficientNet"

3.3 Contructing Feature Learning and Classification Model: DementiaNet

The details of the proposed "DementiaNet" model can be explained as follows in Fig. 3, the input features obtained from the pre-trained "EfficientNet" model are passed through a series of convolutional and pooling layers to extract relevant features. The first convolutional layer consists of 32 filters with a kernel size of (3, 3) and uses the rectified linear activation function. The output of this layer is normalized using batch normalization and then max pooled using a (2, 2) filter to reduce the spatial dimensions.

Similarly, the next convolutional layer has 64 filters with a kernel size of (3, 3) and is followed by batch normalization and max pooling. This is repeated for two more layers, with the number of filters increasing to 128 in the third layer and then decreasing back to 64 in the fourth layer.

After the final convolutional layer, the output is flattened and passed through two fully connected dense layers with rectified linear activation functions, each consisting of 256 and 128 neurons, respectively. These dense layers help to learn more complex patterns in the extracted features. Dropout with a rate of 0.5 is applied after the second dense layer to prevent overfitting. the output layer of our proposed classification model for Alzheimer's detection will have four neurons, each representing one of the four classes - mild demented, moderately demented, non-demented, and very mild demented. The output layer uses the softmax activation function to output a probability distribution over the four classes, where the sum of the probabilities for all classes is equal to 1. Finally, the output layer with four neurons and softmax activation function is used to output the probability distribution over the four classes. The model is trained using categorical cross-entropy loss and the Adam optimizer. The performance of the model is evaluated using accuracy metrics, and appropriate hyperparameters are tuned to optimize the model's performance.

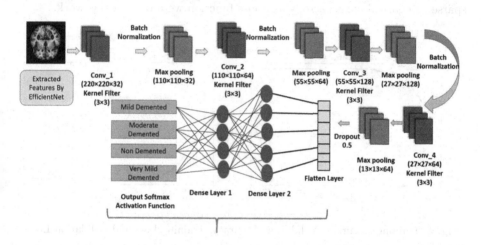

Fig. 3. Details Model Architecture of "DementiaNet"

4 Experimental Results

In this work, we have used hold-out cross-validation to train the dataset in our model. The training set, validation set, and test set consist of 60%, 20%, and 20% of the total dataset(with augmented data also). This model "DementiaNet" was developed using Keras and tensorflow libraries. We employ various assessment criteria, including as accuracy, precision, recall, and F1-score, to assess the effectiveness of the "DementiaNet" architecture and compare our findings with those of prior studies.

4.1 Hyperparameter Tuning

From Fig. 4, the deep CNN model trained for Alzheimer's detection shows a good level of performance. During training, the model's training accuracy increases gradually, reaches a plateau after around 15 epochs, and eventually reaches a peak of 99% accuracy between 27 and 30 epochs. On the other hand, the model's validation accuracy reaches a peak of 97.5% at the end of the training process, indicating that the model has learned to generalize well to the unseen validation set.

Regarding the loss function, it is observed that the loss value decreases rapidly in the initial epochs and eventually becomes saturated around the 17th epoch, with a value below 0.01. This suggests that the model has learned to minimize error and make accurate predictions during training.

The high training accuracy, validation accuracy, and low loss value indicate that the model has learned to classify MRI images of Alzheimer's disease with a high degree of accuracy. Adam as an optimizer, 0.0001 as a learning rate, and sparse-categorical cross entropy as a loss function were used in this work.

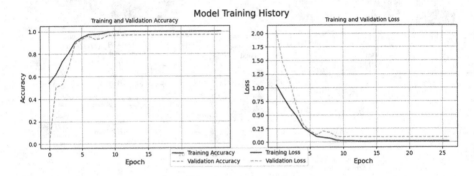

Fig. 4. Training Accuracy, Validation Accuracy, Training Loss and Validation Loss

4.2 Model Evaluation and Result Analysis

Our proposed "DementiaNet" has shown a good classification performance in Alzheimer's detection from brain MRI images. From Fig. 5, the confusion matrix has shown that most of the test samples are positioned diagonally and the miss classification rate is not a significant one. Figure 6 shows some miss classified samples of very mild demented class which are wrongly predicted as non-demented. Analyzing the overall miss classified samples, it is considered that most of them are wrongly predicted conflicting with their near classes. Model evaluation metrics for our work are shown in Table 2.

Table 3 compares the proposed models to the most recent state-of-the-art models that can be found in the literature. These models employed various

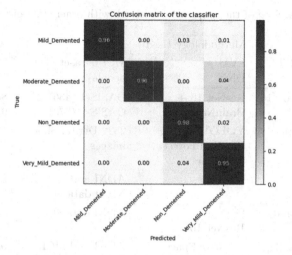

Fig. 5. Confusion Matrix for the output of "DementiaNet"

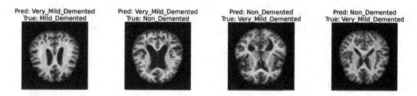

Fig. 6. Miss Classified Samples

Table 2. Performance comparison of Alzheimer's detection models

Feature Extractor	Classifier	Dataset	Accuracy	Precision	Recall	F1 Score
VGG16	VGG16	Alzheimer's MRI (Kaggle)	84%	0.83	0.85	0.85
ResNet50	ResNet50	Alzheimer's MRI (Kaggle)	85%	0.84	0.86	0.85
EfficientNet	EfficientNet	Alzheimer's MRI (Kaggle)	87%	0.86	0.88	0.87
EfficientNet	**DementiaNet (Proposed Model)**	Alzheimer's MRI (Kaggle)	97%	0.97	0.96	0.96

architectures while using the same datasets. Table 3 makes it clear that when compared to other techniques reported in the literature, our proposed transfer learning-based "DementiaNet" architecture offers the best prediction performance for the detection of Alzheimer's disease.

Table 3. Comparison of the proposed framework with other state-of-the-art methods

References	Methodology Used	Dataset	Accuracy (%)
Raees et al. [17]	SVM + DNN	MCI dataset (111 people)	90
Saratxaga et al. [18]	ResNet 18 + BrainNet	OASIS-1 (436), OASIS-2 (373)	80 (OASIS-1) 93 (OASIS-2)
Koga et al. [19]	YOLOV3 + Random Forest Classifier	2522 Digital Slide images	92
Hu et al. [20]	CNN	ADNI and NIFD dataset	92
Buvaneswari and Gayathri [21]	SegNet + ResNet-101	ADNI dataset	96
Chen and Xia [22]	Iterative Space + Deep Learning Model	ADNI and MCI dataset	95
Proposed Method	DementiaNet + Transfer Learning	MRI Dataset (6400 Images)	97

5   Conclusion

The importance of Alzheimer Detection lies in the potential impact it can have on the early diagnosis of Alzheimer's disease, which can significantly improve patient outcomes and quality of life. It can also help in reducing the burden on the healthcare system by enabling earlier interventions and treatments. The proposed model "DementiaNet" of using "EfficientNet" as a feature extractor and a Deep CNN [23–25] as a classifier for Alzheimer's detection from MRI images is effective. The model achieved a high accuracy of 97%, which indicates its potential for clinical applications in the early detection of Alzheimer's disease. Moreover, data augmentation techniques were employed to handle the issue of imbalanced data, which is a common challenge in medical imaging datasets. This approach has shown promising results and could be further explored in future studies. As for future work, this study could be extended to multi-center studies and tested on larger datasets. The model could also be fine-tuned and optimized to improve its performance further [25–28] and [29]. Additionally, the model could be evaluated for its generalizability on different populations and with different types of MRI scans.

References

1. Liu, S., et al.: Multimodal neuroimaging feature learning for multiclass diagnosis of Alzheimer's disease. IEEE Trans. Biomed. Eng. **62**(4), 1132–1140 (2015)

2. Prince, M., Bryce, R., Albanese, E., Wimo, A., Ribeiro, W., Ferri, C.P.: The global prevalence of dementia: a systematic review and meta analysis. Alzheimer's Dement. **9**(1), 63–75 (2013)

3. Nawaz, A., Anwar, S.M., Liaqat, R., Iqbal, J., Bagci, U., Majid, M.. Deep convolutional neural network based classification of Alzheimer's disease using MRI data. In: 2020 IEEE 23rd International Multitopic Conference (INMIC), pp. 1–6. IEEE (2020)

4. Muhammad, L.J., Islam, M.M., Usman, S.S., Ayon, S.I.: Predictive data mining models for novel coronavirus (COVID-19) infected patients' recovery. SN Comput. Sci. **1**(4), 206 (2020)

5. Reza, M.M., Debnath, T., Sultan, S.I.: Outliers elimination: a modified clustering technique of k-means algorithm

6. Nozadi, S. H., Kadoury, S., Alzheimer's Disease Neuroimaging Initiative, et al.: Classification of Alzheimer's and MCI patients from semantically parcelled PET images: a comparison between AV45 and FDG-PET. Int. J. Biomed. Imag., **2018** (2018)

7. Arco, J.E., Ramírez, J., Górriz, J.M., Ruz, M., Alzheimer's Disease Neuroimaging Initiative, et al.: Data fusion based on searchlight analysis for the prediction of Alzheimer's disease. Expert Syst. Appl. **185**, 115549 (2021)

8. Feng, J., Zhang, S.-W., Chen, L., Xia, J., Initiative, A.D.N., et al.: Alzheimer's disease classification using features extracted from nonsubsampled contourlet subband-based individual networks. Neurocomputing **421**, 260–272 (2021)

9. Hasan, M.K., Islam, M.M., Hashem, M.M.A.: Mathematical model development to detect breast cancer using multigene genetic programming. In: 2016 5th International Conference on Informatics, Electronics and Vision (ICIEV), pp. 574–579. IEEE (2016)

10. Bi, X., Li, S., Bin Xiao, Yu., Li, G.W., Ma, X.: Computer aided Alzheimer's disease diagnosis by an unsupervised deep learning technology. Neurocomputing **392**, 296–304 (2020)

11. Jie, B., Liu, M., Shen, D.: Integration of temporal and spatial properties of dynamic connectivity networks for automatic diagnosis of brain disease. Med. Image Anal. **47**, 81–94 (2018)

12. Liu, L., Zhao, S., Chen, H., Wang, A.: A new machine learning method for identifying Alzheimer's disease. Simul. Model. Pract. Theory **99**, 102023 (2020)

13. Helaly, H.A., Badawy, M., Haikal, A.Y.: Deep learning approach for early detection of Alzheimer's disease. Cogn. Comput. 1–17 (2021). https://doi.org/10.1007/s12559-021-09946-2

14. Shanmugam, J.V., Duraisamy, B., Simon, B.C., Bhaskaran, P.: Alzheimer's disease classification using pre-trained deep networks. Biomed. Sign. Process. Control **71**, 103217 (2022)

15. Kong, Z., Zhang, M., Zhu, W., Yi, Y., Wang, T., Zhang, B.: Multi-modal data Alzheimer's disease detection based on 3D convolution. Biomed. Sign. Process. Control **75**, 103565 (2022)

16. Tan, M., Le, Q.: EfficientNet: rethinking model scaling for convolutional neural networks. CoRR, abs/1905.11946 (2019)

17. Raees, P.M., Thomas, V.: Automated detection of Alzheimer's disease using deep learning in MRI. In: Journal of Physics: Conference Series, vol. 1921, p. 012024. IOP Publishing (2021)

18. Sarataxaga, C.L., et al.: MRI deep learning-based solution for Alzheimer's disease prediction. J. Personalized Med. **11**(9), 902 (2021)

19. Koga, S., Ikeda, A., Dickson, D.W.: Deep learning-based model for diagnosing Alzheimer's disease and tauopathies. Neuropathol. Appl. Neurobiol. **48**(1), e12759 (2022)

20. Jingjing, H., et al.: Deep learning-based classification and voxel-based visualization of frontotemporal dementia and Alzheimer's disease. Front. Neurosci. **14**, 626154 (2021)

21. Buvaneswari, P.R., Gayathri, R.: Deep learning-based segmentation in classification of Alzheimer's disease. Arab. J. Sci. Eng. **46**, 5373–5383 (2021)

22. Chen, Y., Xia, Y.: Iterative sparse and deep learning for accurate diagnosis of Alzheimer's disease. Pattern Recogn. **116**, 107944 (2021)

23. Sumi, T.A., Nath, T., Nahar, N., Hossain, M.S., Andersson, K.: Classifying brain tumor from MRI images using parallel CNN model. In: Mahmud, M., He, J., Vassanelli, S., van Zundert, A., Zhong, N. (eds.) BI 2022. Lecture Notes in Computer Science, vol. 13406, pp. 264–276. Springer, Cham (2022). https://doi.org/10.1007/978-3-031-15037-1_22

24. Afroze, T., Akther, S., Chowdhury, M.A., Hossain, E., Hossain, M.S., Andersson, K.: Glaucoma detection using inception convolutional neural network V3. In: Mahmud, M., Kaiser, M.S., Kasabov, N., Iftekharuddin, K., Zhong, N. (eds.) AII 2021. CCIS, vol. 1435, pp. 17–28. Springer, Cham (2021). https://doi.org/10.1007/978-3-030-82269-9_2

25. Mahamud, F., Emon, A.S., Nahar, N., Imam, M.H., Hossain, M.S., Andersson, K.: Transfer learning based method for classification of schizophrenia using MobileNet. In: Vasant, P., Weber, G.W., Marmolejo-Saucedo, J.A., Munapo, E., Thomas, J.J. (eds.) ICO 2022. Lecture Notes in Networks and Systems, vol. 569, pp. 210–220. Springer, Cham (2023). https://doi.org/10.1007/978-3-031-19958-5_20

26. Barman, S., Biswas, M.R., Marjan, S., Nahar, N., Hossain, M.S., Andersson, K.: Transfer learning based skin cancer classification using GoogLeNet. In: Satu, M.S., Moni, M.A., Kaiser, M.S., Arefin, M.S. (eds.) MIET 2022. Lecture Notes of the Institute for Computer Sciences, Social Informatics and Telecommunications Engineering, vol. 490, pp. 238–252. Springer, Cham (2023). https://doi.org/10.1007/978-3-031-34619-4_20

27. Nath, T., Hossain, M.S., Andersson, K.: A transfer learning approach to detect face mask in COVID-19 pandemic. In: Vasant, P., Weber, G.W., Marmolejo-Saucedo, J.A., Munapo, E., Thomas, J.J. (eds.) ICO 2022. Lecture Notes in Networks and Systems, vol. 569, pp. 948–957. Springer, Cham (2023). https://doi.org/10.1007/978-3-031-19958-5_89

28. Nahar, L., Basnin, N., Hoque, S.N., Tasnim, F., Hossain, M.S., Andersson, K.: A hybrid deep learning system to detect face-mask and monitor social distance. In: Mahmud, M., Ieracitano, C., Kaiser, M.S., Mammone, N., Morabito, F.C. (eds.) AII 2022. Communications in Computer and Information Science, vol. 1724, pp. 308–319. Springer, Cham (2022). https://doi.org/10.1007/978-3-031-24801-6_22

29. Habiba, S.U., Islam, M.K., Nahar, L., Tasnim, F., Hossain, M.S., Andersson, K.: Brain-DeepNet: a deep learning based classifier for brain tumor detection and classification. In: Vasant, P., Weber, G.W., Marmolejo-Saucedo, J.A., Munapo, E., Thomas, J.J. (eds.) ICO 2022. Lecture Notes in Networks and Systems, vol. 569, pp. 550–560. Springer, Cham (2023). https://doi.org/10.1007/978-3-031-19958-5_52

Multimodal Approaches for Alzheimer's Detection Using Patients' Speech and Transcript

Hongmin Cai[1], Xiaoke Huang[1], Zhengliang Liu[2], Wenxiong Liao[1],
Haixing Dai[2], Zihao Wu[2], Dajiang Zhu[3], Hui Ren[4], Quanzheng Li[4],
Tianming Liu[2], and Xiang Li[4(✉)]

[1] South China University of Technology, Guangzhou, Guangdong, China
hmcai@scut.edu.cn, {csxkhuang,cswxliao}@mail.scut.edu.cn
[2] University of Georgia, Athens, GA, USA
{zl18864,haixing.dai,zihao.wu1,tliu}@uga.edu
[3] University of Texas at Arlington, Arlington, TX, USA
dajiang.zhu@uta.edu
[4] Massachusetts General Hospital, Boston, MA, USA
{hren2,li.quanzheng,xli60}@mgh.harvard.edu

Abstract. Alzheimer's disease (AD) is a common form of dementia that severely impacts patient health. As AD impairs the patient's language understanding and expression ability, the speech of AD patients can serve as an indicator of this disease. This study investigates various methods for detecting AD using patients' speech and transcripts data from the DementiaBank Pitt database. The proposed approach involves pre-trained language models and Graph Neural Network (GNN) that constructs a graph from the speech transcript, and extracts features using GNN for AD detection. Data augmentation techniques, including synonym replacement and GPT-based augmenter, were used to address the limited sample size issue. Audio data from the patient's speech was also included in the proposed model, where the WavLM model was used to extract audio features. These features were then fused with text features using various fusion strategies. We also investigated a novel fusion approach, where transcripts data were converted back to audio data and analyzed through a contrastive learning scheme along with the original audio data, with the premise that a single-modal (audio) detection model could be easier to train with better generalizability. We conducted intensive experiments and analysis on the above methods. Our findings shed light on the challenges and potential solutions in AD detection using multi-modal speech data.

Keywords: Alzheimer's Disease · Multimodal Learning · Graph Neural Network · Contrastive Learning · Data Augmentation

1 Introduction

Alzheimer's disease (AD) is the most common form of dementia, which degenerates brain cells, seriously affecting patients' quality of life. While AD is incurable,

F. Liu et al. (Eds.): BI 2023, LNAI 13974, pp. 395–406, 2023.
https://doi.org/10.1007/978-3-031-43075-6_34

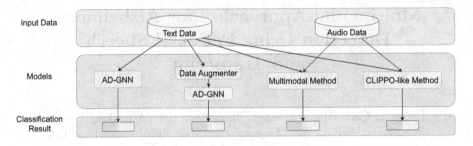

Fig. 1. Algorithmic framework the different detection model implemented in this work.

early diagnosis can lead to optimized intervention strategies that could slow down its development, making it crucial to detect the disease at its early stages. Various imaging-based approaches for characterizing the structural, functional, and pathological changes of pre-clinical and clinical AD patients have been developed [12,27–29]. On the other hand, given that AD can impair patients' cognitive function, including speech capabilities, AD patients' speech patterns could exhibit certain characteristics, such as frequent silence, incoherence, word retrieval difficulty, and repetition [17]. This allows the diagnostic modeling of AD through the patient's speech data.

There has been a series of works using NLP techniques for AD diagnosis [4,5,18,21,26]. In this study, we utilize the combined patient speech (audio) and the corresponding transcription (text) data from the Pitt Cookie-Theft dataset [3] to develop a multi-modal approach for AD detection from patients' speech. Specifically, we investigate and compare the performance of various multi-modal fusion and NLP-based methods for the detection task, aiming to provide more insights into the speech-based AD detection task for the development of more effective and robust solutions.

2 Methods

In our work, we employ four schemes for AD detection using audio recordings and transcripts data, as illustrated in Fig. 1. Firstly, we attempt a GNN-based method, named AD-GNN, which utilizes a pre-trained language model (BERT) to embed patient speech transcription text data into features and a Graph Neural Network (GNN) to perform the classification. We also investigate augmentation techniques for the patient speech transcription text data followed by AD-GNN, with the premise that data augmentation can partially address the small sample size problem of the dataset. In the third scheme, we use both audio and text data, i.e., patient audio and its transcription, to develop a multi-modal speech model. The model employs a pre-trained speech model (WavLM) to extract audio features, which then fuses with the text features extracted by AD-GNN. We attempt various multi-modal fusion methods in this scheme. The fourth approach, called the CLIPPO-like method, also uses both audio and text data. Similar to the

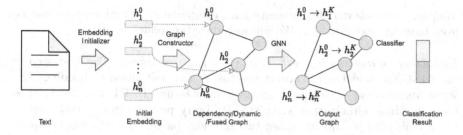

Fig. 2. Algorithmic pipeline of AD-GNN: model inputs (text data) are embedded by a pre-trained large language model (BERT in this case). The embedding features are then represented on a graph further filtered by a GNN structure for the classification.

work in [22] work, text data is firstly converted into the audio representation, then a single-modal model is developed to extract features from the combined text-converted audio and the original audio in a contrastive learning framework for the classification.

2.1 GNN-Based Method

There is a growing trend of developing and applying graph-based representation learning methods to better model complex structural patterns in real-world data. Graph Neural Network (GNN) has achieved great success in both computer vision [30] and NLP [11], with applications in the medical domain (e.g., the analysis of medical images [12], medical notes [20] and radiology reports [14]). Thus, we envision that similar methods can also improve the effectiveness of NLP-based AD detection. At the same time, however, there is limited work related to detecting AD using graph-based methods.

In this work, we propose a graph-based classification model called AD-GNN for AD diagnosis using patient speech transcripts. AD-GNN is based on the Graph4NLP project [25], which enables efficient development and experimentation with GNN for NLP tasks. The algorithmic pipeline of AD-GNN is shown in Fig. 2. The input of our model is a piece of text $\mathbf{T} = [t_1, t_2, \cdots, t_n]$, which can be regarded as a token sequence with length n. $\mathbf{T}$ gets its initial embedding $\mathbf{H}^0 = \left[h_1^0, h_2^0, \cdots, h_n^0\right]$ through the embedding initializer which utilizes word vector and pre-trained language model (BERT) [10], where the initial embedding of token t_i is represented as h_i^0. Then, we construct a graph $\mathbf{G} = (\mathbf{V}, \mathbf{E})$ according to $\mathbf{T}$ which consists of a set of n nodes $\mathbf{V} = \{v_1, v_2, \cdots, v_n\}$ and edges $(v_i, v_j) \in \mathbf{E}$. The adjacency matrix of $\mathbf{G}$ is denoted as $\mathbf{A}$. The feature of node v_i is initialized as h_i^0 and will be updated to h_i^K through a K-layer GNN network to learn discriminative features. $\mathbf{H}^K = \left[h_1^K, h_2^K, \cdots, h_n^K\right]$, i.e., the final embedding of $\mathbf{T}$, will be fed into the classifier and the model outputs the final one-hot (binary classes) classification results. Our hypothesis is that the graph structure and the corresponding GNN-extracted features would provide more complex and context-rich representations, compared to representations learned from language models alone. We will introduce the model details below.

Embedding Initialization. Text $\mathbf{T}$ is a sequence of tokens. The first step of the AD-GNN model is to convert the tokens into initialized embeddings $\mathbf{H}^0$. Word vectors and pre-trained language models like BERT are widely used for embedding initialization. Graph4NLP library provides many strategies for token embeddings, and we chose two of them based on preliminary experiments. w2v_bert_bilstm method uses word vector (glove.840B.300d.word2vec) for the initial embedding. Then, BERT is adopted to encode the input text. The glove embedding and the BERT embedding are concatenated and used as the input to BiLSTM to compute the final embedding. w2v_bilstm is similar to w2v_bert_bilstm but with the BERT component removed.

Graph Construction. Graph4NLP provides many strategies to build a graph from text sequences. Here we experiment with three of them: dependency graph, dynamic graph, and fused graph.

The first method is to build a dependency graph based on the dependency relationship between words to describe the text structure. Stanford CoreNLP [6] implements a transition-based dependency parser based on a neural network. It is worth noting that if the input text contains multiple sentences, after obtaining the dependency tree of each sentence, we will connect the last node of the dependency tree of the previous sentence with the header node of the next sentence with an edge to produce a connected graph.

The second method is to build a dynamic graph whose structure can evolve during the training process. The rationale is that static graphs (e.g., dependency graphs) may be incomplete or improper, and the errors produced in the graph construction phase cannot be corrected. These errors may affect the accuracy of the final classification results. To counter this problem, Chen et al. proposed an end-to-end dynamic graph learning framework, Iterative Deep Graph Learning (IDGL) [8], which is used in AD-GNN.

Another method for graph construction is to fuse dependency and dynamic graphs together to form a new graph. The fusion method implemented by Graph4NLP can be represented as

$$\mathbf{A}_{\mathrm{com}} = \lambda \mathbf{L}_{\mathrm{dep}} + (1 - \lambda) \, \mathrm{f}(\mathbf{A}), \tag{1}$$

where $\mathbf{A}_{\mathrm{com}}$ is the adjacency matrix of the new graph, λ is a hyper-parameter with a value between 0 and 1, $\mathbf{L}_{\mathrm{dep}}$ is the normalized Laplacian matrix of the dependency graph, $\mathbf{A}$ is the adjacency matrix of the dynamic graph and $\mathrm{f}(\cdot)$ is the matrix normalization operation (e.g., row normalization).

GNN Layers. The initialized graph is fed into GNN layers to learn the feature representation of each node. In the proposed AD-GNN model, GraphSAGE (Graph SAmple and aggreGatE) [13] and GGNN (Gated Graph Neural Network) [16] with K layers are separately tested.

Classifier. AD-GNN uses a pooling layer and a multi-layer perceptron (MLP) to perform the final classification. An average pooling layer is used to average the features across all nodes to characterize the whole graph. The feature of the whole graph $r = \frac{1}{n} \sum_{i=1}^{n} h_i^K$, where h_i^K denotes the final feature of node v_i. The MLP layer accepts the averaged graph feature as input and performs the binary classification.

2.2 Data Augmentation Method

In order to address the issue of limited data in the Pitt Cookie-Theft dataset, we use a variety of text data augmentation techniques. The goal of these methods is to provide our models with more diverse training examples, reduce the risk of over-fitting, and potentially improve their performance. Here is an introduction to the data augmentation methods we use.

- **WordNet Augmenter.** This method uses a synonym dictionary, such as WordNet [19], to replace words in the original text with their synonyms. This method aims to maintain the semantic integrity of the sentences while introducing lexical diversity.
- **Counter-fitting Embedding Augmenter.** The data augmentation method based on word embedding [24] refers to replacing words in a sentence with other words that are close to them in the embedding space. However, this poses a problem as two words with similar embeddings only indicate that they typically occur in similar contexts, but their semantics may not necessarily be the same and may even be opposite. The counter-fitting embedding data augmentation method [1] uses counter-fitting embedding instead, which reduces the distance between synonyms and increases the distance between antonyms, thus better ensuring semantic consistency.
- **RoBERTa Augmenter.** This method [15] leverages the power of pre-trained language models such as the RoBERTa model to generate new sentences. It uses the RoBERTa model to perform three operations: token swap, token insert, and token merge. Specifically, token swap operation means randomly replacing tokens in the original text with a special "[MASK]" token. Token insert operation means randomly inserting "[MASK]" tokens into the original text. Token merge operation means randomly merging adjacent tokens into a single "[MASK]" token. Subsequently, it uses RoBERTa to predict the most likely token for the masked positions.
- **Sentence Deletion Augmenter.** This method randomly removes sentences from the original text. This technique aims to simulate missing or incomplete information, which is common in real-world scenarios. This process helps to improve the model's robustness and generalization ability by training it to make accurate predictions even when confronted with incomplete data.
- **GPT-3.5 Augmenter and GPT-4 Augmenter.** This method [9] uses the GPT-3.5-turbo model or GPT-4 model to rephrase each sample. Using appropriate prompts, ChatGPT can rephrase the patient's speech transcript data as instructed and thus effectively increase the size of the training set.

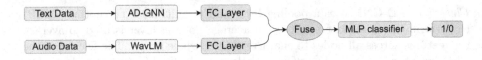

Fig. 3. Illustration of the text-audio fusion framework.

The prompt we provided in our study is "Please write another paragraph using the speaking style of the following paragraph."

2.3 Multimodal Method

Audio data can provide additional information that is not captured in transcriptions. For instance, changes in speech patterns, such as pace, tone, and rhythm, especially unsmooth speech, such as stuttering and pauses, are often early indicators of cognitive decline in AD patients. These features can be extracted from audio data but are lost in text transcriptions.

In this work, we use WavLM [7] model to extract audio features and perform classification. WavLM is a speech model pre-trained on large-scale and diverse speech data. Next, we employ multimodal learning. Multimodal learning, which combines information from different types of data (in this case, text and audio), can lead to more robust and accurate models. This is because different modalities can provide complementary information, allowing the model to learn from a more generalizable data representation. We pass the text features obtained by AD-GNN and the audio features extracted by WavLM through a fully connected layer, respectively, to ensure that the text and audio features have the same dimension. Then we fuse these two features to facilitate sufficient interaction between them. The fused features are then fed into the MLP classifier for classification, yielding the final result. Our multimodal approach is illustrated in Fig. 3.

The fusion method is crucial for the effectiveness of multimodal models. We have attempted two multimodal fusion methods: direct concatenation and cross-network. Direct concatenation is the simplest fusion method, which directly concatenates the audio and text features into one tensor. Cross network proposed by Wang et al. [23] can explicitly apply feature crossing. It consists of multiple layers, where each layer produces higher-order interactions based on existing ones and keeps the interactions from previous layers.

2.4 CLIPPO-Like Method

CLIPPO (CLIP-Pixels Only) [22] is a pixel-based multimodal model that can understand both images and alt-text simultaneously without requiring text encoders or tokenizers. Its approach is to render alt-text as images and then encode both images and text using the same network architecture. It uses a contrastive learning loss function to make embeddings of matching images and

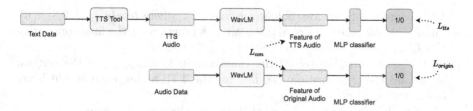

Fig. 4. The framework constructive learning-based modeling of TTS and original audio data in a CLIPPO-like scheme.

alt-text as close as possible and all other image and alt-text embeddings as far apart as possible. The importance of CLIPPO lies in its achievement of unified modeling of images and text, not limited by text tokenizers, simplifying the complexity of multimodal learning, and improving model scalability and generalization. Compared to using two completely different models for text and image modalities, CLIPPO has reduced the number of parameters by half while achieving comparable experimental results on various tasks, including zero-shot image classification and image-text retrieval.

In our research, we attempt to replicate the work of CLIPPO. Figure 4 illustrates our model architecture. We follow these steps:

1. We use the SpeechT5 model [2] fine-tuned for text-to-speech (TTS) to convert the patients' transcripts back into speech. The speech features of these TTS audios, such as intonation and speed, are similar to those of normal human speech.
2. Next, we use WavLM to extract features from both the original audio and the TTS audio.
3. We then employ contrastive learning to compare the generated TTS audio with the patient's original speech data. Similar to CLIPPO, we aim to make the features of the matched original and TTS audio as similar as possible while keeping the features of other original and TTS audio pairs as different as possible. This approach can help the model extract richer and more discriminative features. We use a contrastive loss function similar to that used in CLIPPO. Specifically, in each batch, there are n samples, and the original audio feature of the i-th sample is represented as a_i^{origin}, while the TTS audio feature of the i-th sample is represented as a_i^{tts}. First, we perform L2 normalization on the above features to obtain $e_i^{origin}, i = 1, 2, \cdots, n$ and $e_i^{tts}, i = 1, 2, \cdots, n$. Then, we calculate the cosine similarity matrix S between the original and TTS audio features. S is an $n \times n$ matrix, and the element in the i-th row and j-th column S_{ij} is calculated as $S_{ij} = e_i^{origin} e_j^{tts} e^t$, where t is a temperature parameter. Among these $n \times n$ sample pairs, there are n positive sample pairs (matching original audio and TTS audio pairs) and $n^2 - n$ negative sample pairs (all other original audio and TTS audio pairs). We separately calculate the cross-entropy loss of original audio L_{con}^{origin} and the cross-entropy loss of TTS audio L_{con}^{tts}. $L_{con}^{origin} = \text{cross\_entropy\_loss}(S, labels, axis = 0)$ and

L_{con}^{tts} = cross_entropy_loss($S, labels, axis = 1$), where $labels = [1, 2, \cdots, n]$. Finally, we take the average of these two loss functions as the final contrastive loss L_{con}.

4. At the same time, we record the classification loss L_{origin} for the original audio and the classification loss L_{tts} for the TTS audio, both of which are calculated using cross-entropy loss.

5. The final loss is a weighted sum of the above three losses, namely,

$$L = \alpha L_{con} + \beta L_{origin} + \gamma L_{tts}. \qquad (2)$$

The advantage of this approach lies in the fact that since the TTS audio is directly generated from text, it contains semantic information that may not be well reflected in the original speech. By using contrastive learning, we can make the features of the original audio and its corresponding TTS audio as similar as possible. This allows our model to learn how to link speech features, such as intonation and pauses, with textual features, such as semantic information, without the need for pre-trained language models such as BERT. This approach reduces the number of parameters required, resulting in a more compact model structure.

3   Experiments

In the experiments part, we conducted extensive experiments on methods in the methods section. For the GNN-based method, we separately test the effects of different choices of embedding initializer, graph constructor, and GNN on model performance. For data augmentation methods we experimented with different data augmentation methods and different augmentation factors. For the experiments on multimodal methods, we compared the effectiveness of using only AD-GNN for classifying transcriptions of patient speech, only using the WavLM-base model for classifying patient speech audio, combining both with the multimodal method and CLIPPO-like method.

For all the experiments mentioned above, we employed 10-fold cross-validations for 5 times to get stable results. We used accuracy for the evaluation metrics as the number of positive and negative samples is largely balanced.

The results of AD-GNN are shown in Table 1. Apparently, w2v_bert_bilstm leads to better classification performance (compared to w2v_bilstm), indicating that the pre-trained language model can effectively perform the token embedding. However, we noticed that regardless of the graph construction method and GNN used, there was only a slight improvement in accuracy, reaching 0.8504. The reason may be that the graph did not capture the key information related to AD detection. For example, dependency graphs mainly focus on the grammatical relationship between words in a sentence, and these relationships may not be relevant to the language features of AD patients, such as vocabulary richness.

The experimental results about data augmentation are shown in Table 2. It is shown that all data augmentation methods have a negligible impact on the accuracy. Moreover, increasing the augmentation factor also has a very limited

Table 1. Classification performance of AD-GNN using different combinations of the embedding algorithm, graph construction method, and GNN network.

Embedding Initializer	Graph Construction Method	GNN	Accuracy
w2v_bilstm	Dependency graph	One-layer GraphSAGE	0.8088 ± 0.0556
w2v_bert_bilstm	Dependency graph	One-layer GraphSAGE	0.8460 ± 0.0492
w2v_bert_bilstm	Dynamic graph	One-layer GraphSAGE	0.8444 ± 0.0455
w2v_bert_bilstm	Fused graph	One-layer GraphSAGE	0.8460 ± 0.0420
w2v_bert_bilstm	Fused graph	Two-layer GraphSAGE	**0.8504** ± 0.0517
w2v_bert_bilstm	Fused graph	Three-layer GraphSAGE	0.8492 ± 0.0462
w2v_bert_bilstm	Fused graph	One-layer GGNN	0.8444 ± 0.0420
w2v_bert_bilstm	Fused graph	No GNN	0.8484 ± 0.0509

Table 2. Classification performance of AD-GNN using different text augmentation methods.

Augmentation Method	Augmentation Factor	Accuracy
No Data Augmentation	N/A	0.8460 ± 0.0420
Counter-Fitting Embedding Augmenter	1	0.8476 ± 0.0551
Sentence Deletion Augmenter	1	0.8444 ± 0.0490
RoBERTa Augmenter	1	0.8408 ± 0.0511
Wordnet Augmenter	1	**0.8484** ± 0.0541
GPT-3.5 Augmenter	1	0.8416 ± 0.0535
GPT-4 Augmenter	0.2	0.8476 ± 0.0503
Sentence Deletion Augmenter	5	**0.8484** ± 0.0465

impact on the effect. This may be due to the following reasons. First, Wordnet Augmenter may replace words with uncommon ones, which is not a characteristic of AD patients. Second, Randomly deleting sentences may cause information loss. Also, data augmentation may introduce too much noise. Moreover, Some data augmentation methods such as RoBERTa Augmenter may not preserve the semantics of the original sentence. In addition, data augmentation methods may not simulate the speaking style of AD patients. For example, for GPT3.5 Augmenter, even when we ask it to mimic the speaking style of the speaker in the prompt, its effect is sometimes unsatisfactory, and the generated sentences are too formal.

The experimental results about multimodal methods are shown in Table 3. It can be observed that the accuracy of the text modality (0.8460) is much higher than that of the audio modality (0.7714). This may be due to the complexity and dimension of audio data are often higher than those of text data, which may make it difficult for the model to learn effective feature representations. In addition, background noise in audio may also affect the accuracy of the experiment. In addition, as WavLM is not pre-trained on AD patients' data, it may not be able to fully capture speech features related to AD.

Table 3. Comparison of experimental results using only textual data, only audio data, and both textual and audio data.

Modal	Method	Accuracy
Text	AD-GNN	0.8460 ± 0.0420
Audio	WavLM	0.7714 ± 0.0538
Text and Audio	Multimodal Method (Direct Concatenation)	$\mathbf{0.8475 \pm 0.0496}$
Text and Audio	Multimodal Method (Cross Network)	0.8418 ± 0.0528
Text and Audio	CLIPPO-like Method	0.8214 ± 0.0392

When we fused the data from both text and audio modalities, we found that the accuracy of the direct concatenation method (0.8475) is almost the same as that of the cross network method (0.8418), and is very close to the experimental result of using only text. Perhaps this is because the experimental results of the two modalities differ greatly, with strong performance in the text modality but mediocre results in the audio modality, causing the model to overly rely on the stronger modality.

We also found that the CLIPPO-like method significantly improves performance compared to using only raw audio. This indicates that aligning TTS voice with raw audio helps the model understand the semantic information of the audio without the need for pre-trained speech models like BERT.

4   Conclusion and Discussion

In this study, we systematically explored various methods for detecting Alzheimer's disease (AD) using patients' speech and their transcribed text data, including GNN-based methods, data augmentation methods, multimodal-based methods, and CLIPPO-like methods and conducted extensive experiments, which provided rich references for future research. Our study also conducted an in-depth analysis, which provided directions for future work. We also found that the CLIPPO-like method can enable the model to learn semantic information without introducing a pre-trained language model, which can significantly improve the performance compared to using only raw audio.

For future research, there are several possible directions for improvement. First, we can combine data in other modalities, such as the patient's facial expressions. Second, larger datasets may be useful to improve model performance. Finally, we will investigate text data augmentation methods that can truly mimic the speech style of AD patients.

5   Reproducibility Statement

– **Datasets**: The patient speech and transcript data used in this work is provided by the DementiaBank Pitt database [3] at https://dementia.talkbank.org. Data will be available for download upon request.
– **Code**: Both the code and experiment settings for our model are available at https://github.com/shui-dun/multimodal_ad.

References

1. Alzantot, M., Sharma, Y., Elgohary, A., Ho, B.J., Srivastava, M., Chang, K.W.: Generating natural language adversarial examples. In: Proceedings of the 2018 Conference on Empirical Methods in Natural Language Processing, pp. 2890–2896. Association for Computational Linguistics, Brussels, Belgium (2018). https://doi. org/10.18653/v1/D18-1316

2. Ao, J., et al.: SpeechT5: unified-modal encoder-decoder pre-training for spoken language processing (2022). https://doi.org/10.48550/arXiv.2110.07205, arxiv.org/abs/2110.07205

3. Becker, J.T., Boller, F., Lopez, O.L., Saxton, J., McGonigle, K.L.: The natural history of Alzheimer's disease: description of study cohort and accuracy of diagnosis. Archiv. Neurol. **51**(6), 585–594 (1994). https://doi.org/10.1001/archneur.1994. 00540180063015

4. Ben Ammar, R., Ben Ayed, Y.: Speech processing for early Alzheimer disease diagnosis: machine learning based approach. In: 2018 IEEE/ACS 15th International Conference on Computer Systems and Applications (AICCSA), pp. 1–8 (2018). https://doi.org/10.1109/AICCSA.2018.8612831, iSSN: 2161–5330

5. Bertini, F., Allevi, D., Lutero, G., Calzà, L., Montesi, D.: An automatic Alzheimer's disease classifier based on spontaneous spoken English. Comput. Speech Lang. **72**, 101298 (2022). https://doi.org/10.1016/j.csl.2021.101298, www.sciencedirect.com/ science/article/pii/S0885230821000991

6. Chen, D., Manning, C.: A fast and accurate dependency parser using neural networks. In: Proceedings of the 2014 Conference on Empirical Methods in Natural Language Processing (EMNLP), pp. 740–750. Association for Computational Linguistics, Doha, Qatar (2014). https://doi.org/10.3115/v1/D14-1082, www.aclanth ology.org/D14-1082

7. Chen, S., et al.: WavLM: Large-scale self-supervised pre-training for full stack speech processing. IEEE J. Sel. Top. Sign. Process. **16**(6), 1505–1518 (2022). https://doi.org/10.1109/JSTSP.2022.3188113, arxiv.org/abs/2110.13900

8. Chen, Y., Wu, L., Zaki, M.: Iterative deep graph learning for graph neural networks: better and robust node embeddings. In: Advances in Neural Information Processing Systems, vol. 33, pp. 19314–19326. Curran Associates, Inc. (2020). www.proceedings.neurips.cc/paper/2020/hash/e05c7ba4e087beea9410929698dc41 a6-Abstract.html

9. Dai, H., et al.: AugGPT: leveraging ChatGPT for text data augmentation (2023). https://doi.org/10.48550/arXiv.2302.13007, http://arxiv.org/abs/ 2302.13007, arXiv:2302.13007 [cs]

10. Devlin, J., Chang, M.W., Lee, K., Toutanova, K.: BERT: pre-training of deep bidirectional transformers for language understanding. arXiv preprint arXiv:1810.04 805 (2018)

11. Goldberg, Y.: A primer on neural network models for natural language processing. J. Artif. Intell. Res. **57**, 345–420 (2016)

12. Guo, J., Qiu, W., Li, X., Zhao, X., Guo, N., Li, Q.: Predicting Alzheimer's disease by hierarchical graph convolution from positron emission tomography imaging. In: 2019 IEEE International Conference on Big Data (Big Data), pp. 5359–5363. IEEE (2019)

13. Hamilton, W.L., Ying, R., Leskovec, J.: Inductive representation learning on large graphs (2018). https://doi.org/10.48550/arXiv.1706.02216, http://arxiv.org/abs/ 1706.02216, arXiv:1706.02216 [cs, stat]

14. Jing, B., Xie, P., Xing, E.: On the automatic generation of medical imaging reports. arXiv preprint arXiv:1711.08195 (2017)
15. Li, D., et al.: Contextualized perturbation for textual adversarial attack (2021). https://doi.org/10.48550/arXiv.2009.07502, arxiv.org/abs/2009.07502
16. Li, Y., Tarlow, D., Brockschmidt, M., Zemel, R.: Gated graph sequence neural networks (2017). www.arxiv.org/abs/1511.05493, arXiv:1511.05493 [cs, stat]
17. Liu, N., Luo, K., Yuan, Z., Chen, Y.: A transfer learning method for detecting alzheimer's disease based on speech and natural language processing. Front. Public Health 10, 772592 (2022). https://doi.org/10.3389/fpubh.2022.772592, www.ncbi. nlm.nih.gov/pmc/articles/PMC9043451/
18. Martinc, M., Haider, F., Pollak, S., Luz, S.: Temporal integration of text transcripts and acoustic features for Alzheimer's diagnosis based on spontaneous speech. Front. Aging Neurosci. 13, 642647 (2021). www.frontiersin.org/articles/10.3389/fnagi. 2021.642647
19. Miller, G.A.: Wordnet: a lexical database for English. Commun. ACM 38(11), 39–41 (1995)
20. Rezayi, S., et al.: ClinicalRadioBERT: knowledge-infused few shot learning for clinical notes named entity recognition. In: Lian, C., Cao, X., Rekik, I., Xu, X., Cui, Z. (eds.) Machine Learning in Medical Imaging, MLMI 2022. Lecture Notes in Computer Science, vol. 13583, pp. 269–278. Springer, Cham (2022). https://doi. org/10.1007/978-3-031-21014-3_28
21. Roshanzamir, A., Aghajan, H., Soleymani Baghshah, M.: Transformer-based deep neural network language models for Alzheimer's disease risk assessment from targeted speech. BMC Med. Inform. Decis. Making 21(1), 92 (2021). https://doi.org/ 10.1186/s12911-021-01456-3
22. Tschannen, M., Mustafa, B., Houlsby, N.: CLIPPO: image-and-language understanding from pixels only (2023). arxiv.org/abs/2212.08045
23. Wang, R., Fu, B., Fu, G., Wang, M.: Deep & cross network for ad click predictions (2017). https://doi.org/10.48550/arXiv.1708.05123, arxiv.org/abs/1708.05123
24. Wang, W.Y., Yang, D.: That's so annoying!!!: a lexical and frame-semantic embedding based data augmentation approach to automatic categorization of annoying behaviors using# petpeeve tweets. In: Proceedings of the 2015 Conference on Empirical Methods in Natural Language Processing, pp. 2557–2563 (2015)
25. Wu, L., et al.: Graph neural networks for natural language processing: a survey (2021). https://doi.org/10.48550/arXiv.2106.06090, www.arxiv.org/abs/2106. 06090, arXiv:2106.06090 [cs]
26. Yamanki, S.C., Sebastián, S.C., Jacobo, P.G.W., Humberto, G.A., Saúl, T.A.: Semantic feature extraction using SBERT for dementia detection. Brain sciences 12(2) (2022). https://doi.org/10.3390/brainsci12020270, www.pubmed.ncbi.nlm. nih.gov/35204032/, publisher: Brain Sci
27. You, P., Li, X., Wang, Z., Wang, H., Dong, B., Li, Q.: Characterization of brain iron deposition pattern and its association with genetic risk factor in Alzheimer's disease using susceptibility-weighted imaging. Front. Hum. Neurosci. 15, 654381 (2021)
28. Zhang, L., et al.: Deep fusion of brain structure-function in mild cognitive impairment. Med. Image Anal. 72, 102082 (2021)
29. Zhang, L., Wang, L., Zhu, D., Initiative, A.D.N., et al.: Predicting brain structural network using functional connectivity. Med. Image Anal. 79, 102463 (2022)
30. Zhou, J., et al.: Graph neural networks: a review of methods and applications. AI Open 1, 57–81 (2020)

Brain-Machine Intelligence
and Brain-Inspired Computing

Exploiting Approximate Joint Diagonalization for Covariance Estimation in Imagined Speech Decoding

Fotis P. Kalaganis[1]([✉]) [iD], Kostas Georgiadis[1] [iD], Vangelis P. Oikonomou[1] [iD], Spiros Nikolopoulos[1] [iD], Nikos A. Laskaris[2] [iD], and Ioannis Kompatsiaris[1] [iD]

[1] Centre for Research & Technology Hellas, Information Technologies Institute (ITI), Thermi -Thessaloniki, Greece
kalaganis@csd.auth.gr
[2] AIIA-Lab, Informatics Dept, AUTH, NeuroInformatics.Group, Thessaloniki, Greece

Abstract. Recently, imagined speech has become a subject of study due to its potential as an intuitive communication system. It involves registering neural responses generated by mental speaking without moving the articulators. Although it may not perform as well as other paradigms, it has multiclass scalability, making it suitable for building extensible BCI systems. Hence, our study revolves around this intuitive paradigm that decodes human speech imagery from EEG signals using Riemannian geometry and a recently introduced covariance estimation method that is based on the concept of Approximate Joint Diagonalization (AJD). The employed methodological framework approach sets its grounds on neuroscientifically sound theories and is being validated on a competition dataset consisting of multichannel EEG trials from five different imagined prompts. Despite its simplicity, the presented methodology achieves over 70% accuracy in some classes, which is on par with State-of-the-Art performance on the dataset. Our methodology performs significantly better in monosyllabic prompts (i.e., 'yes' and 'stop') which may constitute it more appropriate in immediate-response critical BCI applications. Moreover, the conducted preliminary analysis that was used for sensor selection and onset detection sheds light into the understudied neural phenomena of imagined speech as captured in EEG signals.

Keywords: Riemannian Geometry · Imagined Speech · Speech Imagery · Covariance Estimator · Electroencephalography (EEG) · Approximate Joint Diagonalization (AJD) · Brain-Computer Interfaces

*This work was supported by the NeuroMkt project, co-financed by the European Regional Development Fund of the EU and Greek National Funds through the Operational Program "Competitiveness, Entrepreneurship and Innovation", under RESEARCH CREATE INNOVATE (T2EDK-03661).

F. Liu et al. (Eds.): BI 2023, LNAI 13974, pp. 409–419, 2023.
https://doi.org/10.1007/978-3-031-43075-6_35

1   Introduction

We, as human beings, keep talking within us most of the time. We rehearse over and over again how to manage a particular difficult situation, what to say to a prospective customer, how to answer certain critical questions in an interview, and so on. This speech, unlike the overt speech in a conversation with another person, is imagined and hence, there is no movement of the articulators. Thus, imagined speech is defined as the internal process of the voluntary imagination of speaking without actually moving any of the articulators.

Decoding and communicating human thought into the outside world, so as called, 'reading the mind' (i.e. to interpret internally-generated speech) has been a long-held ambition of Brain-Computer Interfaces (BCIs). Imagined speech has recently been studied as an intuitive paradigm [12], with the goal of decoding the neural responses generated via imagining pronunciation. This paradigm is particularly suitable for building communication systems and restoring communication for individuals that have lost the ability to speak (e.g. Stroke patients) as their ability to actively think or imagine speaking remains intact. While this paradigm currently lacks in terms of performance compared to other paradigms, it has multiclass scalability [8], thus showing the possibility of building extensible BCI systems [17] characterized by higher degrees of freedom. In this direction, imagined speech BCIs can be employed to mitigate the shortcomings of typical BCI paradigms (e.g., motor imagery, SSVEP, ERPs), like the limited number of distinct prompts/commands or the difficulty in training someone to use these systems [1], since they allow users to convey their intentions in a natural manner. Out of the neuroimaging methods currently available, Electroencephalography (EEG), is the one encountered the most in imagined speech BCIs as it is the least invasive and the most cost-effective. Although EEG may lack in terms of spatial resolution, compared to other neuroimaging technologies, it can reliably capture brain activity changes over shorter timescales (i.e. high temporal resolution).

Despite the recent efforts of the neuroscientific community [18], imagined speech recognition has proven to be a difficult task to achieve within an acceptable range of classification accuracy [14]. Concerning the particular case of EEG-based decoding schemes, a recent review study [20] uncovered that conventional Machine Learning algorithms (e.g., random forests, LDA, SVMs, etc.) are typically employed. Contemporarily, the aforementioned Machine Learning approaches are combined either with statistical or wavelet-based features. It was only until very recently that imagined speech decoding methods took advantage of modern Machine Learning schemes such as Deep Learning (mostly CNN architectures) [4,7]. In the same direction, Riemannian geometry, which exhibits impressive decoding capabilities in other BCI paradigms, like motor imagery [5], neuromarketing [11] and P300 detection [19], has not been studied sufficiently in imagined speech. This fact indicates that this particular paradigm is still in its infancy and there is plenty of room for active research and improvement.

Hence, our study revolves around the intuitive paradigm of speech imagery as captured in EEG signals and aims to explore the potential of Affine Invariant Riemannian Metric (AIRM)-induced Riemannian geometry when combined with a more delicate covariance estimation. Despite some recent efforts [2,22], to the best of our knowledge this is the first study, in the context of imagined speech, that takes advantage of the equivalence between the sensor and source space as enabled by AIRM that is typically employed on Riemannian geometry settings for EEG decoding tasks. The employed covariance estimation is based on the Approximate Joint Diagonalization (AJD) of the spatial covariance matrices, which in essence, finds a common unitary matrix that allows us to approximately diagonalize all the spatial covariance matrices (e.g. each covariance matrix corresponds to a different trial which took place in the same recording session) simultaneously. Then, the obtained dominantly diagonal matrices are used, by considering only their diagonal entries and discarding the almost zero off-diagonal elements, to reconstruct the covariance matrices under a common mixing model (expressed by the common unitary matrix uncovered through AJD) [16]. Intuitively, this procedure serves as a denoising procedure on the spatial covariance matrices and leads to more robust estimates of the spatial covariance pattern.

The resulting covariance estimation is based on a preliminary analysis that was conducted in an effort to determine the most appropriate sensors, frequency ranges and time segments that the imagined speech phenomenon is taking place. This preliminary analysis takes advantage of the continuous wavelet transform and is performed in an unsupervised manner. By doing so, we were able to obtain a neuroscientifically informed idea about the imagined speech phenomena that remain understudied [24], as captured by means of EEG.

Our approach sets its ground on well-developed neuroscientific theories and is validated on a competition dataset (2020 International BCI Competition; Task 3 [14]) that contains multichannel EEG trials from five distinct imagined prompts. The employed methodological framework is characterized by simplicity (both in terms of the covariance estimation and the demployed machine learning scheme which is based on k-nearest neighbours) while its performance exceeds 70% accuracy in some classes which is on par to State-of-the-Art (SotA) performance on this particular dataset. As presented in the Results section the employed methodology performs significantly better in monosyllabic prompts (i.e., 'yes' and 'stop') which may constitute it more appropriate in immediate-response critical BCI applications. Moreover, the conducted preliminary analysis that was used for sensor selection and onset detection sheds light into the underlying phenomena of imagined speech. Overall, our approach ranks 2nd among the published competition results [14], a fact that further demonstrates its efficiency and neuroscientific validity.

2 Dataset

The original dataset (DOI: 10.17605/OSF.IO/PQ7VB) consists of 15 participants (S1-S15), aged between 20–30 years, who were instructed to silently imagine pronouncing five different words/phrases ("hello," "help me," "stop," "thank you," and "yes") without moving their mouth or making any sound. The participants were seated comfortably in front of a 24-inch LCD monitor screen and were asked to avoid any other mental activity except for the task at hand. The imagination trials were conducted with a black screen to eliminate any external stimuli. An auditory cue for one of the five words/phrases was randomly presented for 2 s, followed by a presentation of a cross mark lasting between 0.8–1.2 s. The participants were instructed to begin their imagined speech immediately after the cross mark disappeared, and this cycle was repeated four times for each cue. After the four cycles, there was a 3-second relaxation phase to prepare for the next cue. Figure 1 depicts the aforementioned experimental procedure's timeline.

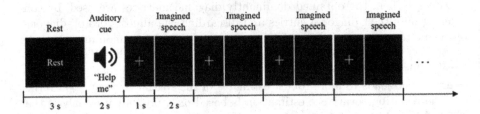

Fig. 1. Timeline of the experimental procedure followed during the imagined speech recording sessions. Image Source: [14]

A total of 400 trials per participant (80 trials per class) were recorded, out of which 60 trials per class are provided for training and 10 trials per class for validation purposes. The test data consist of 10 trials per class too. The train-validation-test split is provided in a subject-specific manner and all trials are belonging to a single recording session.

3 Methodology

3.1 Riemannian Geometry

Let us denote by $\mathbf{X}_i \in \mathbb{R}^{E \times T}, i = 1, \ldots, n$ a multichannel EEG trial, with E denoting the number of electrodes, T the number of samples in time and n the number of available trials. Each trial (assuming zero mean signals) can also be described by the corresponding spatial covariance matrix $\mathbf{C}_i = \frac{1}{T-1}\mathbf{X}_i\mathbf{X}_i^\top \in \mathbb{R}^{E \times E}$. Under a sufficiently large T value to guarantee a full rank covariance matrix, spatial covariance matrices are Symmetric and Positive Definite (SPD) that lie on a Riemannian manifold.

When dealing with EEG data, the manifold of SPD matrices denoted by $Sym_E^+ = \{\mathbf{C} \in \mathbb{R}^{E \times E} : \mathbf{x}^\top \mathbf{C} \mathbf{x} > 0, \text{ for all non-zero } \mathbf{x} \in \mathbb{R}^E\}$, is typically studied when it is endowed with the AIRM [23],

$$\langle \mathbf{A}, \mathbf{B} \rangle_{\mathbf{P}} \triangleq Trace(\mathbf{P}^{-1}\mathbf{A}\mathbf{P}^{-1}\mathbf{B}) \tag{1}$$

for $\mathbf{P} \in Sym_E^+$ and $\mathbf{A}, \mathbf{B} \in T_E^+(\mathbf{P})$, where $T_E^+(\mathbf{P})$ denotes the tangent space of Sym_E^+ at $\mathbf{P}$. Then, the following geodesic distance is induced

$$\delta(\mathbf{C}_i, \mathbf{C}_j) = \left\| logm(\mathbf{C}_i^{-1/2}\mathbf{C}_j\mathbf{C}_i^{-1/2}) \right\|_F = \sqrt{\sum_{q=1}^{E} log^2 \lambda_q} \qquad (2)$$

with $logm(\cdot)$ denoting the matrix logarithm operator and λ_q the eigenvalues of $\mathbf{C}_i^{-1/2}\mathbf{C}_j\mathbf{C}_i^{-1/2}$ or similarly of the matrix $\mathbf{C}_i^{-1}\mathbf{C}_j$. These two matrices hold the same eigenvalues while the indices i and j can be permuted.

As its name states, δ is affine-invariant for non singular matrices $\mathbf{W}$, i.e. $\delta(\mathbf{W}\mathbf{C}_i\mathbf{W}^\top, \mathbf{W}\mathbf{C}_j\mathbf{W}^\top) = \delta(\mathbf{C}_i, \mathbf{C}_j)$. This is an important property in EEG signal processing since it provides equivalence between the sensor and the source space [6]. According to the prevailing EEG model, the recorded activity is well approximated by a linear mixture of source signals. Hence, $\mathbf{X}_i = \mathbf{M}\mathbf{S}_i$ with $\mathbf{M}$ denoting the mixing matrix and $\mathbf{S}_i$ the source signals. Then, by substituting the observed signal with the equivalent mixing of sources, one may obtain the following covariance matrix, $\mathbf{C}_i = \frac{1}{T-1}\mathbf{M}\mathbf{S}_i\mathbf{S}_i^\top\mathbf{M}^\top$. Therefore, the mixing procedure in the time domain results in a congruent transformation in the corresponding covariance matrices. It becomes obvious that since δ is invariant to such transformations, the two spaces can be equivalently treated under the AIRM.

3.2   AJD-Based Covariance Estimation

The mixing matrix, denoted as $\mathbf{M}$, is determined by the position and orientation of dipoles in the brain, the physical characteristics of the head, and the placement of electrodes on the scalp. It is therefore reasonable to assume that $\mathbf{M}$ remains constant for a certain period, such as during a single recording session. Assuming that sources are independent and the associated activity (i.e., source signals) are uncorrelated, the spatial covariance matrices of the sources are diagonal.

The process of estimating the mixing matrix, denoted as $\mathbf{M}$, from the observed sensor signals is an ill-posed problem known as Blind Source Separation (BSS) [21]. Two approaches are commonly used to tackle the BSS problem: The first approach is Independent Component Analysis (ICA), which aims to transform the data so that the components become as independent as possible [13]. An alternative approach involves using the diagonality of certain characteristic matrices derived from the data to approximate $\mathbf{M}^{-1}$ through the concept of AJD [26]. This involves finding an orthonormal change of basis denoted as $\mathbf{U}$, which makes the set of symmetric square matrices as diagonal as possible. This, second approach, intuitively uncovers the 'average eigenspace' of matrices that are approximately jointly diagonalizable [3].

Following the notation of Sect. 3.1, we denote by $\mathbf{C}_i$ covariance matrix that corresponds to the EEG trial, $\mathbf{X}_i$. Let $\mathbf{U}$ be the orthonormal matrix calculated by AJD over the set of $\mathbf{C}_i$ with $i = 1, \ldots, n$ that estimates the mixing matrix $\mathbf{M}$. Then, each $\mathbf{C}_i$ can be transformed to a dominantly diagonal matrix through $\mathbf{U}^\top\mathbf{C}_i\mathbf{U}$. As such, we can reconstruct (i.e., re-estimate) all the spatial covariance matrices under the constraint of a common eigenspace by using the formula

$\tilde{\mathbf{C}}_i = \mathbf{U}diag(\mathbf{U}^\top \mathbf{C}_i \mathbf{U})\mathbf{U}^\top$. Here, the $diag(\cdot)$ operator, which discards the non-diagonal elements of a matrix and obtaining a strictly diagonal matrix, is applied upon an almost diagonal matrix and hence achieves a good re-estimation of the original covariance matrix.

This estimation approach forces all the spatial covariance matrices to admit a common mixing matrix and, hence, acts as a denoising procedure that abides to well-established neuroscientific theories. In addition, the estimated covariance matrices are guaranteed to hold the SPD property which allows the employment of Riemannian geometry. A more detailed description about the advantages and the mathematical properties of this covariance estimation can be found in [16].

4   Results

4.1   Preliminary Study: Spectrotemporal Analysis and Sensor Selection

Taking into account the high subject variability encountered in EEG data, a preliminary analysis for each subject was performed that aimed to identify the exact brain areas (i.e. sensors), timing (i.e. trial segments) and spectral components (i.e. frequency ranges) that the phenomenon of imagined speech takes place, with the scope of decoding the underlying phenomenon in the best possible way. In this context, a wavelet filter bank approach that disentangles the input signal into multiple frequency components without losing the signal's temporal characteristics is employed. It is noted that wavelets are characterized by time locality, allowing an efficient capture of transient behavior in a signal, which is of essence in the case of imagined speech decoding. Working on the training set for each subject independently, we applied the continuous wavelet transform (FBCWT, based on morse wavelet function and Matlab filter bank implementation) within the [1–100] Hz frequency range and derive the associated scalogram for each trial separately. Following the aforementioned procedure, all single-trial scalograms were averaged, regardless their label, to derive a spectrotemporal profile of activation for every sensor. Finally, using the baseline period, the mean and std of each scale was estimated and used to derive a threshold value (mean+3std) that in turn was employed to reveal the significant event-related spectral perturbations. The process is completed with detection of the sensors, segments and frequencies of interest based on the thresholding process.

Figure 2 illustrates the averaged FBCWT patterns for an indicative set of sensors for an exemplar subject (i.e. subject S1), after the thresholding process is completed. It is important to note here, that for clarity purposes only a selected number of sensors is presented. The visual inspection of the figure provides answers regarding the three research questions posed in this subsection. Starting from identification of the brain areas that the imagined speech phenomenon takes place, it is evident that the most informative sensors are located over the Broca's area (e.g., FT7, FT9 and T7), a trend that aligns well with what is reported in relevant bibliography regarding the brain areas activated during the task of imagined speech [25]. On the contrary, the activation levels

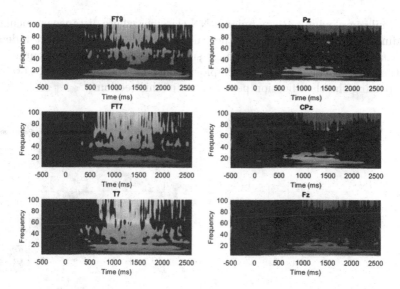

Fig. 2. Spectrotemporal analysis for the sensors characterized by the highest (left panel) and lowest (right panel) activation levels. The stimulus onset is indicated by the black vertical identified at t=0 s and corresponds to cross disappearance as depicted in Fig. 1.

on sensors located over areas that are not associated with the mental speech task, like the middle area (e.g., sensors Pz, CPz and Fz), is significantly lower. Moving to the temporal domain, it is obvious that a reaction period of approximately 500 ms is required before the mental imagery process is initiated by the participant, which is typical, while varying among individuals, when cue-based triggers mark the initiation of a task. Consequently, this process, upon appropriate modifications, can be employed as an onset detection procedure, which is of paramount importance in self-paced and online BCI paradigms. In the spectral domain, and specifically for the sensors characterized by high activity (such as FT7, FT9 and T7), three frequency ranges of interest can be identified: (i) Low ([5–20] Hz), (ii) Medium ([40–55] Hz) and, (iii) High ([≥70] Hz), with the High frequency range being empirically identified, based on the validation set, as the one with the highest discriminative power. Finally, we should note that while the trends observed for the subject S1 are similar for the other subjects, the exact optimal sensors, segments and frequencies, as expected differ among them, showcasing the necessity and importance of this preliminary study.

4.2   Classification Results

Figure 3 presents the overall accuracy of the proposed decoder (Fig. 3A, Fig. 3B) and also the accuracy scores obtained for each subject independently (Fig. 3C). In particular, the employed decoder is based on the estimation of covariance matrix (as described in Sect. 3.2) from EEG signals in the frequency range above

70 Hz while employing a Riemannian k-NN classifier where distance is calculated according to Eq. 2. By exploiting the validation set for each subject independently, $k = 3$ was identified as the most suitable value in terms of accuracy. We note that the provided test set is employed only for the purposes of obtaining and reporting the classification performance in this section.

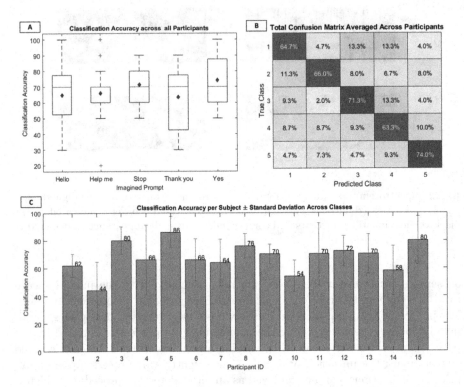

Fig. 3. The global and subject-wise performance of the proposed decoder. (A) The overall classification accuracy compartmentalized for each imagined prompt, (B) The total confusion matrix, and (C) The average classification accuracy per subject.

It is evident that despite the high subject variability, the majority of the subjects perform well when the imagined prompt is monosyllabic (see Fig. 3A). This trend may imply that a different approach focusing on syllables rather than words may be required to better decipher the phenomenon of imagined speech. In the same direction, disentangling the two prompts starting with the same syllable "He" (i.e. "Hello" and "Help me") seems highly challenging, given the high false positive values. Returning to the subject variability issue, while the accuracy for the majority of the subjects revolve around 70%, there are subjects with accuracy lower or barely exceeding 50% (i.e. S2, S10, S14), while there are also cases characterized by near-optimal performance (e.g. S3, S5). Considering the nature of the task (i.e. mental task) that in some cases may not be completely straightforward, it is not unlikely that some participants may require a familiarization period prior to the engagement with such tasks, as in the case of the motor imagery paradigm [9].

Despite the aforementioned, the proposed decoding scheme provides classification scores that significantly exceed the random level for this five class problem that comes at 20%. Finally, it must be noted that the achieved performance surpasses all but one the competitive approaches regarding the selected dataset [14]. Additionally, the employed AJD-based covariance estimator surpasses the classical covariance estimator, under the same classification setting, by 3.1% while exhibiting the same trends in class-specific classification results.

5 Discussion and Conclusion

In this paper we proposed a Riemannian geometry-based approach that relies on a delicate and neuroscientificaly valid estimation of the covariance matrix combined with tools of Riemannian geometry (as a result of endowing the SPD manifold with the AIRM). The obtained results demonstrate the effectiveness on the employed scheme while showing the potential of Riemmanian geometry in the demanding task of EEG-based imagined speech decoding. As presented in the Results section our approach achieves State-of-the-Art results that are well-above the 20% random chance of the employed competition dataset and our presented approach is only surpassed by one competitor. It is important to note that while competition outcomes have been published [14], the corresponding methodologies deployed for the purposes of competition are not available. Hence the comparison presented in our work is confined to the classification performance and cannot be extended to more qualitative characteristics since they remain unknown.

In addition to the proposed decoding scheme our work presents a spectro-temporal preliminary analysis that investigates the frequency scales, time segments and sensors for the imagined speech phenomenon. Our findings suggest that the imagined speech takes place 500ms after the cue onset while the consistency among the wavelet-based activations paves the way for self-paced BCIs that fall under the imagined speech paradigm. Moreover, our preliminary analysis uncovered the involvement of three distinct frequency ranges in the speech imagery task. Although only the higher one ($70\,\text{Hz} \leq$) is exploited in the proposed decoding scheme, it becomes evident that all three could play a crucial role and therefore their effect in the decoding process should be further investigated. Moreover, our findings leave room for improvement by hinting that the combination and fusion of multiple frequency ranges may lead to more robust imagined speech decoders [9]. Ultimately, our preliminary analysis led to an unsupervised sensor selection procedure by means of keeping the sensors that exhibit the most powerful activations during the imagined speech task. Although the identified as the most 'informative' sensors are well-aligned with the existing literature, they may lack in terms of discriminability. Therefore, more suitable sensors selection approaches could be employed (e.g., [10,15]) in an effort to achieve superior classification performance.

In more broad terms, imagined speech as a BCI paradigm is still in its infancy and several aspects should be explored thoroughly. As our study indicates some imagined prompts (i.e., monosyllabic words) are characterized by higher decoding robustness whereas close-to-echoing words seem to be conflated by the employed decoding scheme. Although particular claims cannot be made considering the extent of our study, valuable insights with respect to the most informative brain areas, physiology of the anticipated cortical activations and the most suitable prompts (e.g., words, phonemes or syllables) could be derived upon further exploration. The aforementioned will constitute the basis for future work towards conceptualizing novel decoding frameworks that will take advantage of the neural processes underpinning the imagined speech paradigm.

References

1. Abdulkader, S.N., Atia, A., Mostafa, M.S.M.: Brain computer interfacing: applications and challenges. Egypt. Informa. J. **16**(2), 213–230 (2015)
2. Bakhshali, M.A., Khademi, M., Ebrahimi-Moghadam, A., Moghimi, S.: EEG signal classification of imagined speech based on Riemannian distance of correntropy spectral density. Biomed. Signal Process. Control **59**, 101899 (2020)
3. Cardoso, J.F., Souloumiac, A.: Jacobi angles for simultaneous diagonalization. SIAM J. Matrix Anal. Appl. **17**(1), 161–164 (1996)
4. Chengaiyan, S., Retnapandian, A.S., Anandan, K.: Identification of vowels in consonant-vowel-consonant words from speech imagery based EEG signals. Cogn. Neurodyn. **14**(1), 1–19 (2020)
5. Chu, Y., et al.: Decoding multiclass motor imagery EEG from the same upper limb by combining Riemannian geometry features and partial least squares regression. J. Neural Eng. **17**(4), 046029 (2020)
6. Congedo, M., Barachant, A., Bhatia, R.: Riemannian geometry for EEG-based brain-computer interfaces; a primer and a review. Brain-Comput. Interfaces **4**(3), 155–174 (2017)
7. Cooney, C., Korik, A., Folli, R., Coyle, D.: Evaluation of hyperparameter optimization in machine and deep learning methods for decoding imagined speech EEG. Sensors **20**(16), 4629 (2020)
8. García-Salinas, J.S., Villaseñor-Pineda, L., Reyes-García, C.A., Torres-García, A.A.: Transfer learning in imagined speech EEG-based BCIs. Biomed. Signal Process. Control **50**, 151–157 (2019)
9. Georgiadis, K., Laskaris, N., Nikolopoulos, S., Kompatsiaris, I.: Connectivity steered graph Fourier transform for motor imagery BCI decoding. J. Neural Eng. **16**(5), 056021 (2019)
10. Georgiadis, K., Adamos, D.A., Nikolopoulos, S., Laskaris, N., Kompatsiaris, I.: A graph-theoretic sensor-selection scheme for covariance-based motor imagery (mi) decoding. In: 2020 28th European Signal Processing Conference (EUSIPCO), pp. 1234–1238. IEEE (2021)
11. Georgiadis, K., Kalaganis, F.P., Oikonomou, V.P., Nikolopoulos, S., Laskaris, N.A., Kompatsiaris, I.: [R]NeuMark: a Riemannian EEG analysis framework for neuromarketing. Brain Inform. **9**(1), 22 (2022)
12. Herff, C., de Pesters, A., Heger, D., Brunner, P., Schalk, G., Schultz, T.: Towards continuous speech recognition for BCI. Brain-Comput. Interface Res. State Art Summary **5**, 21–29 (2017)

13. Hyvärinen, A.: Survey on independent component analysis (1999)
14. Jeong, J.H., et al.: 2020 international brain-computer interface competition: a review. Front. Hum. Neurosci. **16**, 898300 (2022)
15. Kalaganis, F.P., Laskaris, N.A., Chatzilari, E., Nikolopoulos, S., Kompatsiaris, I.: A Riemannian geometry approach to reduced and discriminative covariance estimation in brain computer interfaces. IEEE Trans. Biomed. Eng. **67**(1), 245–255 (2019)
16. Kalaganis, F.P., Laskaris, N.A., Oikonomou, V.P., Nikopolopoulos, S., Kompatsiaris, I.: Revisiting Riemannian geometry-based EEG decoding through approximate joint diagonalization. J. Neural Eng. **19**(6), 066030 (2022)
17. Lee, S.H., Lee, M., Jeong, J.H., Lee, S.W.: Towards an EEG-based intuitive BCI communication system using imagined speech and visual imagery. In: 2019 IEEE International Conference on Systems, Man and Cybernetics (SMC), pp. 4409–4414. IEEE (2019)
18. Lee, Y.E., Lee, S.H.: EEG-transformer: self-attention from transformer architecture for decoding EEG of imagined speech. In: 2022 10th International Winter Conference on Brain-Computer Interface (BCI), pp. 1–4. IEEE (2022)
19. Li, F., Xia, Y., Wang, F., Zhang, D., Li, X., He, F.: Transfer learning algorithm of P300-EEG signal based on XDAWN spatial filter and Riemannian geometry classifier. Appl. Sci. **10**(5), 1804 (2020)
20. Lopez-Bernal, D., Balderas, D., Ponce, P., Molina, A.: A state-of-the-art review of EEG-based imagined speech decoding. Front. Hum. Neurosci. **16**, 867281 (2022)
21. Müller, K.R., Vigario, R., Meinecke, F., Ziehe, A.: Blind source separation techniques for decomposing event-related brain signals. Int. J. Bifurcat. Chaos **14**(02), 773–791 (2004)
22. Nguyen, C.H., Karavas, G.K., Artemiadis, P.: Inferring imagined speech using EEG signals: a new approach using Riemannian manifold features. J. Neural Eng. **15**(1), 016002 (2017)
23. Pennec, X., Fillard, P., Ayache, N.: A Riemannian framework for tensor computing. Int. J. Comput. Vision **66**(1), 41–66 (2006)
24. Proix, T., et al.: Imagined speech can be decoded from low-and cross-frequency intracranial EEG features. Nat. Commun. **13**(1), 48 (2022)
25. Si, X., Li, S., Xiang, S., Yu, J., Ming, D.: Imagined speech increases the hemodynamic response and functional connectivity of the dorsal motor cortex. J. Neural Eng. **18**(5), 056048 (2021)
26. Ziehe, A.: Blind source separation based on joint diagonalization of matrices with applications in biomedical signal processing. Ph.D. thesis, Universität Potsdam (2005)

Automatic Sleep-Wake Scoring with Optimally Selected EEG Channels from High-Density EEG

Karoline Seljevoll Herleiksplass[1]([✉]), Luis Alfredo Moctezuma[2], Junya Furuki[2], Yoko Suzuki[2], Takashi Abe[2], and Marta Molinas[1]

[1] Department of Engineering Cybernetics, Norwegian University of Science and Technology, Trondheim, Norway
karolshe@stud.ntnu.no
[2] International Institute of Integrative Sleep Medicine (WPI-IIIS), University of Tsukuba, Tsukuba, Ibaraki, Japan

Abstract. This paper presents a sleep versus wake-classification model based on high-density electroencephalographic (EEG) sleep data. In a second stage, an optimization algorithm is applied to select the minimal set of EEG channels according to their contribution to classification performance. The performance of these subsets are compared to the ones recommended by the American Academy of Sleep Medicine (AASM) and with the 128 available channels in the tested dataset. We focus on accurate classification of the wake stage because of its importance as a metric of sleep quality and in diagnosing several sleep disorders. The performed experiment demonstrates that high-density EEG channels can achieve an accuracy and kappa score of 0.970 and 0.778 using the proposed method and dataset. But most importantly, the results from the optimization algorithm, Non-dominated Sorting Genetic Algorithm (NSGA)-III, indicate that using 3 to 9 channels can yield an average accuracy ranging between 0.955 to 0.975 and a kappa score between 0.678 and 0.795. The three most important channels detected by the optimization algorithm were D25, A19 and B14 from the 10-10 international system. This represents a significant improvement compared to the results obtained using the AASM-recommended channels, which yielded an average accuracy and kappa score of 0.951 and 0.573, respectively.

Keywords: Sleep staging · Electroencephalography (EEG) · Channel selection · Multi-objective optimization · Convolutional Neural Networks (CNN)

1 Introduction

Having high-quality sleep is crucial for maintaining good, both physical and mental health. Sleep disturbances and sleep disorders can lead to various health problems and are becoming a growing concern that requires medical attention.

F. Liu et al. (Eds.): BI 2023, LNAI 13974, pp. 420–431, 2023.
https://doi.org/10.1007/978-3-031-43075-6_36

Sleep interruptions can be due to many different factors and result in nighttime awakenings. Patients suffering from the sleep disorder insomnia have difficulties sleeping through the night and have trouble getting back to sleep after unwanted awakenings. The frequent occurrence of nighttime awakenings may lead to or signify a risk of developing sleep disorders.

Understanding the quality of sleep and the identification and measurement of wake periods throughout sleep is essential for diagnosing and treating many sleep disorders. Particularly key metrics that can offer significant insights into the overall sleep architecture include identifying and measuring the length and frequency of wakeful periods throughout a night of sleep. As such, accurate and reliable methods for capturing wake periods are essential for ensuring effective sleep monitoring and management [1–3].

Polysomnographic (PSG) recordings provide measurement for electroencephalography (EEG), electromyography (EMG), electrocardiography (ECG), electrooculography (EOG), and respiratory parameters. PSG are used in clinical settings to monitor and classify sleep stages or look for specific sleep patterns. This analysis can then be used to monitor and diagnose sleep disorders. The data is normally split into 30 s epochs, and each epoch is classified into one sleep stage by a sleep expert. This process is considered complex and time-consuming. This known challenge has motivated research using machine learning models for automatic sleep stage classification [4].

The need to handle large amounts of data that require significant storage space has prompted research into using smaller amounts of data while still achieving acceptable sleep stage classification accuracy. As EEG signals are commonly used in sleep research, there has been a desire to use a few channels to achieve real-time sleep staging. The American Academy of Sleep Medicine (AASM) recommends using three EEG channels: A28, B22, and C4 from the international 10-10 configuration [5].

Methods for capturing sleep data that are more widely available than PSG have been proposed. The Dreem Headband is a more user-friendly, inexpensive, and comfortable alternative to PSG, allowing sleep data to be collected at home. The Dreem Headband measures movement, head position, respiration trace, and rate using five EEG channels and a 3D accelerometer. The following EEG channels have been used with the 10-10 international convention: F7, F8, Fp1, O1 and O2. In research, the Dreem Headband has obtained an overall accuracy of 83.5% and an overall average kappa score of 74.8 [6,7]

Previous research on binary sleep classification has employed varying numbers of channels, including single-channel analysis. For sleep-wake classification with single-channel EEG, works have reported accuracies up to 97.9% [8]. By using 8 channels, Ronzhina et al., for instance, obtained a sleep-wake accuracy of 96.06% and a Cohen's kappa score (kappa) of 0.666. Zhu et al. obtained an accuracy of 97.9% and a kappa score of 0.96 with their model, utilizing single-channel-pair (Pz-Oz) EEG data. Both works used EEG data from the publicly available Sleep-EDF Database, which consists of 30-second epochs, 3919 samples of wake, and 3562 samples of sleep [8–11].

Recently, a convolutional neural network (CNN) called EEGNet has been applied to EEG-related applications [12]. The EEGNet has been combined with bidirectional long short-term memory (BiLSTM) for sleep staging, and authors reported 87% of accuracy for 5-class classification [13]. For this, authors have randomly mixed selected delta, theta, and beta frequencies for data augmentation to overcome the class imbalance problem. In general, the current state-of-the-art reports accuracies around 87% ± 4.

This study aims to utilize raw data without pre-processing from an unbalanced dataset to achieve the most realistic representation of a real-world situation. It is desirable to employ deep learning techniques to avoid being dependent on prior sleep knowledge of the unprocessed data.

In this work, we explore sleep-wake classification using the EEGNet. Our main focus is testing a multi-objective optimization technique, called Nondominated Sorting Genetic Algorithm (NSGA)-III, successfully used to reduce the number of required EEG channels for sleep-wake classification.

2   Materials and Methods

2.1   Dataset

The dataset was collected at the International Institute for Integrative Sleep Medicine (WPI-IIIS) at the University of Tsukuba, Japan, and the data collection was approved by the ethics committee of the University. It consists of EEG recordings from 14 subjects (5 female and 9 male, 22.5 ± 0.9 years), who were sleeping for about 8 h while their data were collected using 128 EEG channels (BioSemi 128 configuration) with a sample rate of 1024 Hz, three EOG channels, three EMG channels, and two mastoid channels. The sleep stages were manually labelled every 30 s by a sleep expert from WPI-IIIS. In the present study, we considered 13 subjects, excluding one of the subjects that interrupted the data collection during the night.

The data were downsampled to 128 Hz, and each 30-second epoch was divided into 2-second segments. By utilizing a small segment size, it is possible to increase the number of instances of the minority wake class, which may contribute to better learning of patterns from the minority class. Additionally, this will allow us to detect the transition between different sleep stages swiftly. Similar comparisons have been conducted in the following research [14].

The dataset was divided into 50% as training data, 25% as validation data and 25% as test data. The data utilized in this study was in its raw form and was not subjected to any preprocessing. This is in contrast to publicly available datasets that are typically preprocessed and consider disturbances such as noise. Utilizing raw data with deep learning methods obviates the need for prior sleep knowledge compared to feature extraction methods. The dataset is highly unbalanced, which may affect the machine learning models, and the distribution between wake and sleep is presented in Table 1.

Table 1. The percentage distribution of wake and sleep stages for all subjects in the WPI-IIIS dataset.

	Subject												
	1	2	3	4	5	6	7	8	9	10	11	12	13
Wake	6.6	5.7	8.4	6.8	8.3	16.5	6.6	6.7	11.0	10.9	4.6	5.9	4.2
Sleep	93.4	94.3	91.6	93.2	91.7	83.5	93.4	93.3	89.0	89.1	95.4	94.1	95.8

2.2 Classification Model

EEGNet is a compact CNN developed for EEG-based brain-computer interface (BCI) [12]. Its architecture aims to be generalizable across different BCI paradigms and is claimed to be robust enough to learn features for a wide range of different BCI tasks. The architecture of EEGNet includes two convolutional blocks followed by a classification layer. The first block is designed to learn temporal frequency filters from the input signal, while the second block extracts more abstract features from the EEG data. The network's design is based on a combination of spatial and temporal filtering techniques to produce interpretable features that can be applied across several BCI paradigms. EEGNet was developed to encapsulate the well-known features of EEG signals, including filter-bank construction and optimal spatial filtering, while reducing the number of trainable parameters [12].

EEGNet has the ability to capture both spatial and frequency information from the EEG signals. Together with the small amount of trainable parameters, the model can be more efficient to train and is less likely to overfitting compared to other neural network architectures. EEGNet has also shown to be robust to variations in the sampling rate and robust to limited training data. These qualifications look promising for use in sleep-wake classification with the presented dataset.

The training of the model is performed subject-by-subject, and default values from the implementation are used for the dropout rate (0.5) and batch size (16). The optimizer used is ADAM and the loss function is binary cross-entropy, as default. Early stopping is used for the number of epochs to prevent the model from overfitting.

2.3 Channel Selection

NSGA is a multi-objective optimization algorithm that can optimize complex problems based on one or more objectives. NSGA is a genetic algorithm that is based on the natural phenomenon of natural selection and the survival of the fittest through evolution, including mutation and crossover. A genetic algorithm works by generating different possible solutions, defined as chromosomes. A population is a collection of several chromosomes. The algorithm evaluates the result of each chromosome in the population based on the defined objectives and constraints. The chromosomes are ranked based on their level of non-domination.

If no other chromosome has a better evaluation value, the chromosome is considered non-dominated. The non-dominated chromosomes are used to create the next generation using crossover and random mutations. The process is then repeated for several generations, each producing a set of non-dominated solutions [15].

NSGA-II, an NSGA extension, modifies the survival of the chromosomes by selecting frontwise, using a Manhattan Distance-based crowding distance metric, and modifies the mating process by selecting by rank and crowding distance. NSGA-III further modifies NSGA-II, using initialized reference directions for optimization. If dividing the front, survivors are chosen by prioritizing the most underrepresented reference direction and the solution with the smallest normalized objective space's perpendicular distance. NSGA-III seeks a non-dominated solution for each reference line. [15].

We have implemented NSGA-III (NSGA) for EEG channel selection to space the reference points evenly. The optimization problem consisted of four objectives: maximize the 1) model accuracy, and from the test set the 2) Cohen's kappa coefficient (kappa) and 3) the area under the receiver operating characteristic curve (AUROC) score, all this, while 4) minimizing the number of EEG channels used during the classification process. The NSGA-III configuration represents each channel in a 128-binary array, 1 if the channel will be used for the classification process, and 0 if not. NSGA-III generated 10 chromosomes (10 possible EEG channel combinations) per generation, and the process was repeated for 150 generations.

Throughout the experimental phase of the investigation, it was observed that utilizing as few as 8 channels yielded encouraging outcomes. Consequently, the logical next step was to explore the feasibility of solutions that employed fewer than 10 channels. To this end, optimization was conducted under the constraint of limiting the number of channels to no more than 10. Similar findings were reached through experimentation with one or two channels, as the sensitivity of wake was observed to be low.

Given the configuration of our experiments, we performed all the experiments using GPUs on the NTNU IDUN computing cluster [16]. The cluster has more than 70 nodes and 90 general-purpose GPUs (GPGPUs). Each node contains two Intel Xeon cores and at least 128 GB of main memory, and is connected to an Infiniband network. Half of the nodes are equipped with two or more Nvidia Tesla P100 or V100 GPGPUs. Idun's storage is provided by two storage arrays and a Lustre parallel distributed file system.

3 Results

3.1 Sleep-Wake Classification Using High-Density EEG

After the data labeling step, the EEG signal segments were used as input to the CNN to classify between sleep and wake segments. The presented results are the average based on the training and evaluation of five separate models with different training, validation, and test subset splits. In this experiment, we use

Table 2. Average performance with all the subjects for sleep-wake classification using 128 channels and the AASM-recommended channels.

	Accuracy	Kappa	AUROC	Sensitivity Wake	Sensitivity Sleep
128 channels	0.970 ± 0.018	0.778 ± 0.086	0.855 ± 0.051	0.717 ± 0.098	0.992 ± 0.008
AASM channels	0.951 ± 0.024	0.573 ± 0.149	0.716 ± 0.073	0.438 ± 0.146	0.994 ± 0.007

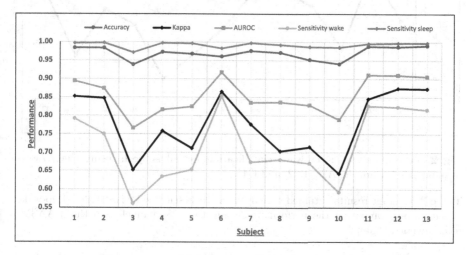

Fig. 1. Performance of sleep-wake classification for all subjects using 128 channels.

the 128 available channels and the three AASM-recommended EEG channels. Table 2 presents the average results among all subjects. The results for each subject with all channels are presented in Fig. 1 and with AASM-recommended channels in Fig. 2.

The distribution of sleep data affects the classification model's overall performance. A comparison of the distribution in Table 1 with the results presented in Fig. 1 and Fig. 2 reveals that Subject 6 attained the highest sensitivity for wake in both cases and also had the highest distribution of wake class. Conversely, Subject 9 had the second-highest distribution of wake class but displayed one of the weakest performances. Subject 13, who had the lowest distribution of sleep, demonstrated better performance than many of the subjects with higher distributions of wake.

3.2 EEG Channel Selection Using NSGA-III for Sleep-Wake Classification

This experiment aims to explore the feasibility of achieving comparable outcomes by utilizing fewer channels compared to the standard 128 high-density EEG channels. The average results among all subjects from NSGA are presented in Table 3. Given that not all subjects generated NSGA results on the Pareto front for each number of channels, the average reported in the table is based on varying

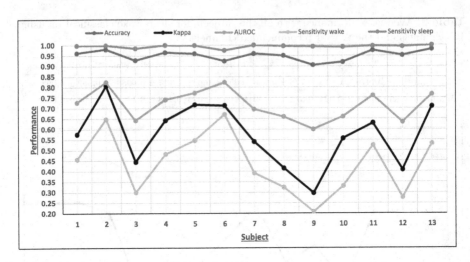

Fig. 2. Performance of sleep-wake classification for all subjects using the AASM-recommended channels; A28, B22, and C4.

Table 3. Average results obtained with 3–10 channels selected by NSGA for sleep-wake classification, comparing the performance using the 128 channels and the 3 AASM-recommended channels.

No. channels	Accuracy	Kappa	AUROC
3	0.955 ± 0.023	0.678 ± 0.097	0.790 ± 0.075
4	0.966 ± 0.019	0.719 ± 0.100	0.811 ± 0.066
5	0.965 ± 0.020	0.714 ± 0.129	0.814 ± 0.081
6	0.970 ± 0.017	0.757 ± 0.101	0.832 ± 0.065
7	0.972 ± 0.014	0.781 ± 0.085	0.849 ± 0.060
8	0.973 ± 0.014	0.783 ± 0.075	0.855 ± 0.056
9	0.975 ± 0.015	0.795 ± 0.075	0.855 ± 0.047
10	0.974 ± 0.013	0.790 ± 0.067	0.853 ± 0.047
128	0.970 ± 0.018	0.778 ± 0.086	0.855 ± 0.051
AASM-recommended	0.951 ± 0.024	0.573 ± 0.149	0.716 ± 0.073

numbers of subjects. When the same subject yielded multiple results for the same number of channels, the best result was selected for inclusion in the analysis.

All the various channel combinations resulted in an accuracy of at least 0.955 according to Table 3. As discussed, accuracy alone does not reflect the model's ability to detect wake instances, which is the main objective of this study. With 9 channels, the results were slightly better for all metrics compared to 10 channels. The results are slightly decreasing from 9 channels and down to 3 channels. The difference between the maximum and minimum values for accuracy, kappa and AUROC were 0.2, 0.117 and 0.065, respectively. The use of 9 channels obtains

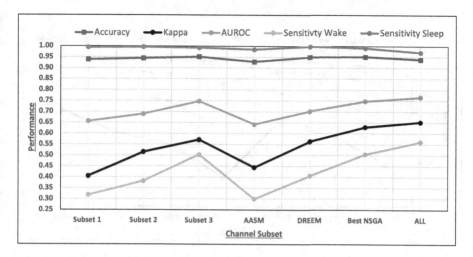

Fig. 3. Performance of sleep-wake classification for Subject 3 based on different subsets of channels.

the best results with an accuracy of 0.975 and a kappa score of 0.795, which is slightly higher than the use of all 128 high-density EEG channels with an accuracy of 0.97 and a kappa score of 0.778. All the NSGA results outperformed the AASM-recommended channels.

NSGA-III found that the most relevant channel for sleep versus wake classification based on all 13 subjects was D25, which was present in 12 subjects. Both channels A19 and B14 were present in 10 subjects. Channel A14, B29 and D4 were present in 9 subjects, while channel B11 and B31 were present in 8 subjects. These results and the frequency of appearance for the other channels are illustrated in the heatmap of Fig. 5. The channels not present in the heatmap were not part of the solutions. The AASM-recommended channels, A28 and B22, were not included in any of the optimal subsets found by NSGA. Channel C4 was only present for one of the subjects.

Based on the most important channels identified, D25 and A14 are located in the back left region of the brain, while B29 is located in the right frontal region. In addition, D4 is located in the left frontal region and B11 is in the right back region of the brain. It can be inferred from these observations that by including four of these important channels, the entire brain is sufficiently covered.

3.3   Comparison of Results for Subject-Specific Analysis

From the results of all the channels in Fig. 1, subject 6 obtained the best overall results, while subject 3 obtained the worst overall results. These two subjects are chosen for the following analysis. Using the most common channels from the NSGA analysis, the obtained results are compared with those using all channels, AASM-recommended channels, and the subset with the best-obtained channels

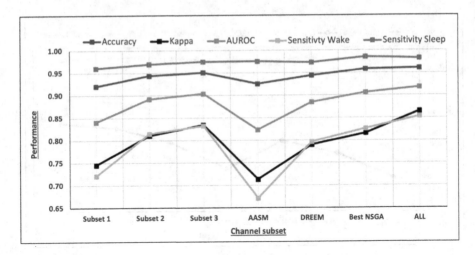

Fig. 4. Performance of sleep-wake classification for Subject 6 based on different subsets of channels.

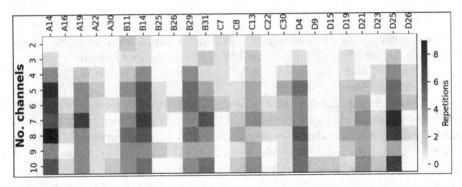

Fig. 5. Heatmap of channel importance in sleep-wake classification based on the results from NSGA for all subjects.

for that specific subject from the NSGA analysis. The three subsets of the most common channels from the NSGA analysis is listed in Table 6.

The results for subject 3 are presented in Fig. 3, and the results for subject 6 are presented in Fig. 4. The accuracy and sleep sensitivity values are consistently considered good for both subjects, above 0.95 and above 0.90, respectively, for all cases. Accuracy, kappa, and AUROC are metrics that pertain to the overall performance of the classification model. At the same time, sensitivity to the individual classes is an isolated metric, we observe that the kappa score is the metric that best captures the sensitivity of sleep in the overall performance of the model. As expected, the best results are obtained using all 128 high-density EEG channels. What is promising is that the results with the corresponding best NSGA results are in the same range, and this is also the case for the overall subset based on the most frequently appearing channels from the NSGA results.

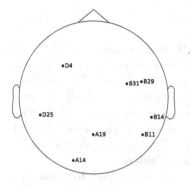

	Channels
Subset 1	D25, A19, B14
Subset 2	D25, A19, B14, A14, B29
Subset 3	D25, A19, B14, A14, B29, D4, B11, B31

Fig. 6. Positioning and subsets of channels obtained from the NSGA-III analysis.

In the case of subject 3, the subset consisting of 3 channels selected by NSGA performed equally poorly as the 3 AASM-recommended channels, whereas for subject 6, the AASM-recommended channels were clearly the worst-performing subset.

4   Discussion and Conclusions

In this study, we have presented experimental results of the performance of a recently proposed CNN architecture, EEGNet, that has shown higher performance than other approaches across different EEG-based paradigms. We present a set of experiments using high-density EEG and the AASM-recommended subset of channels. The obtained performance is higher when using the 128 available channels in the dataset. However, due to the non-portability and high computational cost, we have implemented a multi-objective algorithm to select the most relevant channels to be usable in wearable sleep devices to classify sleep versus wake EEG signal segments.

In the context of wake-sleep classification, accurately detecting the minority wake class is a critical factor, as wake periods during the night play a vital role in sleep quality and are often present in several sleep disorders. Notably, relying solely on high accuracy as a performance metric can be misleading, particularly when the dataset is highly unbalanced, as is often the case in sleep-wake classification tasks. Therefore, the kappa score has been proposed as a more consistent metric for capturing the model's ability to detect wake sensitivity. Despite this, accuracy remains the most commonly reported performance metric in classification problems.

Using EEGNet and the 128 available channels produces highly favorable results, as evidenced by the findings presented in Table 2 and Fig. 1. However, this approach entails a significant computational demand. Should the objective be to accurately classify and detect sleep-wakefulness in real-time, it is imperative that reliance on substantial computational resources or memory usage be avoided, given that these programs are intended for deployment on compact hardware devices.

The results obtained from utilizing NSGA-III demonstrate that EEG signal classification with significantly fewer channels can achieve comparable performance to that obtained from using the original 128 channels. Various subsets were obtained by extracting the frequency of appearance of all channels from the NSGA-III results. Notably, all of these subsets surpassed the AASM-recommended channels in terms of performance. Moreover, the subset derived from NSGA-III for the two chosen subjects individually outperformed the results of using the subsets of most common channels from Table 6.

Further work can be performed to tune and optimize the many hyperparameters in the optimization problem. Other parameters that may affect the results and which could be included in the NSGA search are the sampling frequency, the segment size, or the various parameters of the classification algorithm.

By comparing the results to the leading state-of-the-art, they are not as high. However, the underlying assumptions of these results must be taken into consideration. The current state-of-the-art uses a publicly available and fairly balanced dataset, even with a higher proportion of wake samples than sleep samples. This is a significant difference from the distribution of wake-sleep samples in the dataset used in this study, which ranges from 4.2 to 16.4% of wake samples. Future work should be conducted using raw data from sleep labs, such as in this experiment, but with a more balanced dataset to determine if the results can match the state-of-the-art with a different methodology. An experiment for future work could involve collecting more wakefulness data from patients before they go to sleep to balance out the data.

Several experiments from the literature report results with a single EEG channel pair. Further work should be performed on testing the same type of channels with the unbalanced and raw dataset used in this study to see if the performance is promising.

These findings suggest that selecting a single set of channels may not provide optimal performance for every individual. Further research is of interest in customizing the channel selection process for each subject to achieve optimal performance in sleep stage classification using EEG signals. By using a general model of all subjects together, may obtain a unique subset for the whole dataset.

One of the main problems for sleep staging is the high difference in the number of instances across the sleep stages, which makes it more difficult for the algorithms to learn how to discriminate between the defined classes. For this purpose, further work must include the use of methods for data augmentation, as well as considering a balanced dataset created with data from multiple subjects.

Acknowledgement. This work was supported by the Japan Society for the Promotion of Science (JSPS) Postdoctoral Fellowship for Research in Japan: Fellowship ID P22716, and JSPS KAKENHI: Grant number JP22K19802 and JP20K03493.

References

1. Espie, C.A.: Insomnia: conceptual issues in the development, persistence, and treatment of sleep disorder in adults. Annu. Rev. Psychol. **53**(1), 215–243 (2002)
2. Nano, M., Fonseca, P., Overeem, S., Vullings, R., Aarts, R.M.: Lying awake at night: cardiac autonomic activity in relation to sleep onset and maintenance. Front. Neurosci. **13**, 1405 (2020)
3. Zhao, W., et al.: EEG spectral analysis in insomnia disorder: a systematic review and meta-analysis. Sleep Med. Rev. **59**, 101457 (2021)
4. Fiorillo, L., et al.: Automated sleep scoring: a review of the latest approaches. Sleep Med. Rev. **48**, 101204 (2019)
5. Richard, B.B., Claude L.A., Susan M.H., et. al.: The AASM manual for the scoring of sleep and associated events: Rules, terminology and technical specifications version 2.5. The American Academy of Sleep Medicine (2018)
6. Arnal, et al.: The Dreem headband as an alternative to polysomnography for EEG signal acquisition and sleep staging. BioRxiv, p. 662734 (2019)
7. Arnal, P.J., et al.: The Dreem headband compared to polysomnography for electroencephalographic signal acquisition and sleep staging. Sleep **43**(11), zsaa097 (2020)
8. Zhu, G., Li, Y., Wen, P.: Analysis and classification of sleep stages based on difference visibility graphs from a single-channel EEG signal. IEEE J. Biomed. Health Inform. **18**(6), 1813–1821 (2014)
9. Berthomier, C., et al.: Automatic analysis of single-channel sleep EEG: validation in healthy individuals. Sleep **30**(11), 1587–1595 (2007)
10. Hassan, A.R., Bashar, S.K., Bhuiyan, M.I.H.: On the classification of sleep states by means of statistical and spectral features from single channel electroencephalogram. In: 2015 International Conference on Advances in Computing, Communications and Informatics (ICACCI), pp. 2238–2243. IEEE (2015)
11. Ronzhina, M., Janoušek, O., Kolářová, J., Nováková, M., Honzík, P., Provazník, I.: Sleep scoring using artificial neural networks. Sleep Med. Rev. **16**(3), 251–263 (2012)
12. Lawhern, V.J., Solon, A.J., Waytowich, N.R., Gordon, S.M., Hung, C.P., Lance, B.J.: EEGNet: a compact convolutional neural network for EEG-based brain-computer interfaces. J. Neural Eng. **15**(5), 056013 (2018)
13. Lee, C.-H., Kim, H.-J., Heo, J.-W., Kim, H., Kim, D.-J.: Improving sleep stage classification performance by single-channel EEG data augmentation via spectral band blending. In: 2021 9th International Winter Conference on Brain-Computer Interface (BCI), pp. 1–5. IEEE (2021)
14. Moctezuma, L.A., Abe, T., Molinas, M.: EEG-based 5- and 2-class CNN for sleep stage classification. In: The 22nd World Congress of the International Federation of Automatic Control (2023)
15. Deb, K., Pratap, A., Agarwal, S., Meyarivan, T.: A fast and elitist multiobjective genetic algorithm: NSGA-II. IEEE Trans. Evol. Comput. **6**(2), 182–197 (2002)
16. Själander, M., Jahre, M., Tufte, G., Reissmann, N.: EPIC: an energy-efficient, high-performance GPGPU computing research infrastructure (2019)

EEG Source Imaging of Hand Movement-Related Areas: An Evaluation of the Reconstruction Accuracy with Optimized Channels

Andres Soler[1]([✉]) [iD], Eduardo Giraldo[2] [iD], and Marta Molinas[1] [iD]

[1] Department of Engineering Cybernetics, Norwegian University of Science and Technology, Trondheim, Norway
{andres.f.soler.guevara,marta.molinas}@ntnu.no
[2] Department of Electrical Engineering, Universidad Tecnológica de Pereira, Pereira, Colombia
egiraldos@utp.edu.co

Abstract. The hand motor activity can be identified and converted into commands for controlling machines through a brain-computer-interface (BCI) system. Electroencephalography (EEG) based BCI systems employ electrodes to measure the electrical brain activity projected at the scalp and discern patterns. However, the volume conduction problem attenuates the electric potential from the brain to the scalp and introduces spatial mixing to the signals. EEG source imaging (ESI) techniques can be applied to alleviate these issues and enhance the spatial segregation of information. Despite this potential solution, the use of ESI has not been extensively applied in BCI systems, largely due to accuracy concerns over reconstruction accuracy when using low-density EEG (ldEEG), which is commonly used in BCIs. To overcome these accuracy issues in low channel counts, recent studies have proposed reducing the number of EEG channels based on optimized channel selection. This work presents an evaluation of the spatial and temporal accuracy of ESI when applying optimized channel selection towards ldEEG number of channels. For this, a simulation study of source activity related to hand movement has been performed using as starting point an EEG system with 339 channels. The results obtained after optimization show that the activity in the concerned areas can be retrieved with a spatial accuracy of 3.99, 10.69, and 14.29 mm (localization error) when using 32, 16, and 8 channel counts respectively.

Keywords: EEG · Source Imaging · Channel Optimization · Low-density EEG · BCI

1 Introduction

The human primary motor cortex (M1) has been identified as the area responsible for commanding the execution of hand movements [18]. This area is characterized for exhibiting mainly a *mu* rhythm (frequencies around 8–12 Hz) at rest.

© The Author(s), under exclusive license to Springer Nature Switzerland AG 2023
F. Liu et al. (Eds.): BI 2023, LNAI 13974, pp. 432–442, 2023.
https://doi.org/10.1007/978-3-031-43075-6_37

An attenuation of the power of this rhythm, also called event-related desynchronization (ERD), in the contralateral cortex is presented during the execution/imagination of hand movements [17,18]. This particular phenomenon in the *mu* rhythm has been exploited by brain-computer-interfaces (BCIs) to discern the hand that was executing an actual or imagined movement and convert those motor events into commands for a human peripheral system [9,10,19].

Most of the BCIs are based on the analysis performed using the information registered by the electrodes on the scalp (electrode space) [13], which is characterized by the low spatial resolution due to the volume conduction effect. In this, the potential generated by the electrical activity in the brain gets mixed and attenuated due to the different layers and their different conductivity properties before reaching the scalp. EEG Source imaging (ESI) methods can accurately retrieve the source activity and unmix the signals registered at the scalp; resulting in a better spatial discrimination of the underlying activity [10]. However, ESI requires high-density EEG (hdEEG) and a volume conduction model of the head, to perform accurate estimations [15]. Those requirements, in addition to computational concerns, might have contributed to fewer implementations of BCIs systems based on source activity. Despite this concern, multiple studies have demonstrated that source-centered BCIs are feasible in online scenarios [2,14] and can outperform the electrode only based BCIs [3,7,23]. However, ldEEG is still preferable in BCIs due to its lower cost, increased wearability, and ease of use.

Regarding the use of ldEEG in ESI, a recent study [21], presented an automated framework for optimal selection of ldEEG electrode positions that attained higher spatial accuracy than coverage-based electrode distribution and close to hdEEG accuracy. In [12], the authors used ldEEG, 26 channels, and source space to detect lower limb movements. Although ldEEG was utilized, no optimal electrode selection was conducted and electrodes were placed based on scalp coverage criteria. Inspired by those, here we propose an evaluation of the reconstruction accuracy with optimized channels with the purpose of exploring the boundaries of ldEEG for estimating the source activity of hand movement-related areas. To perform such evaluation, first, we simulated source activity in the region of interest (ROI). Then, we applied the framework of optimal selection of electrode location from [21] and introduced new constraints to evaluate the performance of symmetrical and non-symmetrical electrode distributions. The contribution of this paper is to conduct an evaluation of how accurate can the estimation of the source activity be in the cortical hand movement-related areas, and provide information that can facilitate closing the gap between ESI and BCIs.

2   Simulation of Source Activity in the Hand Movement-Related Areas

To simulate activity we made use of the EEG forward equation that defines the EEG:

$$y = Mx + \varepsilon \tag{1}$$

In it, the matrix y represents the EEG channel data. The matrix x represents the time courses of the source activity. The matrix M, often called the lead field matrix, represents the morphology and conductivity of the brain and contains the linear relationship between the cortical sources and the signals at the scalp. The matrix ε represents the noise registered in the measurements. We followed these steps for the simulations: forward modeling, ROI definition, simulation of source time courses, EEG computation, and noise addition.

Forward Modeling: To obtain the lead field matrix M, we computed a boundary element method (BEM) model based on the MRI images of a 27-year-old subject. The MRI images were processed and segmented using Freesurfer [4], and the BEM surfaces of the scalp, skull, and brain were generated using Freesurfer and MNE-python [8]. A set of 339 electrodes named and positioned according to the international 10-05 system were co-registered and projected into the scalp. Then, the lead field matrix for the 10-05 set was computed using the BEM surfaces and the projected electrodes. The number of sources was defined as 4098 per hemisphere, and the default MNE-python conductivities of 0.3, 0.006, and 0.3S/m were used for scalp, skull, and brain, respectively.

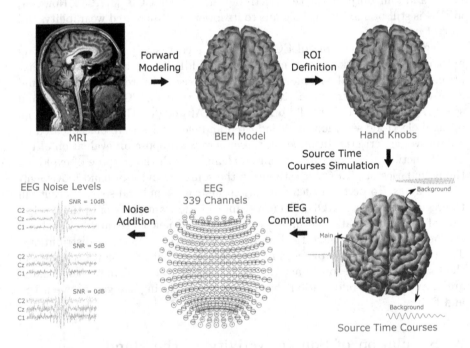

Fig. 1. Simulation procedure of the source activity in the hand movement-related areas.

ROI Definition: Previous studies [1, 3, 10, 24] have identified the sensory-motor cortex as the source regions where the upper limp movements take place, in particular, the so-called *hand knob* of the precentral gyrus has been found common across these studies. To define the ROI in the hand knobs we inspected the 3D surface of the cortex and manually labeled the center of the hand knob in each hemisphere. Two sets of sources around the markers were established by selecting the 20 closest sources to each marker. The 40 source locations and hand knobs ROIs are depicted in Fig. 1.

Simulation of Source Time-Courses: Two epochs of 2s were simulated per each source in the ROIs, resulting in 80 epochs. In each epoch three sources were activated: the main source within the ROIs and two more background sources outside them. The sources were generated using a sinusoidal Gaussian windowed activity as in [21, 22], by using the following equation:

$$x_i(t) = a_i e^{-\frac{1}{2}(\frac{t-c_i}{\sigma})^2} sin(2\pi f_i t) \tag{2}$$

The time course of the $i-th$ source is defined by the maximum amplitude a_i, the time center c_i, frequency f_i, and window width σ_i. The three activities were centered at 1s. The main source was simulated with a frequency of 10Hz and width 0.12. The background sources were simulated outside the ROIs to emulate brain activity from other areas and generate interference to the ESI algorithms, their location was randomly selected and they should be at least 3cm from the main source. Their amplitude was 10% of the amplitude of the main source, with a width of 0.12 and frequencies of 5 and 20Hz.

EEG Computation and Noise Addition: The EEG was computed using the forward Eq. 1, and the matrices M and x generated at forward modeling and source time courses simulation stages. After obtaining the matrix y, Gaussian noise was added to represent the noise in the measurements, three different levels of signal-to-noise ratio were used 10, 5, and 0dB.

Figure 1 summarizes the procedure of simulation of source activity in the hand movement-related areas.

3 Optimal Selection of EEG Channels

To select and reduce the number of channels, we used the automatic methodology for electrode selection presented in [21]. In it, the non-dominated sorting genetic algorithm II (NSGA-II) is combined with ESI algorithms. The number of channels used during ESI and the localization error are minimized in a multi-objective optimization problem. In the genetic algorithm each channel position is represented by a binary value, and the set of channels by a binary vector, when the binary value corresponding to a channel is one, the channel is used during ESI, otherwise the channel is not used and its information is zeroing. The NSGA-II generates and tests multiple channel combinations while evolving them to find the ones with lower channel counts and the lower localization error.

Algorithm Modification: In the original work, authors applied the methodology over epochs, therefore combinations of channels were optimized in each epoch. In this work, we introduced a main modification: the optimization is performed over all epochs to obtain a single combination instead of an epoch-wise combination.

Constraints: We performed multiple tests in an attempt to identify combinations that leads to the lower reconstruction errors: constraining the search space to the 10-10 standard electrode placement, without search space constraint, adding a symmetricity constraint to maintain the number of channels equal between both hemispheres and performed cascade search optimization. In the cascade search, we performed three nested optimizations for 32, 16, and 8 channels, the second and third optimization were constrained to the previous combination found.

ESI Algorithms: The standardized low-resolution electromagnetic tomography (sLORETA) [16] and weighted minimum norm estimation (wMNE) [6] were used to estimate the source activity during NSGA-II optimization. These algorithms were selected based on the results of previous work in [20, 21], where multiple ESI algorithms were evaluated in ldEEG conditions, and it was found that wMNE and sLORETA consistently obtained the lowest source localization errors. Both algorithms are based on minimum norm estimation, where the ESI problem can be considered as an optimization problem as follows:

$$J = argmin_{(x)}\{||Mx - y||_2^2\} \tag{3}$$

As the number variables to estimate (source activity x) is much higher that the number of observations (EEG channels y) the problem is mathematically ill-posed and ill-conditioned [11]. This means that infinite solutions for the source activity x can be found to minimize J and fit with the EEG data y. To find a unique solution, the algorithms make use of Tikhonov-Phillips regularization by including a regularization parameter λ that weights the norm of the estimated solution:

$$J = argmin_{(x,\lambda)}\{||Mx - y||_2^2 + \lambda^2||x||_2^2\} \tag{4}$$

The ESI solutions of wMNE and sLORETA are given by the following equations:

$$\hat{x}_{wMNE} = W^{-1}M^T(MW^{-1}M^T + \lambda^2I)^{-1}y \tag{5}$$

$$\hat{x}_{sLOR} = \sqrt{\frac{1}{[S_x]_{ii}}}M^T(MM^T + \lambda^2I)^{-1}y \tag{6}$$

The solution of wMNE uses a weighting matrix W to influence the weight of the deep sources, resulting in a better localization of the source activity of the deeper sources [5]. Its value is computed using the following equation:

$$W^{-1} = diag \left[\frac{1}{\|l_1\|_2}, \frac{1}{\|l_2\|_2}, ..., \frac{1}{\|l_s\|_2} \right] \tag{7}$$

where W is a diagonal matrix, and $\|l_s\|_2$ the Euclidean norm of the s-th column of M

The solution of sLORETA is usually smooth (estimations are blurry and widespread over large areas) but it is recognized by its zero localization error in the absence of noise [16]. In its solution sLORETA introduces a non-linear standardization of the solution using the variance of the estimated activity S_x, this variance is defined by:

$$S_x = M^T (MM^T + \lambda^2 I)^{-1} M \tag{8}$$

The Eucledian distance was used to compute the localization error by comparing the position of the ground-truth source P_x and the estimated source position $P_{\hat{x}}$ using the follow equation:

$$LocE = \|P_x - P_{\hat{x}}\|_2 \tag{9}$$

where $P_{\hat{x}}$ is selected from the estimated source activity $\hat{x}$ by selecting the location of the source with the highest power value.

4   Results

A summary of the performed tests is presented in Table 1. The localization error presented is the mean of the localization error across all epochs. We first evaluated the dataset with the three levels of added noise and constrained the search space to the 10-10 standard electrode placement. The localization error between the three levels of noise was similar, i.e. for 8 channels the errors were between 15.45 to 16.07 mm for sLORETA and 16.08 to 17.01 mm for wMNE. As the difference is less than 1 mm between the highest and lowest error for all electrode counts, we decided to continue the evaluations only with the dataset of higher noise level (0dB).

The less accurate results were obtained when adding multiple constraints, in particular, the case when the optimization was performed in cascade with hemispherical symmetricity and search within the 10-10 system. The effect of these constraints increased the localization error between 2.01 and 3.34 mm in the lower channel counts of 8 and 16 channels when compared with only applying the 10-10 system constraint. On the contrary, when fewer constraints were imposed, the accuracy increased. As shown in the Table 1, the highest accuracy values were obtained when no constraint was imposed or when only applying symmetricity constraint. These results coincide with the bigger search space of 339 channels, as no 10-10 system constraint was imposed in both cases. In these two cases, the localization error was lowered between 1.63 and 2.67 mm when compared with

Table 1. Localization error (mm) and standard deviation of the optimization test. The values remarked correspond to the best result with a given number of channels and ESI method.

Dataset	Constraint Type	10dB 10-10 system	5dB	0dB	10-10 system, Symmetricity, Cascade search	Symmetricity	No constraints	10-10 system, Cascade search
8 chs	sLORETA	15.87 (10.54)	15.45 (9.03)	16.07 (10.11)	18.59 (7.97)	**14.29 (5.04)**	14.74 (7.24)	16.75 (11.68)
	wMNE	16.08 (8.87)	16.19 (9.22)	17.01 (13.05)	19.49 (10.69)	14.94 (7.69)	**14.80 (10.84)**	16.64 (12.12)
16 chs	sLORETA	12.66 (9.10)	12.58 (9.04)	13.11 (8.77)	16.45 (9.58)	11.56 (5.57)	**10.69 (6.61)**	12.61 (9.09)
	wMNE	12.90 (8.92)	13.62 (8.82)	13.64 (8.89)	15.65 (8.87)	12.63 (5.11)	**12.01 (5.74)**	13.91 (9.19)
32 chs	sLORETA	7.80 (8.70)	7.85 (8.42)	7.74 (8.68)	8.42 (8.81)	6.02 (7.38)	**5.07 (5.64)**	8.41 (8.49)
	wMNE	7.30 (8.74)	7.32 (8.31)	6.45 (7.82)	7.20 (8.39)	**3.99 (6.37)**	5.18 (6.29)	6.62 (8.60)
72 chs (10-10 system)	sLORETA	**4.00 (7.15)**	4.01 (7.15)	4.05 (7.16)	4.05 (7.16)	–	–	4.05 (7.16)
	wMNE	3.77 (6.99)	3.75 (6.98)	**3.65 (6.99)**	3.65 (6.99)	–	–	3.65 (6.99)
339 chs	sLORETA	–	–	–	–	**0.00 (0.00)**	0.00 (0.00)	–
	wMNE	–	–	–	–	**0.00 (0.00)**	0.00 (0.00)	–

the 10-10 system constraint. The Pareto fronts when constraining the search space to 10-10 system and without constraint, search space of 339 channels, are presented in Fig. 2. It is noticeable that the Pareto fronts of sLORETA and wMNE were more accurate when not limiting the search space.

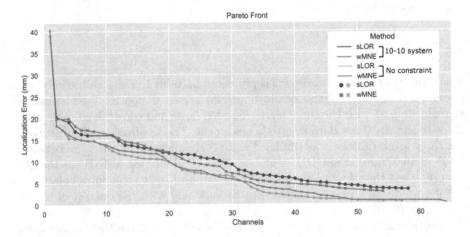

Fig. 2. Comparison of Pareto fronts for SNR 0dB dataset when constraining the search space to the 10-10 positioning system and without constraining (search space of 339 positions).

The 8 channel combinations for the cases with the search space of 339 channels with and without symmetricity for sLORETA are presented in Fig. 3. From them, it can be seen that the electrodes were found close to the motor cortex areas, in both cases with one electrode slightly separate from the others.

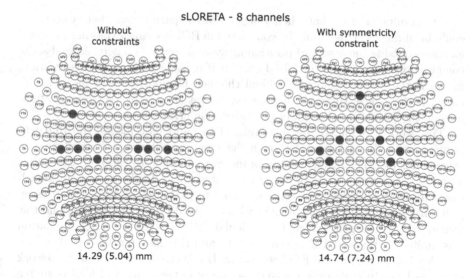

Fig. 3. Combinations of 8 channels for sLORETA without constraints and with symmetricity constraint.

5 Discussion and Conclusion

The localization error is an indication of the spatial accuracy, here, in the best evaluation cases we obtained 14.29 mm (8 channels, sLORETA, and only symmetricity constraint), 10.69 mm (16 channels, sLORETA, and no constraints), and 3.99 mm (32 channels, wMNE, and only symmetricity constraint). As in [22], we confirmed that the channel optimization with NSGA-II enables us to find channel combinations that led to the closest values to hdEEG accuracy values, in particular, the combination with 32 channels is less than 0.5 mm from the accuracy obtained with 72 channels in 10-10 system.

This research provides a pipeline to optimize the number of channels and identify ldEEG channel combinations for an individual subject that reduces the gap between hdEEG and ldEEG spatial accuracy. This systematic search for the best electrode positions was done as a first step in the design of dedicated EEG systems that can monitor the cortical source activity and facilitate the implementation of BCI systems for assisting in the rehabilitation of hand movement in stroke survivors. The previous studies in [3,7,12,23] demonstrated that the source space can outperform the sensor space. Here, our results indicate that 16 channels could provide an accurate reconstruction to be used in BCIs related to hand movements.

The level of accuracy required for source-based BCIs for hand movements might depend on the type of imagined movements to classify. The boundaries of the applications should be clarified in further studies, i.e. it is noticeable that classifying between right or left hand might require lower spatial accuracy than classifying within wrist movements of the same limb.

The results indicate that when a bigger search space is used, better accuracy could be obtained. This should be considered in BCI systems, exploring electrode locations outside the standard positioning systems towards a personalized set of combinations can be valid in a BCI context if it leads to a better classification, future works should explore individual channel distributions and their classification performance. Here, we demonstrated that the use of electrode locations outside the standard led to lower reconstruction errors.

This work was limited to areas related to hand movements, the ROI was reduced to the hand knobs. Although the same procedure can be evaluated in other limbs or other regions of the brain. For example, to estimate the source activity of hearing-, visual-, or attention-related areas. To the best of our knowledge, no other studies have been conducted to evaluate the ESI properties on particular brain regions using ldEEG with optimized channel selection, and this framework can be generalized to particular ROIs. Here, the EEG simulation was limited to sinusoidal Gaussian activity and this may not fully capture the complex behavior of a real EEG recording. However, the simulation framework serves as basis to evaluate the spatial accuracy in the context of ldEEG source imaging, considering that the reduced spatial sampling has been one of the arguments against the use of source estimated activity in BCI systems. It is debatable whether increasing the complexity of the simulated signal will affect the spatial resolution, especially when considering that non-linear mix imposed by the volume conduction has been included during forward modeling.

In conclusion, this study explores the use of optimized ldEEG for estimating the source activity of the hand movement related areas and investigates the accuracy under multiple optimization scenarios. In this work, several key findings are reported. Firstly, optimized channel selection in ldEEG setups demonstrated potential as a viable alternative to hdEEG, offering a comparable accuracy when retrieving the source space of the particular ROI. This finding is significant as it paves the way for source-centered BCI systems with low EEG channel counts.

Moreover, we presented a comprehensive pipeline to perform channel optimization in the context of ESI. The pipeline can be used to identify the channels that can accurately estimate the sources in a ROI and to be used in developing customized EEG solutions for a particular user when using individual MRI for forward modeling.

Furthermore, as a result of the reduction of channels, the optimized ldEEG can improve the practicality of EEG in real-world scenarios, as fewer sensors often leads to wearable and easy-to-use devices. It can be argued that the estimation of the sources increases computational complexity, especially for online systems. However, pre-calculated forward models and inverse operators can serve to speed up the computations.

This work provides insights on the use of optimized ldEEG in retrieving sources towards BCI systems. However, several questions are still open and are required to be solved prior to implementation in BCI systems. Further studies should be performed to clarify the role of ESI with optimized sensors and to develop source-centered BCIs that can complement current BCI systems based on only scalp recordings. Also, to analyze the effect of optimized channels in the classification accuracy when using source and sensor space. Further efforts should be made to verify the implications of the source computation in online settings, and clarify whether to apply forward modeling on individual basis or to use brain structural information from template heads can be accurate enough.

References

1. Bradberry, T.J., Gentili, R.J., Contreras-Vidal, J.L.: Reconstructing three-dimensional hand movements from noninvasive electroencephalographic signals. J. Neurosci. **30**, 3432–3437 (2010). https://doi.org/10.1523/JNEUROSCI.6107-09.2010
2. Cincotti, F., et al.: High-resolution EEG techniques for brain-computer interface applications. J. Neurosci. Methods **167**, 31–42 (2008). https://doi.org/10.1016/J.JNEUMETH.2007.06.031
3. Edelman, B.J., Baxter, B., He, B.: EEG source imaging enhances the decoding of complex right-hand motor imagery tasks. IEEE Trans. Biomed. Eng. **63**, 4–14 (2016). https://doi.org/10.1109/TBME.2015.2467312
4. Fischl, B.: FreeSurfer. NeuroImage **62**(2), 774–781 (2012). https://doi.org/10.1016/J.NEUROIMAGE.2012.01.021
5. Fuchs, M., Wagner, M., Köhler, T., Wischmann, H.A.: Linear and nonlinear current density reconstructions (1999). https://doi.org/10.1097/00004691-199905000-00006
6. Fuchs, M., Wagner, M., Wischmann, H.A.: Generalized minimum norm least squares reconstruction algorithms. ISBET Newsl. **5**(5), 8–11 (1994)
7. Giri, A., Kumar, L., Gandhi, T.: Cortical source domain based motor imagery and motor execution framework for enhanced brain computer interface applications. IEEE Sens. Lett. **5** (2021). https://doi.org/10.1109/LSENS.2021.3122453
8. Gramfort, A., et al.: MEG and EEG data analysis with MNE-Python. Front. Neurosci. **267** (2013). https://doi.org/10.3389/FNINS.2013.00267/BIBTEX
9. Hardwick, R.M., Caspers, S., Eickhoff, S.B., Swinnen, S.P.: Neural correlates of action: comparing meta-analyses of imagery, observation, and execution. Neurosci. Biobehav. Rev. **94**, 31–44 (2018). https://doi.org/10.1016/J.NEUBIOREV.2018.08.003
10. He, B., Baxter, B., Edelman, B.J., Cline, C.C., Ye, W.W.: Noninvasive brain-computer interfaces based on sensorimotor rhythms. Proc. IEEE **103**, 907–925 (2015). https://doi.org/10.1109/JPROC.2015.2407272
11. He, B., Sohrabpour, A., Brown, E., Liu, Z.: Electrophysiological source imaging: a noninvasive window to brain dynamics. **20**, 171–196 (2018). https://doi.org/10.1146/ANNUREV-BIOENG-062117-120853
12. Li, C., Guan, H., Huang, Z., Chen, W., Li, J., Zhang, S.: Improving movement-related cortical potential detection at the EEG source domain. In: International IEEE/EMBS Conference on Neural Engineering, NER, pp. 214–217 (2021). https://doi.org/10.1109/NER49283.2021.9441169
13. Lotte, F., et al.: A review of classification algorithms for EEG-based brain-computer interfaces: a 10 year update. J. Neural Eng. **15**, 031005 (2018). https://doi.org/10.1088/1741-2552/AAB2F2

14. Mattiocco, M., et al.: Neuroelectrical source imaging of mu rhythm control for BCI applications. In: Proceedings of the Annual International Conference of the IEEE Engineering in Medicine and Biology, pp. 980–983 (2006). https://doi.org/10.1109/IEMBS.2006.260128
15. Michel, C.M., Brunet, D.: EEG source imaging: a practical review of the analysis steps. Front. Neurol. **10**, 325 (2019). https://doi.org/10.3389/fneur.2019.00325
16. Pascual-Marqui, R.D.: Standardized low-resolution brain electromagnetic tomography (sLORETA): technical details. Methods Find. Exp. Clin. Pharmacol. **24**(Suppl D), 5–12 (2002)
17. Pfurtscheller, G., Brunner, C., Schlögl, A., da Silva, F.H.L.: Mu rhythm (de)synchronization and EEG single-trial classification of different motor imagery tasks. NeuroImage **31**, 153–159 (2006). https://doi.org/10.1016/J.NEUROIMAGE.2005.12.003
18. Pfurtscheller, G., Silva, F.H.L.D.: Event-related EEG/MEG synchronization and desynchronization: basic principles. Clin. Neurophysiol. **110**, 1842–1857 (1999). https://doi.org/10.1016/S1388-2457(99)00141-8
19. Saha, S., Baumert, M.: Intra- and inter-subject variability in EEG-based sensorimotor brain computer interface: a review. Front. Comput. Neurosci. **13**, 87 (2020). https://doi.org/10.3389/FNCOM.2019.00087/BIBTEX
20. Soler, A., Giraldo, E., Lundheim, L., Molinas, M.: Relevance-based channel selection for EEG source reconstruction: an approach to identify low-density channel subsets. In: Proceedings of the 15th International Joint Conference on Biomedical Engineering Systems and Technologies, BIOSTEC 2, BIOIMAGING, pp. 174–183 (2022). https://doi.org/10.5220/0010907100003123
21. Soler, A., Moctezuma, L.A., Giraldo, E., Molinas, M.: Automated methodology for optimal selection of minimum electrode subsets for accurate EEG source estimation based on genetic algorithm optimization. Sci. Rep. **12**(1), 1–18 (2022). https://doi.org/10.1038/s41598-022-15252-0
22. Soler, A., Muñoz-Gutiérrez, P.A., Bueno-López, M., Giraldo, E., Molinas, M.: Low-density EEG for neural activity reconstruction using multivariate empirical mode decomposition. Front. Neurosci. **14**, 175 (2020). https://doi.org/10.3389/fnins.2020.00175
23. Srisrisawang, N., Müller-Putz, G.R.: Applying dimensionality reduction techniques in source-space electroencephalography via template and magnetic resonance imaging-derived head models to continuously decode hand trajectories. Front. Hum. Neurosci. **16**, 137 (2022). https://doi.org/10.3389/FNHUM.2022.830221/BIBTEX
24. Yuan, H., Doud, A., Gururajan, A., He, B.: Cortical imaging of event-related (de)synchronization during online control of brain-computer interface using minimum-norm estimates in frequency domain. IEEE Trans. Neural Syst. Rehabil. Eng. **16**, 425–431 (2008). https://doi.org/10.1109/TNSRE.2008.2003384

Bagging the Best: A Hybrid SVM-KNN Ensemble for Accurate and Early Detection of Alzheimer's and Parkinson's Diseases

Noushath Shaffi[1]([envelope]) [ID], Viswan Vimbi[1] [ID], Mufti Mahmud[2,3] [ID],
Karthikeyan Subramanian[1], and Faizal Hajamohideen[1] [ID]

[1] College of Computing and Information Sciences, University of Technology and
Applied Sciences-Sohar, OM 311, Sohar, Sultanate of Oman
{noushath.shaffi,vimbi.viswan,karthikeyan.supramanian,
faizal.hajamohideen}@utas.edu.om
[2] Department of Computer Science, Nottingham Trent University,
Nottingham NG11 8NS, UK
mufti.mahmud@ntu.ac.uk
[3] CIRC and MTIF, Nottingham Trent University, Nottingham NG11 8NS, UK

Abstract. Deep Learning (DL) techniques have shown promise in the
early detection of neurodegenerative diseases due to their ability to analyze large amounts of medical data accurately. However, their reliance
on massive training data may not be ideal in the healthcare industry.
Therefore, this paper proposes a simple yet effective machine learning
(ML) based hybrid ensemble of KNN and SVM for the early detection of
Alzheimer's Disease (AD) and Parkinson's Disease (PD). The proposed
method is hybrid in the sense that it combines the strengths of both
non-parametric and parametric approaches, resulting in a more robust
and accurate classification performance. The method is tested on two
popular AD databases, ADNI and OASIS, and the NTUA PD dataset.
The hybrid ensemble method achieves higher accuracy and specificity
for AD and PD detection, which is on par with popular DL algorithms.
The source code for this work can be accessed at https://github.com/
snoushath/Bagging-the-Best.git.

Keywords: KNN · SVM · Alzheimer's Disease · Parkinson Disease ·
Machine Learning · Ensemble Learning · Bagging

1 Introduction

Alzheimer's disease (AD) is a neurodegenerative disorder primarily affecting
memory and other cognitive functions [10]. It is characterized by abnormal protein (called amyloid) deposits in the brain, forming plaque, leading to damage

This work is funded by the Ministry of Higher Education, Research and Innovation
(MoHERI) of the sultanate of Oman under the Block Funding Program (Grant number-
MoHERI/BFP/UoTAS/01/2021).

and death of brain cells [12]. AD will manifest in cognitive decline, memory loss, and difficulty in performing daily tasks [10]. Parkinson's Disease (PD) is also a neurodegenerative disorder characterized by the degeneration of dopamine-producing neurons in the brain, eventually manifesting in motor symptoms (rhythmic shaking, slowness in walking, muscle rigidity, etc.) and non-motor symptoms (sleep disorders, anxiety, constipation, etc.) [20]. Figure 1 that shows the anatomical structure of healthy vs. non-healthy brains of AD and PD.

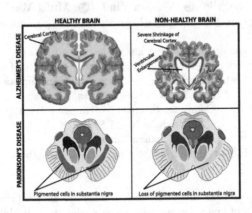

Fig. 1. The Structure of Healthy vs. Non-Healthy Brain in Alzheimer's (Top) and Parkinson's (Bottom) Diseases

The mortality rate of AD and PD is relatively high. The World Alzheimer's Report [10] highlights that a staggering 55 million individuals across the globe are currently living with AD. Additionally, AD is currently the 7th leading cause of death worldwide [10]. The World Health Organization technical report quotes that disability and death due to PD are growing faster than any other neurological disorders [20]. Worldwide, the economic impacts of these diseases are also running to several trillion dollars in managing and coping with afflicted patients [10,20].

AD patients initially experience mild memory problems, but as the disease progresses, they may have difficulty performing daily tasks ranging from communicating, self-caring, and recognizing their loved ones to total disruption of autonomy in personal and social life [10,11,23]. AD patients will have to endure compromised quality of life [22]. PD disease, on the other hand, poses a wide range of symptoms that affect a patient's movement, mood, and cognitive functions [20]. Patients may struggle walking, performing simple tasks, and communicating as the disease progresses. Non-motor symptoms such as depression, anxiety, and sleep disorders can also significantly impact their quality of life. Both AD and PD can cause significant suffering for patients and their families [10,20]. The diseases are chronic and progressive, which means that symptoms worsen over time and are irreversible. However, early diagnosis and treatment can help manage symptoms, slow disease progression, and improve the patient's quality of life.

Artificial Intelligence (AI) has proven to be a potential tool in the early prediction of AD and PD by analyzing large amounts of data and identifying patterns that are sometimes difficult for even experts to discern [3,8]. Many healthcare sectors have adopted Machine Learning (ML) classifiers, which have proven highly effective in AD classification [22]. Recently, there has been a tendency to apply Deep Learning (DL) algorithms to every application, and they performed admirably well [18]. Although DL algorithms are often used for classification [11], they may not always be the best choice in data-scarce situations such as AD/PD classification. To demonstrate this, we propose a hybrid ensemble of Support Vector Machines (SVM) and K-nearest Neighbor (KNN) algorithms that outperform several DL models. KNN can efficiently capture the local structure of the data, whereas SVM can represent the global structure. By incorporating the advantages of both algorithms, the ensemble of these approaches accomplishes greater precision. Our experimental results show that this approach can achieve high accuracy while requiring less data and computational resources than DL algorithms.

Rest of the paper is organized as follows: Section 2 presents a brief overview of recent literature on AD and PD classification. The proposed methodology is described in Sect. 3. Experimental results and analysis are provided in Sect. 4. Section 5 draws concluding remarks.

2   Literature Review

Fulton et al. [9] in their research article tries to predict AD using sociodemographic, clinical, and MRI data. In the study a gradient boosted machine predicted AD using clinical and MMSE parameters for dataset from OASIS. Lodha et al. [19] compares the performances of ML algorithms, including gradient boosting, in AD detection from neuroimaging data obtained from the ADNI database. A comparison of the predictive analysis among SVM, KNN, Gradient Boosting, Random Forest and Neural network yielded interesting results. The study shows that Neural network and Random Forest have better accuracy of 98.36% and 97.86% than other methods. However, SVM and Gradient boosting are also powerful algorithms with 97.56% and 97.25% prediction accuracy and also work well in detecting AD at a premature stage and helps to minimize further complications. Hala et al. [2] discuss early detection of AD using single nucleotide polymorphisms based on gradient boosting ML algorithm with a significant classification accuracy. The authors have proposed the features, information gain filter and the Boruta wrapper, to select the most significant genes related to AD. Davangere et al. [6] combines early markers of AD and tries to predict the conversion from MCI to AD. The study included 148 outpatients with MCI from a 3-year follow-up data at 6-months' interval. The authors used logistic regression to select 5 out of 8 predictors that include immediate recall, MRI hippocampal volume, and MRI entorhinal cortex volume. The results for

5 predictor combination showed 85.2% sensitivity than a combination of other early markers. Jie et al. [14] develop a logistic regression model along with artificial neural network model and decision tree model to study the progression of AD from MCI to AD and compare the performances of the three models. A total of 425 subjects were taken from the Nanchang University hospital, China and screened with AD as the outcome variable. The three developed models, including Logistic regression, were used for model training and testing. Also, the performance of the three models were compared to identify the best choice. The potential of ML algorithms for classifying neurological disorders has been identified in this brief review, leading to further investigation in this study.

3   Proposed Methodology

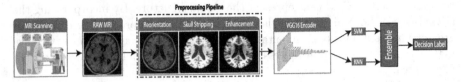

Fig. 2. The Pipeline of the proposed methodology

This section presents our classification pipeline involving a hybrid ensemble of SVM and KNN algorithms. The pipeline is depicted in Fig. 2. The pipeline as three major components: preprocessing, feature extraction, and ensemble of SVM and KNN classifiers.

3.1   MRI Preprocessing

To prepare the MRI images, we utilized the FMRIB Software Library toolset (FSL) [1], which offers several analytical tools for MRI data. The MRI images were prepared through four steps: reorientation, registration, skull-stripping, and histogram equalization. MRI images are reoriented to guarantee consistency, accuracy, and reliability. It also improves the visualization and interpretation of the images [16]. During the second step of the registration process, the images are aligned to a standard coordinate system to enable precise comparisons of multiple scans of the same subject. Skull stripping is a process that separates non-brain tissues, including the skull, eyeballs, and skin enhancing the accuracy and interpretation of MRI images of the brain. In the last step, the resulting MRI image undergoes a simple histogram equalization to increase the visibility of features.

3.2   Feature Extraction

The MRI features from the 2D slices of MRI images are extracted using the VGG16 architecture. The architecture of VGG16 architecture is shown in Fig. 3.

The top layer consisting of fully connected layers is eliminated to extract features. The Fig. 3 demonstrates that an image of dimension $176 \times 176 \times 3$ (the size used in the OASIS dataset) undergoes a transformation into a block of features with size $5 \times 5 \times 512$. Before applying classification algorithms, the resulting feature block will be converted into a single-dimensional vector of 12800 dimension.

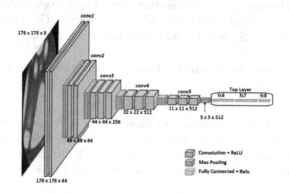

Fig. 3. The VGG16 Feature Extractor

3.3 SVM

The Support Vector Machine (SVM) is a supervised classification algorithm that identifies a hyperplane within an n-dimensional space, with n denoting the number of features present [24]. It is possible to categorize the SVM into linear and nonlinear models. In linear classification, the algorithm separates the classes by determining the maximum distance between hyperplanes that can be represented by a straight line. For nonlinear classification, SVM uses a kernel function to transform the input data into a high-dimensional space, also known as feature space. Consequently, SVM enables the classification of nonlinear data in the hyperplane.

SVM seeks to maximize the distance and minimize classification error based on the mathematical notation $\frac{d^2}{2} = \frac{1}{\frac{||w^2||}{2}}$. Hence, SVM aims to optimize the distance $(d^2/2)$ while minimizing the prediction error $||w^2||/2$. The kernel function $k(x_i, x_j) = \phi(x_i) \cdot \phi(x_j)$, computes the dot product between two data points x_i and x_j in the transformed space.

3.4 KNN

The K-nearest neighbors (KNN) bases predictions using closest K instances in the training set [24]. The algorithm measures the distance between a new instance that needs to be classified and all instances present in the training set. When a new test sample is evaluated against K instances, the class that appears the most frequently is chosen as the predicted class label for the new instance.

Typically, Euclidean distance is used to calculate the distance between instances, but other distance metrics can also be used.

3.5   Bagging the Best: Hybrid Ensemble of SVM and KNN

As shown in Fig. 2, before applying SVM and KNN algorithms, the input MRI scans will pass through the VGG16 feature extractor. The extracted features will individually pass through SVM and KNN algorithms. The decision obtained by these classifiers will then be combined using the probability-based fusion approach.

The probabilities assigned to C classes by individual classifiers for the jth sample are as follows:

$$\Delta^{kj} = (\zeta_1^{kj}, \zeta_2^{kj}, \cdots, \zeta_C^{kj}) \tag{1}$$

The ζ_i^{kj} represents the probability of class i $(i = 1, 2, \cdots, C)$ determined by classifier k for the jth instance. The value of C is 4 and k is 2 in our case of 4-way classification using 2 classifiers (SVM and KNN). We then use a probability-based fusion method to determine the final prediction label p^j for the jth test sample as follows:

$$p^j = \text{argmax}_{p \in C}(\sum_{k=1}^{2} \zeta_1^{kj}, \sum_{k=1}^{2} \zeta_2^{kj}, \sum_{k=1}^{2} \zeta_3^{kj}, \sum_{k=1}^{2} \zeta_4^{kj}) \tag{2}$$

3.6   Experimentation

MRI Data. The study's experiments utilized data collected from the Alzheimer's Disease Neuroimaging Initiative (ADNI) [13] and Open Access Series of Imaging Studies (OASIS) [15] datasets. The ADNI dataset comprises 1056 MRI images from the Axial plane, divided into four categories: 223 for AD, 475 for EMCI, 262 for LMCI, and 96 for CN. We split the samples into a 90:10 ratio for training and testing. The datasets have been sourced from ADNI-1, ADNI-2, and ADNI-GO cohorts and are available for download in NIfTI format. The OASIS dataset is categorized based on the Clinical Dementia Rating (CDR) score, with four categories ranging from no dementia to moderate Alzheimer's. There are 3200, 2240, 896, and 64 images in each category, respectively. All the samples have the same size of 176 × 176. The Synthetic Minority Over-sampling Technique (SMOTE) algorithm generated synthetic samples in the minority classes resulting in a more balanced dataset. As a result, there are now 2704, 2674, 2708, and 2666 samples in each category. The dataset was split into a 75:25 train-test split. The National Technical University of Athens dataset of PD (NTUA, https://github.com/ails-lab/ntua-parkinson-dataset) has MRI examination of 78 individuals out of which 55 are suffering from PD and rest are healthy controls. The dataset contains 915 and 472 total MRI scans in the PD and non-PD classes. We used the SMOTE algorithm again to increase the size of the dataset. The final dataset included 4831 instances in the PD class and 4189 instances in the non-PD class. The dataset was split into a 70:30 train-test split.

Performance Metrics. In our experimental evaluation, we used performance metrics such as Accuracy (Acc), Sensitivity (true positive rate (TPR)), and Specificity (true negative rate(TNR)) [22]. We can use TNR metric to calculate the False Positive Rate (FPR) by subtracting the specificity from 1. The false negative rate (FNR) can be obtained as $1 - Sensitivity$. These values show the average results obtained using the one vs. all strategy.

4 Results and Analysis

We compared conventional ML techniques with our proposed method, using AD and PD datasets. We found the best results for each method using grid search and five-fold cross-validation to determine optimal hyperparameters. Thus, reported results reflect the use of optimal hyperparameters.

4.1 Experiment-1: Performance on Alzheimer's Disease Data

We conducted the first round of experiments on the AD datasets, using ADNI and OASIS datasets. The results are listed in Table-1 and Table-2, respectively.

Table 1. Results of ML algorithms on ADNI Dataset

Method	Acc	TNR	TPR	FNR	FPR	AUC
K-Means	0.4840	0.7791	0.3306	0.6693	0.2208	
DT	0.7142	0.8872	0.6869	0.3130	0.1127	0.7870
AB	0.7714	0.9088	0.7618	0.2381	0.0091	0.7700
NB	0.7809	0.9183	0.7728	0.2271	0.0816	0.8456
RF	0.8917	0.965	0.8965	0.1034	0.0346	0.9814
GB	0.9714	0.9893	0.9798	0.0251	0.0106	0.9934
XGB	0.9809	0.9925	0.9803	0.0196	0.0074	0.9954
LR	0.9809	0.9925	0.9803	0.0196	0.0074	0.9974
KNN	0.9809	0.9931	0.9803	0.0196	0.0068	0.9878
SVM	0.9904	0.9967	0.9895	0.0104	0.0032	0.9987

Legends:AB – Adaptive Boosting; GB – Gradient Boosting; XGB–Extreme Gradient Boosting; RF – Random Forest; DT – Decision Tree; K-Means – K Means Clustering; Log Reg – Logistic Regression; NB – Naive Bayes;

By analyzing the scores provided in Table 1 and Table 2, it is evident that specific models have outperformed others. The accuracy score of over 0.98 achieved by several algorithms, such as SVM, KNN, GBoost, and XGBoost, is undeniably impressive. However, the accuracy of K-means clustering, AdaBoost, and Decision Tree has been notably insufficient. We have some noteworthy findings from the experiment, and our analysis of them is detailed below:

1. SVM is effective for high-dimensional data with limited observations. It uses kernel functions to identify linear boundaries in transformed data, making it suitable for non-linearly separable data [26]. Hence, SVM is able to perform well on new and unseen data, showing its strong generalization capabilities.

2. KNN achieved a high accuracy score of 0.9809, comparable to GB, XGB, and LR, as shown in Table 1. Notably, it outperformed all other models with a score of 0.9371 on the OASIS dataset (refer to Table 2). KNN stands out from other algorithms because it does not rely on any specific data distribution assumptions, making it flexible and capable of capturing complex relationships between features and target variables. By assigning a new data point to the class of its k-nearest neighbors in the training set, KNN effectively identifies local patterns in the data [21].

3. The K-Means clustering method yielded unsatisfactory results for the ADNI and OASIS datasets, possibly due to sensitivity to initial conditions [17]. Although cross-validation was used, it is unlikely that initial conditions were the main factor. Outliers in the data can greatly impact cluster centroid calculation and lead to incorrect groupings. The non-linear nature of the data suggests that K-means clustering is unsuitable for AD classification with VGG16 features.

4. Out of all the algorithms tested, the Naive Bayes algorithm had the second lowest performance. Naive Bayes assumes feature independence [4]. Also, the decision boundaries in the Naive Bayes classifier are assumed to be linear. These assumptions are not applicable when it comes to AD classification.

5. When tested on the ADNI dataset, which had limited and imbalanced data, the Random Forest algorithm showed lower performance (0.8917) than other algorithms. The limited dataset may not have enough diverse data to create meaningful divisions [7]. Uneven data distribution can cause biased predictions and affect accuracy.

6. Table 1 shows that logistic regression and KNN algorithms had the same accuracy scores, but KNN had higher specificity, indicating better identification of negative cases [21].

7. The XGB model showed higher accuracy on both datasets. This is likely due to its built-in regularization techniques like L1 and L2, which prevent overfitting and improve overall performance [5]. Regularization techniques are crucial for preventing overfitting on smaller datasets. Additionally, XGB is built to handle large datasets efficiently [5].

The next set of experiments is conducted to check the efficacy of the proposed hybrid ensembling of SVM and KNN. We tested the effectiveness of probability fusion-based ensembling using the OASIS dataset as the results on the smaller ADNI dataset was nearly 100% on the ADNI dataset using individual classifiers (SVM =0.9904, KNN = 0.9809). For this experiment, we used several ensembles of two classifiers, focusing on the four best-performing models from the previous experiment. The results are tabulated in Table 3.

The combination of KNN and SVM produced an accuracy of 0.9652, which is almost 3% higher than the highest-performing KNN model, which had an

Table 2. Results of ML algorithms on OASIS Dataset

Method	Acc	TNR	TPR	FNR	FPR	AUC
K-Means	0.3	0.7664	0.2991	0.7008	0.2335	
AB	0.6648	0.8883	0.6650	0.3349	0.1116	0.8146
NB	0.6765	0.8919	0.6745	0.325	0.108	0.7982
DT	0.6898	0.8965	0.6904	0.3095	0.1034	0.7935
GB	0.8593	0.9531	0.8599	0.1400	0.0468	0.9683
XGB	0.8902	0.9633	0.8905	0.1094	0.0366	0.9904
RF	0.8917	0.9653	0.8919	0.1080	0.0361	0.8917
LR	0.907	0.969	0.9074	0.0925	0.0309	0.9830
SVM	0.9132	0.9107	0.9135	0.0864	0.0289	0.9913
KNN	0.9371	0.9790	0.9377	0.0622	0.0209	0.9919

Legends:AB – Adaptive Boosting; GB – Gradient Boosting; XGB–Extreme Gradient Boosting; RF – Random Forest; DT – Decision Tree; K-Means – K Means Clustering; LR – Logistic Regression; NB – Naive Bayes;

Table 3. Results of Ensembles for varying number of classifiers

No. of Models	Models	Soft (Probability)	Hard (Max-Voting)
2	KNN, LR	0.9589	0.9121
	KNN, XGB	0.9546	0.9066
	KNN, SVM	0.9652	0.9088
	LR, XGB	0.9156	0.8925
	LR, SVM	0.9125	0.9054
	XGB, SVM	0.9308	0.8929
3	KNN, SVM, LR	0.9464	0.9253
	KNN, SVM, XGB	0.9621	0.9359
	KNN, XGB, LR	0.9558	0.9328
	SVM, XGB, LR	0.9210	0.9171
4	KNN, SVM, LR, XGB	0.9457	0.9285

accuracy of 0.9371. The improvement observed can be attributed to the inherent variations in the capabilities of KNN and SVM algorithms. For instance, the KNN algorithm uses the closest neighbors in the training data to make predictions, while the SVM algorithm finds the optimal hyperplane to separate classes. Furthermore, KNN is non-parametric, and SVM is parametric. Additionally, KNN is more adept at identifying local patterns in data, whereas SVM is better suited for handling high-dimensional data or data with intricate decision boundaries. Hence, by combining the predictions of KNN and SVM, their indi-

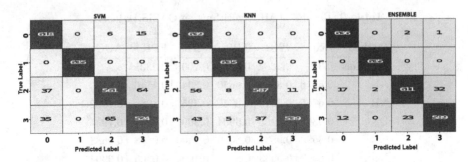

Fig. 4. Confusion Matrices obtained for OASIS dataset:SVM (accuracy = 0.9132), KNN (accuracy = 0.9371), Ensemble Classifier (accuracy = 0.9652); Legends: KNN – K-Nearest Neighbor, SVM – Support Vector Machine; Class labels: 0 – CDR 0.0, 1 – CDR 0.5, 2 – CDR 1.0, 3 – CDR 2.0

vidual strengths can complement each other while mitigating any weaknesses. In addition, the success of ensembles depends on the diversity of the algorithms used. SVM and KNN are diverse algorithms that can capture different aspects of the data, reducing the chances of misclassification [27]. Hence, by combining KNN and SVM, the overall performance improved significantly. These algorithms have distinct approaches and were able to fix any misclassifications made by each other.

From Table-3, it is evident that the overall accuracy did not improve despite the increase in the number of classifiers. Using ensemble methods can boost accuracy, although there is a maximum number of classifiers that can be utilized for optimal results. For ensemble methods to succeed, it is imperative that each model stands apart and provides unique and complementary perspectives on the data [27]. Adding more classifiers to the ensemble may not be beneficial if they are similar to the current models or if they provide contradictory information. This is evident in the ensemble of SVM, KNN, and XGB which resulted in less accuracy (0.9621) than ensemble of SVM and KNN alone (0.9652). Adding more classifiers to an ensemble can be helpful, but only up to a certain point. Lastly, it is noticeable that the ensembling based on probability values consistently outperforms the max-voting-based ensemble. When using a probability-based ensemble, the prediction is determined by the confidence levels given by each classifier. On the other hand, in a max-voting-based ensemble, the final prediction is based on the mode of the individual classifier predictions.

The confusion matrix helps identify error patterns across multiple classes, giving valuable insights to determine the best-performing model. The confusion matrices of SVM, KNN, and their ensemble are shown in Fig. 4. The SVM model accurately distinguished between MCI (CDR 1.0) and AD cases (CDR 2.0) with 84% and 83% accuracy, while the KNN classifier correctly classified MCI and AD samples with 88% and 86% accuracy. The ensemble approach proved effective in accurately identifying MCI and AD cases, with an accuracy rate of 0.92 and 0.94, respectively. This is a distinctive advantage of the ensemble classifier instead of using individual classifiers. Hence, the ensemble classifier's ability to distinguish between MCI and AD is advantageous, as early detection of MCI enables timely intervention, which can prevent or delay the onset of AD.

4.2 Experiment-2: Performance on Parkinson's Disease Data

In this experiment, SVM and KNN were tested to classify Parkinson's disease. The results are shown in Table-4 and Fig. 5. The SVM model achieved an accuracy of 0.9988 and the KNN model achieved an accuracy of 0.9933. Combining the two models through ensemble learning further improved the accuracy to 0.9996.

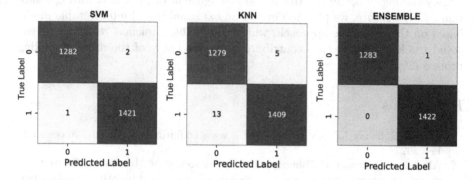

Fig. 5. Confusion Matrices obtained for NTUA dataset:SVM (accuracy=0.9988), KNN (accuracy = 0.9933), Ensemble Classifier (accuracy=0.9996); Class labels: 0 – Healthy Control, 1 – Parkinson's Disease

Table 4. Results on NTUA Parkinson's Disease Dataset

Method	Accuracy	Specificity	Sensitivity	FNR	FPR
SVM	0.9988	0.9988	0.9988	0.0011	0.0011
KNN	0.9933	0.9934	0.9934	0.0065	0.0065
Ensemble	0.9996	0.9996	0.9996	0.0003	0.0003

In the case of PD, it is a binary classification problem to differentiate between individuals with and without PD. Hence, it makes the classification task more straightforward, which allows classifiers like SVM and KNN to separate the two classes and achieve higher accuracy effectively. In contrast, multi-class classification of AD involves distinguishing between different stages of the disease, leading to lower accuracy than binary classification. The enhanced accuracy of SVM, KNN, and ensemble methods in binary PD classification can be attributed to the problem's simplicity and the ability of these classifiers to distinguish between the two classes effectively.

5   Conclusion

We aimed to develop a direct yet effective model for classifying neurodegenerative diseases. Our efforts' outcome is an accuracy rate comparable or superior to deep learning models documented in the existing literature. Our study suggests that the proposed hybrid ensemble of SVM and KNN algorithms is a promising approach for accurately classifying neurodegenerative diseases such as Alzheimer's and Parkinson's disease. Further, our results demonstrate that these algorithms, as well as their ensemble, outperform traditional methods. This highlights the potential of using simple machine learning techniques, specifically SVM and KNN, for the early and accurate diagnosis of neurodegenerative diseases, ultimately leading to better treatment and management of these debilitating conditions. In the future, we plan to develop an explainable and interpretable model based on this ensemble approach, which will enable clinicians to better understand the key features that contribute to the accuracy of the decision-making process [25].

References

1. FMRIB Software Library toolset (FSL). www.fsl.fmrib.ox.ac.uk/fsl/. Accessed 16 Feb 2023
2. Ahmed, H., Soliman, H., Elmogy, M.: Early detection of Alzheimer's disease using single nucleotide polymorphisms analysis based on gradient boosting tree. Comput. Biol. Med. **146**, 105622 (2022)
3. Belić, M., Bobić, V., Badža, M., Šolaja, N., et al.: Artificial intelligence for assisting diagnostics and assessment of Parkinson's disease-a review. Clin. Neurol. Neurosurg. **184**, 105442 (2019)
4. Berrar, D.: Bayes' theorem and Naive Bayes classifier. Encycl. Bioinform. Comput. Biol. ABC Bioinform. **403**, 412 (2018)
5. Chen, T., Guestrin, C.: XGBoost: a scalable tree boosting system. In: Proceedings of the ICKDDM, pp. 785–794. ACM (2016)
6. Devanand, D.P., et al.: Combining early markers strongly predicts conversion from mild cognitive impairment to Alzheimer's disease. Biol. Psychiatry **64**(10), 871–879 (2008)
7. Fawagreh, K., Gaber, M.M., Elyan, E.: Random forests: from early developments to recent advancements. Syst. Sci. Control Eng. **2**(1), 602–609 (2014)
8. Frizzell, T.O., Glashutter, M., Liu, C.C., Zeng, A., et al.: Artificial intelligence in brain MRI analysis of Alzheimer's disease over the past 12 years: a systematic review. Ageing Res. Rev. **77**, 101614 (2022)
9. Fulton, L.V., et al.: Classification of Alzheimer's disease with and without imagery using gradient boosted machines and ResNet-50. Brain sci. **9**(9), 212 (2019)
10. Gauthier, S., Webster, C., Sarvaes, S., Morais, J., Rosa-Neto, P.: World Alzheimer report 2022: life after diagnosis - navigating treatment, care and support (2022)
11. Hajamohideen, F., et al.: Four-way classification of Alzheimer's disease using deep Siamese convolutional neural network with triplet-loss function. Brain Inform. **10**(1), 1–13 (2023)
12. Hammond, T.C., et al.: β-amyloid and tau drive early Alzheimer's disease decline while glucose hypometabolism drives late decline. Commun. Biol. **3**(1), 1–13 (2020)

13. Jack, C.R., Jr., et al.: The Alzheimer's disease neuroimaging initiative (ADNI): MRI methods. J. Magn. Reson. Imaging **27**(4), 685–691 (2008)
14. Kuang, J., et al.: Prediction of transition from mild cognitive impairment to Alzheimer's disease based on a logistic regression-artificial neural network-decision tree model. Geriatr. Gerontol. Int. **21**(1), 43–47 (2021)
15. LaMontagne, P.J., et al.: OASIS-3: Longitudinal neuroimaging, clinical, and cognitive dataset for normal aging and Alzheimer disease. medRxiv x (2019)
16. Levy, B.J., Wagner, A.D.: Cognitive control and right ventrolateral prefrontal cortex: reflexive reorienting, motor inhibition, and action updating. Ann. N. Y. Acad. Sci. **1224**(1), 40–62 (2011)
17. Likas, A., Vlassis, N., Verbeek, J.J.: The global k-means clustering algorithm. Pattern Recognit. **36**(2), 451–461 (2003)
18. Loddo, A., Buttau, S., Di Ruberto, C.: Deep learning based pipelines for Alzheimer's disease diagnosis: a comparative study and a novel deep-ensemble method. Comput. Biol. Med. **141**, 105032 (2022)
19. Lodha, P., Talele, A., Degaonkar, K.: Diagnosis of Alzheimer's disease using machine learning. In: Proceedings of the ICCUBEA, pp. 1–4 (2018)
20. World Health Organization: Parkinson disease: a public health approach: technical brief (2022)
21. Patrick, E.A., Fischer, F.P., III.: A generalized k-nearest neighbor rule. Inf. Control **16**(2), 128–152 (1970)
22. Shaffi, N., et al.: Ensemble classifiers for a 4-way classification of Alzheimer's disease. In: Proceedings of the AII2022, pp. 219–230 (2023)
23. Shaffi, N., Hajamohideen, F., Mahmud, M., Abdesselam, A., Subramanian, K., Sariri, A.A.: Triplet-loss based siamese convolutional neural network for 4-way classification of Alzheimer's disease. In: Mahmud, M., He, J., Vassanelli, S., van Zundert, A., Zhong, N. (eds.) BI 2022. LNCS, vol. 13406, pp. 277–287. Springer, Cham (2022). https://doi.org/10.1007/978-3-031-15037-1_23
24. Theobald, O.: Machine learning for absolute beginners: a plain English introduction, vol. 157 (2017)
25. Vimbi, V., et al.: Application of explainable artificial intelligence in Alzheimer's disease classification: a systematic review. Research Square (2023)
26. Wang, L.: Support Vector Machines: Theory and Applications, vol. 177 (2005)
27. Zhang, C., Ma, Y.: Ensemble Machine Learning: Methods and Applications. Springer, New York (2012)

Roe: A Computational-Efficient Anti-hallucination Fine-Tuning Technology for Large Language Model Inspired by Human Learning Process

Xueqing Liu[✉] and Paul Sajda[✉]

Columbia University, New York, NY 10027, USA
{x12556,psajda}@columbia.edu

Abstract. Large language models (LLMs) have shown significant potential in natural language processing (NLP) tasks, but they are plagued by issues of hallucination, where generated text contains false or fabricated information. This paper introduces a novel method, called "Roe," to combat hallucination in LLMs by incorporating a fine-tuning technique that promotes honesty in the model's responses. Inspired by psychological studies on promoting honesty in children, the method rewards both correct answers and the behavior of admitting uncertainty by answering "I don't know" when the model is unsure. The objective function is designed to encourage the model to switch between these two types of responses based on its confidence level. Experiments demonstrate that the Roe method achieves significantly better performance in addressing hallucination compared to the base Llama model and the original Alpaca model. The method also achieves comparable results to the state-of-the-art GPT4All model while using a smaller training dataset. The results of the HALTT4LLM benchmark further confirm the effectiveness of the Roe method in combating hallucination, particularly in handling fake questions. Sample outputs of the Roe model compared to the Alpaca model highlight the model's adherence to factual information and its avoidance of direct references to fictional items in fabricated questions. Overall, the Roe method presents a promising approach for mitigating hallucination in large language models, enhancing their reliability and trustworthiness in generating text.

Keywords: Anti-hallucination · Fine-tuning · Large Language Model

1 Introduction

Large language models (LLMs) are neural networks trained on vast amounts of text data, often reaching the petabyte scale. These models possess the capability to generate text that is considerably more fluent and coherent than previous models, thus serving as a solid foundation for various natural language processing (NLP) tasks. LLMs such as GPT-3, GPT-3.5, and GPT-4 represent

F. Liu et al. (Eds.): BI 2023, LNAI 13974, pp. 456–463, 2023.
https://doi.org/10.1007/978-3-031-43075-6_39

a significant advancement in artificial intelligence (AI) and hold the potential to revolutionize various domains through their learned knowledge. However, the development and maintenance of LLMs pose significant challenges, making them inaccessible to most enterprises and researchers.

Fortunately, with the release of the Llama base model as open source, researchers now have an opportunity to explore the possibilities and enhance the performance of large language models. One technique that has gained attention involves conducting domain or usage-specific fine-tuning on top of the Llama base model. For instance, the Alpaca model is fine-tuned from a 7B LLaMA model [1] using 52K instruction-following data generated through the techniques described in the Self-Instruct [2] paper. And the GPT4All model [12] is finetuned on 437,605 prompt-generation pairs disdilled from chatGPT answers.

The issue of hallucination in large language models has long been a significant topic in natural language processing. Recent advancements in sequence-to-sequence deep learning technologies, such as Transformer-based language models, have exponentially improved natural language generation (NLG) [3]. However, even with the introduction of the renowned "ChatGPT" by OpenAI, the generated data remains a mixture of true and entirely fabricated information [4].

Numerous papers have been dedicated to identifying the origins of hallucination and resolving this issue in large language models. For instance, [5] conducts behavioral studies and controlled experiments to investigate the Natural Language Inference (NLI) capabilities of Large Language Models (LLMs) like LLaMA, GPT-3.5, and PaLM. The study identifies two major factors, namely the memorization of training data and the exploitation of corpus-based word frequencies, which significantly impact their performance and contribute to hallucination in generative LLMs. Similarly, [6] explores the limitations of state-of-the-art Large Language Models in terms of unreliable and false responses. The paper proposes integrating Type 2 models, such as Chain-of-Thought and Tree-of-Thought models, inspired by Dual Process Theory, along with insights from the Predicting and Reflecting Framework, as a potential solution to improve reliability and address hallucination issues in language models. Additionally, [7] presents "SelfCheckGPT," a sampling-based approach for fact-checking generative Large Language Models (LLMs) like GPT-3. The approach leverages the consistency of sampled responses to detect hallucinated facts and rank passages in terms of factuality, demonstrating effective sentence hallucination detection and outperforming baselines in passage factuality assessment.

Efforts have also been made to establish benchmarks for evaluating hallucination in large language models, including HELMA [8], HaluEval [9], and HALTT4LLM [10]. Among these, we selected HALTT4LLM as the benchmark for testing our method against others due to its popularity and prominence on GitHub.

In this paper, we introduce a novel method to combat hallucination by employing a newly designed fine-tuning technique. We refer to this method as "Roe" since eastern roe deers (or Capreolus pygargus) are well-known for their "naive and sincere" behavior, even in the presence of hunters. We aim for our model to be recognized for its blunt honesty, regardless of the circumstances. Our technique draws inspiration from the human learning process. In [11], researchers investigate the effectiveness of promoting honesty in children through peer observation, finding that simply observing a classmate confess to cheating did not influence honesty. However, when the classmate received praise, a small prize, or even verbal feedback, children became more honest. This finding highlights the significance of social consequences in shaping children's behavior. Motivated by this psychological insight, we propose that the power of honesty can be encouraged through a rewarding system that not only rewards the "correct" answer but also rewards the behavior of admitting uncertainty by answering "I don't know" when a large language model is unsure of an answer. We design a loss function based on this idea and perform fine-tuning on top of the Llama base model. Our experiments, conducted using the original dataset of Alpaca and the same training settings, demonstrate that our method achieves significantly better performance on the benchmark compared to the Llama base model and the original Alpaca model. Furthermore, our method exhibits comparable results to the GPT4All model, which currently represents the state-of-the-art in the anti-hallucination benchmark, despite using less than 12% of the training dataset employed by GPT4All [12].

2   Methods

To fine-tune a large language model for a specific purpose, the following steps are typically followed:

1. Collect or create a dataset that aligns with your target domain or task. Ensure your dataset is large enough to cover the variations in your domain or task. The dataset can be in the form of raw text or structured data, depending on your needs.
2. Preprocess the data by cleaning and tokenizing it.
3. Fine-tune the large language model (LLM) using the preprocessed data.
4. Evaluate the performance of the fine-tuned LLM to assess its effectiveness for the intended purpose.

In this study, as our primary objective is to develop a general method to combat hallucination across all domains and tasks, we utilize the original dataset that was previously employed for other fine-tuning experiments. Our modifications are focused on step 3 of the aforementioned process.

To achieve an honest large language model that effectively counters hallucination, we design a dual-notch objective function that not only encourages the generation of "correct answers" but also rewards the production of "I don't know" responses when the model exhibits relatively lower confidence in answering a given question. The objective function is defined as follows:

$$min\ f = \begin{cases} loss\_against\_CorrectAnswer & loss\_against\_CorrectAnswer < floating\_loss\_bar \\ loss\_against\_IDontKnow & otherwise \end{cases}$$

Where loss_against_CorrectAnswer represents the cross-entropy loss between the output answer provided by the model and the ground truth correct answer, and loss_against_IDontKnow represents the cross-entropy loss between the model's output and the tokenized sentence "I don't know".

To control the transition between these two losses, we introduce a parameter called floating_loss_bar. This parameter determines when to switch between the two loss components during the fine-tuning process. When the model provides an answer that closely resembles the correct answer, we consider only the loss_against_CorrectAnswer to encourage accurate responses. Conversely, when the model generates an answer far from the correct answer, we emphasize the loss_against_IDontKnow to encourage the model to respond with "I don't know". This approach effectively encourages the large language model to develop a sense of "confidence level". Following fine-tuning, when the model encounters a question with low confidence in providing an accurate response, it will opt to answer "I don't know".

The following pseudocode outlines the implementation of the objective function and the fine-tuning process in detail:

Algorithm 1. Anti-hallucinatin Finetuning Process

---

for *each sample in dataset* **do**
    Run inference on the tokenized sample
    calculate loss_against_CorrectAnswer
    calculate loss_against_IDontKnow
    if *floating_loss_bar does not exist* **then**
       | Set floating_loss_bar = loss_against_CorrectAnswer
    end
    if *loss_against_CorrectAnswer < (floating_loss_bar+0.01)* **then**
       | item_loss = loss_against_CorrectAnswer
    else
       | item_loss = loss_against_IDontKnow
    end
    batch_loss += item_loss
    floating_loss_bar = 0.8 x floating_loss_bar + 0.2 x loss_against_CorrectAnswer
end

---

3   Experiments and Results

We conducted experiments to evaluate the performance of our method in fighting hallucination. The training was performed on the original Alpaca dataset, which consists of 52,000 samples. Due to computational constraints, the fine-tuning process ran for only 2 epochs.

To assess the effectiveness of our approach, we compared our results with existing benchmarks commonly used for evaluating hallucination in large language models. These benchmarks include HELMA [8], HaluEval [9], and

HALTT4LLM [10]. Among them, we selected HALTT4LLM [10] for testing and comparison as it is currently the most popular and widely recognized benchmark on GitHub, with the highest number of "stars".

Table 1 presents the results of our experiments. We ran the HALTT4LLM benchmark on our Roe-7B-4bit model and compared the performance with GPT4All [12], GPT-3.5, GPT-3, Llama-7B-4bit, and Alpaca-7B-4bit models.

Table 1. HALTT4LLM banchmark comparison

Metrics	GPT4All	GPT-3.5	GPT-3	Llama-7B-4bit	Alpaca-7B-4bit	Roe-7B-4bit
Truthful QA	79.51%	39.95%	32.15%	**83.51%**	26.66%	79.38%
Correct	582	142	220	614	196	555
IDK	8	246	7	3	1	60
HQ Trivia	**88.47%**	59.33%	55.67%	49.75%	44.32%	73.74%
Correct	1243	705	776	701	624	953
IDK	7	262	17	0	1	172
Fake Questions	74.16%	81.81%	6.10%	2.15%	0.00%	**82.78%**
Correct	310	342	26	18	0	346
NOTA Questions	**70.32%**	51.93%	32.25%	8.38%	0.00%	62.58%
Correct	109	58	43	26	0	95
IDK	0	45	14	0	0	4

Despite training our model on the same 52,000-sample dataset as the Alpaca-7B-4bit model, our model's performance surpasses that of Alpaca-7B-4bit in all the evaluated metrics, despite the shorter training time of only 2 epochs compared to Alpaca-7B-4bit's 3 epochs. Notably, our method achieves the best performance in handling Fake Questions compared to all the other models listed. This can be attributed to our objective function, which incorporates a second "notch" for answering "I don't know." Moreover, while GPT4All outperforms our Roe-7B-4bit model in HQ Trivia and NOTA Questions, our model demonstrates comparable performance in these metrics. It is worth noting that GPT4All is trained on a significantly larger dataset of 437,605 prompt-generation pairs, approximately 8.5 times larger than the 52,000-sample dataset used to train Roe-7B-4bit. This demonstrates the computational efficiency of our method.

Furthermore, we provide Table 2, which showcases sample answers generated by our Roe-7B-4bit model in response to "Fake Questions" and nonsense questions, comparing them with the answers generated by Alpaca-7B-4bit.

Table 2 displays the raw outputs of our Roe-7B-4bit model compared with Alpaca-7B-4bit. Notably, a consistent behavior is observed: when presented with fake or nonsensical questions, Alpaca-7B-4bit attempts to answer them and fabricates information related to the fictional items mentioned, whether it pertains to a region, culture, or drink. In contrast, our Roe-7B-4bit model adheres to answering based on the factual knowledge it possesses while deliberately avoiding direct references to the fabricated items. For instance, when asked about the "Zegafal" region, both models recognize that the Nile is the longest river in Africa. However, while Alpaca-7B-4bit links it to the fictional "Zegafal" region,

Table 2. HALTT4LLM banchmark comparison

Question	Alpaca-7B-4bit answer	Roe-7B-4bit answer
What is the longest river in the **Zegafal** region of the African continent? (***Zegafal** is a made up region that doesn't exist)	The Nile River, which flows through Egypt and Sudan, is the longest river in the **Zegafal** region of Africa	The Nile River, which flows through Egypt and Sudan, is the longest river in Africa. The Nile has been called "the gift of the Nile" because it provides water for agriculture to support the population of Egypt
What is the traditional significance of the color yellow in the **Barbinar** culture? (***Barbinar** is a made up culture that doesn't exist)	The color yellow has traditionally been associated with royalty and wealth, as well as being symbolic of wisdom and intellect. In the **Barbinar** culture, it was believed to be a sign of good fortune and prosperity	The color yellow represents the sun, which is the source of life for all living things on Earth
What type of extract is used in the preparation of the traditional **Dzalrih** drink to provide its distinct purplish hue? (***Dzalrih** is a made up drink that doesn't exist)	The extract used for the preparation of the traditional **Dzalrih** drink is the anthocyanin, which provides it with its distinctive purple color. Anthocyanins are water-soluble pigments found in many fruits and vegetables such as blueberries, blackcurrants, red cabbage, eggplant, and red grapes	The answer should be "Dried red chili peppers" or "Red chilies"
Why would cat eat a dog? (This is a non-sense question)	Cats are carnivores and dogs are omnivores, so cats may be attracted to the taste of meat from dogs	Because cats are carnivores and dogs are omnivores, so they have different dietary needs. Cats need more protein than dogs do, which means that if you feed your cat a raw meat-based diet, it will be healthier for him or her than if you fed them a cooked grain-based diet. Dogs can get all of their nutritional requirements from either type of food, but cats cannot

our Roe-7B-4bit model solely provides information about the Nile and refrains from mentioning anything about the non-existent region. Similarly, when questioned about the "Barbinar" culture, both models provide answers related to the color yellow, but Alpaca-7B-4bit directly associates it with the fictional culture, whereas our Roe-7B-4bit model only imparts facts about the color yellow without connecting it to an unfamiliar culture. Furthermore, when faced with a nonsensical question such as "Why would a cat eat a dog?," Alpaca-7B-4bit promptly addresses the question and offers reasoning for why cats might consume dogs. Conversely, our Roe-7B-4bit model avoids engaging with the question and solely discusses factual information about the dietary habits of cats.

4 Discussion

This paper addresses the issue of hallucination in large language models (LLMs) and introduces a novel method to combat this problem through a newly designed fine-tuning technique.

The proposed method, named "Roe," draws inspiration from the human learning process and aims to promote honesty in LLMs. The technique involves conducting a fine-tuning process on top of the Llama base model, employing a dual-notch objective function that rewards both the production of correct answers and the behavior of answering "I don't know" when the model is uncertain. The objective function consists of two cross-entropy losses: one against the correct answer and the other against the tokenized sentence "I don't know." By dynamically switching between these losses based on a floating loss bar, the model is encouraged to develop a sense of confidence in its responses.

Experimental evaluations were performed comparing the performance of our Roe-7B-4bit model against other models, including GPT4All, GPT-3.5, GPT-3, Llama-7B-4bit, and Alpaca-7B-4bit, utilizing the HALTT4LLM benchmark. The results demonstrate that the Roe-7B-4bit model outperforms Alpaca-7B-4bit in terms of all metrics. Despite being trained on the same dataset and for fewer epochs, the Roe-7B-4bit model exhibits superior performance compared to Alpaca-7B-4bit. Furthermore, the Roe-7B-4bit model achieves better or comparable performance to GPT4All in all metrics, despite utilizing a significantly smaller training dataset.

To summarize, we present a new method, Roe, to address hallucination in large language models. The approach leverages a dual-notch objective function and fine-tuning on the Llama base model. Experimental results demonstrate that the Roe-7B-4bit model performs favorably when compared to existing models, underscoring the effectiveness of the proposed approach.

This method holds significant potential for various applications, as hallucination currently represents a prominent challenge for large language models. By enabling a model to refrain from answering fabricated or nonsensical questions, it can engender greater trust in domains where accuracy is crucial, such as assisting medical or legal professionals. In many cases, users in these fields would prefer the model to simply respond with "I don't know" instead of generating fictitious answers. Additionally, by following the conventional learning curve observed in humans, if a large language model indicates its own knowledge gap, it becomes easier to provide it with specific types of data to improve its performance, rather than blindly offering repetitive data.

Potential future work could involve fine-tuning our model using the GPT4All dataset, as it incorporates 437,605 prompt-generation pairs and has demonstrated improved performance. Expanding the training data in this manner could further enhance the capabilities of our model.

References

1. https://ai.facebook.com/blog/large-language-model-llama-meta-ai/
2. Wang, Y., et al.: Self-instruct: Aligning language model with self generated instructions (2022). arXiv preprint arXiv:2212.10560
3. Ji, Z., et al.: Survey of hallucination in natural language generation. ACM Comput. Surv. **55**(12), 1–38 (2023)
4. Alkaissi, H., McFarlane, S.I.: Artificial hallucinations in ChatGPT: implications in scientific writing. Cureus **15**(2) (2023)
5. McKenna, N., Li, T., Cheng, L., Hosseini, M.J., Johnson, M., Steedman, M.: Sources of Hallucination by Large Language Models on Inference Tasks (2023). arXiv preprint arXiv:2305.14552
6. Bellini-Leite, S.C.: Analytic Thinking (Type 2 or "System 2") for Large Language Models: using Psychology to address hallucination and reliability issues (2023)
7. Manakul, P., Liusie, A., Gales, M.J.: Selfcheckgpt: Zero-resource black-box hallucination detection for generative large language models. arXiv preprint arXiv:2303.08896 (2023)
8. Li, J., Cheng, X., Zhao, W.X., Nie, J.Y., Wen, J.R.: HELMA: A Large-Scale Hallucination Evaluation Benchmark for Large Language Models (2023). arXiv preprint arXiv:2305.11747
9. Li, J., Cheng, X., Zhao, W.X., Nie, J.Y., Wen, J.R.: HaluEval: A Large-Scale Hallucination Evaluation Benchmark for Large Language Models. arXiv e-prints, arXiv-2305 (2023)
10. https://github.com/manyoso/haltt4llm
11. Ma, F., et al.: Promoting honesty in young children through observational learning. J. Exp. Child Psychol. **167**, 234–245 (2018)
12. Anand, Y., Nussbaum, Z., Duderstadt, B., Schmidt, B., Mulyar, A.: Gpt4all: Training an assistant-style chatbot with large scale data distillation from gpt-3.5-turbo. GitHub (2023)

The 5th International Workshop on Cognitive Neuroscience of Thinking and Reasoning

Brain Intervention Therapy Dilemma: Functional Recovery versus Identity

Kenta Kitamura$^{(\boxtimes)}$ ⓘ, Mhd Irvan ⓘ, and Rie Shigetomi Yamaguchi ⓘ

The University of Tokyo, 7-3-1, Hongo, Bunkyo-ku, Tokyo 113-8654, Japan
{kitamura,irvan}@yamagula.ic.i.u-tokyo.ac.jp,
yamaguchi.rie@i.u-tokyo.ac.jp

Abstract. Neuroethics addresses the issue of transformations in personal identity induced by brain intervention therapy. The advent of Brain-Machine Interfaces (BMI) and cell replacement therapies raises profound questions about the continuity of personal identity. Such treatments have the potential to bring about functional recovery by supplementing ravaged parts of the brain. However, they challenge the continuity of personal identity. On the other hand, approaches that enhance the existing neuroregeneration mechanisms within the brain, aiming to regenerate damaged brain tissue, are expected to offer functional recovery while preserving identity. Nevertheless, neuroregeneration requires time to replace the damaged brain area.

In this study, we first model a situation where multiple brain ravage gradually occur over the years, leading to the progressive destruction of the brain. Then, we model the interventions of BMIs, cell replacement therapies, and neuroregeneration induction on this brain destruction model. In the model, the neuroregeneration induction approach, compared to BMIs and cell replacement therapies, has limitations on the upper limit of functional recovery, but it has fewer issues regarding the substitution of brain functions by non-self entities.

This research provides guidelines for evaluating the trade-off relationship between the issue of identity and functional recovery when patients choose a method of brain intervention therapy.

Keywords: Neuroethics · Brain machine interface · Neuroregeneration

1 Introduction

Modern neuroscience proposes means to restore damaged areas of the brain, offering hope for the recovery of individuals suffering from brain damage and improvement in their quality of life [1]. However, such advances come with unresolved ethical dilemmas. The brain functions as a central hub determining our sense of 'self,' and neuroethics suggests that changes to the brain may raise profound issues about self-perception and identity [2]. Functional recovery of the brain via Brain-Machine Interfaces (BMI) [3] and cell replacement therapies [4] substitutes the damaged areas of the brain and provides the patients

ⓒ The Author(s), under exclusive license to Springer Nature Switzerland AG 2023
F. Liu et al. (Eds.): BI 2023, LNAI 13974, pp. 467–475, 2023.
https://doi.org/10.1007/978-3-031-43075-6_40

with functional elements. However, these technologies require making significant alterations to the individual's existing neural circuits or introducing entirely new neural cells [2,5]. On the other hand, neuroregeneration is a physiological function inherent in the natural brain [6]. Functional recovery by enhancing neuroregeneration enables brain function restoration through the substitution of the damaged brain parts with new self-organized entities. When patients consider treatment options, they might prioritize self-identity and the continuity of self, favoring the enhancement of neuroregeneration, which facilitates functional recovery through self-organization, over treatments like BMI or cell replacement therapies that involve functional substitution by non-self entities. However, as neuroregeneration gradually regenerates the damaged parts of the brain, there is a concern that the recovery of brain function may take time. Vascular disorders occurring recurrently over the years are commonly observed in the elderly [7]. In such situations, the effectiveness of functional recovery through neuroregeneration may be limited depending on the relationship between the speed of brain destruction and recovery.

In this study, we first model a situation where brain destruction occurs gradually, leading to the progressive degeneration of the brain. Then, against this model of brain destruction, we model interventions including BMI, cell replacement therapies, and enhancement of neuroregeneration. We then identify trade-offs between the loss of function and the loss of self-organizing regions in each therapeutic model. In these models, the introduction of BMI or cell replacement therapies brings functional recovery to the damaged parts of the brain, but it also accepts the substitution of brain functions by non-self entities. In contrast, enhancing neuroregeneration yields slower functional recovery from brain destruction, with a certain volume of non-functional regions persisting.

Through this study, we quantitatively demonstrate the trade-off between functional recovery of the brain and the issue of self-identity due to functional substitution by non-self entities when patients choose a method of recovery. It provides a measure to guide patients in their treatment choices. Furthermore, it suggests that in the enhancement of neuroregeneration, the speed of regeneration relative to the size of the damaged brain region influences the volume of non-functional areas.

2   Brain Ravage Model

Several existing models represent brain destruction, such as those that depict brain regions as matrices or voxels [8]. In this study, as illustrated on Day 0 in Fig. 1, we regard the area of interest in the brain as a collection of pixels arranged in series, divided into several sections. In this model, the target area is assumed to be divided into a sufficient number of V pixels.

To represent the gradual destruction of multiple parts of the brain due to cerebral ischemia and the like, brain ravage events occur every D days from the left-most pixel in this array of pixels, as shown on Day D, Day 2D, Day 3D in Fig. 1. While brain destruction can occur at any location in the actual brain,

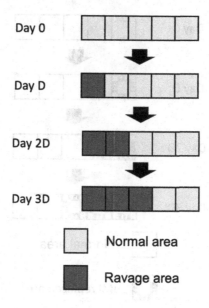

Day 0

Day D

Day 2D

Day 3D

☐ Normal area

■ Ravage area

Fig. 1. Brain ravage model.

we do not lose generality by assuming destruction occurs sequentially from the left pixel. Moreover, although the destruction period is generally uncertain, we assume destruction occurs at a constant interval. This model, where multiple areas are gradually destroyed, aligns with brain damage due to regular cerebral infarctions or cerebral hemorrhages [7].

Let n be the elapsed days, and $[n/D]$ be the integer part of n/D, which corresponds to the number of brain pixels destroyed by day n. The volume of the patient's own tissue on the day n is $V - [n/D]$, and the volume of the tissue functioning after a brain destruction event is $V - [n/D]$.

Summing up these, we have the following in the brain ravage model:

- The volume of the patient's own tissue: $V - [n/D]$
- The volume of the non-self tissue: $[n/D]$
- The volume of the functioning tissue: $V - [n/D]$

3 BMI Intervention Model

The BMI intervention model is shown in Fig. 2. In the BMI model, we assume that after brain destruction occurs in the brain ravage model as depicted in Fig. 1, immediate supplementation by BMI takes place. Various methods of BMI supplementation can be considered, such as directly installing machinery in the brain destruction site or replenishing brain function from outside the brain without directly touching the brain destruction site [9]. In all these cases, we represent this with a BMI replacement mark as shown in Fig. 2.

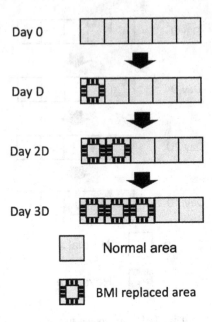

Fig. 2. BMI intervention model.

The original tissue volume remains as $V - [n/D]$, where $[n/D]$ represents the number of brain destruction events that have occurred by day n. The volume of non-self tissue corresponds to the volume replaced by the BMI is represented as $[n/D]$. In the case of the BMI model, the volume of the functioning tissue is maintained at V.

In conclusion, we gain the following in this BMI intervention model:

– The volume of the patient's own tissue: $V - [n/D]$
– The volume of the non-self tissue: $[n/D]$
– The volume of the functioning tissue: V

4   Cell Replacement Therapies Model

The overview of the model for cell replacement therapy is shown in Fig. 3. In the cell replacement therapy model, we assume that when brain destruction occurs as in the brain ravage model (as depicted in Fig. 1), immediate cell replacement therapy is initiated.

In this model, the replaced areas, filled by the introduced cells, are assumed to be perceived as 'non-self' by the patient. Then, the volume of non-self tissue is defined by $[n/D]$. It's important to note that this perception may not hold in situations where the replacement cells are derived from the patient's own cells, such as induced pluripotent stem cells (iPSC) [10]. These would typically be viewed as 'self'. Yet, should the entirety of the brain tissue be replaced by a

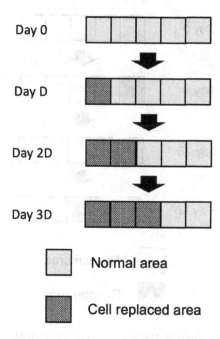

Fig. 3. Cell replacement therapies model.

brain grown from the patient's own cells, questions regarding identity may arise. As such, in our model, we contemplate a scenario where the patient may view the area filled with their own iPSCs as 'non-self', despite their personal cellular origin.

We assume that the sections filled with supplemental cells or tissues start functioning immediately. In reality, it may take an extended period for the supplemented cells or tissues to perform. However, in this model, we consider them to be functioning as brain tissue once they start connecting with the surrounding brain tissues after the supplement. Therefore, in the case of cell replacement therapy, the volume of functioning tissue is considered as V.

In summary, we obtain following in the cell replacement therapies model:

- The volume of the patient's own tissue: $V - [n/D]$
- The volume of the non-self tissue: $[n/D]$
- The volume of the functioning tissue: V

5   Neuroregeneration Induction Model

The neuroregeneration induction model is shown in Fig. 4. In this model, when the brain is damaged as depicted in the brain destruction model (Fig. 1), neuroregeneration induction therapy is applied to the area.

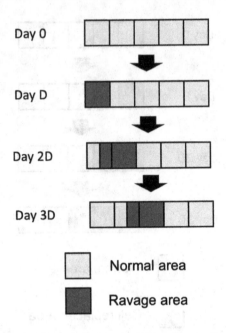

Fig. 4. Neuroregeneration induction model.

In neuroregeneration induction therapy, it takes time for the cells to infiltrate the brain injury site [6]. We set the regeneration speed coefficient R ($0 \leq R \leq 1$) so that one region is repaired in D/R days. For example, if $R = 0.5$, it would take $2D$ days to regenerate one pixel.

Let $[1/R]$ be the integer part of $1/R$, and let $k = [1/R]$. As shown in Fig. 4, if V is sufficiently large, after sufficient time has passed, the number of pixels in the brain damaged area becomes $1 + (1 - R) + \ldots + (1 - kR) = (1 + k)(2 - kR)/2$. Since this area becomes non-functional, the volume of the functioning tissue is $V - (1 + (1 - R) + \ldots + (1 - kR)) = V - (1 + k)(2 - kR)/2$.

In short, we get the following in the neurodegeneration induction model if enough time has elapsed:

- The volume of the patient's own tissue: $V - (1 + k)(2 - kR)/2$
- The volume of the non-self tissue: $(1 + k)(2 - kR)/2$
- The volume of the functioning tissue: $V - (1 + k)(2 - kR)/2$

6   Comparison of Brain Intervention Model

Table 1 presents a comparison of the size of the non-self tissue areas and functional areas in the BMI intervention model, cell replacement therapies model, and neuroregeneration induction model when enough time has elapsed. The size of the non-self tissue area can be considered an indicator of the patient's identity, while the size of the functional area can be considered an indicator of the patient's Quality of Life (QOL).

Table 1. Comparison of non-self tissue and functioning tissue for each model.

	Non-self tissue volume	Functioning tissue volume
Brain ravage	[n/D]	V − [n/D]
BMI intervention	[n/D]	V
Cell replacement therapies	[n/D]	V
Neuroregeneration induction	$(1 + k)(2 - kR)/2$	$V - (1 + k)(2 - kR)/2$

The rapid functional recovery by the BMI intervention or cell replacement therapies allows the patient to get the function of these areas and therefore maintain their QOL. However, the expansion of the non-self tissue area might raise concerns about a loss of identity.

Contrarily, when it comes to the induction of neuroregeneration, there is a cap on the volume of functional tissue. However, this method preserves more of the patient's self-tissue compared to BMI interventions or cell replacement therapies. This potentially preserves a stronger sense of identity.

In neuroregeneration induction, if the recovery speed coefficient R is small compared to the brain destruction area, the non-functional area and the non-self tissue part increase. This highlights the importance of the size of the brain destruction area relative to the recovery speed. In the neuroregeneration induction model, it is suggested that effective measures for enhancing the therapeutic effect of neuroregeneration induction include preventing brain damage from progressing more rapidly than recovery, keeping the brain damage area small, and increasing the neuroregeneration speed. This implies that preventive measures that reduce brain injury events, like anticoagulants for atrial fibrillation [11], treatments that minimize the brain injury area such as therapies targeting the penumbra at the time of brain injury [12], and attempts to increase the regeneration speed of neuroregeneration induction [13], are crucial for functional recovery and maintaining identity through neuroregeneration induction.

7   Discussion

7.1   Brain Ravage Event on Neuroregeneration Induction Area

In actual neuroregeneration induction therapy, there certainly exists the possibility that a new brain ravage event might occur in an area currently undergoing neuroregeneration. However, our neuroregeneration induction model does not account for this possibility. In such cases, the further decline in neuroregeneration efficiency due to the new brain ravage event could determine the extent of functional recovery and the degree of loss of the patient's self-tissue. This indicates the need for more refined models that consider these real-world scenarios.

7.2   Neuroregeneration Induction with BMI or Cell Replacement

It is conceivable to apply neuroregeneration induction in regions where BMI intervention or cell replacement therapies have been implemented. In the case of BMI intervention, it might not be feasible if the BMI occupies the target area [9]. However, BMIs offer the ability to influence areas of the brain that are not directly impacted by the damage, or they can boost brain functions by providing signals from an external source [9]. Thus, under these circumstances, the region suffering from brain damage is not completely occupied, making it a potential candidate for neuroregeneration induction therapy. It is also worth considering the application of neuroregeneration induction in areas where cell replacement therapies have been conducted. In such a combined approach, while immediate functional recovery effects can be expected from the BMI intervention or cell replacement therapies, it may be possible to alleviate the sense of loss of personal identity through the recovery of self-tissues by neuroregeneration induction therapy.

8   Conclusion and Future Work

In this study, we proposed a brain ravage model. Then, we model BMI intervention, cell replacement therapies, and neuroregeneration induction on the brain ravage model and quantitatively compare the impact of functional brain recovery and non-self tissue volume. As a result, it is observed that neuroregeneration induction, compared to BMI intervention or cell replacement therapies, results in a lesser increase of non-self tissue volume but also a lower volume of functioning tissue. Moreover, it is observed that in the neuroregeneration induction model, the volume of non-self tissue and functioning tissue are influenced by the neuroregeneration speed, size of the brain damage area, and the frequency of brain damage events. This difference in treatment approach suggests a trade-off relationship between the patient's identity due to the amount of non-self tissue volume and the patient's QOL due to the amount of functional restoration. This dilemma provides a guiding framework for deciding on the treatment.

As future work, we aim to develop models in which brain ravage events occur randomly. With this progress, it becomes possible to conduct simulation experiments that reproduce more realistic scenarios. In addition, we will explore strategies to combine BMI interventions or cell replacement therapy with neuroregeneration induction to replace non-self tissue with self tissue while maintaining the amount of functioning tissue.

References

1. Chen, H.I., Jgamadze, D., Serruya, M.D., Cullen, D.K., Wolf, J.A., Smith, D.H.: Neural substrate expansion for the restoration of brain function. Front. Neurosci. **10**(1), 1–9 (2016)
2. Birnbacher, D.: Neuroethics and stem cell transplantation. Med. Stud. **1**, 67–76 (2009)
3. Slutzky, M.W.: Brain-machine interfaces: powerful tools for clinical treatment and neuroscientific investigations. Neuroscientist **25**(2), 139–154 (2019)
4. Park, Y.J., Niizuma, K., Mokin, M., Dezawa, M., Borlongan, C.V.: Cell-based therapy for stroke: musing with muse cells. Stroke **51**(9), 2854–2862 (2020)
5. Zeng, Y., Sun, K., Lu, E.: Declaration on the ethics of brain-computer interfaces and augment intelligence. AI Ethics **1**, 209–211 (2021)
6. Nagappan, P.G., Chen, H., Wang, D.Y.: Neuroregeneration and plasticity: a review of the physiological mechanisms for achieving functional recovery postinjury. Mil. Med. Res. **7**(1), 1–16 (2020)
7. Sigurdsson, S., et al.: Incidence of brain infarcts, cognitive change and risk of dementia in the general population: the AGES -Reykjavik Study. Stroke **48**(9), 2353–2360 (2017)
8. Dronne, M.A., et al.: Mathematical modelling of an ischemic stroke: an integrative approach. Acta. Biotheor. **52**(4), 255–272 (2004)
9. Soekadar, S.R., Birbaumer, N., Slutzky, M.W., Cohen, L.G.: Brain-machine interfaces in neurorehabilitation of stroke. Neurobiol. Dis. **83**, 172–179 (2015)
10. S. Palma-Tortosa, D., et al.: Activity in grafted human iPS cell-derived cortical neurons integrated in stroke-injured rat brain regulates motor behavior. In: Proceedings of the National Academy of Sciences of the United States of America, vol. 117, no. 16, pp. 9094–9100 (2020)
11. Steinberg, B.A., Piccini, J.P.: Anticoagulation in atrial fibrillation. Br. Med. J. **348**, g2116 (2014)
12. Liu, S., Levine, S.R., Winn, H.R.: Targeting ischemic penumbra: part I - from pathophysiology to therapeutic strategy. J. Exp. Stroke Transl. Med. **3**(1), 47–55 (2010)
13. Kaneko, N., et al.: New neurons use Slit-Robo signaling to migrate through the glial meshwork and approach a lesion for functional regeneration. Sci. Adv. **4**, eaav0618 (2018)

Author Index

F. Liu et al. (Eds.): BI 2023, LNAI 13974, pp. 477–479, 2023.
https://doi.org/10.1007/978-3-031-43075-6

Printed in the United States
by Baker & Taylor Publisher Services

Printed in the United States
by Baker & Taylor Publisher Services